IFIP Advances in Information and Communication Technology 428

IFIP – The International Federation for Information Processing

IFIP was founded in 1960 under the auspices of UNESCO, following the First World Computer Congress held in Paris the previous year. An umbrella organization for societies working in information processing, IFIP's aim is two-fold: to support information processing within its member countries and to encourage technology transfer to developing nations. As its mission statement clearly states,

> *IFIP's mission is to be the leading, truly international, apolitical organization which encourages and assists in the development, exploitation and application of information technology for the bene t of all people.*

IFIP is a non-profitmaking organization, run almost solely by 2500 volunteers. It operates through a number of technical committees, which organize events and publications. IFIP's events range from an international congress to local seminars, but the most important are:

- The IFIP World Computer Congress, held every second year;
- Open conferences;
- Working conferences.

The flagship event is the IFIP World Computer Congress, at which both invited and contributed papers are presented. Contributed papers are rigorously refereed and the rejection rate is high.

As with the Congress, participation in the open conferences is open to all and papers may be invited or submitted. Again, submitted papers are stringently refereed.

The working conferences are structured differently. They are usually run by a working group and attendance is small and by invitation only. Their purpose is to create an atmosphere conducive to innovation and development. Refereeing is also rigorous and papers are subjected to extensive group discussion.

Publications arising from IFIP events vary. The papers presented at the IFIP World Computer Congress and at open conferences are published as conference proceedings, while the results of the working conferences are often published as collections of selected and edited papers.

Any national society whose primary activity is about information processing may apply to become a full member of IFIP, although full membership is restricted to one society per country. Full members are entitled to vote at the annual General Assembly, National societies preferring a less committed involvement may apply for associate or corresponding membership. Associate members enjoy the same benefits as full members, but without voting rights. Corresponding members are not represented in IFIP bodies. Affiliated membership is open to non-national societies, and individual and honorary membership schemes are also offered.

Nora Cuppens-Boulahia   Frédéric Cuppens
Sushil Jajodia   Anas Abou El Kalam
Thierry Sans (Eds.)

ICT Systems Security and Privacy Protection

29th IFIP TC 11 International Conference, SEC 2014
Marrakech, Morocco, June 2-4, 2014
Proceedings

 Springer

Volume Editors

Nora Cuppens-Boulahia
Frédéric Cuppens
Télécom Bretagne (Campus de Rennes)
2, rue de la Châtaigneraie, 35576 Cesson Sévigné Cedex, France
E-mail: {nora.cuppens, frederic.cuppens}@telecom-bretagne.eu

Sushil Jajodia
George Mason University
4400 University Drive, Fairfax, VA 22030-4422, USA
E-mail: jajodia@gmu.edu

Anas Abou El Kalam
Université Cadi Ayyad, École Nationale des Sciences Appliquées
Avenue Abdelkrim El Khattabi, 40000 Marrakech, Morocco
E-mail: elkalam@hotmail.fr

Thierry Sans
Carnegie Mellon University
Qatar Campus, Doha, Qatar
E-mail: tsans@cmu.edu

ISSN 1868-4238   e-ISSN 1868-422X
ISBN 978-3-662-51541-9   e-ISBN 978-3-642-55415-5
DOI 10.1007/978-3-642-55415-5
Springer Heidelberg New York Dordrecht London

Typesetting: Camera-ready by author, data conversion by Scientific Publishing Services, Chennai, India

Printed on acid-free paper

Springer is part of Springer Science+Business Media (www.springer.com)

Preface

These proceedings contain the papers presented at the 29th IFIP International Information Security and Privacy Conference (SEC 2014). The conference, hosted for the first time in Marrakech, Morocco, June 2–4, 2014, offered outstanding research contributions to the field of security in Internet-related applications, networks, and systems.

In response to the call for papers, 151 papers were submitted to the conference. These papers were evaluated on the basis of their significance, novelty, and technical quality. Each paper was reviewed by four members of the Program Committee. The Program Committee meeting was held electronically with intensive discussion over a period of one week. Of the papers submitted, 27 full papers and 14 short papers were accepted for presentation at the conference. The conference program also included two invited talks by William Caelli Director at IISEC Pty Ltd, Brisbane, Australia, and V.S. Subrahmanian, Professor at University of Maryland, College Park, United States.

Several trends in computer security have become prominent since the beginning of the new century and are considered in the program. These include, the proliferation of intrusions that exploit new vulnerabilities, the necessity to respond to an increasing number of computer security incidents, the emergence of new security threats, and the need to adapt existing approaches, models, and metrics to handle these threats. Reflecting these trends, the conference includes sessions on intrusion detection, data security, privacy, mobile security, metrics and risk assessment, information flow control, identity management, identifiability and decision making, malicious behavior and fraud, organizational security.

The success of this conference was the result of the effort of many people who generously volunteered their time for the various organization tasks. It was a pleasure to work with such dedicated colleagues. We also thank our hosts, the staff from the ENSA Marrakesh and AMAN for their help in day-to-day running of the conference.

We gratefully acknowledge all authors who submitted papers for their efforts in continually enhancing the standards of this conference. It is also our pleasure to thank the members of the Program Committee and the external reviewers for their work and support.

Last but not least, thanks to all the attendees. We hope you will enjoy reading the proceedings.

March 2014   Nora Cuppens-Boulahia
                                                                    Frédéric Cuppens
                                                                    Sushil Jajodia

Organization

Program Committee

Anas Abou El Kalam	Cadi Ayyad University, ENSA of Marrakech, Morocco
Kamel Adi	University of Quebec in Outaouais, Canada
Vijay Atluri	Rutgers University, USA
Fabien Autrel	CNRS-LabSTICC, France
Richard Baskerville	Georgia State University, Atlanta, USA
Abdelmalek Benzekri	Université Toulouse 3 Paul Sabatier, France
Pierre Bieber	Onera, France
Joan Borrell	Universitat Autònoma de Barcelona, Spain
Adel Bouhoula	High School of Communication, Sup'Com, Tunisia
Dagmar Brechlerova	Euromise Prague, Czech Republic
Jonathan Butts	AFIT, USA
William Caelli	IISEC Pty Ltd., Australia
Jan Camenisch	IBM Research, Zurich Research Laboratory, Switzerland
Ana Cavalli	IMT- Telecom SudParis, France
Iliano Cervesato	Carnegie Mellon University, Qatar
Hakima Chaouchi	IMT-Telecom SudParis, France
Abdelghani Chibani	University of Paris Est Créteil, LISSI, France
Nathan Clarke	Plymouth University, UK
Gouenou Coatrieux	IMT-Telecom Bretagne, France
Bruno Crispo	University of Trento, Italy
Frédéric Cuppens	IMT-Telecom Bretagne, France
Nora Cuppens-Boulahia	IMT-Telecom Bretagne, France
Ernesto Damiani	University of Milan, Italy
Christian Damsgaard	Technical University of Denmark, Denmark
Sabrina De Capitani Di Vimercati	Università degli Studi di Milano, Italy
Bart De Decker	KU Leuven, Belgium
Hervé Debar	IMT-Telecom SudParis, France
Mourad Debbabi	Concordia University, Canada
Gurpreet Dhillon	Virginia Commonwealth University, USA
Theo Dimitrakos	British Telecommunications (BT) and University of Kent, UK
Ronald Dodge	United States Military Academy, USA
Josep Domingo-Ferrer	Universitat Rovira i Virgili, Spain
Loic Duflot	ANSSI, France

Jakob Illeborg Pagter	Centre for IT Security, Alexandra Institute Ltd., Denmark
Philippos Peleties	USB BANK PLC, Cyprus
Günther Pernul	Universität Regensburg, Germany
Nicolas Prigent	Supélec Rennes, France
Sihan Qing	School of Software and Microelectronics, China
Kai Rannenberg	Goethe University Frankfurt, Germany
Indrajit Ray	Colorado State University, USA
Indrakshi Ray	Colorado State University, USA
Carlos Reider	Hochschule für Wirtschaft, Switzerland
Yves Roudier	EURECOM, France
Mark Ryan	University of Birmingham, UK
P.Y.A. Ryan	University of Luxembourg, Luxembourg
Pierangela Samarati	Università degli Studi di Milano, Italy
Thierry Sans	Carnegie Mellon University, Qatar
Claire Saurel	ONERA, France
Ingrid Schaumüller-Bichl	University of Applied Sciences Upper Austria, Austria
Anne Karen Seip	Finanstilsynet, Norway
Abderrahim Sekkaki	FS Casablanca, Morocco
Sujeet Shenoi	University of Tulsa, USA
Radu State	University of Luxembourg, Luxembourg
Bhavani Thuraisingham	University of Texas at Dallas, USA
Pedro Veiga	University of Lisbon, Portugal
Rossouw Von Solms	Nelson Mandela Metropolitan University, South Africa
Jozef Vyskoc	VaF, Slovakia
Christian Weber	University of Applied Sciences, Germany

Additional Reviewers

Abbes, Tarek	Bkakria, Anis
Al Khalil, Firas	Blanco-Justicia, Alberto
Alcaraz, Cristina	Boukhtouta, Amine
Alpar, Gergely	Boulares, Sofiene
Ammar, Boulaiche	Boussi, Hanen
Armknecht, Frederik	Chen, Beijing
Asghar, Muhammad Rizwan	Damopoulos, Dimitrios
Ayachi, Mohamed Ali	Daniel, Joshua
Bal, Goekhan	de La Piedra, Antonio
Barbu, Guillaume	Diener, Michael
Batet, Montserrat	Doelitzscher, Frank
Ben Youssef Ben Souayah, Nihel	Dritsas, Stelios
Besson, Frederic	Drogkaris, Prokopios

Dubus, Samuel
Ducatel, Gery
Duquesne, Sylvain
Farràs, Oriol
Fernandez, Carmen
Gaspar, Jaime
Grewal, Gurchetan
Grewe, Sylvia
Hachem, Nabil
Halbich, Cestmir
Hamdi, Mohamed
Hamouid, Khaled
Hassan, Sabri
Hillen, Christiaan
Hu, Jinwei
Idrees, Muhammad Sabir
Jensen, Jonas Lindstrøm
Ji, Qingguang
Joaquim, Rui
Kanoun, Waël
Karyda, Maria
Khambhammettu, Hemanth
Klaoudatou, Eleni
Kondratyeva, Olga
Krasnova, Anna
Kushik, Natalia
Lancrenon, Jean
Lapon, Jorn
Lazouski, Aliaksandr
Lemaire, Laurens
Li, Fudong
Liu, Jia
Lortz, Steffen
Lueks, Wouter
Læssøe Mikkelsen, Gert
Manso, Oscar
Meharouech, Sourour
Meier, Stefan
Milutinovic, Milica
Moataz, Tarik
Mohamed, Aouadi

Moyano, Francisco
Mukherjee, Subhojeet
Mulamba, Dieudonne
Mylonas, Alexios
Netter, Michael
Nielsen, Janus Dam
Nordholt, Peter Sebastian
Ordean, Mihai
Pan, Wei
Pawar, Pramod
Peter, Andreas
Phillips, Joshua
Ray, Sujoy
Rios, Ruben
Rizomiliotis, Panagiotis
Sabouri, Ahmad
Samarji, Léa
Sanchez, David
Santos, Joao
Saracino, Andrea
Savary, Aymerick
Schillinger, Rolf
Sere, Ahmadou
Sgandurra, Daniele
Shen, Qingni
Skjernaa, Berit
Soeanu, Andrei
Soupionis, Yannis
Stergiopoulos, George
Sänger, Johannes
Tang, Qiang
Tesfay, Welderufael
Toumi, Khalifa
Tschersich, Markus
Tsohou, Aggeliki
Veseli, Fatbardh
Virvilis, Nick
Vivas, José Luis
Weber, Michael
Yang, Shuzhe
Yu, Jiangshan

Table of Contents

Privacy I

Metrics and Risk Assessment

Information Flow Control

Identity Management

Identifiability and Decision Making

Malicious Behavior and Fraud

Organizational Security

Privacy II

Mentor: Positive DNS Reputation to Skim-Off Benign Domains in Botnet C&C Blacklists

Nizar Kheir, Frédéric Tran, Pierre Caron, and Nicolas Deschamps

Orange Labs, Issy-Les-Moulineaux, France
{name.surname}@orange.com

Abstract. The Domain Name System (DNS) is an essential infrastructure service on the internet. It provides a worldwide mapping between easily memorizable domain names and numerical IP addresses. Today, legitimate users and malicious applications use this service to locate content on the internet. Yet botnets increasingly rely on DNS to connect to their command and control servers. A widespread approach to detect bot infections inside corporate networks is to inspect DNS traffic using domain C&C blacklists. These are built using a wide range of techniques including passive DNS analysis, malware sandboxing and web content filtering. Using DNS to detect botnets is still an error-prone process; and current blacklist generation algorithms often add innocuous domains that lead to a large number of false positives during detection.

This paper presents a new system called Mentor. It implements a scalable, *positive DNS reputation* system that automatically removes benign entries within a blacklist of botnet C&C domains. Mentor embeds a crawler system that collects statistical features about a suspect domain name, including both web content and DNS properties. It applies supervised learning to a labeled set of known benign and malicious domain names, using its features set in order to build a DNS pruning model. It further processes domain blacklists using this model in order to skim-off benign domains and keep only true malicious domains for detection. We tested our system against a wide set of public botnet blacklists. Experimental results prove the ability of this system to efficiently detect and remove benign domain names with a very low false positives rate.

1 Introduction

The Domain Name System (DNS) constitutes a core infrastructure component of the internet. It provides a global hierarchical service that associates internet domains with their corresponding IP addresses [15]. Today, internet users access the DNS system to locate and retrieve content such as web servers, hosting and mailing services. Because of its global reach, DNS is nowadays being used to share knowledge about malware threats, including infected websites and domain callbacks [7]. As soon as malware infects a terminal, it establishes a Command and Control (C&C) channel with an attacker in order to download updates, retrieve commands and steal data. Yet malware implements multiple mechanisms

N. Cuppens-Boulahia et al. (Eds.): SEC 2014, IFIP AICT 428, pp. 1–14, 2014.

to locate its C&C server, and DNS still constitutes the most widespread technique being used today, including hard-coded domains, DGA [3] and domain flux [10]. A common approach to fight against malware is to use blacklists of botnet C&C domains [2,6]. It observes traffic at system egress points and drops connections towards known malicious domain names. When malware can no longer connect to its C&C server, its effect would be neutralized because it would no longer be accessible to the remote attacker.

Domain C&C blacklists are currently being generated using a wide range of techniques such as passive DNS traffic analysis, malware sandboxing and web content filtering. Yet the wide use of domain blacklists for botnet detection is still confronted with the large amount of false positives included in these blacklists. Hence, security administrators are still reluctant in using domain blacklists as a way to automatically drop botnet C&C communications. In fact these are not reliable enough to be used as a proactive security solution [9], and so they are mostly being used for passive detection and alerting. Yet malware implements multiple obfuscation mechanisms that make difficult the correct identification of its main command and control channels, as follows.

Firstly, extraction of C&C domains during dynamic sandbox analysis is errorprone since malware triggers multiple network connections in addition to its main C&C activity. The conficker.C malware provides a typical example where it randomly selects a C&C domain out of 50 thousand possible domain names created daily for this purpose. The use of similar techniques by malware clearly makes difficult the correct extraction and maintenance of domain blacklists.

On the other hand, negative DNS reputation provides an alternative approach to sandbox analysis as it does not require collecting and executing malware samples. It aims at observing DNS traffic and collecting features that characterize a botnet signaling activity. For instance, the Notos system in [2] uses evidence-based features such as the number of malware that connected to a given domain name in order to measure the reliability of this domain. The Exposure system [6] also defines features that differentiate malicious and benign domains based on botnet C&C artifacts such as short domain TTL and abrupt changes in DNS requests towards a given domain. Unfortunately, modern botnets can easily avert negative DNS reputation systems using techniques such as random delays and noise injection within their main C&C communications. They also increasingly implement hybrid botnet topologies that distribute commands among a larger set of master C&C bots, thus reducing the coverage of DNS features during detection [12,13]. In fact negative DNS reputation observes only artifacts associated with a known botnet signaling activity and so it is efficient only against known botnet C&C topologies. It cannot easily adapt to new botnet obfuscation techniques, thus limiting its coverage and increasing risks of false positives [20].

This paper addresses the limitations of current negative DNS reputation systems through the proposal of a new system called Mentor, that implements positive DNS reputation to separate malicious and benign domain names. Mentor searches for *artifacts that prove the innocuous nature of a domain name*. It acts as a watchdog that processes domain blacklists generated by negative DNS reputation systems. It implements a crawler system that collects artifacts and builds a comprehensive set of features for every single domain in these blacklists. Mentor collects elements that characterize the legitimacy of a given domain name, including the popularity, cross-references, external links and the data hosted on this domain. It further applies machine learning techniques, using this set of features, in order to identify benign domain names and remove these from the initial domain blacklists, keeping only true C&C domains for botnet detection and prevention. Indeed Mentor uses a web crawler that actively connects to remote domains in order to build its features set, as opposed to negative DNS reputation that only uses passive traffic analysis.

To summarize, this paper makes the following two contributions:

- It proposes a comprehensive set of features that characterize the benign nature of a given domain. Our features complete current DNS reputation systems that use artifacts describing only malicious access to a given domain.
- It uses machine learning in order to build an automated, positive DNS reputation system that actively processes domain blacklists and eliminates false positives, with no need for human intervention.

Experimental results prove the ability of Mentor to efficiently identify and discard benign domain names from within domain blacklists, while also satisfying a very low false positives rate. This paper is structured as follows. Section 2 describes related work. Section 3 presents the architecture and workflow of Mentor. Section 4 provides experiments that we used in order to evaluate our system. Section 5 discusses the limitations of our system and finally section 6 concludes.

2   Related Work

DNS is a core service that is widely used to locate content on the internet through association of domain names such as 'www.domainname.com' with routable IP addresses [15]. IP addresses are grouped within autonomous systems (AS) and so they are tightly coupled to a geographical location. On the other hand, domain names are grouped within administrative domains that can be associated with any IP address, regardless of the geographical position of the corresponding resource [17]. DNS is thus widely used by threat actors on the internet to associate IP addresses with domain names that are further used by infected nodes to locate their command servers [19].

Detection and extraction of domain callbacks first consisted of dynamically executing malware and observing its network activity [11,16,12]. After infecting a terminal, malware connects to a command and control server in order to get updates or retrieve commands. By observing network activity of malware in a dynamic analysis environment, we may pinpoint its main C&C channels and add these to domain blacklists. Hence, malware has been constantly developing new techniques to avoid being correctly analyzed, including the use of domain generation algorithms (DGA) [3] and detecting execution inside virtual analysis environments [4]. Although several techniques have been proposed in the literature to thwart malware obfuscation mechanisms [22,21], C&C domains discovered using these techniques are limited only to known malware samples that were correctly executed in sandbox environments. Yet they cannot identify C&C domains for unknown botnets and for malware that can efficiently avert detection during dynamic analysis.

Another trend of research consists of passively observing network activity and using machine learning to detect botnet C&C traffic [2,6,5,13]. While certain techniques such as [5] and [13] observe only netflow data, others are mainly focused on DNS traffic and use negative reputation to detect malicious C&C domains [2,6]. For example, authors in [2] build a dynamic DNS reputation system that uses both network and zone features of a domain. They make the assumption that the malicious use of DNS has unique characteristics and can be separated from benign, professionally provisioned DNS services. Therefore, they passively observe DNS queries and build models of known benign and malicious domains. These models are used to compute a reputation score for a newly observed domain, and which indicates whether this domain is indeed malicious or benign. The main drawback for this approach is that it needs a long enough history for a given domain name in order to assign a correct reputation score. It is inaccurate against frequently changing C&C domains, such as for hybrid botnet topologies that use multiple master C&C nodes to distribute commands.

Authors in [6] propose an alternative approach that applies machine learning to a set of 15 DNS features in order to identify malicious C&C domains. This approach builds a learning set of known benign and malicious domain names that it uses in order to train a DNS classifier. This classifier passively monitors real-time DNS traffic and identifies malware domains that do not appear in existing blacklists. Features in [6] are grouped into four categories, including time-based features, response features, TTL features and syntactical domain name features. Those features characterize anomalies in the way a given domain name is being requested, including abrupt changes in DNS queries towards this domain.

The system that we propose in this paper does not replace negative DNS reputation presented in [2] and [6]. Indeed, Mentor completes negative DNS reputation and it mainly searches for evidence about the benign nature of a domain, as opposed to [2] and [6] that search for evidence about the malicious nature of the same domain. In fact this paper proposes a positive DNS reputation system that processes blacklists of suspicious domains in order to remove false positives and keep only true malicious domains for botnet detection.

3   System Description

The Mentor system includes a training phase where it builds a detection model using a training set of known malicious and benign domains. It further applies this model during detection to unqualified C&C blacklists in order to remove benign false positives and keep only confirmed malicious domains for detection. As in figure 1, the training phase implements a crawler system that builds a

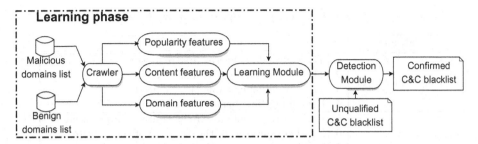

Fig. 1. Architecture and workflow of MENTOR

comprehensive set of features using the initial ground truth dataset. Features extracted by the crawler are further used as input to a supervised learning system. It implements machine learning techniques in order to build a classifier model that is further used during detection. This section provides the details of our features and describes the process that we use to build our detection model.

3.1 Features Selection

As opposed to negative DNS reputation, our system finds evidence about the innocuous nature of a given domain. To determine the features that are indicative of a benign domain, we observed and studied the domain and content features of multiple known benign and malicious C&C domains, and that we obtained using our approach further presented in section 4.1. Following our analysis, we identified several distinctive features that we classify into three main categories, including popularity, content and domain-based features, as shown in figure 1. This section describes our set of features that we summarize in table 1, and explains our view about why they are indicative of benign domains.

Domain Features. Describe empirical time-based observations about a domain name extracted from the public *whois* database. We consider that benign professional domain names are usually not changed and they are expected to remain accessible during the lifetime of their associated business. However, C&C domains are less static in nature. In order to enhance their resilience against detection and takedown, botnet herders frequently modify their callback domains using techniques such as DGA and domain flux. In fact, using the same C&C domain name during an extended period of time adds single nodes of failure in the botnet architecture. Therefore, botnet herders usually register short-lived domain names, along with short TTL values in order to frequently switch for other C&C domains, adding another level of complexity for botnet takedown. Hence, static registration information for professional domains show time-to-live values that are usually longer than other malicious C&C domains. Mentor accounts on this observation in order to introduce 4 domain features. They characterize such time-based differences between professional benign and malicious C&C domains. They include the elapsed time since the domain was first *registered*, the elapsed

Table 1. Features set implemented by Mentor

Category	Id	Feature description
Domain features	1	Time since domain was first registered
	2	Time since domain was first created
	3	Time since domain was last changed
	4	Remaining time before domain expires
Content features	5	Ratio of text content w.r.t overall website content
	6	Number of entries in the site map of the website
	7	Number of entries in the robot file of a website
	8	Number of HTML descriptors metadata
	9	Number of HTML keywords metadata
	10	Number of HTML descriptors in the website title
	11	Number of displayable images hosted by the website
	12	Number of CSS style sheets for a website
Popularity features	13	Number of outbound links towards social networks
	14	Total number of outbound links
	15	Google page rank of the domain
	16	Number of inbound links from social networks

time since the domain was first *created*, the elapsed time since the domain was last *changed*, and the remaining time before the domain *expires*.

Content Features. Characterize differences in the structure and content of websites for both benign and malicious C&C domains. Benign professional domains usually seek higher rankings by the internet search engines such as *Google*, *Yahoo!* and *Bing*. They share rich HTML content, add metadata descriptors, and optimize the structure of their websites, which are all important elements that are used for domain indexing on the internet. On the other hand, C&C domains are used by malware to establish automated control paths between attackers and their remote infected bots. They are usually supplied by the attacker either statically using callback domains that are hard-encoded in malware payloads, or dynamically using domain flux techniques. Hence, malicious C&C domains do not seek good internet rankings. They usually share less human readable content and less metadata descriptors. Mentor capitalizes on these observations by introducing content features that separate benign and malicious C&C domains.

Mentor describes the content of a website using a set of 8 features, all being related to qualitative metrics used for domain indexing on the internet. We consider a domain to be aimed for benign usage when its content is likely to provide a higher indexing by internet search engines. Hence, the first feature provides the website text ratio. It characterizes the amount of human readable content hosted by a domain. It is evaluated as the ratio of textual content with respect to the overall content of a website. The second and third features respectively provide the size of the site map and robot files associated with a website. They are evaluated as the number of entries in these files, and they characterize the structure of this website as seen by robots on the internet. These files determine how a website is displayed by search engines, which is an important property of professional benign domains. The fourth and fifth features provide the number of HTML descriptors and keywords metadata, and that determine the character strings that are most relevant for content indexing on this website. They describe the main area of interest which is being addressed by the website content. For example, a website that is aimed for health insurance would define keywords mostly related with the healthcare system. The sixth feature determines the number of HTML meta descriptors that are also represented in the website title. It provides an indication of whether the website title is randomly generated or if it was defined in compliance with the website content. Last of all, the seventh and eighth features respectively indicate the number of displayable images and css style sheets. They characterize the human friendly aspect and the way content is displayed by a website.

We admit that our features do not provide an exhaustive description of a website content. Nonetheless, they still provide enough evidence about the structure and content of a website. More importantly, they determine whether a website content is rather user friendly and eases human interaction, or if it is more likely to be addressed towards automated robots.

Popularity Features. Describe a domain's popularity, including inbound and outbound links which characterize the user-friendly aspect of a website. As opposed to benign professional domains, malicious C&C domains are mostly aimed at sharing commands with remote infected terminals. They have characteristics that are different from other professional domains which are aimed at sharing content with benign users. For example, professional domains share human-readable content that can be appreciated or commented on social networks. Hence, they can be referenced by, yet they include outbound links towards social networks such as linkedin, twitter and facebook. Besides, the overall internet popularity also provides indicators about the professional or malicious nature of a domain. In fact, professional domains may share business partnerships, sponsors or media articles, which are described with inbound and outbound links towards external domains, and which also increases a domain's popularity. Therefore, we characterize the popularity of a domain using 4 elementary features. They include the number of outbound links towards social networks, the total number of outbound links, the google pagerank as an indicator of the domain's popularity as well as its total inbound links, and the number of inbound links from social networks that we obtain using the moonsy[1] application.

3.2 Detection Model

The use of machine learning for botnet detection constitutes a real challenge as it implements statistical features that can be often bypassed by botnet herders. In fact, modern botnets implement obfuscation mechanisms that make difficult to differentiate benign and malicious C&C activity using only network features.

---

[1] http://www.moonsy.com

Hence, this paper offers a new set of features that leverages artifacts such as popularity, content descriptors, and timeline of a given domain. Indeed it is difficult for an attacker to setup malicious C&C domains that can bypass our features. Attackers need a longer time and effort to build a large enough set of popular domains including rich enough content descriptors in order to avoid detection, while also providing multiple redundant domains for botnet command and control.

In order to build our domain classification system, we tested multiple supervised learning algorithms, including selective bayesian classifiers [14], SVM, J48 and C4.5 decision trees [8,18]. First of all, decision trees offer a way to express structures in data. They provide a classic way to represent information from a machine learning algorithm. Besides, SVM provides an extension to nonlinear models that is based on the statistical learning theory. On the other hand, Bayes models provide a probabilistic classifier based on the Bayes Theorem. In the context of this paper, we evaluated the detection rates, including false positives and negatives, that we obtained by applying each of these learning algorithms, through application to our labeled ground truth dataset. We obtained a higher accuracy using the Bayesian classifier, and therefore we use this algorithm to build our domain classification model.

4   Experiments

This section provides the details of our experiments, including the dataset that we used in order to build and evaluate our system. First, we build a ground truth dataset of malicious and benign domain names that we process, using our crawler system, in order to train our classifier model. Then we evaluate the contribution of our features towards detection, and we adopt a cross-validation process in order to evaluate the accuracy of our system. Last of all, we tested Mentor against real public botnet C&C blacklists in order to evaluate the performance of our system for different malware families, as well as its ability to characterize unknown domain names by the time of building our system.

4.1   Ground Truth Dataset

Mentor applies machine learning to a training set of malicious and benign domain names in order to build a classifier model. The quality of our classifier strongly depends on the coverage of the initial training set and the accuracy of the ground truth labels associated with this training set. In fact Mentor actively connects to the domain names in the training set and builds detection features on the fly before these can be used as input to the training model. Hence, we need a valid blacklist of botnet C&C domains that are all active by the time of building our model. Yet we want to ensure that our blacklist only includes malicious domains and is clear of misclassified benign domain names.

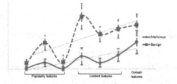

(a) Mentor detection features

Dataset	Training	Evaluation	TP	FP
Benign	400	100	99.02%	0.98%
Malicious	745	185	95.32%	4.68%
Overall	1145	285	97.17%	2.83%

(b) Cross-validation results

Fig. 2. Evaluation of Mentor against the ground truth dataset

Malicious Training Set. In order to build our ground truth malicious dataset, we applied a voting system including Google safe browsing and two publically accessible blacklists: 'malwaredomains.com' and 'malwaredomainlist.com'. We consider that a given domain is more likely to be malicious when it belongs to more than a single blacklist. We obtained a resulting list of 1.849 malicious domains that were matching both blacklists and that were accessible by the time of building our model. Then we discarded domain names in this blacklist that were identified as safe by the Google safe browsing API. This API identified 919 domains out of the initial 1.849 domains as being safe. We thus keep the remaining 930 confirmed malicious domains as input to our classifier model. In fact we applied a conservative filter in order to ensure that our malicious training set does not include safe domains before we build our detection model. Sure we cannot rule out the possibility of few domains being misclassified in our initial training set. However, these would be limited when compared to the confirmed malicious C&C domains and so they would have little impact on our classifier. We further evaluate in this section the accuracy of our classifier, including false positives, by testing against a wide set of malicious and benign domain names.

Benign Training Set. We build our training set of benign domain names using the top domains list in Alexa [1]. The Alexa web site provides the list of most popular domains on the internet. Yet we cannot be sure that all top domains on the list provided by Alexa are indeed benign domains since malicious domains may shortly appear in this list. Therefore, we cross-correlated the Alexa top domains list during a period of one week in order to discard as many suspect domains as possible prior to building our classifier model. In fact we consider that malicious domains may indeed appear in the top domains list, but these would be rapidly detected and so they will be soon removed from this list. According to Alexa, traffic ranks are updated on the website daily, therefore we daily extracted the top domains list from the alexa website during one week of observation. Then we kept only the top 500 domains that were constantly present on this list during the 7 days of observation. Although we cannot formally validate our list of benign domains, we believe that they have a strong evidence of being benign professional domain names since they constantly remained popular on the internet during one week. Our ground truth dataset thus included a list of 930 confirmed malicious and 500 confirmed benign domains that we used to train our classifier.

4.2   Domain Classification Model

We process the training set of malicious and benign domains, using the crawler module, in order to build detection features for our classifier. The crawler took 56 minutes to process the entire list of 1.430 domain names, using a desktop machine with dual core processor and 2Gb of memory. Figure 2a illustrates the distribution of our training set, including benign and malicious domains, against different categories of features provided by our system.

As in figure 2a, content features provide the best detection accuracy with a clear separation of malicious and benign domains. Benign domains in our training set clearly contain rich content, including domain descriptors and metadata that do not exist in malicious domains. For example, most of our malicious C&C domains do not include human friendly HTTP tags such as keywords and rich content descriptors that indeed exist in most benign domains in our training set.

Domain features, including information collected from the *whois* database, provide lower detection accuracy compared to content features. As shown in figure 2a, most of our malicious C&C domains still have lower TTL values than benign domains. However, TTL values for malicious C&C domains have a large standard deviation, which leads to overlap between our set of malicious and benign domains, thus reducing the overall detection accuracy of those features.

Last of all, popularity features also provide an overall good detection accuracy, and so they clearly separate malicious and benign domains. According to our learning set, C&C domains have much less incoming and outgoing links compared to other benign domains. On the other hand, and as shown in figure 2a, features describing the popularity on social networks provide a lower separation between malicious and benign domains in our training set. Hence, they would have a lower detection accuracy compared to other detection features.

In the remaining of this section, we build our classifier system using the detection features described in table 1, and we evaluate the accuracy of our model, including the true hit rate and false positives rate.

Cross-Validation. We first evaluate the Mentor detection system by cross-validating our classifier model against the ground truth dataset at our disposal. We performed multiple experiments, each time randomly splitting our dataset into 80% of data that we used for training, and 20% that we used for evaluation. Then we used our training set as input to the selective Bayesian learning model in order to build our classifier. We further tested this classifier against the remaining evaluation set in order to evaluate the accuracy of our system.

The table of figure 2b summarizes the results of our cross-validation process. Mentor correctly classifies 99.02% of benign domains, with almost 0.98% misclassification rate regarding benign domains. On the other hand, it correctly classifies 95.32% of malicious domains, with an overall classification accuracy of 97.17%. Mentor has a higher accuracy when classifying benign domain names, including a higher hit rate and a lower false positives rate. In fact the features set that we use to build our classifier module characterizes the benign nature of a given domain. It searches for evidence that a given domain is being established

Table 2. Testing Mentor against public blacklists

Blacklist	Date	Nb of entries	Malicious	Benign
Zeus tracker	20-01-2014	90	94.5%	5.5%
Palevo tracker	21-01-2014	26	92.4%	7.6%
SpyEye tracker	21-01-2014	125	96%	4%
Feodo tracker	21-01-2014	25	100%	0%
malwaredomains	20-01-2014	400	97.75%	2.25%

for a professional, human friendly usage. Therefore, most domains in Alexa top domains list are clearly established for professional usage and so they were correctly classified by our system. On the other hand, although it achieved a very good detection accuracy, our system had a *relatively* higher false positives rate against malicious domains. We manually checked malicious domains that were misclassified by our system. Most of these domains are vulnerable benign domains that were exploited by an attacker and used for command and control. These domains were considered by our system as benign as they were first established for professional usage, before they have been hijacked by an attacker. We discuss in section 5 the limitation of our system against such benign domains as they are both used for benign and malicious purposes.

Real-World Evaluation. In order to evaluate the performance of our system, we made real world experiments using public C&C blacklists that we extracted from the *abuse.ch* website[2], including *Zeus*, *SpyEye*, *Palevo* and *Feodo* malware blacklists. We also evaluated the ability of Mentor to detect C&C domains that were unknown by the time of building our system through testing against a more recent blacklist from *malwaredomains.com*. In fact we aim at validating through these experiments the ability of Mentor to correctly skim-off benign domains, and evaluate the consistency of our results for different blacklist categories.

Table 2 summarizes the main results of our experiments, including malicious and benign domains as identified by Mentor. The results in table 2 only include domain names that were accessible by the time of building our experiments. The Feodo blacklist included only 25 accessible domain names, all being identified as malicious C&C domains by our system. Because of the small number of domains in this blacklist, we manually checked each domain, and then we verified these domains using the google safe browsing API. All domains in this blacklist are indeed malicious C&C domains, and therefore Mentor achieves a 0% false positives rate for this blacklist.

On the other hand, Mentor achieved 97.75% true positives rate for the malwaredomains blacklist extracted on the 20th of January 2014. We believe this high matching rate is mainly because we trained the Mentor domain classifier using a similar older version of this blacklist. Indeed Mentor identified 9 benign domains in this blacklist. Yet 7 domains were previously infected websites that

---

[2] http://www.abuse.ch

are currently for rent or back under construction, and so we wouldn't consider them to be misclassified by our system. The remaining two accessible domains include *ankursociety.org* and *keymasconsultancy.co.uk.* We manually checked these two domains, and we scanned them using the Google safe browsing API. The *ankursociety.org* website was identified by the Google robot as previously distributing malicious content. The diagnostic provided by the Google safe browsing API indicates that *no malicious content on this website was detected during the last check.* The other domain was identified as suspicious by Google safe browsing, but it also indicates that no malicious content was recently identified on this website. The manual check of this domain reveals no malicious content, and it looks as a benign professional website for a UK-based company. These are clearly previously infected domains that are still present in the blacklist, and so we would consider them as true positives triggered by Mentor. Hence, Mentor has successfully skimmed-off two benign domains from the malwaredomains list, with no false positives.

As shown in table 2, our system achieved similar detection rates for the 3 remaining C&C blacklists, including *Zeus, Palevo* and *SpyEye.* Mentor detected 12 benign domains out of 241 suspicious domains in these blacklists. Hence, 95.1% of domain names in these blacklists were correctly identified as malicious C&C domains by our system. We checked the remaining 12 domains detected as benign by our system using Google safe browsing, and we manually observed their content for evidence about the malicious or benign nature of these domains. Indeed 6 domains were clearly identified as benign domains by the Google API. The manual analysis of these domains shows two blogsites and 4 professional domains, and so we would consider these as true positives. Four other domains seem to be hosting benign professional content. The Google robot previously detected suspicious content on these domains, but they were all currently identified as benign and so these are also true positives. On the other hand, the two remaining domains (*biozov.ru* and *psgtech72.com*) are clearly malicious domains and these were misclassified by our system. Therefore, Mentor achieved 0.8% false positives rate and skimed-off 10 benign domains during this experiment.

5   Discussion

Our system identifies and eliminates benign domains using content-based features and the popularity of a given domain name. It efficiently detects C&C domains when they are specifically built and established for this purpose. Nonetheless, as shown in our real world experiments described in section 4, Mentor is less efficient when detecting benign domain names that were hijacked and diverted by an attacker. Such compromised domains would be considered by Mentor as benign as long as their popularity and content are not hampered by the attacker. Note that the use of these domains for command and control is risky as they constitute single nodes of failure in the botnet architecture. In fact, administrators of these domains would rapidly take actions, as soon as they detect suspicious usage of their websites, in order to prevent them from being used for malicious purposes. Yet multiple domains were identified as such by our system during our experiments in section 4. Hence, modern botnets increasingly adopt hybrid topologies including master bots that act as C&C servers and distribute commands towards slave bots. Such botnets are more robust as they include a larger set of master C&C nodes. However, they are efficiently detected by Mentor because master servers only act as C&C domains for other slave nodes, and so they would have different characteristics than other professional benign domains.

Mentor applies machine learning techniques to a statistical set of features in order to identify malicious domains. It would be unable to correctly classify C&C domains that share similar features with other benign domains such as high popularity, rich web content and long-lived domain names. These maneuvers would modify the statistical consistency of a malicious domain and so it would be identified as benign by our system. The use of these techniques by an attacker would require to carefully build C&C domains. It would also take a longer time for these domains to increase their popularity so they can no longer be detected by our system. Although being technically possible, these techniques cannot be easily automated. It would be difficult for an attacker to maintain a large enough set of C&C domains to ensure a better botnet resilience while also keeping its C&C domains under the detection radar of our system. Therefore, Mentor adds a new level of complexity for botnet herders in their struggle to keep their C&C domains undetected.

6   Conclusion

This paper presented a new system called Mentor, which implements positive DNS reputation to identify benign domains within a list of malicious C&C domain names. Positive DNS reputation measures the likelihood of a given domain name being innocuous, as opposed to negative DNS reputation that rather observes malicious artifacts for the same domain. Mentor describes a given domain name using three sets of features, including *popularity*, *content* and *domain-based* features. It implements an active crawler system that collects artifacts and content features from the remote domain itself and the public whois database. It groups all features for a given domain within a single vector and further applies machine learning techniques in order to separate benign and malicious domains. Mentor completes current negative DNS reputation systems; it processes domain blacklists generated by these systems and reduces their high false positives rate. Experimental results prove the ability of Mentor to efficiently identify and eliminate benign domains within blacklists of malicious C&C domain names, with a very low false positives rate.

References

1. Alexa web information company (2013), http://www.alexa.com/topsites/
2. Antonakakis, M., Perdisci, R., Dagon, D., Lee, W., Feamster, N.: Building a dynamic reputation system for dns. In: Usenix Security Symposium (2010)

3. Antonakakis, M., Perdisci, R., Nadji, Y., Vasiloglou, N., Abu-Nimeh, S., Lee, W., Dagon, D.: From throw-away traffic to bots: Detecting the rise of dga-based malware. In: USENIX Security Symposium (2012)
4. Balzarotti, D., Cova, M., Karlberger, C., Kruegel, C., Kirda, E., Vigna, G.: Efficient detection of split personalities in malware. In: International Symposium on Network and Distributed System Security, NDSS (2010)
5. Bilge, L., Balzarotti, D., Robertson, W., Kirda, E., Kruegel, C.: Disclosure: detecting botnet command and control servers through large-scale netflow analysis. In: Int. Annual Computer Security Applications Conference, ACSAC (2012)
6. Bilge, L., Kirda, E., Kruegel, C., Balduzzi, M.: Exposure: Finding malicious domains using passive dns analysis. In: Symposium on Network and Distributed System Security (2011)
7. Choi, H., Lee, H., Lee, H., Kim, H.: Botnet detection by monitoring group activities in dns traffic. In: Seventh International Conference on Computer and Information Technology (2007)
8. Cristianini, N., Shawe-Taylor, J.: An introduction to support vector machines and other kernel-based learning methods. Cambridge University Press (2000)
9. Felegyhazi, M., Kreibich, C., Paxson, V.: On the potential of proactive domain blacklisting. In: Third USENIX LEET Workshop (2010)
10. Holz, T., Gorecki, C., Rieck, K., Freiling, F.C.: Measuring and detecting fast-flux service networks. In: Symp. on Network and Distributed System Security (2008)
11. Jacob, G., Hund, R., Kruegel, C., Holz, T.: Jackstraws: Picking command and control connections from bot traffic. In: USENIX Security Symposium (2011)
12. Kheir, N., Han, X.: Peerviewer: Behavioral tracking and classification of P2P malware. In: Wang, G., Ray, I., Feng, D., Rajarajan, M. (eds.) CSS 2013. LNCS, vol. 8300, pp. 282–298. Springer, Heidelberg (2013)
13. Kheir, N., Wolley, C.: BotSuer: Suing stealthy P2P bots in network traffic through netflow analysis. In: Abdalla, M., Nita-Rotaru, C., Dahab, R. (eds.) CANS 2013. LNCS, vol. 8257, pp. 162–178. Springer, Heidelberg (2013)
14. Langley, P., Sage, S.: Induction of selective bayesian classifiers. In: 10th International Conference on Uncertainty in Artificial Intelligence, pp. 399–406 (1994)
15. Mockapetris, P.: Dns encoding of network names and other types. RFC 1101 (April 1989)
16. Moser, A., Kruegel, C., Kirda, E.: Exploring multiple execution paths for malware analysis. In: International Symposium on Security and Privacy (2007)
17. Postel, J.: Domain name system structure and delegation. In: RFC 1591 (1994)
18. Quinlan, J.R.: C4.5: Programs for machine learning. Morgan Kaufmann Publishers (1993)
19. Rajab, M.A., Zarfoss, J., Monrose, F., Terzis, A.: A multifaceted approach to understanding the botnet phenomenon. In: 6th ACM SIGCOMM Conference on Internet Measurement (2006)
20. Sinha, S., Bailey, M., Jahanian, F.: Shades of grey: On the effectiveness of reputation-based "blacklists". In: International Conference on Malicious and Unwared Software, Malware (2008)
21. Wurzinger, P., Bilge, L., Holz, T., Goebel, J., Kruegel, C., Kirda, E.: Automatically generating models for botnet detection. In: Backes, M., Ning, P. (eds.) ESORICS 2009. LNCS, vol. 5789, pp. 232–249. Springer, Heidelberg (2009)
22. Yadav, S., Reddy, A.K., Reddy, A.N., Ranjan, S.: Detecting algorithmically generated malicious domain names. In: 10th ACM SIGCOMM Conference on Internet Measurement (2010)

Game Theory Meets Information Security Management

Andrew Fielder[1], Emmanouil Panaousis[2], Pasquale Malacaria[2],
Chris Hankin[1], and Fabrizio Smeraldi[2]

[1] Imperial College London
{andrew.fielder,c.hankin}@imperial.ac.uk
[2] Queen Mary University of London
{e.panaousis,p.malacaria,f.smeraldi}@qmul.ac.uk

Abstract. This work addresses the challenge "how do we make better security decisions?" and it develops techniques to support human decision making and algorithms which enable well-founded cyber security decisions to be made. In this paper we propose a game theoretic model which optimally allocates cyber security resources such as administrators' time across different tasks. We first model the interactions between an omnipresent *attacker* and a team of system administrators seen as the *defender*, and we have derived the *mixed Nash Equilibria* (NE) in such games. We have formulated general-sum games that represent our cyber security environment, and we have proven that the defender's *Nash strategy* is also *minimax*. This result guarantees that independently from the attacker's strategy the defender's solution is optimal. We also propose *Singular Value Decomposition* (SVD) as an efficient technique to compute approximate equilibria in our games. By implementing and evaluating a *minimax solver with SVD*, we have thoroughly investigated the improvement that Nash defense introduces compared to other strategies chosen by common sense decision algorithms. Our key finding is that a particular NE, which we call *weighted NE*, provides the most effective defense strategy. In order to validate this model we have used real-life statistics from Hackmageddon, the Verizon 2013 Data Breach Investigation report, and the Ponemon report of 2011. We finally compare the game theoretic defense method with a method which implements a *stochastic optimization algorithm*.

Keywords: Information security management, game theory, cyber security.

1 Introduction

Due to the growth of cyber attacks against government agencies and companies, there is a need for more investment to protect networks and platforms which allow the exchange and the storage of important information. Large organizations are more likely to employ a security manager whose main task is to lead *Information Security Management* to mitigate cyber security risks. However many companies do not have dedicated cyber security personnel, but the critical tasks required to

N. Cuppens-Boulahia et al. (Eds.): SEC 2014, IFIP AICT 428, pp. 15–29, 2014.
© IFIP International Federation for Information Processing 2014

mitigate these risks must still be performed. In the latter case these tasks need to be carried out by the system administrators who must allocate part of their time for this. This is determined by other crucial non-security tasks. Since time is a scarce resource for system administrators, the available time to perform cyber security tasks should be ideally optimized. Hence there is a need for a method that gets as an input a time allowance and identifies how much time should be spent on tasks related to the defense of different parts of the infrastructure. The importance of this challenge has also been highlighted by Alpcan and Başar [4] (p. 9). This is a critical challenge given the fact that an attacker usually aims at exploiting one vulnerability of the system whilst the defending party must protect as many cyber security *targets* as possible. System administrators seek to maximize the mitigation of the greatest number of attacks against the various assets while an attacker aims to maximize the probability of penetrating the different "security layers" and complete their attack against a preferable target. This problem falls under the entire class of problems ISO 27001 examines with regards to balancing expenditure to the information security risk.

In this paper, we consider the *global asset* as the collection of all the data assets of an organization. We additionally consider a *target* to be a piece of hardware that has access to a subset of this asset. In our model the process of allocating resources is to improve the performance of the defense of a system. Our model defines the defense in terms of *all the actions that can be performed to improve the defense of a given target*. We assume that each target can be attacked by the exploitation of a vulnerability. The adversary follows a unique path to penetrate into the organization's system and compromise a target. Examples of targets, vulnerabilities, as described by our model, and threats against these targets, can be found in 2013 Data Breach Investigation report [1] published by Verizon. By modeling a cyber security scenario in the form of targets that attacks can be performed against and the set of all actions that can protect that target, we are able to create a more compact and computationally feasible model removing the interdependencies between actions. According to our model, the attacker *probabilistically* chooses a target and plays with probability 1 all the actions required to attack this target. Their decision is based on the different profits they will obtain when they attack this target successfully and the baseline defense applied to each of the attack paths towards the targets. However, we assume that the attacker is not aware of the resource allocation strategy chosen by the defender nor conducts surveillance to identify such strategy.

The research question that this paper attempts to address is *"given that different targets have different weights how do we optimally allocate cyber security resources to defend such targets?"*. The defense of a target is indicated by two security levels, *baseline* and *best practice*. The baseline shows the probability of an attack against a target being mitigated, to guarantee that the basic security functionality of the systems is maintained, when no additional administrators time has been allocated. The *best practice* defense denotes the percentage of attacks that are mitigated assuming that the system is currently running the most up-to-date security software as well as having had all patches applied and any potentially exploitable data removed. These tasks could be carried out by allocating additional system administrators' time. An example of baseline defense and resource allocation towards the provision of extra security is the following. We can assume that an unmonitored *spam filter* stops a certain percentage of junk e-mail, for example 60% which corresponds to the baseline defense. By having an administrator monitoring and upgrading the spam filters, more attacks can be prevented, and for instance 90% of the spam is mitigated. Thus under any resource allocation strategy, in terms of man hours, where an administrator is assigned to perform a spam filter based action, we have an improvement of 50% in stopping junk emails over the baseline defense.

In this paper we use game theory to model the cyber security environment and challenge of resource allocation as described above. Any resource allocation problem must consider the strategies available to the adversary and the cyber security team of the organization thus making game theory an appropriate tool to model such an environment and provide an effective set of solutions. According to [4] (p. 40), *"A game-theoretic framework for defensive decision-making has a distinct advantage over optimization as it explicitly captures the effects of the attacker behavior in the model, in addition to those of the defensive actions. Plain optimization formulations, on the other hand, focus only on the optimization of defensive resources without taking attackers into account."*

The remainder of this paper is organized as follows. Section 2 discusses related work from the state-of-the-art on the intersection of game theory and security. In Section 3, we propose our game theoretic model while in Section 4 we undertake comparisons against alternative methods. Finally, Section 5 concludes this paper by summarizing its main contributions and highlighting future work to be undertaken to further improve the performance and the usability of our model.

2   Related Work

A significant amount of work on the intersection of economics and information security has been published by Grossklags. The authors in [3] discuss the factors that influence the decision process of individuals regarding their information security concerns. They contribute to the formulation of information policies and technologies regarding personal information security and privacy. The work published in [7] examines the weakest target game which refers to the case where an attacker is always able to compromise the system target with the lowest level of defense and not to cause any damage to the rest of the targets. The game theoretic analysis the authors have undertaken shows that the game leads to a conflict between pure economic interests and common social norms. While the former are concerned with the minimization of cost for security investments, the latter imply that higher security levels are preferable. A very thorough work has been published in [5] where the authors model security interactions by choosing different games such as weakest-link or best-shot to represent practical security scenarios. In these games, decision parameters are a protection level determining the security level chosen for the player's resources and a self-insurance level which mitigates damages when a successful attack occurs.

Security problems have been increasingly studied by using Stackelberg games to model the strategic interaction between a defender and an attacker. Some physical security games such as [10] assume the existence of targets that might be covered or uncovered during an attack. In [10], Kiekintveld et al. make the assumption that it is always preferable for the defender to defend as many targets as possible to obfuscate vulnerabilities over a period of time. The resulting players' payoffs depend only on the attacked target and whether this is covered by the defender or not. An important contribution is the work conducted by Korzhyk et al. in [11], showing how a *leader* (defender) should derive their strategy given that the security game could be either a Nash or a Stackelberg game. They also examine the case of a *follower* (attacker) who can attack more than one target. The authors show that Nash and Stackelberg strategies are the same in the majority of cases only when the follower attacks just one target.

Another recent contribution within the field of physical security has been published in [9], where the authors address the problem of finding an optimal defensive coverage. Because of the uncertainty about the attacker's payoffs they define such coverage as the one maximizing the worst-case payoff over the targets in the potential attack set. In a cyber security game we can consider that a defender may not know the payoffs for an attacker and they may be able to infer some bounds for those payoffs. Work published by Lye and Wing [13] uses a non-zero sum stochastic game model where an adversary is attacking an enterprise network and a network security administrator is defending the different network assets (e.g. web server, file server, workstation). A thorough survey of research contributions within the broad field of security and privacy in computer networks modeled by game-theoretic approaches has been carried out in [14].

3   Game Theoretic Formulation

We define a cyber security game as a game-theoretic model that captures essential characteristics of resource allocation decision making (i.e. system administrators' time) to prevent data loss and defend system and network assets of an organization. This is a two-player, non-cooperative static game between a system security team, defender $\mathcal{D}$, which defends an organization's information assets and data against external or insider adversaries who are modeled as an omnipresent attacker $\mathcal{A}$. Our model follows the definitions of the work done by Korzhyk et al. in [11]. The attacker $\mathcal{A}$ might choose to attack any target from the available set of targets $T = t_1, t_2, \ldots, t_n$ whilst $\mathcal{D}$ aims to mitigate attacks by defending targets using resources. In our game the targets are data assets accessible by specific hardware components and system administrators are the limited resources. We consider a schedule as *a unique allocation of system administrators to perform tasks that will update the targets defense from baseline to best practice.* We define the set of available defense schedules as $\mathcal{S}$. The utility of $\mathcal{D}$ when t_i is attacked and has no resources assigned to it equals the *baseline* defense utility $U_{\mathcal{D}}^{bl}(t_i)$. On the other hand, if $\mathcal{D}$ has assigned some resource to defend t_i then their *best practice* defense utility equals $U_{\mathcal{D}}^{bp}(t_i)$. Finally, the utility in case where no attack has taken place equals zero.

Likewise for $\mathcal{A}$, we define their utility values as $U_{\mathcal{A}}^{bl}(t_i)$ and $U_{\mathcal{A}}^{bp}(t_i)$, respectively. Moreover, we denote the difference between best practice and baseline utilities of a target t_i for both players as $\Delta U_{\mathcal{D}}(t_i)$ and $\Delta U_{\mathcal{A}}(t_i)$. We observe that by applying a given resource to a target, the utility of $\mathcal{D}$ for this target increases and the utility of $\mathcal{A}$ decreases; namely $\Delta U_{\mathcal{D}}(t_i) > 0$ and $\Delta U_{\mathcal{A}}(t_i) < 0$. Similarly to the aforementioned example of a spam filter, let's assume that the baseline defense probability of a spam filter is 60% while the best practice defense probability equals 90%. If the damage caused to the organization due to a successful attack against this spam filter is given by $l = -100$ then the baseline utility value equals $U_{bl} = -40$ and the best practice equals $U_{bp} = -10$.

The normal form of this game is described as follows. $\mathcal{A}$'s pure strategy space is the set of targets, while their mixed strategy is denoted by $\mathbf{A} = \langle a_i \rangle$, where a_i represents the probability of attacking a target t_i. A schedule (or pure strategy) of $\mathcal{D}$ is a feasible unique assignment of resources to cover (i.e. provide best practice defense) the different targets. Assuming that one resource is adequate to provide best practice defense for a target, a pure strategy is represented by a tuple $\mathbf{s} = \langle s_i \rangle \in \{0,1\}^n$, where s_i equals 1 when t_i is defended by best practices; or 0 when only baseline defense is in place. Due to limited resources we define the feasible schedules by $\mathcal{S} \subseteq \{0,1\}^n$. The number of schedules available to m administrators in the case of n targets equals $\frac{n!}{(n-m)!m!}$. For example for a scenario with 4 targets, when the number of system administrators equals two then the available schedules are:

$$\mathcal{S} = \{< 1,1,0,0 >, < 1,0,1,0 >, < 1,0,0,1 >,$$

$$< 0,1,1,0 >, < 0,1,0,1 >, < 0,0,1,1 >\}$$

In this paper we assume homogeneous resources, namely each resource can apply best practice defense equally for each of the targets, allowing all the possible resource allocation schedules to be played. The mixed strategy $\mathbf{D} = \langle d_s \rangle$ of the defender is a probability distribution over the different schedules, where d_s is the probability of playing a schedule $s \in \mathcal{S}$. We define the *coverage* induced by the strategy $\mathbf{D}$ to be the vector $C = \langle c_i \rangle$, where the probability c_i of applying the best practice defense for a target i is given by $c_i = \sum_{s \in S} s_i d_s$. Going back to our previous example with 4 targets and 2 system administrators, assuming a mixed strategy $\mathbf{D} = \langle 0.3, 0.2, 0.15, 0.15, 0.1, 0.1 \rangle$ for the defender then the coverage vector equals $C = \langle 0.65, 0.55, 0.45, 0.35 \rangle$. Following [11], we define the utility functions of both players as follows.

Definition 1 (Utilities of the Cyber Security Game). *When a strategy profile $\langle \mathbf{D}, \mathbf{A} \rangle$ is played, the utility values of both players are given by the following:*

$$U_{\mathcal{D}}(\mathbf{D}, \mathbf{A}) = \sum_{i=1}^{n} E_{D,C}(t_i) = \sum_{i=1}^{n} a_i(c_i U_{\mathcal{D}}^{bp}(t_i) + (1 - c_i)U_{\mathcal{D}}^{bl}(t_i)) \qquad (1)$$

$$U_{\mathcal{A}}(\mathbf{D}, \mathbf{A}) = \sum_{i=1}^{n} E_{A,C}(t_i) = \sum_{i=1}^{n} a_i(c_i U_{\mathcal{A}}^{bp}(t_i) + (1 - c_i)U_{\mathcal{A}}^{bl}(t_i)) \qquad (2)$$

If both players act rationally the game theoretic solution, upon their simultaneous moves is the Nash Equilibrium (NE).

Definition 2 (NE of the Cyber Security Game). *A pair of mixed strategies* $\langle \mathbf{D}, \mathbf{A} \rangle$ *forms an NE if the following are satisfied:*

I. $\mathcal{D}$ plays a best-response that is $U_{\mathcal{D}}(\mathbf{D}, \mathbf{A}) \geq U_{\mathcal{D}}(\mathbf{D}', \mathbf{A}), \forall \ \mathbf{D}'$
II. $\mathcal{A}$ plays a best-response that is $U_{\mathcal{A}}(\mathbf{D}, \mathbf{A}) \geq U_{\mathcal{A}}(\mathbf{D}, \mathbf{A}'), \forall \ \mathbf{A}'$

In a game it is possible that there are many NE. However in presence of unknown attack distributions not all Nash defenses perform equally. Therefore we are interested in the particular NE that most favors the targets with the highest defender's utility. We define the *NE's weight* as:

$$\sum_{1 \leq i \leq n} (c_i U_{\mathcal{D}}^{bp}(t_i) + (1 - c_i) U_{\mathcal{D}}^{bl}(t_i)).$$

Definition 3. *The weighted NE has the maximal weight among all NE.*

In the case that there exists than one NE with maximal weight any of these equilibria can be chosen as the weighted NE. Notice the NE's weight differs from the defender's utility in that the attacker's strategy is ignored. In the remaining of this paper, unless otherwise stated, by NE we refer to the weighted NE.

3.1   Characterization of Nash Defense

In a real scenario attackers and defenders often have different preferences and criteria for evaluating the financial impact of a successful attack, as such it is unrealistic to expect that cyber security games are necessarily zero-sum. Thus, in our cyber security game, players typically weigh the same outcomes in different ways. In our model we have made the assumption that both players assess the different targets in a proportionally equivalent manner.

In the following we have proven that *the Nash defense is a minimax strategy for the defender which implies that it minimaximizes the attacker's utility in the cyber security game.* This follows the work reported in [11]. We represent the set of all defender's Nash strategies of a non-zero sum cyber security game G as S_{NE}^{G} and the set of all defender's minimax strategies as S_{MM}^{G}. We define a zero-sum cyber security game $\widehat{G}$ in which the baseline and best practice utilities of the attacker for each target are equivalent to their utilities in G, therefore:

$$\widehat{U}_{\mathcal{A}}^{bp}(t_i) = U_{\mathcal{A}}^{bp}(t_i), \forall t_i \in T, \text{ and } \widehat{U}_{\mathcal{A}}^{bl}(t_i) = U_{\mathcal{A}}^{bl}(t_i), \forall t_i \in T \qquad (3)$$

Since $\widehat{G}$ is a zero-sum game, we know that $\widehat{U}_{\mathcal{D}}^{bp}(t_i) = -\widehat{U}_{\mathcal{A}}^{bp}(t_i)$ and $\widehat{U}_{\mathcal{D}}^{bl}(t_i) = -\widehat{U}_{\mathcal{A}}^{bl}(t_i)$. We define a function μ which maps the attacking probabilities of each target in $\widehat{G}$ to the attacking probabilities in G as defined in [11]:

$$\mu(a_i) = \widehat{a}_i = \lambda a_i \frac{\Delta U_{\mathcal{D}}(t_i)}{\Delta U_{\mathcal{A}}(t_i)}, \forall t_i \in T \qquad (4)$$

where $\mu(a_i)$ is the probability of a target t_i to be attacked in $\widehat{G}$, therefore $\mu(A) = \widehat{A}$. Respectively the set of defender's Nash strategies in G is represented by S_{NE}^{G} and the set of defender's minimax strategies by S_{MM}^{G}.

Proposition 1. $\langle D^\star, A^\star \rangle$ *is NE profile in* G *iff* $\langle D^\star, \mu(A^\star) \rangle$ *is NE profile in* $\widehat{G}$.

Proof. To prove proposition 1, we have combined Lemmas 1 and 2 presented in appendix. We have that $A^\star$ and $\mu(A^\star)$ are the attacker's best responses, in G and $\widehat{G}$ respectively, to the same defender's best response $D^\star$. Therefore the tuple of strategies $\langle D^\star, A^\star \rangle$ is NE profile in G iff $\langle D^\star, \mu(A^\star) \rangle$ is NE profile in $\widehat{G}$. This implies that $D^\star$ is a Nash defense in G iff it is also a Nash defense in $\widehat{G}$.   □

Theorem 1. *A defender's Nash strategy in the non-zero sum cyber security game is also a defender's minimax strategy in the same game.*

Proof. The minimax theorem states that for zero sum games NE and minimax solution coincide. Thus $D^\star$ is a Nash defense in $\widehat{G}$ iff $D^\star$ is a minimax defender's strategy in $\widehat{G}$ namely $D^\star \in S_{MM}^{\widehat{G}}$. This means $D^\star$ minimaximizes the utility of the attacker in the zero-sum game where the defender's strategy is as in G:

$$D^\star = \mathrm{argmin}_D \max_{\widehat{A}} U_\mathcal{A}(D, \widehat{A}).$$

We also have that $U_\mathcal{A}(D, \widehat{A})$ equals:

$$\sum_{i=1}^{n} \widehat{a}_i (c_i U_\mathcal{A}^{bp}(t_i) + (1 - c_i) U_\mathcal{A}^{bl}(t_i)) = \sum_{i=1}^{n} \lambda a_i \frac{\Delta U_\mathcal{D}(t_i)}{\Delta U_\mathcal{A}(t_i)} (c_i U_\mathcal{A}^{bp}(t_i) + (1 - c_i) U_\mathcal{A}^{bl}(t_i))$$

From the above $U_\mathcal{A}(D, \widehat{A}) \leq U_\mathcal{A}(D, \widehat{A'}) \iff U_\mathcal{A}(D, A) \leq U_\mathcal{A}(D, A')$ because the left hand side of the $\iff$ is the right hand side multiplied by the constant(s) $\lambda \frac{\Delta U_\mathcal{D}(t_i)}{\Delta U_\mathcal{A}(t_i)}$. Hence minimum and maximum of the ordering are preserved, therefore a minimax in $\widehat{G}$ is also a minimax in G. Using proposition 1 we conclude that a defense strategy $D^\star$ is NE equilibrium in G and $\widehat{G}$ therefore it is a minimax in $\widehat{G}$ and, by the above argument, it is also a minimax in G.   □

This result guarantees that *independently from the attacker's strategy the defender's solution is optimal.*

3.2   Minimax Solver with Singular Value Decomposition

Given the high number of possible targets within an organization the game formulation is subject to the "state explosion problem" [6]. Therefore there is a need for a method which will compute Nash defenses for large number of targets. This must be computationally fast and provide reasonable precision in the calculation of the equilibrium. A possible approach is to look for an *abstraction* of the payoff matrices where only the most relevant features of such matrices are kept and minor features are discarded. We achieve this by using *Singular Value Decomposition* (SVD) to reduce the rank of the individual payoff matrices. To the best of our knowledge, there are no general results about game solutions for rank reduced payoff matrices. The closest work, undertaken by Kannan and Theobald [8], performs rank reduction of the matrix given by the sum of the payoff matrices of the two players.

Based on the Ponemon report 2013 [12], we have illustrated the payoff matrices in Table 1. We notice that these matrices have a *particular underlying structure* which is mostly captured in the very first singular values. In other words, there are few dominant singular values, usually two or three. By ignoring the singular values after the second or third largest, we obtain reasonably close solutions to the original game solutions and a dramatic speed up of the computation. As an example for a game with 8 targets, 1 security administrator, and payoff matrices illustrated in Table 3, the singular values are $\langle 792, 108, 91, 42, 22, 12, 10, 3 \rangle$. This means the first component already provides a reasonable approximation to the original matrix and the components after the third component can be treated as "noise". The speed-up in performance is mainly caused by the fact that the rank reduction, in our games, results in a large number of strategies becoming dominated. For example in a game with 120 strategies and rank 10, around 3/4 become dominated when the rank is reduced to 6. By comparing the equilibria found in a 10 targets, 2 system administrators game and its SVD rank 2 abstraction (Table 2), we found that there is a *performance improvement of more than 1000 times* while the approximate solution only slightly deviates from the precise solution.

4   Model Comparison

To evaluate our game theoretic model we want to compare the performance of the *Nash resource allocation method* (*Minimax solver with Singular Value Decomposition*) which is given by the NE of the cyber security game, against alternative methods. The methods we have selected for comparison are based on approximations to two common sense approaches that one might consider, called *Uniform* and *Weighted* as well as a stochastic optimization algorithm called *Acceptable Coverage*.

The *Uniform* defense distribution gives no preference to any target that a defender wants to defend meaning that all targets are given equal probability to be defended. This method is a naive approach that assumes no knowledge on the part of the defender to decide how much each target is valued or how likely a target is to be attacked.

The *Weighted* defense distribution creates a probability distribution based on the value of each target that is being defended. According to this approach, the time a defender allocates to protect a target is proportional to its importance. A distribution of time across schedules is calculated such that each target is covered and the sum of the probability for playing each of the particular sets of defenses equals the intended coverage for each target. For example if a target t_1 should be defended with probability 0.2, then all schedules that include a defense of t_1 should sum to 0.2. This results in more time being scheduled to perform tasks which improve the defense of the targets that are either more vulnerable or more valuable to the organization. While this does not necessarily represent the best possible cyber security decision, this method identifies at least an average decision maker, that provides a reasonable defense by which to measure the improvement that the Nash defense introduces.

Acceptable Coverage. We compare the minimax solution to *a stochastic optimization algorithm with uncertainty in the attacker's payoffs*. This approach is similar to the one published in [9] where the authors define a defensive coverage as the one maximizing the worst-case payoff over the targets in the potential attack set[1]. For a given target we have two intervals from which the attacker gets their utility based on the applied defense; baseline or best practice. These are represented as $[U_A^{\min,bl}, U_A^{\max,bl}]$ and $[U_A^{\min,bp}, U_A^{\max,bp}]$, respectively.

When uncertainty about the attacker's payoff is introduced, the concept of attack set gets more involved because we do not know what the maximum expected payoff for the attacker is. One is then led to define a potential attack set for a coverage as *the set of all targets that could give the attacker the maximum expected value*, for any attacker's payoffs that can be extracted from the intervals of the payoffs. Given a coverage C the attacker can be *guaranteed* a payoff of at least the maximum of the minimum values over all targets; $R(C) = \max_{t_i} E_{A,C}^{\min}(t_i)$ where $E_{A,C}^{\min}(t_i) = a_i(c_i U_A^{\min,bp}(t_i) + (1 - c_i)U_A^{\min,bl}(t_i))$. $R(C)$ defines the potential attack set associated to the coverage C as $A(C) = \{t_i | E_{A,C}^{\max}(t_i) \geq R(C)\}$.

Following these ideas we look for a defender's strategy giving the *best utilities guaranteed*. As such the defender will choose a strategy providing best coverage, where a coverage is better than another coverage if the former guarantees both a higher minimum expected utility for the defender and a lower maximum expected utility for the attacker compared to the latter. More formally we define the coverage ordering as follows:

$$C \geq C' \iff \min_i(E_{D,C}(t_i)) \geq \min_i(E_{D,C'}(t_i)) \wedge \max_j(E_{A,C}^{\min}(t_j)) \leq \max_j(E_{A,C'}^{\min}(t_j))$$

Given a set of coverages maximal with respect to the above ordering a coverage is *acceptable* if it is the maximal element, with respect to the defender's utility, of this set. If a coverage is acceptable then we have considered all attacker's payoffs that can be extracted from the payoffs intervals otherwise there would be a coverage above it, contradicting maximality.

Comparisons. We have undertaken simulations to identify how effective a Nash defense performs against distributions created by the *Uniform, Weighted* and *Acceptable Coverage* methods. For the purposes of testing we consider an organization like an online store whose assets include users payment details, website configurations and data related to operational procedures. The most valuable target would be a database server with the most of clients' details. This could be compromised by an SQL injection attack. The second most valuable target would be the store's website that an attacker could deface by modifying data of the web server the website is located at. The rest of the targets could consist of the mail server and different workstations. The device of each user, seen as a target, has a value related to the privileges that a user obtains. To undertake our comparisons, the values of utilities for each target have been taken from a report on data breaches [12], where the utility per target is given by mid-value for each

---

[1] In security games without uncertainty, the attack set is defined as the set of all targets that give the attacker the maximum expected payoff, given some coverage.

Table 1. Financial cost of an organization based on the findings of the Ponemon 2011 report [12]

target ID	t_1	t_2	t_3	t_4	t_5
cost ($)	10k	30k	50k	75k	150k
target ID	t_6	t_7	t_8	t_9	t_{10}
cost ($)	250k	350k	450k	750k	3m

Table 2. Times and defender utilities for a 10 targets 2 system administrators games using SVD

Rank	Time (s)	Value
10 (no SVD)	**204**	-615.744
8	60	-614.854
6	1.8	-617.732
4	0.4	-616.124
2	**0.1**	-616.651

Table 3. Probability of Attack per Target based on Statistics from Hackmageddon [2]

ID	t_1	t_2	t_3	t_4	t_5
8 t.	0.011	0.016	0.016	0.039	0.061
10 t.	0.005	0.005	0.011	0.016	0.016
ID	t_6	t_7	t_8	t_9	t_{10}
8 t.	0.127	0.332	0.398	-	-
10 t.	0.038	0.060	0.125	0.327	0.392

Table 4. Probability of Attack per Target based on Statistics from Verizon [1]

ID	t_1	t_2	t_3	t_4	t_5
8 t.	0.060	0.060	0.060	0.080	0.133
10 t.	0.021	0.021	0.021	0.021	0.063
ID	t_6	t_7	t_8	t_9	t_{10}
8 t.	0.222	0.222	0.244	-	-
10 t.	0.008	0.125	0.208	0.208	0.229

of the ranges of damage reported, and are presented in Table 1. We consider two different sizes of online stores in terms of reputation, number of clients and amount of data held. The larger store has 10 targets while the smaller one has 8. We assume that the organization is limited to the number of system administrators that they have available to them and cannot cover all the targets at one time. We test the defense of a system with up to 3 administrators. These choices seem reasonable for such organizations in our proof-of-concept comparisons.

The utilities for the attacker in this scenario are set at 20% of the value that the defender has for each given target. This is to represent that an attacker will still receive a large payoff for successfully attacking a target. However while the defender may have long term damage, the attacker's profit will generally be given by the immediate impact that their actions have. For the comparisons we have used 2 specific attack distributions given by the Hackmageddon [2] and Verizon data sets [1], where any of the attack distributions, shown in Tables 3 and 4, represents an unknown attacker that is attempting to breach a target.

While we have identified the range of damages that can be expected from a successful attack, the values themselves do not necessarily reflect a single attack, so we consider *varying the utilities both players perceive for each target*. By varying the utility of each target, we are capable of identifying if the Nash method performs better than either of the other methods independently of the cost of each target. We vary the utilities as presented in Table 1 by adjusting the values perceived by the defender, where the experimental bounds allow for a deviation of up to 10% from the stated utilities for each target. The baseline defense has been fixed at a 50% breach rate for each target while the best practice defense reduces that rate to 20%. These numbers have been decided artificially for the model validation.

Performance Evaluation. We define the performance of a solution as the *average amount of damage expected from any single attack*, where the expected damage is calculated as the result of an attack on a given target. In each single attack one or more targets are defended following a schedule determined by the specified defender's strategy. If a target that is being attacked is not defended, then the damage equals the *baseline* damage. If the target is defended, the loss equals the damage with the *best practice* defense. To measure the performance of a solution we have created a simulated environment, in Python, used to perform attack sampling. For all comparisons performed, a sample size of 100,000 attacks was used. Such a sample is referred to as a *run* in the results. In the following we present the results, where 25 runs have been performed in each case and the average of the percentage improvement and the standard deviation seen across the runs have been plotted. We have set the rank values for SVD to 5 in both 8 and 10 target scenarios. These values allow us to minimize the runtime for each of the comparisons while maximizing the accuracy of the results.

The percentage improvement seen in comparison to the uniform defense shows a minimum improvement of approximately 15%. Comparably, the smallest average improvement for Nash defense over the *Weighted* is around 7%. In addition to this, the maximum improvement seen in the Nash solution over the *Uniform* is approximately 50%, where the maximum improvement over a *Weighted* defense does not exceed 25%. The improvements between different numbers of administrators for defending a single system identify the impact that the addition of an administrator has in improving the defense. We see that with 8 targets for both attack distributions the addition of more administrators increases the improvement seen in the defense of the system by more, over the common sense approaches. A large difference in improvement indicates that adding an additional administrator will have a greater impact on the defense of the system than in the case of a lower level of improvement. This growth however saturates, as when the number of administrators tends towards the number of targets the improvement seen tends to zero. This happens because all targets can be covered thus the expected damage is minimized across the whole system for all defender strategies.

When comparing the Nash and *Acceptable Coverage* (AC), we see that unlike the comparisons to the common sense approaches, the Nash defense does not always perform better. In contrast to the approximate performance as measured against the common sense approaches, the average improvement does not exceed 10% for either method. With the 8 target scenario, the results show that the AC performs better for 1 administrator regardless of the data set used; specifically the AC method appears to be approximately 2% to 3% better. However, when there are 2 system administrators, the Nash defense performs between 2% and 6% better depending on the data set. With 3 system administrators the results show that on average, for a Hackmageddon attacker, the AC method performs better, but the Nash defense is preferable with a Verizon attacker. It should be

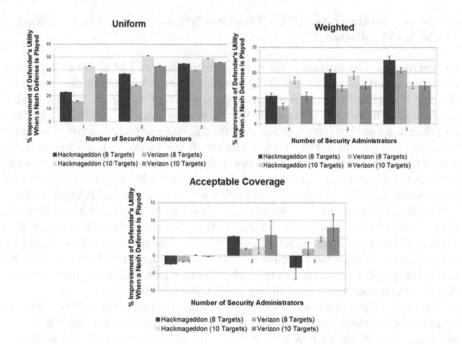

Fig. 1. Improvement of Nash defense over the different methods for both Hackmageddon (H) and Verizon (V) attackers

considered that the deviation of these results shows that in some circumstances the improvement of one method over the other can be less than 1%. For 10 targets and 1 administrator we see that with both datasets there is no improvement in the average performance of the Nash solution over AC, with a very small standard deviation. This indicates that the allocation of system administrators' time to targets is similar for both Nash and AC, where the randomized sampler gives the deviation in the results. For more than 1 administrator it appears to show a relatively large positive improvement for the Nash defense over the AC, where the range improvement is approximately 2% and 5% for 2 and 3 administrators respectively using a Hackmageddon attacker. For a Verizon attacker the improvements are close to 6% and 8% for 2 and 3 administrators. As has been noted above, there is a small deviation in the approximate scheduler used for the AC method, which may account for some of the improvement seen by the Nash defense and the reason for the large deviations in some of the results.

5   Conclusion

In this paper, we have introduced a cyber security model along with game theoretic tools to prove that common sense techniques are not as efficient at providing effective defense schedules as the ones computed by game theory. Our future work includes interviews with system administrators to define levels of values for the different model components. We are also interested in validating the effectiveness of the model when considering an organization where the number of targets available to be attacked will range between 25 and 100. The efficiency of performance for SVD is important given that there is a trade-off in time and accuracy, where we have seen that even for small games it is computationally inefficient to derive the equilibria. As such an interesting extension to this work would be to measure the performance of SVD in terms of efficiency when large games are played. We have described an environment where the defense of a system is pro-active, but we don't consider the scheduling of time in a reactive manner in order to recover systems after a successful attack. In order to recover a system, the time of available system administrators needs to be assigned to this task, which limits the number of system administrators available to maintain the defense of the system. Therefore a further extension of the game considers the concept of optimally dividing the available resources between the recovery of the system and the maintenance of pro-active security. One limitation of the current model, that future work will address, is that in many cases the methods taken by an attacker to break into a system may have steps that are relevant to more than one target. In this case there are specific actions that can be performed by a system administrator that effectively cover multiple targets.

References

1. 2013 data breach investigations report by verizon,
   http://www.verizonenterprise.com/DBIR/2013/
2. Hackmageddon.com, http://hackmageddon.com/ (accessed october 2013)
3. Acquisti, A., Grossklags, J.: Losses, gains, and hyperbolic discounting: An experimental approach to information security attitudes and behavior. In: Proc. of the 2nd Annual Workshop on Economics and Information Security (WEIS 2003), vol. 3 (2003)
4. Alpcan, T., Başar, T.: Network security: A decision and game-theoretic approach. Cambridge University Press (2010)
5. Grossklags, J., Christin, N., Chuang, J.: Secure or insure?: a game-theoretic analysis of information security games. In: Proc. of the 17th International Conference on World Wide Web (WWW 2008), pp. 209–218. ACM (2008)
6. Hankin, C., Malacaria, P.: Payoffs, intensionality and abstraction in games. In: Coecke, B., Ong, L., Panangaden, P. (eds.) Abramsky Festschrift. LNCS, vol. 7860, pp. 69–82. Springer, Heidelberg (2013)
7. Johnson, B., Grossklags, J., Christin, N., Chuang, J.: Nash equilibria for weakest target security games with heterogeneous agents. In: Jain, R., Kannan, R. (eds.) Gamenets 2011. LNICST, vol. 75, pp. 444–458. Springer, Heidelberg (2012)
8. Kannan, R., Theobald, T.: Games of fixed rank: A hierarchy of bimatrix games. Economic Theory 42(1), 157–173 (2005)
9. Kiekintveld, C., Islam, T., Kreinovich, V.: Security games with interval uncertainty. In: Proc. of the 12th International Conference on Autonomous Agents and Multiagent Systems (AAMAS 2013), pp. 231–238. International Foundation for Autonomous Agents and Multiagent Systems, Richland (2013)

10. Kiekintveld, C., Jain, M., Tsai, J., Pita, J., Ordóñez, F., Tambe, M.: Computing optimal randomized resource allocations for massive security games. In: Proc. of the 8th International Conference on Autonomous Agents and Multiagent Systems (AAMAS 2013), pp. 689–696 (2009)
11. Korzhyk, D., Yin, Z., Kiekintveld, C., Conitzer, V., Tambe, M.: Stackelberg vs. nash in security games: An extended investigation of interchangeability, equivalence, and uniqueness. Journal of Artificial Intelligence Research 41(2), 297–327 (2011)
12. Ponemon Institute LLC. State of web application security, http://www.ponemon.org/library/2011-cost-of-data-breach-united-states
13. Lye, K.W., Wing, J.M.: Game strategies in network security. International Journal of Information Security 4(1-2), 71–86 (2005)
14. Manshaei, M., Zhu, Q., Alpcan, T., Basar, T., Hubaux, J.: Game theory meets network security and privacy. ACM Transactions on Computational Logic, 25:1–25:39 (2011)

Appendix

Lemma 1. *An attacker's strategy $A^\star$ is best response to a defender's strategy D in G iff $\widehat{A}^\star = \mu(A^\star)$ is the attacker's best response to D in $\widehat{G}$.*

Proof. To prove this lemma we must prove that

$$U_{\mathcal{A}}^{G}(D, A^\star) - U_{\mathcal{A}}^{G}(D, A') \geq 0 \Leftrightarrow U_{\mathcal{A}}^{\widehat{G}}(D, \widehat{A}^\star) - U_{\mathcal{A}}^{\widehat{G}}(D, \widehat{A}') \geq 0, \forall A'$$

Solving (4) for a_i we have that $a_i = \frac{1}{\lambda} \widehat{a}_i \frac{\Delta U_{\mathcal{A}}(t_i)}{\Delta U_{\mathcal{D}}(t_i)}$ and as we know that $\Delta U_{\mathcal{A}}(t_i), \Delta U_{\mathcal{D}}(t_i), \lambda \geq 0$ the following holds:

$$U_{\mathcal{A}}^{G}(D, A^\star) - U_{\mathcal{A}}^{G}(D, A') \geq 0$$

$$\Leftrightarrow \sum_{i=1}^{n} a_i^\star (c_i U_{\mathcal{A}}^{bp}(t_i) + (1 - c_i) U_{\mathcal{A}}^{bl}(t_i)) - \sum_{i=1}^{n} a_i' (c_i U_{\mathcal{A}}^{bp}(t_i) + (1 - c_i) U_{\mathcal{A}}^{bl}(t_i)) \geq 0$$

$$\Leftrightarrow \sum_{i=1}^{n} (a_i^\star - a_i')(c_i U_{\mathcal{A}}^{bp}(t_i) + (1 - c_i) U_{\mathcal{A}}^{bl}(t_i)) \geq 0$$

$$\Leftrightarrow \sum_{i=1}^{n} \frac{1}{\lambda} \frac{\Delta U_{\mathcal{A}}(t_i)}{\Delta U_{\mathcal{D}}(t_i)} (\widehat{a}_i^\star - \widehat{a}_i')(c_i U_{\mathcal{A}}^{bp}(t_i) + (1 - c_i) U_{\mathcal{A}}^{bl}(t_i)) \geq 0$$

$$\Leftrightarrow \sum_{i=1}^{n} (\widehat{a}_i^\star - \widehat{a}_i')(c_i U_{\mathcal{A}}^{bp}(t_i) + (1 - c_i) U_{\mathcal{A}}^{bl}(t_i)) \geq 0 \Leftrightarrow U_{\mathcal{A}}^{\widehat{G}}(D, \widehat{A}^\star) - U_{\mathcal{A}}^{\widehat{G}}(D, \widehat{A}') \geq 0$$

$\square$

Lemma 2. *A defender's strategy D is best response to an attacker's strategy A in G iff D is also best response to the attacker's strategy* $\widehat{A} = \mu(A)$ *in* $\widehat{G}$.

Proof. To prove this lemma we must prove that $U_D^G(D^\star, A) - U_D^G(D', A) \geq 0 \Leftrightarrow U_D^{\widehat{G}}(D^\star, \widehat{A}) - U_D^{\widehat{G}}(D', \widehat{A}) \geq 0, \forall D'$. We prove this inequality as follows

$$U_D^G(D^\star, A) - U_D^G(D', A) \geq 0$$

$$\Leftrightarrow \sum_{i=1}^{n} a_i(c_i^\star U_D^{bp}(t_i) + (1 - c_i^\star)U_D^{bl}(t_i)) - \sum_{i=1}^{n} a_i(c_i' U_D^{bp}(t_i) + (1 - c_i')U_D^{bl}(t_i)) \geq 0$$

$$\Leftrightarrow \sum_{i=1}^{n} a_i(c_i^\star \Delta U_D(t_i) + U_D^{bl}(t_i)) - \sum_{i=1}^{n} a_i(c_i' \Delta U_D(t_i) + U_D^{bl}(t_i)) \geq 0$$

$$\Leftrightarrow \sum_{i=1}^{n} a_i(c_i^\star - c_i')\Delta U_D(t_i) \geq 0 \Leftrightarrow \sum_{i=1}^{n} \frac{1}{\lambda}\frac{\Delta U_A(t_i)}{\Delta U_D(t_i)}\widehat{a}_i(c_i^\star - c_i')\Delta U_D(t_i) \geq 0$$

$$\Leftrightarrow \sum_{i=1}^{n} \widehat{a}_i(c_i^\star - c_i')\Delta U_A(t_i) \geq 0 \Leftrightarrow \sum_{i=1}^{n} \widehat{a}_i(c_i^\star - c_i') \geq 0$$

$$\Leftrightarrow_{\Delta \widehat{U}_D(t_i) \geq 0} \sum_{i=1}^{n} \widehat{a}_i(c_i^\star - c_i')\Delta \widehat{U}_D(t_i) \geq 0 \Leftrightarrow U_D^{\widehat{G}}(D^\star, \widehat{A}) - U_D^{\widehat{G}}(D', \widehat{A}) \geq 0$$

$\square$

Model-Based Detection of CSRF

Marco Rocchetto[1], Martín Ochoa[2], and Mohammad Torabi Dashti[3]

[1] Università di Verona, Italy
[2] Technische Universität München, Germany
[3] ETH Zürich, Switzerland

Abstract. Cross-Site Request Forgery (CSRF) is listed in the top ten list of the Open Web Application Security Project (OWASP) as one of the most critical threats to web security. A number of protection mechanisms against CSRF exist, but an attacker can often exploit the complexity of modern web applications to bypass these protections by abusing other flaws. We present a formal model-based technique for automatic detection of CSRF. We describe how a web application should be specified in order to facilitate the exposition of CSRF-related vulnerabilities. We use an intruder model, à la Dolev-Yao, and discuss how CSRF attacks may result from the interactions between the intruder and the cryptographic protocols underlying the web application. We demonstrate the effectiveness and usability of our technique with three real-world case studies.

1 Introduction

HTTP and HTTPS, the dominant web access protocols, are stateless. Web servers therefore use Cookies, among other means, to keep track of their sessions with web clients. Cookies are stored by the client's browser; whenever the client sends an HTTP(S) request to the web server, the browser automatically attaches to the request the Cookie that is originated from the web server. This mechanism allows the clients to experience a seamless stateful web browsing, while in fact using an inherently stateless protocol such as HTTP.

Cross-site request forgery attacks (CSRF) exploit the aforementioned mechanism of automatically-attached Cookies. A typical CSRF occurs as explained in the following. The attacker tricks the client into accessing a sensitive web server by making a rogue URL link available to the client: the link instructs the web server to perform a transaction on behalf of the client (e.g. to transfer money). If the client accesses the web server through the rogue link, then in effect the client requests the web server to perform the transaction. The only missing part of the puzzle is a valid Cookie that needs to be attached to the request, so that the web server authenticates the client.

Now, if it happens that the client accesses, via the rogue link, the web server *while* a session between the client and the web server is active, then the client's browser automatically attaches the proper Cookie to the request. The web server would then accept the attacker-generated request as one genuinely sent by the client, and the attack is successful. The web server can deter the attack by checking that critical requests are in fact generated by the client: the requests may have to include an extra random value that is only known to the client and the web server passed as a POST parameter, the

N. Cuppens-Boulahia et al. (Eds.): SEC 2014, IFIP AICT 428, pp. 30–43, 2014.

web server might prompt the client to solve a CAPTCHA to demonstrate that he is aware of the transaction taking place, etc.

However, a number of related vulnerabilities and design flaws might render such countermeasures against CSRF useless. Due to the complexity of modern web applications[1], those vulnerabilities might be difficult to spot. For instance, if the web server uses poorly generated random values, the attacker may open simultaneous sessions with the web server, record the random values, and infer their pattern. It is also well known [7] that state-of-the-art vulnerability scanners do not detect vulnerabilities linked to logical flaws of applications. In general, one should proceed with care when assessing the security of productive servers for vulnerabilities with potential side-effects such as CSRF, since one might affect the integrity of data, making manual testing a challenging task.

Contributions. To address these problems, we propose a model-based technique in order to detect issues related to CSRF during the design-phase. The essence of the formal model is simple: the client acts as an oracle for the attacker. The attacker sends a URL link to the client and the client follows the link. The bulk of the model is therefore centered around the web server, which might have envisioned various protection mechanisms against CSRF vulnerability exploitation. The attacker, in our formal model, is allowed to interact with the web server and exhaustively search his possibilities to exploit a CSRF. The expected result of our technique is, when a CSRF is found, an abstract attack trace reporting a list of steps an attacker has to follow in order to exploit the vulnerability. Otherwise, the specification is safe (under a number of assumptions, as described in Sect. 2.3) with respect to CSRF. We demonstrate the effectiveness and the usefulness of our method through a made-up example (Sect. 2.4) and three real-world case studies (Sect. 3): DocumentRepository and EUBank (two anonymized real-life applications) and WebAuth [11].

More specifically, in this paper, we propose a model-based analysis technique that (i) extends the usage of state of the art model-checking technology for security to search for CSRF based on the ASLan++ language [14]. We also (ii) investigate the usage of the intruder, à la Dolev-Yao [6] (DY from now on), for detecting CSRF on web applications (while it is usually used for security protocols analysis) and, finally, we (iii) show how to concretely use the technique with real web applications.

Structure of the paper. Section 1 gives a general overview of CSRF. In Sect. 2 we describe how to model a web application in order to search for CSRF; there we also introduce the specification language used and our running example. In Sect. 3 we present three case studies, and discuss our findings. In Sect. 4 we discuss related work, and finally in Sect. 5 we conclude the paper proposing future research directions.

2 Modeling CSRF

In this section we describe a technique for modeling web applications in order to search for CSRF. We first give an overview of the CSRF and then we define general guidelines

---

[1] A web application is a software application hosted on one or more web servers.

for writing a specification with the focus on CSRF detection. Finally, we introduce the ASLan++ language used in Sect. 2.3 in which we formally define our technique.

2.1 CSRF

As described in Sect. 1, in order to exploit a CSRF, and attack[2] a web application, mainly three parties have to get involved: an intruder, a client and a web server. The intruder is the entity that wants to find (and then to exploit) the vulnerability and attack the web application hosted on the web server. The web server is thus the entity that represents the web application host and, finally, the client entity is the honest agent who interacts with the web application (i.e. with the web server).

If the web application is vulnerable to CSRF, an attacker can trick the client to perform requests to the web server on his behalf. This attack scenario (depicted in Fig. 1-Left) can be summarized by the following steps:

1. the client logs in to the web application (authentication phase)
2. the web server sends a Cookie (Cookie exchange) to the client who will store it (within the web browser).
3. From this point on, the Cookie will be automatically attached by the web browser to every request sent by the client to the web server (in message 3. of Fig. 1-Left the client sends an honest request along with his Cookie)
4. the intruder sends to the client a malicious link containing a request (Request') for the web application on the web server
5. if the client follows the link, the web browser will automatically attach the Cookie and will send the malicious request to the web server
6. the web application cannot distinguish a request made by the intruder and forwarded by the client from one made and sent by an honest agent; therefore, it accepts the request.

It is important to observe that, from the description of CSRF we have given, an intruder sees the client as an "oracle". The intruder does not see the communication between the client and the web server but it will send a request to the client and wait for it to be executed.

The state-of-the-art protections against CSRF attacks are mainly two (as reported in [10]) and can be used together:

- the web server asks the client for a confirmation at every request the client sends to the web server
- a secret, usually called *CSRF token* (e.g. a pseudo-random token), shared between the client and the web server, has to be attached to every request

In Fig. 1-Right we report the message sequence chart (MSC) of a web application that uses both these CSRF protection mechanisms. In this way, the intruder cannot simply send a request to the client and wait for its execution. In fact, the client will not confirm the request and the browser will not automatically add the secret to the request.

---

[2] In this context, with "attacking a web application" we mean that an intruder can perform requests to the web application that it should not be allowed to do.

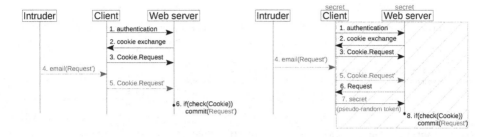

Fig. 1. (Left) CSRF Oracle Message Sequence Chart - (Right) CSRF from the intruder point of view and the barred part is not visible to the intruder

Our goal is to check if protections against CSRF, implemented in a web application, are strong enough; that is, to check if there is a way for the intruder to bypass protections and force the web server to commit a rogue request that it is not allowed to do. Before defining our technique for specifying a web application with the focus on detecting CSRF we show a set of rules (guidelines) that a modeler should be aware of for defining a web application model without trivial flaws that can lead to a CSRF:

- the CSRF token has to be unique for each client
- the CSRF token must be unique for each client-server interaction
- the CSRF token must not be sent with the query string (the part of URL containing data to be passed to the web application) in the URL
- a request has to fail if the CSRF token is missing

2.2 An Introduction to ASLan++

In this section we give a brief presentation of the formal language ASLan++ [14], focusing on the aspects we use for modeling web applications to search for CSRF. This aspects have been used to model our case studies and the running example of Sect. 2.3.

The ASLan++ language is a typed language for formally specifying security-sensitive web servers, web applications and service-oriented architectures. ASLan++ can be used to specify a web system and its security goals, with a modeling language similar to programming languages. The specification will be automatically translated (using a translator [2]) into a more low-level ASLan specification that serves as input of the model checking tools of the AVANTSSAR platform [2]. These will return an abstract attack trace of an attack on the model, if found.

An ASLan++ specification consists in a hierarchy of entity declarations, that are similar to Java classes. The top-level entity is usually called Environment in which commonly the Session entity is defined. The Session entity is composed by sub-entities that are the main principal involved in the system (e.g., clients, servers). Each sub-entity defines the internal behavior of the component it models and the interaction with other entities. For example, the following ASLan++ code represents a simple communication between a client and a server in which the client creates a nonce[3] that he sends to the server. We first focus on the client perspective.

---

[3] Nonce is a freshly generated number, used only once in the execution of the system.

```
1   entity Environment{                14   entity Server(Actor, Client:
2   ...                                        agent){
3    entity Session(U,S:agent){        15     Client -> Actor: Na;
4                                       16   }
5     entity Client(Actor, Server: agent){  17
6      symbols                         18     body{ %of Session
7       Na: text;                      19       new Client(U,S);
8                                       20       new Server(U,S);
9      body{                           21     }
10      Na:=fresh();                   22   }
11      Actor -> Server: Na;           23
12     }                               24   body{ %of Environment
13    }                                25     any U. Session(U, Server);
                                       26   }}
```

The keyword **entity** defines a new component of the model (in this case we consider the Client entity). It accepts arguments, the first one is **Actor** that defines the name of the agent playing the role of the entity Client. The other parameter defines the name of the Server entity that the client wants to communicate with.

Inside the Client entity we have the keyword **symbols** that is used to define the type of all the variables, constants, functions used inside the entity. In our case there is only the Na variable with type text [4].

Inside the **body** section the behavior of the entity is defined. In this example we have the assignment Na:=fresh(); that sets the variable Na to a new constant calculated by the function fresh().

The Server entity is the dual of the Client one, so it will receive the message that the client has sent: Client -> Actor:?Na;. The **Actor** keyword in the server refers to the server entity itself and the ? is used to assign a value to the variable it precedes.

There are several different types of channels in ASLan++ but we are interested in only four types. The plain communication channel -> defines an insecure communication between two entities; that is, no authentication nor confidentiality will be guaranteed for the messages going through the channel. The other three types of communication channels are the authentic one, *->, that ensure messages come from the claimed sender, the confidential one (->*) in which messages can only be received from the intended receiver and the secure channel *->* that combines both authentication and confidentiality.

The Session entity gathers together the two entities Client and Server and in its body section creates the new instances of the two sub-entities (**new** Client(U,S); and **new** Server(U,S);).

The session entity is called by the Environment that instantiates the Session. We now show a shorthand useful for session instantiation that does not bound the client to a particular constant but expresses that each agent of the specification can impersonate the role: **any** U. Session(U, Server);.

The ASLan++ language allows us to also define conditionals. There are the usual if-then-else statements and also a **select**{**on**(statement):{<positive branch>}} that is semantically equivalent to the positive evaluation of if-then-else statement (i.e., the negative branch will not be considered by the model checker). There is also the

---

[4] There are several types: agent, text, message are the main ones. Agent is used to define roles while text and message are for variable and constant. The main difference between text and message is that the former cannot be decomposed by an intruder, while message can.

`while(...)` loop that is used to define that a process (usually a server) is listening for incoming communication.

The last two points we want to briefly discuss are the intruder role and the goal section. The intruder/attacker (à la Dolev-Yao [6]) is intended to control the entire network but every cryptographic algorithm is treated as if cryptography were perfect; that is, the intruder can collect all the messages that are transmitted over the network but cannot break cryptography.

ASLan++ defines several ways to formalize security goals but the one we are interested in is reachability. In the rest of the paper we will use a predicate `commit` over a variable that if is reached with a particular assignment then the CSRF is used by the intruder to attack the web application. We will discuss this last point in details in Sect. 2.3. There are several other aspects of the language that are outside the scope of this paper, however the ones we have briefly defined are enough to understand the ASLan++ code that we have used in the reminder of the paper.

2.3   CSRF in ASLan++: Modeling and Detection

In this section we describe a technique for modeling web applications to check for CSRF. We will use the DocumentRepository specification as a running example. Even if no attack has been detected on this case study it is illustrative for several reasons: it uses the usual client-server paradigm, it models Cookies generation, storage and exchange (using a database) and the server handles login, commit, and malicious requests. Before going into the details of the modeling part we give the system description of the running example.

DocumentRepository Description. The DocumentRepository [5] system is a document repository that implements a document management system for the secure management and sharing of documents via web browser. Its main purpose is then to share and store different documents produced by various group of possibly different institutions. Suppose that both Alice and Bob (from two different institutions) are using the repository system. A typical scenario is the following:

- Alice logs in, via the login page, by providing her credentials (username and password)
- Alice is then forwarded to the system starting page where she can browse to the repositories list. She can now access to all public repositories and to private ones to which she has the permission
- Alice clicks on one of the private repositories she has access to (repository A) and uploads a new document
- Now Bob, who is the administrator of the repository A can download, edit or remove the file Alice has just uploaded and he can also edit Alice's permission on the private repository

---

[5] The DocumentRepository system is a non public industrial case study within the SPaCIoS project. We have then hided the real name of the system and omitted some of the details.

ASLan++ Modeling for CSRF Detection. In order to check for CSRF we consider two entities: *Client/Oracle* entity and *Server* entity, as described in Sect. 2.1.

Client/Oracle. In the Client entity we model a first authentication phase to obtain the Cookie and logging in to the web application. First, in line 2, the client sends its credentials (username and password) and then the server, upon checking the received credentials are correct, sends back a new Cookie to the Client (lines 5, 6).

```
1   % sends his/her name and password to the server's login service
2   Actor ->* Server: Actor.UserName.Password;
3
4   % the server's login service responds to the login request with a Cookie
5   select { on (Server *->* Actor: ?Cookie &
6            ?Cookie=cookie(UserName,?,?)): {} }
```

After this phase, the Client can perform requests to the server asking for services. When a client wants to send a request to the DocumentRepository system, it first loads the web page (usually using a web browser). The server produces the web page and sends it together with a CSRF token (i.e., a fresh pseudo-random token linked to the session ID of the Client). At specification level, skipping line 7 for the moment, we can model this mechanism by creating a variable Request that the Client wants to submit. When the Client sends this Request to the server (line 10), the latter will generate and send the token, CSRFToken, back to the Client (line 11). Now the Client sends (line 12) the Request together with the Cookie and the CSRF token.

```
7    ? -> Actor: ?Request;
8    % load request page with the csrf token
9    % client asks for a web page; server sends it to him including a csrf token
10   Actor *->* Server: Cookie.Request;
11   Server *->* Actor: ?CSRFToken;
12   Actor *->* Server: Cookie.Request.CSRFToken;
```

Between the authentication and the request submission parts, in line 7, we have added a message containing a variable Request. This message is sent from an unknown entity in order to model the scenario in which the Client receives a malicious email from a third party; the email contains a link to submit a request to the web application.

Finally, in line 14, the Client will receive from the server the confirmation that the request has been executed by the web application.

```
13   % the server's frontend sends back to the client the answer
14   Server *->* Actor: Request.?Answer;
```

Server. The server entity accepts three different kinds of requests: authentication, request for a web page and request that it has to commit to the web application.

With *authentication request* a Client (if not already authenticated) sends to the server its username and password asking to log in (line 16). The server will check the received credentials (lines 17, 19) and, if they are correct, it will generate a Cookie (line 25) that will be sent back to the Client (line 30).

```
15   % 1) login service receives the client request and generate a new session
          Cookie
16   on((? ->* Actor: ?UserIP.?UserName.?Password
17        & !dishonest_usr(?UserName)) &
18        % checks if the data are available in the database
19        loginDB->contains((?UserName,?Password,?Role))): {
20        % we have checked, using the password, that the client is legitimate.
```

```
21      % With the query, we extract the role of the legitimate client.
22
23      % creates the Cookie and sends it back to the client
24      Nonce := fresh();
25      Cookie := cookie(UserName,Role,Nonce);
26      % adds the Cookie into the DB associated with the name of the client
27      cookiesDB->add(Cookie);
28
29      % uses the IP address to communicate the Cookie to the correct client
30      Actor *->* UserIP: Cookie;
31   }
```

The second type of request is a *web page request*. The Client asks for a web page before sending a request to the web application. The Client is already logged in and then it sends the request together with the Cookie (line 34). The server will check the Cookie (line 35) and generate a fresh token (line 37) that will send back to the Client (line 39).

```
32   % 2) with a Cookie, a client makes a request to the frontend
33   % without the CSRF token and receives the respective token from the repository
34   on(?UserIP *->* Actor: cookie(?UserName,?Role,?Nonce).?Request &
35   cookiesDB->contains(cookie(?UserName,?Role,?Nonce))): {
36
37        CSRFToken:=fresh();
38        csrfTokenDB->add((UserIP,Request,CSRFToken));
39        Actor *->* UserIP: CSRFToken;
40   }
```

The third case is when a Client sends a *request to the server* (line 43). The server checks both the token (line 46) and the Cookie (line 50) and then commits the request (line 54).

```
41   % 3) a client makes a request (along with a Cookie) to the frontend
42   %and receives the answer from the repository
43   on(?UserIP *->* Actor: cookie(?UserName,?Role,?Nonce).?Request.?CSRFToken &
44
45      % checks if the token is the right one
46      csrfTokenDB->contains((?UserIP,?Request,?CSRFToken)) &
47
48      % checks if the client is allowed to do this request and the link client-
            Cookie
49      checkPermissions(?UserName,?Request) &
50      cookiesDB->contains(cookie(?UserName,?Role,?Nonce))): {
51
52      % if the client has the right credential, then the request
53      % is executed and the answer is sent back to the Client
54      commit(Request);
55      Answer := answerOn(Request);
56      Actor *->* UserIP: Request.Answer;
57    }
58   }
```

Goal. The goal is to check if there is a way for the intruder to commit a request to the web application. We use a predicate `commit` over a constant `intruderRequest` that if true, the intruder has found a CSRF. `csrf_goal: [](!commit(intruderRequest));`

From the specification, the only way that the intruder has to commit a request is to bypass the CSRF protection (i.e., CSRF Token). To model that the intruder wants to submit a request that an honest agent does not, we have introduced a particular request (`intruderRequest`) within the Session entity as follows:

```
59   body { %% of the Environment entity
60      role1->can_exec(request1);
```

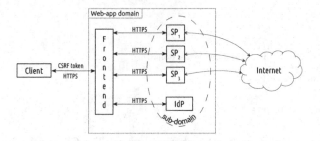

Fig. 2. Application scenario - Example

```
61   role1->can_exec(intruderRequest);
62   role2->can_exec(request2);
63   any UserIP. Session(UserIP, usr1, role1, request1) where !dishonest(UserIP);
64   new       Session(i    , usr2, role2, request1);
65 }
```

Validation. The AVANTSSAR platform has reported that the DocumentRepository specification is safe with respect to the modeled goal. This means that, given a bounded number of sessions, and considering a DY intruder, in this modeled scenario the three model-checkers on which the AVANTSSAR platform relies on have not detected a CSRF.

2.4   A More Complex Example

In this section we present an example, depicted in Fig. 2, to motivate the usage of our technique for more complex architectures. Our aim is to show that, after abstracting away unimportant implementation details, with our modeling technique it is possible to identify CSRF at design phase. We show a design schema of a Service Oriented Architecture (SOA) named Arch1. Arch1 (and a SOA in general) is a distributed system that offers functionalities that are not all hosted within the same server but are distributed on various hosts. Usually, a common interface (e.g., the AVANTSSAR platform web interface available from www.avantssar.eu) is offered to the client for communicating with the system. The architecture structure is then hidden to users who see the SOA as if it were a client-server architecture. It is also a common design choice to provide APIs for directly communicating with one (or a subset) of the services of the SOA so that expert users can develop their own client (or use a customized one if provided). Languages such as WSDL [4] are widely used in SOAs for this purpose.

Architecture description. Arch1 architecture is mainly composed by four parts: Client, Frontend, Service and Identity Providers (from now on SP and IdP respectively).

- the *client* entity represents the client browser. It can only communicate with the frontend via HTTPS, i.e., a secure channel: authenticated and encrypted
- the *frontend* entity provides a common interface to communicate with the system. To avoid CSRF, for each HTML page loaded by the client a CSRFToken (Sect. 2) is attached by the frontend; the client will attach it to its request for guaranteeing

freshness. Upon the receipt of the correct message, composed by request and token, the frontend will forward the request to the correct SP

- *SPs* are the core of the system and provide the services of the SOA
- *IdP* is the entity that handle the client authentication

The frontend, SPs and IdP are all within the same web application domain, i.e., they are grouped in sub-domains that refer to the same domain. As a last remark on the architecture, each SP is also accessible from outside the SOA, and a client can directly communicate with a SP from the Internet.

The scenario we have modeled starts with an authentication phase in which the client logs in using SAML-SSO protocol. After that, it can submit requests to the system by communicating with the frontend that acts as a proxy between the client and SPs. We have also modeled, as motivated in Sect. 2.3, that if the client receives from another (dishonest) entity a request for the Arch1 system, his browser attaches the Cookie and sends the request. This behavior represents that the user clicks on a malicious email sent by a dishonest agent trying to exploit a CSRF on the system.

Authentication phase. As already stated in Sect. 1, HTTP(S) is a stateless protocol and then Cookies are used to ensure authentication. To store a Cookie the client has to authenticate with the SOA. We have chosen one of the state-of-the-art authentication protocols, SAML-SSO[9] but we could have used OpenID or OAuth obtaining the same behavior at this level of abstraction. SAML-SSO uses an IdP to authenticate the credentials (e.g., username and password) given by a client. Here the client can only communicate with the frontend and then the frontend will act as a Proxy between the client and the IdP. The client provides his credentials to the frontend that forwards them to the IdP. The IdP, after validating the client's credentials, creates a Cookie that is sent back to the Client via the frontend. Now the Cookie is stored within the client's browser used and it will be attached to every request he will send to the SOA (because every part of the SOA is inside the same web domain).

Honest client behavior. Once authenticated, the client has a Cookie stored in his web browser. He loads a web page in which a CSRFToken is provided and he sends the request together with the token and the Cookie to the frontend. The frontend forwards the message to the correct SP that, through the frontend, will communicates the result of the commitment of the client's request. An SP will not directly check the Cookie of the request but will ask the IdP to check if the Cookie is a valid one.

Arch1 ASLan++ model and validation. Due to page limit we cannot report the entire ASLan++ model but it follows the structure of the running example of Sect. 2.3.

We have used the AVANTSSAR platform for the verification of the specification obtaining the following attack trace.

```
MESSAGES:
1. frontend *->* <client> : n78(Csrftoken)
2. <?> ->* frontend : Client(80).Cookie(83).Req(83).Csrftoken(84)
3. frontend *->* <sp> : Client(80).Cookie(83).Req(83).Csrftoken(84)
4. <frontend> *->* sp : Client(80).Cookie(83).Req(83).Csrftoken(84)
5. <?> -> client : intruderreq.sp
6. client ->* <sp> : client.client_cookie.intruderreq
7. <?> ->* sp : client.client_cookie.intruderreq
```

We have assumed the Client has already logged in to the web application. In message 1, where the brackets <...> denote the intended communication partner of whose identity the honest communication agent cannot be sure, the frontend sends the CSRF Token to the Client (after having checked the Cookie of the Client). In message 2 the Client sends an honest request to the frontend and in messages 3 and 4 the frontend forwards the request to an SP. In message 5 the intruder sends an email containing a malicious link to the Client with a dishonest request for a SP. The Client clicks on it and in message 6 the request is sent directly to the SP. In message 7 the intruder request is committed and a CSRF is performed.

The attack trace shows that the modeled architecture Arch1 is vulnerable to CSRF. It is clear that, even if protections against CSRF have been (correctly) implemented, the manual detection of CSRF is a difficult and time consuming task. Our technique has permitted the automatic detection of CSRF in a complex architecture as Arch1 is. This extends the AVANTSSAR platform functionalities to check for CSRF.

3   Case Studies and Results

In this section we present results of applying our approach to three case studies. We have used the AVANTSSAR platform [2] to carry out the case studies and for the validation of the CSRF goal.

DocumentRepository. The AVANTSSAR platform model checkers conclude that the specification (described in Sect. 2.3) is safe with respect to the CSRF goal (i.e., no attack trace has been found). This means that the CSRF protection (i.e. CSRF token) cannot be bypassed, in the modeled scenario (i.e., with a bounded number of sessions), by the DY intruder [6]. This result, which has been confirmed by our industrial partner, shows that the combination of SSL and a CSRF token do not permit the intruder to attack the web application using a CSRF.

WebAuth. Authors in [1] have developed a methodology to detect web vulnerabilities using formal methods. In their most extensive case study, WebAuth [11], they show how they have found a CSRF. In order to compare [1] with our methodology we have then chosen to model the same case study.

WebAuth is an authentication system for web pages and web application developed by Stanford University. It consists of three main components: User Agent (UA), WebAuth-enabled Authentication Server (WAS) and WebAuth Key Distribution Center (WebKDC). The first time a UA attempt to access a web page he is redirected to the WebKDC that will ask to the UA for providing his authentication credential. An encryption identity is given to the UA. Now, the UA can use his new encrypted identity to obtain the web pages he wants to browse. The UA identity is stored in a Cookie that the browser will "show" to the WAS in a user transparent way so the UA will simply browse the pages while the browser will use the Cookie to retrieve them.

The result of the analysis shows a flaw in the authentication protocol, rather than a CSRF, in which the intruder convinces the UA to be communicating with the WAS while the UA is communicating with the intruder. In fact, in the attack reported in [1] the token that has to be shown to the WAS in order to retrieve the service is the same used to start the authentication procedure and, due to the stateless property of HTTP, the WAS cannot detect if the two are different.

In order to detect a CSRF, we started from the protocol specification of WebAuth where the possibility of adding a CSRF token is not mandatory nor excluded. We have then modeled two versions: one with CSRF token exchange and the other one without. The model checkers return "NO_ATTACK_FOUND" (that means the specification is safe with respect to the CSRF goal defined) if the token is present, otherwise they report a CSRF as in the attack trace that follows.

```
MESSAGES:
[...]
18. UA(121) *->* <Actor(121)> : n119(Cookie).intruderRequest
19. <UA(121)> *->* Actor(121) : n119(Cookie).intruderRequest
20. Actor(121) *->* <UA(121)> : intruderRequest
```

From message 1 to message 17 there are the needed interactions between the UA and the system in order to obtain the Cookie. Message 18 shows that the intruder sends to the UA a malicious message. In the real case it would be an email with a link containing a request that can be executed only from UA that has access to the system. The intruder is not logged in to the WebAuth application but he wants the honest agent AU to execute the action. In messages 19 and 20 the UA follows the link and then his browser automatically adds the Cookie to the request hidden in the link. In message 21 the system replies with an acknowledge of the execution of the request. We can conclude that with our technique it has been possible to detect both an authentication flaw of the protocol underling the web application and CSRF, while the two were confused in [1].

EUBank. We have analyzed a web application of one of the major European bank searching for CSRF. We have manually analyzed the web application and in particular the money transfer part. The scenario we have modeled can be summarized by the following steps:

1. *Login phase:* a client logs in the web application by providing two numerical codes, a client id and a numerical password over an HTTPS communication
2. *Bank transfer set up:* the user fills in a form with all the necessary data for committing a bank transfer. Once committed, the web application asks for a confirmation. The user has to provide a numerical code that he can retrieve from his EUBank Passa hardware key that displays a numerical code freshly generated every sixty seconds.
3. *Bank transfer conclusion:* after checking the numerical code insert by the user, the web application sends to the client a confirmation page with all the details of the bank transfer

It is important to highlight that all the communication between the client and the server (bank) goes through a secure HTTPS channel, and even if no CSRF token is generated from the web application the EUBank Pass code is used also as a CSRF token

The first model we have implemented follows exactly the steps above, with the assumption that the client has his own EUBank Pass and no CSRF has been detected from the AVANTSSAR platform model checkers. Modeling a scenario in which an intruder has obtained the EUBank Pass key (e.g., through social engineering [12]), we obtain an attack trace reporting a CSRF on the web application. We have not reported it for lack of space and because it is very similar to the abstract attack trace of CSRF of the WebAuth case study.

We have also manually tested it by transferring money from an EUBank account to another (of a different bank) simulating a CSRF exploitation. We have reported the attack and the bank has confirmed it.

4   Related Work

There exist several works that aim to perform model-based testing of Web applications, e.g., [5,1,13]. In particular we want to compare our techniques with works that consider CSRF vulnerabilities.

In [1], authors have presented a (formal) model-based method for the verification of Web applications. They propose a methodology for modeling Web applications and the results of the exploitation of the technique on five case studies, modeled in the Alloy [8] modeling language. Even if the idea is similar, they have defined three different intruder models that should find Web attacks while we have used the standard DY intruder. Also, the detailed way they have used to define the Web application models results in attack traces which are difficult to interpret. In contrast, we have chosen to abstract away from implementation details creating a more abstract modeling technique to easily define a Web application scenario, thus more amenable to human interpretation. The ASLan++ language has permitted us to use the AVANTSAR platform [2] (a state-of-the-art formal analysis tool) and to obtain human-readable attack traces. As a final remark, we have also showed in Sect. 3 that authors in [1] have not found a CSRF on their most extensive case study, confusing an authentication flaw for a CSRF.

Another work close to ours is [3], in which authors have presented a tool named SPaCiTE that, relying on a model checker for the security analysis that uses ASLan++ specifications as input, generates potential attacks with regard to common Web vulnerabilities such as XSS, SQL-i an access control logic flaws. However, they have not explored CSRF.

5   Conclusions

In this work, we have shown that a model-based technique for detecting CSRF related vulnerabilities is feasible and can be of help in complex web applications, by leveraging existing symbolic techniques under the Dolev-Yao adversary models.

In future work, we plan to investigate how to model further web vulnerabilities for the detection of more complex attacks. This is not a trivial task, in fact, the required level of details needed for modeling a specification for the detection of other vulnerabilities, e.g. XSS (Cross-Site Scripting), has a strong impact on the performance of the model checking techniques available.

Acknowledgments. This work was partially supported by the FP7-ICT-2009-5 Project no. 257876, "SPaCIoS: Secure Provision and Consumption in the Internet of Services".

References

1. Akhawe, D., Barth, A., Lam, P.E., Mitchell, J., Song, D.: Towards a Formal Foundation of Web Security. In: 2010 23rd IEEE Computer Security Foundations Symposium (CSF), pp. 290–304 (2010)
2. Armando, A., et al.: The AVANTSSAR Platform for the Automated Validation of Trust and Security of Service-Oriented Architectures. In: Flanagan, C., König, B. (eds.) TACAS 2012. LNCS, vol. 7214, pp. 267–282. Springer, Heidelberg (2012), http://dx.doi.org/10.1007/978-3-642-28756-5_19
3. Büchler, M., Oudinet, J., Pretschner, A.: SPaCiTE – Web Application Testing Engine. In: 2012 IEEE Fifth International Conference on Software Testing, Verification and Validation (ICST), pp. 858–859 (2012)
4. Christensen, E., Curbera, F., Meredith, G., Weerawarana, S., et al.: Web Services Description Language (WSDL) 1.1 (2001)
5. Dias Neto, A.C., Subramanyan, R., Vieira, M., Travassos, G.H.: A Survey on Model-based Testing Approaches: A Systematic Review. In: WEASELTech 2007, pp. 31–36. ACM (2007)
6. Dolev, D., Yao, A.: On the Security of Public-Key Protocols. IEEE Transactions on Information Theory 2(29) (1983)
7. Doupé, A., Cova, M., Vigna, G.: Why Johnny Can't Pentest: An Analysis of Black-Box Web Vulnerability Scanners. In: Kreibich, C., Jahnke, M. (eds.) DIMVA 2010. LNCS, vol. 6201, pp. 111–131. Springer, Heidelberg (2010)
8. Jackson, D.: Software Abstractions: Logic, Language, and Analysis. MIT Press (2012)
9. OASIS. Profiles for the OASIS Security Assertion Markup Language (SAML) V2.0 (2005), http://www.oasis-open.org/committees/tc_home.php?wg_abbrev=security
10. OWASP. OWASP Cross Site Request Forgery (2013), https://www.owasp.org/index.php/Cross-Site_Request_Forgery_(CSRF)
11. Schemers, R., Allbery, R.: WebAuth v3 technical specification (2009), http://webauth.stanford.edu/protocol.html
12. Thornburgh, T.: Social Engineering: The "Dark Art". In: Proceedings of the 1st Annual Conference on Information Security Curriculum Development, InfoSecCD 2004, pp. 133–135. ACM, New York (2004)
13. Tidwell, T., Larson, R., Fitch, K., Hale, J.: Modeling Internet Attacks. In: Proceedings of the 2001 IEEE Workshop on Information Assurance and security, vol. 59 (2001)
14. von Oheimb, D., Mödersheim, S.: ASLan++ — A formal security specification language for distributed systems. In: Aichernig, B.K., de Boer, F.S., Bonsangue, M.M. (eds.) FMCO 2010. LNCS, vol. 6957, pp. 1–22. Springer, Heidelberg (2011)

Lightweight Resource Management for DDoS Traffic Isolation in a Cloud Environment

Ibnu Mubarok[1], Kiryong Lee[1], Sihyung Lee[2], and Heejo Lee[1]

[1] Korea University
{ibnu,krlee,heejo}@korea.ac.kr
[2] Seoul Womens University
sihyunglee@swu.ac.kr

Abstract. Distributed denial-of-service (DDoS) attacks are one of the most difficult issues in network security and communications. This paper is a part of research project that applies distributed defense against distributed attacks. The aim of this project is to provide services by distributing load from one main server to an infrastructure of cloud-based replicas. This paper proposes a lightweight resource management for DDoS traffic isolation in cloud environments. Experimental results show that our mechanism is a viable approach for dynamic resource scaling under high traffic with distributed resource location.

Keywords: Cloud computing, DDoS attack, resource management.

1 Introduction

Existing DDoS mitigation solutions can be categorized by their approach: victim-based and network-based. Victim-based solutions focus on the mitigation of an attack at the client side, while network-based solutions protect the attack at routers. Victim-based solutions suffer from several drawbacks, such as the need for oversized server resources. Network-based solutions often suffer from link congestion and other challenging issues. New types of attacks, such as Layer-7 DDoS attacks, also contribute to the difficulties with network-based solutions. Several methods use a signature-based approach, in which attack signatures are automatically shared among service providers [1]. However, the collection and analysis of these signatures are time consuming. Content delivery network (CDN)-based approaches, such as Akamai [5] and CloudFlare [3], typically use cache servers, and therefore, they are vulnerable to cache pollution attacks such as false-locality and locality-disruption attacks [8], [4]. Attackers might continue to send requests for unpopular data and pollute the cache stored in different locations within the network topology, leading to service disruption and incurring additional costs.

Enormous resource capacity and ease of scalability in cloud computing could be beneficial to protecting services from DDoS attacks. Many companies and researchers are considering the use of a cloud as a shield from DDoS attacks. However, one concern with this approach is the resource usage. Because one component of billing for cloud services is resource usage and most DDoS attacks aim to deplete a servers resource. However, if critical services are being targeted, and those services cannot be shut down, there is no other option but to keep the service alive using the clouds massive power.

N. Cuppens-Boulahia et al. (Eds.): SEC 2014, IFIP AICT 428, pp. 44–51, 2014.

This paper proposes a lightweight resource management for isolating DDoS traffic in a cloud environment. Our work focuses on resource allocation management and provides a mechanism for scaling resources under DDoS attack. In this paper, we describe a simple resource placement based on response time and a modified threshold-based scaling mechanism to ensure resource availability.

The main contribution of this research is to propose and evaluate a simple yet effective mechanism for resource scaling and allocation management in a cloud environment under a DDoS attack. Further, this mechanism can be used when the large bandwidth consumption from other legitimate applications lead to the degradation of the servers quality of service (QoS).

2   Distributed Defense against Distributed Attacks

2.1   DROPFAST

This paper is a part of a research project that is attempting to apply distributed defense against distributed attacks. The project, DROPFAST, is based on the idea of providing efficient and secure service by distributing the load from one main server to an infrastructure of cloud-based replicas of the main protected server [7].

Our project is based on the use of the massive computing power of the cloud infrastructure as well as the distributed nature of the cloud to protect the system from DDoS attacks. Our goal is to distribute DDoS traffic inside the cloud environment, guaranteeing that the main server remains accessible to legitimate users. Anomalous users are directed to a replica server in the cloud, whereas an obvious attacker is directed to the quarantine server.

We define the main server as our primary server in which the services must be protected during a DDoS attack. Replica servers are virtual machine resources in the cloud comprising an image of the original server. Based on traffic classification, legitimate users can access the original server, whereas users are forced to access the replicas. We can not simply drop the suspicious traffic, as it is the gray area in which user might be legitimate. For DDoS detection, we use an open source IDS such as Snort system since detection is not our main research focus. To distribute traffic, we apply DNS-based traffic redirection.

As today's services depend on multiple resources, all the independent resources might be replicated in several locations. Our prototype implementation only mentions about one type of resource, which is a web server, but the concept and idea could be extended as well.

2.2   Problem Statement

In a cloud, computing resources must be allocated and scheduled in such a manner that providers achieve high resource utilization and users meet their applications performance requirements with minimal cost. This task is related to cloud resource management. Based on the idea of providing service by redistributing load from one main server to an infrastructure of cloud-based replicas, in addition to proper traffic isolation and user classification, a clouds resources can be managed to efficiently mitigate DDoS attacks. Therefore, to guarantee service availability, a cloud service provider must provide effective resource management for handling DDoS traffic.

3 Lightweight Resource Management

3.1 Overview

An implicit goal of our work is to minimize cost when serving resource to client. In order to do so, we must ensure that our scaling mechanism works effectively and efficiently. One option is to significantly minimize resource consumption by selecting the best replica locations and allocate a minimum number of resources to each replica. Therefore, our mechanism consists of two main phases: (1) Replica Location Activation; responsible for selecting the best replica placement among these potential locations. (2) Dynamic Scaling; phase when the system triggers an increase or a decrease in the amount of allocated resources in the server, using modified-threshold based scaling.

3.2 Replica Activation and Deactivation

We assume that replica servers are deployed in N predefined locations. In this setting, our objective is to choose M replicas ($M < N$) and activate selected replicas, such that congestion is minimized near the main server. Figure 1 shows the ideal result when we activate one replica ($M = 1$). The high load of attack traffic is redirected to the location furthest from the main server, thus relieving the load near the main server. Legitimate traffic can still access the main server.

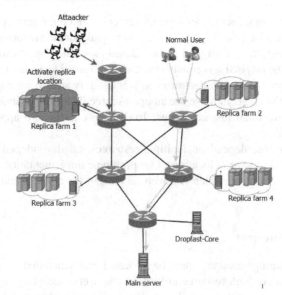

Fig. 1. Replica activation. After activating replica farm 1, traffic from attackers will be redirected from the main server to replica farm 1.

Because our ultimate goal is to minimize congestion near the main server, we need to define a measure of congestion. For our purposes, we use the response time at the main server. The response time is a straightforward metric that represents a servers availability. A benefit of using this metric is that it can be measured by probing the server from the outside, and it does not require installing a probing agent at the server. The installation of additional agents in the server is often a sensitive issue, because such modifications may degrade the servers performance or lead to failure.

According to the objective and the measure of congestion, the optimal solution is to choose an M-subset of replicas with a minimal response time out of all possible M-subsets. However, identifying such a subset is not practical when N is large. The evaluation of all possible M-subsets can take a significant amount of time, and quick decisions are necessary when under DDoS attack. Therefore, we propose an approximation algorithm, a greedy method that performs M iterations and chooses one replica at each iteration. This greedy algorithm works as follows:

1. At the beginning of the iterations, none of the N replicas are activated.
2. At each iteration, we evaluate all of the replicas that are not yet activated. In particular, we compute two metrics: (i) the response time from each replica to the main server, and (ii) the hop count from the replica to the main server.
3. We choose the replica with the highest response time, assuming that the area around this selected replica is more congested than other areas. The response time is measured by sensor agents, which are deployed in every replica farm, and which send TCP SYN and simple HTTP requests to the main server on a regular basis.
4. In step (3), if more than one replica yields the same highest response time, we choose the replica with the highest hop count. Such a selection ensures that the attack traffic is redirected at the farthest possible location from the main server.
5. We activate the selected replica, and then repeat steps (2)-(4), until M replicas are activated.

To summarize, we activate one replica R at a time, selecting the replica with the highest response time and hop count. We expect that this will redirect the largest amount of traffic to R and that this redirection will occur at the location farthest from the server. One advantage of the proposed greedy algorithm is that it does not require the network topology information. Retrieving the latest topology information may not be practical, particularly when the network has thousands of nodes and the topology (and routing) changes frequently.

In the evaluation, we compare the proposed algorithm with two traditional methods that have been used for resource placement: (i) Random placement: randomly chooses M replicas among N potential sites ($M < N$) according to the uniform distribution, and it does not depend on traffic workload. (ii) Hotspot placement: This algorithm selects replicas near the clients that generate the highest load [6]. In particular, the algorithm sorts the N potential sites according to the amount of trafc generated within their area. The algorithm then selects the M sites that generate the largest amount of trafc.

In most cases, DDoS attacks only occur for a certain amount of time. To deactivate the replica location, we check the status of the attack using DDoS detection software/module, whether it is still under attack. The sensor agent then checks the response time. If the response time is gradually returning to normal, there is no congestion, the traffic load returns to normal, and the server health check yields a normal status, the server is in a healthy condition. At this point, we deactivate the replica location. If there are many replica locations, we select the replica location where no congestion is detected or where there is the smallest response time. This purpose of the replica location deactivation is resource saving.

3.3   Scaling Condition

In this section we explain how our scaling mechanism works. Initially, we start with a low number of machines and gradually increase the load to determine the number of resources required. This approach helps us avoid a situation where we need to reduce the number of machines $(M-1)$ at each iteration. The number of resources required must be estimated accurately so that they can be provisioned within the cloud infrastructure.

Normally, a simple threshold consists of two lines, the upper threshold and lower threshold. This simple threshold might not sufficiently capture traffic fluctuation and adapt to changes. Therefore, we use a four-line threshold-based mechanism. We use a modified threshold mechanism to dynamically change the resource allocation for certain threshold configurations. Using a threshold is a straightforward method to scale resources, and it is shown to be effective in any type of scenario. If the performance metric overpassed the invocation threshold, for a certain time, the system will perform invocation. Similarly, when the performance metric is under the revocation threshold, the system will automatically perform revocation. Figure 2 shows the threshold-based approach for invocation. Invocation is a process by which a system increases the resource allocation, whereas revocation decreases the current resource allocation.

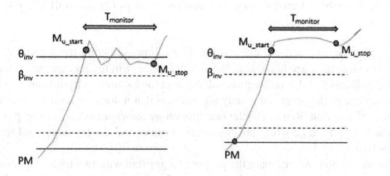

Fig. 2. Invocation condition

The four lines of threshold are: threshold invoke(θ_{inv}), bumper invoke(β_{inv}), bumper revoke(β_{rev}), and threshold revoke(θ_{rev}). We use four lines because a metric that goes beyond the original threshold might only stay momentarily above a certain point, and the additional threshold (bumper) can help us determine if the situation is lasting. For the first interval, if the performance metric value exceeds the invocation threshold, we start the timer to monitor the systems status. During this monitoring period, we collect the performance metric value until the monitoring time ends. If the stop value is located above the bumper invocation threshold, there is a high probability that current resource allocation is stressed. If the last PM (M_{stop}) value is above βinv and below θinv, and the average PM value is also above βinv, we perform invocation with a one-by-one increase. If the average PM value is above θinv, and the $M stop$ value is also above θinv, we conduct invocation with a two-fold increase. This is similar to TCPs slow start, we do 'x 2' to reach the top as soon as possible at the beginning of a DDoS. Once we are near the top, we do "+1" to gradually increase the number of replicas. In addition to the invocation condition, the revocation condition has the same principle for deciding the revocation step, but with a different direction value. The monitoring starts when the performance metric value goes deep below the θrev. This triggers collection of the performance metric value until the monitoring stops. We use response time as performance metric, as we found it sufficient to determine the degradation of a server's performance. Possible threshold and bumper values are 10% for threshold revocation, 25% for bumper revocation, 75% for bumper invocation, and 90% for threshold invocation. This percentage is proportionally scaled with range value from minimum to maximum for the performance metric.

4   Evaluation and Results

For our experiment, we use OMNET++, a simulation environment shown to be efficient for large networks [2]. We also use OverSim and HTTP component from INET module in OMNET++. To emulate Internet topology, we use GT-ITM and BRITE topology generator. We also derive the topology from BGP routing tables. We use the public Web trace of World Cup 1998 as input, which contains flash crowd traffic, a traffic pattern very similar to DDoS attack. The server and network was overloaded by a flash crowd event, and the aggregated volume resembles that of DDoS attack. In total, the web site received more than 1.35 billion requests during the collection period of three months (11,000 requests per minute on average), and almost 5TB of data was sent to clients (41 MB per minute on average). We vary the number of replicas from 1 to 4 for 10-node graphs, from 1 to 10 for 100-node graphs, and from 1 to 100 for 1,000-node graphs.

We ran the simulation several times to obtain a stable result, and these results resemble the normal condition. First, we analyzed the replica placement algorithm. We measured the response time from clients to replicas. As shown in Figure 3.a, which is generated by 100-node graphs, our mechanism achieves shorter response time than random and hot-spot placements. The results are similar in 10-node and 1,000-node graphs. Further, we measured the response time as we increased the number of replicas, starting from 1 to 10. Figure 3.b shows that our mechanism outperforms random and hot-spot placements, and the differences become greater as more replicas are used. This is because hotspot algorithm makes decisions solely based on traffic volume, whereas our mechanism considers multiple factors, (i) response time and (ii) furthest location based on the hop counts. We also measured the efficiency of our scaling mechanism. We assume that one replica can handle one million requests per hour and this may vary depending on the capacity of replicas. Figure 4 compares our approach with the simple threshold and shows that our mechanism much more closely follows the real traffic

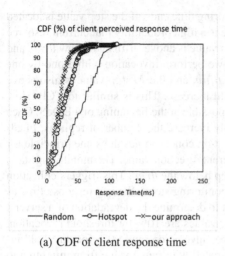
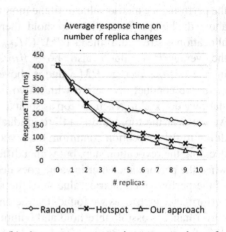

(a) CDF of client response time

(b) Average response time on number of replica changes

Fig. 3. Result of comparison between random, hotspot and our approach

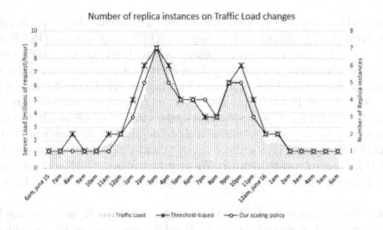

Fig. 4. Replica instances on traffic load changes

load, thereby eliminating the needs to invoke redundant replicas. Compared to the random and hotspot algorithms, our approach demonstrates the following benefits: it will only be active when there is an attack, and it is lightweight and easy to implement.

5   Conclusion

A lightweight scaling mechanism to guarantee service during a DDoS attack. We evaluate a simple and effective mechanism for resource scaling allocation management for

DDoS traffic isolation in a cloud environment. Our work has demonstrated the compelling benefit of the cloud, which can handle high traffic and scale the service dynamically. This research motivation is not to entirely eliminate DDoS attacks, but to provide continuity of a service during a DDoS attack. Other topics, such as a pricing scheme for this mechanism, can be calculated fairly by the cloud service provider as a new type of service, despite the actual resource usage. Inconsistency and synchronization issues procedure would be another problem we should consider be to apply the resource prediction mechanism for dynamic resource scaling.

Acknowledgments. This research was supported by the Public Welfare & Safety Research Program through the National Research Foundation of Korea (NRF) funded by the Ministry of Science, ICT & Future Planning (2012M3A2A1051118).

References

1. ArborNetworks: Fingerprint sharing alliance (2012),
   http://www.arbornetworks.com/careers/53-products/
   4418-fingerprint-sharing-alliance-overview
2. Bless, R.: Using realistic internet topology data for large scale network simulations in omnet++. Tech. rep., University (2002)
3. Cloudflare: An overview of cloudflare (2012),
   https://www.cloudflare.com/overview
4. Muttik, I., Barton, C.: Cloud security technologies. Inf. Sec. Techn. Report 14(1), 1–6 (2009)
5. Nygren, E., Sitaraman, R.K., Sun, J.: The akamai network: a platform for high-performance internet applications. Operating Systems Review 44(3), 2–19 (2010)
6. Qiu, L., Padmanabhan, V.N., Voelker, G.M.: On the placement of web server replicas. In: INFOCOM, pp. 1587–1596 (2001)
7. Rashad, A., Dongwon, S., Heejo, L.: Dropfast: Defending against ddos attacks using cloud technology. In: International Conference on Security and Management (2013)
8. Xie, M., Widjaja, I., Wang, H.: Enhancing cache robustness for content-centric networking. In: INFOCOM, pp. 2426–2434 (2012)

Multi-keyword Similarity Search over Encrypted Cloud Data*

Mikhail Strizhov and Indrajit Ray

Colorado State University
Fort Collins, CO, 80523, USA
{strizhov,indrajit}@CS.ColoState.EDU

Abstract. Searchable encryption allows one to upload encrypted documents on a remote *honest-but-curious* server and query that data at the server itself without requiring the documents to be decrypted prior to searching. In this work, we propose a novel secure and efficient multi-keyword similarity searchable encryption (MKSim) that returns the matching data items in a ranked ordered manner. Unlike all previous schemes, our search complexity is sublinear to the total number of documents that contain the queried set of keywords. Our analysis demonstrates that proposed scheme is proved to be secure against adaptive chosen-keyword attacks. We show that our approach is highly efficient and ready to be deployed in the real-world cloud storage systems.

Keywords: searchable encryption, secure cloud outsourcing, multi-keyword ranked search, homomorphic encryption.

1 Introduction

Cloud computing enables new types of services where the computational and network resources are available online through the Internet. One of the most popular services of cloud computing is data outsourcing. For reasons of cost and convenience, public as well as private organizations can now outsource their large amounts of data to the cloud and enjoy the benefits of remote storage. At the same time, confidentiality of remotely stored data on untrusted cloud server is a big concern. In order to reduce these concerns, sensitive data, such as, personal health records, emails, income tax and financial reports, etc. are usually outsourced in encrypted form using well-known cryptographic techniques. Although encrypted data storage protects remote data from unauthorized access, it complicates some basic, yet essential data utilization services such as plaintext keyword search. A simple solution of downloading the data, decrypting and searching locally is clearly inefficient since storing data in the cloud is meaningless unless it can be easily searched and utilized. Thus, cloud services should enable efficient search on encrypted data to provide the benefits of a first-class cloud computing environment.

Researchers have investigated this problem quite extensively in the context of encrypted documents [1–6, 9, 10, 12, 13, 16, 20, 23, 25, 26]. Solutions generally involve

---

* This work was partially supported by the U.S. National Science Foundation under Grant No. 0905232

N. Cuppens-Boulahia et al. (Eds.): SEC 2014, IFIP AICT 428, pp. 52–65, 2014.

building an encrypted searchable index such that its content is hidden from the remote server yet allowing the corresponding documents to be searched. These solutions differ from each other mostly in terms of whether they allow single keyword search or multi-keyword search and the types of techniques they use to build the trapdoor function. A few of them, most notably [4,5,9,25], allow the notion of similarity search. The similarity search problem consists of a collection of data items that are characterized by some features, a query that specifies a value for a particular feature, and a similarity metric to measure the relevance between the query and the data items. However, these techniques either do not allow searching on multiple keywords and ranking the retrieved document in terms of similarity scores or are very computationally intensive. Moreover, none of these schemes are protected against *adaptive* adversaries [12]. Taking into account large volumes of data available today, there is need in efficient methods to perform secure similarity search over encrypted data outsourced into the cloud. In this work, we propose a novel secure and efficient multi-keyword similarity searchable encryption scheme that returns the matching data items in a ranked order.

Our contributions can be summarized as follows:

1. We present a secure searchable encryption scheme that allows multi-keyword query over an encrypted document corpus and retrieves the relevant documents ranked based on a similarity score.
2. We construct the searchable encryption scheme that is CKA2-secure in the random oracle model [12,17]. Our scheme achieves semantic security against *adaptive* adversaries that choose their search queries as a function of previously obtained trapdoors and search outcomes.
3. We present a construction that achieves the *optimal* search time. Unlike all previous schemes that are glued to the linear search complexity, our search is sublinear to the total number of documents that contain the queried set of keywords. We show that this type of searchable encryption scheme can be extremely efficient.

The rest of the paper is organized as follows: Section 2 gives an outline of the most recent related work. In Section 3 we discuss the threat model for our problem space, give an overview of the system model, notations and preliminaries and introduce the building blocks used in our solution. In Section 4, we provide the framework of the proposed searchable encryption scheme and define the necessary security terms and requirements. The security analysis and comparison to other existing schemes is given in Section 5. Finally, Section 6 is devoted for the concluding remarks.

2   Related Work

Searchable encryption has been an active research area and many quality works have been published [1–6,9–13,16,20–23,25,26]. Traditional searchable encryption schemes usually build an encrypted searchable index such that its content is hidden to the server, however it still allows performing document searching with given search query. Song *et al.* [23] were the first to investigate the techniques for keyword search over encrypted and outsourced data. The authors begin with idea to store a set of plaintext documents on data storage server such as mail servers and file servers in encrypted form to reduce security and privacy risks. The work presents a cryptographic scheme that enables indexed search on encrypted data without leaking any sensitive information to the untrusted remote server. Goh [16] developed a per-file Bloom filter-based secure index, which reduce the searching cost proportional to the number of files in collection. Recent work by Moataz et al. [21] proposed boolean symmetric searchable encryption scheme. Here, the scheme is based on the orthogonalization of the keywords according to the Gram-Schmidt process. Orencik's solution [22] proposed privacy-preserving multi-keyword search method that utilizes minhash functions. Boneh et al. [6] developed the first searchable encryption using the asymmetric settings, where anyone with the public key can write to the data stored remotely, but the users with private key execute search queries. The other asymmetric solution was provided by Di Crescenzo et al. in [11], where the authors propose a public-key encryption scheme with keyword search based on a variant of the quadratic residuosity problem.

All secure index based schemes presented so far, are limited in their usage since they support only exact matching in the context of keyword search. Wang et al. [25] studied the problem of secure ranked keyword search over encrypted cloud data. The authors explored the statistical measure approach that embeds the relevance score of each document during the establishment of searchable index before outsourcing the encrypted document collection. The authors propose a single keyword searchable encryption scheme using ranking criteria based on keyword frequency that retrieves the best matching documents. Cao et al. [9] presented a multi-keyword ranked search scheme, where they used the principle of "coordinate matching" that captures the similarity between a multi-keyword search query and data documents. However, their index structure is uses a binary representation of document terms and thus the ranked search does not differentiate documents with higher number of repeated terms than documents with lower number of repeated terms.

3   Background and Building Blocks

3.1   System and Threat Model

Consider a cloud data hosting service that involves three entities: data owner, cloud server and data user. The data owner may be an individual or an enterprise, who wishes to outsource a collection of documents $D = (D_1, D_2, \ldots, D_n)$ in encrypted form $C = (C_1, C_2, \ldots, C_n)$ to the cloud server and still preserve the search functionality on outsourced data. $C_i = E_S[D_i]$ is the encrypted version of the document D_i computed using a semantically secure encryption scheme E with a secret key S. To enable multi-keyword ranked search capability, the data owner constructs searchable index I that is built on m distinct keywords $K = (k_1, k_2, \ldots, k_m)$ extracted from the original dataset D. Both I and C are outsourced to the cloud server. To securely search the document collection for one or more keywords $\bar{K} \in K$, the authorized data user uses *search trapdoor* (distributed by the data owner) that generates the search request to the cloud server. Once the cloud server receives such request, it performs a search based on the stored index I and returns a ranked list of encrypted documents $L \subseteq C$ to the data user. The data user then uses the secret key S, securely obtained from the data owner, to decrypt received documents L to original view.

We assume a *honest-but-curious* model for the cloud server. The cloud server is *honest*, that is, it is always available to the data user and it correctly follows the designated protocol specification, and it provides all services that are expected. The *curious* cloud server may try to perform some additional analysis to breach the confidentiality of the stored data. In the rest of the paper, the cloud server and the adversary are the same entity. That way, the adversary has access to the same set of information as the cloud server. For this work, we are not concerned about the cloud server being able to link a query to a specific user; nor are we concerned about any denial-of-service attacks.

3.2 Notations and Preliminaries

Let $D = (D_1, D_2, \ldots, D_n)$ be a set of documents and $K = (k_1, k_2, \ldots, k_m)$ be the dictionary consisting of unique keywords in all documents in D, where $\forall i \in [1,m]$ $k_i \in \{0,1\}^*$. $C = \{C_1, C_2, \ldots, C_n\}$ is an encrypted document collection stored in the cloud server. I_i is a searchable index associated with the corresponding encrypted document C_i. If A is an algorithm then $a \leftarrow A(\ldots)$ represents the result of applying the algorithm A to given arguments. Let R be an operational ring, we write vectors in bold, e.g. $\mathbf{v} \in R$. The notation $\mathbf{v}[i]$ refers to the i-th coefficient of $\mathbf{v}$. We denote the dot product of $\mathbf{u}, \mathbf{v} \in R$ as $\mathbf{u} \otimes \mathbf{v} = \sum_{i=1} \mathbf{u}[i] \cdot \mathbf{v}[i] \in R$. We use $\lfloor x \rceil$ to indicate rounding x to the nearest integer, and $\lfloor x \rfloor$, $\lceil x \rceil$ (for $x \geqslant 0$)to indicate rounding down or up.

Cryptographic Notations. A private-key encryption scheme is a set of three polynomial-time algorithms $SKE = (Gen, Enc, Dec)$ such that Gen is a probabilistic algorithm that takes a security parameter k and returns a secret key K_{secret}; Enc is a probabilistic algorithm that takes a key K_{secret} and a message m, and outputs a ciphertext ξ; Dec is a deterministic algorithm that takes a secret key K_{secret} and a ciphertext ξ, and outputs m if K_{secret} is the valid secret key. We say that SKE is CPA-secure if the ciphertexts it outputs do not reveal any partial information about the original plaintext to an adversary that can adaptively query an encryption oracle. We also make use of use pseudo-random function (PRF), which is a polynomial-time computable function that cannot be distinguished from random functions by any probabilistic polynomial-time adversary. We refer the reader [12, 17, 19] for formal definitions of *semantic security*, CPA-security and PRFs.

We now review definitions related to homomorphic encryption. Our definitions are based on Gentry's works [14] and [15], but we slightly relax the definition of decryption correctness, to allow a negligible probability of error.

Definition 1. *Homomorphic encryption: A homomorphic encryption scheme* Hom *consist of four algorithms:*

- KeyGen: *Given security parameter* λ, *returns a secret key* sk *and a public key* pk.
- Enc: *Given the plaintext* $m \in \{0, 1\}$ *and public key* pk, *returns ciphertext* ϕ.
- Dec: *Given the ciphertext* ϕ *and secret key* sk, *returns the plaintext* m.
- Eval: *Given public key* pk, *a* t-*input circuit* C (*consisting of addition and multiplication gates modulo 2*), *and a tuple of ciphertext* $(\phi_1, \phi_2, \ldots, \phi_t)$ (*corresponding to the* t *input bits of* C), *returns a ciphertext* ϕ.

Hom *is correct for a family* $\mathbb{C}$ *of circuits with* $\leqslant t = \text{Poly}(\lambda)$ *input bits if for any* $C \in \mathbb{C}$ *and input bits* $(m_i)_{i \leqslant t}$, *the following holds with overwhelming probability over the randomness of* KeyGen *and* Enc:

$$\text{Dec}(\text{sk}, \text{Eval}(\text{pk}, C, (\phi_1, \phi_2, \dots, \phi_t))) = C(m_1, m_2, \dots, m_t), \qquad (1)$$

where $(\text{sk}, \text{pk}) = \text{KeyGen}(\lambda)$ *and* $\phi_i = \text{Enc}(\text{pk}, m_i)$ *for* $i = 1, \dots, t$.

Hom *is compact if for any circuit* C *with* $\leqslant t = \text{Poly}(\lambda)$ *input bits, the bit-size of the ciphertext* Eval$(\text{pk}, C, (\phi_1, \phi_2, \dots, \phi_t))$ *is bounded by a fixed polynomial* $b(\lambda)$.

3.3 Brakerski's Homomorphic Cryptosystem

Brakerski *et al.* [7, 8] recently proposed encryption schemes that efficiently support low-degree homomorphic computations needed for our constructions. We use the ring-LWE-based variant of Brakerski's homomorphic cryptosystem [7] that operates over polynomial rings modulo a cyclotomic polynomial. One appealing property of Brakerski's homomorphic cryptosystem is to use the "batching mode" where a single ciphertext represent a vector of encrypted values and single homomorphic operation on two such ciphertexts applies the homomorphic operation component-wise to the entire vector. In such way, for the cost of a single homomorphic operation we get the compute on a entire vector of encrypted plaintexts. Let $\Delta_m(x)$ be the mth cyclotomic polynomial and let $R = \mathbb{Z}[x]/\Delta_m(x)$ denote the operational ring. Moreover, let $R_p = \mathbb{Z}_p[x]/\Delta_m(x)$ be our plaintext space and let $R_q = \mathbb{Z}_q[x]/\Delta_m(x)$ be our ciphertext space for some $q > p$. Here, the secret keys are vectors of elements in R_q and the plaintext comprises of elements of R_p. We present the necessary basics of ring-LWE-based homomorphic encryption scheme: key-generation, encryption and decryption mechanisms:

Hom.KeyGen: We sample a polynomial $\bar{s} \in R_q$ from a Hamming weight distribution $\mathbb{HWT}(h)$. Here, h specifies the number of nonzero coefficients in $\bar{s}$ and each nonzero element in $\bar{s}$ is ± 1 with equal probability. The vector $\mathbf{s} = (1, \bar{s}) \in R_q^2$ is the secret key. The public key is generated by sampling uniformly a polynomial $\mathbf{A}$ from R_q and $\mathbf{e}$ from a noise distribution. The noise distribution is set to be the zero-mean discrete Gaussian distribution $\mathbb{DG}(\sigma^2)$ with variance σ^2. The public key is $\mathbf{P} = [\mathbf{b} \| -\mathbf{A}] \in R_q^2$, where $\mathbf{b} = [\mathbf{A} \cdot \bar{s} + \mathbf{e}]_q$.

Hom.Enc($\mathbf{P}, \mathbf{m}$): The algorithm that encrypts the message $\mathbf{m} \in R_p$ with public key $\mathbf{P}$. We sample a polynomial $\mathbf{r}$ with coefficients varying in $\{0, \pm 1\}$ and $\mathbf{e} = (e_0, e_1)$ from the noise distribution $\mathbb{DG}^2(\sigma^2)$. The encryption of message $\mathbf{m}$ using public key $\mathbf{P}$ is a vector of ciphertexts $\mathbf{c} = \left[\mathbf{P}^\mathsf{T}\mathbf{r} + \left\lfloor \frac{q}{p} \right\rfloor \mathbf{m} \right]_q$, where $\lfloor \cdot \rfloor$ is the floor function and $[\cdot]_q$ denotes reduction modulo q.

Hom.Dec($\mathbf{S}, \mathbf{c}$): The algorithm that decrypts a ciphertext $\mathbf{c}$ using the secret key $\mathbf{s}$ as follows: $m = \left[\left\lfloor p \cdot \frac{[\langle \mathbf{c}, \mathbf{s} \rangle]_q}{q} \right\rceil \right]_p$.

Addition: $\mathbf{c}_{sum} = \mathbf{c}_1 + \mathbf{c}_2$. E_{sum} is the result noise in $\mathbf{c}_{sum}$ and $E_{sum} \leqslant E_1 + E_2$, where E_1 and E_2 denote noise for $\mathbf{c}_1$ and $\mathbf{c}_2$.

Multiplication: $c_{prod} = \left\lfloor \frac{p}{q} \cdot (c_1 \otimes c_2) \right\rceil$. E_{prod} here denote the maximum noise in c_{prod} and $E_{prod} \leqslant \delta_1 + \delta_2 + \delta_3$, where $(\delta_i)_{1 \leqslant i \leqslant 3}$ is the noise inflicted by the key switching process. We refer the reader to [7, 8] for more detailed discussion on the properties of Brakerski's homomorphic cryptosystem.

3.4 Term Frequency-Inverse Document Frequency

One of the main problems of information retrieval is to determine the relevance of documents with respect to the user information needs. The most commonly used technique to represent the relevance score in the information retrieval community is Term Frequency-Inverse Documents Frequency measure [18, 27, 28]. It is computed based on two independent measures - the Term Frequency and the Inverse Document Frequency. The Term Frequency (TF) is a statistical measure that represents the frequency of repeated terms in a documents. The TF value calculates the number of times a given term appears within a single document. The Inverse Documents Frequency (IDF) is a measure of a term's importance across the whole document collection. It is defined as the logarithm of the ratio of the number of documents in a collection to the number of documents containing a given term.

We adopt the following equation for TF-IDF measure from [27]:

$$Score = \log\left(f_{i,j} + 1\right) \times \log\left(1 + \frac{n}{\sum\limits_{k=1}^{n} \chi(f_{i,k})}\right) \tag{2}$$

where $f_{i,j}$ specifies the Term Frequency of term j in document D_i, n is the total number of documents in the corpus and $\sum\limits_{k=1}^{n} \chi(f_{j,k})$ denotes IDF value for term j among the entire document collection D.

To provide the ranked results to user's queries we choose to use the dot product as similarity metric. We use vector space model [18], where the documents and search query are represented as high dimensional vectors. The similarity metric is measured by applying the dot product between each document vector and the search query vector as follows: $\mathrm{dotprod}(D_i, Q) = D_i \otimes Q$, where D_i is a vector that represents i-th document and Q is a search query vector.

4   Multi-keyword Similarity Searchable Encryption (MKSim)

Recall that we are targeting the following scenario: the data owner creates secure searchable index and sends it along with encrypted data files to the cloud server. The index is constructed in such a way that it provides enough information to perform the search on the outsourced data, but does not give away any information about the original data. Once the server receives the index and encrypted document files, it performs a search on the index and retrieves the most relevant documents according to data user's query.

4.1   Algorithm Definitions

Definition 2. *Multi-keyword Similarity Searchable Encryption (MKSim) scheme over the set of documents* D *consists of five polynomial-time algorithms, as follows:*

1. $S_1, S_2, PK, SK \leftarrow Gen(1^s)$: *a probabilistic algorithm that is run by the data owner to setup the scheme. The algorithm outputs secret keys S_1, S_2, PK and SK.*
2. $(I, C) \leftarrow BuildIndex(S_1, S_2, PK, D, K)$: *a probabilistic algorithm run by the data owner that takes as input a collection of documents* D, *the keyword dictionary* K *and secret keys S_1, S_2 and PK, and outputs the collection of encrypted documents* $C = \{C_1, C_2, \ldots, C_n\}$ *and the searchable index* I.
3. $\Omega \leftarrow MakeQuery(S_2, PK, K, \bar{K})$: *a (possibly probabilistic) algorithm run by the data user that takes an input a secret keys S_2 and PK, keyword dictionary* K *and multiple keywords of interest* $\bar{K}$, *and outputs the search query* Ω.
4. $L \leftarrow Evaluate(I, \Omega)$: *a deterministic algorithm run by the cloud server. The algorithm inputs a search query* Ω *and the secure index* I. *It outputs the sequence of identifiers* $L \subseteq C$ *matching the search query.*
5. $D_i \leftarrow Decrypt(S_1, SK, C_i)$: *a deterministic algorithm that takes as input secret keys S_1 and SK, and a ciphertext C_i and outputs a document D_i.*

An index-based MKSim scheme is correct if $\forall s \in \mathbb{N}$, $\forall S_1, S_2$, PK,SK *generated by* $Gen(1^s)$, $\forall D$, $\forall (I, C)$ *output by* $BuildIndex(S_1, S_2, PK, D, K)$, $\forall \bar{K} \in K$, *and* $1 \leqslant i \leqslant n$,

$$Evaluate(I, MakeQuery(S_2, PK, K, \bar{K})) = D(\bar{K}) \bigwedge Decrypt(S_1, SK, C_i) = D_i$$
(3)

4.2   MKSim Security Model

Definition 3. *History: Let* $\bar{K}$ *be a collection of keywords of interest,* D *be a collection of documents and* $\Omega = \{\Omega_1, \Omega_2, \ldots, \Omega_q\}$ *be a vector of* q *search queries. The history of is defined as* $H(D, \Omega)$.

Definition 4. *Access Pattern: Let* $\bar{K}$ *be a collection of keywords of interest,* D *be a collection of documents and* $\Omega = \{\Omega_1, \Omega_2, \ldots, \Omega_q\}$ *be a vector of* q *search queries. The access pattern induced by a* q-query *history* $H(D, \Omega)$, *is defined as follows:* $\alpha(H) = (D(\Omega_1), D(\Omega_2), \ldots, D(\Omega_q))$.

Definition 5. *Search Pattern: Let* $\bar{K}$ *be a collection of keywords of interest,* D *be a collection of documents and* $\Omega = \{\Omega_1, \Omega_2, \ldots, \Omega_q\}$ *be a vector of* q *search queries. The search pattern of the history* $H(D, \Omega)$ *is a symmetric binary matrix* $\sigma(H)$ *such that for* $1 \leqslant i, j \leqslant q$, *the element in the ith row and j^{th} column is 1 if $\Omega_i = \Omega_j$, and 0 otherwise.*

Definition 6. *Trace: Let* $\bar{K}$ *be a collection of keywords of interest,* D *be a collection of documents and* $\Omega = \{\Omega_1, \Omega_2, \ldots, \Omega_q\}$ *be a vector of* q *search queries. The trace induced by the history* $H(D, \Omega)$ *is a sequence* $\tau(H) = (|D_1|, |D_2|, \ldots, |D_n|, \alpha(H), \sigma(H))$ *comprised of the lengths of document collection* $D = (D_1, D_2, \ldots, D_n)$, *and the access and search patters induced by the history* $H(D, \Omega)$.

Definition 7. *Randomized query: Let* $\Omega_{1 \leqslant i \leqslant q}$ *be a sequence of* q *generated search queries with the same set of keywords* $\bar{K}$. *We say that the scheme has* (q, ϵ)-*randomized query if:* $\forall i, j \in 1, q$ $Pr(\Omega_i = \Omega_j) < \epsilon$.

Definition 8. *Adaptive Semantic Security: Let* $MKSim$ = (Gen, BuildIndex, MakeQuery, Evaluate, Decrypt) *be an index-based similarity searchable encryption scheme,* s *be the security parameter, and* $A = (A_0, \ldots, A_q)$ *be an adversary such that* $q \in \mathbb{N}$ *and* $S = (S_0, \ldots, S_q)$ *be a simulator. Consider the following probabilistic experiments* $Real_{MKSim,A}^{\star}(s)$ *and* $Sim_{MKSim,A,S}^{\star}(s)$:

$Real_{MKSim,A}^{\star}(s)$:	$Sim_{MKSim,A,S}^{\star}(s)$:
$(D, st_A) \leftarrow A_0(1^s)$	$(D, st_A) \leftarrow A_0(1^s)$
$S_1, S_2 \leftarrow Gen(1^s)$	$(I, C, st_S) \leftarrow S_0(\tau(D))$
$(I, C) \leftarrow BuildIndex(S_1, S_2, D, K)$	$(\bar{K}_1, st_A) \leftarrow A_1(st_A, I, C)$
$(\bar{K}_1, st_A) \leftarrow A_1(st_A, I, C)$	$(\Omega_1, st_S) \leftarrow S_1(st_S, \tau(D, \bar{K}_1))$
$\Omega_1 \leftarrow MakeQuery(S_2, K, \bar{K}_1)$	*for* $2 \leqslant i \leqslant q$
for $2 \leqslant i \leqslant q$	$\quad (\bar{K}_i, st_A) \leftarrow A_i(st_A, I, C, \Omega_1, \ldots, \Omega_{i-1})$
$\quad (\bar{K}_i, st_A) \leftarrow A_i(st_A, I, C, \Omega_1, \ldots, \Omega_{i-1})$	$\quad (\Omega_i, st_S) \leftarrow S_i(st_S, \tau(D, \bar{K}_1, \ldots, \bar{K}_i))$
$\quad \Omega_i \leftarrow MakeQuery(S_2, K, \bar{K}_i)$	*let* $\Omega = \{\Omega_1, \Omega_2, \ldots, \Omega_q\}$
let $\Omega = \{\Omega_1, \Omega_2, \ldots, \Omega_q\}$	*output* $o = (I, C, \Omega)$ *and* st_A
output $o = (I, C, \Omega)$ *and* st_A	

where st_A *is the state of adversary,* st_S *is the state of the simulator. We say that MKSim is adaptively semantically secure if for all polynomial-size adversaries* $A = (A_0, \ldots, A_q)$ *such that* q *is is polynomial in* s, *there exist a non-uniform polynomial-size simulator* $S = (S_0, \ldots, S_q)$ *such that for all polynomial-size* $\mathbb{R}$:

$$|Pr[\mathbb{R}(o, st_A) = 1] - Pr[\mathbb{R}(\bar{o}, s\bar{t}_A)]| \leqslant \epsilon, \qquad (4)$$

where $(o, st_A) \leftarrow Real_{MKSim,A}^{\star}(s)$, $(\bar{o}, s\bar{t}_A) \leftarrow Sim_{MKSim,A,S}^{\star}(s)$ *and the probabilities are over the coins of* Gen *and* BuildIndex *and* MakeQuery.

4.3 MKSim Construction

Our searchable scheme is based on SSE-2 inverted index data construction previously introduced in [12]. We enhance SSE-2 scheme with addition of TF-IDF statistical measurement and dot product for ranked search. We show that our construction is very efficient and it achieves the same semantic security guarantees as SSE-2 scheme. Fig. 1 shows an outline of MKSim scheme.

Our searchable index consist of two main algorithms: building the lookup filter T, based on SSE-2 construction and building the TF-IDF table Φ, based on TF-IDF word importance. We first couple the document collection D with the dictionary K to produce the lookup filter T. For each word k we add an entry in T, there value is the document identifier with the instance of word k. Note, for a given word k and the set of documents that contains the word k, we derive a label for k with j^{th} document identifier. For example, if word k is a "colorado" and there is only one document with this word, then $k\|j$ is "colorado1". We represent the family of k with matching j^{th} documents as follows: $F_k = \{k\|j : 1 \leqslant j \leqslant |D(k)|\}$, where $|D(k)|$ represents the list of matching documents. For instance, if the word $k=$"state" exists in a set of four documents, then family F_k is {"state1", "state2", "state3", "state4"}. In our construction, searching for word k becomes equal of searching for all labels in a form of $k\|j$ in the family F_k.

We guard the unique number of words in each document by adopting the idea of padding the lookup filter T such that the identifier of each document appears in the same number of entries. To protect the keyword content in the table T, we use the pseudo-random permutation π with secret parameter S_2 such as $\{0, 1\}^{S_2} \times \{0, 1\}^{l+\log_2(n+max)} \to \{0, 1\}^{l+\log_2(n+max)}$, where max denote the maximum number of distinct keywords in the largest document in D, n is the number of documents in D and each keyword is represented using at most l bits. Our lookup table T is $(\{0, 1\}^{l+\log_2(n+max)} \times \{0, 1\}^{\log_2(n)} \times \{p\})$, where $p = max \star n$.

In our second step, for each distinct keyword k_j in a document D_i, we calculate the TF-IDF value using equation (2). We then construct a table Φ where each row corresponds to the document id and each column is a keyword in the dictionary K. Each cell element of table Φ contains the TF-IDF value of a keyword k_j. Unfortunately, outsourcing the table elements to the cloud leaks some important information. It is well known fact [24] that an adversary (in our case, the cloud server) may know some of keywords and their TF distributions. Using this information, an adversary can infer the keyword index or even the document content. Based on this observation, we decided to improve the security of our solution. Our table includes the set of dummy keywords Z that are added to the keyword dictionary K. This gives us the randomness that hides the original keyword distribution of TF-IDF values. Finally, we use the "batching mode" encryption of Brakerski's homomorphic cryptosystem to protect the values of TF-IDF table Φ. We apply Brakerski's Hom.Enc() with secret PK on each row of TF-IDF table Φ.

Once both the lookup filter T and TF-IDF table Φ are constructed, we use secure symmetric encryption scheme SKE to encrypt each document D_i with secret key S_1 to form C_i. We outsource searchable index $I = (T, \Phi)$ and encryption collection $C = \{C_1, C_2, \ldots, C_n\}$ to the cloud server.

Now the collection is available for selective retrieval from the cloud server. To search for keywords of interest $\bar{K}$, the data user uses the trapdoor to output the search query Ω to the cloud server. The trapdoor utilizes the pseudo-random permutation π with secret parameter S_2 and Hom.Enc() with secret PK to form the search query Ω. The server then locates the document identifiers id in the filter table T that matches the keywords of interest. For each encrypted document C_j, where $1 \leqslant j \leqslant id$, the cloud server executes the dot product between the search query and the values in TF-IDF table Φ to form the set of polynomials $\{score_{C_1}, score_{C_2}, \ldots, score_{C_{id}}\}$. The data user decrypts these polynomials using Hom.Dec() with secret SK and then he retrieves top-m documents with highest output scores.

$Gen(1^s)$: generate $S_1 \leftarrow SKE.Gen(1^s)$ and $S_2 \xleftarrow{R} \{0,1\}^s$. Sample **SK**, **PK** $\leftarrow Hom.KeyGen()$.
Output S_1, S_2, **SK** and **PK**.

$BuildIndex(S_1, S_2, PK, D, K)$:

Initialization:
1. Scan document corpus D, extract $k_1, k_2, \ldots, k_p \leftarrow$ from D_i.
2. Construct dictionary K with dummy Z.
3. For each $k \in K$, build $D(k)$ (i.e., the sequence of documents with k).

Build lookup filter T:
1. for each $k_i \in K$:
   - for $1 \leqslant j \leqslant |D(k_i)|$:
     - value $= id(D_{i,j})$, where $id(D_{i,j})$ is the jth identifier in $D(k_i)$.
     - set $T[\pi_{S_2}(k_i\|j)] =$ value.
2. let $\bar{p} = \sum_{k_i \in K} |D(k_i)|$. If $\bar{p} < p$, assign value $= id(D)$ for all $D_i \in D$ for exactly max entries, set the $address$ to random values.

Build TF-IDF table Φ:
1. for each $D_i \in D$
   - for each $k_j \in K$
     - $z_j \leftarrow TFIDF(k_j)$ (i.e., calculate TF-IDF value for keyword k_j).
   - $\Phi_i = Hom.Enc(PK, z)$.

Output:
1. for each $D_i \in D$, let $C_i \leftarrow SKE.Enc(S_1, D_i)$.
2. output (I, C), where $I = (T, \Phi)$ and $C = \{C_1, C_2, \ldots, C_n\}$.

$MakeQuery(S_2, PK, K, \tilde{K})$:
1. for each $k_i \in \tilde{K} \in K$, $t_i = (\pi_{S_2}(k_i\|1), \ldots, \pi_{2_i}(k_i\|n))$, $b_i \leftarrow TFIDF(k_i)$.
2. $x = Hom.Enc(PK, b)$.
3. output: $\Omega = (t, x)$.

$Evaluate(I, \Omega)$:
1. $id \leftarrow T[t]$.
2. for all $1 \leqslant j \leqslant id$, $score_{C_j} \leftarrow \Phi_{C_j} \otimes x$.
3. output $\{score_{C_1}, score_{C_2}, \ldots, score_{C_{id}}\}$.

$Decrypt(S_1, SK, C_i)$:
1. $score_{D_i} = Hom.Dec(SK, score_{C_i})$.
2. $(score_{D_i})_m \xleftarrow{top\text{-}m} \{score_{D_1}, score_{D_2}, \ldots, score_{D_{id}}\}$.
3. output $(D_i)_m \leftarrow SKE.Dec(S_1, (C_i)_m)$.

Fig. 1. MKSim Construction

5   Security Analysis and Complexity Results

5.1   Security

Theorem 1. *If* $MKSim = (Gen, BuildIndex, MakeQuery, Evaluate)$ *is a index-based searchable encryption scheme, then it is adaptively semantically secure.*

Proof. We are going to describe a polynomial-size simulator $\mathbb{S} = \{\mathbb{S}_0, \mathbb{S}_1, \ldots, \mathbb{S}_q\}$ such that for all polynomial-size adversaries $A = \{A_1, A_2, \ldots, A_q\}$, the outputs of $Real^\star_{MKSim,A}(s)$ and $Sim^\star_{MKSim,A,\mathbb{S}}(s)$ are computationally indistinguishable. Consider the simulator $\mathbb{S} = \{\mathbb{S}_0, \mathbb{S}_1, \ldots, \mathbb{S}_q\}$ that adaptively generates the output $o^* = (I^*, C^*, \Omega^*)$ as follows:

- $\mathbb{S}_0(1^s, \tau(D))$: the simulator has a knowledge of history H that includes the number and the size of the documents. $\mathbb{S}_0$ start with generating $C_i^* \xleftarrow{R} \{0,1\}^{|D_i|}$ where $i \in \{1, 2, \ldots, n\}$ and index $I^* = (T^*, \Phi^*)$. Here $T^* \xleftarrow{R} \{0,1\}^{1+\log_2(n+max)}$ is a lookup filter, and $\Phi^* \xleftarrow{R} \{0, 1\}^K$ is TF-IDF table. $\mathbb{S}_0$ now includes I^* in st_S and outputs (I^*, C^*, st_S). Since st_A does not include secrets S_1 and **PK**, I^* is indistinguishable from the real index. Otherwise $\mathbb{S}_0$ can distinguish between the output of pseudo-random permutation π and a random values of size $l + \log_2(n + max)$ and K. At the same time, st_A does not include secret S_2, thus the output C^* is indistinguishable from the real ciphertext

- $\mathbb{S}_1(st_S, \tau(D, \Omega_1))$: now the simulator $\mathbb{S}_1$ has a knowledge of all document identifiers corresponding to the search query. However the search query does not disclose its structure and the content. Recall that $D(\Omega_1)$ is the set of all matching document identifiers. For all $1 \leqslant j \leqslant |D(\Omega_1)|$, the simulator first makes an association between each document identifier $id(D_j)$ and a generated search query such that $(D(\Omega_1)_i, I_i^*)$ are pairwise distinct. $\mathbb{S}_1$ then creates $\Omega_1^* = (t^*, x^*)$, where $t^* \xleftarrow{R} (id(D_1), \ldots, id(|D(\Omega_1)|))$ and $x^* \xleftarrow{R} \{0, 1\}^K$. $\mathbb{S}_1$ stores the association between Ω_1^* and Ω_1 in st_S, and outputs (Ω_1^*, st_S). Since st_A does not include secret S_1, the output t_1^* is indistinguishable from the real generated query t_1, otherwise one could distinguish between the output of π and a random string of size $l + \log_2(n + max)$. Similarly, since st_A does not include secret **PK**, the output x^* is indistinguishable from the real x, otherwise one could distinguish between the output of $Hom.Enc()$ and a random string of a size K. Thus, Ω_1^* is indistinguishable from Ω_1.

- $\mathbb{S}_i(st_S, \tau(D, \Omega_1, \Omega_2, \ldots, \Omega_q))$ for $2 \leqslant i \leqslant q$: first $\mathbb{S}_i$ checks if the search query Ω_i was executed before, that is, if it appeared in the trace $\sigma[i, j] = 1$, where $1 \leqslant j \leqslant i - 1$. If $\sigma[i, j] = 0$, the search query has not appeared before and $\mathbb{S}_i$ generates the search query as $\mathbb{S}_1$. If $\sigma[i, j] = 1$, then $\mathbb{S}_i$ retrieves previously searched query, and constructs Ω_i^*. $\mathbb{S}_i$ outputs (Ω_i^*, st_S), where Ω_i^* is indistinguishable from real Ω_i. The final output $\Omega = (\Omega_1^*, \ldots, \Omega_q^*)$ is indistinguishable from generated query $(\Omega = \Omega_1, \ldots, \Omega_q)$, and outputs of experiments $Sim_{MKSim,A,S}^*(s)$ and $Real_{MKSim,A}^*(s)$ are indistinguishable.

$\square$

Theorem 2. *Injection of dummy keywords provides randomized search queries.*

Proof. Let us consider two search queries Ω_1 and Ω_2, both constructed from the same keyword set K and a randomly chosen set of dummy keywords Z_1 and Z_2 from a dictionary $\mathscr{Z}$ of a size $n = |\mathscr{Z}|$. We are aiming to prove that: $\forall i, j \ i \neq j \ Pr(\Omega_i = \Omega_j) < \epsilon$ where ϵ tends to zero as n increases.

We first estimate the probability $Pr(k)$ that the intersection Z of two sets $Z_1, Z_2 \subseteq \mathscr{Z}$ is equal to some value k. We have:

$$Pr(k) = \frac{\# of \ ways \ of \ choosing \ Z_1, Z_2 \ with \ |Z| = k}{\# \ of \ ways \ of \ choosing \ Z_1, Z_2} \qquad (5)$$

Note, there are $\binom{n}{k}$ choices for Z. If Z_1 has size k, then there is one choice for Z_1, and we can choose Z_2 arbitrarily from 2^{n-k} possibilities. If Z_1 has size $k + 1$, then there are $\binom{n-k}{1}$ choices for Z_1 and 2^{n-k-1} choices for Z_2. Let $m = n - k$, then there are $\sum_{j=0}^{m} 2^{m-j} \binom{m}{j} = 3^m$ possible choices for Z_1, Z_2 with intersection Z. Thus, there are

$3^{n-k}\binom{n}{k}$ possible ways of choosing the subsets. Since there are 4^n ways of choosing any two subsets of $\mathscr{X}$, we have the following: $Pr(k) = \frac{3^{n-k}\binom{n}{k}}{4^n}$. We now evaluate $Pr(k)$ with input $k \to 0$: $\lim_{k \to 0} Pr(k) = \lim_{k \to 0} \frac{3^{n-k}\binom{n}{k}}{4^n} = \left(\frac{3}{4}\right)^n$. As n increases, $\lim_{k \to 0} Pr(k) \to 0$ and hence Theorem 2 is preserved. $\qquad\square$

5.2 Complexity

We compare MKSim scheme with previous searchable encryption solutions in Table 1. Our comparison is based on few simple metrics: matching technique, query randomization, security notions and search complexity. We use security notations from [12]. Note that all previous work able to achieve the linear search complexity within the total number of documents in the collection. In contrast, the search in our solution is proportional to the number of files that contain a certain set of keywords.

Table 1. Comparison of several searchable encryption schemes. n is the document collection, $|n|$ denotes its bit length, #n is the number of files in the collection n, $\#n_{\bar{K}}$ is the number of files that contain keywords of interest $\bar{K}$.

Scheme	Matching	Query randomization	Security	Search complexity
Song *et al.* [23]	Exact	no	CPA	$O(|n|)$
Goh *et al.* [16]	Exact	no	CKA1	$O(\#n)$
Cao *et al.* [9]	Similarity	yes	CKA1	$O(\#n)$
Moataz *et al.* [21]	Exact	yes	CKA2	$O(\#n)$
Curtmola *et al.* [12]	Exact	no	CKA2	$O(\#n_{\bar{K}})$
Orencik *et al.* [22]	Exact	no	CKA2	$O(\#n)$
MKSim	**Similarity**	**yes**	**CKA2**	$O(\#n_{\bar{K}})$

6 Conclusion

Searchable encryption is a technique that enables secure searches over encrypted data stored on remote servers. We define and solve the problem of multi-keyword ranked search over encrypted cloud data. In particular, we present an efficient similarity searchable encryption scheme that supports multi-keyword semantics. Our solution is based two building blocks: Term Frequency - Inverse Document Frequency (TF-IDF) measurement and ring-LWE-based variant of homomorphic cryptosystem. We use the dot product to quantitatively evaluate similarity measure and rank the outsourced documents with their importance to the search query. We show that our scheme is adaptive semantically secure against adversaries and able to achieve optimal sublinear search time. As future work, we plan to optimize the index construction algorithm and continue to research on usable and secure mechanisms for the effective utilization over outsourced cloud data.

References

1. Abdalla, M., Bellare, M., Catalano, D., Kiltz, E., Kohno, T., Lange, T., Malone-Lee, J., Neven, G., Paillier, P., Shi, H.: Searchable encryption revisited: consistency properties, relation to anonymous ibe, and extensions. Journal of Cryptology 21(3), 350–391 (2008)

2. Agrawal, R., Kiernan, J., Srikant, R., Xu, Y.: Order-preserving encryption for numeric data. In: Proceedings of the ACM SIGMOD International Conference on Management of Data, Paris, France (June 2004)

3. Bellare, M., Boldyreva, A., O'Neill, A.: Deterministic and efficiently searchable encryption. In: Menezes, A. (ed.) CRYPTO 2007. LNCS, vol. 4622, pp. 535–552. Springer, Heidelberg (2007)

4. Blanton, M.: Achieving full security in privacy-preserving data mining. In: Proceedings of the 3rd IEEE International Conference on Privacy, Security, Risk and Trust, Boston, MA, USA (October 2011)

5. Blanton, M., Atallah, M.J., Frikken, K.B., Malluhi, Q.: Secure and efficient outsourcing of sequence comparisons. In: Foresti, S., Yung, M., Martinelli, F. (eds.) ESORICS 2012. LNCS, vol. 7459, pp. 505–522. Springer, Heidelberg (2012)

6. Boneh, D., Waters, B.: Conjunctive, subset, and range queries on encrypted data. In: Proceedings of the 4th IACR Theory of Cryptography Conference, Amsterdam, The Netherlands (February 2007)

7. Brakerski, Z.: Fully homomorphic encryption without modulus switching from classical gapsvp. In: Safavi-Naini, R., Canetti, R. (eds.) CRYPTO 2012. LNCS, vol. 7417, pp. 868–886. Springer, Heidelberg (2012)

8. Brakerski, Z., Gentry, C., Vaikuntanathan, V.: Fully homomorphic encryption without bootstrapping. In: Proceedings of the 3rd Innovations in Theoretical Computer Science Conference, Cambridge, MA, USA (2012)

9. Cao, N., Wang, C., Li, M., Ren, K., Lou, W.: Privacy-preserving multi-keyword ranked search over encrypted cloud data. In: Proceedings of the 30th IEEE International Conference on Computer Communications, Shanghai, China (April 2011)

10. Chang, Y.-C., Mitzenmacher, M.: Privacy preserving keyword searches on remote encrypted data. In: Ioannidis, J., Keromytis, A.D., Yung, M. (eds.) ACNS 2005. LNCS, vol. 3531, pp. 442–455. Springer, Heidelberg (2005)

11. Di Crescenzo, G., Saraswat, V.: Public key encryption with searchable keywords based on jacobi symbols. In: Srinathan, K., Rangan, C.P., Yung, M. (eds.) INDOCRYPT 2007. LNCS, vol. 4859, pp. 282–296. Springer, Heidelberg (2007)

12. Curtmola, R., Garay, J., Kamara, S., Ostrovsky, R.: Searchable symmetric encryption: Improved definitions and efficient constructions. In: Proceedings of the 13th ACM Conference on Computer and Communications Security, Alexandria, Virginia, USA (October 2006)

13. di Vimercati, S.D.C., Foresti, S., Jajodia, S., Paraboschi, S., Samarati, P.: Private data indexes for selective access to outsourced data. In: Proceedings of the 10th Annual ACM Workshop on Privacy in the Electronic Society, Chicago, IL, USA (October 2011)

14. Gentry, C.: A fully homomorphic encryption scheme. PhD thesis, Stanford University (2009), http://crypto.stanford.edu/craig

15. Gentry, C.: Fully homomorphic encryption using ideal lattices. In: Proceedings of the 41st Annual ACM Symposium on Theory of Computing, Bethesda, MD (2009)

16. Goh, E.-J.: Secure indexes. Cryptology ePrint Archive, Report 2003/216 (2003), http://eprint.iacr.org/2003/216/

17. Goldreich, O.: The foundations of cryptography. Basic Applications, vol. 2. Cambridge University Press (2004)

18. Grossman, D.A., Frieder, O.: Information retrieval: algorithms and heuristics. Kluwer international series on information retrieval. Springer (2004)
19. Katz, J., Lindell, Y.: Introduction to Modern Cryptography. Chapman & Hall/CRC Cryptography and Network Security Series. Chapman & Hall/CRC (2007)
20. Kuzu, M., Islam, M.S., Kantarcioglu, M.: Efficient similarity search over encrypted data. In: Proceedings of the 28th IEEE International Conference on Data Engineering, Washington, DC, USA (April 2012)
21. Moataz, T., Shikfa, A.: Boolean symmetric searchable encryption. In: Proceedings of the 8th ACM SIGSAC Symposium on Information, Computer and Communications Security, Hangzhou, China (May 2013)
22. Orencik, C., Kantarcioglu, M., Savas, E.: A practical and secure multi-keyword search method over encrypted cloud data. In: Proceedings of the 6th IEEE International Conference on Cloud Computing, Santa Clara, CA, USA (June 2013)
23. Song, D.X., Wagner, D., Perrig, A.: Practical techniques for searches on encrypted data. In: Proceedings of the 2000 IEEE Symposium on Security and Privacy, Berkeley, CA, USA (May 2000)
24. Swaminathan, A., Mao, Y., Su, G.-M., Gou, H., Varna, A.L., He, S., Wu, M., Oard, D.W.: Confidentiality-preserving rank-ordered search. In: Proceedings of the ACM Workshop on Storage Security and Survivability, Alexandria, Virginia, USA (2007)
25. Wang, C., Cao, N., Ren, K., Lou, W.: Enabling secure and efficient ranked keyword search over outsourced cloud data. IEEE Transactions on Parallel and Distributed Systems 23(8), 1467–1479 (2012)
26. Wang, C., Ren, K., Yu, S., Urs, K.M.R.: Achieving usable and privacy-assured similarity search over outsourced cloud data. In: Proceedings of the 31st Annual IEEE International Conference on Computer Communications, Orlando, FL, USA (March 2012)
27. Witten, I.H., Moffat, A., Bell, T.C.: Managing gigabytes: compressing and indexing documents and images, 2nd edn. Morgan Kaufmann, San Francisco (1999)
28. Zobel, J., Moffat, A.: Exploring the similarity space. SIGIR FORUM 32, 18–34 (1998)

Security of the Multiple-Key Blom's Key Agreement Scheme for Sensor Networks

Mee Loong Yang[1], Adnan Al Anbuky[2], and William Liu[1]

[1] School of Computer and Mathematical Sciences
[2] School of Engineering
Auckland University of Technology
Auckland, New Zealand
http://www.aut.ac.nz

Abstract. The security of the Multiple-Key Blom's (MKB) key agreement scheme is analysed. We considered how the scheme may be broken by a very powerful and well resourced adversary who is able to capture any number of nodes to extract all the sensitive keying material. We showed that by choosing suitable keying parameters, the captured private keys cannot be used directly to break the scheme. Each captured key must first be correctly associated with the public key and master key used to compute it. The chances of finding this private-public-master-key association (PPMka) can be made extremely small and would require the attacker to capture a very large number of nodes, or try an extremely large number of possible solutions. This allows the scheme to be secure for use in large networks, overcoming the limitations in the original Blom's scheme. We obtained some analytical results and compared them to those from computer simulated attacks on the scheme.

1 Introduction

In our previous works [1] [2], we presented the Multiple-Key Blom's (MKB) key agreement scheme for sensor networks. This scheme is fast, efficient and frugal, making it specially attractive for low power devices in ad hoc mobile networks. In this paper we show that it is also resilient against a powerful and well resourced adversary who is able capture a large number of nodes and extract all keying material.

For ad hoc mobile networks, an identity-based cryptographic (IBC) key establishment protocol would be very useful for pairs of node to derive their pairwise keys when needed. As defined in [3] an IBC key establishment protocol uses an entity's identity (*ID*) information (e.g. name and address, identifying index, etc.) as its public key. While its origin is usually attributed to Shamir [4] where the *ID* can be the node's name and address, according to Menezes, Oorschot & Vanstone [3], Blom was first to propose the identity-based (or more accurately, index-based) key establishment scheme in [5][6]. The Blom's scheme is unconditionally-secure in the information-theoretic sense if less than a certain number of nodes are compromised. Once this threshold is exceeded, the scheme

N. Cuppens-Boulahia et al. (Eds.): SEC 2014, IFIP AICT 428, pp. 66–79, 2014.

can be completely broken. Recognising this limitation, Blom [5] said "It would be nice to have systems that degrade more gracefully but more research is needed". We believe that our scheme is able to fulfil this requirement.

This Contribution. We considered the security of the Multiple-Key Blom's scheme in the three aspects – the strength of the keys, the security of the underlying Blom's scheme as it applies to our scheme, and the probabilities of the scheme being completely broken by a very powerful adversary. We presented analytical results to compute the probability of success in breaking the scheme and compared it with computer simulated attacks on some implementations.

The paper is structured as follows: In Section 2, we described briefly some related works and the necessary background material. Section 3 dealt with the security of the keys and how our scheme would improve the security of the original Blom's scheme. In Section 4 we presented some analytical results on the effort required and the probabilities of breaking the scheme. We gave our conclusions in Section 5.

Notations and Terms Used

K – private key, a secret $(1 \times m)$ row vector unique to the node
M – master key, an $(m \times m)$ secret symmetric matrix
N – number of master keys
R – pairwise key-set, the set of numbers used to form the pairwise key
V – public key, a $(m \times 1)$ column vector unique to the node
m – the size of the master key matrix
η – number of public keys assigned to each node
p – prime modulus for key operations
q – prime modulus for public key operations only
s – public key seed, an integer $\in [0, q-1]$

2   Related Works

The original Blom's scheme has limitations in that to be secure, it would require substantial memory for storage of keying material when used in large networks. The work in [7], improved on its scalability by using a clustered topology where only the cluster-heads implemented the Blom's scheme. The probabilistic scheme in [8] used multiple key-spaces where nodes would first discover their shared key space to implement the scheme. A recent work in [9] added some constrained random perturbations to the private keys to break its direct relationship with the master key, thereby increasing the resilience against the master key being computed from sufficient number of stolen private keys. All these works did not address the issue of the pairwise key sizes which would be same as the data size used for the master key elements.

The BYka Scheme

The basic concepts of our Multiple-key Blom's key agreement scheme, now called the Blom-Yang key agreement (BYka) scheme, has been presented in [1] [2]. Due to space constraint only a brief description suffice for this paper is given here.

Trusted Authority and Master Keys. The Trusted Authority (TA) is responsible for all keying material. It generates N secret master keys $\mathbf{M}_1, \mathbf{M}_2, \cdots,$ $\mathbf{M}_N$, each one being a random $(m \times m)$ symmetric matrix $\mathbf{M}$ over the prime field $\mathbb{F}_p$.

Public Key-Tag (ID). The TA assigns each node one set of public keys called the "public key-set" consisting of η column vectors over the prime field $\mathbb{F}_q$, where $q \gg p$. For example, for node A, the public key-set is $\{\mathbf{V}_{A_1}, \cdots, \mathbf{V}_{A_\eta}\}$. These vectors are columns of the Vandermonde matrix, i.e.,

$$\mathbf{V}_{A_i}^T = \begin{bmatrix} 1 & s_{A_i} & s_{A_i}^2 & \cdots & s_{A_i}^{m-1} \end{bmatrix} \pmod{q}, \text{ for } i = 1, \cdots, \eta$$

The values s_{A_i} are called the public key "seeds". The seeds $s_{A_1}, \cdots, s_{A_\eta}$ are consecutive such that the smallest seed, s_{A_1} is a multiple of η. In this way, each node's public key-set is unique and can be concisely represented by just the smallest seed. This serves as the node's identity ID, also called the "public key-tag". For example, node A's public key-set can be represented by its public key-tag $ID_A = s_{A_1}$.

Private Keys. The TA computes the private keys for each node using all permutations of their η public keys with the N master keys. For node A, the private keys are a set of ηN $(1 \times m)$ row vectors, called the "private key-set" computed as follows,

$$\mathbf{K}_{A_{ij}} = \mathbf{V}_{A_i}^T \mathbf{M}_j \pmod{p}, \text{ for } i = 1, \cdots, \eta, \ j = 1, \cdots, N$$

Consider the uth element of the private key $\mathbf{K}_{A_{ij}}$,

$$K_{A_{ij_u}} = \sum_{n=1}^{m} s_{A_i}^{n-1} \pmod{q} \ M_{j_{nu}} \pmod{p}$$

$$= M_{j_{1u}} + s_{A_i}^1 M_{j_{2u}} + \cdots + s_{A_i}^{m-1} M_{j_{mu}} \pmod{p} \tag{1}$$

The public key operations are modulo q, while all other key operations are modulo p. It is possible for multiple public keys to map to the same key in Eqn. (1), a phenomenon we call "key aliasing".

To prevent key aliasing, a seed s is chosen such that at least one vector element is $> q$ and $\not\equiv 0 \pmod{p}$, i.e.,

$$\left. \begin{array}{c} \text{for some } w \leqslant m, \quad s^{w-1} > q \\ \text{i.e. } s^{w-1} \equiv r \pmod{q} \\ \text{and } r \not\equiv \begin{cases} 0 \pmod{p}, \text{ or} \\ s \pmod{p} \end{cases} \end{array} \right\} \tag{2}$$

The TA installs into each node their keying material comprising the global keying parameters $\{m, N, \eta, p, q\}$, the node's individual public key-tag ID, and its private key-set $\mathbf{K}_{1,\cdots,N_\eta}$. Crucially, the private keys in the key-set are stored in a random order. All these are static and can be stored in the ROM or flash memory.

Pairwise Key Derivation. After deployment, any pair of nodes can derive their common secret pairwise key after exchanging their IDs, a very small amount of bits. For example, A and B have obtained each other's IDs. Next, each node generates their counterpart's public keys. For example, node A generates B's public keys,

$$\left. \begin{array}{l} s_{B_k} = ID_B + (k - 1), \\ \mathbf{V}_{B_k}^T = \begin{bmatrix} 1 & s_{B_k} & s_{B_k}^2 & \cdots & s_{B_k}^{m-1} \end{bmatrix} \pmod{q} \\ \text{for } k = 1, \cdots, \eta \end{array} \right\} \tag{3}$$

Then, using all the permutations with its own private keys, the nodes computes (modulo p), the "pairwise key-sets" R_A and R_B as follows,

$$\text{Node A:} \quad R_{A_{ijk}} = \{\mathbf{K}_{A_{ij}} \mathbf{V}_{B_k}\} = \{(\mathbf{V}_{Ai}^T \mathbf{M}_j) \mathbf{V}_{B_k}\}$$

$$\text{Node B:} \quad R_{B_{ijk}} = \{\mathbf{K}_{B_{ij}} \mathbf{V}_{A_k}\} = \{(\mathbf{V}_{Bi}^T \mathbf{M}_j) \mathbf{V}_{A_k}\}$$

$$\text{for } i, k = 1, \cdots, \eta, \quad \text{and} \quad j = 1, \cdots, N$$

Transposing all the elements in the set R_B we have,

$$R_{B_{ijk}} = \{((\mathbf{V}_{B_i}^T \mathbf{M}_j) \mathbf{V}_{A_k})^T\} = \{(\mathbf{V}_{A_k}^T \mathbf{M}_j^T) \mathbf{V}_{B_i}\}$$

Since $\mathbf{M}_j$ is symmetric, $\mathbf{V}_{Ai}^T \mathbf{M}_j \mathbf{V}_{B_k}$ is scalar, and i, j, k are merely independent counters, the sets R_A and R_B each contain $N\eta^2$ identical numbers, though not in the same order. These numbers would be used by both nodes to form a pairwise key using a preconfigured method.

In our scheme, the sequence formed from the number of occurrences of the integers $0, 1, \cdots, p - 1$ is used as input to a hash function to obtain a 128-bit pairwise key.

3   Security of the BYka Scheme

3.1   Security Model

System Model. The system comprises nodes belonging to one administrative unit under the TA. The TA has access to a good random number generator for generating the master key matrices. Before deployment, each node uses a secure connection with the TA to obtain its keying material.

The nodes have very limited computing power, memory, and battery life. They have access to strong cryptographic services such as hash functions, pseudo random number generators, and strong symmetric encryption techniques such as the AES algorithm. They are highly mobile, are deployed in an ad hoc manner, and communicate with each other using low power radio with a limited range.

Adversary Model. The adversary is a very powerful agent capable of moving about freely in the deployment space to monitor and insert messages. In addition, it is capable of capturing any number of nodes to extract all the keying material including the public and private keys from ROM and RAM. It also has access to unlimited computing resources. It cannot compromise the TA.

System Breakdown. The scheme is consider broken if the adversary is able to, by monitoring messages and/or obtaining sensitive information from captured nodes, compute the pairwise keys of any pair of un-compromised nodes, fabricate new valid public and private keys, or compute the master keys of the TA. Identity theft attacks are not considered in this paper.

3.2   Vulnerabilities

The vulnerabilities of the BYka scheme can be studied in three main aspects:

1. Resistance of the keys against brute force attacks,
2. Security of the Blom's scheme on which is is based, and
3. Resilience against node capture

3.3   Security of Keys against Brute Force

Master Keys. Each master key is an $m \times m$ symmetric matrix. It has $\frac{m(m+1)}{2}$ unique elements, each one being a random number $\in [0, p-1]$. The brute force attacker would have to try all the $p^{\frac{m(m+1)}{2}}$ possible keys. For example, even with small values of $m = 12$, $p = 13$, there are 7.72×10^{86} possible keys, equivalent to 288 bits.

Private Keys. In Eqn. (1), the elements of the private keys, being products and sums of random numbers, are also random. Hence, each private key is just a row vector of random numbers and is indistinguishable from each other.

There are $\eta N m$ elements in each private key-set. Even with small values of $m = 12, N = 6, \eta = 6$ and $p = 13$, there are about 1.673×10^{481} possible keys, or equivalent to $1,599$ bits. This is large enough to defeat the brute force attempt to fabricate a node's private key-set.

Pairwise Key. The BYka scheme can be viewed as a mechanism for two nodes to derive identical (unordered) key-sets R_A and R_B which contains $N\eta^2$ integers $\in [0, p-1]$. The numbers in the key-set, for example, $R_{A_{ijk}} = \mathbf{K}_{A_{ij}} \mathbf{V}_{B_k} = \sum_{n=1}^{m} K_{A_{ij}} s_{B_k}^{n-1}$ (mod p), where s_{B_k} satisfy Eqn. (2), are also random numbers $\in [0, p-1]$. Hence the number of occurrences of the integers $1, 2, \cdots, p-1$ in the key-set R_A is also random.

Pairwise Key Size. The pairwise-key set contains $N\eta^2$ integers $\in [0, p-1]$. These can be combined together to form a pairwise key of up to $N\eta^2 b$ bits, where b is the data size of p. For example with $N, \eta = 6$, and $p = 31$, the key size can be up to 1080 bits.

Pairwise Keyspace. The number of possible pairwise keys, or the keyspace size, must be at least as large as the desired key size. It is however, limited by the number of possible combinations of the $N\eta^2$ integers in the key-sets R. The keyspace size can be determined by considering the number of possible combinations of the integers $1, 2, \cdots, p-1$, such that the total number of integers in each combination is exactly $N\eta^2$. This can be obtained by considering the following partitioning problem.

Given a row of $N\eta^2$ items, we wish to partition them such that there are p groups, $g_0, g_1, \cdots, g_{p-1}$, each containing the integers $0, 1, \cdots, p-1$ respectively. To create the partitions, we first insert $(p-1)$ items into the row so that there are now $(N\eta^2 + p - 1)$ items. If any $(p-1)$ items are now removed, it would leave $(p-1)$ gaps separating the remaining items into p groups as desired. The number of ways to remove $(p-1)$ items from $(N\eta^2 + p - 1)$ gives the keyspace size as follows,

$$K_{space} = \binom{N\eta^2 + p - 1}{p - 1} \tag{4}$$

Using suitable values of N, η, and p, keyspace sizes of 64, 80, 96, and 128 bits are possible, as shown in Table (1).

Table 1. Key space sizes in bits

η	N	Values of p				
		13	17	19	23	31
6	6	64	80	88	102	127
	7	67	84	92	106	134
	8	69	87	95	111	139
7	6	69	87	95	111	140
	7	72	91	99	116	146
	8	74	94	103	120	152
8	6	74	93	102	119	151
	7	77	97	106	124	157
	8	79	100	109	128	163

3.4   Security of the Underlying Blom's Scheme

In our previous work [2], we showed how the Blom's scheme would be completely broken if the number of nodes compromised is m, the "capture threshold". The scheme is said to be unconditionally secure if no more than $(m-1)$ nodes are compromised, and all the public key vectors are linearly independent of each other [3]. Otherwise, using the captured private keys from m or more nodes, the attacker would be able to either mount the Sybil attack by fabricating new public and private keys using linear combinations of the m captured keys, or attack the master key $\mathbf{M}$ by solving the system of $m \times m$ linear equations, $\mathbf{K}_X = \mathbf{V}_X^T \mathbf{M}$.

The security of the BYka scheme would appear to be similar to the original Blom's scheme. Apparently, the capture threshold is lower at $\lceil \frac{m}{\eta} \rceil$ since each node has η private keys associated with each master key. However, the attacker would first have to associate each private key with the public key and master key used to compute it, i.e. discover the private-public-master-key associations (PPMka).

Each private key computed in Eqn. (1) is a row vector of random integers $\in [0, p-1]$ and has no information about the public key and master key used to compute it. Without the PPMka information each key can be correctly associated with the public key and master key with a probability of $\frac{1}{N\eta}$. To mount the Sybil or master key attack, all the m private keys must be used together. This will result in a very large number of possible solutions as shown later.

4 Attacks to Discover the PPMka

4.1 Using Brute Force

Using One Captured Node. Consider that the attacker has obtained the public and private keys from one captured node. The attacker generates an arbitrary master key, and using one of the public keys, computes a trial private key using Eqn. (1). This is then compared with each of the captured keys to find a match. After trying all the possible master keys, there will be N matches and eventually all the master keys will be found. The number of possible master keys to try is $p^{\frac{m(m+1)}{2}}$ which is a very large number with typical keying parameters.

Using Sufficient Captured Nodes. Consider that $\frac{m}{\eta}$ nodes have been captured. Each node has $N\eta$ private keys. There is enough information to construct the N systems of $m \times m$ equations to solve for all the master keys, using for example, the following procedure.

From each node, the $N\eta$ keys are grouped into $\binom{N\eta}{\eta}$ possible groups each associated with one of the master keys. Within each group, each private key can be associated with the η public keys in $\eta!$ ways. Therefore for each node there are $\binom{N\eta}{\eta}\eta!$ ways to obtain the set of ηm equations for solving one master key, say $\mathbf{M}_1$. Using a total of $\frac{m}{\eta}$ nodes, it is possible to obtain a set of $m \times m$ equations to solve for $\mathbf{M}_1$.

After obtaining the first master key, the η private keys associate with $\mathbf{M}_1$ is removed and the process is repeated for $\mathbf{M}_2$, and so on. Overall, the total number of attempts required to obtain all the master keys is

$$\Phi = \sum_{i=0}^{N-1} \left[\binom{N\eta - i\eta}{\eta} \eta! \right]^{\frac{m}{\eta}}$$

The number of iterations required, even with small parameter values is very large. For example with $m = 12$, $N = 6$, $\eta = 6$, there are 2.16×10^{18} possible master keys solutions.

4.2   Pairing Attack to Discover the PPMka

A better approach would be to get pairs of nodes, e.g. nodes A and B, to compute their pairwise key-sets R_A and R_B using each other's public keys. The $N\eta^2$ numbers in the two key-sets will be identical, and if they are unique, the attacker would be able to, by matching them, associate the related private keys to the same master key. We call this the "pairing attack".

A more efficient pairing attack would use only one of each other's public keys to compute the partial key-sets R_{rA} and R_{rB} which now contains only $N\eta$ elements. This is illustrated in Fig. (1) for the simple case using $N, \eta = 2$. Here, since $\mathbf{K}_{A_1}\mathbf{V}_{B_2} = \mathbf{K}_{B_3}\mathbf{V}_{A_1}$, both must be associated with the same master key say, $\mathbf{M}_1$. The PPMka for the private keys can then be found, i.e. $\mathbf{K}_{A_1} = \mathbf{V}_{A_1}^T\mathbf{M}_1$, $\mathbf{K}_{B_3} = \mathbf{V}_{B_2}^T\mathbf{M}_1$ and similarly, $\mathbf{K}_{A_2} = \mathbf{V}_{A_1}^T\mathbf{M}_2$, $\mathbf{K}_{B_2} = \mathbf{V}_{B_2}^T\mathbf{M}_2$.

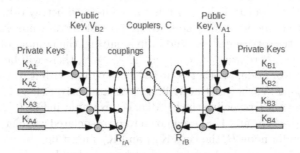

Fig. 1. Pairing attack for case $N = 2, \eta = 2$

Collisions. If all the numbers in R_r are unique, the above attack would be successful. However, if they are not, we say there are "collisions", and there are more than one possible PPMka's for the affected private key.

Couplers and Couplings. We call the numbers that are identical across both partial key-sets R_{rA} and R_{rB}, "couplers". In Fig. (1), the set C contains the couplers. The links connecting the couplers to the numbers in R_{rA} and R_{rB} are called "couplings". The number of couplings linking R_r to the couplers is denoted as N_c.

In the ideal case where there is no collision, there would be exactly $N_c = N$ couplings on each side of C, each one linking the private key to the associated master key and public key, revealing their PPMka. However, if the couplers are not distinct, then the PPMka's for the related private keys are ambiguous.

The probability of having all distinct couplers in the partial key-set of $N\eta$ numbers is $P_u = (\frac{p}{p})(\frac{p-1}{p}) \cdots (\frac{p-N\eta-1}{p})$. This can be made very small by choosing suitable values of p, N and η. For example, with $p = 31$, $\eta = 6$, $N = 5$, we have $P_u = 2.49 \times 10^{-12}$. If $N\eta \geqslant p+1$, the probability P_u is zero as there is not enough numbers to go round without repetition.

Pairing Attack Approaches. We consider two extreme approaches to discover the PPMka. In the first case, the "unlimited capture" attack, the attacker is able to capture as many nodes as necessary until finally the PPMka can be exposed. At the other end of the spectrum, in the "limited capture" attack, the attacker has just enough nodes to compute the master keys.

4.3   Unlimited Capture Attack

Traitor Node. The pairing attack would be successful if each pairing results in key-sets R in which all the numbers are unique. However with suitable choice of keying parameters this probability is very small. Nevertheless, the attack would have a better chance of success if a node is available such that all the N private keys associated with one of the public keys is known or "exposed". This set of private keys can be used to reduce the ambiguities in subsequent pairings. We call this node the "traitor node" since it can be used to betray other nodes. For example in Fig.(1), nodes A and node B are possible traitor nodes.

In general, a traitor node T is found if, in a pairing, the number of couplings it has is $N_c = N$ i.e. there are $\leqslant N$ couplers. If $N_c > N$, there will be ambiguities.

Using the traitor node, another node say B, is paired with it. If the number of couplings in R_{rB} is N, they distinctly link the related private keys in B to the exposed private keys in T revealing the PPMka. For example, in Fig. (2), T is a traitor node and the keys $\mathbf{K}_{T1}$ and $\mathbf{K}_{T2}$ are known to be associated with $\mathbf{M}_x$ and $\mathbf{M}_y$ respectively. Then for node B, the keys $\mathbf{K}_{B1}$ and $\mathbf{K}_{B2}$ must be associated with $\mathbf{M}_x$ and $\mathbf{M}_y$ respectively, and both associated with public key $\mathbf{V}_{B2}$.

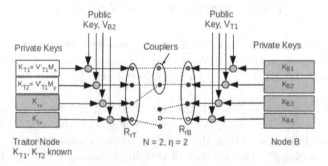

Fig. 2. Traitor Node can be used to attack the PPMka

This is not so straightforward if the number of couplings or couplers in R_{rB} is $\neq N$. The PPMka of the keys related to colliding couplers will be ambiguous, as in Fig. (3). Fig. (3a) shows the partial key-set R_{rB} having only 1 coupler. While $\mathbf{K}_{B1}$ and $\mathbf{K}_{B2}$ can both be associated with $\mathbf{V}_{B2}$, their associations with the master keys are ambiguous. In Fig. (3b), R_{rB} has more than N couplings, i.e. 3 instead of 2. Now it not clear whether $\mathbf{K}_{B2}$ or $\mathbf{K}_{B3}$ is associated with $\mathbf{V}_{B2}$ and master key $\mathbf{M}_y$.

Probability of Finding a Traitor Node. To determine the probability of finding a traitor node, we can consider the following problem. In the Fig. (4a), the

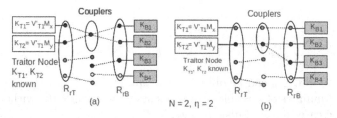

Fig. 3. Traitor Node cannot be used to discover the PPMka

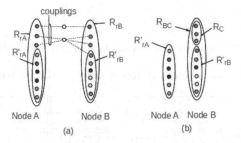

Fig. 4. Partial key-sets

pairing attack produces partial key-sets R_{rA} and R_{rB}. We remove the couplers from R_{rA} to form the set R_c, leaving the reduced partial key-sets R'_{rA} and R'_{rB} in Fig. (4b). A traitor node is found if the reduced set R'_{rA} is disjoint with $(R'_{rB} \cup R_c)$, or R'_{rB} is disjoint with $(R'_{rA} \cup R_c)$. In addition, the sets R'_{rA}, R'_{rB} and R_c can all be disjoint.

The probability of these occurrences can be found by counting the number of arrangements for the above cases. Let N_a, N_b and N_c be the number of elements in sets R'_{rA}, R'_{rB} and R_c respectively. Here, $N_a = N_b = N\eta - N$ and $N_c = N$. The number of elements in $(R'_{rB} \cup R_c)$ is $N\eta$.

First, consider the general case of arranging N_a numbers given r numbers, such that each arrangement has **all** the r numbers. For example, in arranging 4 numbers given the 3 numbers $\{6, 7, 8\}$, permutations like $\{6, 6, 7, 8\}$ and $\{6, 7, 7, 8\}$ would be included, but excludes permutations such as $\{6, 6, 6, 7\}$ and $\{6, 6, 7, 6\}$, etc. Let the number of arrangements be $Q_{N_a r}$. It can be shown that

$$Q_{N_a r} = r^{N_a} - \sum_{i=1}^{r-1} \binom{r}{i} Q_{N_a i} \quad \text{where} \quad Q_{N_a 1} = 1 \tag{5}$$

The total number of arrangements where R'_{rA} is disjoint with $(R'_{rB} \cup R_c)$ is then,

$$\theta_u = \sum_{r=1}^{N_a} \binom{p}{r} Q_{N_a r} (p - r)^{N\eta} \tag{6}$$

It is also possible that the sets R'_{rA}, R'_{rB} and R_c are all disjoint. The number of such arrangements θ_d, can be similarly shown to be,

$$\theta_d = \sum_{r=1}^{N_c} \left[\binom{p}{r} Q_{N_c r} \times \left(\sum_{k=1}^{N_a} \binom{p-r}{k} Q_{N_a k} (p-r-k)^{N_b} \right) \right] \tag{7}$$

where $Q_{N_c r}$ and $Q_{N_a k}$ can be obtain as in Eqn. (5).

The total number of possible arrangements is $\theta_t = 2\theta_u - \theta_d$, without double counting the cases for all 3 disjoint sets.

The probability of finding a traitor node is then,

$$P_t = \frac{\theta_t}{p^{2N\eta - N}} = \frac{2\theta_u - \theta_d}{p^{2N\eta - N}} \tag{8}$$

The values of P_t for various keying parameters is given in Table (2).

Table 2. Probabilities of finding a Traitor Node P_t, and expected capture sizes n_c

η	N	$p=13$		$p=17$		$p=31$	
		P_t	n_c	P_t	n_c	P_t	n_c
6	6	1.07×10^{-16}	2.29×10^7	1.70×10^{-15}	5.75×10^6	5.62×10^{-12}	1.00×10^5
	7	5.25×10^{-19}	1.02×10^9	8.71×10^{-19}	2.51×10^8	5.01×10^{-15}	3.31×10^6
	8	2.57×10^{-23}	4.68×10^{10}	4.37×10^{-22}	1.12×10^{10}	3.72×10^{-18}	1.23×10^8
7	6	2.40×10^{-20}	1.29×10^9	4.07×10^{-19}	3.16×10^8	2.45×10^{-15}	4.07×10^6
	7	2.88×10^{-24}	1.20×10^{11}	5.01×10^{-23}	2.88×10^{10}	4.68×10^{-19}	2.95×10^8
	8	3.47×10^{-28}	1.10×10^{13}	6.17×10^{-27}	2.57×10^{12}	7.59×10^{-23}	2.34×10^{10}
8	6	5.50×10^{-24}	7.59×10^{10}	9.55×10^{-23}	1.82×10^{10}	8.71×10^{-19}	1.91×10^8
	7	1.62×10^{-28}	1.38×10^{13}	2.88×10^{-27}	3.31×10^{12}	3.63×10^{-23}	2.95×10^{10}
	8	4.79×10^{-33}	2.57×10^{15}	8.51×10^{-32}	6.03×10^{14}	1.32×10^{-27}	4.90×10^{12}

Expected Node Capture. We assume that attacker is able to capture any number of nodes. As a new node is captured, it is paired with each of the previous ones to find the traitor, if not another new node is captured and the process repeated. Since the probability of finding a traitor node is P_t, the expected number of pairing attempts to find one is $\frac{1}{P_t}$. Each node has η public keys to try, so each pair gives η^2 attempts. If the number of nodes captured is n_c, the number of pairs that can be formed is $\binom{n_c}{2}$ giving a total of $\eta^2\binom{n_c}{2}$ pairing attempts. To find a traitor node we have,

$$\eta^2 \frac{n_c!}{2!(n_c-2)!} \geqslant \frac{1}{P_t}$$

$$\text{i.e.} \quad n_c \geqslant \frac{1}{2}\left(1 + \sqrt{1 + \frac{8}{\eta^2 P_t}}\right) \tag{9}$$

The values of n_c for some keying parameters is also given in Table (2). It can be seen that for these cases, thousands of nodes need to be captured just to find a traitor node. Finding a traitor does not break the scheme. The chance of finding a node which has exactly N couplers when paired with the traitor node is as improbable as finding the traitor node itself.

4.4   Limited Capture Pairing Attack

In this attack only $\lceil \frac{m}{\eta} \rceil$, but sufficient, number of nodes has been captured. Using the pairing attack, the partial key-set is obtained. If there are $N_c > N$ couplings due to collisions, there are N_c possible ways choose the private key related to one of the master keys, say $\mathbf{M}_1$. Using all the η public keys one at a time, the number of sets of equations from one node is $[N_c]^\eta$. To obtain the $m \times m$ equation, $\frac{m}{\eta}$ nodes are required. The number of possible solutions for the master key $\mathbf{M}_1$ is $[N_c]^m$.

After obtaining the first master key, the associated private key is removed leaving $N_c - 1$ keys to choose for solving the next master key. In total, to solve for all the master keys, the total possible number of sets of equations, i.e. the number of iterations required is, $\Phi = \sum_{i=0}^{N-1} [N_c - i]^m$.

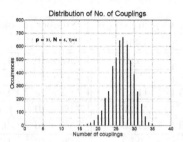

Fig. 5. Distribution of number of couplings for $p = 31, N = 6, \eta = 6$

Binomial Distribution Approximation. Fig. (5) shows the typical distribution of the number of couplings in the pairing attacks, in this case for $p = 31, N = 6, \eta = 6$. It suggests that the distribution can be approximated by the binomial distribution,

$$P(X = x) = \binom{N\eta}{x} p_r^x (1 - p_r)^{(N\eta - x)} \tag{10}$$

where the x is the number of couplings, and $\mu = N\eta p_r$ is the mean. From Eqn. (8), we can compute the probability when there are N couplings, i.e. $P(X = N)$. Then solving for p_r in Eqn. (10), we can obtain the mean μ. Writing the expected number of couplings in a pairing as $N_c = \mu$, then the probable number of possible solutions for all the master keys is,

$$\Phi = \sum_{i=0}^{N-1} [N_c - i]^m = \sum_{i=0}^{N-1} [\mu - i]^m \tag{11}$$

Table (3) gives the probable number of master keys solutions, Φ for various keying parameters.

Table 3. Probable number of Master key solutions, Φ

η	N	$m = 12$			$m = 24$		
		13	17	31	13	17	31
6	6	$3.55{\times}10^{17}$	$2.34{\times}10^{17}$	$9.55{\times}10^{16}$	$1.26{\times}10^{35}$	$5.37{\times}10^{34}$	$9.12{\times}10^{33}$
	7	$2.40{\times}10^{18}$	$1.66{\times}10^{18}$	$7.94{\times}10^{17}$	$5.75{\times}10^{36}$	$2.75{\times}10^{36}$	$6.17{\times}10^{35}$
	8	$1.23{\times}10^{19}$	$1.23{\times}10^{19}$	$4.79{\times}10^{18}$	$1.55{\times}10^{38}$	$1.55{\times}10^{38}$	$2.24{\times}10^{37}$
7	6	$1.66{\times}10^{18}$	$1.66{\times}10^{18}$	$5.37{\times}10^{17}$	$2.75{\times}10^{36}$	$2.75{\times}10^{36}$	$2.82{\times}10^{35}$
	7	$1.23{\times}10^{19}$	$1.23{\times}10^{19}$	$4.79{\times}10^{18}$	$1.55{\times}10^{38}$	$1.55{\times}10^{38}$	$2.24{\times}10^{37}$
	8	$8.91{\times}10^{19}$	$6.92{\times}10^{19}$	$3.02{\times}10^{19}$	$8.13{\times}10^{39}$	$4.79{\times}10^{39}$	$9.12{\times}10^{38}$
8	6	$9.12{\times}10^{18}$	$6.61{\times}10^{18}$	$3.39{\times}10^{18}$	$8.13{\times}10^{37}$	$4.37{\times}10^{37}$	$1.15{\times}10^{37}$
	7	$6.92{\times}10^{19}$	$6.61{\times}10^{19}$	$3.02{\times}10^{19}$	$4.79{\times}10^{39}$	$2.75{\times}10^{39}$	$9.12{\times}10^{38}$
	8	$3.89{\times}10^{20}$	$3.09{\times}10^{20}$	$1.91{\times}10^{20}$	$1.51{\times}10^{41}$	$9.55{\times}10^{40}$	$3.63{\times}10^{40}$

Table 4. Comparison between analytical and experimental results for $p = 31$

η	N	Traitor Capture size n_c		Number of solutions, Φ	
		Eqn.(9)	Expt.	Eqn.(11)	Expt.
4	4	5.59	5.23	7.97×10^{22}	1.06×10^{24}
	5	23.23	21.48	5.43×10^{26}	8.46×10^{26}
	6	128.05	113.53	7.92×10^{28}	1.10×10^{29}
5	4	24.45	21.37	7.95×10^{26}	8.16×10^{26}
	5	237.99	215.63	7.93×10^{28}	$9.95{\times}10^{29}$
6	3	10.76	9.62	1.00×10^{24}	1.17×10^{25}
	4	155.91	135.88	1.68×10^{28}	1.42×10^{29}
7	3	37.57	33.04	7.95×10^{25}	7.17×10^{26}

4.5   Experimental Results of Simulated Pairing Attacks

A computer programme was used to implement the pairing attacks to determine the traitor capture sizes n_c and the probable number of master key solutions Φ.

The programme first generates the master keys. It then randomly creates new nodes with unique IDs to simulate captured nodes. Each node is paired with each of the previously "captured" nodes until a traitor node is found. At the same time the number of couplings is accumulated for the first $\frac{m}{\eta}$ nodes. This is the probable number of couplings in the limited captured attack. When a traitor node is found, a new implementation is done using a new set of master keys and this is repeated for 1000 times.

These are real attacks on real systems as the public and private keys can be implemented in real sensor nodes. They are "simulated" in the sense that capturing the nodes and extracting the keys are done in the computer programme, greatly accelerating the attacks.

Due to the large traitor capture sizes, only cases which gives results within a reasonable time is given in Table (4). These results are the mean values for 1000 implementations for each case. As an indication, one run for the case using

$N = 6$, $\eta = 4$ took over $2\frac{1}{2}$ hours to find a traitor node, requiring about 135 captured nodes.

5 Conclusion

The security of our BYka key agreement scheme was analysed in term of the resistance of its keys against brute force attacks, the security of the Blom's scheme on which it is based, and its resilience against node capture. We showed that the keys are random and large enough to resist brute force attacks. The scheme inherits the unconditionally security of the original Blom's scheme and also allows it to break free from the limitations therein. This is because, by using multiple keys in permutations, the relationships of the private keys with the master keys and public keys becomes indiscernible, and they cannot be used directly to break the scheme. We calculated the probabilities of discovering the correct private-public-master-key association information and showed that, with suitable keying parameters, these probabilities are very small. Consequently, to break the scheme, it would require a very large number of nodes to be captured, or an infeasibly large number of solutions are possible. Our analytical results were verified by comparing them with results obtained from simulated attacks on the scheme using a computer programme. Our BYka scheme is thus secure against very powerful adversaries and being fast, efficient and frugal, would be useful for large ad hoc mobile sensor networks.

References

1. Yang, M.L., Al-Anbuky, A., Liu, W.: A Fast and Efficient Key Agreement Scheme for Wireless Sensor Networks. In: International Conference on Wireless and Mobile Communications, Venice, pp. 231–237 (2012)
2. Yang, M.L., Al-Anbuky, A., Liu, W.: The Multiple-Key Blom's Scheme for Key Establishment in Mobile Ad Hoc Sensor Networks. In: The 19th Asia-Pacific Conference on Communications, Bali, Indonesia, pp. 422–427 (2013)
3. Menezes, A.J., Oorschot, P.C., Vanstone, S.A.: Handbook of Applied Cryptography (2001)
4. Shamir, A.: Identity-Based Cryptosystems and Signature Schemes. In: Blakely, G.R., Chaum, D. (eds.) CRYPTO 1984. LNCS, vol. 196, pp. 47–53. Springer, Heidelberg (1985)
5. Blom, R.: Non-Public Key Distribution. In: Advances in Cryptology, Proceedings of Crypto 1982, pp. 231–236 (1983)
6. Blom, R.: An Optimal Class of Symmetric Key Generation Systems. Linkopping University, Tech. Rep. (1984)
7. Chen, N., Yao, J.-B., Wen, G.-J.: An Improved Matrix Key Pre-distribution Scheme for Wireless Sensor Networks. In: International Conference on Embedded Software Systems, pp. 40–45 (2008)
8. Du, W., Han, S.Y., Deng, J., Varshney, P.K.: A pairwise key pre-distribution scheme for wireless sensor networks. In: Proceedings of the Conference on Computer and Communications Security (October 2003)
9. Yu, C.-M., Lu, C.-S., Kuo, S.-Y.: Noninteractive Pairwise Key Establishment for Sensor Networks. IEEE Transactions on Information Forensics and Security 5(3), 556–569 (2010)

New Algorithmic Approaches
to Point Constellation Recognition

Thomas Bourgeat[1], Julien Bringer[2], Hervé Chabanne[2], Robin Champenois[1],
Jérémie Clément[1,3], Houda Ferradi[1,2], Marc Heinrich[1], Paul Melotti[1],
David Naccache[1], and Antoine Voizard[1]

[1] École normale supérieure
Équipe de cryptographie, 45 rue d'Ulm, F-75230 Paris CEDEX 05, France
{given_name.name}@ens.fr
[2] Morpho
11 boulevard Gallieni, F-92130 Issy-les-Moulineaux, France
{given_name.name}@morpho.com
[3] Crocus Technology
4 place Robert Schuman, F-38025 Grenoble Cedex, France
jclement@crocus-technology.com

Abstract. Point constellation recognition is a common problem with many pattern matching applications. Whilst useful in many contexts, this work is mainly motivated by fingerprint matching. Fingerprints are traditionally modelled as constellations of oriented points called *minutiae*. The fingerprint verifier's task consists in comparing two point constellations. The compared constellations may differ by rotation and translation or by much more involved transforms such as distortion or occlusion.

This paper presents three new constellation matching algorithms. The first two methods generalize an algorithm by Bringer and Despiegel. Our third proposal creates a very interesting analogy between mechanical system simulation and the constellation recognition problem.

1   Introduction

Fingerprints are traditionally modelled as feature-sets called *minutiae*. Each minutia m_i is composed of two cartesian coordinates and an orientation $\{x_i, y_i, \theta_i\}$. Matching algorithms return a score expressing the similarity between the candidate minutiae set $M = \{m_1, \ldots, m_\ell\}$ and the template minutiae set $M' = \{m'_1, \ldots, m'_{\ell'}\}$. The main difficulty met while trying to compute such similarity scores is that many experimental parameters may affect the minutiae comparison task. The easiest obstacles to deal with are simple transforms such as translation and rotation but minutiae may also disappear (occlusion), appear *ex nihilo* (noise) or be subject to nonlinear distortion. Most matching algorithms usually try to translate and rotate M' to obtain an optimal superimposition with M (while dealing with nonlinear transforms using a variety of heuristics). In general, matching algorithms use a $\{x_i, y_i, \theta_i\}$ representation standardized in ISO/IEC 19794-2 [1].

In [2] Bringer and Despiegel (BD) define the notion of *vicinity*. Instead of using minutiae to compare M and M', [2] groups minutiae into vicinities V_i. A vicinity V_i is

N. Cuppens-Boulahia et al. (Eds.): SEC 2014, IFIP AICT 428, pp. 80–90, 2014.

defined as a center minutia $m_i = \{x_i, y_i, \theta_i\}$ and all the minutiae m_j whose distance to m_i does not exceed a certain range. The advantage of this representation is that each vicinity V_i carries its own coordinate system, whose center is $\{x_i, y_i\}$ and whose x-axis is θ_i. Thereby, rotation and translation issues are naturally avoided.

This paper presents three new point constellation matching algorithms. The first two techniques generalize BD's algorithm. Section 2 recalls BD's ideas and notations, which will serve as a basis for our two first algorithms. Section 3 describes a technique based on *second-order vicinities*, which are vicinities of vicinities. Second-order vicinities allow to extract more information from constellations by exploiting the information present in the relative distances separating vicinities. Section 4 describes *missing minutiae analysis*, a technique allowing to extract useful information from... missing minutiae. Section 5, introduces a matching method that stems from a very interesting analogy between mechanical system simulation and the constellation recognition problem.

2 Fingerprints, Minutiae and Vicinities

2.1 From Minutiae to Vicinities

As we have already mentioned, a vicinity V_i consists of all the minutiae m_j whose distance from m_i does not exceed some range ρ, *i.e.*:

$$m_j \in V_i \Leftrightarrow \sqrt{(x_i - x_j)^2 + (y_i - y_j)^2} < \rho$$

Each V_i has its own coordinate system. $\{x_i, y_i\}$ is the center of this coordinate system and θ_i provides the orientation of V_i's x-axis. All the $m_j \in V_i$ have their coordinates recomputed with respect to $\{x_i, y_i\}$. Now a fingerprint M can be regarded as a set of vicinities instead of a set of minutiae. If M contains n minutiae then M will also yield n vicinities. To compare two vicinities (hereafter A and B, respectively containing the minutiae a_i and b_j) we will compare the a_is to the b_js pairwise. For each a_i vs. b_j comparison a matching score will be computed. Here we use the simplified scoring formula:

$$s(a_i, b_j) = (x_{a_i} - x_{b_j})^2 + (y_{a_i} - y_{b_j})^2 + \frac{\sigma_x}{\sigma_\theta}(\theta_{a_i} - \theta_{b_j})^2$$

where σ_x represents the variance of the position (we assume that $\sigma_x = \sigma_y$), and σ_θ is the variance of the orientation. Experimentally measured vicinities are used to tune these parameters.

Each pair of minutiae yields a score. A matrix containing all these scores is built. Then, the Hungarian algorithm [3] is applied to this matrix to find the best association between the minutiae of A and B. The final matching score between the two vicinities will be computed as follows :

$$S_{A,B} = \sum_{f(a_i)=\{b_j\}} s(a_i, b_j) - (\mathrm{NAR}(A, B) + \mathrm{NAS}(A, B))K_{\mathrm{NA}}$$

$$\text{where } f(a_i) = \begin{cases} \{b_j\} & \text{if } a_i \text{ is associated to } b_j \\ 0 & \text{otherwise} \end{cases}$$

NAR represents the number of minutiae of A that do not have any association in B and NAS is the number of minutiae of B that do not have any association in A. K_{NA} is a penalty coefficient for non associated minutiae.

Once we have the scores corresponding to the comparisons between the template's and candidate's vicinities, we can compute the binary *feature vector* which will represent our fingerprint.

2.2 From Vicinities to the Binary Feature Vector

To create a *feature vector* that will represent a fingerprint we will need N representative vicinities. This set of representative vicinities, denoted DB_R, contains N vicinities R_i that fulfill several conditions:

- The R_is are not related to the main fingerprint database. The R_is come from generated fingerprints or external databases.
- The R_is contain more than ℓ_{min} and less than ℓ_{max} minutiae. ℓ_{min} and ℓ_{max} are chosen so the R_is are not too discriminative.
- Each R_i isn't similar to other R_js (according to a certain threshold criterion).

The vector V, of length N, representing the candidate fingerprint is computed as follows:

- Extract all the vicinities (denoted F_j) from the candidate fingerprint.
- For $1 \leq i \leq N$ compute the matching scores $S(F_j, R_i)$
- Given a certain threshold t, create the vector V:

$$V_i = \begin{cases} 1 & \text{if } \exists j \in \{1, \dots, n\} \text{ such as } S(F_j, R_i) < t \\ 0 & \text{otherwise} \end{cases}$$

To compare two fingerprints, compute the hamming distance of their feature vectors.

This can be used both for authentication (compare a candidate fingerprint to a database of fingerprints, this database contains only the binary vectors of each fingerprint) and for identification (compare the candidate fingerprint to one template fingerprint to check the identity). This method has three main advantages :

- Avoiding rotation and translation problems usually met by alternative algorithms.
- Feature vector comparison is an easy binary operation.
- Feature vectors' length depends on N. A small DB_R is less expensive in terms of memory. In fact if ρ is small, we won't need a lot of representative vicinities to cover all possibilities. If ρ is large, we will need more representative vicinities, but achieve a better matching accuracy.

We now show how to improve this algorithm in two different ways.

3 Second-Order Vicinities

The algorithm that we have just described is insensitive to the relative positions of vicinities. *i.e.* two fingerprints containing the same vicinities at *different* locations will be considered equivalent. It is hence natural to try to squeeze more information out of point constellations by considering the relative positions of vicinities.

Second-order vicinities are defined as vicinities of vicinities. Run the algorithm as before and extract (first-order) vicinities. Replace each vicinity by its barycenter and get a new scatter plot. Group each plot into new vicinities, larger than previous ones. These new vicinities are our *second-order vicinities*. This takes into account the position of a vicinity with respect to the other vicinities and hence eases the discrimination of two constellations containing identical vicinities at different places.

The program doing this, available from the authors, computes vicinities as before and then filters them to keep only "significant" vicinities, having more than ℓ_{min} and less than ℓ_{max} vicinities. We delete vicinities whose central minutiae belong to other vicinities to keep vicinities pairwise distinct. Once done, we reduce the vicinity representation to their central minutiae. Finally, we run the BD algorithm, except that we now use the vicinity barycenters instead of the center minutiae, and a radius ρ_2 larger than the ρ_1 used for the first-order vicinities. We can notice that at first sight, the final representation of second-order vicinities is not that different from a larger first-order vicinity. The difference is in the recognition. In fact, we make a double pass recognition, one for first-order vicinities (in second-order vicinities) and one for minutiae (in first-order vicinities). The same algorithm is hence run twice with different parameters. A fingerprint will match if both its first-order and second-order vicinities match the target template. With proper parameter tuning, this algorithm experimentally improves recognition accuracy.

Higher order vicinities can be defined as well. But the higher is the order, the larger will the (higher-order) vicinity be. Hence, the information increment brought by higher order vicinities quickly decreases with the order.

4   Missing Minutiae Analysis

Let's go back to BD's classical (first-order) vicinities. We will now extract information from accidentally missing minutiae. Infering the missing minutiae and taking them into account reduces the algorithm's False Reject Rate. As shown in Figure 1, a given minutia may simultaneously belong to (*i.e.* be at the intersection of) several vicinities.

If several candidate vicinities present a missing minutia with respect to their template vicinities, we may suspect that a minutia common to these vicinities was omitted accidentally. In other words the *simultaneous disappearance* of m in Figure 1 would be a "smoking gun" indicating an "explainable error". The computational strategy implementing this intuitive observation turns out to be a nontrivial exercise[1].

The Hungarian algorithm compares vicinities (hereafter A and B) pairwise. To do so, the Hungarian algorithm takes as input a square matrix containing the matching scores $s(a_i, b_j)$ computed between the minutiae of A (lines) and B (columns). If B has less minutiae than A, a virtual column is created. All the elements of this virtual column are set to the value $\max_{i,j} s(a_i, b_j)$. After associations are found, the associations corresponding to the virtual column are removed from the list of associations between the minutiae of A and B.

The score $S(A, B)$ is the sum of the matrix elements corresponding to the associations, plus a penalty for non-associated elements. If the associated minutiae match each

---

[1] The Mathematica code is available from the authors.

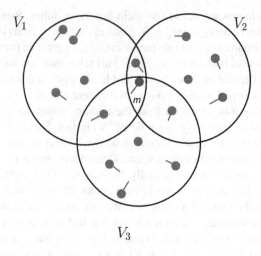

Fig. 1. Example of a Missing Minutia

other, $S(A, B)$ is essentially equal to the penalty. In that case, we can plausibly assume that one of the vicinities (A or B) presents a missing minutia.

This scheme can be generalized to more missing minutiae but claims time exponential in the number of missing minutiae. It is hence useful for assessing the occlusion (disappearance) of one or two minutiae only.

5   Can Nuts and Bolts Compare?

This section presents a rather unusual point constellation recognition algorithm. One advantage of this scheme is the fact that it can be easily implemented using physical engines. A physics engine is a computer software that provides an approximate simulation of certain physical systems, such as rigid body dynamics (including collision detection), soft body dynamics, and fluid dynamics, of use in the domains of computer graphics, video games and films. Physical engines are mainly used in video games (typically as middleware), in which case the simulations are in real-time.

Let $a_i = (a_{i,x}, a_{i,y}) \in \mathbb{R}^2$ and $b_i = (b_{i,x}, b_{i,y}) \in \mathbb{R}^2$ denote points in $\mathbb{R}^2$. The reader may consider each such point as the barycenter of a specific vicinity or as the $\{x_i, y_i\}$ coordinates of minutiae to compare.

Let $\mathcal{A} = \{a_1, \ldots, a_\ell\}$ and $\mathcal{B} = \{b_1, \ldots, b_\ell\}$ be two sets of points.

Our goal is to *measure the geometrical similarity* between the point constellations $\mathcal{A}$ and $\mathcal{B}$.

Define the operator Γ by:

$$a_i' = \Gamma(a_i, \Delta x, \Delta y, \theta) = \begin{pmatrix} a_{i,x}' \\ a_{i,y}' \end{pmatrix} = \begin{pmatrix} \cos\theta & -\sin\theta \\ \sin\theta & \cos\theta \end{pmatrix} \begin{pmatrix} a_{i,x} \\ a_{i,y} \end{pmatrix} + \begin{pmatrix} \Delta x \\ \Delta y \end{pmatrix}$$

In other words, Γ translates a point by Δx, Δy and rotates it by the angle θ.

We define the *similarity* between the constellations $\mathcal{A}$ and $\mathcal{B}$ by:

$$\text{sim}(\mathcal{A}, \mathcal{B}) = \min_{\Delta x, \Delta y, \theta} \left(\sum_{i=1}^{\ell} \text{dist}(\Gamma(a_i, \Delta x, \Delta y, \theta), b_i) \right) \in \mathbb{R}$$

Where $\text{dist}((x, y), (x', y')) = \sqrt{(x - x')^2 + (y - y')^2}$.

Informally, $\text{sim}(\mathcal{A}, \mathcal{B})$ measures the total distance remaining between the points of $\mathcal{A}$ and $\mathcal{B}$ after the best possible translation and rotation attempting to match $\mathcal{A}$ and $\mathcal{B}$. It is easy to see that $0 \leq \text{sim}(\mathcal{A}, \mathcal{B}) < \infty$ where $\text{sim}(\mathcal{A}, \mathcal{B}) = 0 \Leftrightarrow \mathcal{A} = \mathcal{B}$ (perfect match).

In applications requiring a $[0, 1]$ score, one can use $c^{-\text{sim}}$ for some constant $c > 1$ (e.g. the base of natural logarithms e).

The analytical determination of $\text{sim}(\mathcal{A}, \mathcal{B})$ turns out to be a complex task. We hence replace sim by a function sim_ϕ which effect approximates sim. As will be explained in the next section, the ϕ in sim_ϕ denotes the fact that this new similarity measurement function is inspired by *physics*.

5.1 Elastic Potential Energy Matching

The two point constellations $\mathcal{A}$ and $\mathcal{B}$ are modeled as fully rigid physical solids (illustrated by the red and black objects in Figure 3). We link each couple of related points (i.e. a_i and b_i) with physical springs (Figure 4), release the objects and simulate the resulting evolution of the mechanical system using linear integral interpolation to get the result shown in Figure 5.

Recall that elastic potential energy is the potential energy stored following the deformation of a spring. This energy is the work necessary to stretch the spring by x length units. According to Hooke's law, the force $F = -kx$ required to stretch a spring is proportional to x. Since the change in spring's potential energy between two positions is the work required to move the object from point 0 to point x, the spring's potential energy at distance x is $\frac{kx^2}{2}$. We assume that the springs used in our model start extending from a length of zero.

With well-chosen parameters, the system converges quickly to a minimal-energy position (measured by the potential energy stored by the springs). The higher this stable energy is, the further apart the sets are.

Figure 2 shows the convergence between the red (candidate vicinities $\mathcal{A}$) and the blue plots (template vicinities $\mathcal{B}$). The green plots represent the initial position of $\mathcal{A}$ before the release of the system. The blue plots are assigned an infinite mass and hence don't move. We can see in this figure that after the release of the system, the red plots are really close (and at times even superimposed on) to blue plots. The system's potential energy or the sum of the distances between red and blue plots after system convergence provide two possible similarity scores.

Let $\mathcal{A}'$ be the solid obtained by placing a fixed unitary mass $m_{a,i}$ at each of the ℓ coordinates given by $\mathcal{A}$. All the unitary masses of $\mathcal{A}'$ are linked together by weightless rigid bars. Exactly the same construction is applied to $\mathcal{B}$ to yield a mechanical structure $\mathcal{B}'$ composed of infinite masses $m_{b,i}$. Fixing $m_{b,i} = \infty$ makes $\mathcal{B}'$ immovable.

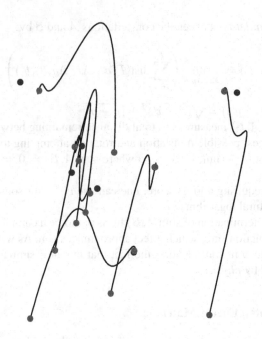

Fig. 2. Convergence Plot

We then add for all i a spring linking $m_{a,i} \rightsquigarrow m_{b,i}$ and release the system. Following this release, $\mathcal{A}'$ and $\mathcal{B}'$ will move to a position minimizing the sum of spring energies, while preserving the spatial offsets between the mass points composing $\mathcal{A}'$ and $\mathcal{B}'$.

We can manipulate two parameters : the strength coefficient of the spring, and the friction coefficient. The friction force we apply is $F = -k_v V$ where V is the speed. If we choose a friction coefficient which is too low, the springs become too strong and the system keeps oscillating for too long. If we choose a too low force coefficient, the figures will never match in reasonable time. By using well-chosen parameters, the system stabilizes in less than a second. After defining a proper stop condition (*cf. infra*), we get Algorithm 1.

Algorithm 1. The Mechanical Comparator

1: "Assemble" rigid objects $\mathcal{A}'$ and $\mathcal{B}'$ from the point sets $\mathcal{A}$ and $\mathcal{B}$ assigning an infinite mass to $\mathcal{B}'$.
2: Compute the moment of inertia of $\mathcal{A}'$
3: **while** stop condition is not met **do**
4:    Compute springs forces and moments
5:    Compute the next position of $\mathcal{A}'$ using integral linear interpolation
6: **end while**

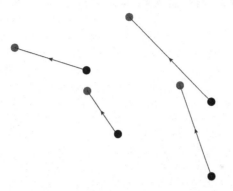

Fig. 3. Two Point Constellations (Black & Red) to Match

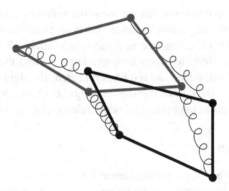

Fig. 4. Rigidified Constellations Attached with Springs Before Release

Fig. 5. Rigidified Constellations Attached with Springs Stabilized After Release

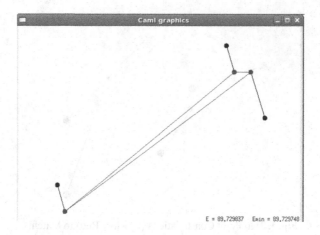

Fig. 6. The Mechanical Matching Software

For now, the only stop condition that we use is the stabilization of the system, but as further improvements we may consider having other stop conditions.

The software (Figure 6), developed in Ocaml, is available from the authors. The blue plots represent the (infinite mass) template minutiae and the red plots represent the (mobile) candidate minutiae. The red lines represent the rigid structure formed by the candidate minutiae. Black lines represent springs. E shows the system's energy at time t and E_{min} is the minimum potential energy released by the system.

5.2   Further Research

This work opens a number of interesting research perspectives:
- Is it possible to leverage physical attraction-repulsion phenomena to build concrete *analog* point constellation comparison hardware? *i.e.* cheap and disposable analog image recognition coprocessors? Because opposite electrical particles essentially act as springs this might not be impossible. However, it remains to somehow neutralize the "crosstalk attraction" between unrelated points (*i.e.* the attraction of a_i by b_j for $i \neq j$). Note that such *physically built* systems can also serve as real-life alert systems: by equipping a bridge with sensors and consolidating the global system energy, an alert can be launched if the mechanical strain on the bridge becomes dangerously high.
- Add to the simulation system perturbations to avoid meta-stable states. Experimentally, such meta-stable states appeared when extreme physical coefficient values were chosen.
- Match point-sets more accurately (by making the moving system partially flexible. This will capture the intuition that a finger or a face are soft masses whose forms could have slightly been stretched if we wanted to. Hence, by allowing the mobile

object some flexibility we reproduce a slight "grimace" that the user could have naturally done if we would have asked him to. Flexibility can be naturally implemented by embedding in each solid bar an inner spring or by replacing edges by mechanical articulations with two degrees of freedom.

– Matching non-tagged points with multiple springs. Here the idea consists in finding the proper assignment between the a_i and the b_j using multiple springs before comparing the tagged point constellations. We note that if $\mathcal{A}$ and $\mathcal{B}$ only differ by an unknown rotation (of a known center), a forced rotation of $\mathcal{A}$ during which we monitor the system's potential energy will reveal the unknown angle by a sudden global system energy drop. While this amounts to exhaustively searching the unknown angle, it is probable that coarse-grain interpolation could be used to avoid testing useless configurations. For instance one possibility would be to sample angles with a $10°$ increment, select those having the smallest energy and refine the search. We did not try this so far and it is pretty probable that artificially crafted (or maybe naturally encountered objects) would fail to be detected. Finding and/or approximating the optimal Δx, Δy using this method is another open problem.

– Optimize friction, force and mass coefficients as a function of correlation between sim_ϕ and sim using simulated annealing. Simulated annealing is a generic probabilistic metaheuristic for the global optimization problem of locating a good approximation to the global optimum of a given function in a large search space. It is often used when the search space is discrete (*e.g.*, all tours that visit a given set of cities). For certain problems, simulated annealing may be more efficient than exhaustive enumeration — provided that the goal is merely to find an acceptably good solution in a fixed amount of time, rather than the best possible solution. This seems to be case here. One possibility could be to generate a library of objects $\mathcal{A}_i$, slightly distort the $\mathcal{A}_i$s to obtain $\mathcal{B}_i$s, randomly rotate and translate the $\mathcal{B}_i$s and compute the Pearson correlation coefficient $\rho[\text{sim}_\phi, \text{sim}]$ between the data sets $\{\text{sim}_\phi(\mathcal{A}_i, \mathcal{B}_i)\}$ and $\{\text{sim}(\mathcal{A}_i, \mathcal{B}_i)\}$. Using simulated annealing determine the friction, force and mass coefficients that maximize $\rho[\text{sim}_\phi, \text{sim}]$.

– The viscosity of a fluid is a measure of its resistance to gradual deformation by shear stress or tensile stress. For liquids, it corresponds to the informal notion of "thickness". For example, honey has a higher viscosity than water. Viscosity is due to the friction between neighboring particles in a fluid that are moving at different velocities. When the fluid is forced through a tube, the fluid generally moves faster near the axis and very slowly near the walls; therefore, some stress (such as a pressure difference between the two ends of the tube) is needed to overcome the friction between layers and keep the fluid moving. For the same velocity pattern, the stress required is proportional to the fluid's viscosity. A liquid's viscosity depends on the size and shape of its particles and the attractions between the particles. Replacing mechanical friction by viscosity (*i.e.* simulating the behavior of the system immersed in water or honey) can be explored.

– Finally, apply this approach to image face recognition (the characteristic points of the face are known and easy to detect and are thus easy to match).

90   T. Bourgeat et al.

References

1. ISO/IEC 19794-2:2005. Information technology, biometric data interchange formats, part 2: Finger minutiae data. Technical report, ISO/IEC (2005)
2. Bringer, J., Despiegel, V.: Binary feature vector fingerprint representation from minutiae vicinities. In: Biometrics: Theory, Applications, and Systems, BTAS (2010)
3. Kuhn, H.: The Hungarian method for the assignment problem. Naval Research Logistics Quarterly 2, 83–97 (1955)

Protection Profile for PUF-Based Devices

Andrea Kolberger[1], Ingrid Schaumüller-Bichl[1],
Verena Brunner[2], and Martin Deutschmann[2]

[1] University of Applied Sciences Upper Austria
Department Secure Information Systems, Softwarepark 11, A-4231 Hagenberg
{andrea.kolberger,ingrid.schaumueller-bichl}@fh-hagenberg.at
[2] Technikon Forschungs- und Planungsgesellschaft mbH
Burgplatz 3a, A-9500 Villach
codes@technikon.com

Abstract. Physically Unclonable Functions (PUFs) are a promising technology in cryptographic application areas. The idea of PUFs is to make use of the unique "fingerprint" of the IC, to enable generation of secrets or keys without storing sensitive data permanently in memory. Since PUFs are "noisy" functions, some kind of post processing is required to reliably reconstruct the respective PUF response. Based on potential threats and vulnerabilities as well as the security requirements for PUF-based tokens we developed a draft version of a Protection Profile according to Common Criteria. This paper discusses the central parts of this Protection Profile, namely the Target of Evaluation (TOE), PUF-specific security functional requirements (SFRs), and requirements on the operational environment regarding the whole life cycle of the TOE.

1 Introduction

The security of IT systems in various domains, such as consumer electronics, automotive, avionics or control systems is gaining in importance more and more. On the other hand nobody is willing to pay extra for a higher level of security. Therefore, designers of security solutions have to build systems, which offer a reasonable level of security, while being economically attractive. The technology of Physically Unclonable Functions (PUFs) [8] promises to be a good candidate to serve both demands, as the idea can be realized cost-effectively, while still providing a higher level of security than state-of-the-art solutions.

PUFs are special challenge-response entities, which make use of intrinsic variations in the integrated circuit (IC) - which are out of the control of the manufacturer - to build cryptographic applications such as secure key storage or authentication protocols. The technology is explained in more detail in section 2. In order to collect and formalize the requirements for PUF-based systems we prepared a draft version of a Protection Profile (PP) according to Common Criteria (CC). Thus the present paper targets the crypto community, dealing with PUF applications and industry partners considering PUFs as a potential technology. Section 3 gives a brief overview of the CC and some information

N. Cuppens-Boulahia et al. (Eds.): SEC 2014, IFIP AICT 428, pp. 91–98, 2014.
© IFIP International Federation for Information Processing 2014

regarding PPs whereas section 4 describes the intended TOE and its components. The PUF-specific requirements defined and selected from CC to ensure a secure operation of the TOE are summarized in section 5. The paper comes to an end with a conclusion and outlook on our ongoing work in section 6.

2   PUF Technologies

One basic principle of cryptographic applications is that the security of a system relies on the secrecy of the used key (Kerckhoff's principle). Therefore the question where and how to store a secret key is essential for the level of security a system can provide. The usage of Physically Unclonable Functions (PUFs) allows designing cryptographic systems, where the key is not present in memory at all. Only the combination of some non-sensitive information, called helper data, and the intrinsic, unclonable properties of the PUF instantiation allows the reconstruction of the key.

The basic principle of PUFs is to exploit unique information which originates from submicron variations in the manufacturing process in integrated circuits (ICs), which are out of the control of the manufacturer. One established technique is to utilize the start-up behaviours of SRAM cells to serve as the digital fingerprint. If we view each SRAM cell as a single bit, the resulting bit string will tend to have the same value every time the device is powered, however, owing to time, temperature variations and voltage ramp-up variations, some bits tend to flip [9]. Another widespread PUF instantiation is the so-called Arbiter PUF, which belongs to the group of delay-based intrinsic PUFs [7]. The basic idea is to conduct a race on two paths on a chip and then let an Arbiter circuit decide, which path "won" the race. The challenges consist of a vector shaping the path of the "race". For further PUF constructions we refer to Maes and Verbauwhede [11] who present an extensive overview of all PUFs and PUF-like proposals.

Responses generated by PUFs are noisy by nature, i.e. when a single PUF is challenged with one and the same challenge several times it always returns a slightly different response. Such responses cannot be directly used for cryptographic applications. Thus post processing methods are used to reliably produce and reproduce a certain PUF response or to derive a cryptographic key. The post processing includes a procedure to perform information reconciliation which is mostly realized by some error correcting algorithm and a procedure to extract nearly uniform randomness, which can be realized with help of cryptographic hash function. The combination of these two procedures is called a fuzzy extractor (FE). For more information about FE realizations, we refer to [5].

PUF instantiations are amongst others characterized by the so-called inter- and intra-distance. For a particular challenge, the inter-distance between two PUF instantiations is the distance between the two responses resulting from applying this challenge once to both PUFs. On the other hand, we define for a particular challenge, the intra-distance between two evaluations on one single PUF instantiation as the distance between two responses resulting from applying this challenge twice to one PUF.

3   Common Criteria and Protection Profiles

The Common Criteria for Information Technology Security Evaluation (CC) are internationally accepted criteria to evaluate the security functionality of a product and the correctness of its design and implementation (assurance). Part 1 of Common Criteria [1] provides an introduction to CC and describes the general model. Requirements that might be fulfilled by a certain product are specified in Part 2 [2] and 3 [3]. Part 2 contains requirements intended to provide the security functionality of a product, the so-called security functional requirements (SFRs). In order to be able to evaluate the security functionality provided by a product the CC have defined security assurance requirements (SARs) in Part 3.

The central documents of CC are the Protection Profile (PP) and Security Target (ST). Protection Profiles describe the SFRs and SARs for a product class, i.e. a PP describes which requirements a certain product has to fulfill but it is not defined how these requirements are implemented. In comparison to that a Security Target contains security requirements for a specific product and defines how these requirements are implemented. The development and evaluation of a Security Target is mandatory for certification issues against CC.

4   Protection Profile for PUFs - The TOE

In the CODES project[1] we worked out a draft version of a Protection Profile for Physically Unclonable Functions (PUFs). Our PP contains all required parts, however this paper is confined to the TOE definition, the security functional requirements and the requirements on the operational environment of the TOE.

Figure 1 provides an overview of the TOE design that is intended to realize two use cases, namely *Mutual Authentication* [10] and *Secret Key Generation/Session Key Exchange* [6]. In the authentication process both verifier and PUF-based device are capable to (re-)construct a PUF response and verify the authenticity of each other. The second use case is intended to encrypt the initial communication between two entities with an error corrected PUF response (common secret, symmetric key) agreed upon in the enrolment phase. Part of the encrypted messages is a session key that is used for further communication.

The **pre-operational environment** includes procedures that are performed during the development process of the TOE. One major part in this environment is the initialization, personalization and enrolment of the TOE where data like the ID of the TOE, challenge-response pairs (CRPs) and helper data are generated and stored. This information is unique and essential for the security functionality of the TOE (TSF). The **operational environment** contains components like database and terminals that will be combined with the TOE in the composite product integration. The **TOE** itself shall be implemented on one single IC. Below, the components providing the security functionality are

---

[1] Project CODES: Research activities are on post processing methods like error correction codes and anti-ageing techniques to raise the stability of PUF-based responses and thereby the reliability of PUF-based security modules.

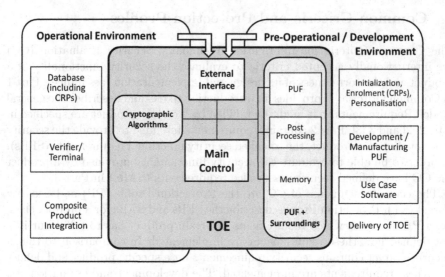

Fig. 1. TOE with its surrounding environment within the whole life cycle

briefly described. The **main control** is the central component which controls communication between and access to all other TOE components. In order to communicate with the TOE's environment an **external interface** needs to be implemented. The **PUF** type itself is not specified in this TOE. Depending on the use case, either a memory- or delay-based PUF can be used. The PUF can only be accessed by the main control which then returns a response that will directly serve as an input to the post processing. Due to the fact that PUFs are noisy functions some post processing procedure is necessary in order to correct occurred errors and reconstruct certain information. Depending on the intended use case the post processing can be realized by one of the following features:

- **Secure Sketch:** The reproduction step of the secure sketch uses helper data to reconstruct the original PUF response. The helper data is regarded non-sensitive, as it provides only negligible information about the actual secret.
- **Fuzzy Extractor:** The reconstruction step of the fuzzy extractor uses helper data generated in the pre-operational environment to reproduce a secret that has also been enrolled in the pre-operational environment.

Memory is used to store some information which is necessary to provide the TOE's security functionality. These data might be helper data or the ID of the TOE. The protection of the memory space of the IC against attacks is not in the scope of this PP. **Cryptographic functions** will be necessary in order to realize the complete use case. In case of key generation it is necessary that the respective symmetric or asymmetric cipher is available on the TOE in order to be able to en- or decrypt information.

5   Security Requirements and Extended Components

A risk analysis on the use cases described in section 4 highlighted the main threats that have to be countered for PUF-based devices and showed that the usage of a weak fuzzy extractor or secure sketch as well as PUF failures cause the highest risks. As a consequence the developed post processing methods must not reveal any information regarding the PUF response. At the same time these methods have to reliably reconstruct secrets from an errorprone PUF response.

5.1   Security Functional Requirements

Our PP includes numerous security functional requirements concerning detection of and reaction on malicious activities, control of the internal workflow, and selftests to provide an initial secure start-up of the TOE. Below we concentrate on SFRs [2] that focus on the specific needs of PUF-based security schemes.

PUF and Cryptographic Functions. The TSF challenges the PUF using a predefined challenge from the CRP database. Depending on the underlying PUF construction a PUF response is generated. According to the intended use case the PUF response is transferred between the TOE's components and might be directly used as a cryptographic key after post processing or it serves as an input to a cryptographic key generation algorithm. Therefore generated secrets shall meet defined quality metrics (e.g. number of required bits).

FPT_PUF.1 Physically unclonable function, requires that according to a challenge a PUF response is generated.

FCS_CKM.1 Cryptographic key generation, requires cryptographic keys to be generated in accordance with a specified algorithm and key sizes which can be based on an assigned standard.

FCS_COP.1 Cryptographic operation, requires a cryptographic operation to be performed in accordance with a specified algorithm and with a cryptographic key of specified sizes. The specified algorithm and cryptographic key sizes can be based on an assigned standard.

FIA_SOS.2 TSF Generation of secrets, requires the TSF to be able to generate secrets that meet defined quality metrics.

Reliable Post Processing Methods. Post processing methods are used to reconstruct secrets/keys from a noisy PUF response. The error correction mechanism shall be implemented in such a way that with the help of helper data a secret/key can be reconstructed reliably, i.e. it shall be capable to correct a certain number of errors even though of environmental variations or ageing effects of a PUF. Helper data extracted by the fuzzy extractor needs to be generated in the pre-operational environment and must not reveal any information about the response. Depending on the use case helper data are generated by the TOE itself, by an external entity or they are already stored in the TOE's memory.

FCS_CPP.1 Secure Sketch, requires helper data to reconstruct a PUF response.

FCS_CPP.2 Fuzzy extractor, requires helper data to reconstruct a cryptographic key or secret.

5.2 Extended Component Definition

PUF-based security schemes provide functionalities that are not based on components specified in CC Part 2. For the use of PUFs and the according post processing methods new families were defined.

Definition of the Family FPT_PUF. This family defines requirements that a PUF is used to derive a PUF response according to a challenge. The PUF response is subsequently used for authentication procedures or generation of cryptographic keys or secrets.

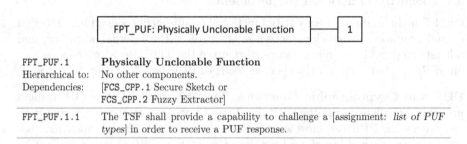

FPT_PUF.1   **Physically Unclonable Function**
Hierarchical to: No other components.
Dependencies: [FCS_CPP.1 Secure Sketch or
                        FCS_CPP.2 Fuzzy Extractor]

FPT_PUF.1.1   The TSF shall provide a capability to challenge a [assignment: *list of PUF types*] in order to receive a PUF response.

Definition of the Family FCS_CPP. This family defines requirements for the post processing step necessary for PUF-based applications. Depending on the use case, helper data is used either in combination with a secure sketch to reproduce a PUF response or in combination with a fuzzy extractor to reconstruct a cryptographic key or secret.

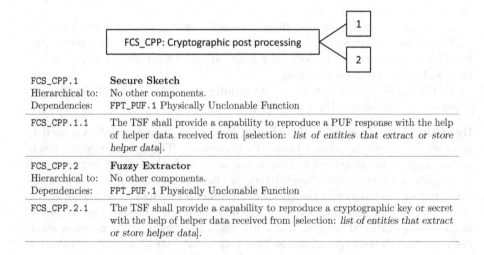

FCS_CPP.1   **Secure Sketch**
Hierarchical to: No other components.
Dependencies: FPT_PUF.1 Physically Unclonable Function

FCS_CPP.1.1   The TSF shall provide a capability to reproduce a PUF response with the help of helper data received from [selection: *list of entities that extract or store helper data*].

FCS_CPP.2   **Fuzzy Extractor**
Hierarchical to: No other components.
Dependencies: FPT_PUF.1 Physically Unclonable Function

FCS_CPP.2.1   The TSF shall provide a capability to reproduce a cryptographic key or secret with the help of helper data received from [selection: *list of entities that extract or store helper data*].

In addition to the two families described above we also defined extended components concerning limited capability (FMT_LIM.1) and limited availability (FMT_LIM.2) of functions [7].

5.3   Requirements and Assumptions on the Operational Environment

Requirements defined in this section are addressed to the TOE's operational environment. That implies requirements which cannot be fulfilled by the TOE's security functionality and therefore have to be realized by the operator/enduser to ensure the secure, correct and effective operation of the TOE. The most important requirements and assumptions are described below.

Manufacturing, Enrolment and Delivery of PUF-Based Tokens. In the contract concluded between the manufacturer of the TOE and operator has to be stated that the manufacturer is not allowed to add any functionality that enables prediction or specific manipulation of the PUF response anyway. Further the operator should be capable to verify the correct implementation of the PUF. In the enrolment phase the database, including CRPs as well as common secrets or helper data for a specific TOE uniquely identified by an ID, shall be generated in a secure manner and secure environment. The database including PUF-specific and consequently confidential data has to be transferred in a secure manner between the enrolment facility and the customer. Therefore authenticity, confidentiality and integrity of the stored data has to be ensured. Further the enroller has to make sure that only the intended person receives the CRP database.

Selection of Challenges. Enrolment shall take place in secure environment as mentioned before. During enrolment a PUF shall be challenged with randomly chosen and unpredictable challenges. Further the challenges for different PUF-based token must not be equal and should be made of a sufficient length in order to make brute force attacks harder or inefficient.

Temperature/Voltage. It is assumed that the temperature of the TOE's operational environment is within the range of $-40\ ^\circ C$ up to $+85\ ^\circ C$ [12]. Regarding the variation of voltage PUF technologies react differently. Therefore an assumption on the range of voltage, within that a certain PUF construction works reliable, has to be made in the ST. Thus the operator shall ensure that the temperature of the TOE's operational environment and the variation of voltage is within the specified range otherwise the TOE might not work reliably.

6   Conclusion and Outlook

To the best of our knowledge no Protection Profile for the technology of PUFs exists at the moment. Our draft version is going to be followed up in the ongoing project. Especially the requirements defined so far might be refined, replaced or some further security functionality might be added. Since the goal of the project is not to certify a "real world" TOE, our draft PP is not object to evaluation activities in order to judge its suitability. The aim is to elaborate a Protection Profile for PUFs that might form the basis for future work on PPs to enable certification of PUF-based devices against Common Criteria.

Acknowledgements. This work is co-financed by the Austrian Research Promotion Agency (FFG) in the FIT-IT line within the project CODES (835932): Algorithmic extraction and error correction codes for lightweight security anchors with reconfigurable PUFs. The project partners are Technikon Forschungs- und Planungsgesellschaft mbH, Alpen-Adria Universität Klagenfurt and University of Applied Sciences Upper Austria - Campus Hagenberg.

References

1. Common Criteria for Information Technology Security Evaluation, Part 1: Introduction and General Model. CCMB-2012-09-001, Version 3.1, Revision 4 (September 2012)
2. Common Criteria for Information Technology Security Evaluation, Part 2: Security Functional Components. CCMB-2012-09-002, Version 3.1, Revision 4 (September 2012)
3. Common Criteria for Information Technology Security Evaluation, Part 3: Security Assurance Components. CCMB-2012-09-003, Version 3.1, Revision 4 (September 2012)
4. Eurosmart Security IC Platform Protection Profile. Version 1.0, BSI-PP-0035 (June 2007)
5. Bösch, C., Guajardo, J., Sadeghi, A.-R., Shokrollahi, J., Tuyls, P.: Efficient Helper Data Key Extractor on FPGAs. In: Oswald, E., Rohatgi, P. (eds.) CHES 2008. LNCS, vol. 5154, pp. 181–197. Springer, Heidelberg (2008)
6. Dodis, Y., Ostrovsky, R., Reyzin, L., Smith, A.: Fuzzy Extractors: How to Generate Strong Keys from Biometrics and Other Noisy Data. SIAM Journal on Computing, 38(1):97–139 (2008)
7. Fruhashi, K., Shiozaki, M., Fukushima, A., Murayama, T., Fujino, T.: The arbiter-PUF with high uniqueness utilizing novel arbiter circuit with Delay-Time Measurement. In: IEEE International Symposium on Circuits and Systems (ISCAS) 2011, pp. 2325–2328 (2011)
8. Gassend, B., Clarke, D., van Dijk, M., Devadas, S.: Controlled Physical Random Functions. In: IEEE (ed.) Proceedings of the 18th Annual Computer Security Applications Conference (ACSAC 2002), USA (2002)
9. Handschuh, H.: Hardware-Anchored Security Based on SRAM PUFs, Part 1. IEEE Security Privacy 10(3), 80–83 (2012)
10. Van Herrewege, A., Katzenbeisser, S., Maes, R., Peeters, R., Sadeghi, A.-R., Verbauwhede, I., Wachsmann, C.: Reverse Fuzzy Extractors: Enabling Lightweight Mutual Authentication for PUF-Enabled RFIDs. In: Keromytis, A.D. (ed.) FC 2012. LNCS, vol. 7397, pp. 374–389. Springer, Heidelberg (2012)
11. Maes, R., Verbauwhede, I.: Physically Unclonable Functions: A Study on the State of the Art and Future Research Directions. In: Sadeghi, A.-R., Naccache, D. (eds.) Towards Hardware-Intrinsic Security, Information Security and Cryptography, pp. 3–37. Springer, Heidelberg (2010)
12. Schrijen, G.-J., van der Leest, V.: Comparative analysis of SRAM memories used as PUF primitives. In: Design, Automation Test in Europe Conference Exhibition (DATE), pp. 1319–1324 (2012)

Text-Based Active Authentication for Mobile Devices

Hataichanok Saevanee[1], Nathan Clarke[1,3], Steven Furnell[1,3], and Valerio Biscione[2]

[1] Centre for Security, Communications and Network Research,
[2] Centre for Robotics and Neural Systems,
Plymouth University, Plymouth, United Kingdom
[3] Security Research Institute, Edith Cowan University,
Perth, Western Australia
info@cscan.org

Abstract. As modern mobile devices are increasing in their capability and accessibility, they introduce additional demands in terms of security – particularly authentication. With the widely documented poor use of PINs, Active Authentication is designed to overcome the fundamental issue of usable and secure authentication through utilizing biometric-based techniques to continuously verify user identity. This paper proposes a novel text-based multimodal biometric approach utilizing linguistic analysis, keystroke dynamics and behavioral profiling. Experimental investigations show that users can be discriminated via their text-based entry, with an average Equal Error Rate (EER) of 3.3%. Based on these findings, a framework that is able to provide robust, continuous and transparent authentication is proposed. The framework is evaluated to examine the effectiveness of providing security and user convenience. The result showed that the framework is able to provide a 91% reduction in the number of intrusive authentication requests required for high security applications.

Keywords: Active authentication, Transparent authentication, Continuous authentication, Multimodal, Biometric, Mobile devices.

1 Introduction

Mobile devices are commonplace with over 6 billion subscribers worldwide [1]. With the rapid development of mobile network technology and the increasing popularity of mobile devices, modern devices are capable of providing a wide range of services and applications over multiple networks. The plethora of functionalities offered by the mobile device enables users to store increasing amounts of a wider variety of information from business to personal and sensitive data. A series of studies have highlighted the potential risk of mobile device misuse through the storing of personal information (e.g. home address), security credentials (e.g. PIN codes, user names and passwords) and business data (e.g. customer data) [2,3].

Although PIN or password authentication is available on most mobile devices, a survey conducted by [4] demonstrated that a third of mobile users do not protect their devices with this simple technique. Furthermore, the poor use of PIN or password

N. Cuppens-Boulahia et al. (Eds.): SEC 2014, IFIP AICT 428, pp. 99–112, 2014.
© IFIP International Federation for Information Processing 2014

techniques when they are used is also widely documented in several studies [4,5]. A fundamental weakness of the PIN is that as a point-of-entry approach, once the user has been successfully authenticated, they obtain access to the system without having to re-authenticate. Several studies [6,7] proposed Active Authentication or transparent authentication to overcome the fundamental issue and more closely associate the authentication and access control decisions. There are a number of biometric techniques that have the potential to be used for authentication in a transparent and thus continuous fashion, such as keystroke dynamics, behavioral profiling, gait recognition, speaker verification and facial recognition. Unfortunately, research has demonstrated that using a single biometric may be inadequate for verification due to a variety of reasons, such as noise in the sample data, the unavailability of a sample at a given time and the underlying performance of the technique [8]. To overcome this limitation within traditional the point-of-entry domain, several researchers have proposed the use of multiple biometric modalities, which have demonstrated increased accuracy of verification [9,10,11].

This paper presents the findings of a research study exploring the application of multimodal biometric authentication in a transparent fashion to text-based entry. As users frequently use their mobile device to send SMS text messages (over 9.8 trillion in 2012), social network posts, emails and tweets, it was felt this medium provided a frequent opportunity to capture samples [12]. The focus upon text-based entry provides the possibility to apply keystroke dynamics, linguistic analysis and behavioral profiling. It is the aim of this paper to present the results of an exhaustive investigation into optimizing the recognition performance and an evaluation of the security processes required to maximize the security of the approach whilst minimizing user inconvenience. Section 2 presents the state of the art in behavioral biometrics that have been applied in the mobile domain. Section 3 describes the feasibility study of multimodal biometric. Based upon the results, a novel text-based multimodal framework that will provide the verification of a mobile user's identity in a continuous and transparent manner is proposed in Section 4 and then evaluated through simulation in Section 5. The paper concludes by highlighting the future direction of research in Section 6.

2   Text-Based Behavioral Biometric for Mobile Devices

With the rapid evolution of mobile devices, utilizing biometrics on them has become a reality. Many mobile devices come equipped with a number of hardware components that are able to be used for capturing a variety of biometric traits, enabling several biometric approaches to be deployed – such as keystroke dynamics, behavioral profiling and voice recognition. For example, Apple has now incorporated TouchID, a fingerprint-based approach, and Google has Face Unlock for its Android Operating System [13,14]. To date, however, these are point-of-entry solutions that focus upon usability rather than security. Of interest in this research is the use of three behavioral biometric techniques: linguistic profiling, keystroke dynamics and behavioral profiling. It is hypothesized that the integration of these three techniques together offers the opportunity to improve upon the usability through transparent capture, improve the overall recognition performance and mitigate the unavailability of samples at a given time.

Linguistic profiling is a behavioral biometric that identifies people based upon linguistic morphology. Previous studies have investigated the feasibility of linguistic profiling for several tasks such as text categorization, authorship identification and authorship verification. In the authorship verification domain, examples of writing from a single author are given to the system, which is then asked to confirm if the given texts were written by this author. According to previous studies [15], almost 1000 writing styles have been analyzed and both statistical and machine learning methods were used in the analytical process. Many studies have confirmed the good discriminating capability of linguistic features. Through using a machine learning method, the performance accuracies were in the range of 80%-100% [16,17]. However, there is no agreement on a best set of features for authorship verification and historically large volumes of text are required for the training dataset. The performance of linguistic profiling technique highly depends upon the combination of the selected features and classification models utilized.

Behavioral profiling aims to identify users based upon the way in which they interact with the services on their mobile device. Previous behavior-based studies have mainly focused upon the area of fraud detection. Research in mobile IDSs can be divided into two categories: call-based and mobility-based mechanisms. The former monitors user's calling behavior (e.g. start date of call and dial telephone number) that have been collected over a service provider's network during a period of time [18,19]. Based upon the theory that people have a predictable travelling pattern when they travel from one location to another, the mobility-based approach monitors a mobile user's location activities to detect abnormal behavior [20]. Through monitoring a user's calling or location activities, behavioral-based IDS can offer a high detection rate and ability to detect unforeseen attacks [18,19,20,21]. Depending upon application types, profiling techniques and classification approach, a study by [7] showed that behavioral profiling could be used for authentication on mobile devices with accuracies of between 87% and 98%.

Keystroke dynamics identifies a user based upon the typing pattern of a user, looking at characteristics of their interaction with a keyboard. Based upon previous studies, two main characteristics were identified: inter-key and hold time [24]. The inter-key is the duration between two successive keys. The hold-time represents the duration between the press down and releasing of a single key. Many studies have shown it is feasible to authenticate users successfully based upon usernames and passwords (i.e. in parallel with a typical Windows login request), with a commercial product on the market utilizing this technology [22, 23]. More recent studies [6, 24] investigated the possibility of using keystroke dynamics on mobile devices, showing the possibility of keystroke dynamic based authentication can be deployed in practice to provide an extra layer of security for mobile devices with an average accuracy of 87%.

Based upon the prior-art, these three techniques provide valuable discriminative information to permit identity authentication. All of the biometric traits of these three techniques can be captured during user interactions with a mobile device without a user explicit interaction to authenticate. In addition, no additional hardware is required to deploy these techniques. As a result, these approaches arguably provide a cost effective and a non-intrusive solution for mobile handset authentication. Furthermore, a significant amount of prior research within the point-of-entry authentication domain [9,10,11] has concluded that using multiple biometric modalities can improve accuracy and reliability of single-modal systems. For example, using combination of fingerprint and face modality can achieve better performance than using single biometric, improving the accuracy of 2.3% at 0.1% FAR [25].

3   A Feasibility Study of Text-Based Multimodal Biometrics

Since no multimodal database availability where the above three biometric modalities are measured within the same individual, a standard practice employed within multibiometrics is to combine the modalities from different datasets and create a virtual person [11]. The SMS corpus collected by the authors, a public mobile usage dataset provided by [26] and keystroke dataset provided by [24] were used in this experiment. An individual user from the linguistic profiling database was associated with an individual of keystroke and behavioral profiling database to create a virtual subject. As a result, a final database consisting of 30 users, each user having their SMS messages, keystroke and text messaging activity data was created and utilized in this experiment.

3.1   Experiment Procedure

The experiments investigated the performance both of the individual techniques and their combination. To investigate the linguistic profiling's effectiveness; four types of linguistic features were examined: word profiling, lexical, syntactic and structural. The frequency distribution of a total 133 abbreviations and emotional words were used to create a user's word profiles, including 64 discriminating characteristics of every possible type of feature. To create a user profile, the t-test ranking measure was utilized to rank input features according to its discriminative capability. From the ranking list, features with a p value less than 0.05 were selected to create input vectors. The key to utilizing the t-test was to ensure a set of features that was as unique to the individual authorized user in comparison to the wider population. Therefore, the number of linguistic features required for discrimination will vary between users. Three different classification techniques: K-Nearest Neighbor (K-NN), the Radial Basis function (RBF) and Feed-Forward Multi-Layered Perceptron (FF-MLP) neural networks were utilized with differing network configurations - looking to optimum performance.

In the keystroke dynamics experiment, the hold time vector constructed from five letters: E, T, A, O and N were extracted. A number of analyses were undertaken using the FF-MLP neural network as it had demonstrated the better performance in previous studies over other techniques [24].

For the behavioral profiling technique, the following features were extracted: receiver's telephone number and location of texting. A number of analyses were undertaken, using a Radial Basis Function (RBF) neural network as it had performed the best in the prior study [7].

Table 1. Final dataset used in the experiments

	Training size	Testing size
Linguistic profiling	316	171
Keystroke dynamics	3339	171
Behavior profiling	1178	171

To perform the classification for the individual techniques, the dataset was divided into two groups: 171 data samples were used for the testing set and the remainder was used for training (as illustrated in Table 1). The pattern classification test was performed with one user acting as the valid user, while all others are acting as impostors (a standard procedure in this type of test) [6-8]. The Equal Error Rate (EER) was calculated to evaluate the system. The EER is the value where False Acceptance Rate (FAR) crosses the False Rejection Rate (FRR), and is typically used as a comparative measure within the biometric industry [28].

The multimodal experiment was conducted using all possible combination of three techniques. The results of each technique were combined at the matching-level - as each technique utilized different classifiers and a different range of outputs, the min-max score normalization method was applied to scale the results of each technique into the range between 0 and 1. Based upon prior research, two fusion methods were utilized: simple sum and matcher weighting [11], [29]. For the Simple Sum fusion, the raw score of each individual technique were simple added and rescaled into the 0 to 1 range. For the Matcher Weighting approach, weights are assigned to the individual matchers based on their individual EER. The weights are inversely proportional to the corresponding errors; the weights for less EER are higher than those of with a high EER.

3.2 Experiment Results

The results of using individual biometrics and the multimodal approach are shown in Table 2. The results illustrated an average of all the users' EERs by using a single optimized neural network. The results showed that the individual techniques can be used to discriminate users with relatively low error rates for a good proportion of participants. However, further analysis showed that the individual user is able to achieve a better overall EER when each user is permitted to use a different network configuration. By using individually optimized network configurations for individual user, the overall performance was an EER of 8.9%. Behavioral profiling demonstrated the best individual performance using a single network configuration, with keystroke dynamics being the worst performer.

A further analysis of individual performances raises a number of interesting points. Foremost, that the best-case EERs are extremely good. However, it is noticeable that there are some users that experience very high error rates, reiterating the importance of multimodal approaches.

Table 2. Experiment results for text-based authentication

	Equal Error Rate (EER)%		
	Average	Best Case	Worst Case
Linguistic Profiling (LP)	12.8	0.0	40.0
Behavioral Profiling (BP)	9.2	0.0	50.0
Keystroke Dynamics (KA)	20.8	0.0	50.7
Fusion by Sum			
Multimodal (LP+BP)	5.5	0.0	30.6
Multimodal (KA+BP)	6.2	0.0	20.0
Multimodal (LP+KA)	11.2	0.0	45.0
All techniques	4.4	0.0	18.1
Fusion by Matcher Weighting			
Multimodal (LP+BP)	3.6	0.0	20.0
Multimodal (KA+BP)	5.3	0.0	20.2
Multimodal (LP+KA)	8.5	0.0	44.7
All techniques	3.3	0.0	19.3

As seen in the Table 2, both of the two fusion methods lead to better performance than any of the individual classifiers. Generally, the Matcher Weighting technique outperforms simple sum method. Whilst the results show that on average the use of more modalities leads to a better performance, this is not reflected within the individual user results. On occasions, it was noticed that users performed better when using two inputs (typically LP+BP) rather than three. Therefore in an operational environment case must be taken on selecting the most appropriate classifier. Examining the individual worst-case performance, it can be seen that the multimodal models have significantly improved upon the error rates – further supporting the use of multimodal approaches.

4   A Novel Framework for Active Authentication

The concept of Transparent Authentication System (TAS) on mobile devices was first proposed in 2002 [30]. The framework utilizes a mixture of biometric techniques to verify a mobile user's identity in a continuous and transparent manner. The framework is able to:

− to increase the authentication security beyond that offered by the password based approach;
− to provide transparent non-intrusive authentication for the user (rather than intrusive) to maximize user convenience;
− to provide continuous verification of the user, ensuring that the protection can be maintained throughout the duration of the device usage;
− to provide an authentication architecture that automatically works on all mobile devices regardless of hardware configuration, processing capability and network connectivity.

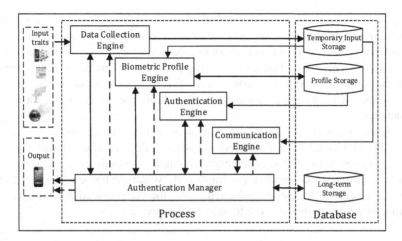

Fig. 1. Text-based multimodal framework

A number of process engines and a security manager have been devised to achieve these objectives (as demonstrate in Fig.1). A detailed description of these processes is presented in the following sections.

4.1   Processing Engines

The primary role of the Data Collection Engine is to capture a user's input text. When a user utilizes a text-based application on the mobile, information about the user's typing, message writing style and the application usage are automatically collected by the Data Collection Engine and transformed into various biometric input samples. The captured input samples are then stored in the Temporary Input Storage to be used further in the authentication process by the authentication engine.

The main duty of the biometric profiling engine is to generate the various biometric profile templates by using the combination of the user's historical data and a number of template generation algorithms. The generated biometric templates will be stored in the Profile Storage and will be used in the verification process.

The main functionality of the Authentication Engine is to perform the user authentication process. The Authentication Engine has the ability to perform authentication for every permutation of inputs to ensure that authentication can be performed even if all of the three biometric samples are not presented (e.g. location may be not be able to be determined). When a verification process is required by the Authentication Manager, the Authentication Engine compares the input samples with the biometric templates to determine the legitimacy of the user. Once the verification process is completed, the verification result is appropriately processed by the Authentication Manager. If the verification result indicates the sample(s) came from authorized user, the sample(s) will be stored within the Profile Storage to be used for profile (re)generation; otherwise it will be deleted. A multibiometric authentication technique may produce a verification result that accepts the samples as coming from the authorized user even though the sample from one individual technique might be rejected as coming from an imposter. Since the overall decision was that the sample comes from the authorized user, the failed samples are deemed to be, in fact, from the authorized user and incorrectly failed. As such, these samples are added to the profile and are not deleted. In this way, the template re-training process can produce a more accurate profile that could provide better performance. This process overcomes a fundamental issue with biometric template re-training and ensuring the correct inclusion of relevant samples.

The framework can operate in both standalone and distributed modes to allow the framework to be useful for non-wireless and wireless devices. If the framework operates in client-server mode, the communication engine works as a bridge between the capture device and the comprehensive framework. When the framework operates in a standalone mode and the device is locked down, the communication engine sends a code to the user which they can use to unlock their device.

4.2   Security Manager

The Authentication Manager is the central controller of the framework and provides the "intelligence". The key task of the Authentication Manager is to monitor the security level and make authentication decisions when the user requests access to an application. It is the responsibility of the Authentication Manager to handle the security and user convenience trade-off. In order to achieve this, the Authentication Manager utilizes two processing algorithms: the System Security (SS) Level Automatic Update Algorithm and the Application Request Algorithm to manage the balance between the security of the mobile device and user convenience. These processes have been designed based upon a well-known study [24].

The SS level is a sliding numerical value in the range of 0 and +5 with 0 indicating a low security level and +5 indicates a high security level[1]. The SS level changes depending upon the outcomes of the authentication processes and the time that has elapsed between authentication requests. In this proposed framework, each application will have its own security level. The high value application will have a high security level and a normal application will have a low security level. This can be achieved either manually by the user or automatically by the system, using a database stored in the Long-term Storage. Prior research has investigated simple mechanisms by which these risk-based evaluations for applications can be made [30].

The Authentication Manager utilizes the SS Level Automatic Update Algorithm in order to periodically update the SS level based on the results of authentication decisions based upon the user's input samples. The Authentication Manager periodically sends an authentication request to the Authentication Engine in order to update the SS level. The time interval in which the authentication should be requested depends upon the user's preference (i.e. every 5 minutes). Initially, the Authentication Manager requires the Authentication Engine to perform authentication using the best set of the user's input samples (i.e. utilizes the classifier with the lowest EER that samples exist

---

[1]   The boundaries defined on the numerical scale are only provided as a suggestion. In practice, these values maybe redefined.

for) from the last x minutes (i.e. 5 minutes). In a case where no user's input data is presented, the Authentication Manager maintains the SS level at its latest updated value. However, if the Authentication Engine responds with a pass then the Authentication Manager updates the SS level and subsequently reverts back to monitoring mode. If not, the Authentication Manager decreases the SS level and sends an authentication request again by using the next best set of user's input samples. The Authentication Manager will try three times to send an authentication request, every time with the next best available sample being employed. The Authentication Manager updates the SS level based upon the authentication result. The SS value is increased or decreased based on the type of sample used. For example, a sample using the keystroke dynamics technique will have an increment/decrement value of 0.5; a sample which contains both linguistic profiling and behavior profiling will have an increment/decrement value of 2. This numbers are based on the performance of the technique or combination of techniques. In scenarios where the updated SS level is less than 0, the Authentication Manager will set the SS level back to 0, meaning that the user will be able to access only the applications that do not required security. The process gives bias toward the user as they are given three non-intrusive chances to authenticate correctly and no intrusive authentication requests. This enables the system to minimize inconvenience to its user. Should the user attempt to access applications that require a SS level greater than the current SS level, the Authentication Manager will utilize the Application Request Algorithm to check the legitimacy of the user as shows in Fig.2.

The current SS level of the user is compared with the security level of the requested application. If the level is equal to or greater than the security level of the required application, the user can automatically access the application. Otherwise the

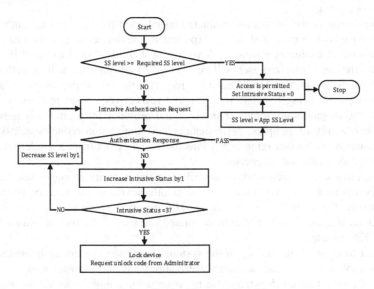

Fig. 2. Application Request Algorithm

user will be asked intrusively to authenticate. If the authentication response to this intrusive request fails to pass, the device is locked. Otherwise, the level of the user will be updated to the security level of the requested application and access will be granted.

5   Evaluation

To examine the effectiveness of the framework in providing security and user convenience, the proposed framework was evaluated through a simulation. The simulation process involves implementing a virtual user and applying the SS Level Automatic Update Algorithm and the Application Request Algorithms.

To evaluate the performance of the security mechanisms to an authorized user, three different usage levels (infrequent, moderate and frequent) will be investigated - as the level of usage will have a direct impact on the availability of biometric samples and thus the capability of the system to maintain the security level. The use of the mobile device is simulated using a flow of timeslots. Each time slot can be seen as a minute in real life. Within each time slot the user can do one of two actions, or both: provide an input sample (thus simulating a text-based entry) or the use an app. Within each timeslot, the probability for the user to provide an input sample or accessing an application will set to 0.05, 0.15 and 0.50 in order to simulate an infrequent, moderate and frequent user respectively. There are 6 different types of application that can be chosen by the user (reflecting the possible security levels of an application from 0 to 5). Each type of application has the same probability of being accessed. Similarly, there are 7 different non-intrusive techniques (refer to Table 2). Given that within a time slot the user provides an input sample, each type of technique has the same probability of occurring.

All non-intrusive techniques are evaluated based upon the EER of each authentication technique as demonstrated in the experimental result section. This means that, when the system evaluates a sample, there is a probability (equal to the EER of the technique) that an authorized user will be rejected or an imposter will be authorized. With regards to the intrusive authentication requests, the probability of an authorized user and impostor being rejected and accepted respectively is set to 0.03. This approach to the methodology removes any bias and provides for a randomly generated dataset with a mix of samples, performances and application requests across three usage scenarios. To further remove any bias that would exist from a single run of the simulation, the simulation is repeated.

The security system will work as described in the Security Manager session. The SS will be updated every 10 minutes. If the mobile device is not used for 10 minutes consecutively, the SS will be decreased by 0.05 for every following minute, until the system is used again. The simulation simulated the use of the mobile phone for 12 hours or 720 minutes.

In order to examine the ability of the system security to prevent an imposter from using the mobile device, two scenarios were simulated: an imposter using a mobile device at the initial state (SS =0) and the imposter using a mobile device starting from a high level of security (SS=5). This can simulate an imposter taking control a mobile device which has just been used by the authorized user.

5.1   Simulation Results

The result for all scenarios is represented using the average of running the simulation 10 times. The simulation results for an infrequent, moderate and frequent authorized user are presented in Table3.

Table 3. Simulation results for different types of authorized user

App Level	Infrequent User		Moderate User		Frequent User	
	#App Request	#Intrusive Request	#App Request	# Intrusive Request	#App Request	# Intrusive Request
5	7.2	4.2	16.2	1.5	60.0	1.50
4	5.1	0.4	17.9	0.5	60.1	0.50
3	7.3	0.3	20.0	0.2	61.3	0.30
2	5.9	0.2	16.8	0.3	59.6	0.10
1	6.0	0.0	19.5	0.2	55.2	0.00
0	6.7	0.0	19.3	0.0	57.6	0.00
Total	38.2	5.1	109.7	2.7	353.8	2.40

Based upon the simulation results, it can be shown that the security system can provide a high level of security whilst minimizing user inconvenience in all three scenarios. Analysing the proportion between intrusive authentication request and application access permits an insight into how often the user experiences an intrusive authentication request. Ideally, this proportion would be zero meaning that the user would not be required to perform an intrusive authentication request when they access an application. In our simulation these values are 13%, 2% and 0.6%, for the infrequent, moderate and frequent user respectively. The infrequent user experiences a higher intrusive request because it will probabilistically have fewer samples in the system and the system decreases the SS level if the device is not used for 10 consecutive minutes. Therefore, when this user want to access an application, it is more likely that its SS will not be sufficient to be granted immediate access. Throughout the complete 720 minute simulation the device was never incorrectly blocked for the authorized user. Further analysis of the results demonstrates for a level 5 app (which is arguably sensitive enough to warrant authentication of the user), this transparent approach results in a 97.5% reduction in intrusive authentication requests (for a frequent user).

The simulation results of the imposter scenarios showed that the security system blocks the imposter from using the mobile device after few minutes in both cases (as illustrated in Table 4). The reasons for this is that when the imposter tried to access an application that required a security level greater than 0, the system requested the imposter to authenticate themselves using an intrusive technique three times. There is a really small chance for the imposter to successfully authenticate, so after three requests the device will be blocked. As expected, the system will take more time to block the device if the imposter starts using the device when the SS is high.

Table 4. Simulation results for imposter user start using device at SS=0 and 5

App Level	Device at SS= 0		Device at SS= 5	
	#App Request	# Intrusive Request	#App Request	# Intrusive Request
5	0.6	0.4	1.0	0.2
4	0.3	0.1	1.8	0.6
3	0.4	0.4	1.5	0.0
2	0.4	0.2	1.3	0.1
1	0.3	0.1	1.9	0.1
0	0.4	0.0	1.0	0.0
Total	2.4	1.2	8.5	1.0
Time In Use	5.0 minutes		14.7 minutes	

5.2 Discussion

The simulations show how the proposed framework can provide a good compromise between improving the level of security provided and without increasing the user convenience. Indeed, it can be argued that user convenience under this model is also significantly improved over existing approaches. However, further investigations are required in order to better examine the values of the parameters. For example, it seems clear that the verification time does play an important role of providing security and user convenience. By regularly authenticating the user, the user will suffer more intrusive authentication requests but the system will be able to recognize an imposter in a relatively short period of time. On the other hand, users will find the device more convenient to use with longer time periods between user authentications but the system will take longer to recognize an imposter and lock down the system. In our simulation the verification time was 10 minutes. However, this may not be the optimum compromise between convenience and security.

Similarly, decreasing SS level was not examined, but it is expected to play a relevant role in the system. The infrequent user will experience less challenges from the intrusive authentication technique when the time period of the degradation function gets longer. However, the imposter will have more chance of accessing a high level application in cases where the device was initially left with a high level SS. In this simulation, a linear function is used to decrease the SS level but it is suggested that the function for degrading the SS level should be implemented using an exponential function as it decrease slowly at first and then more rapidly.

6   Conclusions and Future Work

The first part of this paper presented a feasibility study that demonstrated the ability of utilizing text-based entry to authenticate users. The use multimodal biometrics, specifically the combination of linguistic profiling, behavior profiling and keystroke dynamics showed an excellent level of recognition performance, validating the feasibility that multimodal text-based has the ability to authenticate user on mobile devices.

The novel multimodal authentication framework subsequently presented to support text-based biometrics was designed to add additional security to a mobile handset, providing transparent and continuous authentication. The system is designed using a variety of single and multimodal biometric techniques without any additional hardware. The users can benefit from the framework in terms of both device security and convenience of use. By setting various security requirement levels for different applications/services based upon their risk, the framework is capable of controlling the impact on each application/service. The simulation results clearly showed that the proposed authentication framework is able to provide continuous and transparent authentication to protect mobile devices.

Future work will focus upon the development of a more representative and larger biometric corpus from which to further examine the level of recognition performance that can be achieved. To accompany this work, an operational prototype will also be developed to enable an end-user evaluation to be undertaken so that user acceptance and operational performance can be established.

References

1. Ericsson.: Traffic and market report on the pulse of the networked society, http://www.ericsson.com/res/docs/2012/traffic_and_market_report_june_2012.pdf

2. Kaspersky Lab.: European Users Mobile Behaviour and Awareness of MobileThreats, http://www.kaspersky.com/news?id=207576289

3. Dimensional Research.: The impact of mobile devices on information security: A survey of IT professionals, http://www.checkpoint.com/downloads/products/check-point-mobile-security-survey-report.pdf

4. McAfee.: McAfee Reveals Consumers Fail To Protect Their Mobile Devices, http://www.mcafee.com/us/about/news/2013/q1/20130224-01.aspx

5. Clarke, N., Furnell, S.M.: Authentication of users on mobile telephones – A survey of attitudes and practices. Computer & Security 24(7), 519–527 (2005)

6. Karatzouni, S., Clarke, N., Furnell, M.: Utilising Biometric for transparent user authentication on mobile devices. In: 2nd Internet Technologies and Applications, pp. 549–557 (2007)

7. Li, F., Clarke, N., Papadaki, M., Dowland, P.: Behaviour Profiling for Transparent Authentication for Mobile Devices. In: Proceedings of the 10th European Conference on Information Warfare (ECIW), Tallinn, Estonia, pp. 307–314 (2011)

8. Sim, T., Zhang, S., Janakiraman, R., Kumar, S.: Continuous verification using multimodal biometrics. Pattern Analysis and Machine Intelligence 29(4), 687–700 (2007)

9. Kittler, J., Matas, J., Jonsson, K., Ramos Sanchez, M.U.: Combining Evidence in Personal Identity Verification Systems. Pattern Recognition Letters 18, 845–852 (1997)

10. Poh, N., Korczak, J.: Hybrid Biometric Person Authentication Using Face and Voice Features. In: Bigun, J., Smeraldi, F. (eds.) AVBPA 2001. LNCS, vol. 2091, pp. 348–353. Springer, Heidelberg (2001)

11. Snelick, R., Uludag, U., Mink, A., Indovina, M., Jain, A.K.: Large-Scale Evaluation of Multimodal Biometric Authentication Using State-of-the-Art Systems. IEEE Transactions on Pattern Analysis and Machine Intelligence 27(4), 450–455 (2005)

12. Cmo Council, http://www.fastcompany.com/3010237/bottom-line/texting-is-the-new-email-does-your-company-do-it-right

13. ComputerWeekly, http://www.computerweekly.com/news/2240205200/Apple-adopts-hands-off-approach-to-iPhone-fingerprint-scanner

14. MIT Technology Review, http://www.technologyreview.com/news/425805/new-google-smart-phone-recognizes-your-face/

15. Rudman, J.: The state of authorship attribution studies: Some problems and solutions. Computers and the Humanities 31, 351–365 (1998)

16. Halteren, V.H.: Linguistic Profiling for Author Recognition and Verification, In: 42nd Annual Meeting on Association for Computational Linguistics (ACL 2004). Association for Computational Linguistics, Morristown (2004)

17. Zheng, R., Li, J., Chen, H., Huang, Z.: A Framework for Authorship Identification of Online Messages: Writing-Style Features and Classification Techniques. Journal of the American Society for Information Science and Technology 53, 378–393 (2006)

18. Boukerche, A., Nitare, M.S.M.A.: Behavior-based intrusion detection in mobile phone systems. J. Parallel Distrib. Comput. 62(9), 1476–1490 (2002)

19. Damopoulos, D., Menesidou, S., Kambourakis, Papadaki, M., Clarke, N., Gritzalis, S.: Evaluation of Anomaly-Based IDS for Mobile Devices Using Machine Learning Classifiers. Security and Communication Networks 5(1), 3–14 (2012)

20. Buschkes, R., Kesdogan, D., Reichl, P.: How to increase security in mobile networks by anomaly detection. In: Proceedings of the 14th Annual Computer Security Applications Conference, pp. 3–12 (1998)

21. Hall, J., Barbeau, M., Kranakis, E.: Anomaly based intrusion detection using mobility profiles of public transportation users. In: Proceeding of IEEE International Conference on Wireless and Mobile Computing, Networking and Communications, vol. 2, pp. 17–24 (2005)

22. Biopassword.: the keystroke dynamics approach, http://www.biopassword.com/bp2/welcome.asp

23. Behaviosec, http://www.behaviosec.com/products/enterprise/

24. Clarke, N., Furnell, S.M.: Authenticating Mobile Phone Users Using Keystroke Analysis. International Journal of Information Security, 1–14 (2006) ISSN: 1615-5262

25. Indovina, M., Uludag, U., Snelick, R., Mink, A., Jain, A.: Multimodal biometric authentication methods: a COTS approach. In: Proc. MMUA, pp. 99–106 (2003)

26. Eagle, N., Pentland, A., Lazer, D.: Inferring Social Network Structure using Mobile Phone Data. Proceeding of National Academy of Sciences (PNAS) 106, 15274–1578 (2009)

27. Ashbourne, J.: Biometric, Advanced identity verification. The complete guide. Springer (2000)

28. Jain, A.K., Nandakumar, K., Ross, A.: Score normalization in multimodal biometric systems. Pattern Recognition 38(12), 2270–2285 (2005)

29. Clarke, N., Furnell, S.M. and Reynolds P.L.: Biometric Authenticating for Mobile Devices. In: 3rd Australian Information Warfare and Security Conference, Western Australia, (2002)

30. Lederm, T., Clarke, N.L.: Risk assessment for mobile devices. In: Furnell, S., Lambrinoudakis, C., Pernul, G. (eds.) TrustBus 2011. LNCS, vol. 6863, pp. 210–221. Springer, Heidelberg (2011)

Styx: Design and Evaluation of a New Privacy Risk Communication Method for Smartphones

Gökhan Bal[1], Kai Rannenberg[1], and Jason Hong[2]

[1] Goethe University Frankfurt, Germany
{goekhan.bal,kai.rannenberg}@m-chair.de
[2] Carnegie Mellon University, Pittsburgh, PA, USA
jhong@cs.cmu.edu

Abstract. Modern smartphone platforms are highly privacy-affecting but not effective in properly communicating their privacy impacts to its users. Particularly, *actual* data-access behavior of apps is not considered in current privacy risk communication approaches. We argue that factors such as frequency of access to sensitive information is significantly affecting the privacy-invasiveness of applications. We introduce Styx, a novel privacy risk communication system that provides the user with more meaningful privacy information based on the actual behavior of apps. In a proof-of-concept study we evaluate the effectiveness of Styx. Our results show that more meaningful privacy warnings can increase user trust into smartphone platforms and also reduce privacy concerns.

1 Introduction

Technological innovations in the area of consumer electronics developed by far faster than our ability to assess their implications on our social lives. Information privacy is one of the facets in consumer life that experiences the most substantial change. For the sake of innovation and utility, consumers have unconcernedly (or unknowingly) given away the control over their personal data. Most designers of privacy-affecting systems[1] don't define the protection of consumer privacy as a primary goal and thus, privacy-awareness or privacy-protection mechanisms usually are not a prominent feature in most technologies.

Modern smartphone platforms have unique properties that make them highly privacy-affecting, i.e. they are always on, they are connected to the Internet, they follow their users in space and time, they are open to third-party applications, and they provide those applications with access to a multiplicity of sensitive resources such as the GPS module, the user's contacts, call log, or browsing history. The dynamics and the quantity of sensitive information flows on smartphone platforms require sophisticated approaches for giving back the consumers the control over their data. According to the *Privacy Space Framework*, information privacy protection is a process that starts with *awareness* and

---

[1] Based on Lederer et al. (2005) [26], we define privacy-affecting systems as any interactive system whose use has personal privacy implications.

N. Cuppens-Boulahia et al. (Eds.): SEC 2014, IFIP AICT 428, pp. 113–126, 2014.

detection of privacy issues [5]. Consequently, solutions have also to improve these two mechanisms.

The use of personal data by third-party applications affects the users' privacy in varying extent. Factors influencing the extent are e.g. the type of data that is processed, the frequency of access, or the destination of sensitive information flows. Ideally, privacy-awareness solutions reflect those dependencies in their underlying mechanisms. In practice, the users are too often not even aware that sensitive resources have been accessed by applications. Privacy-related notices are in most cases not successful in informing the users appropriately about the actual privacy risks of the services. One major explanation for this is that in most cases the underlying model for privacy risks is limited to access-control information such as granting an application access to some resources. Other commonly known explanations are the extensive length of privacy policies, the frequent use of technical or legal terminology, or the inappropriate timing of privacy notices. We argue that privacy-awareness measures should move from *access-control level* to *privacy-impact level*. In other words, privacy-awareness systems should not (solely) inform users about single information flows. Instead, the mechanisms should reason about multiple information flows that happen over time and look at the actual privacy-impacting behavior of an app. The (user-facing) outcome of those mechanisms should be concrete privacy-impact information that relate to the individual behavior of apps. In this paper we propose *Styx*[2], which is such a privacy-awareness system for smartphone platforms. We use *privacy-impacting behavioral patterns (PIBP)* [2] as the conceptual basis for our system. PIBPs are a model for privacy impacts that bridge the gap between multiple information flows and their impact on user privacy.

The contributions of this paper are as follows: 1. we present the design principles and a proof-of-concept implementation of Styx, a novel privacy-awareness system for the Android smartphone platform, 2. we present results from an experimental evaluation of Styx to demonstrate its utility, focusing on human factors. We contribute to the knowledge base of information privacy technology design, especially regarding privacy risk communication methods.

The paper is structured as follows. Section 2 summarizes and integrates relevant concepts and theories from the knowledge base. Section 3 provides some key definitions and subsequently presents design principles for Styx that we have identified from information privacy literature. Section 4 then introduces and elaborates in more detail the conceptual basis for Styx, namely the privacy-impacting behavioral patterns. Following on that, Section 5 proposes an architectural design for Styx. The components of Styx that we have developed as proof-of-concept are introduced in Section 6. Details about the evaluation are presented in Section 7. We conclude this paper with a discussion on the results (Section 8).

---

[2] Inspired by the river "Styx" from Greek mythology, which formed a boundary between the world of the living and the Underworld. We use this as a metaphor for sensitive information flows between the user's "realm" and the hidden, "dark side" of the smartphone device.

2   Related Work

This section provides an overview of the relevant literature in smartphone privacy research, which will help to understand how our research on Styx was informed by the body of knowledge. Due to space restrictions, we do not describe single research results in detail.

The Nature of Privacy Risks of Smartphone Usage. On the very basic level, the privacy risks of smartphone app usage are about the leakage of sensitive information from the user's device [31]. With *TaintDroid*, Enck et al. [14] revealed that privacy-breach incidents are not rare, many apps are sending sensitive data to their servers without informing the user. On a more semantic level, privacy risks result due to the long-term usage of apps. Data mining-based approaches demonstrate the potentials of inferring user identity-related information based on data that is available on the devices or collected by apps over time. Kwapisz et al. show how collected accelerometer data can be used to uniquely identify the user [24]. Weiss et al. [33] show how the same source of information can even be used to identify user traits such as sex, height, and weight of the user. Similar results can be found in [8], [28], [11], [30], and [19].

Smartphone Users' Perception of Privacy Risks. Privacy indicators or warnings should both motivate users to respond, and help them understand the risk of the used services [4]. Besides privacy policies that exist for some apps, Android's permission request screen, which shows up each time the user wants to install an application, can be regarded as Android's main indicator for the potential impacts on user privacy. However, researchers have demonstrated that permission screens are not effective privacy indicators. Often users don't notice this screen or they have difficulties in understanding the risk signals [23]. Chia et al. showed that none of the existing risk signals in the smartphone app ecosystem are effective as indicators for the privacy risks [7].

Alternative Privacy Indicators. Kelley et al. [22] used the nutrition-label approach to represent privacy information taken from privacy policies of online services. Another approach to improve privacy information on the Android platform is to use attribution mechanisms which is a method to indicate which source (i.e. app) was responsible for a security or privacy-related action on the device, e.g. which app last changed the wallpaper of the device [32]. The approach taken by Lin et al. [27] to increase the usefulness of Android permissions is to add empirical information about how other users feel about the respective request, e.g. "95% of users were surprised this app sent their approximate location to mobile ads providers". Egelman et al. (2009) could show that the timing had a significant impact on the behavior of users in the context of online shopping [13]. Alternative designs for privacy indicators have an effect on the user's behavior, but yet so far there is no approach that considers the multiplicity of potential sensitive information flows and their very dynamic nature on smartphone platforms when modeling privacy risks.

Technologies for Enhanced Privacy Control. Many tools have been developed in recent years that aim to analyze or enhance the privacy level of smartphone platforms. One category of such tools are *information flow analyzers* that analyze smartphone applications regarding potential privacy breaches before they are installed on users' devices. Some of the more prominent examples are *Kirin* [15], *AppInspector* [18], *Stowaway* [16], *SCanDroid* [17], *PiOS* [12], *TaintDroid* [14], and *XManDroid* [6]. Except for Kirin, the mentioned approaches have a limited model for the actual privacy risk.

Enhanced Information Flow Control. Some privacy tools provide the users a more fine-grained or context-sensitive control over their data. Examples are *TISSA* [34], *Apex* [29], *CRePE* [9], and *ConUCON* [1]. Another form of enhanced information flow control for smartphone users is replacing real data with mocked data when apps want to access sensitive resources [21] and [3]. The concepts listed here are useful approaches for the prevention and response phases of information privacy control. Our focus is on the awareness and detection phases of the privacy space framework.

3   Design Principles and Guidelines

Existing literature on privacy theories and tools provide valuable guidelines for the design of privacy mechanisms. Our requirements analysis for Styx resulted in a set of principles and guidelines that we present in the following. Also, we introduce some key terms that will help the reader in integrating our contributions into the bigger picture of privacy research.

3.1   Working Definitions and Relevant Concepts

We see information privacy rather as a process as defined in the Privacy Space Framework [5]. The proposed phases of information privacy management are *awareness, detection, prevention, response,* and *recovery.* With Styx we target the phases awareness and detection. Another important concept that informed our research was the concept of *Exoinformation.* Generally speaking, exoinformation is *new* information that is gathered by putting together and analyzing *available* information [5]. The PIBP approach introduced in Section 4 can be regarded as a specific implementation of the exoinformation concept.

3.2   Design Principles

From the usable privacy literature we have identified a set of design guidelines that inform the design of Styx:

- avoid the use of privacy jargons (DP1),
- communicate the existence of a threat (DP2) [26],

- filter information and alert users only to potentially important or new concerns and threats (DP3),
- minimal distraction (DP4),
- do not obscure actual and potential information flow (DP5) [20],
- provide educational opportunities to users (DP6) [10],
- provide meaningful summaries of privacy information (DP7),
- consider exoinformation (DP8).

4 Privacy-Impacting Behavioral Patterns

As the conceptual basis for Styx we use privacy-impacting behavioral patterns [2]. The basic idea behind the PIBP concept draws on the concept of exoinformation. The most common approach for privacy notices is to inform users about single, potentially privacy-impacting, information flows. In this case, privacy risks are modeled as a single data leakage[3]. The assumption here is that consumers are able to map that specific information flow instance to the impact it will have on their privacy. The information-flow level approach does not consider long-term aspects such as *frequency of access* or *combinations* with information flows of other type. Location information for example is dynamic, thus it is a function of time. A one-time access to the resource will not exploit the full potentials of knowledge extraction. Rather, the more often an application accesses the user's current location, the more information can be extracted about the user. An app that accesses the user's location every 30 minutes could infer where the user lives, where he works or goes to school, which locations he visits in his leisure time, and so on. In this case, the specific PIBP would be "accessing geo-location every 30 minutes or more often". One could think of much more complex examples where for example different sensitive resources are combined.

5 Styx

In this section we present the conceptual architecture of Styx, a PIBP-implementing, privacy-awareness system for the Android platform. We will further present a proof-of-concept implementation of Styx and demonstrate how the requirements of Section 3 are met.

5.1 Styx Architecture

Figure 1 shows the proposed components for a PIBP-implementing system. These components are introduced in the following.

Styx Monitoring. This component is responsible for dynamically monitoring sensitive information flows between the device and applications. TaintDroid [14] could be used as the implementation of this component.

---

[3] Simple example: "Application *A* wants to access your location".

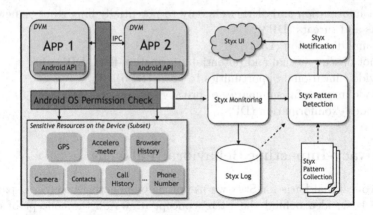

Fig. 1. Conceptual architecture of Styx

Styx Log. Information about information flows will be stored here. The monitoring component is responsible for creating new log entries.

Styx Pattern Collection. Since we model privacy impacts as behavioral patterns of apps, Styx must have access to a set of such privacy-impacting behavioral patterns in order to match application behavior with privacy impacts. Pre-defined patterns are stored in the pattern collection database.

Styx Pattern Detection. The actual matching between observed app behavior and PIBPs is performed by the Styx Pattern Detection engine. This component is triggered by the monitoring component after a new entry has been stored in the log. The pattern detection mechanisms then takes the Styx Log (including the new entry) and the pattern collection as input and tries to match patterns with application behavior.

Styx Notification. This component is responsible for notifying the user about matches that have been identified by the pattern detection. Ultimately, this is the user-facing component of the system and therefore its design is of key importance. It uses the notification mechanisms of the smartphone platform to show the Styx UI to the user. The UI will present information about privacy-impacting behavior of the respective app.

6   Proof-of-Concept

We have implemented a proof-of-concept of Styx for the purpose of evaluating its effectiveness. As stated in the beginning of this paper, Styx targets the awareness and detection phases of the information privacy process. Consequently, we focused our implementation on the user-facing part of the architecture, namely the notification component and its respective user interfaces. The Styx monitoring, logging, and pattern detection mechanisms are simulated in the proof-of-concept. The Styx UI is composed of six different screens that represent different types and levels of privacy information. The respective purposes of the screens are described in the following.

a) Styx Notification   b) Styx Inference Screen   c) Styx Basis Screen   d) Styx Dashboard

Fig. 2. Styx screenshots

1. **Styx Notification.** The first screen that the user sees is the notification and the respective entry in the notification menu (a. in Figure 2).
2. **Styx Inference Screen.** This is the landing page of Styx after the user clicks on a notification entry. The purpose is to visually communicate what identity-related inference the currently used app could make about the user (in the simple example it's the user's gender; b. in Figure 2).
3. **Styx Rating.** The purpose is to help users understand whether the applications behavior is unusual or rather something expected. Factors that influence this rating are the functionality of the app and also a comparison with apps of the same category (e.g., "Are similar apps also able to determine the user's gender?").
4. **Styx Basis Screen.** We want to make the underlying mechanisms of Styx transparent to the user by also informing him about the privacy-impacting behavior of the app (i.e., which resources did it access in what manner?). At the same time, this is an educational part of Styx (DP6). The users will be able to better understand the relation between concrete privacy impacts and access to sensitive information (c. in Figure 2). In the example, the app has accessed the list of installed applications and is able to see the high number of sports-related apps on the device.
5. **Styx Detailed Pattern Information.** In its approach to provide on-demand access to more detailed information, Styx shows the user more detailed information when he clicks on the "Learn more..." part of the inference screen.
6. **Styx Dashboard.** This screen is essential to communicate the overall privacy-invasiveness of an application. It summarizes what other identity-related information the current app has already inferred in the past (DP7). Each information item can be clicked on to open the detailed information screens. The goal was to make this screen very concise, intuitive, and visually attractive. The Styx Dashboard plays an important role in enabling the comparison of privacy-related properties of different apps (d. in Figure 2).

6.1   Meeting the Requirements

Styx is an implementation of the PIBP concept. As such, actual and potential information flows are considered when assessing the privacy impacts of app behavior (DP5). Furthermore, the PIBP concept can be regarded as an instantiation of the exoinformation concept, thus exoinformation are considered by design (DP8). The ultimate goal of Styx is communicating the existence of privacy threats. It does so by analyzing what potential identity-related inferences an app can make about the user, based on what is has accessed so far and then inform the user about these specific threats (DP2). Another advantage of the PIBP approach is that it does not notify the user on information-flow level. Rather, multiple information flows are observed, aggregated and analyzed (DP3). Only when a certain privacy-impacting behavior has been detected, the user gets notified, so the number of distractions from the user's primary task is reduced (DP4). In the Styx UI, we avoid technical terms (DP1), educational opportunities are provided by the Styx Basis Screen and the Styx Detailed Information Screen (DP6). A privacy summary of an app is provided by the Styx Dashboard (DP7).

7   User Study

We evaluated the Styx proof-of-concept in a user study in spring of 2013. We set up an in-lab experiment at Carnegie Mellon University. We recruited participants through the *CBDR Participant Portal*[4] of the university. We invited people to "A User Study about Smartphone apps". Participants were compensated with a $10 gift card for their time.

7.1   Participants

In total, 77 participants registered for the user study. 50 of those showed up during the two-week experiment phase. 18 of the participants were female (36%), 32 were male (64%). M_{age}=25.56 (SD=7.18). 27 of the participants had permanent residence in the U.S. (54%), 23 had permanent residence in another country (46%). 2% of the participants owned a smartphone for less than 1 month, 6% for 1-3 months, 20% for 3-12 months, 14% for 1-2 years, 26% for 2-3 years, 8% for 3-4 years, and 24% for more than 4 years. The participants had installed M=25.54 apps (SD=25.32) on their devices and used M=9.12 apps regularly (at least once a week; SD=7.13).

7.2   Experimental Design

The experiments have been conducted in the Human-Computer Interaction Institute at Carnegie Mellon University. We invited one participant at a time to do

---

[4] The CBDR Participant portal is an online system that help researchers in organizing their user studies.

the experiment, which took approximately one hour per participant. We used a *between-subjects* design for the experiment, since we wanted to test Styx against an alternative approach that is based on current risk communication schemes. Before starting the experiment, participants were randomly assigned to one of the two conditions. We handed the participants a smartphone[5] on which the respective tool was running in the background. After introducing them to the key UI concepts of the device, we handed them an instruction sheet containing a step-by-step description of what they should do with the device. The tasks were mainly about starting specific apps[6] and using some of their core features. In pre-defined points in time, the device showed notifications in the notification bar and played a sound while showing up. Participants in the *experimental condition* have been shown the Styx privacy user interfaces, participants in the *control condition* have been faced with an alternative run-time privacy UI that will provide the user with a chronologically ordered information flow history. By introducing a run-time component to the control condition, we made the comparison fair[7]. The participants were free to examine the notifications. Only in the case of the weather and the running app we explicitly instructed them to examine the notification and the respective user interfaces.

7.3 Collected Data

During the experiments, we collected a variety of data that would allow us to evaluate the effectiveness of Styx according to our evaluation targets.

Questionnaire. The main goal of the user study was evaluating the new privacy risk communication method regarding *comprehension* of the communicated privacy information. However, it is also important to look at the impact of the new approach on user trust and privacy concern. We believe that effective transparency mechanisms can increase *trust* into the smartphone platform and reduce privacy *concern*. Therefore, we added these two variables as dependent variables to the questionnaire. We proposed Styx as an innovative approach to communicate privacy risks of smartphone apps. To assess novelty, we used the respective scale from the *User Experience Questionnaire (UEQ)* (Laugwitz et al. [25]). Participants had to complete the questionnaire after the experiment on a computer in the lab. All items were rated on a 6-point Likert scale ranging from "strongly disagree" to "strongly agree". Example items: "The privacy information was self-explanatory" (comprehension), "I trust this smartphone to protect the user's data against harmful apps" (trust), "I'm concerned that the apps have accessed personal data without informing me" (concern), "The presented privacy user interfaces were innovative" (novelty).

---

[5] Samsung Galaxy S3 LTE.

[6] We used five types of apps during the experiment: flashlight, weather, dice, running tracker, and a kids memory game.

[7] Otherwise, the pure existence of privacy information in the experimental group would lead to biased data.

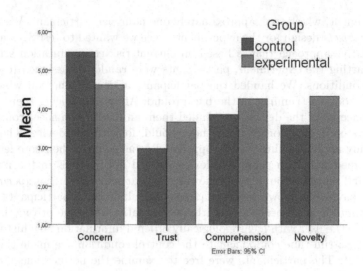

Fig. 3. Mean values of the questionnaire scales

Qualitative Data. As part of the evaluation, we also asked the participants in the questionnaire what they particularly liked and did not like about the new privacy user interface. Participants could enter up to five aspects per question.

7.4 Data Analysis

Questionnaire. Figure 3 shows the mean scores for the concern, trust, comprehension, and novelty scales for the two conditions. The experimental group scores better in all four scales, while the differences in the concern (M_{exp}=4.62, M_{ctrl}=5.46) and novelty (M_{exp}=4.33, M_{ctrl}=3.58) scales are statistically significant (p<.05). There are strong tendencies in the mean values of the trust (M_{exp}=3.66, M_{ctrl}=2.97) and comprehension (M_{exp}=4.26, M_{ctrl}=3.86) scales.

Qualitative Data. When looking at the responses to the question "what did you *not* like about the privacy user interface?", four responses were related to the comprehensibility of the information (example answer: "It just took some time to figure out what Styx was about"). Eight responses on the other hand were about how annoying the notifications were during the experiment (example answer: "I disliked the constant notification")[8]. Three responses were about the usability of the UI (example answer: "I also did not like the graphical interface"). Nine responses were about some functionality that participants would additionally expect (example answers: "I would have loved if the app could suggest me another app with same functionality but lesser data access", "It should pop up

---

[8] The issue with the notifications is due to the experimental design where multiple notifications were simulated in a short time frame. In a real setting, these notifications would occur less frequently.

before the app starts sending data"). Looking at the responses to the question "what *did* you like about the privacy user interface?", there were noticeably more responses that refer to the comprehensibility and usability of the UI. In total, 13 responses can be classified as such (example answers: "The notifications were self-explanatory", "The notifications covered all the information regarding the app using personal info in brief sentences"). Nine responses can be classified as relating to the usefulness or the perceived purpose of the privacy user interfaces (example answers: "I liked that I could see a list of these icons and use that list to compare one app to another", "I liked the icons categorizing the types of data that Styx detected"). In sum, the analysis of the qualitative data revealed some existing issues with Styx (e.g. people expect additional information or instructions on what to do next), some of them being caused by the experimental design, however, regarding the comprehension and usefulness of the privacy user interfaces, Styx was quite successful in achieving its goals.

8 Discussion and Conclusion

Styx is our proposed approach to provide smartphone users with more intuitive and semantic privacy information about their apps. Our aim was to increase the comprehensibility of privacy risks, and at the same time increase trust and reduce concern towards the smartphone. Our data shows that Styx scores very well regarding these aspects. Compared to traditional privacy risk-communication approaches, the Styx privacy user interfaces were more comprehensible and participants also appreciated it being an innovative approach for privacy warnings. The qualitative data further revealed that Styx is easy to understand and use. At the same time, the data clearly shows that such an privacy-awareness system should only be deployed in combination with privacy control mechanisms. This is in-line with the Privacy Space Framework, where the phases prevention, response, and recovery immediately follow the phases of awareness and detection. Our results further show that more effective transparency mechanisms can increase user trust towards the smartphone and significantly reduce privacy concerns when interacting with the device. We believe that smartphone vendors could use such trust mechanisms as competitive advantage in future when even more operating systems and apps will be available in the smartphone ecosystem. We also want to note that run-time privacy warnings should not be the ultimate way to communicate privacy information to the user. Privacy risk communication should happen as early as possible (e.g. in the app discovery phase). However, the basic principle behind the PIBP approach is monitoring application behavior during run-time and thus, run-time notifications are a suitable method to detect and communicate privacy-impacting application behavior. We further propose that gathered privacy information about apps should be fed back into the privacy risk communication in the app discovery phase, e.g. they could be integrated into the app markets. This will further help users in making safer decisions at the right time. With Styx we contribute to the knowledge base of human factors in privacy by developing and testing a new method to model and communicate the privacy-related impacts of smartphone usage. We also contribute to the design knowledge for more intuitive privacy-awareness mechanisms.

Acknowledgments. This research was partially funded by the *Vereinigung von Freunden und Förderern der Johann Wolfgang Goethe-Universität* and the Faculty of Economics and Business Administration at Goethe University Frankfurt. We further thank Tahmine Tozman for her advice concerning the experimental design and Ralf Strobel for his support in implementing the prototype.

References

1. Bai, G., Gu, L., Feng, T., Guo, Y., Chen, X.: Context-Aware Usage Control for Android. In: Jajodia, S., Zhou, J. (eds.) SecureComm 2010. LNICST, vol. 50, pp. 326–343. Springer, Heidelberg (2010)
2. Bal, G.: Revealing Privacy-Impacting Behavior Patterns of Smartphone Applications (Short Paper). In: MoST 2012 - Proceedings of the Mobile Security Technologies Workshop 2012, San Francisco, USA (2012),
   http://mostconf.org/2012/papers/15.pdf
3. Beresford, A.R., Rice, A., Sohan, N., Skehin, N., Sohan, R.: MockDroid: trading privacy for application functionality on smartphones. In: Proceedings of HotMobile 2011, ACM (2011)
4. Bravo-Lillo, C., Cranor, L.F., Downs, J., Komanduri, S., Sleeper, M.: Improving Computer Security Dialogs. In: Campos, P., Graham, N., Jorge, J., Nunes, N., Palanque, P., Winckler, M. (eds.) INTERACT 2011, Part IV. LNCS, vol. 6949, pp. 18–35. Springer, Heidelberg (2011), http://www.springerlink.com/content/q551210n08h16970/
5. Brunk, B.: A User-Centric Privacy Space Framework. In: Cranor, L.F., Garfinkel, S.L. (eds.) Security and Usability - Designing Secure Systems that People Can Use, ch. 21, pp. 401–420. O'Reilly (2005)
6. Bugiel, S., Davi, L., Dmitrienko, A., Fischer, T., Sadeghi, A.R.S.: XManDroid: A New Android Evolution to Mitigate Privilege Escalation Attacks. Tech. rep. (2011)
7. Chia, P.H., Yamamoto, Y., Asokan, N.: Is this App Safe? A Large Scale Study on Application Permissions and Risk Signals. In: Proceedings of WWW 2012 (November 2012)
8. Chittaranjan, G., Blom, J., Gatica-Perez, D.: Mining large-scale smartphone data for personality studies. Personal and Ubiquitous Computing (December 2011), http://www.springerlink.com/index/10.1007/s00779-011-0490-1
9. Conti, M., Nguyen, V.T.N., Crispo, B.: CRePE: Context-related Policy Enforcement for Android. In: Burmester, M., Tsudik, G., Magliveras, S., Ilić, I. (eds.) ISC 2010. LNCS, vol. 6531, pp. 331–345. Springer, Heidelberg (2011)
10. Cranor, L.F., Garfinkel, S.L.: Security and Usability - Designing Secure Systems that People Can Use. O'Reilly (2005)
11. Eagle, N., Pentland, A.S., Lazer, D.: Inferring Social Network Structure using Mobile Phone Data. Tech. Rep. usually 1 (2009)
12. Egele, M., Kruegel, C., Kirda, E.: PiOS: Detecting Privacy Leaks in iOS Applications. In: NDSS 2011 Network and Distributed System Security Symposium Proceedings (2011)

13. Egelman, S., Tsai, J., Cranor, L.F., Acquisti, A.: Timing is everything?: the effects of timing and placement of online privacy indicators. In: Proceedings of the 27th International Conference on Human Factors in Computing Systems, CHI 2009, p. 319. ACM Press, New York (2009),
http://dl.acm.org/citation.cfm?id=1518701.1518752

14. Enck, W., Gilbert, P., Chun, B.G., Cox, L.P., Jung, J., McDaniel, P., Sheth, A.N.: TaintDroid: An Information-Flow Tracking System for Realtime Privacy Monitoring on Smartphones. In: Proc. of USENIX Symposium on Operating Systems Design and Implementation, OSDI (2010)

15. Enck, W., Ongtang, M., McDaniel, P.: On Lightweight Mobile Phone Application Certification. In: Proceedings of the 16th ACM Conference on Computer and Communications Security, CCS 2009, p. 235. ACM Press, New York (2009)

16. Felt, A.P., Chin, E., Hanna, S., Song, D., Wagner, D.: Android permissions demystified. In: Proceedings of the 18th ACM Conference on Computer and Communications Security, CCS 2011, p. 627. ACM Press, New York (2011)

17. Fuchs, A.P., Chaudhuri, A.: SCanDroid: Automated Security Certification of Android Applications. Tech. rep., University of Maryland (2009),
http://citeseerx.ist.psu.edu/viewdoc/summary?doi=10.1.1.148.2511

18. Gilbert, P., Chun, B.G., Cox, L.P., Jung, J.: Vision: automated security validation of mobile apps at app markets. In: Proceedings of the Second International Workshop on Mobile Cloud Computing and Services, MCS 2011, p. 21. ACM Press, New York (2011)

19. González, M.C., Hidalgo, C.A., Barabási, A.L.: Understanding individual human mobility patterns. Nature 453(7196), 779–782 (2008),
http://www.ncbi.nlm.nih.gov/pubmed/18528393

20. Hong, J.I.: An Architecture for Privacy-Sensitive Ubiquitous Computing. Ph.D. thesis, UNIVERSITY OF CALIFORNIA (2005)

21. Hornyack, P., Han, S., Jung, J., Schechter, S., Wetherall, D.: These aren't the droids you're looking for: retrofitting android to protect data from imperious applications. In: CCS 2011 - Proceedings of the 18th ACM Conference on Computer and Communications Security, p. 639. ACM, New York (2011)

22. Kelley, P.G., Bresee, J., Cranor, L.F., Reeder, R.W.: A "nutrition label" for privacy. In: Proceedings of the 5th Symposium on Usable Privacy and Security, SOUPS 2009, p. 1. ACM Press, New York (2009),
http://dl.acm.org/citation.cfm?id=1572532.1572538

23. Kelley, P.G., Consolvo, S., Cranor, L.F., Jung, J., Sadeh, N., Wetherall, D.: A Conundrum of Permissions: Installing Applications on an Android Smartphone. In: Proceedings of USEC 2012, pp. 1–12 (2012)

24. Kwapisz, J.R., Weiss, G.M., Moore, S.A.: Cell phone-based biometric identification. In: 2010 Fourth IEEE International Conference on Biometrics: Theory, Applications and Systems (BTAS), pp. 1–7. IEEE (September 2010),
http://ieeexplore.ieee.org/articleDetails.jsp?arnumber=5634532

25. Laugwitz, B., Held, T., Schrepp, M.: Construction and Evaluation of a User Experience Questionnaire. Tech. rep. (2008)

26. Lederer, S., Dey, A.K., Mankoff, J.: A Conceptual Model and a Metaphor of Everyday Privacy in Ubiquitous Computing Environments. In: Ubiquitous Computing Computer S (2002), http://www.cs.cmu.edu/~io/publications/old-pubs/privacy-techreport02.pdf

27. Lin, J., Amini, S., Hong, J., Sadeh, N., Lindqvist, J., Zhang, J.: Expectation and Purpose: Understanding Users Mental Models of Mobile App Privacy through Crowdsourcing. In: Proceedings of the 14th ACM International Conference on Ubiquitous Computing - Ubicomp 2012 (2012)

28. Min, J.K., Wiese, J., Hong, J.I., Zimmerman, J.: Mining Smartphone Data to Classify Life-Facets of Social Relationships. In: Conference on Computer Supported Cooperative Work and Social Computing 2013 (2013)

29. Nauman, M., Khan, S., Zhang, X.: Apex: Extending Android Permission Model and Enforcement with User-defined Runtime Constraints. In: Proceedings of the 5th ACM Symposium on Information, Computer and Communications Security, ASIACCS 2010, pp. 328–332. ACM Press (2010)

30. Phithakkitnukoon, S., Horanont, T., Di Lorenzo, G., Shibasaki, R., Ratti, C.: Activity-Aware Map: Identifying Human Daily Activity Pattern Using Mobile Phone Data. In: Salah, A.A., Gevers, T., Sebe, N., Vinciarelli, A. (eds.) HBU 2010. LNCS, vol. 6219, pp. 14–25. Springer, Heidelberg (2010), http://www.springerlink.com/index/10.1007/978-3-642-14715-9

31. Thampi, A.: Path uploads your entire iPhone address book to its servers, http://mclov.in/2012/02/08/path-uploads-your-entire-address-book-to-their-servers.html

32. Thompson, C., Johnson, M., Egelman, S., Wagner, D., King, J.: When it's better to ask forgiveness than get permission. In: Proceedings of the Ninth Symposium on Usable Privacy and Security, SOUPS 2013, p. 1 (2013), http://dl.acm.org/citation.cfm?doid=2501604.2501605

33. Weiss, G.M., Lockhart, J.W.: Identifying user traits by mining smart phone accelerometer data. In: Proceedings of the Fifth International Workshop on Knowledge Discovery from Sensor Data - SensorKDD 2011, pp. 61–69. ACM Press, New York (2011), http://portal.acm.org/citation.cfm?doid=2003653.2003660

34. Zhou, Y., Zhang, X., Jiang, X., Freeh, V.W.: Taming information-stealing smartphone applications (on android). In: McCune, J.M., Balacheff, B., Perrig, A., Sadeghi, A.-R., Sasse, A., Beres, Y. (eds.) Trust 2011. LNCS, vol. 6740, pp. 93–107. Springer, Heidelberg (2011)

A Trusted UI for the Mobile Web

Bastian Braun[1], Johannes Koestler[1], Joachim Posegga[1], and Martin Johns[2]

[1] Institute of IT Security and Security Law (ISL), University of Passau, Germany
[2] SAP Research, Karlsruhe, Germany
{bb,jp}@sec.uni-passau.de, martin.johns@sap.com,
koestler@fim.uni-passau.de

Abstract. Modern mobile devices come with first class web browsers that rival their desktop counterparts in power and popularity. However, recent publications point out that mobile browsers are particularly susceptible to attacks on web authentication, such as phishing or clickjacking. We analyze those attacks and find that existing countermeasures from desktop computers can not be easily transfered to the mobile world. The attacks' root cause is a missing trusted UI for security critical requests. Based on this result, we provide our approach, the MobileAuthenticator, that establishes a trusted path to the web application and reliably prohibits the described attacks. With this approach, the user only needs one tool to protect any number of mobile web application accounts. Based on the implementation as an app for iOS and Android respectively, we evaluate the approach and show that the underlying interaction scheme easily integrates into legacy web applications.

1 Introduction

Since the introduction of the original iPhone in 2008, mobile devices are first class citizens in the world of computing. Due to the impressive advances in energy consumption, mobile processor power, and display quality, the majority of the common computing tasks can nowadays be done as easily on a mobile device as on a "real" computer on the desktop.

However, while the computational power of the mobile devices is almost comparable to their desktop counterparts, other key differences, in areas such as screen estate, UI paradigms, or operating system induced limitations, remain for the foreseeable future. These differences have a significant impact on the device's security characteristics: Reduced screen estate results in significant less space for visual security indicators that could help combating phishing attacks [1, 2]. Changed user interaction paradigms allow for different clickjacking variants [3]. Virtual keyboards on mobile devices lead to choosing insecure passwords, due to necessary, uncomfortable context switches between letters, numbers, and special characters [2]. And finally, the current restrictions in mobile operating systems and the lack of an extension model for iOS' mobile browser render most of the currently proposed attack mitigation tools impossible on mobile devices.

As we will explore in Section 2, these limitations especially amplify security threats against mobile web authentication. For this reason, we propose a novel

N. Cuppens-Boulahia et al. (Eds.): SEC 2014, IFIP AICT 428, pp. 127–141, 2014.
© IFIP International Federation for Information Processing 2014

authorization delegation scheme using a native application, the MobileAuthenticator, that functions as a companion application to the mobile web browser. In this paper, we make the following contributions:

- We analyze how common web authentication attacks, such as phishing or clickjacking, manifest themselves in mobile scenarios and identify a common root cause – the lack of a trusted UI of the browser.
- We propose a novel authorization delegation scheme for mobile web applications that leverages a native companion application. It serves as a trust anchor for the mobile web application's client side through providing the missing trusted UI capabilities.
- We report on a practical implementation of our system as an app for the two currently dominating mobile operating systems, iOS and Android. In this context, we show how the concept can be realized through leveraging the platform-specific facilities for inter-app cooperation.

In the remainder of this paper, we first cover relevant attack classes that target web authentication mechanisms and discuss their specific characteristics in mobile web scenarios (Sec. 2). Then, we present our solution in Sec. 3. In Sec. 4, we document our practical implementations for iOS, Android, and Wordpress. The security and usability properties of our scheme are evaluated in Sec. 5. After revisiting related work in Sec. 6, we conclude the paper in Sec. 7.

2   Security Threats

In the last decade, numerous security problems in the field of web applications have been discovered and documented, among them phishing, cross-site scripting (XSS), cross-site request forgery (CSRF), session fixation, or clickjacking. In this section, we discuss the listed security threats in respect to how they apply to mobile web applications. Furthermore, we explore if previously proposed solutions can be adopted in a mobile environment.

2.1   Threat Classes

In general, mobile web applications are susceptible to the same class of threats as their desktop counterparts. However, it has been shown that several attack types, such as phishing or clickjacking, are harder to solve in the mobile scenario, due to their direct interplay with the available screen estate and web browser chrome [2, 4, 1]. In this section, we list applicable security issues and briefly discuss special aspects of the mobile case.

Phishing. The term *phishing* subsumes all attacks that aim to obtain the user's password via tricking the user to interact with a web resource that claims to be a legitimate part of the targeted web application but in fact is under the control of the attacker. It has been shown [5, 2, 1] that mobile web applications expose a higher level of susceptibility to such attacks, mainly due to the significantly reduced availability of optical indicators, such as browser chrome or SSL indicators.

Clickjacking. A *clickjacking* attacker deludes the user concerning the context and target of her actions to make her click in the attacker's interest. For the mobile case, Rydstedt et al. [4] coin the term *tapjacking* for this attack vector as users do not click but tap on their mobile devices. One of their techniques is zooming elements of the target web page. They found that the hosting (i.e., attacking) page can set a zoom factor overriding the iframe's own scaling. This way, an attacker can include a transparent "Like" or "Tweet" button fitting the entire width of the screen.

CSRF. A *CSRF* attacker inserts a crafted link into some website that makes the browser send a request to the target web application, seemingly on behalf of the user. The mobile case is similar to the desktop scenario with a slight exception: Client-side protection approaches like CsFire [6] do not work because mobile browsers have no or not sufficient extension support.

XSS. The *XSS* attacker is able to inject malicious script code into benign web pages. The code runs in the context of the benign domain and can impersonate the user. There is actually no difference between XSS attacks on mobile browsers and desktop browsers.

Session Fixation. During a *session fixation* attack, the attacker sets a session identifier before the user logs in. The attack is successful if the SID is not changed during the login. The attacker's window of opportunity lasts until the user logs out. The mobile case is very similar to the desktop case. However, sessions in some mobile web applications expire later [4], or do not expire at all but only delete the client-side session cookie upon logout [7]. This extends the attacker's control over the user's account.

2.2   On the Infeasibility of Existing Mitigation Approaches in Mobile Web Scenarios

In this section, we discuss several potential solutions to the outlined security problems and show their insufficiency in the realm of mobile web applications.

Client-side SSL Authentication. The current generation of – at least Android – smart phones is missing proper tools support for certificate management. Furthermore, the usage of this authentication method only solves a subset of the identified security implications, i.e., all issues that exist in connection with the potential stealing of passwords (i.e., mainly phishing). However, security problems that concern attacker-initiated state changes (e.g. caused by XSS, CSRF, or clickjacking) remain unprotected.

Browser Extensions or Plugins. A potential approach to overcome shortcomings of web browser-based applications is to include the security mechanism directly into the browser using a browser extension or plugins, such as Silverlight or Flash. However, the web browsers in current smart phones do not support plugins[1], and the only browser offering support for extensions is Firefox Mobile for Android with only a limited number of APIs[2].

---

[1] The Android platform offered limited support for Flash on a subset of existing devices. Adobe discontinued support by Aug 15, 2012. See `http://adobe.ly/1a1EpPH`

[2] See `http://mzl.la/1fwQNoX` and `http://bit.ly/1k7NQOE` for details.

Dedicated Modified Browsers. It is possible to deploy dedicated web browsers to mobile devices, which incorporate enhanced security mechanisms. However, they can not be used within applications that offer an integrated web-view, nor can they be set to serve as the default browser on iOS platforms, thus, excluding roughly half of all users. Finally, developing and maintaining a special browser variant is of high effort and cost, which is also a major roadblock for this potential approach.

Local Network-Layer Helpers. Finally, there are several approaches that rely on local network-layer utilities, such as HTTP proxies. Such tools cannot be deployed to the current generation of mobile devices.

2.3   Root Cause Analysis

Generally speaking, a web application is a reactive system. The web server receives incoming HTTP requests and reacts according to the implemented business logic of the application. A subset of the incoming requests lead to changes in the server-side state while others only retrieve data stored on the server. If received as part of an authenticated session, the first case may represent security sensitive actions on the application data. The handling of such requests requires special attention. Within this paper, we will repeatedly utilize the term *authorized action*.

Definition 1. *Authorized Action An authorized action is a security sensitive event on the server that is triggered by an incoming authenticated request, meaning that the user authorized the web application to perform the requested action on her behalf.*

Which events have to be considered security sensitive highly depends on the internal logic of the application. Hence, the applicable set of authorized actions has to be determined on a per-application basis. Frequently encountered examples include the login into the application, changing the user's data record, and ordering and purchasing of services or goods. For all such actions, the underlying assumption is that the owner of the credential (password or authenticated SID) is the originator of the triggering event and that the details of the action have not been tampered with by unauthorized third parties. All discussed security issues have in common, that the application's back-end component (i.e., the web server) cannot distinguish authorized actions, which have been conducted intentionally by the user, from authorized actions, that have either been conducted directly by the attacker (e.g., through credentials that have been stolen via phishing or XSS) or have been initiated by the attacker via tricking the user (through clickjacking or CSRF). What web applications are missing is a *trusted path* between the user and the back-end system. The back-end system needs reliable evidence, that the initiated security sensitive actions have indeed been deliberately conducted by the user:

Definition 2. *Trusted Path An application provides a trusted path, if it can be verified on the server-side that all incoming authorized actions are caused with the user's explicit consent and that their integrity is ensured.*

3   Mobile Authenticator

The general idea of our approach is to establish a
trusted path between the user and the web application in order to protect the user against the attacks given in Sec. 2.1. We implement the approach
as an app but we envisage it as an integral feature of mobile operating systems. The mobile application enables the user to communicate securely
with the web application's server side using authorized actions that (1) have been explicitly initiated
by the user, (2) thus are fully intended by the user,
instead of being created without her consent (i.e.,
through clickjacking or XSS), and (3) have not been
tampered with. This way, the security functionality is strongly separated from the web application's

Fig. 1. Solution Overview

browser-based front-end, and hence, the web-specific weaknesses and limitations
do not apply anymore. The actual application logic can still be implemented as
a cross-platform web application which can be accessed on any web-enabled mobile device. The only part that needs to be implemented as a native application
for each mobile platform is the MobileAuthenticator. The MobileAuthenticator
itself provides generic security functionality. As a consequence, it can serve as a
trusted interface for more than one mobile web application.

3.1   Providing a Trusted Path through an App

We propose to introduce the MobileAuthenticator as a dedicated system app
that serves as a trust anchor for the user in the communication with the web
application. It establishes a trusted path between the UI and the application's
back-end. However, as extending modern mobile operating systems is out of our
scope, we describe the approach as an app that can be installed by the user.

Concept. The MobileAuthenticator is a dedicated application that encapsu-
lates the user's credentials and authorization state and that maintains a trust
relationship with the web server. Authorized actions are routed through the
MobileAuthenticator on behalf of the web application. The mobile web browser
never receives, processes, or sends credentials that can be utilized for conducting
authorized actions. This way, the MobileAuthenticator serves both as a trusted
UI for the mobile web interface as well as a second authentication factor, effectively elevating all supporting web applications to using an implicit two-factor
authentication scheme.

Interaction Pattern. For most purposes, the interaction between the web
browser and the mobile web application remains unchanged. Only in cases,
when the user initiates an authorized action, the control flow is routed via the
MobileAuthenticator, implementing a challenge/response scheme to capture the
user's intend.

1. Using a dedicated interaction bridge between the web browser and the MobileAuthenticator, the authorized action, which is supposed to be triggered,
   as well as all needed parameters including the server's challenge are passed
   over to the app.
2. The user explicitly acknowledges the authorized action in the trusted UI of
   the MobileAuthenticator. This causes the MobileAuthenticator to compute
   the response to the server's challenge.
3. The MobileAuthenticator passes the control back to the browser including
   a dedicated credential which allows the triggered authorized action to be
   conducted.
4. This credential is passed from the web front-end to the server.

Please note: This process is only executed when authorized actions are conducted. For the vast majority of a user's web interaction, the web application
remains unchanged (see Sec. 5.3). This also entails, that general authentication
tracking is done the regular way, i.e., using HTTP cookies, and that application
handling does not change significantly from a user's perspective.

3.2 Components

The overall architecture consists of three main components: The actual MobileAuthenticator that runs on the mobile device and provides the trusted UI,
a server-side module that evaluates incoming requests and checks the integrity
of the authentication token, and a JavaScript library that is delivered to the
browser and takes care of delegation between all participants.

MobileAuthenticator. The client-side component, the MobileAuthenticator,
maintains a repository of preconfigured authorized actions (see Sec. 3.3) including a human understandable description of each action's impact. Upon receiving
a security critical request from the browser, it looks up the respective action's
details in its repository, displays the description to the user, and asks for consent.
The MobileAuthenticator signs the request using a shared secret (see Sec. 3.3)
with the web application, and passes it back to the browser, if the user agreed.

Server-Side Module. On the web application's server side a counterpart is
needed that maintains a trust relationship with the user's MobileAuthenticator instance and implements the challenge/response process to accept incoming
authorized actions.

AuthenticationBroker. The AuthenticationBroker is a small JavaScript library that provides the necessary interface to the application's web front-end
to delegate authorized actions to the MobileAuthenticator for obtaining user
consent. Upon receiving the MobileAuthenticator's response, the acknowledged
request is routed to the web application for processing. It is evident that the
AuthenticationBroker itself is not security critical. This is an important fact because otherwise malicious injected script code might be able to manipulate or
disable the AuthenticationBroker and, thus, run an attack. The worst impact of
an attack against the AuthenticationBroker, however, is a denial-of-service that
prevents authenticated requests from being routed towards the MobileAuthenticator.

3.3   Initial Enrollment on the Mobile Device

Each instance of the MobileAuthenticator that the user wants to use has to be enrolled individually. In this process, the web application's server-side and the application instance initiate a device specific trust context, represented through a shared secret. This enrollment process works as follows:

After account setup, the web application provides the user with a unique URL pointing back to the application, which carries parameters that identify the enrollment process. The user copies this URL to the MobileAuthenticator. The MobileAuthenticator displays the application's domain to ask the user for confirmation. The user confirms by entering her password which is then used by the MobileAuthenticator for authentication. If the initial authentication step terminated successfully, the MobileAuthenticator and the web application compute a shared secret using the Diffie-Hellman key exchange. This secret is not only specific for the user but also for this particular MobileAuthenticator instance. The MobileAuthenticator then discards the user password as it is no longer needed. All further app-to-server interaction uses the shared secret for authentication. As long as this secret is valid, the user will not be required to enter her password again. Finally, the web application supplies a repository of configured authorized actions, including parameters and actionID, and a human understandable description of each request's impact. The MobileAuthenticator is able to maintain several of such (shared key,repository) records and can thus protect all user accounts for compatible web applications on the device.

3.4   User Login

After the MobileAuthenticator and the web application are synchronized, the overall login procedure adheres to the following protocol: The user first accesses the web application's login page in her mobile browser. As the user is not authenticated yet, the server can not utilize user-specific credentials at this step. Instead, it issues a challenge consisting of its AppID, the login's ActionID and a timestamp (see Sec. 3.7). The challenge is signed using the web application's private key. The respective public key is stored in the MobileAuthenticator during enrollment (see Sec. 3.3). When tapping the login button, the control is delegated by the AuthenticationBroker (see Sec. 3.2) to the MobileAuthenticator. In this step, the server challenge is pushed to the MobileAuthenticator that takes over and asks the user whether she wants to login to this web application. A phishing attack would fail at this point, as the password is never entered to the mobile device for login. If the signature is valid, the MobileAuthenticator compiles the response from the server's challenge, the username, and the device ID and signs it using HMAC with the shared secret, and control is transferred back to the browser. Finally, the AuthenticationBroker sends the signed login request to the web application.

Upon receiving this request, the web server extracts the username and device ID and verifies that the request was indeed signed using the shared secret and, thus, finishes the user's login process. Username and device ID are required to pick the correct shared secret for signing and verification.

3.5   Conducting Authorized Actions

The process for conducting further authorized actions is similar to the login process (see Sec. 3.4). For the login, the MobileAuthenticator witnesses the user's consent and proves the request's integrity and its own authentication by signing the request using the shared secret. The same features are necessary for authorized actions: First, in the browser, the user taps a link or a button requesting an authorized action. The respective request is then relayed to the MobileAuthenticator that obtains the user's consent, signs, and returns the request to the browser. The AuthenticationBroker forwards the request to the web application that checks the signature and performs the requested authorized action.

3.6   Unknown Authorized Actions

During enrollment, the server pushes a list of allowed authorized actions to the MobileAuthenticator. If the web application has been updated since the enrollment of the MobileAuthenticator instance, it can happen that the MobileAuthenticator receives a request for an unknown authorized action. In this case, the MobileAuthenticator updates its local repository by a new list from the web application. This update process can also be triggered in a regular manner or based on push messages. After receiving the updated list from the web server, the MobileAuthenticator verifies that the requested authorized action is indeed contained in the list. If this is not the case, the app rejects the action request.

3.7   Challenge and Response Formats

In this section, we briefly specify the challenge/response formats.

Server Challenge. For a given authorized action challenge, the server compiles a tuple consisting of: $CTuple = \{AppID, UserID, ActionID, timestamp\}$. The server HMAC-signs this tuple with the user-specific shared secret to allow the MobileAuthenticator to verify the challenge's authenticity. The values in this tuple have the following meanings:

- $AppID$ & $UserID$: Identifiers of the web application and the user account, to allow the MobileAuthenticator to choose the correct authentication context.
- $ActionID$: Unambiguous identifier of the requested authorized action.
- $timestamp$: To mitigate potential replay attacks, each challenge can be assigned a dedicated lifespan.

The resulting challenge consists of the tuple and the corresponding HMAC signature: $SChallenge = HMAC(CTuple, shared\ secret)$. On the server-side, the challenge is bound to the user's session and, thus, to her session identifier.

Client Response. After interacting with the user to capture her explicit consent, the MobileAuthenticator creates the response by assembling the response tuple: $RTuple = \{SChallenge, (Parameter_1), ..., (Parameter_i)\}$. Again, this tuple is HMAC-signed using the shared secret: $CResponse = HMAC(RTuple, shared\ secret)$. The existence and number of the *parameters* depends on the authorized action. For instance, the login procedure requires the username and device ID (see Sec. 3.4), while the transfer of money in a banking application will most likely include the amount and the receiving account number in the signed response value.

4 Implementation

To practically evaluate the feasibility of our concept, we implemented the solution for the two leading mobile operating systems, iOS and Android. Furthermore, we outfitted the popular CMS Wordpress with server-side support for our system.

4.1 Client-Side Implementation

In this section, we point out the platform dependent differences between the implementations for iOS and Android respectively. Our implementation shows that the approach can be put into practice without support by platform providers though we favor an integration into the mobile platforms.

Implementation for iOS. On iOS, communication between apps, such as the web browser and the MobileAuthenticator is severely limited. The only - for our purpose - usable channel is leveraging custom URL schemes: An iOS app can register a URL scheme, such as `mobileauth:`, which is registered with the operating system on app installation. When a different app accesses a URL that starts with this custom URL scheme, iOS conducts a context switch and activates the application that has registered the scheme while pushing the calling app into background. The activated app receives the full URL in form of a string for further processing.

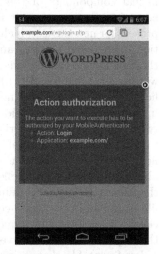

Fig. 2. Triggering an authorized action

We use this mechanism to delegate the authorized action from the web browser to the MobileAuthenticator: The AuthenticationBroker (see Sec. 3.2) compiles a `mobileauth`-URL which carries the server's challenge and the required parameters. Furthermore, the location of the active web document is attached to the URL as the callback URL. Then, the script makes the browser request the compiled `mobileauth` URL via assigning it to `document.location`. This, in turn, causes the operating system to activate the MobileAuthenticator. After user acknowledgment, the MobileAuthenticator calls the callback (`http-`)URL and appends the `CResponse` as a hash identifier. This prevents a page reload in the browser and submits the response to the AuthenticationBroker.

Implementation for Android. The MobileAuthenticator provides a background service that is started right after the boot process completed. This service hosts a WebSocket server and is therefore accessible from the device's browser using the AuthenticationBroker and the HTML5 WebSocket API. The Authentication Broker establishes a WebSocket connection to the MobileAuthenticator's background service when it hooks an attempt for an authorized action. It obtains the challenge from the action's HTML meta data and pushes the request together with the challenge to the background service. The background service then launches an activity bringing the MobileAuthenticator to foreground (see Fig. 2). After the user took a decision (either consent or denial, see Fig. 3), the app computes the HMAC on the entire request, including the challenge, appends it and sends the whole string back to the AuthenticationBroker using the established WebSocket connection.

4.2 Server-Side Implementation

We implemented server-side components to support the MobileAuthenticator and integrated them into the popular PHP weblog Wordpress as a plug-in. This allows to support legacy web applications without changing the existing codebase. There are three logical components of the plug-in: First, a client administration component manages the enrollment process for new devices, including a device confirmation in the user account, and the revocation of authorized device connections, e.g. because the device was lost or stolen (see Sec. 5). Second, an action verification component issues new challenges and checks incoming requests for valid response tokens. These two components are generic and need no adaption to the particular web application. The last component, however, is application specific. It glues the above components into the legacy code, incorporates the client administration function into the user profile pages, and activates a central request filter that

Fig. 3. Obtaining user consent to perform an authorized action

checks if an incoming request targets an authorized action. If so, it forwards the request to the action verification component. The AuthenticationBroker is a JavaScript file that is included with every web page. It is roughly 10kb, is stored in the browser's LocalStorage together with a list of authorized actions, and hooks requests for those actions.

5 Evaluation

We evaluate the MobileAuthenticator with respect to its security and protection properties as well as to its usability.

5.1 Security Evaluation

Phishing. An attack can only succeed if the user enters credentials on a phishing site ignoring the fact that this is not necessary on her device. Expecting a redirect to the MobileAuthenticator, users become suspicious if their used comfort is missing.

Clickjacking. An attacker can still lure his victim into clicking on links but the target web application then redirects the victim to the MobileAuthenticator where, of course, the attack becomes obvious and the victim does not acknowledge the targeted authorized action.

CSRF. An attack is only detectable for a potential victim if the attacker can forward his payload to the MobileAuthenticator (see Sec. 4). Even if the attacker manages to do so, the victim suddenly faces the MobileAuthenticator asking for permission to perform an authorized action on a different website.

XSS. Injected JavaScript code can perform all actions on the user's behalf. It can raise new authorized actions and redirect the respective requests to the MobileAuthenticator. However, due to the missing shared secret, it can not sign the requests. So, as long as users do not acknowledge unintended actions, no authorized action can be triggered. The only damage an XSS attacker can cause is a denial-of-service by discarding all signed requests and, thus, preventing intended authorized actions.

Session Fixation. The attacker can still get access to the user's account. The login step elevates the session cookie to an authorized state granting access to the owner. However, the attacker can not perform authorized actions because he has no access to the shared secret.

No More Password Entry. Felt and Wagner discussed the fact that mobile keyboards actively discourage the usage of complicated, and thus secure, passwords, as the entry of numbers or special characters require cumbersome context switches [2]. Our scheme obliterates the necessity of entering passwords completely. Hence, the password cannot be stolen, as it is neither stored nor entered again. Moreover, this process allows the usage of arbitrarily complicated application (master) passwords, as the usability drawbacks upon password entry do not apply for our system.

Device-specific Credentials. As a matter of fact, mobile devices get lost or stolen from time to time. A thief or finder can use the MobileAuthenticator to log into accounts and conduct authorized actions, once he vanquished the display lock. However, there is built-in protection against this threat: During enrollment (see Sec. 3.3), the MobileAuthenticator and the web application compute a shared secret. The MobileAuthenticator does not store the user password. So, the user only has to revoke the shared secret in her account to prevent any access using the lost device. A thief, in contrast, can not exclude the user as changing the password is not possible without knowing the old password.

5.2 Attacking the MobileAuthenticator

We briefly discuss attacks that might apply directly to our implemented mechanism. The proposed solution as a system app is not susceptible to these attacks.

App Spoofing. An attacker may offer a malicious app via the respective platform's market, i.e., Apple's App Store or Google Play. When installed on a user's device, it could try to obtain user credentials pretending to be the legitimate

MobileAuthenticator. The only occasion is the registration of new accounts in the MobileAuthenticator. This, however, is initialized by the user, usually by shortcuts on her home screen. So, as long as this malicious app is not able to replace the legitimate app shortcut with its own, the attacker can not gain confidential knowledge. We want to emphasize that spoofing the legitimate app when the AuthenticationBroker forwards them for signing does not reveal any credentials to the malicious app, because the user only confirms or denies but does not enter anything. The implementation as a system app can register an exclusive protocol scheme such that the registration URL is instantly forwarded to the MobileAuthenticator.

Task Interception. There is a task interception attack on Android devices. A malicious app having the necessary permissions (given by the user at installation time) can poll running tasks and display a phishing screen as soon as the target app is started. The user, expecting this screen, would probably enter the credentials. Finally, the malicious app can exit and call the genuine app. This kind of attack is not promising when run on the MobileAuthenticator because the background service is permanently running, thus, revealing no indication for the moment to spoof the MobileAuthenticator screen.

5.3   Usability

Felt et al. phrase crucial criteria for user-friendly interaction with respect to questions and user-based decisions [8]. We generalize and apply their criteria though they study mobile apps and their questions for permissions. In fact, the MobileAuthenticator is similar because it needs a user's decision on the permission to perform an authorized action. We show that the MobileAuthenticator complies with their criteria.

Their first point is to conserve user attention and only ask if the respective question has severe consequences. The MobileAuthenticator only comes into play when such confirmation is necessary. This way, we limit user interaction to the absolute minimum while, in the end, the web application determines the actual authorized actions (see Sec. 2.3).

Second, a usable security mechanism avoids interrupting the user's primary task with explicit security decisions. We achieve this by integrating the user question into the usual workflow. For instance, the MobileAuthenticator can ask the user for consent while presenting an overview of the purchase, including payment information, goods, shipping, etc. The user expects such a final inquiry. So, the integration of the MobileAuthenticator does not interrupt the user's primary task.

Finally, Felt et al. recommend using a trusted UI for *non-revertible*, *severe*, and *user initiated* actions. The authorized actions are generally *not revertible*, which means that the MobileAuthenticator can not let them happen and revert if needed. They are *severe*, meaning that carelessness is not an option and drawing the user's attention is justified. Finally, authorized actions are generally *user initiated*. This is an important point why one can expect the user to confirm her intent. Other, i.e., implicit, actions can not be confirmed that easily because the user does not know what to decide and why that dialogue popped up.

For instance, a usual shopping workflow and an online banking transaction only require one acknowledgment using the MobileAuthenticator respectively. This acknowledgment can be smoothly embedded in the workflow as a last step being expected by the user anyway. Social networks need to assess their users' risk: publicly posted messages on the one hand are deletable (i.e., revertible), so there is no need for a trusted UI. On the other hand, however, annoying or insulting posts might damage the victim's reputation which is non-revertible and severe. This decision could also be left to each customer weighing her personal or business interests respectively. As a rule of thumb, an acknowledgment step using the MobileAuthenticator is at least necessary when a re-authentication (providing the password again) or second factor authentication (e.g., via Google Authenticator, one-time passcodes, flicker codes) has been in place.

6 Related Work

There is no other approach covering the whole range of authentication-based attacks. Existing approaches either protect the login process against phishing [9–11] or target session-based attacks [6, 12–15] Finally, the related body of work includes authentication and authorization protocols in the web [16–18]. GuarDroid [19] aims at establishing a trusted path between the user and the web application using a modified execution platform (firmware). It protects against malicious apps installed on the mobile device and prevents leakage of the user's password. GuarDroid does not require changes of the installed apps nor of the remote web application, however, it can not protect against session-based attacks which still allow a malicious app to impersonate the user towards the web application. GuarDroid causes considerable network latency and requires the user to set, remember, and check a secure passphrase that authenticates the secure login form and delays the system boot process. Finally, the user is responsible to verify the target URL for login requests to prevent phishing attacks, thus, demanding a high level of awareness and increasing the risk that users just click through the dialog. Other existing approaches for trusted paths concerning user login [7] and user actions in authenticated sessions [20] focus on surfing web applications using desktop browsers.

7 Conclusion

In this paper, we presented a web authorization delegation scheme for mobile devices that utilizes a native companion app, the MobileAuthenticator, to realize a trusted UI. For a set of predefined *authorized actions*, our system reliably mitigates state changing effects of currently known user impersonation attacks, such as phishing, CSRF, or clickjacking.

Furthermore, the MobileAuthenticator effectively becomes the user's authentication credential, obliterating the necessity to frequently enter passwords on the mobile device, thus, correcting the usability drawbacks that are observed when entering secure passwords on mobile keyboards.

The MobileAuthenticator itself is independent from specific characteristics of the protected web application and, thus, can serve as the central trust anchor for many different, independent applications. In consequence, a future integration of such a service on a platform-level into the mobile operating system is a compelling option.

Acknowledgements. The research leading to these results was supported by the "Bavarian State Ministry of Education, Science and the Arts" as part of the FORSEC research association.

References

1. Amrutkar, C., Traynor, P., van Oorschot, P.C.: Measuring SSL Indicators on Mobile Browsers: Extended Life, or End of the Road? In: Gollmann, D., Freiling, F.C. (eds.) ISC 2012. LNCS, vol. 7483, pp. 86–103. Springer, Heidelberg (2012)
2. Felt, A., Wagner, D.: Phishing on Mobile Devices. In: W2SP (2011)
3. Luo, T., Jin, X., Ananthanarayanan, A., Du, W.: Touchjacking attacks on web in android, iOS, and windows phone. In: Garcia-Alfaro, J., Cuppens, F., Cuppens-Boulahia, N., Miri, A., Tawbi, N. (eds.) FPS 2012. LNCS, vol. 7743, pp. 227–243. Springer, Heidelberg (2013)
4. Rydstedt, G., Gourdin, B., Bursztein, E., Boneh, D.: Framing Attacks on Smart Phones and Dumb Routers: Tap-jacking and Geo-localization Attacks. In: wOOt (2010)
5. Niu, Y., Hsu, F., Chen, H.: iPhish: Phishing Vulnerabilities on Consumer Electronics. In: UPSEC (2008)
6. De Ryck, P., Desmet, L., Heyman, T., Piessens, F., Joosen, W.: CsFire: Transparent Client-Side Mitigation of Malicious Cross-Domain Requests. In: Massacci, F., Wallach, D., Zannone, N. (eds.) ESSoS 2010. LNCS, vol. 5965, pp. 18–34. Springer, Heidelberg (2010)
7. Bursztein, E., Soman, C., Boneh, D., Mitchell, J.C.: SessionJuggler: Secure Web Login from an Untrusted Terminal Using Session Hijacking. In: WWW (2012)
8. Felt, A., Egelman, S., Finifter, M., Akhawe, D., Wagner, D.: How to Ask for Permission. In: HotSec (2012)
9. Chou, N., Ledesma, R., Teraguchi, Y., Boneh, D., Mitchell, J.C.: Client-side Defense against Web-Based Identity Theft. In: NDSS 2004 (2004)
10. Dhamija, R., Tygar, J.: The Battle Against Phishing: Dynamic Security Skins. In: SOUPS (2005)
11. Balfanz, D., Smetters, D., Upadhyay, M., Barth, A.: TLS Origin-Bound Certificates. IETF Draft, http://tools.ietf.org/html/draft-balfanz-tls-obc-01
12. Huang, L.S., Moshchuk, A., Wang, H.J., Schechter, S., Jackson, C.: Clickjacking: Attacks and Defenses. In: 21st USENIX Security Symposium (2012)
13. Jovanovic, N., Kruegel, C., Kirda, E.: Preventing cross site request forgery attacks. In: Securecomm (2006)
14. Sterne, B., Barth, A.: Content Security Policy. W3C Working Draft (2012), http://www.w3.org/TR/2011/WD-CSP-20111129/ (November 2012)

15. Johns, M., Braun, B., Schrank, M., Posegga, J.: Reliable Protection Against Session Fixation Attacks. In: ACM SAC (2011)
16. Mozilla: Persona, `https://developer.mozilla.org/en-US/docs/Mozilla/Persona` (November 19, 2013)
17. Lockhart, H., Campbell, B.: SAML V2.0, `https://www.oasis-open.org/committees/download.php/27819/sstc-saml-tech-overview-2.0-cd-02.pdf` (March 2008)
18. Internet2: Shibboleth, `http://shibboleth.net/`
19. Tong, T., Evans, D.: GuarDroid: A Trusted Path for Password Entry. In: Mobile Security Technologies, MoST 2013 (2013)
20. Braun, B., Kucher, S., Johns, M., Posegga, J.: A User-Level Authentication Scheme to Mitigate Web Session-Based Vulnerabilities. In: Fischer-Hübner, S., Katsikas, S., Quirchmayr, G. (eds.) TrustBus 2012. LNCS, vol. 7449, pp. 17–29. Springer, Heidelberg (2012)

Detecting Code Reuse in Android Applications Using Component-Based Control Flow Graph

Xin Sun, Yibing Zhongyang, Zhi Xin, Bing Mao, and Li Xie

State Key Laboratory for Novel Software Technology
Department of Computer Science and Technology
Nanjing University, China
{sunxin508,Sophie.xuer,zxin.nju}@gmail.com, {maobing,xieli}@nju.edu.cn

Abstract. Recently smartphones and mobile devices have gained incredible popularity for their vibrant feature-rich applications (or apps). Because it is easy to repackage Android apps, software plagiarism has become a serious problem. In this paper, we present an accurate and robust system DroidSim to detect code reuse. DroidSim calculates similarity score only with component-based control flow graph (CB-CFG). CB-CFG is a graph of which nodes are Android APIs and edges represent control flow precedence order in each Android component. Our system can be applied to detect repackaged apps and malware variants. We evaluate DroidSim on 121 apps and 706 malware variants. The results show that our system has no false negative and a false positive of 0.83% for repackaged apps, and a detection ratio of 96.60% for malware variants. Besides, ADAM is used to obfuscate apps and the result reveals that ADAM has no influence on our system.

Keywords: Mobile Applications, Code Reuse, Repackaging, Malware Variants.

1 Introduction

Smartphones have played a more and more important role in people's life due to abundant and feature-rich smartphone applications (or apps) that people can download and experience from app repositories such as Apple's App Store [2] and Google's Google Play [3]. Recent statistics show that till the second quarter of 2013, Android dominates the mobile device market with 79.3% of market shares while the next closest platform iOS accounts for 13.2% of overall share [1]. Now Google Play has officially reached over 1 million apps and it has finally outgrown App Store [4]. Since users are no longer satisfied with a few functionalities like making phone calls or sending messages, they are willing to browse and download apps which can meet their other various demands.

Code reuse occurs when different apps share the same code. It is often found in repackaged apps and malware variants.

Users browse and download apps from markets. Developers submit apps to markets to make them available to users and accordingly gain profits from submitted apps. Therefore, a healthy ecosystem comes into being. Unfortunately,

N. Cuppens-Boulahia et al. (Eds.): SEC 2014, IFIP AICT 428, pp. 142–155, 2014.

this ecosystem is mostly threatened by repackaged apps. A repackaged app emerges when a plagiarist unpacks a legitimate app, modifies certain code and redistributes it violating the intellectual property of original developer. Developers can directly charge for their apps, but many instead offer free apps and gain monetary profits from in-app billing or third-party ad libraries. Apps are repackaged for two motivations. First, a plagiarist can modify the ad library's client ID or embed new ad libraries to steal or re-route ad revenues [10]. Second, malicious payloads or exploits may be injected into popular apps to increase propagation. Once installed, this kind of apps can leak privacy, send messages to premium numbers and even turn the infected phones into bots. A recent work indicates that 86% of Android malwares repackage other legitimate (popular) apps [11], which is the main vehicle for propagation. Malware authors tend to enclose malicious payloads to as many apps as possible, which leads to different variants that should be classified into one malware family.

Due to the huge amount of Android apps, researchers have proposed several detection algorithms based on static analysis [12] [13] [14] [17] [18]. Till now, no dynamic algorithm has been proposed because dynamic detection is too slow to bear and Android specific input is hard to feed. While static analysis is fast, it is not robust enough to detect repackaged apps or malware variants especially when they are obfuscated. These algorithms generally sacrifice robustness for scalability. Simple obfuscation techniques can cause considerable false negative rates [15]. In practice, several obfuscation techniques have been used to successfully evade 10 state-of-the-art commercial mobile anti-malware products [16]. Without doubt, these obfuscation techniques can be easily applied to hinder the existing algorithms.

In this paper, we propose an accurate and robust system called DroidSim to effectively detect code reuse. DroidSim performs pare-wise comparison based on component-based control flow graph (CB-CFG). CB-CFGs are generated by static analysis for every component. Nodes in them are Android APIs and edges reflect the control flow precedence relationship of APIs. We propose CB-CFG based on three insights. First, Android APIs can represent semantic information. All the sensitive behaviors must interact with Android phone hardware through different APIs. Hence, Android APIs are effective to denote behaviors. Second, there are no superfluous APIs. It is hard to modify APIs without modifying the original behaviors. Third, the control flow can clearly clarify the relationship between two APIs. We notice that several problems occur when constructing CB-CFGs. Java inheritance and reflection usually make us ambiguous about which method is to invoke. Multi-threading and callbacks are also big challenges for static analysis.

We present DroidSim and apply it to detect repackaged apps and malware variants. For repackaged app detection, a dataset which contains 25 pairs of repackaged apps and other 61 irrelevant apps is customized from the Android Malware Genome Project [11] and the Internet. Our system shows that all the repackaged apps are detected and only 1 irrelevant app is falsely detected as repackaged, indicating a false negative of 0.00% and a false positive of 0.83%.

For malware variant detection, we evaluate our system on 706 variants and gain a detection ratio of 96.60%.

Our contributions are two folds:

☐ We propose a novel approach to detect code reuse in Android. DroidSim performs the pair-wise comparison and computes the similarity score only by CB-CFGs. CB-CFGs consist of Android APIs and reflect the relationship between different APIs. It can represent the semantic information of apps and is able to denote the behaviors of a component. Our system can be applied to detect repackaged apps and malware variants.

☐ Since an app has no superfluous APIs and the Android system has no redundant API to replace, we believe CB-CFG is not easy to modify and is able to resist common obfuscations. In our experiment, we leverage ADAM [22] to obfuscate the samples and the result shows that ADAM has no influence on our system.

The rest of the paper is organized as follows: section 2 introduces the system overview. In section 3, we describe the design and implementation for static code reuse detection, followed by evaluation in section 4. Section 5 presents the limitations of DroidSim and future work. Finally we describe related work in Section 6 and conclude in section 7.

2   System Overview

2.1   Threat Model

We aim to detect code reuse in Android apps. For repackaged apps, plagiarists usually don't modify the functionalities of legitimate apps, so the code must be very similar to the legitimate apps intuitively. A similarity score can be calculated to discern the repackaged apps. Malware variants in one family share the same malicious code snippets in most cases. And these shared code can be extracted as the signature of one malware family. With the evolution some obfuscation techniques are applied to repackaged apps and malware variants to escape detection. For instance, a real-world malware Gamex [6] has been found to apply some simple obfuscation techniques.

2.2   Assumption

In this paper we consider only *classes.dex* and the author information of an app. To detect repackaged apps, two assumptions must be satisfied. First, the signing key of a developer is not leaked. Once guaranteed, the repackaged app must be signed by a different key from the original one. Second, we measure the similarity score based on the DEX code and leave native code alone because native code only occupies a small portion of real-world apps and is much harder to modify than dalvik bytecode.

2.3 Methodology

DroidSim contains 4 steps as depicted in Figure 1. First, it pre-processes the whole dataset (section 3.1). For each app, it extracts two key features: *classes.dex* and the author information. *Classes.dex* is the main basis to calculate the similarity score while the author information is used to mark each app for excluding similarity comparison from the same author. Second, it constructs CB-CFGs from *classes.dex* (section 3.2). In general, Android apps consist of different components (e.g. Activity, Service, Broadcast Receiver and Content Provider). DroidSim generates CB-CFG for each component. Finally, it computes the similarity score according to the former features (section 3.3).

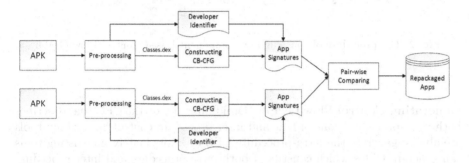

Fig. 1. Overview of our design

3   Design and Implementation

3.1 Pre-processing

Android apps are distributed in markets in the form of APK. An APK is a compressed archive of the program's Dalvik bytecode, resources and a XML manifest file. Two features are extracted first. One is *classes.dex* which contains the Dalvik bytecode for execution. The other is $META - INF$ which contains the detailed author information.

DroidSim utilizes *Keytool* utility [8] (included in the Android SDK) to extract the author information from *cert.rsa* in $META - INF$ and uses the public key as the identifier for each developer. In the following steps, this identifier will be integrated into signatures and used to determine whether two apps are from the same author.

For ease of constructing CB-CFGs, we leverage *baksmali* [7] to disassemble the DEX format. After disassembling, the DEX files are transformed to *smali* files. Disassembling is lossless. However, it may fail in rare circumstances. The *smali* files support the full functionality of the original dex format and are much friendlier to read. DroidSim takes advantage of Android-apktool [5], a tool that already integrates *baksmali* and is able to decompress APKs. At the end of this step, DroidSim transforms an APK into a developer identifier and a set of *smali* files which will simplify the next few steps.

3.2 Constructing Component-Based Control Flow Graph (CB-CFG)

The second step is the core of DroidSim. It takes a developer identifier and *smali* files as input and outputs a signature for each app. Figure 2 shows the detailed process of how to construct a signature.

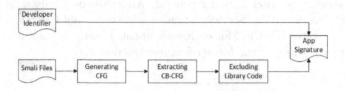

Fig. 2. The procedure of construction Component-Based Control Flow Graph

Generating Control Flow Graph. DroidSim relies on the CFG that describes both intra-procedure control flow and inter-procedure control flow. Many tools are able to generate the intra-procedure CFGs. Unfortunately no existing tools can generate CFGs which consists of both intra-procedure and inter-procedure control flow. Therefore we implement a tool to generate this specific CFG based on the *smali* files.

To achieve this, DroidSim first identifies all the components in an app. For each method in a component, we divide the method body into many Basic Blocks. A Basic Block is a straight-line piece of code without any jump instructions or jump targets. It is easy to construct intra-procedure control flow. For inter-procedure control flow, method invocations in *smali* code always start with *invoke∗* or *execute∗* instructions. Resolving method invocations is hard when we meet the java characteristics such as polymorphism and inheritance. Besides, java reflection is also a challenge. It allows programs to invoke a method according to its string name. While it is easy to determine which method to invoke during runtime, it is not easy for static analysis. In this paper, we make a conservative approach that connects all the possible paths for reflections. Multi-threading and callbacks are often found in Android apps and hard to analyze for static analysis. In the same way, we conservatively connect all possible paths. Although conservative approaches may cause imprecision, we believe that it will make little influence because the same approach must be made for both the repackaged and the legitimate apps when meeting the same ambiguous method invocation.

Extracting CB-CFG. CB-CFG is a graph of which nodes are Android APIs and edges represent control flow precedence relationship. It is extracted for each component. The node of CFG generated above represents a Basic Block and the directed edge represents control flow relationship. In this step DroidSim extracts APIs in Basic Blocks and omits other statements to generate nodes of CB-CFGs.

If a Basic Block has more than one API, we divide it into different nodes in CB-CFG to make sure that each node has only one API. However, not all of Android APIs are suitable and only APIs that represent the app functionalities e.g. file operations, sending messages, making phone calls etc are reserved. We use APIs instead of Basic Blocks based on the insight that APIs usually have enough information to represent the program behaviors and are difficult to modify. The precedence order of different APIs is preserved in our CB-CFGs. Obtaining the precedence order is not easy because some Basic Blocks may have no APIs and more than one subsequent basic blocks. In this case, the precedence relationships should be stored until we find all the subsequent Basic Blocks which have APIs. Hence, a data structure is created to store the order and a depth-first traversal is implemented in the original CFG. Once nodes and edges are determined, CB-CFG is completed. Each node in CB-CFG corresponds to a unique type. And it is efficient to decide whether two nodes are of the same type when DroidSim calculates similarity score through subgraph isomorphism. Figure 3 is a simple example of CB-CFG generated from the *smali* code below.

Example of smali code

```
1. invoke-direct {v0, v1}, Landroid/content/Intent;-><init>(...;)V
2. if-gtz v17, :cond_0
3. invoke-virtual {v3, v4, v5}, Lcom/example/b/B;->display(II)I
4. goto/16 :goto_0
5. :cond_0
6. invoke-virtual {p0, v0}, Lcom/GoldDream/zj/zjService;->startActivity
   (Landroid/content/Intent;)V
7. :goto_0
8. invoke-virtual/range {v0 .. v5}, Landroid/telephony/SmsManager;
   ->sendTextMessage(...;)V
```

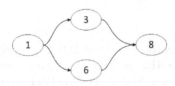

Fig. 3. Generated CB-CFG from smali code above. The content in each node is a digit for brevity. In real cases, it is the Android API.

Excluding Library Code. Third-party libraries are often embedded in Android apps. For example, most free apps insert ad libraries like admob to compensate for their work. After pre-processing, these libraries are still reserved. In this case, computing the similarity score will likely bring about a misleading result due to the shared libraries. In case of it, DroidSim excludes the common library code by a white-list.

Ultimately DroidSim gets a set of CB-CFGs and a developer identifier for each app and integrates them into one signature for further detection.

3.3   Similar App Detection

For repackaged app detection, DroidSim performs pair-wise comparison for each app and calculates the similarity score by signatures. A signature contains a developer identifier and a set of CB-CFGs. The concrete process is as follows. For an app A, we want to detect whether app B is repackaged from A. DroidSim first checks whether two apps' identifiers are the same. If so, it neglects this pair, because they are written by the same author. Otherwise, it calculates the similarity score for B according to equation 1.

$$Sim(B) = \frac{\sum_{b \in B} |b|}{min(|A|, |B|)} \tag{1}$$

In Equation 1, the similarity score of B is calculated in comparison with A. In the denominator, the symbol $|A|$ represents the number of CB-CFGs in A and $|B|$ represents the number of CB-CFGs in B, $min(|A|, |B|)$ chooses the minor value in $|A|$ and $|B|$. In numerator, the symbol b stands for each CB-CFG in B. $|b|$ equals to 1 if b is subgraph isomorphic to any CB-CFG in A and equals to 0 otherwise.

For malware variant detection, an intuitive approach is proposed. The shared CB-CFGs are automatically extracted as signatures because variants of one family share the same malicious code. If an app contains the signature of certain malware family, it is regarded as the variant of this family.

Subgraph isomorphism is NP-complete. Fortunately because there are only limited nodes in CB-CFGs and each node has the unique API type, it is often efficient to perform subgrpah isomorphism mappings. And we leverage VF2 algorithm [19] to perform these mappings.

4   Evaluation

We have implemented a prototype system called DroidSim in Linux. In this section we first take a false positive and false negative measurement about detecting repackaged apps in a customized dataset. To elaborate the robustness, we measure how the prototype is resistant to several common obfuscation techniques. Then we leverage DroidSim to generate signatures for known malware families and apply these signatures to detect malware variants.

4.1   Experimental Setup

While it is easy to measure the false positive through manual verification, it is the opposite case for measuring the false negative. So we determine to customize a dataset from Android Malware Genome Project [11]. To measure the false

negative, we randomly select several repackaged apps and find their corresponding legitimate apps via the Internet. What's more, we download irrelevant apps
from a third-party market [1] to measure the false positive. For detecting malware variants, we also select 8 malware families from Android Malware Genome
Project [11]. All apps are obfuscated by ADAM [22] to measure the obfuscation-
resistance. The whole experiment is performed on a desktop PC with 3.4 GHz
Intel Quad-cores CPU, 12GB RAM and Ubuntu 13.10 as OS.

4.2   Dataset Statistics

In total the dataset for repackaged app detection contains 121 apps. Among
them, 25 are malwares from Android Malware Genome Project [11] and 25 are
the corresponding legitimate apps. The rest 61 are downloaded from one third-
party market. Callbacks are usually used in event handling process of widgets like
buttons. Multi-threading is often applied in time-consuming tasks like network
connecting and file downloading. Reflection is often used in malwares to escape
detection. All the three specific features are included in our benchmark. In the
first step, it takes 1214.87 seconds to generate all the signatures, in average,
10.04 seconds per app.

In practice, DroidSim removes CB-CFGs that are smaller than a specified size
(< 5 nodes), because small graphs are more likely to be the same by chance.
As illustrated on Figure 4, 95.9% of apps have less than 45 CB-CFGs. Among
them, 57.8% have less than 15 CB-CFGs, which will reduce the frequence of
comparison.

Figure 5 shows that 98.3% of CB-CFGs have more than 10 nodes. It is hard
to get through subgraph isomorphism test by coincidence, which is also proved
by our experiment that most of unrelated apps have 0 CB-CFG in common.
Besides, 95.0% of nodes in CB-CFG are in the range between 10 and 70, which
also guarantees the efficiency of subgraph isomorphism.

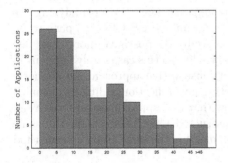

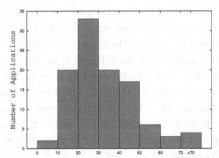

Fig. 4. Distribution of CB-CFG number

Fig. 5. Distribution of the average node
number in CB-CFG

---

[1] http://www.appsapk.com/

4.3   Repackaged App Detection

We measure the false positive and false negative on the dataset described in section 4.2. To measure the robustness of DroidSim, an obfuscation tool called ADAM [22] is used. ADAM is initially used to transform an original malware sample to different variants. It targets Dalvik bytecode and is often used as an automated obfuscation tool. The obfuscation techniques in ADAM include, (1) repacking such as realigning, re-signing and rebuilding APKs, (2) junk code insertion such as adding new methods that perform invalid operations, (3) method renaming, (4) code reordering such as inserting goto instruction to modify the control flow graph, (5) constant string encryption. There are also other obfuscation tools such as Proguard and Dexguard. However, Proguard directly targets java source code. Dexguard targets Dalvik bytecode, but is not free to get. Both tools are not adopted in our experiment.

Table 1. Experiment Result

Apps in Dataset	Detected before Obfuscation	Detected after Obfuscation
121	26	26

The first column in Table 1 indicates the number of apps in our dataset. The second column lists the number of apps detected as repackaged by DroidSim before obfuscation. The third indicates the number detected as repackaged after obfuscation. In our experiment, the threshold of similarity score is set to 0.3. If the similarity score is higher than 0.3, the app will be inferred as repackaged. We note that it is a tradeoff to determine the threshold. If we raise the threshold, the false positive will rise and the false negative will decrease.

Our manual verification shows that 25 apps are repackaged. Table 1 indicates that the false negative rate is 0.00% because all the repackaged apps have been detected successfully. And the false positive rate is 0.83%. 1 out of 121 is detected incorrectly. The mistaken one is named *xiangpeizhishu* [2]. After analyzing, we find that it only contains one Activity and its unique CB-CFG happens to be isomorphic to another app [3]. Most of the Android apps have more than one components and the APIs in them often vary a lot, so this case rarely happens in practice. As we mentioned in section 3.2, a conservative approach that connects all the possible paths is adopted when meeting java reflection, callbacks or multithreading. And the experiment results show that this approximate approach can work well. For two similar apps, the constructed CB-CFGs remain the same because the same paths are connected when meeting the same ambiguous method invocation.

Table 1 also shows that ADAM has no influence on our experiment because DroidSim computes the similarity score only by CB-CFGs. Simple transformation techniques in ADAM such as repacking, methods renaming, and constant

---

[2] xiangpeizhishu. http://os-android.liqucn.com/rj/29261.shtml

[3] Free File Manager. http://www.appsapk.com/free-file-manager/

string encryption obviously do not change the control flow. As for junk code insertion, only inserting Android APIs can modify generated CB-CFGs, and thus lower the similarity score. Currently we don't distinguish the dead code in DroidSim and rely on a low threshold value to reduce the influence. It proves to be effective in our experiment for no existing obfuscation tool can do this. If a tool that automatically injects APIs as junk code is available, a semantic investigation must be employed to eliminate the unreachable code. With respect to code reordering, it can change the control flow. But the CB-CFG remains untouched because the precedence order of APIs is not modified. Overall, obfuscation techniques in ADAM have no effect on DroidSim.

4.4   Malware Variant Detection

Besides detecting repackaged apps, our system can also be used to detect malware variants. Previous work [11] shows that one malware family often has many variants. The variants share the same malicious code snippets, which can be the signature of this malware family. CB-CFG consists of Android APIs and their relationship, and is able to represent the functionality of shared code snippets. Hence we use DroidSim to extract a set of CB-CFGs as the signature of one malware family. To measure the validity and robustness, we analyze 8 malware families and extract signatures from several malware variants of each malware family. Then signatures are tested on 706 malware variants.

Table 2. Detection Results of Malware Variants

Malware Family	CB-CFGs (signature)	Samples	Detected before obfuscation	Detected after obfuscation	Percentage
AnserverBot	9	187	186	186	99.47%
DroidKungFu1	5	28	28	28	100.00%
DroidKungFu2	3	28	15	15	53.57%
DroidKungFu3	3	300	299	299	99.67%
DroidKungFu4	3	96	88	88	91.67%
DroidDream	2	14	13	13	92.86%
DroidDreamLight	1	41	41	41	100.00%
Zsone	1	12	12	12	100.00%
total	27	706	682	682	96.60%

As illustrated on Table 2, the first column lists the malware family name. The second column is the signature extracted by DroidSim. The third lists the number of malware variants for test. The fourth indicates the malwares detected before ADAM is used. The fifth is the number of malware variants detected after ADAM is used. And the sixth represents the detection ratio. Among the 8 malware families, the detection ratio varies much. For AnserverBot, only 1 out of 187 escapes our detection. For further analysis, we notice that apktool [5] we employ does not generate the *smali* code corresponding to the signature.

Thus it does not have the corresponding CB-CFGs. For the DroidKungFu series, only all variants of DroidKungFu1 are detected. The detection rate of Droid-KungFu2 is the worst, which just exceeds a half. By analyzing the experiment log, we note that all the 13 missing variants are different versions of the same app named OnekeyVPN. Their behaviors are pretty different from the others. They do not access Wi-Fi state or open Internet connection while others do. Later we add the signature of this kind into the signatures, the detection ratio instantly rise to 100%. As for DroidKungFu3, one variant [4] escapes our detection. Manual analysis reveals that its malicious payload is modified exclusively for this app, which results in different CB-CFGs from others. 8 variants of DroidKungFu4 escape our detection. Among them, seven are different versions of the same app. All missing apps have different behaviors from the others. We believe that Droid-Sim can extract additional signatures to cover them if necessary. DroidDream shares the same situation with AnserverBot. Only one variant escape our detection due to the same reason with AnserverBot. As for the last two malware families, all their variants have been detected successfully.

5   Discussion

We try to detect code reuse by CB-CFGs. CB-CFG is essentially a graph. And we compare them with subgraph isomorphism. In DroidSim, we implement VF2 algorithm [19] to compare two graphs. Although subgraph isomorphism is NP-complete, it is still efficient because the node number is not that much and each node has a unique type. In our experiment, the average node number of 96.7% apps is less than 70. Hence the comparison is practical.

If an obfuscation tool that can automatically inject APIs as junk code is developed to attack our system, a semantic investigation on the program will be made to discern the unreachable code and drastically get rid of the influence.

DroidSim performs pair-wise comparison, indicating a time complexity of $O(n^2)$. Lots of algorithms try to decrease the time complexity and therefore sacrifice the robustness for scalability. In this paper, we focus on the robustness and the obfuscation techniques that may escape the detection of existing algorithms. To detect code reuse in a large scale, DroidSim should be implemented in a paralleled way and we leave it for future work.

6   Related Work

There are several approaches proposed to detect the repackaged apps. In general, these approaches can be divided into two categories: syntactic-level analysis and semantic-level analysis.

Juxtapp [20] is a scalable infrastructure for syntactic-level code similarity analysis among Android apps. It pre-processes the DEX files to obtain the opcode and discard the operands. Similarity score is calculated based on the feature

---

[4] d99165d50a17d5678b13e0e7f70605f9fd4b7e9a.apk in Android Malware Genome Project [11].

vectors extracted every k-grams of opcode. And it is vulnerable to trivial obfuscation techniques e.g. injecting junk code every few instructions. DroidMoss [12] is also a syntactic-level detection algorithm. It generally employs the basic thoughts of MOSS [21], a well-known software similarity measurement algorithm. DroidMoss adopts fuzzy hashing to generate fingerprints from the opcode (excluding the oprands) for each app. It has the same shortcomings of Juxtapp that a consecutive opcode modification can easily escape the detection. [13] is a scalable algorithm that can detect the "piggybacked" apps. A "piggybacked" app refers to the app that plagiarists attach the malicious payloads in an independent package. It can't detect the payload in the original packages. What's more, it uses feature fingerprinting to represent the primary module, which is vulnerable to simple obfuscation techniques.

DNADroid [17] is more robust than the algorithms above. It uses the semantic information to detect repackaged apps. In detail, it uses PDG (only data dependency) to represent a method and computes pair-wise similarity score. Hence the robustness of DNADroid is equal to that of PDG. Obfuscation techniques such as adding data related variables can be utilized to change the data dependency in PDG, which will effectively cause false negative. AnDarwin [14] is the advanced version of DNADroid. It still uses PDG to uniquely represent a method. To meet scalability, it clusters similar apps based on the semantic vectors extracted from PDGs and thus is more vulnerable to obfuscation than DNADroid.

As various detection algorithms are proposed, [15] provides a framework for evaluating the obfuscation resilience. It applies this framework to evaluate AndroGuard [9] to find out that even simple obfuscation techniques can be applied to potentially cause false negative.

With respect to malware variant detection, a few static algorithms can work to some extent [13] [14] [20]. However, they all unintentionally find some variants when detecting repackaged apps. But our work can automatically extract the signatures and make a systematic examination on malware families. [23] proposes a malware variant detection algorithm in the desktop environment. It leverages the high-level models abstracted from the control flow graphs. This work differs from ours mainly in three aspects. First, our system can detect repackaged apps besides malware variants. Second, DroidSim works on a different platform Android. We develop a tool that constructs the control flow graphs from the *smali* code because of the lack of similar tools in Android. And some specific features like reflection, callbacks and multi-threading bring new challenges to us. Third, Android malwares often implement the malicious payload in relatively independent components, using CB-CFGs is more efficient.

7 Conclusion

We present DroidSim, a tool that can detect code reuse in an accurate and robust way. In contrast with the earlier approaches, our system aims to detect code reuse in a more accurate way. DroidSim extracts CB-CFGs and author information to uniquely represent an app. It computes the similarity score based on CB-CFGs.

We apply DroidSim to respectively detect repackaged apps and malware variants. Our results indicate that it can effectively detect the repackaged apps with no false negative and considerably low false positive rate. For malware variants, it automatically extracts signatures for 8 malware families and gains a detection ratio of 96.60% in average. All the results have demonstrated the effectiveness and robustness of our system.

Acknowledgments. We would like to thank the anonymous reviewers for their comments. This work was supported in part by grants from the Chinese National Natural Science Foundation (61073027, 60773171, 90818022, 61272078, and 61321491), and the Chinese National 863 High-Tech Program (2007AA01Z448, 2011AA01A202).

References

1. Android Nears 80% Market Share in Global Smartphone Shipments, `http://techcrunch.com/2013/08/07/android-nears-80-market-share-in-global-smartphone-shipments-as-ios-and-blackberry-share-slides-per-idc/`
2. Apple Inc., `https://itunes.apple.com/us/genre/ios/id36?mt=8`
3. Google Inc., `https://play.google.com/store?hl=en&tab=w8`
4. Android's Google Play beats App Store with over 1 million apps, now officially largest, `http://www.phonearena.com/news/Androids-Google-Play-beats-App-Store-with-over-1-million-apps-now-officially-largest_id45680`
5. Android-apktool, `https://code.google.com/p/android-apktool/`
6. Lookout Inc. Gamex Trojan, `https://www.lookout.com/resources/top-threats/gamex-trojan`
7. Smali - An assembler/disassembler for Android's dex format, `http://code.google.com/p/smali/`
8. Google Inc. Signing Your Applications, `http://developer.android.com/tools/publishing/app-signing.html`
9. AndroGuard: Reverse engineering, Malware and goodware of Android applications, `http://code.google.com/p/androguard/`
10. Clint, G., Ryan, S., Jonathan, C., Hao, C., Hui, Z., Heesook, C.: AdRob: Examining the Landscape and Impact of Android Application Plagiarism. In: 11th International Conference on Mobile Systems, Applications and Services (Mobisys), pp. 431–444. ACM Press, Taipei (2013)
11. Zhou, Y., Jiang, X.: Dissecting android malware: Characterization and evolution. In: The 2012 IEEE Symposium on Security and Privacy (S&P), pp. 95–109. IEEE Press, Oakland (2012)
12. Wu, Z., Yajin, Z., Xuxian, J., Peng, N.: DroidMoss: Detecting Repackaged Smartphone Applications in Third-party Android Marketplaces. In: 2nd ACM Conference on Data and Application Security and Privacy (CODASPY), pp. 317–326. ACM Press, San Antonio (2012)
13. Wu, Z., Yajin, Z., Michael, G., Xuxian, J., Shihong, Z.: Fast, Scalable Detection of Piggybacked Mobile Applications. In: 3rd ACM Conference on Data and Application Security and Privacy (CODASPY), pp. 185–196. ACM Press, San Antonio (2013)

14. Crussell, J., Gibler, C., Chen, H.: AnDarwin: Scalable Semantics-Based Detection of Similar Android Applications. In: Crampton, J., Jajodia, S., Mayes, K. (eds.) ESORICS 2013. LNCS, vol. 8134, pp. 182–199. Springer, Heidelberg (2013)
15. Huang, H., Zhu, S., Liu, P., Wu, D.: A framework for evaluating mobile app repackaging detection. In: Huth, M., Asokan, N., Čapkun, S., Flechais, I., Coles-Kemp, L. (eds.) TRUST 2013. LNCS, vol. 7904, pp. 169–186. Springer, Heidelberg (2013)
16. Vaibhav, R., Yan, C., Xuxian, J.: DroidChameleon: Evaluating Android anti-malware against transformation attacks. In: 8th ACM SIGSAC Symposium on Information, Computer and Communications Security (ASIACCS), pp. 329–334. ACM Press, Hangzhou (2013)
17. Crussell, J., Gibler, C., Chen, H.: Attack of the Clones: Detecting Cloned Applications on Android Markets. In: Foresti, S., Yung, M., Martinelli, F. (eds.) ESORICS 2012. LNCS, vol. 7459, pp. 37–54. Springer, Heidelberg (2012)
18. Potharaju, R., Newell, A., Nita-Rotaru, C., Zhang, X.: Plagiarizing smartphone applications: Attack strategies and defense techniques. In: Barthe, G., Livshits, B., Scandariato, R. (eds.) ESSoS 2012. LNCS, vol. 7159, pp. 106–120. Springer, Heidelberg (2012)
19. Liugi, P., Pasquale, F., Carlo, S., Mario, V.: A (sub)graph isomorphism algorithm for matching large graphs. IEEE Transactions on Pattern Analysis and Machine Intelligence (TPAMI), 1367–1372 (2004)
20. Hanna, S., Huang, L., Wu, E., Li, S., Chen, C., Song, D.: Juxtapp: A Scalable System for Detecting Code Reuse among Android Applications. In: Flegel, U., Markatos, E., Robertson, W. (eds.) DIMVA 2012. LNCS, vol. 7591, pp. 62–81. Springer, Heidelberg (2013)
21. Saul, S., Danial, S., Alex, A.: Winnowing: Local Algorithms for Document Fingerprinting. In: 2003 ACM SIGMOD International Conference on Management of Data (SIGMOD), pp. 76–85. ACM Press, New York (2003)
22. Zheng, M., Lee, P.P.C., Lui, J.C.S.: ADAM: An Automatic and Extensible Platform to Stress Test Android Anti-virus Systems. In: Flegel, U., Markatos, E., Robertson, W. (eds.) DIMVA 2012. LNCS, vol. 7591, pp. 82–101. Springer, Heidelberg (2013)
23. Silvio, C., Yang, X.: Malware Variant Detection Using Similarity Search over Sets of Control Flow Graphs. In: 10th International Conference on Trust, Security and Privacy in Computing and Communications (TrustCom), pp. 181–189. IEEE Press, Changsha (2011)

Privacy Risks from Public Data Sources

Zacharias Tzermias[1], Vassilis Prevelakis[2], and Sotiris Ioannidis[1]

[1] Institute of Computer Science,
Foundation for Research and Technology - Hellas (FORTH)
{tzermias,sotiris}@ics.forth.gr,
[2] Institute of Computer and Network Engineering,
Technical University Carolo-Wilhelmina zu Braunschweig
prevelakis@ida.ing.tu-bs.de

Abstract. In the fight against tax evaders and other cheats, governments seek to gather more information about their citizens. In this paper we claim that this increased transparency, combined with ineptitude, or corruption, can lead to widespread violations of privacy, ultimately harming law-abiding individuals while helping those engaged in criminal activities such as stalking, identity theft and so on.

In this paper we survey a number of data sources administrerd by the Greek state, offered as web services, to investigate whether they can lead to leakage of sensitive information. Our study shows that we were able to download significant portions of the data stored in some of these data sources (scraping). Moreover, for those datasources that were not ammenable to scraping we looked at ways of extracting information for specific individuals that we had identified by looking at other data sources. The vulnerabilities we have discovered enable the collection of personal data and, thus, open the way for a variety of impersonation attacks, identity theft, confidence trickster attacks and so on. We believe that the lack of a big picture which was caused by the piecemeal development of these datasources hides the true extent of the threat. Hence, by looking at all these data sources together, we outline a number of mitigation strategies that can alleviate some of the most obvious attack strategies. Finally, we look at measures that can be taken in the longer term to safeguard the privacy of the citizens.

1 Introduction

The increasing computerization of government departments and state organizations often places in jeopardy the confidentiality of the private information of the citizens. Moreover, there exists an additional incentive in collecting as much data, financial or otherwise, into central databases and improving the interconnection of existing databases, namely that the information from all these sources can be combined to discover illegal activities. Examples of this holistic approach abound: the US Drug Enforcement Agency checks electricity bills because high electricity consumption without an obvious reason, may indicate an underground marijuana plantation [19]. The Greek government wants to gain

N. Cuppens-Boulahia et al. (Eds.): SEC 2014, IFIP AICT 428, pp. 156–168, 2014.

access to water utility bills to discover unregistered swimming pools (in Greece, swimming pools above a certain size are levied a special wealth tax, as well as increasing the minimum taxable income that the owner must declare).

Nevertheless, these actions run counter to basic privacy principles (which, by the way, the private sector is expected to follow), and may lead to widespread leakage of information that can then be used for fraud or other illegal activities. For example, the widespread use in the US of the social security number as a unique identification number has been implicated in numerous cases of fraud, such as identity theft[1]

Another example would be the case where the state requires that citizens submit inventories of valuable articles in their possession (e.g. paintings, works of art, electronic equipment etc.) together with the physical address, name and telephone number of the owner. If such lists are ever leaked, they will constitute a guide to potential thieves or other scammers that may use this information to defraud the owners.

In this paper we look at the information stored in various repositories and look at how the unintended use of the information, or services offered by these repositories can affect the privacy of the citizens. We will use the Greek state as an example of the case where the lack of commonly applied data protection rules and the casual disregard for such rules when they exist, allows infringement of privacy in a massive scale. Miscreants, can extort valuable private information from the aforementioned repositories, that can be used in targeted attacks.

The rest of the paper is organized as follows. In Section 2 we survey a wide number of data sources operated by the Greek state describing their purpose and what data is available from them. Section 3 presents our crawling methods and infrastructure that we used towards the aforementioned data sources. We present the evaluation of our approach in Section 4. In Section 5 we propose countermeasures than can be incorporated to repulse future attacks. Related work is presented in Section 6. Finally we conclude in Section 7.

2   Public Datasources

The Greek government has offered a variety of data to the public, either to accommodate taxpayers' need to access their own personal information, or in terms of transparency. The most prominent example is Diavgeia [6], a government repository where every public entity is obliged to upload its decisions. This section depicts every public datasource that contains sensitive information about individuals as well as enumerates a variety of identification numbers used by the Greek government for various transactions with citizens.

2.1   The Greek Tax Registration Number

Greek Tax Registration Number (in Greek, "ΑΦΜ"), is a unique number provided by the Greek Ministry of Finance to every person or legal entity exhibiting

---

[1] http://www.consumer.ftc.gov/articles/0271-signs-identity-theft

financial activity in Greece. Every transaction with public sector services, like tax offices, require this number among others. The ubiquitous nature of Greek Tax Registration Number (TRN), made other institutions, such as banks or insurance services to incorporate it in their transactions as an additional means of identification. The Greek TRN is a non-sequential number consisting of 9 digits and generated by an algorithm. This algorithm has been published and used in forms of state websites to detect mistyped TRNs.

Greek Tax Registration Numbers are separated in two main categories. The former includes numbers issued to wage earners and pensioners, while the latter includes freelancers, legal entities, organizations, institutions and businesses. In an effort to aid transactions among entities belonging in the second category, the General Secretariat of Information Systems (GSIS) [2] responsible of computerization of the public sector, introduced a web service that given an TRN that belongs to the second category, provides an abbreviated version of the record of the entity which matches that TRN. The information provided includes name and commercial title of business, location of headquarters, telephone number as well as the type of business activity. [11]. If the submitted number does not belong in the second category, the system returns an error which indicates the reason for the refusal, such as unregistered Tax Registration Number, number belongs to a wage earner or pensioner (and hence information about that TRN cannot be released), and so on. This information, as we shall see later, can be used to determine which TRNs to look for in other on-line datasources

Generally self-employed people and single-person businesses (e.g. farmers, plumbers, electricians and many other categories) tend to submit their residential addresses and phone numbers as their contact information, during the TRN registration procedure. Some even submit mobile telephone numbers. Consequently, the TRN search web service can inadvertently expose potentially private data to the public.

2.2   Greek Identification Card Number

Along with the Tax Registration Number, every Greek citizen is issued with an Identification (ID) card. It holds information about its owner, namely first name, last name, father's name, date of birth, as well as a unique Identification Card Number. Each Identification Card Number (ID) consists of 1 or 2 Greek capital letters and a 6-digit sequence. The ID card number is the primary form of person identification, and is widely used by whenever a government ID is required. Hence, its ubiquity can be considered similar with the Social Security Number (SSN) in the US. Unlike the social security number and the Tax Registration Number, the Identification Card Number identifies the ID card, not the person, hence changes each time a new ID card is issued. This means that there may well be multiple ID card numbers corresponding to a given person. In many cases organisations such as banks, request the TRN along with the ID card number, implying that there numerous databases

---

[2] http://www.gsis.gr

in both the private and the public sector that may be used to match TRNs to ID card numbers and vice versa.

2.3 Greek Social Security Number

In 2009, the Greek state, introduced the Social Security Registration Number (AMKA) aiming to unify transactions among insurance and healthcare institutions in Greece. Every Greek national is required to have an AMKA number. AMKA is a structured number consisting of 11 digits. The first six encode the person's date of birth while the following 4 is an incremental sequence number. The last digit usually indicates the sex of the owner. During registration for an AMKA, the Identification Card Number is required. Optionally, one may provide his TRN, as well [1]. Individuals can find their AMKA, by supplying their first name, last name, father's and mother's name as well as their full date of birth to a government operated website [4]. If the supplied information does not match exactly the corresponding information in the AMKA database, the site returns a message to the effect that the person does not exist. The only exception is the date of birth. If only the year of birth is supplied, the site may ask for additional information (such as person's TRN or Identification Card Number) towards validation. If all information is correct, the AMKA of the person is returned.

2.4 Phone Directory

As in many countries, the use of telephones in Greece (both fixed and cellular) is widely established. OTE, the main telecommunications provider in Greece, offers a phone directory service from its site [3] for landline phones. A newly updated version of the directory website offers features such as reverse search (using the phone number itself instead of the name), and location search using specific addresses, postal codes or even cities. Additionally, the directory includes cellular numbers, from OTE's subsidiary mobile telecommunication company, Cosmote. A cellular entry also exhibits the address that the cellphone owner had declared during number registration. This address usually points to owners residence.

2.5 Greek Voter Registration

The Ministry of the Interior, deployed a new web service to help voters find their electoral center on election day [8]. Voters, enter their first name, last name, father's name, mother's name and their year of birth and get back a screen with information from the Registrar General specifying their assigned electoral center. While this service is only useful during elections, it is available continuously.

2.6 Tax Card for Recording Transactions

The Greek state, in an effort to monitor retail transactions and force shop owners to issue receipts, introduced a "tax receipt card" that the customer presents to the shop owner as part of the payment. This allows the customer to declare the transaction to the tax authority on-line, thus earning some tax discount at the end of the year, while the tax authorities get instant notification of the transaction.

The disadvantage of this method is that the shops can use the number in the "receipt card" to track customers, thus dispensing of the need for loyalty cards. Moreover, if the use of these cards becomes obligatory (through, for example the imposition of financial penalties if an insufficient number of receipts is collected) then the customers will lose their right to refuse to identify themselves when making certain purchases.

2.7 Governmental Documents

From October 1, 2010, any organization receiving funding from the Greek government, is obliged to upload decisions and other documents to a publicly available repository, called Diavgeia [6] (in Greek, transparency). According to Diavgeia statistics, [3] so far, more than 10 million documents have been published by approximately 3,500 public organizations. Documents include hiring or purchasing decisions, detailed payroll lists, balance sheets and so forth. Hence it is an obvious source of private data such as names, Identification Card Number, Tax Registration Number, etc.

2.8 Other Public Resources

Without effective guidance, or coordination, the various systems are developed in an ad hoc manner with a shocking disregard of the preservation of private and confidential data on Greek nationals. Hence sensitive information can be easily collected from many sources. The following serve as examples of this trend:

Municipalities and other institutions upload lists of persons who have been hired. Like Diavgeia, these lists contain a wealth of personal information.

Moreover, lists of persons that are selected to work programmes and are published by ministries or other state organizations, are rarely anonymized [2, 5] from any identification numbers. Worse, they include information that can be misused. In particular, such lists contain selection criteria like martial status, time of unemployment or disability degree. Each criterion is assigned a discrete score. Thus, it is easy to infer one's disability degree using the assigned score on that criterion. As email addresses can be collected using social networks [24], a spammer could send targeted spam to that individual. As of the writing of this paper, these lists still remain available to public.

Data security in such sites is also a problem. Even in the flagship IT system of the Greek state, the Taxis system operated by GSIS (which stores tax data for every company or person that has income or property in Greece), recently, had an extensive breach of security. This resulted in the leak of large parts of the database with tax returns and real estate ownership. In an unprecedented move,

---

[3] http://et.diavgeia.gov.gr/f/all/stats

the Hellenic Data Protection Authority (HDPA) fined GSIS for the security breach. The HDPA report [4] indicates that large chunks of the database (about 70GB) had been copied and made available to private companies who processed the data and stored it in a MySQL database.

3 Data Crawling Infrastructure

As we have noted in the previous section, a lot of private data is held in publicly accessible repositories protected with weak authentication mechanisms. The common assumption is that only the owner of this information can access it, because the systems rely on knowledge of personal information that only the owner can know. This assumption can be broken by, on one hand, searching for the required information in other sites, and by guesswork (trying out repeated guesses until we hit the correct value). In this section we describe various techniques used and methodology followed towards collecting data from a variety of sources.

Our first target was the Tax Registration Number web service, described in the previous section. Our objective was to submit all possible TRNs and thus get all the records that were accessible to public. As stated in section 2, the algorithm for generating TRNs is used in form validation of state websites. Therefore, we generated every valid Tax Registration Number, using the TRN generation algorithm. This resulted in approximately 90 million valid Tax Registration Numbers. For each one, we queried the Tax Registration Number web service and recorded the returned information. To make our collection mechanism more efficient, we segregated the set of valid Tax Registration Numbers into 10 subsets using the first digit as a filter. Each subset contained approximately 9 million elements. As Greece's population does not exceed 11 million residents, it is obvious that the search space would be sparse. From empirical observations, we concluded that registered TRNs are those starting from 0, 1, 2 and 99. Hence, we requested numbers from these ranges first and then search for the remaining space for completeness. To avoid triggering any detection mechanism we implemented the collection mechanism in a distributed fashion; A searcher component performs requests to the service using a set of TRNs, while results are stored in a centralized machine. Searchers were deployed on multiple PlanetLab nodes located in Greece. To avoid possible lockouts from the web-service, we requested random TRNs from each subset using an interval of 100ms between consecutive requests.

The Diavgeia document repository was our second target. Although, it employs indexing mechanisms to document data, it does not index the documents' contents. Luckily a third-party service called yperdiavgeia [10], indexes both data and metadata of documents posted on Diavgeia. Moreover, it incorporates faster search mechanisms as well as applies OCR techniques to scanned documents, broadening the scope of potential results. In order to automate the process of locating and extracting Identification Card Numbers that appear in documents we used the following heuristic; Many instances of Identification Card Numbers are preceded by the string $A\Delta T$ (the initials of Identification Card Number in

---

[4] HDPA, decision 98/2013.

Greek). Moreover, we observed that the person's name, surname usually follow the Identification Card Number in the text. We, therefore, searched the yperdiageia documents for instances of the string "AΔT" (a possible reference to identification numbers) and download them locally. Using pattern matching we identified each Identification Card Number location within the document, and tried to find person's name that may have been located near the ID reference via common syntax patterns. A valid reference to a name along with an Identification Card Number would be "John Papadopoulos, son of George, with AΔT AB-123456". This heuristic produced very good yields, because most official documents follow set patterns for stating the name, Identification Card Number, and address of individuals.

In the case of the telephone directory (white pages) crawling, we used the location search feature offered by the OTE website. One could search for phones using street names, postal codes or even names of cities (e.g Athens). In cases where the name and telephone number fields were left blank, the engine returned every phone number from the specified area or region. In such cases the results were limited to 1,000 records. To extract the telephone numbers and their owners from the website, we relied to scraping mechanisms along with headless browsers provided by Selenium. Queries were constructed using a combination of known addresses, postal codes and cities. To extract the information we wanted (telephone numbers and owners) from the HTML text, we used the crawling and screen-scraping framework, Scrapy in conjunction with the headless browser framework, Selenium. We implemented a Scrapy spider that issued synthesized queries to the telephone number directory website, and extracted our data from the results. Queries were constructed using a combination of known addresses, postal codes, and cities provided by the Greek Postal Service. To avoid being blocked for potential rate-limiting mechanisms, queries were performed periodically using a fixed 90-second interval.

Despite the fact that crawling utilizes multiple machines to throttle data collection, a malicious user without adequate collection resources, could still considered as a threat, by targeting specific individuals of his interest and collecting only the relevant data for them. Therefore, the collection effort is minimized.

4 Data Analysis

In this section we perform a coarse-grained analysis of collected data in order to prove our hypothesis that the combination of discrete datasources results in greater information leakage for individuals. We also present some proof-of concept data mining attacks that may be implemented against these repositories.

4.1 Data Completeness

The first question, concerns the quantity of data we were able to acquire using our design. In particular we seek to answer, what is the size of each data source, hence answering what is the portion of data we have collected. Data collection

Table 1. Data collected from public sources

Datasource	Results
Active Business Tax Registration Numbers	1,900,035
Phones (cellphones and landlines)	3,326,658
Identification numbers (total)	74,760
Voters	720,255
AMKA numbers	108,867

results are depicted on Table 1. According to a report issued by the General Secretariat for Information Systems[5], 2,082,396 Tax Registration Numbers are assigned to businesses and persons working free lance. Our crawling mechanism gathered 1,900,035 business Tax Registration Numbers covering the 91.2 % of the aforementioned set. Regarding non-business related TRNs (i.e. those assigned to salaried persons and pensioners), even if no actual record was returned, the GSIS web service gave a big hint. In particular, it is possible to discriminate between a Tax Registration Number belonging to an individual and an unassigned TRN, using the returned error code. Despite providing no additional information, the indication that the TRN is valid allows us to reduce the set of TRNs that would be used in a future brute force attack. In total we have discovered 7,397,876 Tax Registration Numbers belonging to individuals.

Regarding the acquisition of information on telephone numbers, we have gathered 1,676,195 PSTN and 1,650,377 cellphone numbers. There were 4,927,000 PSTN and 15,254,000 subscribers in Greece at the end of 2012 [6] [7] . Hence we located the 34.2 % of PSTN numbers and the 10.81 % of cellphone numbers.

Harvesting Identification Card Numbers from documents in the Diavgeia repository, resulted in 9,370 unique numbers. We were able to identify the person associated with the specific Identification Card Number in half of our set. If we add Identification Card Numbers leaked by documents published from municipalities, the total number rises to 74,760 records. As every Greek citizen is obliged to have an Identification Card, we can assume that the set of Identification Card Numbers is at least the size of the population which is 10,815,197 according to the Greek demographics [9]. Thus, our collected data concerning Identification Card Numbers cover the 0.69 % of the aforementioned set.

The Greek Ministry of the Interior [7], reported that in the recent elections held in June 2012, there were 9,947,876 registered voters. Our crawling methodology resulted in acquiring information for 720,255 voters, thus covering 7.2 % of the set.

4.2 A Taxonomy of Tax Registration Numbers

Each record of the Tax Registration Number database includes information about business activity that the owner of the TRN is engaged in. Thus we can

---

[5] http://www.gsis.gr/gsis/export/sites/default/gsis_site/ PublicIssue/ documents_Statistics/statdeltio2011.pdf

[6] http://www.3comma14.gr/pi/?survey=15701

[7] http://www.3comma14.gr/pi/?survey=13821

identify persons according to their line of work. For example, we can identify journalists or newspaper publishers based on the business activity identifier in their tax record. Such information could be misused for malevolent purposes. As the home address of these journalists becomes public knowledge, a terrorist or a crook, could use it for blackmailing or terrorist attacks.

4.3   A Closer Look at Diavgeia Documents

The Diavgeia document repository contains miscellaneous documents mostly about the public sector. Despite, the obvious benefits of Diavgeia in promoting transparency in government decisions, we believe that specific and serious privacy concerns arise from the publication of such documents on the Internet.

Diavgeia includes contracts of individuals with specific organizations. The contract usually specifies first and last name as well as the monthly wage. Therefore, we can acquire information about one's income. However, not all contracts are been published in Diavgeia.

Furthermore, many municipalities publish construction permits. Each permit contains information about its owner, namely full name as well as Tax Registration Number. As every individual can acquire a construction permit, the referred Tax Registration Number, could potentially point to a wage earner or pensioner, mappings between non-commercial TRNs and names. The fact that most of these documents are scanned (hence bitmaps) is only a minor obstruction, as OCR software can easily convert them to searchable form.

Moreover, documents may contain Identification Card Numbers. The prevalence of Identification Card Number as a primary means of identification (such as the SSN in the US), could lead to impersonation attacks. One could leverage Identification Card Number and owner names, performing a social engineering attack to phone customer services.

5   Mitigation

The problem of balancing transparency against the protection of privacy is very hard indeed, and to a large extent philosophical, rather than technical. Nevertheless, there are numerous techniques that, if deployed, would diminish the extent of leaks by limiting or eliminating the effectiveness of our methods. In this section we discuss countermeasures that could be adopted by government entities towards prevention of similar information leaks in the future.

Rate-Limiting. Rate-limiting techniques are widely used to throttle the number of requests originating from a specific user or host. Despite its primary use in thwarting Denial-of-Service (DoS) attacks, rate-limiting can be also used to prevent rapid-fire requests of the type that we described earlier in this paper. For example, the TRN web service can introduce a daily limit on the number of requests that can be issued from a given IP address. The granularity of this limit can be adjusted to accommodate legitimate uses of the facility. From our crawling experience, we faced lock-outs from the TRN web service after a long period of crawling and only to the extent that specific IP addresses we used for our crawler were blocked. We are not aware as to whether this block was manually enforced, or automatically, triggered by a rate limiting mechanism. Since we were not the only ones downloading the contents of that particular service (we are aware of at least one company which apparently did something similar) we were not surprised when the service was eventually discontinued temporarily, with no specific justification.

CAPTCHA. Such methods can be applied to web services to prevent brute-force attacks. After a number of successive requests originating from the same IP address, a CAPTCHA must be solved. This would spurn most automated brute force attempts. During our crawling, we did not encounter any website incorporating CAPTCHA techniques. For some web services, such as the TRN service, the root of the problem was lack of any user authentication. By authenticating users and asking them to be bound by some guidelines on the use of the service, there would be little scope for the kind of massive data downloads we have carried out. In many cases, the mere fact that the client has been identified will be sufficient to deter abuse.

Data Sanitization. As we have observed, much sensitive information was hidden inside Government documents found either on the Diavgeia repository or on municipality websites. With the introduction of the yperdiavgeia search engine [10], this unstructured information can be indexed. Thus an attacker may search for specific names or TRNs of his interest, performing a more targeted attack. As a countermeasure, Diavgeia document repository can sanitize references to names or surnames prior to document publication. Instead of displaying the full name of an individual, only a portion may be visible. For example, a reference to "John Papadopoulos" would be sanitized to "J. Papad.". Moreover, governments can enforce a stricter policy, for making Personally Identifiable Information (PII) available from sources outside Diavgeia. As we have shown, major privacy leaks were effected though municipal or other institutions linked to the public sector. Decisions containing sensitive information must be sanitized or anonymized and sent to Diavgeia.

Coordination. The plethora of data sources and the disparities in their design and operation significantly contributed to the creation of the vulnerabilities we exploited during our crawling.

Since 2011, the UK government has been trying, with some success, to bring state-run websites into the fold of gov.uk. In this way redundant websites can be axed while the rest can be made to comply with a common set of rules[8].

Greece has to do something similar to prevent each new website from the pitfalls experienced by other, older, web sites. Already the GSIS site is providing single log-on services to a very small number of websites (e.g. companies wishing to register with the appropriate Chamber of Commerce can authenticate via GSIS). Soon every Greek citizen will have log-on credentials with the GSIS website which means that GSIS will be able to function as an authentication service for other state-run websites. However, this assumes that at least the

---

[8] http://www.bbc.co.uk/news/uk-politics-25950004

GSIS site is itself secure. However, we have not seen any announcements to the effect that the recommendations offered by the HDPA after the security breach we discussed earlier have been implemented. Moreover, all sites authenticating via GSIS will have to meet some common privacy and security guidelines and undergo security audits at regular intervals.

Accountability. By identifying civil servants who are responsible of PII leaks, we envisage that proper vigilance will be observed on the part of the authorities who publish documents on public websites. To that effect, analysis of document metadata (e.g. Word documents storing the name of the author or the modification date) may produce valuable information leading to the source of disclosures of PII to the public [12, 18]. Finally, Government can also use decoy documents [14], with "bait" information like TRNs or AMKAs, as a method to identify leaks.

6   Related Work

The concept on privacy exposure through public available data is not new. United States Social Security Numbers (SSN) is susceptible to conduct fraudulent actions through social engineering. Their prevalence as a means of identification made them a prime target for someone attempting identity thefts. Studies [13, 16] have indicated that the use of SSNs to identify individuals should be discouraged.

The first research, concerning privacy leakage from a Greek State datasource was conducted by Gessiou et al. [17]. The authors investigated whether personal identifiable information are publicly available on Greek web sites and documents, and if they are sufficient to extract a person's AMKA number for the AMKA web service [4]. Using these past results as a starting point, the work presented in this paper carries it a step forward. Our study is also related with the article [20], where various governmental open databases are discussed in terms of preserving citizen privacy. A similar study has been conducted by Simpson [25] for the UK government repository, `data.gov.uk`, showing how public data can be misused in terms of a privacy breach. Whang and Garcia-Molina [26] showed that adversaries can collect various private data from diverse sources and combine them resulting in a more precise piece of information for individuals. They proposed a model that can quantify the amount of a person's information leakage from a collection of data sources.

Personally Identifiable Information (PII) are present not only in the text of a document, but also to its embedded metadata. The first work investigating the problem was conducted by Byers [15] where Microsoft Word documents were crawled on the Web and searched for hidden words or deleted SSNs within document metadata. Gessiou et al. [18] collected over 10 million Microsoft Office documents from Google using synthesized queries. Using information present only on document metadata (such as documents contributors), constructed the relation graph of document contributors and searched Twitter to investigate whether such relationships are retained on social networks. Aura et al. [12] implemented a tool capable of identifying PII in documents that can potentially be used for tracing document authors or organizations. The tool automatically harvests sensitive information using heuristics from the user's computer, and searches for their presence in a collection of documents. Our work focuses on the document's context instead. In particular, we focus on documents like hiring lists or public documents uploaded on the Diavgeia repository to extract sensitive information like Identification Card Number and associate it with their respective owners. Narayanan and Shmatikov [23] denote that typical de-identification techniques are not sufficient for privacy, as information that distinguish one person from another (commercial transactions, browsing and search histories) can be used to re-identify anonymous data. They discuss that privacy cannot be guaranteed solely by anonymizing the data, but rather by enforcing policies concerning their usage.

A rich source of Personally Identifiable Information are social networks. Mao et al. [22] indicated that users can inadvertently release sensitive information to the public, such as vacation plans or disclosure of one's medical condition. Authors showed how a miscreant count leverage such information to perform automated attack on specific victims. Krisnamurthy et al. [21] showed that social networks can leak PII of their users to third-parties, like ad services. Wondracek et al. [27] introduced an attack to deanonymize social network users. They indicated that memberships to groups of a user can act as a fingerprint and can be exploited using history stealing attacks.

7 Conclusion

In this paper we discussed ways that information from multiple government sites or lists available on-line may be combined to create profiles of Greek citizens. As this sensitive information is publicly available, a miscreant may exploit it for malevolent purposes. Furthermore, ethical questions arise from the publication of this type of sensitive information. We looked at specific examples related to terrorism, identity theft, stalking, and spam, but these are only the obvious cases of the unauthorised use of the information provided by state institutions. As more private data are released on the Internet, there will be many more novel abuses of this information.

Acknowledgments. This work was supported in part by the project ForToo, funded by the Directorate-General for Home Affairs under Grant Agreement No. HOME/2010/ISEC/AG/INT-002 and by FP7 project SysSec, funded by the European Commission under Grant Agreement No. 257007.

References

1. http://www.amka.gr/odigos4.html
2. http://www.asep.gr/asep/site/home/Tabs/
   autepistasia/autepistasia-sub1.csp
3. 11888.gr (Greek Phone Catalogue), http://11888.ote.gr/web/guest/home
4. AMKA Web Service, https://www.amka.gr/AMKAGR/
5. Charitable Work Programme, http://www.epanad.gov.gr/
6. Diavgeia Document Repository, http://diavgeia.gov.gr

7. Greek Elections 2012 - Ministry of Interior,
   http://ekloges.ypes.gr/v2012b/public/
8. Greek Electorate Web Service, http://www.ypes.gr/services/eea/eea.htm
9. Hellenic Statistical Authority, http://www.statistics.gr
10. UltraCl@rity - Search in the depths of the Cl@rity program,
    http://www.yperdiavgeia.gr
11. VAT Registration Numbers Web Service, http://www.gsis.gr/wsnp/wsnp.html
12. Aura, T., Kuhn, T.A., Roe, M.: Scanning Electronic Documents for Personally
    Identifiable Information. In: Proceedings of the 5th Annual ACM Workshop on
    Privacy in the Electronic Society. ACM (2006)
13. Berghel, H.: Identity Theft, Social Security Numbers, and the Web. Communica-
    tions of the ACM 43(2), 17–21 (2000)
14. Bowen, B.M., Hershkop, S., Keromytis, A.D., Stolfo, S.J.: Baiting Inside At-
    tackers Using Decoy Documents. In: Chen, Y., Dimitriou, T.D., Zhou, J. (eds.)
    SecureComm 2009. LNICST, vol. 19, pp. 51–70. Springer, Heidelberg (2009)
15. Byers, S.: Information Leakage Caused by Hidden Data in Published Documents.
    Security & Privacy 2(2), 23–27 (2004)
16. Garfinkel, S.: Risks of Social Security Numbers. Communications of the
    ACM 38(10), 146 (1995)
17. Gessiou, E., Labrinidis, A., Ioannidis, S.: A Greek (privacy) Tragedy: The Intro-
    duction of Social Security Numbers in Greece. In: Proceedings of the 8th Annual
    ACM Workshop on Privacy in the Electronic Society. ACM (2009)
18. Gessiou, E., Volanis, S., Athanasopoulos, E., Markatos, E.P., Ioannidis, S.: Digging
    up Social Structures from Documents on the Web. In: Proceedings of the Global
    Communications Conference (GLOBECOM). IEEE (2012)
19. Glenn, S.: Marijuana bust shines light on utilities,
    http://www.postandcourier.com/article/20120129/PC1602/301299979
    (January 29, 2012)
20. Keenan, T.P.: Are They Making Our Privates Public?–Emerging Risks of Govern-
    mental Open Data Initiatives. In: Camenisch, J., Crispo, B., Fischer-Hübner, S.,
    Leenes, R., Russello, G. (eds.) Privacy and Identity 2011. IFIP AICT, vol. 375,
    pp. 1–13. Springer, Heidelberg (2012)
21. Krishnamurthy, B., Wills, C.E.: On the Leakage of Personally Identifiable Infor-
    mation via Online Social Networks. In: Proceedings of the 2nd ACM Workshop on
    Online Social Networks. ACM (2009)
22. Mao, H., Shuai, X., Kapadia, A.: Loose Tweets: An Analysis of Privacy leaks on
    Twitter. In: Proceedings of the 10th Annual ACM Workshop on Privacy in the
    Electronic Society. ACM (2011)
23. Narayanan, A., Shmatikov, V.: Myths and Fallacies of Personally Identifiable In-
    formation. Communications of the ACM 53(6), 24–26 (2010)
24. Polakis, I., Kontaxis, G., Antonatos, S., Gessiou, E., Petsas, T., Markatos, E.P.:
    Using Social Networks to Harvest Email Addresses. In: Proceedings of the 9th
    Annual ACM Workshop on Privacy in the Electronic Society. ACM (2010)
25. Simpson, A.: On Privacy and Public Data: A study of data.gov.uk. Journal of
    Privacy and Confidentiality 3(1), 4 (2011)
26. Whang, S.E., Garcia-Molina, H.: A model for Quantifying Information Leakage. In:
    Jonker, W., Petković, M. (eds.) SDM 2012. LNCS, vol. 7482, pp. 25–44. Springer,
    Heidelberg (2012)
27. Wondracek, G., Holz, T., Kirda, E., Kruegel, C.: A Practical Attack to De-
    Anonymize Social Network Users. In: Proceedings of 2010 IEEE Symposium on
    Security and Privacy (2010)

Security and Privacy in Video Surveillance: Requirements and Challenges*

Qasim Mahmood Rajpoot and Christian Damsgaard Jensen

Department of Applied Mathematics & Computer Science
Technical University of Denmark
DK-2800 Kgs. Lyngby, Denmark
{qara,cdje}@dtu.dk

Abstract. Use of video surveillance has substantially increased in the last few decades. Modern video surveillance systems are equipped with techniques that allow traversal of data in an effective and efficient manner, giving massive powers to operators and potentially compromising the privacy of anyone observed by the system. Several techniques to protect the privacy of individuals have therefore been proposed, but very little research work has focused on the specific security requirements of video surveillance data (in transit or in storage) and on authorizing access to this data. In this paper, we present a general model of video surveillance systems that will help identify the major security and privacy requirements for a video surveillance system and we use this model to identify practical challenges in ensuring the security of video surveillance data in all stages (in transit and at rest). Our study shows a gap between the identified security requirements and the proposed security solutions where future research efforts may focus in this domain.

Keywords: Video Surveillance, Security, Privacy, Monitoring, Storage, Access Control, Encryption.

1 Introduction

Video surveillance is often considered one of the first applications of pervasive computing [1]. Its usage has significantly increased over the last two decades, firstly due to continuously decreasing hardware costs including camera, storage or networking and secondly due to the increased sense of insecurity caused by incidents like 9/11 and the Madrid and London bombings.

Traditional video surveillance systems are either simple recording systems or they are monitored by human observers without automated technological assistance. This makes them very expensive in terms of installation and operation. They are mainly used as deterrents and the recordings help investigation once an incident has occurred. Compared to these traditional solutions, modern digital solutions are less expensive while offering much better quality. Modern systems make use of advanced techniques such as object-detection, -identification, -tracking and event-detection, exploiting algorithms

---

* The work presented in this paper is supported by a grant from the Danish National Advanced Technology Foundation.

N. Cuppens-Boulahia et al. (Eds.): SEC 2014, IFIP AICT 428, pp. 169–184, 2014.

from the fields of computer vision, image processing and pattern recognition [2]. These techniques potentially allow recognizing a target object e.g. a vehicle, or even automatically tracking an individual spanning over multiple areas in a surveillance network [1], with trivial effort. Having such systems installed throughout the major public places in a city, for example, at bus stops, in train stations, near ATMs, in shopping malls, streets, etc., may lead to a big brother society in which all the activities of an individual can be profiled, allowed legally by law enforcement authorities or performed out of curiosity by an operator. Doing so requires a significant amount of time and effort in traditional surveillance systems, so the privacy concerns are obviously much more serious in modern video surveillance systems compared to traditional ones.

Consequently, there have been a lot of research efforts on developing privacy enhancing technologies (PETs) in video surveillance during last few years. This is achieved by hiding privacy sensitive regions like faces by means of obfuscation [3] or scrambling [4]. However, little research has focused on effectively making use of these techniques in ensuring privacy and controlling access to the data [1], [5]. Similarly, little research is found in literature that addresses the security of video streams and the associated data while they are transmitted or stored. In this paper, we propose a general model of video surveillance to help identify a list of security and privacy requirements in a video surveillance system. We provide an overview of existing solutions proposed to fulfill the major requirements identified through our model and point out their problems. Our study identifies a potential gap where research efforts need to be put in by pointing out challenges that need to be considered while designing security solutions in this regard.

The rest of the paper is organized as follows. In section II, we present the architecture of a video surveillance system to help the reader understand the security and privacy requirements identified through our model in section III. An overview of privacy enhancing technologies is presented in section IV. We examine the existing work related to security requirements in video surveillance and outline the associated challenges in section V. Section VI concludes the paper.

2   Architecture of a Video Surveillance System

In this section we present a simplified architecture of a modern video surveillance system. The aim of this section is to give a brief overview of a video surveillance system, and its related issues, which serves as background to understand the model and the security and privacy requirements that we identify in the next section.

Modern video surveillance systems primarily use the internet as a channel to transfer data to intermediary servers, storage systems and the users. Such a system normally employs a network of several cameras which capture video data at their respective locations, as depicted in Fig. 1. This data is sent to the storage server responsible for securely storing the data. Depending on the application requirements, this could be a centralized or distributed storage solution. The data may be accessed by users, wishing to see the live or recorded data of a desired location, e.g. live video feeds are often sent to a special monitoring room, and this live or stored data may also be watched on hand-held devices or a workstation. We refer to such users as observers. The control unit handles access requests from the observers and allows them to access data as per the specified policy.

Consider the video surveillance system deployed at Technical University of Denmark (DTU). This system consists of several cameras which are employed on the entrances of different departments and in the parking lots. The captured data is continuously monitored manually, along with the technological assistance by the system which generates an alarm upon detection of an anomalous event e.g. crossing a fence or gate in a parking lot. The observers are associated with different areas in the university and on generation of an alarm they investigate closely what happened and call security, if required. The observers may access the data in the monitoring room or on their hand-held devices when they are approaching towards the place of incident. However, notice that the observers are normally pre-associated with the specific areas and are already granted access to watch videos of those areas, independent of the alarm generation. This static access control leads to privacy issues where observers are always allowed to access the data.

An alternative approach could make use of dynamic access control where access to data is granted to the nearest available mobile observers upon detection of an event. Considering the proportionate access principle, observers in the monitoring room may be given regular access with less privileges (low resolution) in normal situations and higher privileges in an emergency situation.

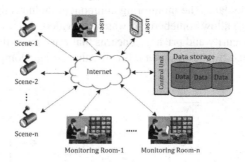

Fig. 1. Architecture of a video surveillance system

Allowing access of data to certain individuals only in case a specific event occurs or an emergency situation, addresses the privacy concerns raised because of continuous video surveillance. Using these techniques can prove to be immensely useful in public video surveillance too, conducted by Birmingham city council, for instance. In this video surveillance system, cameras are deployed in the major public places all over the city. Suppose there is a fire incident reported in the city center. Upon detection of this emergency situation, along with the observers assigned to this location, the nearest fire-brigade and police stations are also informed about the event and the system allows access of data to the respective employees of these stations. Allowing access to the video stream to the fire-brigade and police station would help them understand the severity of the situation and to come prepared with appropriate tools and man-power to better combat such situations. Although the system should allow advanced functionalities such as searching, tracking an individual and automatically identifying an individual, however, appropriate access control mechanisms must be adopted in order to minimize the chances of performing voyeurism by the observers, reduce privacy invasion and to make these systems widely acceptable.

3   Video Surveillance Model

In this section, we generalize the architecture, presented in Section 2, into an abstract model of video surveillance as a method to identify the manifold security and privacy requirements in a video surveillance system. Fundamentally, a video surveillance system must include elements to capture video, to store/record video and to display video to the users, as well as a mechanism to transport video data between these elements. Figure 2(a) shows the main elements of our model, which includes four components, namely: video capture, -transport, -monitoring, and -storage. The video capture component includes the cameras, their local infrastructure, and the area which can be captured by the cameras. Once the data is captured, it needs to be securely transported; this is typically done over the internet, so we have included this as a component in our model. It is important that video transport is done in a way that ensures the confidentiality and integrity of data while in-transit. The transport component considers transport of data from cameras to storage servers, between storage servers, and while watching either live- or stored video data. The monitoring component includes the different elements that are necessary to allow somebody to watch the video. The monitoring component must consider all security and privacy concerns that arise when the captured data (live or stored) is watched by the observers. Finally, the storage component is responsible

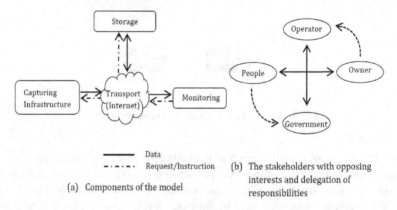

Fig. 2. Video surveillance model

for securely storing the data and restricting the access of stored data to the authorized individuals only. Monitoring includes any automatic or manual processing for the purpose of observing live or stored data, therefore when the stored data is watched by the observers, it falls under the monitoring component.

The four components identified in Fig. 2(a), allow us to identify the domain and scope for many of the security and privacy requirements that may arise in video surveillance systems. We do, however, also need to consider the different stakeholders and interests in order to identify all the security and privacy requirements in video surveillance systems. There are two principal stakeholders in all video surveillance systems, the owner, who commissions and is responsible for the system, and the people who are being watched by the system; these are shown as principal opposing forces in Fig. 2(b) In practice, however, normally owners do not operate the video surveillance systems themselves, but instead delegate this task to another organization, e.g. a guard company; this organization is referred as operator. Similarly, most people are unable to determine whether video surveillance is fair and warranted or excessive, so it is typically an elected government which regulates video surveillance through legislation and guidelines. This means that, in practice, the video surveillance operator and the government become the real opposing forces in a video surveillance system. The term observer used in the previous section holds a subset of responsibilities of the operator, as the operator may have additional responsibilities other than merely watching the video streams. For the sake of simplicity, we will use the term operator in rest of the paper.

People are the core of our model, because they may have certain expectations from each component of the video surveillance system, whereas the other entities strive to live up to the expectations of the people. It is the combined responsibility of the owner and the operator to ensure the security of the system and the privacy of the people as it is defined by the government. Privacy of people should be protected both from outside attackers and the personnel within the owner and operator organizations. The operator is responsible for performing his duties while being least intrusive as far as the privacy of people is concerned. Based on our model, requirements capturing consists of two stages. In the first stage, we map the requirements from the perspective of each of the stakeholders for each of the four components in the model. In the second stage, we remap these requirements in terms of privacy and security aspects. The first stage ensures that we identify the requirements that can be specified by the people and/or the government, owner and operator in the form of security and privacy related functionalities and features in the system.

Based on the requirements specified by the people/government, owner and operator, we then derive further requirements from the implementation point of view. For instance, the proportionate access requirement specified by the owner is divided into multiple requirements including data hiding, dynamic access control and voyeurism protection when looked in the implementation perspective. Table 1 presents the security and privacy requirements in video surveillance identified as a result of the first stage.

Based on our model, the first stage produces a large number of requirements. However, it contains certain overlapping and repetitive requirements too. This is because our model identifies each requirement in the perspective of the individual stakeholders. Thus in the second stage, we remap those requirements considering the conventional security and privacy aspects that allows us to combine the repetitive requirements together. Table 2 depicts this mapping. We briefly describe these requirements in greater details below.

Privacy

Consent and Signage: Consent of the people who can potentially be recorded by the video surveillance system needs to be taken in advance, either explicitly or implicitly.

Table 1. Security and privacy requirements in different phases of video surveillance corresponding to all the stakeholders. The last column derives implementation requirements from the ones
on left.

Phase/ Stakeholders	People/ Government	Owner	Operator	Implementation requirements
Capture	c1. Consent c2. Signage c3. Anonymity	c4. No data missing c5. Availability c6. Video properties	None	c7. Security of software and hardware infrastructure
Transport	t1. Confidential-ity t2. Integrity t3. Authenticity	t1. Confidential-ity t2. Integrity t3. Authenticity	None	t4. Camera authentication t5. Data encryption t6. Key management t7. No deletion of data
Monitoring	m1. Privacy safeguards m2. Authorized access m3. Public access to their data	m4. Continuous monitoring m5. Proportionate access m6. Occasional access m2. Authorized access	m7. Data freshness m8. Time-stamping m9. Easy to search	m10. Dynamic access control m11. Data hiding m12. Voyeurism protection m13. User management m8. Time-stamping
Storage	s1. Secure storage	s2. Secure data storage as per law s3. Deletion after retention period	None	s3. Deletion after retention period c7. Security of software and hard-ware infrastructure t2. Integrity t6. Key management

One way to take consent is by informing the people about video surveillance through
signage i.e. displaying clear and visible symbols in the area where video surveillance
takes place.

Anonymity, Data Hiding and Privacy Safeguards: While the system is supposed to monitor the behavior of the people, it should strive to maintain the *anonymity* of the people
by hiding their identity using certain *privacy safeguarding mechanisms*. Therefore the
system must implement *data hiding* techniques which obfuscate the identity-revealing
regions in the images when the operators monitor video streams in a normal situation.
Needless to say, these data hiding techniques should be reversible such that identity
could be revealed if required, for example while investigating a murder.

Video properties: The owner needs to determine whether cameras with advanced functionalities such as pan-tilt-zoom, night-vision and high-resolution are really required to
be used, with respect to the purpose of the surveillance conducted.

Voyeurism protection: In order to restrict voyeurism, advanced functionalities such as
searching, identifying and tracking an individual are only to be made available when an

Table 2. Remapping of the requirements in Table 1 in terms of privacy & security aspects

Components/ P&S Aspects		Capture	Transport	Monitoring	Storage
Privacy	**1. Privacy**	*1a.* Consent (c1) *1b.* Signage (c2) *1c.* Anonymity (c3) *1d.* Video properties (c6)	None	*1e.* Privacy safeguards (m1) *1f.* Data hiding (m11) *1g.* Voyeurism protection (m12) *1c.* Anonymity (c3)	*1g.* Voyeurism protection (m12)
Security	**2. Confidentiality**	Covered by 7a, below	*2a.* Data encryption (t5) *2b.* Key management (t6)	None	*2a.* Data encryption (t5) *2b.* Key manageent (t6)
	3. Integrity	Covered by 7a, below	*3a.* No deletion of data (t7) *3b.* Integrity (t3)	*3c.* Data freshness (m7)	*3b.* Integrity (t3)
	4. Authenticity	Covered by 7a, below	*4a.* Camera authentication (t4) *4b.* Time-stamping (m8)	*4b.* Time-stamping (m8)	None
	5. Availability	*5a.* No data missing (c4)	None	*5b.* Fast search (m9) *5c.* Continuous monitoring (m4)	Covered by 7a, below
	6. Access authorization	None	None	*6a.* Authorized access (m2) *6b.* Public access to their data (m3) *6c.* Occasional access (m6) *6d.* Dynamic access control (m10) *6e.* User management (m13) *6f.* Logging (m14) *6g.* Proportionate access (m5)	None
	7. Others	*7a.* Security of software and hardware infrastructure (c7)	None	None	*7a.* Security of software and hardware infrastructure (c7) *7b.* Deletion after retention period (s3)

operator explicitly requests them. While granting these privileges the system logs the request along with the information about the circumstances.

Confidentiality

The people and owner desire that the data is accessible only to the intended recipients. *Confidentiality* ensures privacy protection against outsiders mainly when data is in transit, whereas *privacy* is a much broader concept that covers privacy protection against insiders too. *Confidentiality* can be ensured by using appropriate *encryption algorithms* and taking care of *key management* issues. Because of the nature of the system, the encryption mechanism should be efficient enough enabling the data to reach the other end in real-time.

Integrity

Any unauthorized change in the data should be detectable. Appropriate measures should be taken to ensure the *integrity* of data. Moreover, it should not be possible to *delete chunks of data* while leaving other data intact so as to hide the data captured in a specific time interval.

Authenticity

Camera authentication: In order to ensure the authenticity of the captured data, each camera may be required to authenticate itself to the server.
Data freshness: The operator requires newly captured data in live streaming rather than previously captured data being replayed. *Time-stamping:* The recorded data must include verifiable time-stamping helping to ensure that the data was captured at a specific time and also to search videos specifying the time interval later on.

Availability

The services offered by the system should of course be *available* when needed. If surveillance takes place upon detection of an event e.g. motion detection then such a mechanism is to be made perfectly reliable such that no event goes uncaptured i.e. *data missing should not be possible.*
Continuous monitoring: The owner requires that the captured data is continuously monitored manually and/or by using automated tools.
Easy search: The operators require that advanced functionalities such as searching, identifying and tracking an individual are available whenever required so they can effectively perform their duties.

Access Authorization

Public access to their data: Certain countries, for example Canada and France, allow an individual to watch their own images captured by the surveillance system. Therefore, people should be able to get access to the images containing them, through a predefined procedure.
Proportionate access: In order to protect the privacy of people, the owner requires that the proportionate access principle is implemented in the system and that the operators are given the minimum access to the data required to fulfill their duties. This can be achieved by implementing dynamic access control.
Dynamic Access Control: The system must take the context pertinent to a situation into account when authorizing access to data so that different access levels (e.g. blurred,

original images) are maintained in different situations (e.g. normal, emergency) and privacy of people is preserved to the maximum extent. In short, the access level should change appropriately depending upon the situation.

User management: This involves all the issues related to the users of the system including user enrollment, permission assignment, changing permissions, permission revocation, user deletion etc.

Occasional access: As explained in section 2, occasional access to the data might need to be given to certain public organizations; the system needs to build a mechanism to enable such access.

Occasional access: As explained in section 2, occasional access to the data might need to be given to certain public organizations; the system needs to build a mechanism to enable such access.

Logging: All activities performed by the operators should be securely logged, especially those permissions requested explicitly.

Others

Deletion after retention period: Depending upon the regulations of the region where video surveillance takes place, the captured data must be automatically deleted as soon as the retention period expires.

Security of software and hardware infrastructure: It is to be ensured that the security of the underlying infrastructure is well protected against the attacks exploiting software vulnerabilities or physical access to the hardware.

Considering the concerns of each party involved to maintain security and privacy, it is reasonable to expect that our model has identified a comprehensive set of requirements, though a complete set of requirements is not guaranteed. As mentioned previously, there exists a large amount of work on protecting privacy in video surveillance. The next section briefly summarizes the major types of available techniques for protecting privacy, followed by the state of the art of security research in video surveillance system and the associated challenges.

4   Privacy in Video Surveillance

A pervasive video surveillance system may be exploited by the operators for unauthorized collection of data on the activities of an individual [6]. In the United Kingdom, a report discovered that operators have used video surveillance for voyeurism [7]. In another report by the BBC, council workers in Liverpool spied on a womans apartment using a CCTV street camera. Possibilities for such misuse are further increased with the advent of modern video surveillance systems that facilitate rapid data retrieval enabled by indexing and searching and advanced imaging technology allowing high-resolution and zooming-in. Moreover, pervasive surveillance networks may enable linking the activities of a target in multiple video streams [1].

Considering the above-mentioned issues, several techniques to protect the privacy of the observed individuals have been proposed. In order to hide the identity of observed subjects, identity revealing sensitive areas are first determined and then removed or de-identified depending upon the approach used. Several types of techniques to hide privacy-sensitive areas have been proposed. A simple technique is to fully remove the sensitive regions but this not only hides the identity but in some cases also the behavior, see for example [8] [9] [10]. Another type of approach is to reduce the level of detail of privacy-sensitive areas, with the help of blurring or pixilation, leaving the subject unidentifiable yet the behavior remains recognizable, [3] [11] [12] to name only a few. The third approach, called abstraction, is to remove the sensitive regions and replace them with dummy objects such as silhouettes or skeletons. Some of the key works in this area are [5] [13] [14]. Yet another technique proposed in literature, called scrambling, is to encrypt the sensitive regions with a key allowing the area to be decrypted only by authorized personnel possessing the key, see for instance [4] [15] [16]. As compared to other techniques, this approach offers the benefit of perfectly reconstructing the original image.

This section explored the major privacy enhancing techniques in order to enable us to identify the research gaps, in the next section. Addressing the identified research gaps may also need to exploit these techniques while suggesting new security and access control mechanisms.

5 Security in Video Surveillance

A study of the relevant literature so far, reveals that many solutions, discussed below, addressing the security requirements including integrity, authentication and confidentiality have been proposed in multimedia systems e.g. video on demand and business video conferencing. However the factors involved in video surveillance systems are quite different than multimedia systems hence these solutions cannot be directly applied in video surveillance systems, although a few commonalities exist.

Due to the communication over public networks, the security aspects are to be addressed when data is transferred from camera to server, server-to-server and server to handheld devices or monitoring room. We discuss here why the security requirements in video surveillance systems are important and identify the challenges to be addressed when designing security solutions for them.

Integrity and Authenticity

An important security consideration is integrity protection and authentication of recorded video data. This is important for two reasons [17]: i) to accept the recordings as evidence in a court of law, and ii) to avoid framing an individual by tempering with the recordings of a crime scene, for example. Two major techniques to address integrity exist [18]: using cryptographic hash functions along with digital signatures or by making use of watermarks in the video recordings. Solutions proposed in multimedia systems mostly use cryptographic techniques [18] [19]. The integrity protection solution is desired to be robust against certain modifications such as scaling and compression and images should be verifiable despite such benign modifications [19]. In order to ensure authenticity, cameras need to authenticate themselves to the server. Some of the key solutions proposed in this respect require to use Trusted Platform Module in each camera [20] [21] [22]. This approach is prohibitively expensive. Furthermore, performance and scalability remain issues to be resolved too.

Confidentiality

Similar to integrity and authentication, there are several solutions presented for confidentiality mainly targeting multimedia applications [23] [24] [25]. In order to fulfill these requirements, the existing solutions essentially use cryptography. However, the conventional cryptographic algorithms used in these solutions are not especially designed to encrypt video data [26]. Their usage on video data, although compressed, requires significant processing power, for instance, an MPEG-2 video stream requires a bit rate ranging between 4 to 9 Mbps [27]. Because of the huge amount of data and real-time requirement, efficient usage of cryptography is far from the desired efficiency level in conventional multimedia applications [26], whereas its usage in video surveillance introduces further challenges. In video surveillance systems, unlike multimedia applications, there are several video producers (cameras) with limited processing capabilities. A major challenge, therefore, is to devise encryption algorithms which may efficiently encrypt the large amounts of continuously produced video data, transferred in real-time to the server side, by the cameras. Another relevant issue is key management. Along with encrypting the data from each camera with a different key, the keys may also need to differ for each chunk of data, for instance different key for each 24 hours of data recorded by a camera.

A few solutions addressing confidentiality in video surveillance systems have been proposed in [28] [29] [30]. In order to protect the privacy of individuals and to ensure efficient retrieval of data, modern video surveillance systems extract metadata such as object identification, number of objects and the object types contained in the video streams in real-time [2]. This data is normally extracted at the server, therefore the server must be able to access decrypted data. Solutions proposed in [28] and [30] fail to consider this aspect and share the keys among operators requiring them to collaborate when data is to be decrypted. Another reason for the server to access plain data contents is to be able to send modified video streams (low resolution, obfuscated privacy regions) to different users depending on their access authorization, discussed later in this section. Once metadata has been extracted at the server, another interesting research issue is to securely store the data along with the associated metadata in a manner that it is possible to efficiently retrieve metadata and its associated video streams later, based on query language, for example.

Access Authorization

Another important challenge which we believe requires major research effort is access authorization in video surveillance systems. Controlling the access to data is of critical importance, as the potential capabilities offered by modern video surveillance systems such as searching for an individual or an event, and monitoring the activities of an individual spanning over multiple locations [1], makes it very easy to invade the privacy of individuals. Clearly video surveillance is expected to become more pervasive and this leaves us with only two choices: either entrust the operators or to devise a mechanism for watching the watchers and minimizing the chances to use such systems abusively [31].

Similar to the above-mentioned security requirements, there exist several solutions regarding access control mechanisms for online and other payment-based video databases such as [32] [33] [34]. Bertino et al. [32] argue that an effective and efficient access control mechanism in video databases requires advancements in extraction of meaningful metadata, furthermore, such mechanism must take benefit of the indexing structure used to store the video data. This is even more important in video surveillance systems as the access control mechanisms are to be applied to live video streams, continuously produced by several cameras, in real-time. With advancements in indexing and metadata extraction techniques in video databases, we believe that the research efforts now need to focus on devising access authorization techniques for video surveillance systems.

There are only a few research attempts that address the challenge of access authorization in video surveillance. Senior et al. [5] present the idea of using multiple privacy levels in video surveillance systems where different operators are provided different levels of information and actions to be performed, depending on the access privileges of the operator. Different information levels may include for example access to behavioral information where objects are replaced with silhouettes. Similarly different levels of actions to be performed include restrictions over playback, zooming-in and searching functions, offered by the system. The authors suggest using a privacy-preserving console manager that makes use of encryption and access control mechanisms and reveals the data to the operator by extracting information components from video streams as per the authorization level of the operator. In order to use this approach, a large-scale video surveillance system requires a sophisticated access control model. However, the paper presents only the concept without providing details of the privacy-preserving console manager, encryption and access authorization.

Moncrieff et al. [1] argue that using static security policies in video surveillance is either too intrusive for privacy or it hinders the usability of the system. They identify the challenge of utilizing the video surveillance system by exposing sufficient need-specific data to the operators while preserving the privacy of people. The authors suggest that one possible way of protecting privacy in video surveillance while retaining its useful functionality is to use dynamic access control mechanisms. They propose to incorporate the context of the requestor in the access authorization, where privacy is maintained using data hiding techniques in normal situations, whereas a request to data in certain situations, e.g. emergency cases, would enable the operators to access full information with less focus on protecting privacy. Similar to [5], this paper also does not provide an access control mechanism. The main contribution of this paper is presenting the idea of dynamic access control in video surveillance while leaving the designing of dynamic access control model as a goal to be achieved in future research. Our model emphasizes this challenge and demands that the context of requestor is taken into consideration while granting the access.

To the best of our knowledge, no comprehensive access control mechanism in video surveillance has been proposed. An access control model proposed by Thuraisingham et al. [35] makes use of metadata extracted from the video streams. It presents a grammar that allows referring to video streams by the information contained within them, such as timestamp, location, events occurred and objects. Access privileges for operators can be specified using predefined credential expression templates based on their id, group and/or a set of credentials. The solution, however, offers a static access control model and does not allow the access privileges of an operator to be changed dynamically based on the changing context.

Finally, in a large-scale video surveillance systems requiring occasional access by multiple public organizations such as the police and fire-brigade, management of users is also a challenge. This may require using federated identity management allowing each participating organization to manage its own users. Existing federated identity and access management solutions like SAML [36] and WS-Federation [37] may be investigated for this purpose.

Table 3 provides a list of future challenges in security of video surveillance systems. Each challenge refers to the related requirements given in Table 2. Based on our model and the discussion, it is evident that many security requirements in video surveillance systems still require further research in this domain. Certain privacy requirements are dependent on some security requirements as a result it is not possible to effectively ensure privacy without the security requirements being addressed. Protecting the privacy of individuals without compromising the functionality of the system demands an access control mechanism that makes use of privacy enhancing technologies in order to hide the privacy sensitive regions in the video frames while making them available when required. Clearly there exists a gap demanding further research in this domain in order to satisfy the security requirements in video surveillance systems and to increase their acceptability in society.

Table 3. Future research challenges in security of video surveillance systems

Security aspect	Future research challenges
1. Confidentiality	*1.1.* Novel efficient real-time encryption algorithms for large-scale video data from multiple sources (2a) *1.2.* Duration-specific key management techniques for data produced by several cameras (2b) *1.3.* Secure storage of video data and the associated metadata while enabling efficient retrieval (5b, 6a)
2. Integrity & Authenticity	*2.1.* Integrity protection solutions having robustness against benign modifications (3b, 3c) *2.2.* Scalable and efficient authenticity mechanisms for large-scale video surveillance data (4a, 4b)
3. Access authorization	*3.1.* Multiple privacy levels in the video surveillance data, making use of existing privacy enhancing techniques, with each level accessible to different access privileges (1c, 1e, 1f, 6g) *3.2.* Dynamic access control that enable preserving the privacy of people yet exposing maximum data to the operators when needed (6a, 6c, 6d, 6g) *3.3.* Novel access control mechanisms utilizing the indexing structure of video data and the extracted metadata (6a, 6b) *3.4.* Federated identity and access management solutions for access authorization of video surveillance data (6c, 6e)

6   Conclusion

Modern video surveillance systems provide an effective mechanism to combat security threats. Advanced functionalities offered by these systems, however, greatly threaten the privacy of the individuals under surveillance. Aside from protecting privacy from outside attackers by securing the video streams using cryptographic mechanisms, it is equally important to protect the privacy of individuals from the insider personnel involved in monitoring surveillance data. We identify the security and privacy requirements in a video surveillance system and outline a number of challenges and directions for future research to accomplish these requirements. Our study unveils that existing solutions for security and access authorization in multimedia systems cannot be used in video surveillance hence further research efforts are required to devise security solutions in video surveillance. We have also outlined the further research challenges to be solved for ensuring the security of video surveillance systems.

References

1. Moncrieff, S., Svetha, V., Geoff, A.W.: Dynamic Privacy in Public Surveillance. Journal of Computer 42, 22–28 (2009)
2. Hampapur, A.: Smart Video Surveillance for Proactive Security. IEEE Signal Processing Magazine 25, 136 (2008)
3. Saini, M.K., Atrey, P.K., Mehrotra, S., Kankanhalli, M.S.: Privacy Aware Publication of Surveillance Video. International Journal of Trust Management in Computing and Communications 1, 23–51 (2013)
4. Frederic, D., Ebrahimi, T.: Scrambling for Privacy Protection in Video Surveillance Systems. IEEE Transactions on Circuits and Systems for Video Technology 18, 1168–1174 (2008)
5. Senior, A., Sharath, P., Arun, H., Lisa, B., Ying-Li, T., Ahmet, E., Jonathan, C., Chiao, F.S., Max, L.: Enabling Video Privacy Through Computer Vision. Journal of Security & Privacy 3, 50–57 (2005)
6. Cavallaro, A.: Privacy in Video Surveillance. IEEE Signal Processing Magazine 24, 168–169 (2007)
7. Norris, C., Armstrong, G.: The Maximum Surveillance Society. Berg (1999)
8. Criminisi, A., Perez, P., Toyama, K.: Object Removal by Exemplar-Based Inpainting. In: 13th IEEE Computer Visioin and Pattern Recognition, pp. 721–728. IEEE (2003)
9. Criminisi, A., Prez, P., Toyama, K.: Region Filling and Object Removal by Exemplar-Based Image Inpainting. IEEE Transactions on Image Processing 13, 1200–1212 (2004)
10. Tang, F., Ying, Y., Wang, J., Peng, Q.: A novel texture synthesis based algorithm for object removal in photographs. In: Maher, M.J. (ed.) ASIAN 2004. LNCS, vol. 3321, pp. 248–258. Springer, Heidelberg (2004)
11. Schiff, J., Meingast, M., Mulligan, D.K., Sastry, S., Goldberg, K.: Respectful cameras: Detecting visual markers in real-time to address privacy concerns. In: Senior, A. (ed.) Protecting Privacy in Video Surveillance, pp. 65–89. Springer (2009)
12. Yu, X., Chinomi, K., Koshimizu, T., Nitta, N., Ito, Y., Babaguchi, N.: Privacy Protecting Visual Processing for Secure Video Surveillance. In: 15th IEEE International Conference on Image Processing, pp. 1672–1675. IEEE (2008)
13. Haritaoglu, I., Harwood, D., Davis, L.S.: W4: Real-Time Surveillance of People and their Activities. IEEE Transactions on Pattern Analysis and Machine Intelligence 22, 809–830 (2000)
14. Koshimizu, T., Toriyama, T., Babaguchi, N.: Factors on the Sense of Privacy in Video Surveillance. In: 3rd ACM Workshop on Continuous Archival and Retrieval of Personal Experiences, pp. 35–44. ACM (2006)
15. Boult, T.E.: Pico: Privacy through Invertible Cryptographic Obscuration. In: IEEE Computer Vision for Interactive and Intelligent Environment, pp. 27–38. IEEE (2005)

16. Carrillo, P., Kalva, H., Magliveras, S.: Compression Independent Object Encryption for Ensuring Privacy in Video Surveillance. In: 9th IEEE International Conference on Multimedia and Expo, pp. 273–276. IEEE (2008)

17. Atrey, P.K., Yan, W., Kankanhalli, M.S.: A Scalable Signature Scheme for Video Authentication. Journal of Multimedia Tools and Applications 34, 107–135 (2007)

18. Schneider, M., Chang, S.: A Robust Content Based Digital Signature for Image Authentication. In: International Conference on Image Processing, pp. 227–230 (1996)

19. Sun, Q., He, D., Tian, Q.: A Secure and Robust Authentication Scheme for Video Transcoding. IEEE Transactions on Circuits and Systems for Video Technology 16, 1232–1244 (2006)

20. Winkler, T., Rinner, B.: Securing Embedded Smart Cameras with Trusted Computing. EURASIP Journal on Wireless Communications and Networking 2011, 20 (2011)

21. Winkler, T., Rinner, B.: TrustCAM: Security and Privacy-Protection for an Embedded Smart Camera Based on Trusted Computing. In: 7th IEEE Advanced Video and Signal Based Surveillance, pp. 593–600. IEEE (2010)

22. Winkler, T., Rinner, B.: A Systematic Approach Towards User-Centric Privacy and Security for Smart Camera Networks. In: 4th ACM/IEEE International Conference on Distributed Smart Cameras, pp. 133–141. ACM (2010)

23. Liu, X., Ahmet, M.E.: Selective Encryption of Multimedia Content in Distribution Networks: Challenges and New Directions. In: 2nd IASTED Conference on Communications, Internet & Information Technology (2003)

24. Liu, F., König, H.: Puzzle - A Novel Video Encryption Algorithm. In: Dittmann, J., Katzenbeisser, S., Uhl, A. (eds.) CMS 2005. LNCS, vol. 3677, pp. 88–97. Springer, Heidelberg (2005)

25. Socek, D., Magliveras, S., Marques, O., Kalva, H., Furht, B.: Digital Video Encryption Algorithms Based on Correlation-Preserving Permutations. EURASIP Journal on Information Security (2007)

26. Liu, F., Hartmut, K.: A Survey of Video Encryption Algorithms. Journal of computers & security 29, 3–15 (2010)

27. Haskell, B.G., Puri, A., Netravali, A.N.: Digital Video: An Introduction to MPEG-2. Kluwer Academic Publishers (1998)

28. Schaffer, M., Schartner, P.: Video Surveillance: A Distributed Approach to Protect Privacy. In: Dittmann, J., Katzenbeisser, S., Uhl, A. (eds.) CMS 2005. LNCS, vol. 3677, pp. 140–149. Springer, Heidelberg (2005)

29. Liu, Z., Peng, D., Zheng, Y., Liu, J.: Communication Protection in IP-Based Video Surveillance Systems. In: 7th IEEE International Symposium on Multimedia, pp. 69–78. IEEE (2005)

30. Castiglione, A., Cepparulo, M., De Santis, A., Palmieri, F.: Towards a Lawfully Secure and Privacy Preserving Video Surveillance System. In: Buccafurri, F., Semeraro, G. (eds.) EC-Web 2010. LNBIP, vol. 61, pp. 73–84. Springer, Heidelberg (2010)

31. Brin, D.: The Transparent Society: Will Technology Force Us to Choose Between Privacy and Freedom. Perseus Publishing (1999)

32. Bertino, E., Fan, J., Ferrari, E., Hacid, M., Elmagarmid, A.K., Zhu, X.: A Hierarchical Access Control Model for Video Database Systems. ACM Transactions on Information Systems 21, 155–191 (2003)

33. Bertino, E., Moustafa, A.H., Walid, A.G., Elmagarmid, A.K.: An Access Control Model for Video Database Systems. In: 9th International Conference on Information and Knowledge Management, pp. 336–343. ACM (2000)

34. Pan, L., Zhang, C.N.: A Web-Based Multilayer Access Control Model for Multimedia Applications in MPEG-7. International Journal of Network Security 4, 155–165 (2007)

35. Thuraisingham, B., Lavee, G., Bertino, E., Fan, J., Khan, L.: Access Control, Confidentiality and Privacy for Video Surveillance Databases. In: 11th ACM Symposium on Access Control Models and Technologies, pp. 1–10. ACM (2006)
36. Security Assertion Markup Language, OASIS Standard, http://saml.xml.org/wiki/saml-introduction
37. Web Services Federation Language (WS-Federation) Version 1.2, http://docs.oasis-open.org/wsfed/federation/v1.2/os/ws-federation-1.2-spec-os.html

Playing Hide and Seek
with Mobile Dating Applications

Guojun Qin, Constantinos Patsakis, and Mélanie Bouroche

Distributed Systems Group, School of Computer Science & Statistics,
Trinity College, Dublin, Ireland

Abstract. Recently, a wide range of dating applications has emerged
for users of smart mobile devices. Besides allowing people to socialize
with others who share the same interests, these applications use the location services of these devices to provide localized mapping of users. A
user is given an approximation of his proximity to other users, making
the application more attractive by increasing the chances of local interactions. While many applications provide an obfuscated location of the
user, several others prefer to provide quantifiable results.

This paper illustrates that the user's location can be disclosed, with
various degree of approximation, despite the obfuscation attempts. Ex-
perimenting with four of these applications, namely MoMo, WeChat,
SKOUT and Plenty of Fish, we show that an attacker can easily bypass
the fuzziness of the results provided, resulting in the full disclosure of a
victim's location, whenever it is connected.

Keywords: Location privacy, online social networks, information reve-
lation, geosocial networks.

1 Introduction

Modern smartphones are more than just mobile phones. Due to their processing resources they are closer to mobile information systems that have access to
the Internet and are location-aware, either through an embedded GPS module or through network resources. Quickly, all major social networks ported
their applications to these new devices. Soon afterwards, a new species evolved,
the location-based social networks, often also referred to as geosocial networks
(GSNs). These applications are enriching the widely-used online social networks
with location-based services. By exploiting the location awareness of users or
their knowledge of proximity to points of interest, these applications are providing more fine-grained and personalised services to their users.

It is clear that this shift has not only created a whole new market, but simultaneously has drastically changed the way in which people regard their location
privacy. While almost three quarters (74%) of adult smartphone owners use their
phones to get directions or other information based on their current location [1],
their trust in the provided privacy is not that high. This can be understood by
the number of users concerned about location sharing privacy, as the sharing of

N. Cuppens-Boulahia et al. (Eds.): SEC 2014, IFIP AICT 428, pp. 185–196, 2014.

their location could be abused to disclose more sensitive personal information, such as home addresses and user identities. Similarly, another 58% of all teens have downloaded applications to their cell phone or tablet computer and 51% of teen applications users have avoided certain applications due to privacy concerns [2]. Moreover, 46% of teen applications users have turned off tracking features on their cell phone or in an application and 26% of teen applications users have uninstalled an application because they were worried about the privacy of their information.

Those research reports clearly illustrate that the privacy of location-based services is a serious concern for most smart devices users. In the past few years, many researchers have proposed several solutions to preserve users' location privacy such as location k-anonymity and cloaking granularity [3–6]. However, the location privacy threats in digital life are changing as the popularity of mobile and online dating applications is growing. According to another report, 11% of Internet users have personally used an online dating site and 7% of cell phone applications users have used a mobile dating application [7]. Additionally, 40% of online daters have used a site or an application for people with shared interests or backgrounds. The dating applications typically not only share users' pictures and interests, but also the distance between users. The latter manages to enhance even more the engagement of users to the application, as they feel that they can really meet other users, and that potentially interesting other users are in their vicinity.

The fact that users can know almost in real-time their distance to other users, motivated us to investigate whether and to what extend this feature could be used to trace other users' location, and the effort required. Our hypothesis is that these applications can provide a reliable metric, or that certain pattern would emerge which an adversary can exploit to track down a user's actual location by using simple and widely-used trilateration algorithms. It is clear that if a malicious user has more background knowledge, other users' sensitive information such as their real identities, home and work locations might be revealed as well.

The rest of this paper is organised as follows. In the next section we provide an overview of the related work, mainly focusing on attacks on online social networks and geosocial networks. In Section 3 we describe how trilateration works and Section 4 is devoted to the experimental results. We describe how we generated the experimental environment along with the individual results and impact for four of the most widely used applications of this field. In Section 5 we discuss possible counter measures that would prevent such attacks. Finally the article concludes in Section 6 with a brief summary and ideas for future work.

2   Related Work

Due to the wide use of Online Social Networks (OSN), many attacks have emerged targeting their users or even the OSN infrastructure. An adversary may try to manipulate users in many ways, either using shared information, social engineering or even by creating malicious applications [8].

In many instances, OSNs are used to harvest user email addresses and send them spam messages [9–12]. Going a step further than spam, malicious users might launch phishing attacks, which have better click-through rates than typical spamming as reported in [13]. The "freemium" model under which the vast majority of OSNs operate, allows users to easily create multiple accounts, launching what is known as sybil attacks [14]. The goals of the adversary typically vary and range from a simple voting scenario to a de-anonymization attack [15]. A malicious user can also launch an attack to the reputation of a user [16], usually anonymously, or try to extort the victim with the gathered information.

Overall, information about the user location can be inferred from OSNs and be exploited in many malicious ways[1], however, the location awareness opens up the possibility for even more attacks. For instance, based on collected location data, the home and work location of users or even their identities can be recovered [17–20].

Similar attacks can be launched from geospacial networks [21–23]. Nevertheless, even if some solutions have already been proposed [24], they have not been adopted. The interested reader may also refer to [25–27].

3   Trilateration Attack

The trilateration attack is the application of the geometric process of trilateration which determines the location of an object based on its distance from other known points. Therefore, in the trilateration attack an adversary tries to find some points from which the distance to the target is known.

To understand the attack, we assume that the attacker co-ordinates with two more entities or that he can impersonate as two other entities. To succeed, the attacker has to select three points A_1, A_2, A_3 that are not collinear and manage to trick his victim to disclose his distance from these points (d_1, d_2, d_3). The attacker then finds the exact location of his target, as the victim V, will reside on the intersection of three circles with centers A_1, A_2, A_3 and radii d_1, d_2, d_3 respectively, as illustrated in Figure 1.

Following the same methodology, even if the distances are not exact, the location of the victim can be very well bounded. Let us assume that the accuracy of the measurement is τ, then the actual location of the user is not known, however, it resides within the area of the intersection of the three circles, see Figure 2.

Indeed, even using only the distance of three known points, the victim's location can by approximated with an error bounded by roughly by $\tau/2$. However, this bound can be further improved if more measurements are made.

As seen, the accuracy of the positioning depends on the accuracy of the distance to the known points. The experiments described below focus on investigating the accuracy with which we can determine the distance from an attacker. This can then be used to derive the achievable accuracy for the positioning.

---

[1] `seeforexamplehttp://www.pleaserobme.com/`

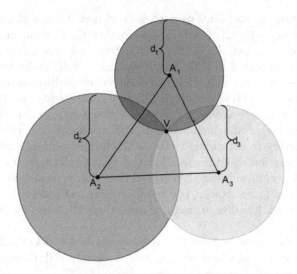

Fig. 1. Trilateration attack with exact distances

4   Experiments

In what follows, we describe analytically how the experiments were made, their findings and the impact for each of the applications.

4.1   Experimental Methodology

In order to conduct our experiments, we needed to create a well-constrained environment for the applications, given that access to their internals or reverse engineering is not possible or legal. To avoid privacy issues that can be triggered by trying to trace individuals, we created some fake accounts on the applications that would be tested. From now on, we will only refer to two of these accounts that are going to be used, one representing the victim and the other the attacker. For convenience, we will refer to them as Alice and Bob respectively. An additional problem was that the measurements should be generic and replicable. In addition, the measurements should be independent of any kind of external noise. All these requirements can simply be met by using fake location. By setting the exact locations of Alice and Bob, one can

- replicate the exact same measurements,
- the mobile phones report always the same location and are not subject to GPS skewness or faults imposed by other antennas or lack of signal,
- the true distance between Alice and Bob can be easily recovered.

The rationale of the experiments is the following: Bob selects Alice as his target and every time he notes the distance to Alice D' as reported by the application. This is compared to the actual distance D (known from the use of

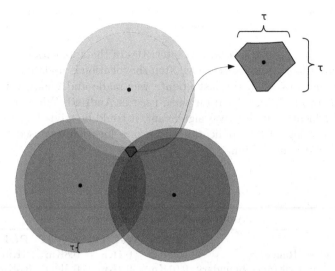

Fig. 2. Trilateration attack with approximate distances

the fake location), to derive a patterns between D and D' that enable Bob to deduce the actual distance from an unknown reported distance.

We found that all the applications try to obfuscate the results by reporting either rounded or randomized distances. To extract the required information, we examine the actual distance when the reported distances change. More precisely, we assume that Alice is at point A and Bob at B_0, so their distance is D_0 and the reported distance is D'_0. Bob chooses another point B_1, closer to Alice so their distance is D_1 and checks the reported distance if it is still D'_0 or it is a new value D'_1. The tests are repeated with new points A and B_0, but with the same actual initial distance D_0.

The assumption that the experiments aim to verify is the following:

Assumption: Bob can always find a points B so that when his reported distance with Alice is D', then the actual distance is always $D \pm \epsilon$.

The attack is then very straight forward: Bob records his initial distance from his target, and he starts moving until he finds that the reported distance approximates the target D'. Then performing small steps, Bob finds a turning point, where the application reports D'' rather than D' that it was previously reporting. Bob now has found a point whose actual distance is $D \pm \epsilon$.

4.2   Experimental Environment

The tests were made using two iOS devices running on a jailbroken version of iOS7. For faking the location, we have used the "LocationFaker" application from Cydia version 1.5-2. The applications that were tested are:

– MoMo version 4.8,
– WeChat version 5.1.0.6,

  – SKOUT version 4.0.2,
  – Plenty of Fish (POF) version 1.71

In Table 1 we summarize several characteristics of the applications. These characteristics are the distance range, how often the location is updated, whether the application displays when the last update was made and finally whether they detect usage of mock GPS location when used in Android. While in some cases the delay for location update was significant, it could be trivially bypassed. The attacker had to log off the application so his new location was used to calculate the distance with the victim.

Table 1. Dating mobile application

Application Characteristics				
	MoMo	WeChat	SKOUT	POF
Distance Range	0.01Km	0.1Km	0.8Km	1Km
Minimum distance boundary	0.01Km	0.1Km	0.8Km	0.5Km
Location update frequency	Run time	Run time	10 mins	30 mins
Last update time	✓	✗	✗	✗
Mock GPS location detected	✓	✗	✗	✓

4.3   Experimental Results

To calculate the true distance between Alice and Bob we have used the well-known haversine formula, where the radius of the Earth is set to 6371Km. In the following paragraphs we analyse the findings and their implications for each application specifically.

MoMo Findings. The experimental results, an example of which is depicted in Figure 3, clearly indicate that MoMo is reporting the actual distance to the users, in groups of 10 meters. The formula that MoMo seams to use in order to report the distances is the following:

$$10 \left\lceil \frac{d_{True}}{10} \right\rceil$$

This means that the distances of the users are bounded by an error of 5 meters.

Implications. Using the trilateration attack, Bob can trace Alice with an accuracy of around 2.5 meters.

SKOUT Findings. The experimental results for SKOUT at first glance indicate that the reported distances are not correct. The application attempts to obfuscate the results, probably to provide some additional security to the users from such attacks. However, as shown in Figure 4, some patterns emerge. More

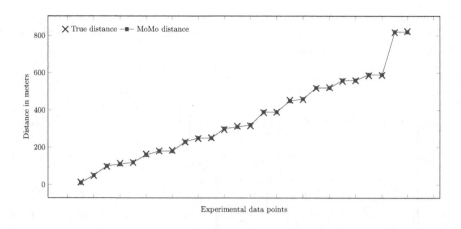

Fig. 3. A typical experiment for MoMo, the actual and reported distances coincide

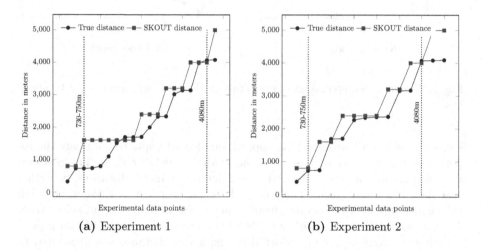

Fig. 4. Graphical representation of the actual vs the reported distances for SKOUT

precisely, as Bob moves in the range of 730-750 meters from Alice, he will see that the reported distance in the application will change from 800 to 1600 meters. The same behavior is repeated in other cases as well. Figure 4 illustrates these patterns, by showing the results of two typical experiments, comparing the reported from the application distance to the actual.

Implications. Bob can easily find a point which reports a distance of 800m. Moving around this point, Bob can find when the reported distance changes to 1600m. At that point, Bob will know that Alice's true position is 730-750 meters. It becomes apparent, that Bob can find another such point, thus the trilateration attack can be performed, tracking Alice with an accuracy of 10 meters. It is worthwhile to notice that the same behavior is noticed in the transition from 4Km to 5Km, where the actual distance is 4080 meters. Therefore, the victim's location can be almost accurate.

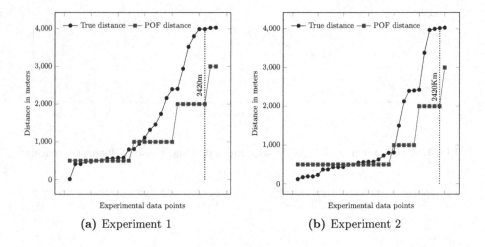

(a) Experiment 1   (b) Experiment 2

Fig. 5. Graphical representation of the actual vs the reported distances for Plenty of Fish

Plenty of Fish Findings. This application also attempts to obfuscate the reported distances, more or less in the same way as SKOUT does. The reported distances might not reflect the actual rounded to kilometer distances, nevertheless, there are again specific patterns that emerge. For instance, the application will change the reported distance from 2Km to 1Km while Bob approaches Alice. At that point, their actual distance is 2420 meters. The results of two typical experiments, comparing the reported to the actual distance are illustrated in Figure 5, and clearly indicate the aforementioned patterns.

Implications. Using the same steps as in SKOUT, Bob can trace Alice using the trilateration attack with almost absolute accuracy.

WeChat Findings. From the applications that were tested, WeChat was the one that tried to obfuscate the results the most. The initial results indicated that the application is not returning the actual distances. Moreover, the application is reporting the distance between Alice and Bob in a non standard way. For instance, the reported distance might be 500m when the actual distance might be 160m or 260m. Additionally, if Bob decides to track Alice, even if they are at the same positions as before, the reported distance might be different over time. Therefore, we may assume that WeChat is trying to detect probable attacks and

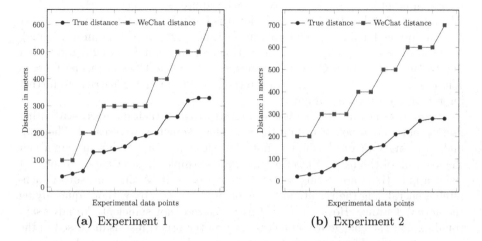

(a) Experiment 1   (b) Experiment 2

Fig. 6. Graphical representation of the actual vs the reported distances for WeChat

stop them, by reporting inaccurate distances. Nevertheless, even if Bob cannot find an exact and stable point where his distance from Alice will change, there is some information that can be extracted. In all our experiments we noticed that when the reported distance between Alice and Bob is 200m, their actual distance is less than 150m. Figure 6 illustrates the results of two such experiments, indicating the reported behavior.

Implications. Exploiting the last comment, Bob can try to find points which are reported 200m away from Alice. This means that Alice will be at most 150 meters away from him. Exploiting this fact along with more points, Bob can accurately find Alice's location.

5   Discussion and Counter Measures

The results from the previous section demonstrate that users' position can be estimated very accurately from the distances provided by the applications. Those experiments, however, assume ideal GPS positioning (i.e. the GPS position reported to the application by both users is completely accurate). Due to the urban morphology, as well as the fact that users are often indoors, GPS is actually inaccurate, with an an error that can reach several meters in dense urban areas. The official study from the US government[2] clearly indicates this fact. In rural settings, however, the positioning is expected to be very accurate, and even in urban settings, using map information about the area (residential vs office building, public spaces etc.), would allow to improve the estimation. In addition, since these users are sharing their photographs, they can be identified amongst a set of

---

[2] http://www.gps.gov/systems/gps/performance/accuracy/

people in a public space. While this attack requires several steps, the use of the fake location by the attacker means that it is fairly fast, and users typically stay at some places for a significant amount of time (e.g., office, restaurant, home), rendering the attack highly practical. However, it should be highlighted that due to this well known GPS inefficiency, many mobile OSes are using GPS in combination with wifi networks or even the signal from mobile carriers to further improve the position accuracy.

As we have shown, allowing users to arbitrarily test their distances with other users is not a good policy, even if the results are somehow obfuscated. The optimal, in terms of privacy, would be not to disclose any kind of information about the location of the users. However, this would cripple the user engagement that these applications are trying to get via displaying it. A first measure is definitely generalizing the results in terms of "far", "close" etc, without quantifying the actual distance. However, even this measure is not sufficient. An adversary could exploit the change from one category to the other, just as discussed in the previous section. Therefore, the best policy would be to fuzz the results in order to report more random distances between the users. If users could decide on the amount of fuzziness, they could provide their desired level of privacy and create safe "areas" or a specific radius of tracing.

Private proximity schemes, such as [28, 24], could also be considered. These schemes allow two parties to exchange privately whether they are close or not, without disclosing any further information to each other, the server or any eavesdropper. The adoption of these schemes is not very straight forward, as these schemes require the two parties to have some sort of trust to each other, which translates to key exchange. Therefore, dating sites that operate with arbitrary users that do not already know each other and just want to flirt does not fit well within this application scenario. Nevertheless, it would be worthwhile to consider escalating information, so that proximity for instance is only disclosed to authenticated "friends" and not to all subscribed users. This approach could certainly provide more privacy to the users while limiting the computational effort significantly.

6   Conclusions

The quest for finding one's other half leads many people to use online dating applications. While this engages people to another way of communication, they are exposed in many ways, mainly due to the nature of Internet. However, as we highlighted in this work, users are exposed to an additional risk due to the location awareness of the smart phone applications. By spoofing his location, a malicious user can manipulate these applications in order to disclose the actual location of an honest user using simple and well known methods. This way, not only private information can be leaked, but cyber-stalking can become real-life, automated stalking exposing users even physically. It is shown that currently applied methods, even if they attempt to somehow obfuscate the results, fail and that a user's actual location can be disclosed very accurately.

Acknowledgments. This work was supported by Science Foundation Ireland under the Principal Investigator research program 10/IN.1/I2980 "Self-organizing Architectures for Autonomic Management of Smart Cities".

References

1. Zickuhr, K.: Location-based services. Pew Internet and American Life Project (2013)
2. Madden, M., Lenhart, A., Cortesi, S., Gasser, U.: Teens and mobile apps privacy. Pew Internet and American Life Project (2013)
3. Gedik, B., Liu, L.: Protecting location privacy with personalized k-anonymity: Architecture and algorithms. IEEE Transactions on Mobile Computing 7(1), 1–18 (2008)
4. Beresford, A.R., Stajano, F.: Location privacy in pervasive computing. IEEE Pervasive Computing 2(1), 46–55 (2003)
5. Cheng, R., Zhang, Y., Bertino, E., Prabhakar, S.: Preserving user location privacy in mobile data management infrastructures. In: Danezis, G., Golle, P. (eds.) PET 2006. LNCS, vol. 4258, pp. 393–412. Springer, Heidelberg (2006)
6. Damiani, M.L., Silvestri, C., Bertino, E.: Fine-grained cloaking of sensitive positions in location-sharing applications. IEEE Pervasive Computing 10(4), 64–72 (2011)
7. Smith, A., Duggan, M.: Online dating and relationships. Pew Internet and American Life Project (2013)
8. Patsakis, C., Asthenidis, A., Chatzidimitriou, A.: Social networks as an attack platform: Facebook case study. In: ICN, 245–247 (2009)
9. Brown, G., Howe, T., Ihbe, M., Prakash, A., Borders, K.: Social networks and context-aware spam. In: Proceedings of the 2008 ACM Conference on Computer Supported Cooperative Work CSCW 2008, pp. 403–412 (2008)
10. Huber, M., Mulazzani, M., Weippl, E., Kitzler, G., Goluch, S.: Friend-in-the-middle attacks: Exploiting social networking sites for spam. IEEE Internet Computing 15(3), 28–34 (2011)
11. Abu-Nimeh, S., Chen, T., Alzubi, O.: Malicious and spam posts in online social networks. Computer 44(9), 23–28 (2011)
12. Huber, M., Mulazzani, M., Weippl, E., Kitzler, G., Goluch, S.: Exploiting social networking sites for spam. In: Proceedings of the 17th ACM Conference on Computer and Communications Security CCS 2010, pp. 693–695 (2010)
13. Jagatic, T.N., Johnson, N.A., Jakobsson, M., Menczer, F.: Social phishing. Communications of the ACM 50(10), 94–100 (2007)
14. Douceur, J.R.: The sybil attack. In: Druschel, P., Kaashoek, M.F., Rowstron, A. (eds.) IPTPS 2002. LNCS, vol. 2429, pp. 251–260. Springer, Heidelberg (2002)
15. Backstrom, L., Dwork, C., Kleinberg, J.: Wherefore art thou r3579x?: Anonymized social networks, hidden patterns, and structural steganography. In: Proceedings of the 16th International Conference on World Wide Web, pp. 181–190. ACM (2007)
16. Hoffman, K., Zage, D., Nita-Rotaru, C.: A survey of attack and defense techniques for reputation systems. ACM Computing Surveys (CSUR) 42(1), 1 (2009)
17. Krumm, J.: Inference attacks on location tracks. In: LaMarca, A., Langheinrich, M., Truong, K.N. (eds.) Pervasive 2007. LNCS, vol. 4480, pp. 127–143. Springer, Heidelberg (2007)

18. Gambs, S., Killijian, M.O., del Prado Cortez, M.N.: Show me how you move and i will tell you who you are. Transactions on Data Privacy 4(2), 103–126 (2011)

19. Gambs, S., Killijian, M.O., del Prado Cortez, M.N.: De-anonymization attack on geolocated data. In: TrustCom/ISPA/IUCC, pp. 789–797 (2013)

20. Golle, P., Partridge, K.: On the anonymity of home/Work location pairs. In: Tokuda, H., Beigl, M., Friday, A., Brush, A.J.B., Tobe, Y. (eds.) Pervasive 2009. LNCS, vol. 5538, pp. 390–397. Springer, Heidelberg (2009)

21. Pontes, T., Vasconcelos, M.A., Almeida, J.M., Kumaraguru, P., Almeida, V.: We know where you live: privacy characterization of foursquare behavior. In: UbiComp, pp. 898–905 (2012)

22. Kostakos, V., Venkatanathan, J., Reynolds, B., Sadeh, N., Toch, E., Shaikh, S.A., Jones, S.: Who's your best friend?: Targeted privacy attacks in location-sharing social networks. In: Proceedings of the 13th International Conference on Ubiquitous Computing, UbiComp 2011 pp. 177–186 (2011)

23. He, W., Liu, X., Ren, M.: Location cheating: A security challenge to location-based social network services. In: 2011 31st International Conference on Distributed Computing Systems (ICDCS), pp. 740–749. IEEE (2011)

24. Mascetti, S., Freni, D., Bettini, C., Wang, X.S., Jajodia, S.: Privacy in geo-social networks: Proximity notification with untrusted service providers and curious buddies. The VLDB Journal 20(4), 541–566 (2011)

25. Zheleva, E., Getoor, L.: To join or not to join: The illusion of privacy in social networks with mixed public and private user profiles. In: Proceedings of the 18th International Conference on World Wide Web, pp. 531–540. ACM (2009)

26. Carbunar, B., Rahman, M., Pissinou, N., Vasilakos, A.: A survey of privacy vulnerabilities and defenses in geosocial networks. IEEE Communications Magazine 51(11), 114–119 (2013)

27. Ruiz Vicente, C., Freni, D., Bettini, C., Jensen, C.S.: Location-related privacy in geo-social networks. IEEE Internet Computing 15(3), 20–27 (2011)

28. Narayanan, A., Thiagarajan, N., Lakhani, M., Hamburg, M., Boneh, D.: Location privacy via private proximity testing. In: Network & Distributed System Security Symposium (2011)

Towards a Framework for Benchmarking Privacy-ABC Technologies*

Fatbardh Veseli[1], Tsvetoslava Vateva-Gurova[2], Ioannis Krontiris[1],
Kai Rannenberg[1], and Neeraj Suri[2]

[1] Chair of M-Business & Multilateral Security, Goethe University Frankfurt,
Germany
{firstname.lastname}@m-chair.de
[2] Department of Computer Science, Technische Universität Darmstadt, Germany
{lastname}@deeds.informatik.tu-darmstadt.de

Abstract. Technologies based on attribute-based credentials (Privacy-
ABC) enable identity management systems that require minimal disclosure of personal information and provide unlinkability of user's
transactions. However, underlying characteristics of and differences between Privacy-ABC technologies are currently not well understood. In this
paper, we present our efforts in defining a framework for benchmarking
Privacy-ABC technologies, and identifying an extensive set of benchmarking criteria and factors impacting such benchmarks. In addition, we identify important challenges in the adoption of Privacy-ABC technologies,
indicating directions for future research.

1   Introduction

In the digital world, users are often required to authenticate towards service
providers in order to use their services. In many interactions with different service providers, users must disclose personally identifying information in order
to use these services, resulting in the loss of control over such information, and
a direct impact on their privacy. Privacy-enhancing attribute-based credentials
(Privacy-ABCs) enable an identity management system that takes into consideration both the privacy interests of the User, and the security requirements of
the Service Providers. They eliminate the need for an active participation of the
identity service provider during the authentication of the user, and enable minimal disclosure of personal information for authentication purposes. However,
despite existence of implementations of such technologies, such as Microsoft's
U-Prove [1] or IBM's Idemix [2], there are additional challenges towards their
wider adoption in practice, one of which is the lack of understanding of their
differences.

Privacy-ABC technologies are mainly investigated as part of anonymous credential systems. As the underlying technology relies heavily on cryptographic

---

* The research leading to these results has received funding from the European Com-
munitys Seventh Framework Programme (FP7/2007-2013) under Grant Agreement
no. 257782 for the project Attribute-based Credentials for Trust (ABC4Trust).

N. Cuppens-Boulahia et al. (Eds.): SEC 2014, IFIP AICT 428, pp. 197–204, 2014.

primitives [3,4], much of the work has been focused on individual aspects, such as efficiency [3,5,6,7,8,9], or support for additional features [10,11]. In addition, there are a number of proposed mechanisms for revocation of anonymous credentials, which also need to be benchmarked. An analysis on revocation schemes for PKI is presented in [12], but it does not take into account the specific aspects of Privacy-ABCs (e.g. privacy features). In this regard, tradeoffs between revocation schemes for anonymous credentials have been analysed in [13,8,9]. From a methodological perspective, elicitation of benchmarking criteria in general is studied also in other areas, e.g. on benchmarking security [14,15,16], although not particularly focusing on Privacy-ABC technologies. However, there is no comprehensive work on benchmarking Privacy-ABC technologies with a broader perspective covering a wider range of aspects.

In this paper, we provide results of an ongoing work towards a framework for benchmarking Privacy-ABC technologies, identifying an extensive set of criteria covering main aspects of Privacy-ABC technologies. We organise these criteria into four main dimensions and identify relevant factors that could influence the benchmarks. We base our work on the unified architecture, concepts and features of Privacy-ABCs [17,18], and build on both the relevant literature on these technologies, as well as experiences during the deployment of these technologies in real-world pilots [19]. Besides for benchmarking Privacy-ABC technologies, this work can also be used as an indicator to the specific challenges and important considerations in their deployment in real life applications.

This paper is organized as follows. First we briefly introduce Privacy-ABC technologies. Then we present the proposed framework for benchmarking these technologies, describing also typical factors that may influence benchmarks. Finally, we conclude the paper with a summary of our results, and a discussion on the potential utility of this work, and give future research directions.

2   Privacy-ABCs - Overview of Features and Concepts

This section gives a very brief introduction on the Privacy-ABC technologies. The interested reader is referred to [18,17], where a comprehensive description of these technologies is provided. Privacy-ABC technologies address the privacy implications of existing identity management schemes, by supporting *selective disclosure* of identity information, and enabling *unlinkability* of user's transactions. Through Privacy-ABCs users can be authenticated without being identified due to the anonymous zero-knowledge proofs support.

The architecture of Privacy-ABCs [18] recognizes the entities: User, Issuer, Verifier, Revocation Authority and Inspector. The *User* is a central entity mainly interacting with the *Issuer* to get Privacy-ABC in an issuance protocol, and with the *Verifier* when accessing services. A Verifier accepts verifiable proofs by the User in forms of *presentation tokens*, and trusts the proofs generated by the credentials of the User, which are issued by the Issuer. Following the Privacy-ABCs architecture [18] and the interactions between the entities [17], we consider the following stages in the lifecycle of Privacy-ABCs, namely *issuance, presentation, inspection,* and *revocation.*

Issuance. During this initial stage of the lifecycle, an Issuer issues a credential to the User. Privacy-ABC technologies support different forms of issuance, also more "advanced" ones e.g., reflecting the relation of a new credential to an existing one. Examples are "carrying-over attributes" or "key binding".

Presentation. In a presentation protocol the User can prove the possession of credentials and disclose certain information to the Verifier using Privacy-ABC. The Verifier sends a *presentation policy* to the User, specifying the type of proof the User must present. This may include proof of possession of a certain type of credential, disclosure of a subset of attributes, proof of not being revoked, etc., which the User presents in the form of a *presentation token* to the Verifier. Finally, the Verifier can verify the validity of the presented proof.

Inspection. In scenarios where an identity management system aims at conditionally "anonymous" transactions with conditional accountability, Privacy-ABCs support the optional feature of *inspection*, which enables revocation of anonymity in exceptional cases, and is performed by a trusted entity, the Inspector. The fact that a particular presentation token may potentially be subject to inspection in the future should be clearly explained to the User in the presentation policy, along with a strict description of the potential reasons that require inspection to take place.

Revocation. Revocation is the last stage in the lifecycle of Privacy-ABCs, invalidating the credential(s). It is a crucial component of an identitiy management system. The reasons for revocation might be scenario-specific, but revocation is considered normally in cases of misuse, lost or compromised credentials or their storage medium, etc. Responsible for revocation is the Revocation Authority, which maintains the list of (in)valid credentials, and disseminates the latest information on this list to the other entities.

3   Benchmarking Criteria and Impact Factors

We have organised the extensive set of identified benchmarking criteria into four main subsets: *Functionality, Efficiency, Security Assurance,* and *Practical Viability.* Each of these subsets represent a separate benchmarking dimension and contains a list of criteria, organised following the lifecycle of Privacy-ABCs, as presented in Figure 1. Furthermore, we identify typical impact factors for the benchmarks related to given criteria, following a user-centered approach.

3.1   Functionality

The functionality criteria are mostly qualitative and they aim at benchmarking different Privacy-ABC technologies based on their native support for different features, as well as on the additional factors that could be valuable in practice.

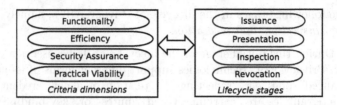

Fig. 1. The organisational structure of the benchmarking criteria

Table 1 summarizes the list of criteria which could be used for functionality benchmarking, organised following the Privacy-ABC lifecycle approach.

Support for the advanced privacy features of the *issuance* phase, such as "key binding", or "attribute carry-over" (blindly, from another credential), or *presentation* features, such as pseudonymity, (types of) predicates, inspection, or non-revocation proof, provide basic criteria for benchmarking functionality aspects of different Privacy-ABC technologies. For *inspection* it is important to recognize whether the technology provides certain features that would minimise the potential for authority abuse by an Inspector, such as four-eyes principle or requiring k out of n inspectors to be present for inspection. Finally, as *revocation* is usually a challenging aspect of Privacy-ABCs, the support for immediate revocation is a key benchmarking criterion, whereas additional advantage is gained if a revocation scheme enables revocation of the secret key instead of a credential attribute (for instance, to revoke all credentials based on a given key at once).

3.2   Efficiency

Privacy-ABC technologies can be built using different cryptographic building blocks, such as signature schemes, encryption, zero-knowledge proofs, commitments, and revocation schemes. Efficiency has been identified as an important factor for Privacy-ABCs already in previous research [3,5,6,7,8,9,11], as it directly affects the performance of the applications using these technologies, which is a crucial factor for their wider acceptance. In our work, we identify a set of criteria for benchmarking the efficiency, which are mostly quantitative, and organise them in three main aspects, namely into *computational, communication* and *storage* efficiency criteria.

Computational efficiency is expressed in time units (in seconds) required to perform a given operation, whereas **communication efficiency** deals with the

Table 1. Functionality benchmarking criteria

Stage	Functionality Criteria
Issuance	-Supported advanced issuance features
Presentation	-Unlinkability of multiple presentations
	-Supported advanced presentation features
Inspection	-Support for multi-party inspection
Revocation	-Support for immediate revocation
	-Key- vs. attribute revocation

Table 2. Efficiency benchmarking criteria

Stage	Criteria	Impact Factors
Issuance	-CCE of issuance	-Number of attributes
		-Use of "advanced" issuance features
Presentation	-CCE of presentation	-Number of credentials proven
		-Use of advanced presentation features
Inspection	-Overhead on presentation	-Number of inspectable attributes
Revocation	-Overhead on presentation	-Number of revocable credentials
All stages		-Security level (key size)

data sizes exchanged during different operations. Both efficiency metrics depend on the underlying cryptographic operation that are performed. Table 2 presents the main criteria for benchmarking different Privacy-ABCs on these two metrics, and the most important factors, which influence both of these efficiency aspects along the lifecycle of Privacy-ABCs. The use of advanced features during the *issuance* and *presentation*, such as key binding or (type of) predicates, should impact both efficiency figures, as they incurr additional crypto operations. However, the actual impact on on different Privacy-ABC technologies may vary. On top of that, a significant overhead on the presentation efficiency can be the use of *inspection*, which may also vary depending on the number of inspectable attributes. Finally, *revocation* has a similar overhead on presentation, which may depend on the type of revocation scheme used. Finally, the security level, which corresponds to the cryptographic key length used, has a direct impact on the efficiency of presentation.

Storage efficiency is important, as storage requirements can have impact on the choice of storage medium for the user. Besides the Privacy-ABCs, a number of other information might need to be stored in practice, such as revocation-related information to credentials, pseudonyms, and other static information about other entities (public key of the issuer, revocation authority, inspector). Hence, it is important to benchmark the different storage requirements of different Privacy-ABC technologies, and the factors impacting it.

3.3 Security Assurance

To be able to assess the security assurance provided by a specific Privacy-ABC technology, we propose the usage of security assurance criteria for the different stages of the lifecycle of Privacy-ABCs. The aim of these criteria is to assess the effectiveness of the technology-specific security assurance mechanisms in order to evaluate how the security requirements are met by the respective Privacy-ABC technology. Table 3 presents the security assurance benchmarking criteria we are proposing. As can be seen from the table, security assumptions and security proofs are involved in all the stages of the lifecycle and have to be taken into account. It has to be considered whether the security proofs and assumptions of the issuance protocol and the presentation token, as well as the security proofs and assumptions of the inspection-related and revocation-related mechanisms are information

Table 3. Security assurance benchmarking criteria

Stage	Criteria
Inspection	-Preventive measures against authority misuse
Revocation	-Mechanisms to guaraantee the authenticity and integrity of RI
	-Access to the Revocation Handles
All stages	-Security proofs and assumptions

theoretic, computational or without security reduction. In case they are computational, the hardness assumptions have to be described. In each of the lifecycle's stages the underlying security proofs and assumptions have to be listed.

In addition, means to assess the security of the conventional mechanisms, which are specifically applied and customized to enhance the security assurance of Privacy-ABCs (e.g. access control mechanisms for the Revocation Information), are necessary; therefore security assurance benchmarks for these mechanisms are to be considered. With regard to Inspection, the security assurance for preventing authority misuse by the person in charge of inspection has to be investigated. It has to be assessed whether the technology supports measures for preventing this, e.g. by applying key sharing mechanisms, where k out of n keys must be combined in order to be able to conduct inspection. Additional security assurance criteria are needed also for the Revocation. The guarantees the the Privacy-ABC technology provides for the protection of integrity and authenticity of the Revocation Information have to be studied and the applied protection mechanisms need to be specified. Moreover, the access restrictions to the Revocation Handles that are posed through the technology have to be analyzed. The different possibilites, e.g. public vs. private access and whether the Revocation Handles are learnt only by the Verfier or also by the Revocation Authority have to be studied.

3.4 Practical Viability

Practical viability benchmarking deals with a group of criteria that may inhibit or enable adoption of Privacy-ABC technologies in the ever-more mobile world. These criteria are listed in Table 4 and relate to the workarounds in overcoming potential lack of support for certain Privacy-ABC features, limiting restrictions on the deployment platforms, or challenges in maintaining privacy in potentially unforeseen application requirements.

Reissuance of Linkable Credentials. Certain Privacy-ABC technologies do not provide multiple presentations unlinkability. In case this feature is required, a workaround could be to use Privacy-ABCs only one time, requiring re-issuance

Table 4. Benchmarking criteria for practical viability

Stage	Practical Viability Criteria
Issuance	-Reissuance of linkable credentials
Presentation	-Feasibility of smart card deployment
Revocation	-Offline non-revocation proof

of such credentials (before every presentation). In order to overcome potential privacy implications, it is possible to automate the process of issuance by issuing a batch of such credentials at once. However, this approach has not only storage implications for the User, but also the usability impact for the fact that the User needs to engage in additional issuance instances with the Issuer (which also may require the User needs to be online).

Feasibility of Smart Card Deployment. Many scenarios where Privacy-ABCs could be deployed, such as new e-IDs or e-tickets, could benefit from the use of smart cards. Except for storing Privacy-ABCs, it may be useful to be able to perform presentation proofs in the card, which can be challenging, considering the computing power of current smart cards. In addition to that, as smart cards are offline devices, Privacy-ABC technologies must enable offline presentations. This factor is important for the wider acceptance and usability of the Privacy-ABC technologies in such scenarios, as also recognized in the the efforts to efficiently implement them on smart cards [5,6,7,13].

Offline Non-revocation Proof. Proving non-revocation comes challenging for Privacy-ABCs, as this needs to be done without losing privacy. Schemes that support immediate revocation rely on accumulators [11,9], and this typically involves some overhead on the presentation, who needs to provide an additional proof of not being revoked. This makes the presentation less efficient (longer), but also requires periodical connectivity of the User with the Revocation Authority during the presentation in order to refresh the "evidence" that her credentials are not revoked, limiting the deployability of these technologies on devices with network capabilitiy (making them infeasible such as smart cards). A number of studies in this area show the different overhead distribution of revocation (non-revocation proof) on the presentation [13,8], whereas the importance of non-interactive schemes is obviously acknowledged [9].

4 Conclusion

Privacy-ABC technologies enable user-centric, privacy-preserving identity management. This paper summarizes ongoing work in providing a framework for benchmarking Privacy-ABC technologies, enabling a transparent identification of their differences in terms of functionality, efficiency, security assurance, and practical viability. It identifies a number of challenges in the adoption of these technologies in practice, which can also be used to identify open research directions. Next steps in completing the proposed framework include identifying additional factors that could influence the benchmarks and performing actual benchmarks to evaluate the actual impact of these factors on different Privacy-ABC technologies.

References

1. Paquin, C., Zaverucha, G.: U-prove Cryptographic Specification v1.1 (Revision 2). Technical report, Microsoft Corporation (2013)

2. Bichsel, P., Binding, C., Camenisch, J., Gro, T., Heydt-Benjamin, T., Sommer, D., Zaverucha, G.: Cryptographic Protocols of the Identity Mixer Library. Technical Report RZ 3730 (99740), IBM Research GmbH (2008)
3. Camenisch, J.L., Lysyanskaya, A.: A Signature Scheme with Efficient Protocols. In: Cimato, S., Galdi, C., Persiano, G. (eds.) SCN 2002. LNCS, vol. 2576, pp. 268–289. Springer, Heidelberg (2003)
4. Brands, S.A.: Rethinking Public Key Infrastructures and Digital Certificates: Building in Privacy. MIT Press (2000)
5. Vullers, P., Alpár, G.: Efficient Selective Disclosure on Smart Cards Using Idemix. In: Fischer-Hübner, S., de Leeuw, E., Mitchell, C. (eds.) IDMAN 2013. IFIP AICT, vol. 396, pp. 53–67. Springer, Heidelberg (2013)
6. Mostowski, W., Vullers, P.: Efficient U-Prove Implementation for Anonymous Credentials on Smart Cards. In: Rajarajan, M., Piper, F., Wang, H., Kesidis, G. (eds.) SecureComm 2011. LNICST, vol. 96, pp. 243–260. Springer, Heidelberg (2012)
7. Schnorr, C.P.: Efficient signature generation by smart cards. Journal of Cryptology 4, 161–174 (1991)
8. Lapon, J., Kohlweiss, M., De Decker, B., Naessens, V.: Performance Analysis of Accumulator-Based Revocation Mechanisms. In: Rannenberg, K., Varadharajan, V., Weber, C. (eds.) SEC 2010. IFIP AICT, vol. 330, pp. 289–301. Springer, Heidelberg (2010)
9. Camenisch, J., Lysyanskaya, A.: Dynamic Accumulators and Application to Efficient Revocation of Anonymous Credentials. In: Yung, M. (ed.) CRYPTO 2002. LNCS, vol. 2442, pp. 61–76. Springer, Heidelberg (2002)
10. Belenkiy, M., Chase, M., Kohlweiss, M., Lysyanskaya, A.: P-signatures and Noninteractive Anonymous Credentials. In: Canetti, R. (ed.) TCC 2008. LNCS, vol. 4948, pp. 356–374. Springer, Heidelberg (2008)
11. Li, J., Li, N., Xue, R.: Universal accumulators with efficient nonmembership proofs. In: Katz, J., Yung, M. (eds.) ACNS 2007. LNCS, vol. 4521, pp. 253–269. Springer, Heidelberg (2007)
12. Aarnes, A., Just, M., Knapskog, S., Lloyd, S., Meijer, H.: Selecting Revocation Solutions for PKI (2000)
13. Lapon, J., Kohlweiss, M., De Decker, B., Naessens, V.: Analysis of Revocation Strategies for Anonymous Idemix Credentials. In: De Decker, B., Lapon, J., Naessens, V., Uhl, A. (eds.) CMS 2011. LNCS, vol. 7025, pp. 3–17. Springer, Heidelberg (2011)
14. Luna, J., Langenberg, R., Suri, N.: Benchmarking Cloud Security Level Agreements Using Quantitative Policy Trees. In: CCSW, pp. 103–112. ACM (2012)
15. Luna, J., Ghani, H., Vateva, T., Suri, N.: Quantitative Assessment of Cloud Security Level Agreements: A Case Study. In: SECRYPT, pp. 64–73. SciTePress (2012)
16. Parrend, P.: Security benchmarks of OSGi platforms: toward Hardened OSGi. Softw., Pract. Exper. 39(5), 471–499 (2009)
17. Camenisch, J., Dubovitskaya, M., Lehmann, A., Neven, G., Paquin, C., Preiss, F.-S.: Concepts and Languages for Privacy-Preserving Attribute-Based Authentication. In: Fischer-Hübner, S., de Leeuw, E., Mitchell, C. (eds.) IDMAN 2013. IFIP AICT, vol. 396, pp. 34–52. Springer, Heidelberg (2013)
18. Camenisch, J., Krontiris, I., Lehmann, A., Neven, G., Paquin, C., Rannenberg, K., Zwingelberg, H.: D2.1 Architecture for Attribute-based Credential Technologies - Version 1. ABC4TRUST - Deliverable to the European Commision (2011), https://abc4trust.eu/index.php/pub
19. ABC4Trust: Abc4trust pilots, https://abc4trust.eu/index.php/home/pilots/ (last accessed on December 14, 2013)

Evaluating the Security of a DNS Query Obfuscation Scheme for Private Web Surfing*

Dominik Herrmann, Max Maaß, and Hannes Federrath

University of Hamburg, Computer Science Department, Germany

Abstract. The Domain Name System (DNS) does not provide query privacy. Query obfuscation schemes have been proposed to overcome this limitation, but, so far, they have not been evaluated in a realistic setting. In this paper we evaluate the security of a random set range query scheme in a real-world web surfing scenario. We demonstrate that the scheme does not sufficiently obfuscate characteristic query patterns, which can be used by an adversary to determine the visited websites. We also illustrate how to thwart the attack and discuss practical challenges. Our results suggest that previously published evaluations of range queries may give a false sense of the attainable security, because they do not account for any interdependencies between queries.

1 Introduction

DNS is an integral part of the Internet infrastructure. Unfortunately, it does not offer privacy, i. e., the so-called resolvers (recursive nameservers) can see all queries sent to them in the clear. Resolvers can learn about users' habits and interests, which may infringe their privacy if the resolver is not run by a trusted party, but by a third party such as Google, whose resolver 8.8.8.8 serves more than 130 billion queries per day on average [11]. The discussions about limiting tracking via cookies spurred by the "Do not track" initiative may result in DNS queries becoming the next target for tracking and profiling purposes [7]. According to [12] behavior-based tracking based on DNS queries may be feasible.

Integrating mechanisms for confidentiality into DNS is difficult because of the need for compatibility with existing infrastructure. Fundamental changes to the protocol are implemented very slowly, as previous attempts have shown: Although the initial DNSSEC security extensions have been proposed in 1999 [9], the majority of users still can not profit from their benefits today. Unfortunately, DNSSEC does not address privacy issues due to an explicit design decision [1].

Currently, there is no indication that facilities for privacy-preserving resolution will be integrated into the DNS architecture in the short term. Previous research efforts have focused on interim solutions, i. e., add-ons and tools that enable users who care for privacy to protect themselves against profiling and tracking efforts. The objective consists in designing and evaluating suitable privacy enhancing techniques in such a way that users do not have to rely on or

---

* This paper is based on the BSc thesis [14] of the second author.

N. Cuppens-Boulahia et al. (Eds.): SEC 2014, IFIP AICT 428, pp. 205–219, 2014.

trust the existing DNS infrastructure. The "range query" scheme by Zhao et al. [17] is one of those efforts. The basic idea consists in *query obfuscation*, i.e., sending a set of dummy queries (hence the term "range") with random hostnames along with the actual DNS query to the resolver.

So far the security of range query schemes has only been analyzed within a simplistic theoretical model that considers the obtainable security for *singular queries*. In this paper we study the security offered by range queries for a more complex real-world application, namely *web surfing*, which is one of the use cases Zhao et al. envision in [17]. In contrast to singular queries, downloading websites typically entails a number of inter-related DNS queries. Our results indicate that the range query scheme offers less protection than expected in this scenario, because dependencies between consecutive queries are neglected.

The main contribution of this paper is to **demonstrate that random set range queries offer considerably less protection than expected in the web surfing use case.** We demonstrate that a curious resolver (the adversary) can launch a semantic intersection attack to disclose the actually retrieved website with high probability. We also show how the effectiveness of the attack can be reduced, and we identify a number of challenges that have to be addressed before range query schemes are suitable for practice.

The paper is structured as follows. In Sects. 2 and 3 we review existing work and fundamentals. Having described our dataset in Sect. 4, we continue with theoretical and empirical analyses in Sects. 5 and 6. We study countermeasures in Sect. 7 and discuss our results in Sect. 8. We conclude in Sect. 9.

2   Related Work

The basic DNS range query scheme was introduced by Zhao et al. in [17]; there is also an improved version [18] inspired by private information retrieval [6]. Although the authors suggest their schemes especially for web surfing applications, they fail to demonstrate their practicability using empirical results.

Castillo-Perez and Garcia-Alfaro propose a variation of the original range query scheme [17] using multiple DNS resolvers in parallel [3,4]. They evaluate its performance for ENUM and ONS, two protocols that store data within the DNS infrastructure. Finally, Lu and Tsudik propose PPDNS [13], a privacy-preserving resolution service that relies on CoDoNS [15], a next-generation DNS system based on distributed hashtables and a peer-to-peer infrastructure, which has not been widely adopted so far.

The aforementioned publications study the security of range queries for singular queries issued independently from each other. In contrast, [10] observes that consecutively issued queries that are dependent on each other have implications for security. They describe a timing attack that allows an adversary to determine the actually desired website and show that consecutive queries have to be serialized in order to prevent the attack.

3   Fundamentals

3.1   Random Set DNS Range Query Scheme

In this paper we focus on the basic "random set" DNS range query scheme as introduced in [17]. Zhao et al. stipulate that each client is equipped with a large database of valid domain names **(dummy database)**. Each time the client wants to issue a DNS query to a resolver, it randomly draws (without replacement) $N - 1$ *dummy names* from the database, and sends N queries to the resolver in total. When all replies have been received from the resolver, the replies for the dummy queries are discarded and the desired reply is presented to the application that issued the query.

Zhao et al. claim that this strategy leaves the adversary with a chance of $\frac{1}{N}$ to guess the desired domain name. The value of N is a security parameter, which is supposed to be chosen according to the user's privacy expectations and performance needs.

3.2   Query Patterns

The semantic intersection attack exploits the fact that typical websites embed content from multiple servers, causing clients to issue a burst of queries for various domain names in a deterministic fashion, whenever they visit the site. For example, visiting *google.com* will also trigger a DNS request for *ssl.gstatic.com*, as the site includes some resources from that domain. We call the set of domain names that can be observed upon visiting a site its *query pattern p*, i. e., $p(\text{google.com}) = \{\text{google.com}, \text{ssl.gstatic.com}\}$. In Sect. 4, we will show that many popular websites do have query patterns that can be used for this attack.

Using range queries, each individual query from a pattern p is hidden in a set of $N - 1$ randomly chosen queries, leading to $|p|$ sets, each containing N queries, being sent to the resolver in order to retrieve all the domain names required to visit the corresponding website. We refer to N as the *block size* of the range query scheme and to each individual range query as a *block*.

Note that the client uses standard DNS queries to deliver the range query, because it uses a conventional DNS resolver, i. e., a single range query with a block size of N causes N individual DNS queries.

3.3   The Semantic Intersection Attack

An adversary, who is in possession of a database that contains the query patterns for a set of websites he is interested in **(pattern database)**, can check whether one of these patterns can be matched to consecutive query blocks received by the client. As all the dummy names are drawn independently from each other from the dummy database, it is quite unlikely that the client will draw the pattern of a different website by chance. Therefore, the adversary can be optimistic that he will only find a single pattern in the set of consecutive range queries he receives from the client, i. e., the pattern of the actually desired website.

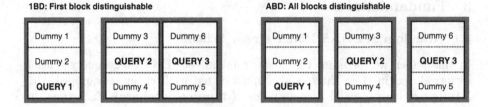

Fig. 1. Distinguishability of blocks for the resolver

From the viewpoint of the adversary there are two different scenarios, depending on how well the adversary can distinguish consecutive blocks (cf. Fig. 1). The adversary may either be able to identify all the queries that belong to the first block, but be unable to determine which of the remaining queries belongs to which of the remaining blocks (**1BD**, 1st block distinguishable), or be able to distinguish all individual blocks, i. e., be able to determine for all queries to which block they belong (**ABD**, all blocks distinguishable). The difference between the 1BD and the ABD scenario becomes evident by considering the following example. When a user visits the site *http://www.rapecrisis.org.uk*, her browser will issue a query for *www.rapecrisis.org.uk*. Moreover, it will issue two additional queries, for *twitter.com* and *www.rapecrisislondon.org*, once the HTML page has been parsed. For illustrative purposes we assume that range queries with $N = 3$ are used. In the **ABD scenario** the adversary might, for instance, observe a first block of queries for (*cnn.com, www.rapecrisis.org.uk, img.feedpress.it*), then a second block for (*github.com, twitter.com, s.ebay.de*), and finally a third block for (*www.rapecrisislondon.org, ytimg.com, conn.skype.com*). In contrast, in the **1BD scenario** the adversary might observe a first block with (*cnn.com, www.rapecrisis.org.uk, img.feedpress.it*) and a second block with (*github.com, twitter.com, www.rapecrisislondon.org, s.ebay.de, ytimg.com, conn.skype.com*).

The first block is distinguishable in both scenarios, because the web browser has to resolve the *primary domain name* in order to learn the IP address of the main web server. This IP address is received within the replies that belong to the first block of queries. After the browser has downloaded the HTML file from the main web server, it will issue queries for the *secondary domain names* in order to retrieve all embedded content hosted on other web servers.

Given a *pattern database DB* that contains primary and secondary domain names of websites, the adversary proceeds as follows in order to carry out the intersection attack in the **ABD scenario**:

1. From *DB* the adversary selects all patterns, whose primary domain name is contained in the first block, obtaining the set of candidates C.
2. The adversary selects all patterns with length $|p|$, which is the number of observed blocks, from C to obtain $C_{|p|}$.
3. For each pattern q in $C_{|p|}$ the adversary performs a *block-wise set intersection*: q is a *matching pattern*, if all of its domain names are dispersed among the blocks in a plausible fashion, i. e., iff

(a) each block contains at least 1 element from q, and
(b) each element of q is contained in at least 1 block, and
(c) q can be completely assembled by drawing one element from each block.

In the **1BD scenario** the adversary has to use a different approach, because there are only two blocks observable:

1. From the pattern database the adversary selects all patterns, whose primary domain name is contained in the first block, thus obtaining the set of candidate patterns C.
2. For each pattern q in C the adversary performs a *block-wise set intersection*: q is a *matching pattern*, if all of its secondary domain names are contained within the second block.

Note that due to caching, the adversary cannot reliably determine $|p|$ in the 1BD scenario. Due to variations in the lookup time of different domain names, the stub resolver on the client may already receive replies (and cache the results) for some domain names before all range queries have been submitted to the resolver. However, if the range query client happens to draw one of the cached domain names as a dummy, the stub resolver will not send another query, but answer it immediately from its cache. As a result, some queries will not reach the adversary and the effective size of consecutive blocks will vary. Therefore, the adversary cannot easily determine $|p|$ in the 1BD scenario in order to filter the set C. For now, we neglect the fact that caching may also affect the desired queries (cf. Sect. 8 for a discussion of this issue).

In the remainder of the paper we focus on the **1BD scenario**, which we deem to be more realistic than the ABD scenario. Contemporary web browsers issue the queries for the secondary queries in parallel. Thus, when the range query client constructs range queries for each of the desired domain names, the individual queries of all the blocks will be interleaved, causing uncertainty about the composition of the individual blocks. On the other hand, the ABD scenario is relevant for range query schemes that submit all queries contained in a block in a single message. We will consider the effect of this approach in Sect. 6.4.

4 Dataset

In order to evaluate the feasibility of the semantic intersection attack, we performed probabilistic analyses and implemented a simulator that applies the attack to the patterns of actual websites. For this purpose we obtained the query patterns of the top 100,000 websites of the "Alexa Toplist" (http://www.alexa.com) with the headless Webkit-based browser PhantomJS (http://phantomjs.org).[1] As PhantomJS was not able to reach and retrieve all of the websites contained in the Toplist at the time of the data collection (May

---

[1] The source code of our crawler and simulator as well as all experimental data is available at https://github.com/Semantic-IA

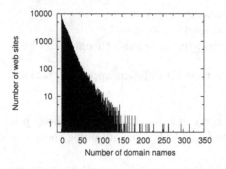 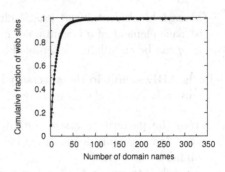

Fig. 2. Histogram and cumulative distribution of pattern lengths

2013) the cleaned dataset contains $|P| = 92{,}880$ patterns and $|Q| = 216{,}925$ unique queries. The average pattern length (*mean value*) is 13.02 with a standard deviation of 14.28. The distribution of pattern lengths as displayed in Fig. 2 shows that, while patterns of the length 1 are frequent, patterns of higher lengths make up the majority of the dataset. The longest pattern consists of 315 queries.

5   Probabilistic Analysis

Before we carry out any practical evaluation using our simulator, we want to get an expectation of the likelihood of **ambiguous results**, which occur if the client happens to draw all the domain names of another website from the dummy database while the range queries needed for the desired website are assembled. If the client draws all domain names of a different pattern by chance and distributes the individual names among the blocks in a plausible fashion, the adversary will observe two patterns: the pattern of the actually desired website as well as the **random pattern**.

5.1   Modeling the Probability of Ambiguous Results

In the 1BD scenario an ambiguous result occurs if the primary domain name of a random pattern (the domain name of the corresponding website) is selected as a dummy in the first block, and all remaining elements of the pattern are contained in the union of the remaining blocks.[2] The probability for an ambiguous result can be modeled as a series of hypergeometric distributions. A hypergeometric distribution $h(k|N; M; n)$ describes the probability of drawing k elements with a specific property when drawing n elements out of a group of N elements, of which M have the desired property:

$$h(k|N; M; n) := \frac{\binom{M}{k}\binom{N-M}{n-k}}{\binom{N}{n}} \tag{1}$$

---

[2] In the 1BD scenario the query distribution between the remaining blocks is irrelevant, as long as all needed queries occur at least once in the union of the blocks.

First, we need to obtain the probability to draw the first element of a pattern of the correct length n into the first block of queries. As the variables of the hypergeometric distribution overlap with those we use to describe the properties of a range query, we substitute them for their equivalents in our range query notation. N is equal to $|Q|$, the number of names in the dummy database. M equals to the number of patterns of the correct length, which we will write as $|P_n|$. In our case, the parameter n of the hypergeometric distribution corresponds to $N-1$, as we will draw $N-1$ dummy names into the first block. By substituting these values into Eq. 1, we obtain the probability $p(n, k)$ of drawing exactly k beginnings of patterns of the length n:

$$p(n, k) := \frac{\binom{|P_n|}{k}\binom{|Q|-|P_n|}{(N-1)-k}}{\binom{|Q|}{N-1}} \tag{2}$$

In addition to that, we need to determine the probability of drawing the remaining $k*(n-1)$ queries into the second block, which contains the remaining $(n-1)*(N-1)$ randomly drawn dummy names in the 1BD scenario. To complete our k patterns, we need to draw $k*(n-1)$ specific dummy names. The probability of success is described by the function $q(n, k)$, which is given in Eq. 3.

$$q(n, k) := \frac{\binom{n-1}{n-1}^k\binom{|Q|-(n-1)*k}{(n-1)*(N-1)-(n-1)}}{\binom{|Q|}{(n-1)*(N-1)}} = \frac{\binom{|Q|-(n-1)*k}{(n-1)*(N-1)-(n-1)*k}}{\binom{|Q|}{(n-1)*(N-1)}} \tag{3}$$

The two probabilities $p(n, k)$ and $q(n, k)$ can now be combined to receive the probability of drawing k complete patterns of the correct length n:

$$P(n, k) := p(n, k) * q(n, k) \tag{4}$$

In this context, the expected value of $P(n, k)$ for different values of n is of interest, as it describes the average number of patterns we expect to see. The expected value, in general, is defined as:

$$E(X) := \sum_{i \in I}(x_i p_i) \tag{5}$$

In our case, x_1 is k, as it describes the number of patterns, and p_i equals $P(n, k)$ as the probability of drawing k patterns, i.e., the expected value is

$$E(n) := 1 + \sum_{k=1}^{N-1}(P(n, k) * k) \tag{6}$$

We are adding 1 to the result, as the original pattern will always be present. Equation 6 will only calculate the expected value for patterns of a specific length. However, as the adversary does not know the length of the pattern with certainty in the 1BD scenario, we have to consider patterns of any length. For that, we have to use a modified variant of Eq. 3:

Table 1. Expected avg. number of detected patterns $F(N)$ for varying block sizes N

N	10	50	100
$F(N)$	1.35	2.93	4.83

$$q(n, k, M) := \frac{\binom{|Q|-(n-1)*k}{(M-1)*(N-1)-(n-1)*k}}{\binom{|Q|}{(M-1)*(N-1)}} \tag{7}$$

In Eq. 7, n is the length of the random pattern, while M is the length of the original pattern. Accordingly, we modify Eq. 4 and Eq. 6:

$$P(n, k, M) := p(n, k) * q(n, k, M) \tag{8}$$

$$E(M) := 1 + \sum_{n=1}^{M} \sum_{k=1}^{N-1} (P(n, k, M) * k) \tag{9}$$

Finally, to determine the expected mean value of the number of detected patterns given a specific block size N, we calculate

$$F(N) = \frac{1}{|P|} * \sum_{M=1}^{L} (E(M) * |P_M|) \tag{10}$$

where L is the length of the longest pattern, and $|P_M|$ the number of patterns having length M.

5.2   Analytical Result

The results (cf. Table 1) indicate that an adversary will, on average, detect only very few random patterns. As expected, the privacy expectation for singular queries ($\frac{1}{N}$) does not apply to the web surfing scenario.

Note that for reasons of conciseness we have provided a slightly simplified model, which disregards overlaps between patterns. Actually, the adversary must expect to find a slightly *higher* number of patterns, because a domain name that is contained within multiple patterns has to be drawn only once to be detected as part of all patterns. Nevertheless, the analysis is instructive and provides us with a baseline for the empirical evaluations that we will describe in the following.

6   Evaluation

In order to evaluate the effectiveness of the semantic intersection attack in a realistic scenario, we developed a simulator that enables us to efficiently test different attack strategies and various assumptions about the knowledge of the adversary. In the following we present results for the 1BD scenario.

Methodology Given a dataset the simulator will generate range queries for all the patterns from the dataset and perform the semantic intersection attack. We are interested in the influence of two factors on the effectiveness of the attack, namely the *block size N*, and the *size of the dummy database* $|Q|$ that contains the dummy names. If the range query scheme was to be used in practice, these two factors could be easily influenced by the user. Thus, it is worthwhile to analyze their effect on the attainable privacy.

In the following, we will use the metric of k-**identifiability**, which is derived from the well-known metric k-anonymity [16]: A set of consecutively observed range queries is said to be k-identifiable, if the adversary finds *exactly* k matching patterns of websites in his pattern database. For conciseness we will show the cumulative distribution of the fraction of k-identifiable patterns, i. e., the fraction of patterns that are k-identifiable or less than k-identifiable.

6.1   Results of Experiment 1: Variation of Block Size

For the purpose of this analysis, we consider three different block sizes: $N = 10$, $N = 50$, and $N = 100$. [10] has shown that the median latency exceeds 1200 ms for a block size of $N = 100$, rendering higher values impractical for practical use.

Based on the result of Sect. 5, we expect to receive some, but not many ambiguous results, i. e., instances where the whole pattern of a different website appears in a set of consecutively observed range queries by chance. Intuitively, the larger the block size, the more random patterns will occur. Accordingly, we expect the effectiveness of the attack to degrade with increasing block sizes.

As can be seen in Table 2 and Fig. 3, the smallest block size provides little privacy, with 62 % of patterns being 1-identifiable. Consequently, the median of the observed k-identifiability values is 1. 99 % of patterns are 5-identifiable or better. No pattern is more than 6-identifiable. For a larger block size of $N = 50$, only 8 % of patterns are 1-identifiable, but the cumulative distribution quickly approaches 100 %. All patterns are 14-identifiable or less, and the median of all observed k-identifiability values is 3, i. e., for 50 % of the websites the adversary can narrow down the actually desired site to a set of 3 or less sites, which is far smaller than the baseline probability of $\frac{1}{50}$ for finding the desired domain name in the first block. As expected, $N = 100$ is most effective: 0.8 % of patterns are 1-identifiable, but still 43 % of patterns are at most 5-identifiable.

Generally, we can observe diminishing returns when the block size is increased. While the increase from $N = 10$ to 50 leads to 54 % less 1-identifiable patterns, adding another 50 queries per block only decreases the fraction by 7.2 percentage points. The same is true for the maximum k-identifiability, which increases by eight and four, respectively. On overall, the results indicate that range queries provide far less privacy than suggested by Zhao et al. in the web surfing scenario.

1BD-improved. We also considered an improved attack algorithm that guesses the length of the desired patterns based on the total number of observed queries in the second block, resulting in a range of possible pattern lengths. This allows the adversary to reject all patterns that do not fall into this range. As a result

Table 2. Results for varying block sizes N given the whole dummy database

N	S	1-identifiable	$\leq$ 5-identifiable	median(k)	max(k)
10	216,925	62 %	99 %	1	6
50	216,925	8 %	88 %	3	14
100	216,925	1 %	43 %	6	18

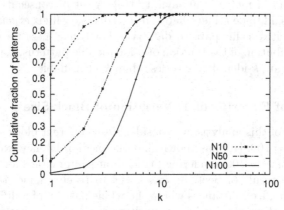

Fig. 3. Distribution of k-identifiability for varying block sizes N (whole database)

80 % ($N = 100$) and 94 % ($N = 10$) of all patterns are 1-identifiable. Due to space constraints, we are unable to adequately cover the calculations to estimate the length in this paper, but we have released an implementation including the relevant documentation in the source code repository (see Footnote 1).

6.2   Results of Experiment 2: Variation of Dummy Database

Generating and maintaining a dummy database is a non-trivial task for the client, which gets harder the larger the database is supposed to be. Accordingly, the importance of the size of the dummy database is of interest. We assume that the client's dummy database is always a subset of the pattern database of the adversary, because, in general, the adversary will have access to more resources than the client, and collecting patterns scales very well.

We compare the effectiveness of three different database sizes ($S = 2000$, 20,000 and 200,000). The domain names are chosen by drawing patterns from the full pattern database (without replacement) and adding all domain names of each pattern to the dummy database. This process continues until exactly S unique domain names have been found. We select full patterns to increase the chance that the client randomly chooses a full pattern when drawing dummies. We used a fixed block size of $N = 50$ for this experiment.

Table 3. Results for varying dummy database sizes S given the block size $N = 50$

N	S	1-identifiable	$\leq$ 5-identifiable	median(k)	max(k)
50	2,000	19 %	92 %	3	14
50	20,000	16 %	95 %	3	11
50	200,000	9 %	88 %	3	13

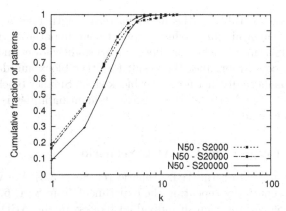

Fig. 4. Distribution of k-identifiability for varying dummy database sizes S; $N = 50$

Fig. 4 shows that the differences are quite small on overall. Thus, the biggest effect of varying the database is the change in the percentage of 1-identifiable patterns: The percentage of 1-identifiable patterns drops by three percentage points when the dummy database size is increased from $S = 2000$ to $S = 20,000$, and by another 7 points on the second increase to $S = 200,000$. The observed changes have a much smaller effect than the variation of the block size; however, regardless of these results, a larger database is always desirable to prevent other attacks, such as the enumeration of the client's database.

6.3   Effect of Pattern Length on Site Identifiability

Now that we know the effect of varying the block size, the composition of the different k-identifiabilities is of interest. With this information, we can determine **whether websites with longer or shorter patterns are more at risk** to be identified. Intuitively, shorter patterns should generally have lower k-identifiabilities, as comparatively few dummies are drawn to obfuscate them, decreasing the chance of drawing a whole pattern. Conversely, longer patterns should generally achieve higher k-identifiabilities, as they use a higher number of dummy domain names. We will now test this hypothesis by analyzing the composition of the different k-identifiabilities, using the results of our simulation with a block size of $N = 50$ and the full dummy database ($S = 216{,}925$).

Table 4. Number of patterns n_k, mean length $\overline{|p|}$ and standard deviation SD aggregated by resulting k-identifiability ($N = 50$, $S = 216{,}925$)

k	1	2	3	4	5	6	7	8	9	≥ 10
n_k	7,693	18,790	23,184	19,784	12,497	6,532	2,875	1,077	336	121
$\overline{|p|}$	10.59	11.43	12.52	13.54	14.43	15.45	16.22	17.65	17.09	19.47
SD	12.16	13.24	13.65	14.55	15.02	16.14	16.65	17.71	15.35	19.68

As can be seen in Table 4, the mean pattern length rises almost linearly with increasing k-identifiability, which supports our hypothesis. The standard deviation exhibits a similar behavior, albeit with a slightly lower and less uniform growth rate. We could reproduce this result for other block and database sizes. The correlation is more distinct for larger block sizes. Smaller block sizes do not show this behavior as clearly, as the range of k-identifiabilities is too small to show any distinct trend.

6.4   Results of Experiment 3: ABD Scenario

So far, we concentrated on the 1BD scenario (cf. Sect. 3.3). We will now consider the ABD scenario by repeating the experiment from Sect. 6.1, simulating an adversary that can distinguish individual blocks: In the ABD scenario the adversary is able to 1-identify between 87 % ($N = 100$) and 97 % ($N = 10$) of all domain names, vastly improving on the results of 1BD (1 % and 62 %, respectively).

The increased accuracy is due to two effects: Firstly, in the ABD scenario the adversary can derive $|p|$, the length of the obfuscated pattern, and filter the set of candidate patterns accordingly (cf. Sect. 3.3). Secondly, the probability that another matching pattern is drawn from the dummy database by chance is much smaller when it has to meet the three ABD conditions.

The contribution of these two effects to the overall effectiveness obtained for ABD can be analyzed by reviewing the results obtained for the baseline (1BD) in comparison to 1BD-improved (cf. Sect.6.1) and ABD: The results for 1BD-improved, which filters candidate patterns using a vague estimation of $|p|$, already show a significant increase: For $N = 50$ the fraction of 1-identifiable sites is 83 % for 1BD-improved, while it is only 8 % for 1BD. On the other hand, the fraction of 1-identifiable websites obtained for ABD, where matching patterns have to meet the additional conditions and the exact value of $|p|$ is known, rises only by another 6 percentage points (reaching 89 %) compared to 1BD-improved.

While this sort of analysis can not conclusively prove that the effect of filtering by length is larger than the effect of filtering via the ABD conditions, we note that the additional benefit of these conditions is comparatively small when the adversary can estimate the length of the obfuscated pattern.

This result indicates that range query schemes that are supposed to provide privacy in a web surfing scenario have to be devised and implemented in a way that the adversary cannot infer the length of the obfuscated query pattern.

Table 5. Statistics for varying block sizes N using the pattern-based dummy construction strategy

N	S	1-identifiable	$\leq$ 5-identifiable	median(k)	max(k)
10	216,925	0%	0%	10	10
50	216,925	0%	0%	50	50
100	216,925	0%	0%	100	100

7 Countermeasures

Having shown the weaknesses of the range query scheme against a pattern-based attack strategy, we will now discuss possible countermeasures. First, we will discuss and evaluate a pattern-based dummy selection strategy. Afterwards, we will consider other strategies that could be used to hinder the adversary.

7.1 Pattern-Based Dummy Selection Strategy

In the original dummy selection strategy, the client sampled the dummies independently and randomly from his dummy database. In contrast, the client will now draw *whole patterns* from his database. When querying the resolver for a desired pattern, the client will draw $N-1$ random patterns of the same length and use them as dummies. If not enough patterns of the correct length are available, the client will combine two shorter patterns to obtain a concatenated pattern with the correct length. Intuitively, this approach ensures that the adversary will always detect N patterns. The results of our evaluation, shown in Table 5, confirm this conjecture. All patterns are exactly N-identifiable.

However, in real-world usage scenarios, the length of the pattern the client is about to query cannot be known in advance. As the dummies for the first element of the pattern have to be chosen before the query can be sent, the client has no way to be sure of the pattern length of the desired website, as these values may change over time when a website changes. This leads to uncertainty about the correct length of the dummy patterns. A wrong choice of pattern length may be used by the adversary to identify the original pattern. Future research could study more sophisticated dummy selection strategies, drawing from experience gained in the field of obfuscated web search [2].

7.2 Other Countermeasures

As described in the previous section the pattern-based dummy selection strategy is subject to practical limitations. We will briefly cover other countermeasures that may be used to improve the privacy of clients. This list is not exhaustive.

The first option is to use a variable value for N that changes on each block. This will raise the difficulty of determining the length of the original pattern, as long as the adversary cannot distinguish individual blocks. This change would render 1BD-improved useless, as it depends on a fixed number of chosen dummies per block (although similar optimizations could be found that would still improve on the performance of the trivial algorithm). However, this would not impact the performance of the ABD algorithm, as it does not rely on uniform block sizes.

Another improvement that may make the pattern-based strategy more feasible would be to round up the length of the target pattern to the next multiple of a number $x > 1$. The additional queries ("padding") could be chosen randomly, or by choosing patterns of the correct length.

Finally, other privacy-enhancing techniques, such as mixes and onion routing [5,8], can be employed to counter monitoring and tracking efforts. However, these general-purpose solutions are not specifically designed for privacy-preserving DNS resolution and may introduce significant delays into the resolution process.

8   Discussion

We designed our experimental setup to stick as closely as possible to reality. However, for reasons of conciseness and clarity we have neglected some effects. In the following we will discuss whether they affect the validity of our conclusions.

Firstly, the results are implicitly biased due to a closed-world assumption, i.e., our results have been obtained on a dataset of limited size. However, as the Toplist of Alexa contains a large variety of websites we are confident that the results are valid for a large fraction of sites in general. Moreover, we have only evaluated the effectiveness of the attack for the *home pages*; the evaluation of the attack on individual sub-pages is left for future work.

Secondly, while we considered the effects of caching of dummy queries in the 1BD scenario, we disregarded caching of the desired queries: The client may still have (parts of) a pattern in his local cache, resulting in incomplete patterns being sent to the resolver. However, the adversary may adapt to caching by remembering the TTL of all responses he sent to a client and matching the patterns against the union of the received domain names and the cached entries.

Moreover, an adversary who wants to determine all websites a user visits needs the patterns of all websites on the Internet. Such a database would be non-trivial to generate and maintain. However, a *reactive* adversary may visit any domain name he receives a query for and store the pattern for that domain name in its pattern database, making a slightly delayed identification possible.

Finally, we disregarded changing patterns as well as DNS prefetching techniques, which cause longer and more volatile patterns. However, a determined adversary will have no problems in addressing these issues.

9   Conclusion

We demonstrated that random set range queries offer considerably less protection than expected in the use case of web surfing. Our attack exploits characteristic query patterns, which lead to greatly reduced query privacy compared to the estimations made by Zhao et al. in their original work. Moreover, we proposed and evaluated an improved range query scheme using query patterns to disguise the original pattern. We encourage researchers to consider the effects of semantic interdependencies between queries when designing new schemes for query privacy, as the rising pervasiveness of social networking buttons, advertising and analytics makes singular queries less and less common for web surfing.

References

1. Arends, R., Austein, R., Larson, M., Massey, D., Rose, S.: DNS Security Introduction and Requirements. RFC 4033 (March 2005)
2. Balsa, E., Troncoso, C., Díaz, C.: OB-PWS: Obfuscation-Based Private Web Search. In: Symposium on Security and Privacy, pp. 491–505. IEEE (2012)
3. Castillo-Perez, S., Garcia-Alfaro, J.: Anonymous Resolution of DNS Queries. In: Meersman, R., Tari, Z. (eds.) OTM 2008, Part II. LNCS, vol. 5332, pp. 987–1000. Springer, Heidelberg (2008)
4. Castillo-Perez, S., García-Alfaro, J.: Evaluation of Two Privacy–Preserving Protocols for the DNS. In: International Conference on Information Technology: New Generations (ITNG 2009), pp. 411–416. IEEE (2009)
5. Chaum, D.: Untraceable electronic mail, return addresses, and digital pseudonyms. Communications of the ACM 24(2) (1981)
6. Chor, B., Goldreich, O., Kushilevitz, E., Sudan, M.: Private Information Retrieval. In: Symposium on Foundations of Computer Science, pp. 41–50. IEEE (1995)
7. Conrad, D.: Towards Improving DNS Security, Stability, and Resiliency (2012), http://internetsociety.org/sites/default/files/ bp-dnsresiliency-201201-en_0.pdf
8. Dingledine, R., Mathewson, N., Syverson, P.: Tor: The Second-Generation Onion Router. In: USENIX Security Symposium, pp. 303–320 (2004)
9. Eastlake, D.: Domain Name System Security Extensions. RFC 2535 (March 1999)
10. Federrath, H., Fuchs, K.-P., Herrmann, D., Piosecny, C.: Privacy-Preserving DNS: Analysis of Broadcast, Range Queries and Mix-Based Protection Methods. In: Atluri, V., Diaz, C. (eds.) ESORICS 2011. LNCS, vol. 6879, pp. 665–683. Springer, Heidelberg (2011)
11. Google Online Security Blog (2013), http://googleonlinesecurity.blogspot.com/2013/03/ google-public-dns-now-supports-dnssec.html (accessed March 18, 2014)
12. Herrmann, D., Banse, C., Federrath, H.: Behavior-based Tracking: Exploiting Characteristic Patterns in DNS Traffic. Computers & Security 39A, 17–33 (November 2013)
13. Lu, Y., Tsudik, G.: Towards Plugging Privacy Leaks in the Domain Name System. In: International Conference on Peer-to-Peer Computing, pp. 1–10. IEEE (2010)
14. Maaß, M.: Schnittmengenangriffe auf DNS Range Queries. Bachelor Thesis, University of Hamburg, http://nbn-resolving.de/urn:nbn:de:gbv:18-228-7-1989 (2013)
15. Ramasubramanian, V., Sirer, E.: The Design and Implementation of a Next Generation Name Service for the Internet. In: SIGCOMM, pp. 331–342. ACM (2004)
16. Sweeney, L.: k-Anonymity: A Model for Protecting Privacy. International Journal of Uncertainty, Fuzziness and Knowledge-Based Systems 10(5), 557–570 (2002)
17. Zhao, F., Hori, Y., Sakurai, K.: Analysis of Privacy Disclosure in DNS Query. In: International Conference on Multimedia and Ubiquitous Engineering, pp. 952–957. IEEE (2007)
18. Zhao, F., Hori, Y., Sakurai, K.: Two–Servers PIR Based DNS Query Scheme with Privacy–Preserving. In: International Conference on Intelligent Pervasive Computing, pp. 299–302. IEEE (2007)

A Novel Metric for the Evaluation of IDSs Effectiveness

Khalid Nasr[1] and Anas Abou El Kalam[2]

[1] Electrical Eng. Dept., Faculty of Engineering, Minia University, Egypt
khalid.nasr79@hotmail.com
[2] OSCARS Laboratory, UCA/ENSA of Marrakesh, Morocco
anas@ensa.ac.ma

Abstract. Nowadays intrusion detection system (IDS) has a considerable attention as a crucial element in network security. The question that arises is which IDS is effective for our system? The answer should inevitably take into account the evaluation of IDSs effectiveness. Dealing with this challenge, many valuable evaluation metrics have been introduced such as *receiver operating characteristic (ROC) curve, Bayesian detection rate, intrusion detection capability, intrusion detection operating characteristic, cost-based metrics,* etc. The benefits and drawbacks of these metrics are discussed in this paper. We subsequently propose a novel metric called *intrusion detection effectiveness* (E_{ID}) that manipulates the drawbacks of the existing ones, taking into account all essential and related parameters. We demonstrate the utility of E_{ID} over the previously proposed ones, and how it realizes the measurement of the actual effectiveness rather than the relative effectiveness as followed by the existing ones. E_{ID} can be used for evaluating the wired or wireless IDSs effectiveness. Additionally, we conduct experimental evaluation of two popular wireless IDSs (WIDSs), *Kismet* and *AirSnare*, to illustrate the benefits of E_{ID}.

Keywords: IDSs effectiveness, evaluation metrics, intrusion detection, false alarms.

1 Introduction

Despite the importance of intrusion detection systems (IDSs) in network security, their performance is sometimes not satisfying in practice. Thus, evaluating the IDSs performance is a pressing necessity. Many attributes judge the IDSs performance such as *effectiveness, efficiency, interoperability* [1], *redundant alerts correlation, attack type recognizing, the impact on the supervised system resources, scalability and flexibility, etc.* No doubt that the IDSs effectiveness is considered the main attribute and basic factor in evaluating the IDSs performance, where it reflects the ability of the IDS to detect the intrusive activities and the absence degree of the false alarms; they are considered the main great challenges facing the IDSs performance.

Evaluation metrics play the significant role in measuring and evaluating the IDSs effectiveness. In this paper, we study the well-known existing metrics for the IDSs effectiveness evaluation, such as *receiver operating characteristic (ROC)* [2] [3], *Bayesian detection rate ($P(I|A)$)* [1], *cumulative cost* [4], *expected cost* [5], *intrusion*

N. Cuppens-Boulahia et al. (Eds.): SEC 2014, IFIP AICT 428, pp. 220–233, 2014.

detection capability (C_{ID}) [6], and *intrusion detection operating characteristic* (*IDOC*) [7]. Each of these metrics is based on a different theoretical approach such as *decision theory* [5], *information theory* [6], *cost-based analysis* [4] [5], etc. The strengths and weaknesses of these metrics are discussed in this paper, and consequently we propose a novel evaluation metric called *intrusion detection effectiveness* (E_{ID}) that manipulates the drawbacks of the existing ones, especially the common main drawback that is manifested in their main notion of measuring the IDSs effectiveness on the basis of comparing two IDSs or more to select the best one, whereas this selected one may be ineffective.

Our developed metric E_{ID} helps in measuring the actual effectiveness of IDSs rather than measuring the relative effectiveness as followed by the previously proposed metrics. The notion of E_{ID} is based on comparing the operation curve of the IDS under test to the optimal operation curve (i.e., created as a zero reference curve for the optimal operation state) by calculating the variation between the two curves. The variation value interprets the deviation of the IDS operation from the intended optimal operation.

The rest of this paper is organized as follows. Section 2 studies the existing metrics, their benefits, and their drawbacks. Section 3 introduces the novel proposed metric E_{ID} for evaluating the IDSs effectiveness. Section 4 presents the proof of the concept to achieve a credible evaluation of two popular WIDSs (*Kismet* and *AirSnare*). Finally, section 5 presents our conclusion and perspective.

2   Related Work

Various appreciable efforts have been exerted in the recent past for developing reliable evaluation metrics. In this section, we are concerned with analyzing the most valuable and well-known metrics for evaluating the IDSs effectiveness. *Bayesian detection rate* has a great concern in this paper, where we manipulate it to extract the base equation for our proposed metric E_{ID} (*intrusion detection effectiveness*).

Receiver Operating Characteristic (*ROC*). The first unified metric used in the experimental evaluation of IDSs is the *receiver operating characteristic* (*ROC*) curve, as applied by DARPA evaluations [2] [3]. *ROC* curve is used to analyze the trade-off between *detection rate* and *false alarms rate*. The notion of using *ROC* curve in IDSs evaluation is based on comparing the IDSs curves to select the best one. If *ROC* curves don't cross, then the upper curve with the higher values of *detection rate* is considered better than the lower ones. But, if *ROC* curves are crossed, then the differentiation between them is based on the area under each curve. One of the drawbacks of *ROC* curve is its disregard of *base-rate* parameter [1] that is considered a significant parameter in the IDSs evaluation, where it reflects the hostility of the operating environment (i.e., represented by the *prior probability of intrusion*).

Bayesian Detection Rate (*P(I\A)*). *Bayesian detection rate* [1] defines a mathematical relation between the main parameters related to the intrusion detection effectiveness, i.e., *detection rate, false alarms rate,* and *base-rate*. The main advantage of this metric is its consideration of the *base-rate* parameter or probability of intrusion ($P(I)$). *Bayesian detection rate* ($P(I|A)$) (Eq. 1) was mainly derived from the Bayes' theorem by considering the possible events related to IDSs.

$$P(I|A) = \frac{P(I) \cdot P(A|I)}{P(I) \cdot P(A|I) + P(\neg I) \cdot P(A|\neg I)}$$ Eq. 1

Where I, $\neg I$, A, $P(A|I)$, and $P(A|\neg I)$ denote intrusions, normal traffic, alarms, detection rate, and false alarms rate respectively. Axelsson in [1] studied the effect of the base-rate fallacy on the intrusion detection, and he demonstrated that the limiting factor for IDS performance is not the ability to correctly identify the intrusions, but rather its ability to suppress the false alarms. We totally agree with this conclusion.

Unfortunately, despite the prominence of *Bayesian detection rate* and its consideration of the significant parameters for the IDSs effectiveness evaluation, it is not completely expressive metric for measuring the IDSs effectiveness. We analyze $P(I|A)$ (Eq. 1) mathematically to reach the following results:

Case 1: if $P(A|I) = P(A|\neg I) = 1$
Combining these values with equation Eq. 1, then;

$$P(I|A) = \frac{P(I)}{P(I) + P(\neg I)}$$

Since $P(I) + P(\neg I) = 1$, then;

$$P(I|A) = P(I)$$ Eq. 2

Case 2: if $P(A|I) = 0$
Combining this value and equation Eq. 1, then;

$$P(I|A) = 0$$ Eq. 3

$P(I|A)$ gives reasonable expressions for the IDSs effectiveness, just in the above two cases. In *case* 1 of passing all the traffic with raised alarms ($P(A|I) = P(A|\neg I) = 1$), $P(I|A)$ equals $P(I)$ (Eq. 2) that is considered the perfect expression in this case; where the ratio of the detected intrusions to the generated alarms corresponds to the ratio of the intrusions to the input traffic. In *case* 2, $P(I|A)$ equals zero when the *detection rate* $P(A|I)$ comes to nought (Eq. 3), where $P(A|I)$ is the predominant parameter in equation Eq. 1. However, the drawback of *Bayesian detection rate* $P(I|A)$ is manifested when the *false alarms* or *false positive rate* $P(A|\neg I)$ is equal or close to zero as shown in the following *case* 3.

Case 3: as $P(A|\neg I)$ approaches 0, then equation Eq. 1 can be written as;

$$\lim_{P(A|\neg I) \to 0} P(I|A) = \lim_{P(A|\neg I) \to 0} \frac{P(I) \cdot P(A|I)}{P(I) \cdot P(A|I) + P(\neg I) \cdot P(A|\neg I)} = 1$$ Eq. 4

As we observe from equation Eq. 4, when $P(A|\neg I)$ equals or approaches "0", $P(I|A)$ is equal to constant value "1" for any value of $P(A|I)$; this unfortunately seems illogical. How the IDSs effectiveness can be evaluated in disregard of the *detection rate* $P(A|I)$? Merely considering the complete absence of false alarms is insufficient. Thus $P(I|A)$, in this case, is inexpressive metric for the IDSs effectiveness or even the detection rate. However, we propose a reasonable solution for this drawback through our manipulation of $P(I|A)$ to become completely expressive in a new form called *enhanced Bayesian detection rate (EBD)* (section 3.1). We use *EBD* as a base equation for our proposed metric E_{ID} (section 3.2).

Cost-Based Metrics. Cost-based metrics analyze the intrusion detection from the perspective of costs. Stolfo et al. [4] proposed *cumulative cost* metric for evaluating the fraud and intrusion detection in the financial information systems. They defined three types of costs; *operational, damage,* and *challenge costs. Operational cost* refers to the resources needed to run the IDS. *Damage cost* is the amount of damage caused by the leaked undetected intrusions. *Challenge cost* is the cost of acting upon an intrusion when it is detected. $CumulativeCost(S)$ metric (Eq. 5) is derived by considering the challenge and damage costs on the outcome events of IDSs plus the operational cost to evaluate the IDSs over test set "S" of labeled connection "c". One of the drawbacks of this metric is its disregard of the *base-rate* parameter.

$$CumulativeCost(S) = \sum_{c \in S} (Cost(c) + OpCost(c)) \qquad \text{Eq. 5}$$

The second noted metric is *expected cost* metric that was proposed by Gaffney and Ulvila [5] who argued that both *ROC* analysis and *cumulative cost* metric are incomplete metrics. They used decision analysis techniques to combine and extend *ROC* analysis and cost-based analysis to provide *expected cost* metric that considers the *base-rate* parameter. More details about this metric are available in [5].

Intrusion Detection Capability (C_{ID}). Gu et al. [6] proposed an information-theoretic measure of the intrusion detection capability. They depended on the notion of having less uncertainty about the IDS input, given the IDS output. They introduced C_{ID} metric (Eq. 6) as the mutual information between the IDS input X and output Y normalized by the entropy (or self-information) of the input $H(X)$. C_{ID} is maximized by calculating the operating point that minimizes the uncertainty of the input.

$$C_{ID} = \frac{I(X;Y)}{H(X)} = \frac{H(X) - H(X|Y)}{H(X)} \qquad \text{Eq. 6}$$

Where $H(X|Y)$ is the entropy of X given Y. We believe that the notion of C_{ID} for minimizing the uncertainty of the input is inapplicable in the IDSs evaluation domain.

Intrusion Detection Operating Characteristic (*IDOC*). Cardenas et al. [7] used $P(I|A)$ (Eq. 1) and introduced the *intrusion detection operating characteristic (IDOC)* as a trade-off curve between the $P(I|A)$ and the *probability of intrusion detection* $P(A|I)$. As a consequence of the dependence of *IDOC* on the *Bayesian detection rate* equation, it carries all its drawbacks.

The common drawback of most existing metrics lies in their main notion of comparing two or more IDSs to select the best one, although this selected one may be ineffective. This is considered a deficient approach that leads to measuring the *relative effectiveness* rather than the *actual effectiveness*. We are concerned with manipulating this drawback and the above mentioned ones.

3   Intrusion Detection Effectiveness (E_{ID})

The logical approach for measuring the *actual effectiveness* is comparing the IDS under test to the optimal operation level (as a reference). We thus propose a new evaluation metric E_{ID} (*intrusion detection effectiveness*) that is based on the notion of comparing the operation curve of the IDS under test to the optimal operation curve (created as a zero reference curve) by calculating the variation between the two curves. The variation value interprets the deviation of the IDS from the intended optimal operation. We believe that the main parameters which the IDS effectiveness depends on are *detection rate, false alarms rate,* and *base-rate.* To realize the notion of E_{ID}, we need an expressive formula or equation that considers these parameters to be used as a base for E_{ID}. As a result of our research, we discovered that *Bayesian detection rate (Eq. 1)* regards the needed parameters, but it is inappropriate as a base equation due to its drawback when the *false alarms rate* equals or approaches "0" (Eq. 4). Consequently, we manipulate this drawback to derive a new completely expressive formula called *enhanced Bayesian detection rate (EBD)* to become the base for E_{ID}.

3.1   Deriving the Enhanced Bayesian Detection Rate (*EBD*)

As a brief summary of our analysis of *Bayesian detection rate* $P(I|A)$ (section 2), in *case 1* ($P(A|I) = P(A|\neg I) = 1$) and *case 2* ($P(A|I) = 0$), $P(I|A)$ gives reasonable expressions, but it is inexpressive in *case 3* (as $P(A|\neg I)$ equals or approaches "0"). Accordingly, we are concerned with manipulating *case 3*. By analyzing *case 3*, we conclude that the logical expressive formula for $P(I|A)$, as $P(A|\neg I)$ equals or approaches "0", should be equal to $P(A|I)$. This can be achieved by modifying the denominator of equation Eq. 4 to produce the following new formula.

$$\lim_{P(A|\neg I) \to 0} P(I|A) = \lim_{P(A|\neg I) \to 0} \frac{P(I) \cdot P(A|I)}{P(I) \cdot P(A|I)_{\sim=1} + P(\neg I) \cdot P(A|\neg I)}$$

$$= \frac{\cancel{P(I)} \cdot P(A|I)}{\cancel{P(I)} \cdot P(A|I)_{\sim=1}} = P(A|I) \qquad \text{Eq. 7}$$

From equations Eq. 1, Eq. 2, Eq. 3 and Eq. 7 we produce the *enhanced Bayesian detection rate (EBD)* (Eq. 8) that is completely expressive under all operation conditions.

$$EBD = \frac{P(I) \cdot P(A|I)}{P(I) + P(\neg I) \cdot P(A|\neg I)} \qquad \text{Eq. 8}$$

Property 1
    EBD can be defined as the posterior probability of the detected intrusions (*TP*) given the total output of intrusion related responses (*TP + FN*) and false alarms (*FP*).

Proof
    The intrusion detection can be summarized by the simple model shown in Fig. 1, where $I, \neg I, A, \neg A, TP, FP, FN,$ and TN denote intrusions, normal traffic, alarms, no alarms, true positives, false positives, false negatives, and true negatives respectively.

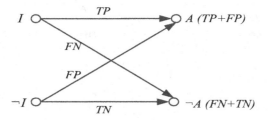

Fig. 1. Intrusion Detection Model

Basically,
$$P(I) = I/(\neg I + I)$$
$$P(\neg I) = \neg I/(\neg I + I)$$
$$P(A|I) = TP/I = TP/(TP + FN)$$
$$P(A|\neg I) = FP/\neg I = FP/(FP + TN)$$

Recalling equation Eq. 8 and solving it by these parameters, then;

$$EBD = \frac{P(I) \cdot P(A|I)}{P(I) + P(\neg I) \cdot P(A|\neg I)} = \frac{1}{\dfrac{1}{P(A|I)} + \dfrac{P(\neg I) \cdot P(A|\neg I)}{P(I) \cdot P(A|I)}}$$

$$= \frac{1}{\dfrac{TP + FN}{TP} + \dfrac{\neg I \cdot FP/(FP + TN)}{I \cdot TP/(TP + FN)}} = \frac{TP}{TP + FN + FP} \qquad \text{Eq. 9}$$

Equation Eq. 9 shows the significance of *EBD* for measuring the proportion of the intrusion related responses ($TP + FN$) and false alarms (FP) that correspond to the detected intrusions (TP). This is considered one of the great advantages of *EBD* over $P(I|A)$ that ignores the *false negatives* (FN), as demonstrated in the following.

By recalling $P(I|A)$ (Eq. 1) and solving it in the same way, then;

$$P(I|A) = \frac{P(I) \cdot P(A|I)}{P(I) \cdot P(A|I) + P(\neg I) \cdot P(A|\neg I)} = \frac{1}{1 + \dfrac{P(\neg I) \cdot P(A|\neg I)}{P(I) \cdot P(A|I)}}$$

$$= \frac{1}{1 + \dfrac{\neg I \cdot FP/(FP + TN)}{I \cdot TP/(TP + FN)}} = \frac{TP}{TP + FP} \qquad \text{Eq. 10}$$

Equation Eq. 10 clarifies that $P(I|A)$ disregards *FN* parameter that influences the expressiveness of the metric.

To clarify more the benefit of *EBD* over $P(I|A)$ regarding taking the whole false responses ($FP+FN$) into account, the relationships between the IDS input and output events are depicted through Venn diagram (Fig. 2). The intersections between the different events are represented by the areas denoted by numbers from 1 to 4. Area 1 represents the tranquil area of no intrusion and no alarm, but areas 2, 3 and 4 represent the challenge areas of false responses (areas 2 and 4) and detected intrusions (area 3). These events in the areas 2, 3 and 4 have a great significance in the IDSs effectiveness evaluation, and they should be considered by the evaluation metric. This is attained by *EBD* as shown in equation Eq. 9. On the contrary, $P(I|A)$ considers only the events of the areas 3 and 4 as shown by Eq. 10.

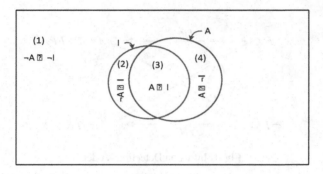

Fig. 2. The Relationships between the IDS Input and Output Events

Property 2

EBD is an expressive metric under different operation conditions.

Proof

EBD agrees with $P(I|A)$ on the aforementioned *case* 1 (Eq. 2) and *case* 2 (Eq.3), and gives the same expressive results. As well, *EBD* gives an expressive value in the third case (Eq. 7) according to its mathematical manipulation. For the other rest conditions, *EBD* can be analyzed as follows.

Case 4: if $P(A|\neg I) = 1$

Combining this value with equation Eq. 8, then;

$$EBD = \frac{P(I) \cdot P(A|I)}{P(I) + P(\neg I)}$$

Since $P(I) + P(\neg I) = 1$, then;

$$EBD = P(I) \cdot P(A|I) = \frac{\cancel{I}}{(\neg I + I)} \cdot \frac{TP}{\cancel{I}} = \frac{TP}{TP + FN + FP} \qquad \text{Eq. 11}$$

Equation Eq. 11 demonstrates the expressiveness of *EBD* in the worst case of false alarms $(P(A|\neg I) = 1)$.

Case 5: if $P(A|I) = 1$

Combining this value with equation Eq. 8, then;

$$EBD = \frac{P(I)}{P(I) + P(\neg I) \cdot P(A|\neg I)} = \frac{1}{1 + \frac{\neg I \cdot FP/(FP + TN)}{TP}} = \frac{TP}{TP + FP} \qquad \text{Eq. 12}$$

As shown in equation Eq. 12, *EBD* equals the proportion of the generated alarms that correspond to the detected intrusions. This is the expressive formula in this case of the absence of false negatives $(P(A|I) = 1 \Leftrightarrow FN = 0)$. The above analysis concludes the expressiveness of *EBD* under different operation conditions.

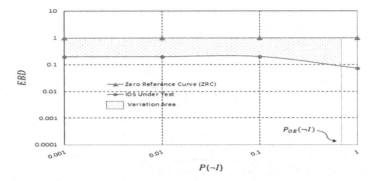

Fig. 3. The trade-off between *EBD* and *P(¬I)*

3.2   Deriving the Intrusion Detection Effectiveness (E_{ID})

Following the main notion of our metric E_{ID}, we consider the trade-off between *EBD* and $P(\neg I)$ that helps in developing the expressive metric E_{ID}. To simplify dealing with *EBD* (Eq. 8), we adapt it to be a function of $P(\neg I)$ as shown in Eq. 13.

$$EBD = \frac{P(A|I) - P(\neg I) \cdot P(A|I)}{1 - P(\neg I) \cdot (1 - P(A|\neg I))} \qquad \text{Eq. 13}$$

The first step in deriving E_{ID} is calculating and plotting the *zero reference curve* (*ZRC*) as a trade-off between *EBD* and $P(\neg I)$ with assumption of the optimal operation case of the IDS under test. To clarify the idea of calculating and plotting *ZRC*, we assume an IDS installed in an operating environment with hostility or probability of intrusion $P(I)=3*10^{-4}$. Then, the probability of no intrusion $P(\neg I) = 1 - P(I) = 0.9997$. First, we assume that the IDS under test operates at the optimal case with perfect *detection rate* ($P(A|I)=1$) and complete absence of *false alarms* ($P(A|\neg I) = 0$). We combine these values with *EBD* (Eq. 13) to plot *ZRC* (Fig. 3). As a note, the axes are set to logarithmic scale. The second step, we plot the real operation curve of the IDS with the actual values of the *detection rate* and *false alarms*; we assume their values as $P(A|I) = 0.2$ and $P(A|\neg I) = 0.0035$. Now we have two operation curves; one as a *ZRC* curve for the optimal operation and the other represents the actual operation curve (Fig. 3). The variation between the two curves is represented by the dotted area. $P_{OE}(\neg I)$ denotes the probability of no intrusion in the operating environment, and it refers to the upper limit of the variation area.

We normalize this variation by the area under *ZRC* (only through $P(\neg I) = [0, P_{OE}(\neg I)]$) to have a representative metric E_{ID} of values in the range [0, 1]; where "0" indicates zero deviation from the intended optimal operation and then perfect effectiveness, but "1" indicates the maximum deviation and then zero effectiveness. E_{ID} is represented by equation Eq. 14, where EBD_{ZRC}, $P_{ZRC}(A|I)$, and $P_{ZRC}(A|\neg I)$ denote *EBD*, detection rate, and false alarms of *ZRC* respectively. As well, EBD_{ID}, $P_{ID}(A|I)$, and $P_{ID}(A|\neg I)$ denote *EBD*, detection rate, and false alarms of IDS under test respectively. $P(\neg I)$ is considered the integration variable.

$$E_{ID} = \frac{1}{\int_0^{P_{OE}(\neg I)} EBD_{ZRC}\, dP(\neg I)} \left(\int_0^{P_{OE}(\neg I)} EBD_{ZRC}\, dP(\neg I) \right.$$

$$\left. - \int_0^{P_{OE}(\neg I)} EBD_{ID}\, dP(\neg I) \right) \qquad \text{Eq. 14}$$

Where,

$$EBD_{ZRC} = \frac{P(I) \cdot P_{ZRC}(A|I)_{\rightsquigarrow=1}}{P(I) + P(\neg I) \cdot P_{ZRC}(A|\neg I)_{\rightsquigarrow=0}} = 1 \qquad \text{Eq. 15}$$

$$EBD_{ID} = \frac{P_{ID}(A|I) - P(\neg I) \cdot P_{ID}(A|I)}{1 - P(\neg I) \cdot (1 - P_{ID}(A|\neg I))} \qquad \text{Eq. 16}$$

Then equation Eq. 14 becomes;

$$E_{ID} = 1 - \frac{\int_0^{P_{OE}(\neg I)} EBD_{ID}\, dP(\neg I)}{P_{OE}(\neg I)} \qquad \text{Eq. 17}$$

Equation Eq. 17 can be solved mathematically [8], and E_{ID} becomes;

$$E_{ID} = 1 - \frac{P_{ID}(A|I) \cdot \left(P_{OE}(\neg I) + \left(\frac{1}{(1 - P_{ID}(A|\neg I))} - 1 \right) ln|1 - P_{OE}(\neg I) \cdot (1 - P_{ID}(A|\neg I))| \right)}{P_{OE}(\neg I) \cdot (1 - P_{ID}(A|\neg I))} \qquad \text{Eq. 18}$$

Property 3

E_{ID} is an expressive metric for measuring the actual effectiveness of IDSs by values in the range [0,1], where "0" indicates the ideal case of supreme effectiveness, but "1" indicates the worst case of zero effectiveness.

Proof

Case 1: when the IDS detects all the intrusive activities $(P(A|I) = 1)$ and generates no false alarms $(P(A|\neg I) = 0)$, then its deviation from the optimal operation case can be measured by E_{ID} (Eq. 18) as follows.

$$E_{ID} = 1 - \frac{P_{ID}(A|I)_{\rightsquigarrow=1} \cdot (P_{OE}(\neg I) + 0)}{P_{OE}(\neg I) \cdot (1 - P_{ID}(A|\neg I)_{\rightsquigarrow=0})} = 1 - \frac{P_{OE}(\neg I)}{P_{OE}(\neg I)} = 0 \qquad \text{Eq. 19}$$

Equation Eq. 19 demonstrates the supreme effectiveness of the IDS by its zero deviation from the optimal operation case.

Case 2: when the IDS fails to detect the intrusions $(P(A|I) = 0)$, its deviation from the optimal operation case can be measured by E_{ID} (Eq. 18) as follows.

$$E_{ID} = 1 - \frac{0}{P_{OE}(\neg I) \cdot (1 - P_{ID}(A|\neg I))} = 1 \qquad \text{Eq. 20}$$

Equation Eq. 20 demonstrates the maximum deviation of the IDS from the optimal operation case and accordingly its ineffectiveness.

Besides *property* 1 and *property* 2 of *EBD* that is the base equation of E_{ID}, it becomes clear from equations Eq. 19 and Eq. 20 that E_{ID} is an expressive metric for measuring the actual effectiveness. E_{ID} can be used for evaluating the effectiveness of wired or wireless IDSs.

4   Proof of the Concept

As a proof of the concept, we conduct an experimental evaluation of two popular wireless IDSs (WIDSs) *Kismet* (for Linux) [9] and *AirSnare* (for Windows) [10], and measure their effectiveness using E_{ID}. We used RF shielded testbed, an access point Linksys WRT54GL, and workstations (Linux and Windows) with Wi-Fi adapters ALFA awus036h and D-Link DWA-110 with respect to the compatibility with the operating systems and the WIDSs. We resorted to use the RF shielded testbed to circumvent the problem of the uncontrolled 802.11 traffic from the adjacent wireless stations that obstructs the accurate measurements of the considered parameters. We are concerned with the wireless infrastructure mode with two possible scenarios for the installation of WIDSs (Fig. 4); *scenario* 1: the WIDS was installed on the access point, and *scenario* 2: the WIDS was installed on a terminal machine as a victim. As for the normal background traffic, we generated real traffic by capturing the operational traffic during the normal operation of a private network installed for this purpose, and then replaying the collected traffic into the testbed. This private network (Fig. 4) consists of an access point, three workstations (i.e., two machines operate under Windows and the third one operates under Linux) and two mobile phones (i.e., Android system). Table 1 shows the statistics of the collected benign traffic.

As for the generated attacks, the credible evaluation of WIDSs necessitates taking into account all possible attacks. While this is operationally impossible, it is necessary to select representative attack test cases that are extracted mainly from a holistic classification of wireless attacks. Dealing with this challenge, we used our developed taxonomy of wireless attacks from the perspective of the WIDSs evaluator [11] and we generated the attacks listed in Table 2 according to the representative attack test cases shown in Fig. 5. As well, the attack detection of each WIDS is shown in Table 2. For calculating the detection rate, if we follow the ordinary method that was used in the previous evaluations of IDSs, then Table 2 is sufficient for the calculations and then the detection rate is $P(A|I) = 0.61$ for *Kismet*, and $P(A|I) = 0.167$ for *AirSnare*. These values are not real expressive values for the detection rate, and subsequently have a negative effect on the calculation of the real effectiveness. The best way for calculating the expressive detection rate is considering the probability of occurrence of the attack test cases under the operating environment conditions.

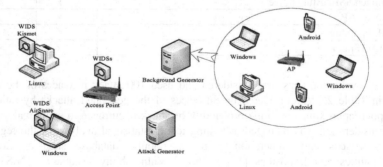

Fig. 4. Evaluation Testbed

Table 1. The Collected Normal Traffic

Frame Subtype	Frame Count
Association request	38
Association response	43
Reassociation request	172
Reassociation response	142
Probe request	227081
Probe response	218602
Beacon	378
Disassociation	332
Authentication	169
Deauthentication	80
Action frames	3484
Null data	89920
QoS data	1723
QoS null data	19868
Total	562032

Table 2. The Attack Detection

Generated Attacks	Kismet	AirSnare
	TP	TP
Deauthentication/Disassociation Flood (< 10 Request)	✓	x
Deauthentication/Disassociation Flood (< 20 Request)	✓	x
Deauthentication/Disassociation Flood (> 30 Request)	✓	✓
Deauthentication/Disassociation Flood (> 100 Request)	✓	✓
Deauthentication/Disassociation (Amok mode)	✓	x
Fake Authentication	✓	x
Authentication Flood	✓	x
Beacon Flood (evil duplicate AP DoS)	✓	x
MITM attack	x	x
ARP Request Replay Attack	x	x
WPA Downgrade	✓	x
WPA Cracking	✓	x
WEP Cracking	x	x
Chopchop	x	x
Hidden SSID Brute Force	x	x
Rogue AP	x	x
RF Jamming	✓	x
MAC Spoofing	x	✓

In our evaluation tests, we considered and used 100 attack instances of the attacks listed in Table 2. We considered the instances of the generated attacks by ratios that correspond approximately to the probability of attack occurrence in some real systems. This consideration was managed according to our statistical analysis of the registered wireless attacks and vulnerabilities in the popular database such as Common Vulnerabilities and Exposures [12], National Vulnerability Database – NIST [13],

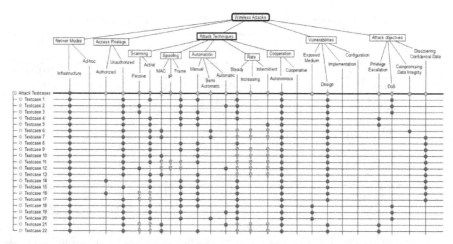

Fig. 5. Representative Attack Test Cases

Table 3. The Generated Attacks and the Corresponding Test Cases

Generated Attacks	Representative Attack Test Cases
Deauthentication/Disassociation Flood	1, 2, 3
Deauthentication/Disassociation (Amok mode)	3
Fake Authentication	4, 5
Authentication Flood	2,3
Beacon Flood (evil duplicate AP DoS)	3
MITM attack	6,7
ARP Request Replay Attack	8
WPA Downgrade	3
WPA Cracking	9
WEP Cracking	10, 11, 12
Chopchop	13
Hidden SSID Brute Force	11
Rogue AP	14, 15, 16, 17
RF Jamming	18, 19, 20
MAC Spoofing	21, 22

and others. It is worth mentioning that we considered in our calculations the deauthentication/disassociation flood attack instances with deauthentication requests > 30 (Table 2); we generated it by 8 instances from total of 100 instances of all the generated attacks. We classified the generated attacks under the representative test cases (Fig. 5 and Table 3), and adjusted the estimated probability of occurrence as shown in Table 4. Then, the expressive detection rate is $P(A|I) = 0.65$ for *Kismet*, and $P(A|I) = 0.13$ for *AirSnare*. In our evaluation environment, the used 100 attack instances generated approximately 1500 malicious frames, in addition to the generated background normal traffic (Table 1). Then, we have hostility or intrusion probability $P(I)=1500/562032=2.66889*10^{-3}$, and no intrusion probability $P(\neg I)=0.99733$. As well, the registered false alarms for the two WIDSs are $P(A|\neg I)=0.008967$ for *Kismet*

Table 4. Probability of Occurrence of the Generated Attack Instances

Attack Test Cases	Estimated Probability	WIDSs Detection Ratio	
		Kismet	AirSnare
1, 2, 3, 4, 5	0.46	✓	✓ (0.08)
6, 7	0.05	x	x
8	0.04	x	x
9	0.13	✓	x
10, 11, 12	0.1	x	x
13	0.04	x	x
14, 15, 16, 17	0.07	x	x
18, 19, 20	0.06	✓	x
21, 22	0.05	x	✓
Total	1	0.65	0.13

and $P(A|\neg I)=0.0014946$ for *AirSnare*. Combining these obtained results with our proposed evaluation metric E_{ID} (Eq. 18), then;

$$E_{ID} \ (kismet) = 0.37$$
$$E_{ID} \ (AirSnare) = 0.871$$

In the same way, as described in section 3.2, we can plot the operation curves of the two WIDSs, besides the *zero reference curve* (*ZRC*) as shown in Fig. 6. E_{ID} of the two WIDSs and Fig. 6 show that *Kismet* operation doesn't deviate much more from the optimal case *ZRC*, in contrast to *AirSnare* that has a great deviation from the optimal case. Then, *Kismet* is more effective than *AirSnare*.

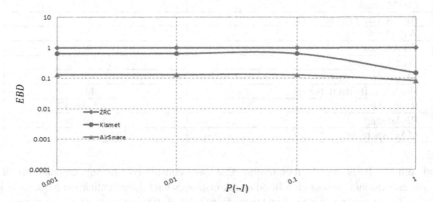

Fig. 6. The Trade-off between *EBD* and *P(¬I)* of *Kismet*, *AirSnare*, and *ZRC*

5   Conclusion

Our proposed metric E_{ID} manipulated the drawbacks of the existing metrics and it realizes the measurement of the actual effectiveness, taking into account the main related parameters. We conducted credible evaluation of two popular WIDSs (*Kismet* and *AirSnare*) using E_{ID} and considered some important aspects that were ignored in the existing work such as the probability of occurrence of attacks and selecting the attacks on the basis of representative attack test cases. The results demonstrated that *Kismet* is more effective than *AirSnare*. We are interested in deriving other evaluation metrics for the rest attributes of IDSs/WIDSs performance.

References

1. Axelsson, S.: The Base-Rate Fallacy and its Implications for the Difficulty of Intrusion Detection. In: Proceedings of the 6th ACM Conference on Computer and Communications Security (CCS 1999), pp. 1–7. ACM Press (1999)
2. Lippmann, R., Fried, D., Graf, I., Haines, J., Kendall, K., McClung, D., Weber, D., Webster, S., Wyschogrod, D., Cunningham, R., Zissman, M.: Evaluating Intrusion Detection Systems: The 1998 DARPA Off-line Intrusion Detection Evaluation. In: Proceedings of DARPA Information Survivability Conference and Exposition (DISCEX 2000), Los Alamitos, CA, USA, pp. 12–26 (2000)
3. Lippmann, R., Haines, J.W., Fried, D., Korba, J., Das, K.: Analysis and Results of the 1999 DARPA Off-Line Intrusion Detection Evaluation. In: Debar, H., Mé, L., Wu, S.F. (eds.) RAID 2000. LNCS, vol. 1907, pp. 162–182. Springer, Heidelberg (2000)
4. Stolfo, S., Fan, W., Lee, W., Prodromidis, A., Chan, P.: Cost-based modeling for fraud and intrusion detection: Results from the JAM project. In: Proceedings of DARPA Information Survivability Conference and Exposition (DISCEX 2000), pp. 130–144 (2000)
5. Gaffney, J.E., Ulvila, J.W.: Evaluation of intrusion detectors: A decision theory approach. In: Proceedings of IEEE Symposium on Security and Privacy (S&P 2001), Oakland, CA, USA, pp. 50–61 (2001)
6. Gu, G., Fogla, P., Dagon, D., Lee, W., Skoric, B.: Measuring Intrusion Detection Capability: An Information-Theoretic Approach. In: Proceedings of ACM Symposium on InformAtion, Computer and Communications Security (ASIACCS 2006), Taipei, Taiwan (2006)
7. Cardenas, A.A., Baras, J.S., Seamon, K.: A Framework for the Evaluation of Intrusion Detection Systems. In: Proceedings of IEEE Symposium on Security and Privacy (S&P 2006), Oakland, CA, USA, pp. 63–77 (2006)
8. Zill, D.G., Wright, W.S.: Advanced Engineering Mathematics. Jones & Bartlett Learning (2012)
9. Kismet: Kismet–WIDS, http://www.kismetwireless.net/
10. AirSnare: AirSnare-WIDS, http://home.comcast.net/~jay.deboer/airsnare/
11. Nasr, K., Abou El Kalam, A., Fraboul, C.: An IDS evaluation-centric taxonomy of wireless security attacks. In: Wyld, D.C., Wozniak, M., Chaki, N., Meghanathan, N., Nagamalai, D. (eds.) CNSA 2011. CCIS, vol. 196, pp. 402–413. Springer, Heidelberg (2011)
12. CVE Wireless: Common Vulnerabilities and Exposures - Wireless, http://cve.mitre.org/cgi-bin/cvekey.cgi?keyword=wireless
13. NVD-NIST: National Vulnerability Database, National Institute of Standards and Technology (NIST), http://nvd.nist.gov/home.cfm

How to Assess Confidentiality Requirements
of Corporate Assets?

Gabriela Varona Cervantes and Stefan Fenz

University Carlos III of Madrid, Madrid, Spain and Vienna University of Technology and SBA
Research, Vienna, Austria
gvarona@pa.uc3m.es, stefan.fenz@tuwien.ac.at

Confidentiality is an important property that organizations relying on information technology have to preserve. The purpose of this work is to provide a structured approach for identifying confidentiality requirements. A key step in the
information security risk management process is the determination of the impact level arisen from a loss of confidentiality, integrity or availability. We deal
here with impact level determination regarding confidentiality by proposing a
method to calculate impact levels based on the different kind of consequences
typically arisen from threats. The proposed approach assesses the impact arisen
from confidentiality losses on different areas separately and uses a parameter-
ized model that allows organizations to adjust it according to their specific
needs. A validation of the developed approach has been conducted in a small
software development company.

1   Introduction

Nowadays Information Technology (IT) plays a crucial role in society. Organizations
depend on it to successfully carry out their business missions and functions. In our
interconnected and digitized world, confidentiality becomes an important asset to
preserve for companies and individuals. The National Institute of Standards and
Technology (NIST) defines confidentiality as "preserving authorized restrictions on
information access and disclosure, including means for protecting personal privacy
and proprietary information."

Companies typically have information that should kept secret in order to maintain
their business' competitive advantage. Confidentiality requirements must be incorporated in the business processes of a company, along with the implementation of the
corresponding security measurements. The 2013 edition of the biennial information
security breaches survey carried out by Infosecurity Europe in UK (Department for
business innovation and skills, United Kingdom, 2013), has confirmed the upward
trend in the number of security breaches affecting UK businesses. Affected companies experienced on average roughly 50% more breaches than a year ago. The number
of organizations critically depending on externally hosted services has slightly increased since the last survey. Increasing numbers of companies are now storing
confidential or highly confidential data on the cloud, which makes confidentiality
compliance more complex. 10% of respondent companies had their worst security
incident related with the theft or unauthorized disclosure of confidential information,
the majority of which had a serious impact for the organization.

N. Cuppens-Boulahia et al. (Eds.): SEC 2014, IFIP AICT 428, pp. 234–241, 2014.

In information security risk management (ISRM), IT managers have to identify and evaluate possible risks before deciding what security measures to implement. In this process, a balance has to be found between the impact of potential breaches and the operational and economic costs of protective measures. Regarding confidentiality, it is important to accurately define confidentiality requirements on data, resources and business processes. While no restrictions can cause confidential information leaks, setting everything as confidential will complicate the processes and result in higher economic costs for the company. Therefore, the research question of this paper is: How can confidentiality requirements be determined for corporate assets?

Our work approaches confidentiality determination by proposing a structured method for companies to determine their resources' confidentiality. In this paper we present our developed approach on confidentiality determination and validate it in the context of a small software development company.

2   Related Work

Related work includes business process-based approaches (cf. (Accorsi et al., 2011a), (Accorsi et al., 2011b), (Accorsi et al., 2012), (Fenz et al., 2009), (Lehmann et al., 2012), (Lehmann et al., 2013), and (Lohmann et al., 2009)) and confidentiality determination methods implemented as part of different risk assessment methods (e.g., NIST (Barker et al., 2008a), Magerit (Spanish Ministry for Public Administrations, 2006), and Mehari (CLUSIF, 2010)). When dealing with confidentiality requirements in business processes one of the first decisions to make is the level to which each asset should be protected. This is part of the risk assessment phase of the ISRM process, which aims at identifying and evaluating risks affecting confidentiality, integrity and availability. Standards, methods and tools supporting security categorization and ISRM in general have been developed (e.g. (NIST, 2012; ISO/IEC, 2013; Spanish Ministry for Public Administrations, 2006; CLUSIF, 2010).

The National Institute of Standards and Technology (NIST) defines security categorization as the first step in the risk management process. Security categories used by NIST SP 800-60 are defined in the Federal Information Processing Standard Publication 199 (FIPS 199) (NIST, 2004):

Table 1. Potential impact levels by FIPS 199

Potential impacts	Definitions
Low	The potential impact is **low** if—The loss of confidentiality, integrity, or availability could be expected to have a **limited** adverse effect on organizational operations, organizational assets, or individuals (e.g., minor damage to organizational assets).
Moderate	The potential impact is **moderate** if—The loss of confidentiality, integrity, or availability could be expected to have a **serious** adverse effect on organizational operations, organizational assets, or individuals (e.g., significant financial loss).
High	The potential impact is **high** if—The loss of confidentiality, integrity, or availability could be expected to have a **severe or catastrophic** adverse effect on organizational operations, organizational assets, or individuals (e.g., severe or catastrophic harm to individuals involving loss of life or serious life threatening injuries).

In Magerit's (Spanish Ministry for Public Administrations, 2006) terminology, confidentiality, availability and integrity, together with authenticity are dimensions of an asset that together determine its value. Furthermore, the "valuation of an asset in a certain dimension is the measurement of the prejudice the organization may suffer if the asset is damaged in that dimension", i.e. the impact level. For valuation of assets a scale of 10 values is used. Criteria to value the assets consider adverse consequences in the following aspects: the security of persons, personal information, obligations arising from the law, capacity for following up offences, commercial and financial interests, interruption of the service, public order, corporate policy, and other intangible values. As a result from the valuation process, assets are assigned one of four confidentiality labels: secret, confidential, restricted or unclassified. Magerit's risk analysis process takes into account dependencies between assets when calculating the security impact.

Mehari (CLUSIF, 2010) uses a four-value scale to measure the impact level should a security breach occur:

Level 4 - Vital: existence and survival of the entity is in danger.

Level 3 - Very Serious: The impact is considered very serious at the level of the entity, although its future would not be at risk.

Level 2 - Serious: Malfunctions at this level would have a clear impact on the entity's operations, results or image, but are globally manageable.

Level 1 - Not significant: At this level, any resulting damage would have no significant impact on the results or image of the entity.

3   Confidentiality Impact Level Determination

Confidentiality determination refers to how restricted access to a certain resource must be in order to preserve its confidentiality. It can be expressed as a meaningful label or category. How to combine this categorization with other risk information and translate it to security measures is subject of another part of the risk management process. As mentioned earlier, the confidentiality label that must be assigned to an asset depends directly on the impact if the asset's confidentiality is compromised. This impact should be assessed independently of the implemented security measures and not with respect to any particular threat. Instead, the overall impact for the organization in case the asset is publicly available should be considered.

Consider for instance a company that keeps a file containing the details of a planned advertising campaign of which only the marketing team and the managers are aware. The file disclosure by other staff members would probably have a negligible impact for the company, while its disclosure by competitors could reduce the effectiveness of the campaign and negatively affect the company. The confidentiality of such a file should be then determined by the higher potential impact resulting from any possible situation.

In general, adverse impact is related to a degradation of the following:

- Laws and regulations compliance
- Commercial and financial interests
- Company's reputation
- Privacy and security of individuals

Note that they are not independent from each other and are interrelated in a cause-effect manner. Thus, a compromise to the privacy of individuals may affect the company's reputation and directly lead to a noncompliance with the law, which in turn may cause the company to be fined and affect financial interests. Nevertheless this relation may sometimes be difficult to determine and so the approach we propose evaluates each factor independently.

Furthermore, organizations may find damage to some of the above mentioned factors to have a greater impact than others. For instance, a company acting as a trusted third party managing the electronic transactions between absent participants will find a minimum damage to its reputation to have a stronger impact on it than, for instance, the noncompliance to a minor regulation.

3.1 Impact Level Determination

To determine the overall impact level derived from the loss of confidentiality of a certain resource x, we propose the following formula:

$$I(x) = \alpha * A_1(x) + \beta * A_2(x) + \gamma * A_3(x) + \delta * A_4(x)$$

where each of the A_i represent the level of damage to one of the mentioned areas (in this order): laws and regulations, commercial and financial interests, company's reputation and privacy and security of individuals. The coefficients allow adjusting the relevance each factor has with respect to the others.

Each of the consequences should be assessed in a scale from 0 to 4, being

0 – No damage to the organization
1 – Minimum damage with no significant impact on the organization
2 – Damage with clear impact on the organization
3 – Serious damage to the organization (future of the organization is not at risk)
4 – Maximum damage to the organization (bankruptcy, etc.)

Coefficients should range from 0 to 1, all of them summing up to 1. Aspects having stronger impact on the company's mission and business activity will be accompanied by higher coefficients. Note that organizations are free to add to the formula additional terms representing factors they might find missed. It is not advisable to neglect any of the factors, i.e. assigning a value very close to 0 to any of the accompanying coefficients, as that would cause to ignore potential impacts affecting the particular factor. Coefficients should be used to tune the final result by adding information of the specific company context to the model. According to our estimations, it is not recommended to have any coefficient being more than twice the value of any other one. We recommend equally distributing the coefficients (i.e., 0.25 at each coefficient) and only adjust if there is clear evidence to do so.

Notice that the coefficients (α, β, γ, δ) are part of the general model built by the company to evaluate potential impact, while the damage on each factor (A_i) should be determined for each resource for which the potential damage wants to be calculated.

Here are some questions that can help in the determination of each of the Ai factors regarding the disclosure of a specific asset x. Notice that in case a certain fact affects more than one aspect, damage to each of them should be estimated independently.

Laws and Regulations Compliance

Is the disclosure likely to lead to an important/serious breach of legal or regulatory obligations? Consider not only external laws affecting the organization's activity but also internal regulations the company or the group to which it belongs can be subject to.

Commercial and Financial Interests

Does it facilitate significant improper gain or advantage for individuals or other organizations? Is x of high/medium interest to a competitor? Would the disclosure result in significant monetary or productivity losses?

Company's Reputation

Is it likely to adversely affect relations with other organizations, the public, or other countries? To what extent? Is it likely to result in widespread adverse publicity? Could it lead to loss of public confidence in the organization? Could it lead to loss of current or potential employees trust? Could it lead to a serious breach of contractual undertakings to maintain the security of information provided by third parties?

Privacy and Security of Individuals

Does x contain sensitive information such as financial account number or medical records that can be linked to individuals? Is it likely to lead to the life of an individual or group of individuals being threatened?

Recall that this whole process should be carried out in the specific context of the organization in question. The same financial loss (in terms of absolute monetary units) won't have the same impact in a big and in a small company. Also, some aspects will be more critical to some kinds of companies. For instance, the impact a hospital would face if its customers' (i.e. patients) records are disclosed are higher than the impact faced by a dancing company giving up its customers' data. For this reason it is important that impact determination process is guided by managers and staff involved in the company's activity and with some experience in the sector. It may be the case that the consequences of a confidentiality breach are rated differently by different stakeholders within the company. Therefore the proposed method requires a consolidation phase for the impact ratings (0-4). In this phase the organization has to identify the reasons for the deviations and has to harmonize the impact ratings. Furthermore, confidentiality categories might vary as part of the regular lifecycle of a process. For instance, the disclosure of an advertising campaign could have a considerable impact while is still being planned, but once it has been implemented the impact will be minimal, if not zero.

3.2 Validation - Field Test

To validate the approach, we conducted a field test in a 4-year-old software development company in Austria. The company develops information security software and has therefore a high interest in protecting the confidentiality of the products' source code. Because of its business activities, the company relies on its reputation and trustworthiness and because it is a young company, it is critical for them to maintain a quality service and gain its customers loyalty.

For validation purposes, the members of the management team were informed about the developed confidentiality determination method and asked to determine the required parameters. The management team discussed the weighting of the impact categories and decided to focus on the financial interest and reputation category (i.e. these categories were weighted higher than the remaining ones). The following weights were applied:

> Laws and regulations: 0.2
> Commercial and financial interests: 0.3
> Reputation: 0.3
> Privacy and security for individuals: 0.2

Therefore, the general formula used by the company to assess the impact level derived from the loss of confidentiality is:

$$I(x) = 0.2 * A_1(x) + 0.3 * A_2(x) + 0.3 * A_3(x) + 0.2 * A_4(x)$$

After the category weighting we asked the management board to estimate the damage derived from the disclosure of the source code (0: no damage, ..., 4: maxiumum damage to the organization):

> Laws and regulations (A_1): 3
> Commercial and financial interests (A_2): 4
> Reputation (A_3): 4
> Privacy and security for individuals (A_4): 1

Thus, the overall impact level derived from the disclosure of the source code is 3.2. Based on their experience, the calculated impact level has been approved by the management board. Within this field test we conducted 14 calculations regarding different assets to check if the calculation results comply with managements' opinion. 9 calculations provided obvious results (like the source code confidentiality calculation shown above). 5 calculations provided results which were not obvious to the management team (e.g., disclosure of personal data on invoices or e-mails). In these cases the method helped to think in a structured way about the confidentiality impact and plan appropriate countermeasures.

4   Conclusions and Further Work

Impact level determination is a complex and context-dependent process and a crucial step in security risk management processes. When approaching confidentiality, impact level estimations are more complex as the kinds of possible damage involved are of different nature and thus affect in different ways.

Approaching our original research question: "How can confidentiality requirements be determined for corporate assets?" we proposed here a method of impact level determination regarding confidentiality. The peculiarity of the method is that it estimates negative impact on different areas separately. That is, damage to laws and regulations, finance, or reputation are assessed independently and then combined to calculate the overall impact to the organization. The model also allows organization to give more relevance to some aspects than to others thus making the process more flexible and customizable.

Although this method leads to more accurate results in the context of each organization, it requires a lot of effort from qualified and experienced personnel. In further research we aim at automating the proposed method (e.g., by analyzing business processes and their interaction with the corporate assets).

References

Accorsi, R., Wonnemann, C.: InDico: Information flow analysis of business processes for confidentiality requirements. In: Cuellar, J., Lopez, J., Barthe, G., Pretschner, A. (eds.) STM 2010. LNCS, vol. 6710, pp. 194–209. Springer, Heidelberg (2011)

Accorsi, R., Wonnemann, C.: Strong non-leak guarantees for workflow models. In: Proceedings of the 2011 ACM Symposium on Applied Computing, New York, USA, pp. 308–314 (2011)

Accorsi, R., Lehmann, A.: Automatic information flow analysis of business process models. In: Barros, A., Gal, A., Kindler, E. (eds.) BPM 2012. LNCS, vol. 7481, pp. 172–187. Springer, Heidelberg (2012)

Barker W., Stine K., Kissel R., Fahlsing J., Gulick J.: Volume I: Guide for mapping types of information and information systems to security categories. In: NIST Special Publication 800-60 Volume I Revision 1, NIST, Gaithersburg, MD 20899-8930 (2008a)

Barker, W., Stine, K., Kissel, R., Fahlsing, J., Lee, A.: Volume II: Appendices to Guide for Mapping Types of Information and Information Systems to Security Categories" in NIST Special Publication 800-60 Volume II Revision 1, Gaithersburg, MD 20899-8930 (2008b)

Club for the Security of Information in France (CLUSIF). Method for Harmonized Analysis of Risk (Mehari) (2010)

Department for business innovation and skills, United Kingdom. Information security breaches survey.Technical report (2013)

Fenz, S., Ekelhart, A., Neubauer, T.: Business process-based resource importance determination. In: Dayal, U., Eder, J., Koehler, J., Reijers, H.A. (eds.) BPM 2009. LNCS, vol. 5701, pp. 113–127. Springer, Heidelberg (2009)

ISO/IEC, ISO/IEC 27001:2013, Information technology - Security techniques -Information security risk management (2013)

Lehmann, A., Fahland, D.: Information flow security for business process models -just one click away. In: Lohmann, N., Moser, S. (eds.) Proceedings of the Demo Track of the 10th International Conference on Business Process Management 2012, Tallinn, Estonia (2012)

Lehmann, A., Lohmann, N.: Modeling wizard for confidential business processes. In: La Rosa, M., Soffer, P. (eds.) BPM Workshops 2012. LNBIP, vol. 132, pp. 675–688. Springer, Heidelberg (2013)

Lohmann, N., Verbeek, E., Dijkman, R.: Petri net transformations for business processes – A survey. In: Jensen, K., van der Aalst, W.M.P. (eds.) ToPNaC II. LNCS, vol. 5460, pp. 46–63. Springer, Heidelberg (2009)

McCallister, E., Grance, T., Scarfone, K.: Guide to Protecting the Confidentiality of Personally Identifiable Information (PII) in NIST Special Publication 800-122, NIST Gaithersburg, MD 20899-8930 (2010)

National Institute of Standards and Technology, Standards for Security Categorization of Federal Information and Information Systems. In: Federal Information Processing Standards Publication 199, NIST, Gaithersburg, MD 20899-8930 (2004)

National Institute of Standards and Technology, Guide for conducting risk assessment in NIST Special Publication 800-30 Revision 1, NIST, Gaithersburg, MD 20899-8930 (2012)

Spanish Ministry for Public Administrations, Methodology for Information Systems Risk Analysis and Management (MAGERIT) v2 (2006)

Towards Developing SCADA Systems Security Measures for Critical Infrastructures against Cyber-Terrorist Attacks

Suhaila Ismail, Elena Sitnikova, and Jill Slay

Information Assurance Research Group,
School of Information Technology and Mathematical Sciences,
University of South Australia, Adelaide, Australia
{suhaila.ismail,elena.sitnikova,jill.slay}@unisa.edu.au

Abstract. Security is essential in protecting confidential data, especially in Supervisory Control and Data Acquisition (SCADA) systems which monitor and control national critical infrastructures, such as energy, water and communications. Security controls are implemented to prevent attacks that could destroy or damage critical infrastructures. Previous critical infrastructure surveys point out the gaps in knowledge, including the lack of coordination between sectors, inadequate exchange of information, less awareness and engagement in government critical infrastructure protection (CIP) programs. Consequently, private sector and government organizations feel less prepared. This paper highlights existing vulnerabilities, provides a list of previous attacks, discusses existing cyber security methodologies and provides a framework aiming to improve security in SCADA systems to protect them against cyber-attacks.

Keywords: Critical Infrastructure, SCADA, Cyber Security, Security Assessment, SCADA vulnerabilities.

1 Introduction

Supervisory Control and Data Acquisition (SCADA) systems are used to monitor and remotely control critical infrastructure (CI) processes, such as electricity transmission, water supply and distribution, gas pipelines, government facilities and power generation plants. SCADA systems facilitate remote access to monitoring of real-time data and execute instructions or commands to remote devices and field devices [29]. As such, SCADA systems are essential and important in sustaining daily activities. Traditionally, SCADA systems were isolated systems that were not connected to or accessed by other networks. Each site or operation had its own SCADA system which originated in the 1960s [26]. Due to the need for shared information between the isolated SCADA systems network and cyber interdependencies that are part of the inescapable computerization and automation of infrastructures, the SCADA systems are now connected as a network. Pressures of modernization, integration, cost, and security have forced SCADA systems to migrate from closed proprietary systems

N. Cuppens-Boulahia et al. (Eds.): SEC 2014, IFIP AICT 428, pp. 242–249, 2014.

and networks to commercial off-the-shelf products and hardware, standard network protocols, and shared communications infrastructure [8]. This opens up SCADA systems in terms of security and their vulnerabilities.

According to a 2004 study on the Critical Infrastructure Protection (CIP) Survey of the Worldwide Activities, the main problem was the lack of coordination and inadequate exchange of information [3]. Symantec Corp. reported in the 2011 Critical Infrastructure Protection (CIP) Survey, that there was a decrease in awareness and engagement globally, as measured by the CIP Participation Index. Findings of the survey were organisations less aware, engaged and slightly more ambivalence about government CIP programs and global organizations feel less prepared [23]. The surveys indicated the government's CI plan and controls that protect SCADA systems are implemented by organizations providing the service. However, they are not fully aware of CI planning as a whole. Further discussions throughout the paper could be used to provide better understanding of SCADA systems security. More importantly, the paper provides an insight into developing a framework that can be used to assist critical infrastructure sectors.

The paper is organized as follows. It outlines some of the SCADA systems' vulnerabilities in section 2. Section 3 outlines previous attacks on SCADA systems as well as the impact of the attacks. Section 4 discusses the current security issues specific to SCADA systems, explains existing approaches for security assessments and proposes an initial framework for measuring security for SCADA Systems. Finally, section 5 concludes the entire paper and discusses future research.

2   SCADA Systems Vulnerabilities

The growing demands of connectivity between corporate networks and SCADA systems have created much vulnerability. Private and confidential information is widely accessible to the general public on the Internet, including structural maps networks, network systems configurations and names, etc. By obtaining this information, an intruder can then access the systems and manipulate the SCADA systems [11]. Access control might also be an issue if it is not properly administered. Appropriate skills and expertise as well as level of understanding of the systems security issues are essential. The documented cases show that most attacks originated from disgruntled employees who have the authority to access the systems, and arrange attacks without being easily detected. Another growing concern is the lack of real time monitoring because of the enormous amount of data that is being used in controlling the SCADA systems. Mobile communication systems that are integrated and used with the existing systems also pose a threat, and are quite difficult to consolidate [20]. Due to their vulnerabilities, critical infrastructures can be penetrated through application exploits, backdoor attacks, exploitation of operating systems, unauthorized access, exploitation of systems configurations, tampering, etc.

Cyber-Terrorism in the SCADA Systems context; Cyber-terrorism is defined as the use of Information Communications Technology (ICT) by terrorist groups and agents to promote extremist or aggressive tendencies, usually politically motivated and designed to leave a forceful or catastrophic impact. The perpetrator must use information systems or other electronic means to launch a cyber-attack against critical information infrastructures [28]. Also defined as "non-state actors' use of ICTs to attack and control critical information systems with political motivation and the intent to cause harm and spread fear to people or at least with the anticipation of changing domestic, national or international events" [1].

3   Previous Attacks on SCADA Systems

Table 1 provides a list of previously documented cases of deliberate or undeliberate attacks, or malfunctions of SCADA systems, as well as discusses the methods and the impacts of cyber-attacks. Initially based on [16], the survey has been expanded by further research on more recent cases that have been arranged in chronological order.

Table 1. Summary of Previous Attacks on SCADA Systems (adapted from Miller et al., 2012)

ATTACK/ YEAR	ATTACKER	ATTACKED	HOW ATTACK HAPPENED	THE IMPACT OF ATTACKS
Flame (2012)	Unidentified	Iran, Lebanon, Syria, Sudan,	Flame computer virus. Managed to evade detection by 43 different anti-virus, despite its size; 20MB [27]	Stole large quantities of information from various Iranian government agencies, and disrupted oil exports by shutting down oil terminals [27]
Gauss Malware (2012)	Unidentified	Lebanon, Israel, Palestinian, United States, United Arab Emirates	Collect information on infected systems, and steal credentials for banking and social network, email and IM accounts.	The Gauss code includes commands to intercept data required to work with Bank of Beirut, Byblos Bank, and Fransabank [13]
Night Dragon (2011)	Unidentified	Five global energy and oil firms	Using a combination of attacks including social engineering, Trojans and Windows-based exploits.	5 global energy and oil firms companies that operate SCADA were attacked. Operational blueprints were stolen [18]
DUQU (2011)	Unidentified	Iran, Europe	Windows-exploiting code similar to Stuxnet to attack Siemens industrial software [7]	Unidentified
Stuxnet (2010)	Unidentified	Iranian nuclear facility at Natanz. Stuxnet used four 'zero-day vulnerabilities	The worm employs Siemens' default passwords to access Windows operating systems that run WinCC and PCS7 programs.	Stuxnet altered the frequency of the electrical current to the drives causing it to switch between high and low speeds. The centrifuges fail at a higher than normal rate. [9]
Polish Trams (2008)	A teenage boy hacker	Polish Tram Systems	Unauthorized access by adapting a remote control to change the track points	12 people were injured in one derailment
Red October (2007)	Unidentified. Russian used in codes	Diplomatic and government, research institutes, energy nuclear, aerospace	Malware infiltrates computers and smartphones to obtain sensitive documents through email attachment	Infiltrated over 1000 high level government computers. Sensitive information being stolen; 7TB stolen data & 55,000 connection targets across Switzerland, Kazakhstan & Greece [19]

Table 1.(*Continued.*)

Tehama Colusa Canal (2007)	A former electrical supervisor	Tehama Colusa Canal Authority	Installed unauthorized software on the TCAA's SCADA systems.	Unidentified
Daimler Chrysler (2005)	Unidentified	Manufacturing plants and business	Zotob infected laptop connected to Daimler Chrysler's network	Infected business and industrial control network causing 13 manufacturing plants to shut production lines, loss $1.4m [5]
Davis-Besse Nuclear Power Plant (2003)	Unidentified	Power plants	SQL Slammer worm infected the Davis Besse nuclear power plant	Safety Parameter Display Systems and Plant Process Computer were disabled for several hours
CSX Corporation (2003)	Unidentified	CSX Corporation, Transportation Supplier in Florida, U.S.	A virus (email attachment) was reported to have shut down train signalling systems	No major incidents but trains were delayed. It shut down the signalling, dispatching and other systems at CSX Corporation
California Systems Operator (2001)	Unidentified attackers	California Independent Systems	Gained access into one of the computer networks	Unsuccessful attempt to penetrate systems, however, it lasted for 2 weeks [21]
Maroochy Water Systems (2000)	Disgruntled ex-employee	Maroochy Water Systems, Maroochy Shire	Hacked into a water control system. A series of attacks over a prolonged period	Flooded the grounds of a hotel and a nearby river with one million litres of sewage waste.
Gazprom (1999)	Disgruntled ex-employee	Gas company in Russia	Trojan Horse gain control of central switchboard, that controls gas flow in pipelines	Unidentified
Bellingham, WA Gas Pipeline (1999)	Failure of SCADA Systems	Bellingham, WA Gas Pipeline	The pipeline failed because the control systems did not during database development on the pipes while the pipes were in operation [25]	237,000 gallons of gasoline leaked from a 16" pipeline into a creek. The gasoline ignited and burned nearly 1 1/2 miles along the creek causing 3 deaths and 8 injuries [25]
Worcester, MA Airport (1997)	Hacker	Telephone Services Company	Hacker penetrated and disabled a telephone company computer that serviced Worcester Airport in Massachusetts	The telephone service to FAA control tower, airport security, weather service and several private airfreights were cut off. Financial losses & public safety
Salt River Project, Phoenix (1994)	An attacker	Government	Unauthorized access. Installed a backdoor. Altered login, password, computer systems files, root privilege	Critical data was accessed by attackers including water and power monitoring and delivery, financial, and customer and personal information.
Chevron Emergency Alert System (1992)	Disgruntled employee	Company and users	Unauthorized hacking of computers and programs and disabled the alarm	The systems did not operate for 10 hours and left affected people in 22 states at risk, including 6 unspecified areas of Canada
Siberian Pipeline Explosion (1982)	Vladimir Vetrov, KGB colonel	Siberian Pipeline	Unauthorized hacking and distribution of Trojan	Estimated at one-seventh the magnitude of bombs in World War II. Vaporized part of the Soviet Union's Trans-Siberian Pipeline [15]

4   Security of SCADA Systems

SCADA is described as a wide geographic distribution system. Stringent availability requirements and a heavy reliance on legacy systems introduce significant cyber security concerns while constricting the feasibility of many security controls [12]. The systems that govern these infrastructures must be able to highlight five main factors: ensuring security of the systems; emphasis on the reliability; ability to provide protection; ensuring the sustainability; and validating the cost effectiveness of the SCADA systems. Attacks on SCADA systems can be divided into three categories; attacks against or through the central controller, field units or the communication networks [10].These attacks could be physical attacks, malicious settings, malicious alterations, malicious alarms, denial of services, sniffing and/or spoofing.

Bearing in mind that in a typical SCADA System, availability of the system is emphasized and followed by integrity as well as confidentiality[6]. An earlier study [14] focused on compartmentalizing policies, to avoid overlap and ensure that each policy is effective including communication, personnel, data, physical and platform security as well as configuration and application management, manual operations and audit. [24] proposed a Real-time Monitoring, Anomaly Detection, Impact Analysis and Mitigation Strategy (RAIM) Framework, mainly for electric power generation and it consists of four main components: monitoring of the systems and devices; extracting and analysing data from the power instruments and devices; assess the system's vulnerability and potential attack impact; and mitigate risks based on previous intrusion attempts, intrusion scenario, or ongoing denial of service (DoS) attacks. In this paper, we propose a framework for SCADA cyber security measures (see Fig 1). It is derived from both Cyber-Terrorism SCADA Risk Framework [2] and NIST 2011 standards [22] as described in more detail further in the text.

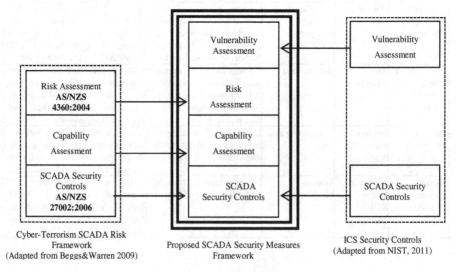

Fig. 1. Proposed SCADA Security Measures Framework

Vulnerability Assessment; is conducted to identify the vulnerabilities and security weakness in a system, and this means reviewing codes, settings, and logs for known security weakness [4]. A variety of security tools and techniques are used to identify and validate vulnerabilities, in order to secure the systems. The ICS Security Controls 2011 documentation outlined that the vulnerabilities for ICS could be grouped into Policy and Procedure, Platform and Network categories. These will assist in determining optimal mitigation strategies [22], and maximize the security of SCADA systems.

Risk Assessment; is used to identify, quantify and prioritize risks against criteria for risk acceptance and objectives relevant to an organization, specifically to those organizations that employ SCADA systems. The outcome of a risk assessment could be used to determine the appropriate action in managing the information security risks to the SCADA system networks, which will then lead to appropriately selecting the best security controls to implement. The key areas in assessing risks are: communicate and consult SCADA; establish the context and framework; identify the risks associated; analyse and treat risks; and finally, monitor and review SCADA systems.

Capability Assessment; [2] stated that the capability model was designed to identify, examine and analyse the level of cyber-capability that a terrorist attacker needs to acquire in order to attack SCADA systems. The assessment model consists of eight levels to indicate the terrorist's cyber-capability with: political/motivation; advanced ICT skills; required tools and techniques; access to new advanced ICT; advanced knowledge of SCADA systems; ability to use internal resources and knowledge; ability to reconnaissance (scanning or probing); sufficient financial ability to attack SCADA systems [2]. Further research will be done to incorporate the three levels of cyber terror capability as aligned by [17] which include Simple-Unstructured, Advanced-structured and Complex-Coordinated. The indications will be developed after further research is conducted based on different cases of attacks compared to the previous work done.

SCADA Security Controls; in their framework, Beggs and Warren (2009) defined the SCADA Security controls according to AS/NZS 270002:2006, which covers SCADA Security Policy. This includes, security policy, organization information security, human resource security, physical and environmental security, communications and operations management, access control, information systems acquisition, development and maintenance, IS incident management, SCADA business continuity management and finally SCADA compliance. This paper adopts the SCADA security controls in the NIST 2011, which categorizes these controls into three groups, namely management controls, operational controls and technical controls.

5   Conclusion and Future Work

Based on understanding the importance of assessing security and ensuring organizations are well informed on security measures, this paper investigated issues in critical infrastructures and SCADA systems security. It highlights SCADA systems vulnera-bilities and provides a comprehensive list of cases of cyber-attacks and their impact on society, economy and environment. It further describes existing approaches and some best practices on SCADA security assessments and proposes a framework for SCADA security measures.

Our research aims to further study and enhance initial framework for measuring SCADA Systems security and its resilience against cyber-terrorist attacks. The first step is to define the existing standards, regulations and process in SCADA security systems and to examine the standards that have been defined in the national security policies. The next step is to evaluate the current SCADA systems security by measur-ing the SCADA security controls that have been implemented and assess their effec-tiveness, including:

- SCADA systems' vulnerability assessment;
- SCADA systems' risk assessment;
- SCADA systems' capability assessment; and
- SCADA systems' security controls.

By merging the four assessments criteria, it is hoped the framework will enhance the awareness and security levels, by assessing the vulnerabilities and risks involved as well as indicating the level of capability that a terrorist to penetrate the systems and security controls that needs to be put forward to ensure the security in organisations. This will be done by integrating the available procedures and guidelines and enhanc-ing it to improve security. The final step will be to validate the framework through conducting focus groups sessions with the experts from the industry in order to verify that the framework could assist in increasing awareness and reducing security risks in an organisation. In order to address the issues and gaps arising from previous surveys, further research will focus on the three dimensions (people, process and technology) in improving security in SCADA systems.

References

1. Beggs, C.: Cyber-terrorism: a threat to Australia? In: Managing Modern Organisation with Information Technology- Information Resources Management Association (IRMA), pp. 472–475. Idea Group Publishing, San Diego (2005)
2. Beggs, C., Warren, M.: Safeguarding Australia from Cyber-terrorism: A Proposed Cyber-terrorism SCADA Risk Framework for Industry Adoption Keywords. In: Proc. 10th Aust. Inf. Warf. Secur. Conf., pp. 369–384. Ed. Cowan Univ., Perth (2009)
3. Brömmelhörster, J., et al.: Critical Infrastructure Protection: Survey of World-Wide Ac-tivities (2004)
4. Centre for the Protection of National Infrastructure (CPNI): Cyber Security Assessments of Industrial Control Systems: Good Practice Guide (2010)
5. Combs, M.M.: Impact of the Stuxnet Virus on Industrial Control System. In: XIII Interna-tional Forummodern Information Society Formation Problems, Perspectives, Innovation Approaches, pp. 5–10 (2011)
6. Dawson, R., et al.: SKMA – A Key Management Architecture for SCADA Systems. In: Proceedings of the 2006 Australasian Workshops on Grid Computing and e-Research, pp. 183–192. Australian Computer Society Inc. (2006)

7. Espiner, T.: McAfee: Why Duqu is a big deal, http://www.zdnet.com/mcafee-why-duqu-is-a-big-deal-3040094263/

8. Farris, J.J., Nicol, D.M.: Evaluation of Secure Peer-to-Peer Overlay Routing for Survivable SCADA Systems. In: 2004 Winter Simulation Conference, pp. 300–308 (2004)

9. Farwell, J.P., Rohozinski, R.: Stuxnet and the Future of Cyber War. Surviv. Glob. Polit. Strateg. 53(1), 23–40 (2011)

10. Fernandez, E.B., et al.: On building secure SCADA systems using security patterns. In: Proceedings of the 5th Annual Workshop on Cyber Security and Information Intelligence Research Cyber Security and Information Intelligence Challenges and Strategies - CSIIRW 2009, p. 17. ACM Press, New York (2009)

11. Fernandez, J.D., Fernandez, A.E.: Scada systems: vulnerabilities and remediation. J. Comput. Sci. Coll. 20(4), 160–168 (2005)

12. Hahn, A., et al.: Development of the PowerCyber SCADA Security Testbed (Extended Abstract). In: Proceedings of the Sixth Annual Workshop on Cyber Security and Information Intelligence Research, pp. 1–4 (2010)

13. Kaspersky Lab: Gauss: Abnormal Distribution, http://www.securelist.com/en/downloads/vlpdfs/kaspersky-lab-gauss.pdf

14. Kilman, D., Stamp, J.: Framework for SCADA Security Policy (2005)

15. Melito, S.: Software and Cold War: The Siberian Pipeline Explosion, http://defsecnet.com/software-and-cold-war-the-siberian-pipeline-explosion/

16. Miller, B., Rowe, D.: A Survey of SCADA and Critical Infrastructure Incidents. In: Proceedings of the 1st Annual Conference on Research in Information Technology, RIIT 2012, p. 51. ACM Press, New York (2012)

17. Nelson, B., et al.: Cyberterror Prospects and Implications, Monterey, CA (1999)

18. Nicholson, A., et al.: SCADA security in the light of Cyber-Warfare. Comput. Secur. 31(4), 418–436 (2012)

19. Prigg, M.: The hunt for Red October, http://www.dailymail.co.uk/sciencetech/article-2263322/Operation-Red-October-revealed-The-astonishing-hacker-attack-infiltrated-55-000-high-level-government-computers.html#ixzz2KAIDcX4G

20. Rautmare, S.: SCADA System Security. In: Annual IEEE India Conference (INDICON), pp. 1–4 (2011)

21. Stamp, J., et al.: Sustainable Security for Infrastructure SCADA (2003)

22. Stouffer, K., et al.: Guide to Industrial Control Systems (ICS) Security, US (2011)

23. Symantec: Symantec Critical Infrastructure Protection Survey (2011)

24. Ten, C., et al.: Cybersecurity for Critical Infrastructures: Attack and Defense Modeling. IEEE Trans. Syst. Man, Cybern. A System Humans. 40(4), 853–865 (2010)

25. Tsang, R.: Cyberthreats, Vulnerabilities, and Attacks of SCADA Networks, http://gspp.dreamhosters.com/iths/Tsang_SCADAAttacks.pdf

26. White, J.: 12 Steps toward Cyber Resilience, https://www.isc2.org/infosecurity-professional-insights.aspx

27. Yaron, O.: Flame virus had massive impact on Iran, http://www.haaretz.com/news/diplomacy-defense/flame-virus-had-massive-impact-on-iran-says-israeli-security-firm-1.433222

28. Yunos, Z., et al.: Safeguarding Malaysia's critical national information infrastructure (CNII) against cyber terrorism: Towards development of a policy framework. In: 2010 Sixth Int. Conf. Inf. Assur. Secur., pp. 21–27 (2010)

29. Zhu, B., et al.: A Taxonomy of Cyber Attacks on SCADA Systems. In: 2011 Int. Conf. Internet Things 4th Int. Conf. Cyber, Phys. Soc. Comput., pp. 380–388 (2011)

Compatibility of Safety Properties
and Possibilistic Information Flow Security
in MAKS*

Thomas Bauereiss and Dieter Hutter

German Research Center for Artificial Intelligence (DFKI)
Bremen, Germany
{firstname.lastname}@dfki.de

Abstract. Motivated by typical security requirements of workflow management systems, we consider the integrated verification of both safety properties (e.g. separation of duty) and information flow security predicates of the MAKS framework (e.g. modeling confidentiality requirements). Due to the refinement paradox, enforcement of safety properties might violate possibilistic information flow properties of a system. We present an approach where sufficient conditions for the compatibility of safety properties and information flow security are derived by performing an information flow analysis of a monitor enforcing the safety property and applying existing compositionality results for MAKS security predicates. These conditions then guarantee that the composition of a target system with the monitor satisfies both kinds of properties. We illustrate our approach by deriving sufficient conditions for the security-preserving enforcement of separation of duty and ordered message delivery in an asynchronous communication platform.

1 Introduction

In large, distributed systems that facilitate the collaboration of multiple users there are different types of relevant security requirements. The confidentiality and integrity of data items that are processed in the system needs to be protected, and there are security requirements regarding the users involved in the process, e.g. the requirement that at least two users must agree on a joint decision before the corresponding action can be taken (this requirement is commonly known as separation of duty). Process requirements such as separation of duty can be modeled as safety properties [1]. For confidentiality and integrity requirements, there are various proposals of information flow hyperproperties [5] that go beyond mere access control by taking into account the behavior of the system. The MAKS framework [8], for example, allows to express a range of information flow properties, including several properties proposed in the literature, as a combination of certain basic security predicates.

---

* This research is supported by the Deutsche Forschungsgemeinschaft (DFG) under grant Hu737/5-1, which is part of the DFG priority programme 1496 "Reliably Secure Software Systems."

N. Cuppens-Boulahia et al. (Eds.): SEC 2014, IFIP AICT 428, pp. 250–263, 2014.

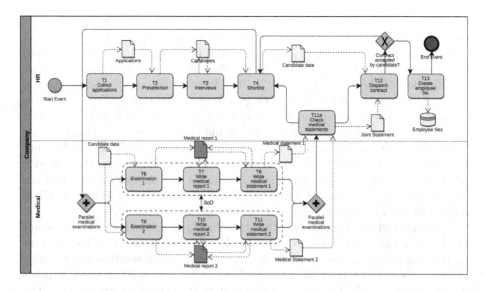

Fig. 1. Example workflow used in [3]

Due to the well-known refinement paradox, the enforcement of a safety property by prohibiting system runs violating it can potentially invalidate possibilistic information flow security: For example, consider a workflow system where a separation of duty constraint between a confidential and a non-confidential activity is enforced. Someone who can observe the non-confidential activity and sees a certain user perform it can deduce that this user has not participated in the confidential activity. This might be an information leak in itself (if anonymity is a concern), and if different users are allowed to perform different actions it might even leak information about the exact sequence of actions that could have been performed in the confidential activity.

In a case study on the verification of information flow security of workflow management systems on an abstract level [3], we considered a hiring process as a running example (Fig. 1). It involves medical examinations of job candidates, and the medical details of these examinations are considered confidential information. We considered two types of separation of duty constraints: We require that the medical examinations must be performed by different persons than the rest of the hiring process due to the need-to-know principle, and we require that there must be two independent medical examinations for each candidate performed by different persons for high assurance of physical fitness of the candidates. The information flows in this example are not entirely trivial, because even though the medical details have to be kept confidential from anyone not involved in the examinations, the final decisions (and only the decisions) must be released to the human resources department so that the workflow can continue. Hence, there is some information flow in the presence of separation of duty constraints, and it is not immediately clear whether there might be subtle interrelations between confidentiality and separation of duty. This motivated us to formally investigate the compatibility of information flow security and safety properties.

Existing approaches such as [10] on security-preserving refinement can be used to construct a system that satisfies both kinds of properties, but the mechanic modification of the safety property so that it preserves an unwinding relation can lead to unexpected results. We propose to use compositionality [11] for this purpose. A safety property can be enforced using an execution monitor that runs in parallel with the target system and inhibits executions that would violate the safety property. We can analyze such a monitor and verify that it does not leak confidential information under certain conditions, and then compose it with the target system. The composed system satisfies the safety property, and the compositionality theorems of the MAKS framework give us sufficient conditions under which this composition preserves information flow security.

The contribution of this paper is to state this approach formally. It can be applied to arbitrary safety properties, although manual effort seems to be necessary for deriving sufficient conditions for compatibility with information flow security. However, we believe that this manual effort can be very efficient when compatibility results for whole classes of important safety properties are derived. The two example properties that we use for illustration, namely separation of duty and the enforcement of ordered delivery of messages between asynchronously communicating systems, are relevant for many systems, and our results can be instantiated for them simply by replacing the sets of underlying events accordingly. If such a compatibility results exists for a safety property of interest and its side conditions are satisfied, it allows us to prove information flow security for a simplified system that does not need to satisfy the safety property, and then enforce safety by composition with a monitor while preserving security.

The rest of this paper is structured as follows. In Section 2, we recall definitions of state-event systems, information flow security and safety properties from the literature. Section 3 describes our approach of using compositionality for the security-preserving enforcement of safety properties and illustrates it with two examples. Section 4 discusses related work and Section 5 concludes the paper.

2 Preliminaries

2.1 System Model

We briefly recall the definitions of (state-) event systems and security predicates from the MAKS framework for possibilistic information flow [8] that we use in this paper. An event system $ES = (E, I, O, Tr)$ is essentially a (prefix-closed) set of traces $Tr \subseteq E^*$ that are finite sequences of events in the event set E. The disjoint sets $I \subseteq E$ and $O \subseteq E$ designate input and output events, respectively. We denote the empty trace as $\langle \rangle$, the concatenation of traces α and β as $\alpha.\beta$, and the projection of a trace α onto a set E as $\alpha|_E$. In the composition $ES_1 \| ES_2$ of two event systems ES_1 and ES_2, the set of traces is the set of interleaved traces of the two systems, synchronized on events in $E_1 \cap E_2$:

$$Tr(ES_1 \| ES_2) = \{\alpha \in (E_1 \cup E_2)^* \mid \alpha|_{E_1} \in Tr(ES_1) \wedge \alpha|_{E_2} \in Tr(ES_2)\}$$

Input events of one system matching output events of the other system are connected (and vice versa) and thus become internal events of the composed system. Note that we drop the assumption of [11] that all shared events of the two components must be an output event of one component and an input of the other. This allows us to formulate execution monitors for safety properties as event systems with no input and output events of their own, such that the composition of the monitor with a target system retains the input and output events of the original target system. This notion of composition is in line with the generalized parallel composition operator of CSP [15]. All proofs of compositionality of security predicates remain valid, as the concrete sets of input and output events are not used in the proofs at all.[1]

Example 1. In [3], we defined the behavior of workflow systems in terms of the behaviors of communicating subsystems representing individual activities of the workflow. In our example workflow, activities correspond to nodes of the graph in Figure 1. This approach makes the verification simpler and more scalable, as it allows us to use the decomposition methodology of [6] to verify the security of the overall system by verifying security properties of the subsystems. Each activity a is modeled as an event system with a set of events E_a of the form

- $Start_a(u)$, starting the activity a and assigning it to the user $u \in U$,
- $End_a(u)$, marking the end of the activity,
- $Send_a(a', msg)$ and $Recv_a(a', msg)$, representing activity a sending message msg to another activity a' (or a receiving msg from a', respectively),
- $Setval_a(u, i, val)$ and $Outval_a(u, i, val)$, representing a user $u \in U$ writing (or reading, respectively) the value val of data item i during activity a, and
- a set of internal events τ_a.

The behavior of these activities is modeled using internal states S_a and a transition relation $T_a \subseteq S_a \times E_a \times S_a$, inducing the set of possible traces. The overall workflow system $ES_W = (\|_{a \in \mathcal{A}} ES_a) \| ES_P$ emerges from the composition of these event systems ES_a for every activity $a \in \mathcal{A}$, together with a communication platform ES_P. The communication platform asynchronously forwards messages between the activities. Upon composition with the platform, the communication events between the activities become internal events of the composed system. Only the communication events between activities and users remain input and output events. These events form the user interface of the workflow system. □

2.2   Information Flow Security

The MAKS framework defines a collection of basic security predicates (BSPs). Many existing information flow properties from the literature can be expressed as a combination of these BSPs. Each BSP is a predicate on a set of traces with

---

[1] We verified this using an existing formalization of the MAKS framework for the interactive theorem prover Isabelle. Removing the assumption of matching input and output events has no effect on the validity of the proofs.

$$BSD_{\mathcal{V}}(Tr) \equiv \forall \alpha, \beta \in E^*.\forall c \in C.\,(\beta.c.\alpha \in Tr \wedge \alpha|_C = \langle\rangle)$$
$$\Rightarrow \exists \alpha' \in E^*.\,(\alpha'|_V = \alpha|_V \wedge \alpha'|_C = \langle\rangle \wedge \beta.\alpha' \in Tr)$$
$$BSIA_{\mathcal{V}}^{\rho}(Tr) \equiv \forall \alpha, \beta \in E^*.\forall c \in C.\,(\beta.\alpha \in Tr \wedge \alpha|_C = \langle\rangle \wedge \beta.c \in Tr \wedge Adm_{\mathcal{V}}^{\rho}(Tr, \beta, c))$$
$$\Rightarrow \exists \alpha' \in E^*.\,(\alpha'|_V = \alpha|_V \wedge \alpha'|_C = \langle\rangle \wedge \beta.c.\alpha' \in Tr)$$
$$FCIA_{\mathcal{V}}^{\rho,\Gamma}(Tr) \equiv \forall \alpha, \beta \in E^*.\forall c \in C \cap \Upsilon.\forall v \in V \cap \nabla.$$
$$(\beta.\langle v\rangle.\alpha \in Tr \wedge \alpha|_C = \langle\rangle \wedge \beta.c \in Tr \wedge Adm_{\mathcal{V}}^{\rho}(Tr, \beta, c))$$
$$\Rightarrow \exists \alpha' \in E^*.\exists \delta' \in (N \cap \Delta)^*.$$
$$(\alpha'|_V = \alpha|_V \wedge \alpha'|_C = \langle\rangle \wedge \beta.c.\delta'.\langle v\rangle.\alpha' \in Tr)$$

Fig. 2. The MAKS basic security predicates BSD, $BSIA^{\rho}$, and $FCIA^{\rho,\Gamma}$

respect to a view $\mathcal{V}$. A view $\mathcal{V} = (V, N, C)$ on an event system $ES = (E, I, O, Tr)$ is defined as a triple of event sets, where the set V defines the set of events that are visible for an observer, C are the confidential events, and the events in N are assumed to be neither visible nor confidential. A view is *valid* if V, N and C are pairwise disjoint, and it is *valid for ES* if V, N and C form a disjoint partition of E. Notable examples for BSPs, that we will use in this paper, are backwards-strict deletion of confidential events (BSD), backwards-strict insertion of admissible confidential events ($BSIA^{\rho}$), and forward-correctable insertion of admissible confidential events ($FCIA^{\rho,\Gamma}$)[2], defined in [11] as given in Figure 2. Intuitively, BSD requires that the occurrence of confidential events must not be deducible, while $BSIA$ and $FCIA$ require that the *non*-occurrence of confidential events must not be deducible. Technically, they are closure properties of sets of traces. For example, if a trace in Tr contains a confidential event, then BSD requires that a corresponding trace without the confidential event exists in Tr that yields the same observations. This means the two traces must be equal with respect to visible V-events, while N-events might be adapted to correct the deletion of the confidential event.

In [11], compositionality results for these basic security predicates are presented. They give sufficient conditions under which security of a composed system is implied by the security of its subsystems. Let us consider the composition of two event systems ES_1 and ES_2 with event sets E_1 and E_2 and trace sets Tr_1 and Tr_2, respectively. First, the views $\mathcal{V}_i = (V_i, N_i, C_i)$ for the subsystems must form a *proper view separation* of the view $\mathcal{V} = (V, N, C)$ for the composed system, i.e. $V \cap E_i = V_i$, $C \cap E_i \subseteq C_i$ and $N_i \cap N_j = \emptyset$. Second, the components must be well-behaved wrt. the views, i.e. if a shared event is used for corrections in one component, then the other component must accept it at any time without interfering with visible observations. We slightly reformulate the notion of well-behaved composition given in Definition 6.3.6 of [12] as a well-behavedness condition on the individual components to be composed:

---

[2] The parameters ρ and $\Gamma = (\nabla, \Delta, \Upsilon)$ control at which positions in traces it must be possible to insert confidential events and which corrections are allowed, and admissibility is defined as $Adm_{\mathcal{V}}^{\rho}(Tr, \beta, e) \equiv \exists \gamma \in E^*.\,(\gamma.\langle e\rangle \in Tr \wedge \gamma|_{\rho(\mathcal{V})} = \beta|_{\rho(\mathcal{V})})$.

Definition 1. *The component ES_i is well-behaved for $\mathcal{V}_i$ wrt. $\mathcal{V}_j$, with $i, j \in \{1, 2\}$ and $i \neq j$, if*

- $N_j \cap E_i \neq \emptyset$ *implies* $total(ES_i, C_i \cap N_j) \wedge BSIA_{\mathcal{V}_i}^{\rho_E}(Tr_i)$, *and*
- $N_j \cap E_i \neq \emptyset \wedge N_i \cap E_j \neq \emptyset$ *implies* $FCIA_{\mathcal{V}_i}^{\rho_E, \Gamma_i}(Tr_i)$,

where $\rho_E((V, N, C)) = V \cup N \cup C$ and $\Gamma_i = (E_i \cap E_j, E_i \setminus E_j, C_i \cap N_j)$.

The composition of ES_1 and ES_2 is well-behaved wrt. $\mathcal{V}_1$ and $\mathcal{V}_2$ if ES_1 is well-behaved for $\mathcal{V}_1$ wrt. $\mathcal{V}_2$ and ES_2 is well-behaved for $\mathcal{V}_2$ wrt. $\mathcal{V}_1$.

Third, specific side conditions for the security predicate in question must be satisfied. For BSD and $BSIA$, this is summarized in the following corollary:

Corollary 1 (of Theorem 6.4.1 in [12]). *Let $\mathcal{V}_1$ and $\mathcal{V}_2$ be a proper separation of V and let the composition of ES_1 and ES_2 be well behaved wrt. $\mathcal{V}_1$ and $\mathcal{V}_2$. Then the following holds:*

- $BSD_{\mathcal{V}_1}(Tr(ES_1)) \wedge BSD_{\mathcal{V}_2}(Tr(ES_2))$ *implies* $BSD_{\mathcal{V}}(Tr(ES_1 \| ES_2))$.
- *If $BSD_{\mathcal{V}_j}(Tr(ES_j))$ and $\rho_j(\mathcal{V}_j) \subseteq \rho(\mathcal{V}) \cap E_j$ for all $j \in \{1, 2\}$, then $BSIA_{\mathcal{V}_1}^{\rho_1}(Tr(ES_1)) \wedge BSIA_{\mathcal{V}_2}^{\rho_2}(Tr(ES_2))$ implies $BSIA_{\mathcal{V}}^{\rho}(Tr(ES_1 \| ES_2))$.*

For details of the compositionality of other basic security predicates, see [12].

Example 2. In our example workflow, we consider the contents of the medical reports as confidential information. Hence, we classify system events representing the input our output of medical reports (i.e. events of the form $\text{Setval}_a(u, i, v)$ and $\text{Outval}_a(u, i, v)$ with $i \in \{\text{MedReport1}, \text{MedReport2}\}$ and a being on the medical activities) as confidential events. The events belonging to activities of the human resources department that do not handle medical information can be considered as potentially visible to an observer. This gives rise to a security view on the overall system, and the security predicates BSD and $BSIA$ formalize the requirement that someone who observes or participates in visible activities cannot deduce information about the occurrence or non-occurrence of confidential events and, hence, the values of confidential data items. See [3] for detailed definitions of the security views and predicates. We used compositionality for the verification of information flow security by applying the methodology of [6] to decompose the overall security property into properties of the subsystems, and verifying those using an unwinding technique [9]. □

2.3 Safety Properties

A safety property can be characterized by a "bad thing" that must not happen [1]. Hence, it can be formalized as the set of traces where this bad thing does not occur. For example, consider a separation of duty constraint between two activities. The bad thing happens when the same user performs both activities.

Example 3. Consider a system that includes several activities to be performed with user interaction, such as our workflow system of Example 1. Let a and a' be two activities between which a separation of duty constraint shall be enforced, for example the medical examinations T6 and T9 in Figure 1. Let E_a and $E_{a'}$, respectively, denote the sets of events belonging to these activities, let E_W denote the set of all events of the workflow system, let U be a set of users, and let E_u denote the events of interaction between user $u \in U$ and the system. Separation of duty between a and a' is represented by the set of traces

$$\{\alpha \in E_W^* \mid \forall u, u' \in U. \; \forall e_1, e_2 \in \alpha.(e_1 \in (E_a \cap E_u) \wedge e_2 \in (E_{a'} \cap E_{u'})) \rightarrow u \neq u'\}$$

It contains only traces where the users participating in a are different from those participating in a'. We denote this safety property as $P_{SoD}^{a,a'}$. □

Such a safety property can be enforced by an execution monitor that is run in parallel with the target system and inhibits executions that would violate the property. Note that the above property is defined solely in terms of events in $(E_a \cup E_{a'}) \cap E_U$, where $E_U = \bigcup_{u \in U} E_u$ denotes the set of all user interaction events. Hence, other events are irrelevant for this property and can be ignored by an execution monitor. This is captured in the following notion of relevant events:

Definition 2. *Let $P \subseteq E^*$ be a safety property, i.e. a set of traces composed of events in E. The set $E_P \subseteq E$ is a* relevant set of events *for P iff for all $\tau \in E^*$ it holds that $\tau|_{E_P} \in P$ implies $\tau \in P$.*

A monitor can then be defined as an event system with a relevant set of events and a set of traces that satisfies the property:

Definition 3. *Let P be a safety property. A* monitor *for P is an event system $ES = (E, I, O, Tr)$ such that E is a relevant set of events for P and $Tr \subseteq P$.*

Composing a target system with the monitor yields a system that satisfies the safety property:

Lemma 1. *Let $ES = (E, I, O, Tr)$ be an event system and $ES_P = (E_P, I_P, O_P, Tr_P)$ be a monitor for a safety property P. Then $Tr(ES \| ES_P) \subseteq P$. Furthermore, if $E_P \subseteq E$, then $Tr(ES \| ES_P) \subseteq Tr(ES) \cap P$.*

This follows directly from the definitions of relevant events, monitor, and set inclusion. For simplicity, we assume below that the set of monitor events is a subset of the events of the target system.[3] In this case, the composed system is a refinement of the original system, in the sense that the set of traces of the composition is a subset of the traces of the original system, and it satisfies the safety property.

3   Secure Composition with Safety Monitors

Now that we have cast the enforcement of a safety property as a composition of the target system with a monitor, we can leverage compositionality results for

---

[3] Internal monitor events modeling enforcement could be added in a subsequent refinement.

information flow predicates to obtain conditions under which the enforcement of the safety property preserves information flow security. Consider the situation that we have a target system that we have already proven secure, but that does not yet satisfy a safety property, and we have a monitor for that safety property. The idea is that with a proof that the monitor itself is secure wrt. a suitable security view for the monitor,[4] we can derive the security of the composed system via compositionality of the security predicate, provided that

- the security views for the monitor and the target system form a proper view separation wrt. a view for the composed system,
- the monitor and the target system are well-behaved for their view wrt. the view of the other component, and
- the side conditions for the compositionality of the desired security predicate are satisfied.

In this paper, we consider not a single target system, but we aim to find sufficient conditions under which the composition of the monitor with arbitrary target systems preserves security. We approach this problem by focusing on the monitor first and searching for sufficient conditions on the security view that guarantee that the monitor is well-behaved and secure. These conditions give rise to a *set* of views for potential target systems and corresponding views for the monitor:

Definition 4. *Let P be a safety property, ES_P be a monitor for P and SP be a security predicate. A* view-aware monitor *for P is a tuple $(ES_P, \mathcal{V}s_P, \pi_P)$, where $\mathcal{V}s_P$ is a set of views for potential target systems ES, and π_P is a function from views for target systems to views for the monitor. A view-aware monitor is*

- valid *if for every view $\mathcal{V} \in \mathcal{V}s_P$, it holds that $\mathcal{V}$ is valid, $\pi_P(\mathcal{V})$ is valid for ES_P, and $\mathcal{V}$ and $\pi_P(\mathcal{V})$ form a proper view separation for some $\mathcal{V}'$.*
- well-behaved *if for every view $\mathcal{V} \in \mathcal{V}s_P$, ES_P is well-behaved for $\pi_P(\mathcal{V})$ wrt. $\mathcal{V}$.*
- secure wrt. *SP if for every $\mathcal{V} \in \mathcal{V}s_P$, ES_P satisfies SP for $\pi_P(\mathcal{V})$.*

Intuitively, a view-aware monitor is enriched with a set of compatible security views for potential target systems and corresponding views for the monitor. Once we have shown a view-aware monitor for P to be well-behaved and secure wrt. a security predicate SP, and we have a concrete target system at hand that satisfies SP wrt. a compatible view $\mathcal{V} \in \mathcal{V}s_P$, we just have to show the remaining conditions on the target system: that ES is well-behaved for $\mathcal{V}$ wrt. $\pi_P(\mathcal{V})$, and the side conditions for the compositionality of SP are satisfied. The resulting composed system satisfies *both* the safety property P (by Lemma 1) and the security predicate SP wrt. a view $\mathcal{V}'$, for which $\mathcal{V}$ and $\pi_P(\mathcal{V})$ form a proper view separation (by Corollary 1). As a trivial example, a monitor for an arbitrary safety property is well-behaved and

---

[4] Which is typically different to the view for the target system because it is restricted to the set of relevant monitor events, and because monitored events that are neutral N-events for the target system have to be considered confidential C-events for the monitor (or vice versa) due to the constraints in the definition of proper view separation (particularly $N_i \cap N_j = \emptyset$, i.e. an event cannot be used for corrections in both components). See Section 3.2 for an example where this plays a role.

secure wrt. (almost) any security predicate if the relevant events are all confidential or all visible in the target system.

Theorem 1. *Let $ES_P = (E_P, I_P, O_P, Tr_P)$ be a monitor for a safety property P. The view-aware monitor $(ES_P, \mathcal{V}s_P, \pi_P)$ with*

$$\mathcal{V}s_P = \{(V, N, C) \mid valid\,((V, N, C)) \wedge E_P \subseteq V \vee E_P \subseteq C\}$$

$$\pi_P\,((V, N, C)) = (V \cap E_P, \emptyset, C \cap E_P)$$

is valid, well-behaved and secure wrt. BSD and $FCIA^{\rho,\Gamma}$, and it is secure wrt. $BSIA^\rho$ if $\rho(\pi_P(V)) \supseteq C \cap E_P$ for any $V \in \mathcal{V}s_P$.

This follows directly from Theorems 3.5.7 and 3.5.16 of [12] about trivially satisfied BSPs and the fact that well-behavedness is trivially satisfied if there are no shared N-events. We now illustrate our approach with two more specific examples of safety properties, namely separation of duties between activities in a workflow system, and the enforcement of ordered delivery of messages by an asynchronous communication platform.

3.1 Separation of Duty

We have seen in Example 3 how to formalize separation of duty as a safety property. We could enforce this property using a monitor with event set $E_{SoD}^{a,a'} = (E_a \cup E_{a'}) \cap E_U$ and the traces in $P_{SoD}^{a,a'}$ projected onto these events. However, it is useful to refine our monitor by adding two parameters that give us more flexibility for formulating conditions for security.

- We designate a set $E^{assign} \subseteq E_{SoD}^{a,a'}$ of events that are used to assign a user to an activity. The monitor then enforces that a single user is not assigned to both a and a', and that any interaction between a user and an activity is only allowed to happen after that user has been assigned to the activity.
- The set $E^{disabled} \subseteq E_{SoD}^{a,a'}$ contains events that do not occur at runtime at all. This can be used to make explicit static knowledge of disabled events, e.g. a subset of users not being allowed to perform certain actions.

Lemma 2. *The event system $ES_{SoD}^{a,a'} = \left(E_{SoD}^{a,a'}, \emptyset, \emptyset, Tr_{SoD}^{a,a'}\right)$ is a monitor for $P_{SoD}^{a,a'}$, where $E_{SoD}^{a,a'} = (E_a \cup E_{a'}) \cap E_U$ and*

$$Tr_{SoD}^{a,a'} = \Big\{\alpha \in \left(E_{SoD}^{a,a'}\right)^* \mid \forall u, u' \in U. \; \forall e, e' \in set(\alpha).$$
$$((e \in (E_a \cap E_u) \wedge e' \in (E_{a'} \cap E_{u'}) \longrightarrow u \neq u')$$
$$\wedge \left(set(\alpha) \cap (E_a \cap E_u \cap E^{assign}) = \emptyset \longrightarrow set(\alpha) \cap (E_a \cap E_u) = \emptyset\right)$$
$$\wedge \left(set(\alpha) \cap E^{disabled} = \emptyset\right) \Big\}$$

This follows from $Tr_{SoD}^{a,a'} \subseteq P_{SoD}^{a,a'}$ and $E_{SoD}^{a,a'}$ being a relevant event set. We can show that this monitor satisfies BSD, $BSIA$ and $FCIA$ if

- user assignment is non-confidential, or
- only confidential or only visible user interaction events are enabled, or
- the separation of duty constraint is enforced statically (i.e. the sets of users for whom interaction events with a and a' are enabled, respectively, are disjoint) and dynamic user assignment is permissive (i.e. $E^{assign} = E^{a,a'}_{SoD}$).

Formally, these conditions are captured in $Vs^{a,a'}_{SoD}$ of the following definition:

Lemma 3. *The view-aware monitor* $\left(ES^{a,a'}_{SoD}, Vs^{a,a'}_{SoD}, \pi^{a,a'}_{SoD}\right)$ *with*

$$Vs^{a,a'}_{SoD} = \{(V, N, C) \mid valid((V, N, C)) \wedge E^{a,a'}_{SoD} \subseteq V \cup C$$
$$\wedge \left(E^{assign} \subseteq V\right.$$
$$\vee \left(V \cap E^{a,a'}_{SoD} \subseteq E^{disabled} \vee C \cap E^{a,a'}_{SoD} \subseteq E^{disabled}\right)$$
$$\left.\vee \left(users(E_a) \cap users(E_{a'}) = \emptyset \wedge E^{assign} = E^{a,a'}_{SoD}\right)\right\}$$

$$\pi^{a,a'}_{SoD}((V, N, C)) = \left(V \cap E^{a,a'}_{SoD}, \emptyset, C \cap E^{a,a'}_{SoD}\right)$$

where $users(E) = \{u \in U \mid \exists e \in ((E \setminus E^{disabled}) \cap E_u)\}$, *is valid, well-behaved and secure wrt.* BSD, $BSIA^\rho$ *and* $FCIA^{\rho,\Gamma}$ *if* $\rho(V) \supseteq E^{assign}$.

Due to space constraints, we place the proofs of this and the following lemmas and theorems into an extended version of this paper [2].

For this monitor, the security predicates BSD, $BSIA^\rho$ and $FCIA^{\rho,\Gamma}$ (for suitable ρ) are preserved upon composition as follows:

Theorem 2. *Let* $ES = (E, I, O, Tr)$ *be an event system and* $V \in Vs^{a,a'}_{SoD}$ *be a view for ES. Then*

- *$BSD_V(Tr)$ implies $BSD_V(Tr(ES \| ES^{a,a'}_{SoD}))$, and*
- *$BSD_V(Tr) \wedge BSIA^\rho_V(Tr)$ implies $BSIA^\rho_V(Tr(ES \| ES^{a,a'}_{SoD}))$ if $\rho(V) \supseteq E^{assign}$.*
- *$BSD_V(Tr) \wedge BSIA^\rho_V(Tr) \wedge FCIA^{\rho,\Gamma}_V(Tr)$ implies $FCIA^{\rho,\Gamma}_V(Tr(ES \| ES^{a,a'}_{SoD}))$ if $\rho(V) \supseteq E^{assign}$.*

This means that if the target system satisfies one of the above combinations of security predicates, then the monitored system $ES \| ES^{a,a'}_{SoD}$ still satisfies it, and it additionally satisfies the separation of duty property (by Lemma 1).

Example 4. In our workflow scenario, we only considered the values of data items confidential, not the identity of participants in the workflow. We therefore simply used the events of the form $Start_a(u)$ as assignment events and chose a view that considers these events as visible. Hence, the case $E^{assign} \subseteq V$ applies[5]

---

[5] Note that $E^{assign} \subseteq V$ does not mean that these events *have to be* visible for an observer of the system, it just means that if we are able to prove security wrt. this view, then the system is secure *even if* user assignment were visible for an observer. This notion of strengthening views is captured formally in Theorem 1 of [11], for example.

and we can use Theorem 2 for the security-preserving enforcement of arbitrary separation of duty constraints.   □

3.2   Ordered Delivery of Asynchronous Messages

Another safety property we encountered while working on [3] is the guarantee of ordered delivery of messages by the asynchronous communication platform. When we specified our workflow system in terms of communicating subsystems in [3], we did not include any guarantees regarding message delivery in the specification of the communication platform. This simplified the specification of the platform and the proof of compositionality, but it made the specifications of the communicating subsystems more complex. We had to introduce explicit acknowledgment messages and make the subsystems wait for acknowledgments before continuing with a communication protocol in some cases. Message delivery ordering per sender-receiver pair, i.e. the guarantee that messages between two components are received in the order that they are sent, makes these explicit acknowledgments unnecessary in the cases we encountered. It turns out that we can use the same compositional approach as above to analyze the impact that this refinement of the communication platform has on the requirements regarding information flow.

We first formulate ordered delivery as a safety property. Let $\text{sentMsgs}(a, b, \alpha)$ and $\text{rcvdMsgs}(b, a, \alpha)$ denote the sequences of messages m contained in the sequences of events of the form $\text{Send}_a(b, m)$ or $\text{Recv}_b(a, m)$, respectively, in a trace α, and let $\preceq$ be the prefix order on traces. Ordered delivery can be formulated as

$$Tr_{CD} = \{\alpha \mid \forall a, b. \ \text{rcvdMsgs}(b, a, \alpha) \preceq \text{sentMsgs}(a, b, \alpha)\}$$

The event system $ES_{CD} = (E_{CD}, \emptyset, \emptyset, Tr_{CD})$ with the relevant set of events

$$E_{CD} = \{e \mid \exists a, b, m. \ e = \text{Send}_a(b, m) \vee e = \text{Recv}_b(a, m)\}$$

is a monitor for ordered delivery, assuming communication between components is represented by Send and Recv events of the form given above.

It turns out that, in order for the refined communication platform to be secure, we have to treat Recv events corresponding to confidential Send events as N-events. The reason is that we might have to correct the deletion or insertion of a confidential Send event by removing or inserting a corresponding Recv event at the correct position in the trace in order to preserve the correct order of delivery.

Lemma 4. *The view-aware monitor* $(ES_{CD}, \mathcal{V}s_{CD}, \pi_{CD})$ *with*

$$\mathcal{V}s_{CD} = \{(V, N, C) \mid valid\,((V, N, C)) \wedge E_{CD} \subseteq V \cup N \cup C$$
$$\wedge Send_a(b, m) \in V \longleftrightarrow Recv_b(a, m) \in V$$
$$\wedge Send_a(b, m) \notin V \longleftrightarrow Recv_b(a, m) \in C\}$$

$$N_{CD}(C) = C \cap \{e \mid \exists a, b, m. \ e = Recv_a(b, m)\}$$
$$\pi_{CD}\,((V, N, C)) = (V \cap E_{CD}, N_{CD}(C), E_{CD} \setminus (V \cup N_{CD}(C)))$$

is valid, well-behaved and secure for BSD and BSIA$^\rho$ and FCIA$^{\rho,\Gamma_{CD}}$ for any ρ and $\Gamma_{CD} = (\nabla_{CD}, \Delta_{CD}, \Upsilon_{CD}) = (E_{CD}, \emptyset, E_{CD})$.

In this case, there are further side conditions on the target system that follow directly from the requirement of well-behavedness. Moreover, confidential Recv events become neutral in the security view of the composed system. Confidential Send events, however, and thus the message contents, remain confidential.

Theorem 3. *Let $ES = (E, I, O, Tr)$ be an event system and $\mathcal{V} = (V, N, C)$ be a view for ES such that*

- *$\mathcal{V} \in \mathcal{V}s_{CD}$, and*
- *$total(ES, N_{CD}(C))$, and*
- *$BSD_\mathcal{V}(Tr) \wedge BSIA^\rho_\mathcal{V}(Tr)$ holds for some ρ, and*
- *$N \cap E_{CD} \neq \emptyset$ implies $FCIA^{\rho,\Gamma}_\mathcal{V}$ for some $\Gamma = (\nabla, \Delta, \Upsilon)$ with $E_{CD} \subseteq \nabla$, $E_{CD} \subseteq \Upsilon$, and $E_{CD} \cap \Delta = \emptyset$.*

Then $BSD_{\mathcal{V}'}(Tr(ES\|ES_{CD})) \wedge BSIA^\rho_{\mathcal{V}'}(Tr(ES\|ES_{CD}))$ holds for $\mathcal{V}' = (V, N \cup N_{CD}(C), C \setminus N_{CD}(C))$, and $FCIA^{\rho,\Gamma}_\mathcal{V}(Tr)$ implies $FCIA^{\rho,\Gamma}_{\mathcal{V}'}(Tr(ES\|ES_{CD}))$.

Example 5. In [3], we have already proven *BSD* and *BSIA* for our workflow system wrt. a view such that most of the preconditions of Theorem 3 are satisfied, i.e. non-visible Recv events are treated as confidential and are accepted at any time by the individual subsystems. However, we had to use some Send events for corrections in our proofs. Hence, $N \cap E_{CD} \neq \emptyset$ holds and in order to apply Theorem 3, we get *FCIA* as an additional proof obligation.[6] As *FCIA* is relatively similar to *BSIA* and we had already proven *BSIA* for the activities in our example workflow, it turns out to be easy to prove in this case.   □

4   Related Work

The connection between safety properties and execution monitors is elaborated in [17]. Information flow security is of a different nature than safety properties. In [8], possibilistic information flow properties are characterized as closure properties on the whole sets of traces of a system. Hence, removing traces in order to enforce a safety property can invalidate such a closure property. This explains the refinement paradox, which was already observed in early works such as [7].

The idea of using composition for the security-preserving enforcement of safety properties also occurs in [14, Section 3.2] for the framework of McLean's selective interleaving functions. We apply and elaborate this idea in the context of the MAKS framework [8], which has been shown to be more expressive than McLean's framework [13]. We demonstrate the approach by deriving three results giving explicit and succinct conditions for the security-preserving enforcement

---

[6] Intuitively, this means that we may use Send events for corrections, but not in direct response to the insertion of a Recv event, in order to avoid a non-terminating sequence of communication events. See [12, pages 132f] for a discussion of this issue.

of safety properties (Theorems 1 to 3). For this purpose, we heavily rely on the well-developed MAKS framework, in particular its compositionality results [11].

In the context of MAKS, a paper with a goal very similar to ours is [10]. The approach is different, however. It requires a proof of security of the target system via unwinding, and then modifies the safety property to be enforced by removing or adding traces so that the unwinding conditions are preserved. It works with arbitrary safety properties, but the result can be hard to predict, as it depends heavily on the unwinding relation that is used. We see this approach as complementary to ours. It can be used if compatibility results as we presented them above are not available for the safety property in question.

There are approaches for security-preserving process refinement (i.e. reducing the set of possible traces) also for other notions of information flow security. [16] considers confidentiality-preserving refinement for probabilistic information flow. [18] builds upon the MAKS framework, but modifies the notions of system specification and security predicates to make the distinction between underspecification and unpredictability explicit. [4] uses a similar approach to [10], but in the context of a process algebra and bisimulation-based notions of security. Which of the available approaches is best suited for a concrete application depends on the precise security requirements at hand.

5   Conclusion

In this paper, we have focused on the compatibility of possibilistic information flow security and safety properties. We have described how existing compositionality results for information flow predicates can be used to derive sufficient conditions for compatibility with a given safety property. We found this approach to be useful in our case study of verifying the specification of a distributed workflow management system [3].

While Theorem 1 applies to arbitrary safety properties, results like our Theorems 2 and 3 have to be derived for each safety property of interest individually. However, it is worth pointing out that the compatibility result for separation of duty is parametric in the event sets and can therefore be instantiated for arbitrary systems where users participate in distinct activities in the presence of separation of duty constraints. Similarly, ordered delivery can be applied to any system with asynchronous message passing. This demonstrates that compositional reasoning can be used to derive compatibility results for whole classes of common safety properties.

In this paper, we have considered systems and properties on a high level of abstraction. In order to move to a more concrete level of implementation detail, we intend to focus on action refinement in future work. Combined with the compositional reasoning described in this paper and in [3], this facilitates a stepwise development process. Eventually, we hope to integrate these techniques into a development tool for provably secure workflow management systems.

Acknowledgments. We thank Richard Gay, Sylvia Grewe, Steffen Lortz, Heiko Mantel and Henning Sudbrock for providing a formalization of the MAKS framework in Isabelle/HOL that allowed us to verify our main results in Isabelle, and the anonymous reviewers for helpful comments.

References

1. Alpern, B., Schneider, F.B.: Recognizing safety and liveness. Distributed Computing 2(3), 117–126 (1987)
2. Bauereiss, T., Hutter, D.: Compatibility of safety properties and possibilistic information flow security in MAKS. Tech. rep. (2014), http://bauereiss.name/papers/SEC2014_TR.pdf
3. Bauereiss, T., Hutter, D.: Possibilistic information flow security of workflow management systems. In: GraMSec 2014. To appear in EPTCS (2014)
4. Bossi, A., Focardi, R., Piazza, C., Rossi, S.: Refinement operators and information flow security. In: SEFM, pp. 44–53. IEEE Computer Society (2003)
5. Clarkson, M.R., Schneider, F.B.: Hyperproperties. Journal of Computer Security 18(6), 1157–1210 (2010)
6. Hutter, D., Mantel, H., Schaefer, I., Schairer, A.: Security of multi-agent systems: A case study on comparison shopping. J. Applied Logic 5(2), 303–332 (2007)
7. Jacob, J.: On the derivation of secure components. In: IEEE Symposium on Security and Privacy, pp. 242–247. IEEE Computer Society (1989)
8. Mantel, H.: Possibilistic definitions of security - an assembly kit. In: CSFW, pp. 185–199. IEEE Computer Society (2000)
9. Mantel, H.: Unwinding possibilistic security properties. In: Cuppens, F., Deswarte, Y., Gollmann, D., Waidner, M. (eds.) ESORICS 2000. LNCS, vol. 1895, pp. 238–254. Springer, Heidelberg (2000)
10. Mantel, H.: Preserving information flow properties under refinement. In: IEEE Symposium on Security and Privacy, pp. 78–91. IEEE Computer Society (2001)
11. Mantel, H.: On the composition of secure systems. In: IEEE Symposium on Security and Privacy, pp. 88–101. IEEE Computer Society (2002)
12. Mantel, H.: A uniform framework for the formal specification and verification of information flow security. Ph.D. thesis (2004)
13. Mantel, H.: The framework of selective interleaving functions and the modular assembly kit. In: Atluri, V., Samarati, P., Küsters, R., Mitchell, J.C. (eds.) FMSE, pp. 53–62. ACM (2005)
14. McLean, J.: A general theory of composition for a class of "possibilistic" properties. IEEE Trans. Software Eng. 22(1), 53–67 (1996)
15. Roscoe, A.: Parallel operators. In: Understanding Concurrent Systems. Texts in Computer Science, pp. 45–66. Springer, London (2010)
16. Santen, T.: Preservation of probabilistic information flow under refinement. Inf. Comput. 206(2-4), 213–249 (2008)
17. Schneider, F.B.: Enforceable security policies. ACM Trans. Inf. Syst. Secur. 3(1), 30–50 (2000)
18. Seehusen, F., Stølen, K.: Maintaining information flow security under refinement and transformation. In: Dimitrakos, T., Martinelli, F., Ryan, P.Y.A., Schneider, S. (eds.) FAST 2006. LNCS, vol. 4691, pp. 143–157. Springer, Heidelberg (2007)

Ghostrail: Ad Hoc Control-Flow Integrity for Web Applications

Bastian Braun, Caspar Gries, Benedikt Petschkuhn, and Joachim Posegga

Institute of IT Security and Security Law (ISL), University of Passau, Germany
{bb,jp}@sec.uni-passau.de, cgries@in-doc.de, petschku@fim.uni-passau.de

Abstract. Modern web applications frequently implement complex control flows, which require the users to perform actions in a given order. Users interact with a web application by sending HTTP requests with parameters and in response receive web pages with hyperlinks that indicate the expected next actions. If a web application takes for granted that the user sends only those expected requests and parameters, malicious users can exploit this assumption by crafting harming requests. We analyze recent attacks on web applications with respect to user-defined requests and identify their root cause in the missing enforcement of allowed next user requests. Based on this result, we provide our approach, named *Ghostrail*, a control-flow monitor that is applicable to legacy as well as newly developed web applications. It observes incoming requests and lets only those pass that were provided as next steps in the last web page. Ghostrail protects the web application against race condition exploits, the manipulation of HTTP parameters, unsolicited request sequences, and forceful browsing. We evaluate the approach and show that it neither needs a training phase nor a manual policy definition while it is suitable for a broad range of web technologies.

1 Introduction

Over the past two decades, the Web has evolved from a simple delivery mechanism for static content to an environment for powerful distributed applications. In spite of these advances, remote interactions between users and web applications are still handled using the stateless HTTP protocol, which has no protocol-level session concept. Handling session state is fully left to the web application developer or to high-level web application frameworks.

Web applications often include complex control flows that span a series of multiple distributed interactions. The application developer usually expects the user to follow the intended control flow, i.e., to first access the website on an entry page and then proceed by clicking on links and buttons and fill provided forms. However, if a web application does not carefully ensure that interactions adhere to the intended control flow, attackers can easily abuse the web application by using unexpected interactions. Our previous work showed that common web application frameworks provide hardly any protection means a developer could rely on [1], meaning that developers must ensure control-flow integrity manually.

N. Cuppens-Boulahia et al. (Eds.): SEC 2014, IFIP AICT 428, pp. 264–277, 2014.
© IFIP International Federation for Information Processing 2014

Several known attacks have exploited missing protection in the past. The attacks' impact ranges from sending more free SMS text messages than actually allowed [2], and unauthorized access to user accounts [3–5], to shopping for expensive goods with arbitrarily low payments [6]. This paper presents a novel approach for avoiding problems related to control-flow integrity in web applications. Based on the assumption that all client-side requests are potentially compromised, the approach replicates a user's mouse clicks and form input in a server-side sandbox. Requests triggered by the sandbox are trustworthy because they adhere to the assumed user interaction with the web application. We show that this approach provides ad hoc protection against attacks on the web application's control flow without the need for a learning phase or a manual policy definition. It functions as a reverse proxy and is thus independent of the server-side technology. No adaptations are required on the web application making the approach applicable to new and legacy applications. The induced load can be outsourced to scalable, e.g. cloud-based, platforms if necessary.

This paper is structured as follows. The next section provides an in-depth discussion of technical aspects of control-flow integrity in web applications and explains known attacks and vulnerabilities. Section 3 presents our novel approach for controlling flow integrity at the server-side, and Section 4 gives details about the implementation. We evaluate the approach in Section 5, discuss related work in Section 6, and finally conclude in Section 7.

2   Control-Flow Integrity

In this section, we investigate in more detail the problem of control-flow integrity of web applications, analyze several real-world attacks, and discuss their root causes.

2.1   Technical Background

In a typical web application, the user's web browser interacts with the remote application by sending HTTP requests. HTTP is a stateless protocol without session concept. This means that each request is independent of all others. The protocol does not inherently link one request to the next. Dynamic web applications, however, have workflows that are composed of multiple steps, which corresponds to multiple HTTP requests from the user to the web application. For each step, the client receives a web page with hyperlinks that offer possible next steps to a user. Upon clicking a link, the user's browser sends a particular HTTP request to the web application, which then performs actions in order to progress to the next step in the workflow. The actions are defined by the URI of the HTTP request, the request parameters, and the server-side session record.

2.2   The Attacks

Several kinds of attacks on web applications exploit the fact that attackers can craft arbitrary requests instead of clicking on provided hyperlinks. Real-world examples of control-flow integrity violations are race conditions, manipulated HTTP parameters, unsolicited request sequences, and forceful browsing.

Race Conditions. In order to exploit race conditions [7] in web applications, attackers can send several crafted requests almost in parallel. If the web application does not handle concurrent requests by proper synchronisation, the actual application semantics can be changed in this way. In one real-world example, a web application provided an interface to send a limited number of SMS text messages per day [2]. The web application first checked the current amount of sent messages (*time-of-check*), then delivered the message according to the received request, and finally updated the number of sent messages in the database (*time-of-use*). Attackers were able to send more messages than allowed by the web application by crafting a number of HTTP requests, each containing the receiver and text of the message to be sent. These requests were sent almost in parallel and the multi-threaded web application processed the incoming requests concurrently. This way, the attacker exploited the fact that the messages were sent before the respective database entry was updated, leading to the delivery of all requested messages. The developers' underlying assumption was that users finish one transmission process before sending the next message and do not request one operation of the workflow several times in parallel.

HTTP Parameter Manipulation. HTTP requests can contain parameters in addition to the receiving host, path, and resource. As the parameters are sent by the client, the user can control the parameters' values and which parameters are sent to the web application. Wang et al. [6] found a bunch of logic flaws in well-known merchant systems and Cashier-as-a-Service (CaaS) services. These flaws allowed them to buy any item for the price of the cheapest item in the store. In 2011, the Citigroup faced an attack on their customers' data [4]. The attackers were able to access names, credit card numbers, e-mail addresses and transaction histories. All the attackers had to do was simply changing the HTTP parameters in the web browser. By automation, they obtained confidential data of more than 200,000 customers.

File Inclusion Attacks are a special kind of HTTP parameter manipulation. The successful attacker gains access to protected resources be it static documents or application functions. For instance, an application might offer the URL `http://example.com/?view=welcome.html` as a hyperlink. In this case, the `view` parameter holds the name of a file that is supposed to be included in the output. An attacker can change the parameter value to `/etc/passwd`. He succeeds if the application fails to detect the manipulation. A successful file inclusion attack allows to access all files that are readable to the web server process.

Unsolicited Request Sequences. Attackers can not only modify the requests' parameters but also craft requests to any method of the web application. Besides manipulated HTTP parameters, web applications might face unexpected requests to any method. For instance, in another given scenario by Wang et al. [6], a malicious shopper was able to add items to her cart between checkout and payment. She was only charged the value of her cart at checkout time. The recently added items were shipped but not invoiced.

Forceful Browsing. A forceful browsing attacker exploits predictable naming schemes in combination with insufficient access control. For instance, left installation scripts for PHP-based web applications are popular targets for forceful browsing attacks. An administrator uploads such a script to the web server and calls it via her browser in order to install a web application. Attackers can call the installation script and reconfigure the application if the administrator forgets to delete it. In 2010, a group of attackers gained access to 114,000 user records of iPad owners by requesting a server-side script that was supposed to embed user details into a web page [5]. The attackers could easily guess the naming scheme and access restricted application functions.

2.3 Root Causes

All described attacks share common root causes. Web application developers assume that users first request one of possibly several application entry points, e.g. the base directory at `http://www.example.com`. Upon the first request, the web application sends a given response containing a set of hyperlinks or a redirect instruction to the client. As users tend to click on hyperlinks in order to navigate through the application, developers might assume that only the given requests will be accessed next. However, the user is technically not bound to click on one of the provided hyperlinks but she can still send requests that are not provided within this response. Sent requests can differ from provided hyperlinks in terms of addressed methods and HTTP parameters. Vulnerable web applications fail to handle unintended user behavior in terms of sequences of requests.

More formally, web application developers implement implicit control-flow graphs. In each state, sending a request leads to a subsequent state in the graph. Executing a step corresponds to changing the server-side state. Control-flow weaknesses occur if an attacker is able to address at least one method, i.e. cause a state-changing action, that is not meant to be addressed in the respective session state. In the respective control-flow graph, this transition does not exist due to the developer's assumption that the request does not happen at that time. Vice versa, a web application implementing a control-flow graph with transitions for all requests in every state is not susceptible to control-flow weaknesses.

Forceful browsing attacks and some cases of HTTP parameter manipulation can be overcome with access control. The other attack vectors, however, include only requests that are in the scope of the user's rights. Access control mechanisms prevent users from accessing sensitive API methods at all time while control-flow integrity protection prohibits access to regular API methods at the wrong time.

3   Preserving Control-Flow Integrity Ad Hoc

In this section, we present *Ghostrail*, our approach to overcome the attacks described in Sec. 2. We give details on the implementation in Sec. 4.

3.1   High-Level Overview

The idea behind Ghostrail is the ad hoc enforcement of control-flow integrity based on the developer's assumptions phrased in Sec. 2.3: Users first request one entry point of the web application, e.g. `www.example.com`, and then click on links and buttons or fill in forms. We assume that the attacker is a web user that controls all client-side data and applications within his domain. However, he can not bypass reverse proxies. He can send messages to the server but does not control the server-side platform.

Ghostrail operates as a traffic monitor on the server side. It protects a web application against the attacks described in Sec. 2.2 by filtering out incoming requests that are not generated by user clicks and form entries. In order to determine whether a request arises from regular interaction between the user and the current web page, Ghostrail analyzes the last web page delivered by the web application. A request is accepted if the web page contained the respective link. Otherwise – the page did not contain the requested URL – the request is considered crafted and, thus, possibly malicious because it violates the assumption that the user only interacts with the web application using clicks and filling in forms. Ghostrail has a three-tier whitelisting approach to derive regular requests:

- First, Ghostrail queries an application-wide whitelist of always allowed requests. The list contains the application's entry points, e.g. the start page, and possibly all requests to public resources that do not change the application's state.
- Second, Ghostrail parses the last web page delivered by the web application. It compiles a list of static references found in HTML and CSS documents. Those references denote hyperlinks, i.e., possible next user clicks, or embedded resources that are needed by the browser to render the web page, e.g. images. We give more details on static reference extraction in Sec. 3.2.
- Third, Ghostrail renders web pages in server-side sandboxes to determine dynamically generated requests, e.g. using AJAX and JavaScript. Those requests can not be determined by the static parser in step 2. Ghostrail accepts requests from client side if the sandbox triggered the same request. We describe the sandbox-based request detection in Sec. 3.3.

Ghostrail lets only requests found in any of these three lists pass. This way, it enforces the assumption that users do only interact with the web application using mouse clicks and form input. Due to the fact that the whitelists in step 2 and step 3 are compiled ad hoc, Ghostrail neither needs a pre-release learning phase to generate its control-flow policy nor a hand-crafted control-flow definition. However, as Ghostrail operates on automatically generated whitelists of references, every reference it fails to extract may degrade the usability of the web application. It is therefore crucial to extract as many references as possible. By extraction we mean the analysis, classification and storage of reference information that is embedded in content delivered by the web application. In the remainder of this section, we provide details on how Ghostrail extracts references statically and dynamically.

3.2 Extraction of Static References

In this section, we give details on how Ghostrail extracts static URLs from delivered web pages. Static references usually occur in HTML and CSS files. Other web resources like JavaScript and Flash, i.e., ActionScript, mainly utilize dynamic URL generation. They assemble the requests based on user input or client-side state. We explain dynamic URL tracking in the next section. Finally, media files like images are ignored because they do not contain links for subsequent requests.

HTML is a tag-based language, i.e., the elements of a web page are described as tags. There is a limited number of HTML tags that may contain URLs: `<a>`, `<link>`, `<iframe>`, `<script>`, `<img>`, `<area>`, `<embed>`, `<form>`, `<base>`, and `<meta>`. Ghostrail parses these tags and extracts URLs found. However, not all HTML content is trustworthy. Web applications often allow users to provide own content, e.g. in the form of comments that are embedded in the HTML output. An attacker could easily abuse such a feature by posting the URLs he wants to request next. It is therefore possible and necessary to configure Ghostrail so that it excludes user-provided content from reference extraction within HTML documents. The second type of static content that may contain references is CSS data. As this is limited to only one syntax element (`url()`), an adequate regular expression performs the reference extraction.

There can be different URLs that are semantically identical, e.g. `http://exa mple.org/?par1=foo&par2=bar` and `http://example.org/?par2=bar&par1= foo`. Ghostrail normalizes URLs in order to prevent misclassification.

During reference extraction, Ghostrail tags whitelisted URLs either as a *transition* or as an *extension*. Transitions make the browser replace the current web page while extensions only update a part of the page, e.g. in a iframe or by an AJAX request, or load an additional page in a new browser window (or tab) without modifying the parent window. A transition invalidates all previous whitelisted URLs whereas an extension adds new URLs to the whitelist.

3.3 Replication of Client-Side Execution

Beside the static references, dynamically generated requests play an important role within modern web applications. Applications that used to be installed and executed on a local machine, for instance office apps, move to the Web and become accessible via a web browser. The synchronization of client and server state as well as seamless interface updates require dynamic request generation and response processing, known as AJAX. The same is true for the search-as-you-type feature during user input. Such dynamically generated requests can not be determined using the static reference extraction described in Sec. 3.2 because the static analysis of JavaScript code is fault-prone and requires manual code annotations [8]. Ghostrail, however, aims to protect web applications without the need to change the application code. Instead, we equipped Ghostrail with a server-side replica of the user's browser to track the execution of JavaScript and derive the respective requests. Ghostrail maintains one replica for each user

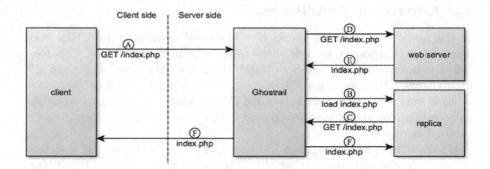

Fig. 1. Initial loading of a web page in the sandbox

session. Each replica runs in a sandbox and virtually performs the same actions that happen in the user's browser.

In order to monitor a user's actions, Ghostrail injects a few lines of JavaScript code into every delivered web page. This code monitors all user actions that can trigger JavaScript events. This is necessary because JavaScript has an event-driven execution paradigm: Code is not executed linearly but triggered by user actions, timing, or state changes of the web page. While timing and state changes also happen in the server-side replica without further ado, user actions must be transmitted to keep track. Interesting user actions include mouse movements, mouse clicks, and keystrokes.

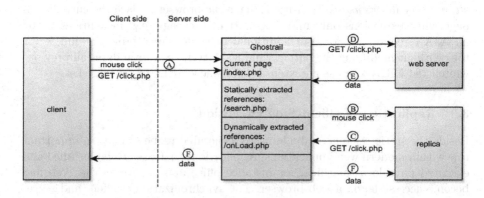

Fig. 2. Dynamic reference extraction by replicating an user's action

The server-side replica virtually renders the same web page as the user, it executes the same JavaScript code, and it simulates the user's mouse movements, clicks, and form input, i.e., only expected – thus benign – user actions. The requests from the replica are the condensed set of expected user requests. So, Ghostrail adds them to the user's whitelist. It is important to stress that Ghostrail only receives user actions from client side but not the respective state change in the user's browser. This is a crucial point because it limits a malicious user's scope: transmitting state changes allows an attacker to modify his browser such that it finally generates an attack request. For instance, a hash function may compute a URL parameter. The modified browser would always output /etc/passwd, independent of the input. Transmitting the output would allow the attacker to inject crafted requests into Ghostrail's whitelist. Limited to user actions, he can only spoof mouse clicks, movements and keystrokes on the web page. However, all these actions are within the scope of expected user interaction so there is no attack even if these actions are spoofed.

Fig. 1 shows the initial loading of a web page in the sandbox. The replica is initiated with the start of the user session (steps A/B). After the page has been fetched from the web application (steps D/E), it is send as a response to the client and the replica (step F). The replica does not interact directly with the web application to prevent double impact on the application state. Also, the duplication of the application's response (step F) ensures that both the client and the replica share the same content. After the page load, the user can interact with the web page. Fig. 2 shows an example how Ghostrail classifies dynamic references. The user clicks on an element (step A). The details are transmitted to Ghostrail and forwarded to the replica (step B) which simulates the same mouse click. The subsequent request to click.php (step C) is recorded by Ghostrail as legitimate because it is the result of intended user interaction. So, Ghostrail accepts and forwards the user request (step D).

4 Implementation

In this section, we describe the implementation of Ghostrail and the sandboxed replica. We implemented Ghostrail as a reverse proxy using Node.js (version 0.10.0) [9]. This reverse proxy manages all requests and responses and directs the replicas (see Sec. 3.3) as well as the static reference parser (see Sec. 3.2). This design allows to outsource CPU- or memory-intensive processes to other machines. The reverse proxy buffers incoming requests, queries the three-tiered list of regular requests (see Sec. 3.1) and finally accepts or rejects the request. It forwards the web application's responses to the static reference parser and the respective replica for further analysis. In the remainder of this section, we focus on the implementation of the replicas and the handling of client-side data.

4.1 The Sandboxed Replica

Ghostrail initiates a fresh replica for each user session – and destroys replicas when the session ends. We implemented the replicas using PhantomJS [10], a fully-fledged, GUI-less, and WebKit-based browser. Due to the WebKit basis, the replicas support all major web technologies like JavaScript, AJAX, CSS, JSON and SVG. Replicas do not need to run on the same machine as Ghostrail. They can be distributed to cloud-based computing platforms to scale with varying load. The communication between the replicas and Ghostrail is based on HTTP and WebSockets.

Ghostrail injects a small piece of JavaScript code into every web page that is delivered to the user. This code establishes a WebSocket connection with Ghostrail to transmit user actions. Ghostrail records three kinds of user actions:

- **Mouse Clicks:** Ghostrail records mouse clicks by injecting the `onclick` event handler for the whole web page. In order to simulate the click in the right page area, the (x, y) coordinates relative to the browser window are appended. Also, the dimensions of the browser window must be transmitted to configure the replica with the same size.
- **Mouse Movements:** Mouse movements can trigger `onmouseover` events on a web page. Hence, Ghostrail records mouse movements above a configurable threshold using the `onmousemove` event handler. The threshold is necessary to avoid an overload of Ghostrail.
- **Key Strokes:** Requests can contain user-defined data from an HTML form. Ghostrail must record every key stroke (using `onkeypress` and `onkeyup` event handlers) to simulate the user input. This is the only option to relate the resulting request to regular user behavior, i.e., entering data into form fields.

While Ghostrail injects new event handlers into the web page, there could be other event handlers that fire first and bypass Ghostrail's events. For instance, an event handler that redirects the browser to another page is executed first such that Ghostrail loses track and forbids future regular requests. We overcome this issue the following way: There are two options for the order of cascading event handlers, namely *event bubbling* and *event capturing* [11]. Event bubbling triggers the innermost event of the DOM tree first, i.e., for nested elements where each has an `onclick` event handler, the event of the inner element fires first when the user clicks. Event capturing has the reverse execution order. Ghostrail enforces event capturing and assigns its event handlers to the outermost element of the DOM tree, i.e., `document`.

4.2   Handling Browser Cache and History

In order to improve performance, browsers cache web content locally. Upon the next page access, they first query their local cache and restore the page without the need to request it again from the website. This, however, poses a problem to Ghostrail if it can not observe the local page load and extract the references from the cached page. We implemented a twofold cache management in Ghostrail to overcome this issue: First, Ghostrail adds the `Cache-Control: no-cache` HTTP header [12] to each response to prevent caching on client side. More precisely, the browser may cache the respective content but must revalidate every usage with the server. However, we found that the Chrome and the Firefox browser still cache at least the last visited page and reuse it without revalidation. Second, the client-side code detects the click that loads the cached resource. Then, the replica performs the same click and loads the same content from the local cache provided by PhantomJS. Beside the local cache, browsers also maintain a local browsing history. This history allows users to navigate back and forth. PhantomJS supports the browsing history since version 1.8 such that the replica can emulate the navigation through the browsing history.

5   Evaluation

We evaluate the security gain by Ghostrail, investigate a possible impact of Ghostrail on the protected web application's availability, and give results of our performance measurements.

5.1   The Security Gain by Ghostrail

In order to evaluate the security gain by Ghostrail, we first describe how Ghostrail protects web applications against the attacks described in Sec. 2.2. Then, we explain our practical evaluation using the intentionally vulnerable web application Google Gruyere [13].

An attacker who exploits race conditions in web applications must send the same request many times in parallel. If the request is compiled dynamically, he must prepare the respective input in his browser and send the form using a mouse click to make the request be also sent by the replica and thus be whitelisted. In any case, as soon as Ghostrail accepts the attacker's first request, it immediately discards the whitelist of requests and waits for the application response to refill the list of expected requests. So, Ghostrail rejects the second request unless it is extracted from the subsequent page.

HTTP parameter manipulation attacks rely on the user's ability to freely change the parameters of a given request, e.g. to change the given account ID or message ID. While an attacker can still craft arbitrary requests in his browser's address line, Ghostrail rejects all requests that do not match an extracted request from the current page.

Unsolicited request sequences occur if an attacker can assemble a request to call application functions when they are not supposed to be called. In the example given in Sec. 2.2, the attacker knows the request that adds items to his shopping cart. As Ghostrail discards previously allowed requests, the crafted request is not whitelisted after checkout and thus rejected.

A forceful browsing attacker also needs to craft a targeted request that is not part of the current web page. So, Ghostrail rejects forceful browsing attempts by design.

In order to evaluate Ghostrail's protection in practice, we set up Google Gruyere that is vulnerable to forceful browsing, file inclusion, and reflected cross-site scripting (XSS) attacks. With Ghostrail in place, none of the attacks on Gruyere worked. However, we want to emphasize that injection attacks like XSS and SQL injection are out of scope for Ghostrail. If the attacker enters the payload into a form field, Ghostrail regards the resulting request as benign. So, protected applications still need to sanitize user input from free text form fields. Nevertheless, Ghostrail limits possible user input via drop-down menus or radio buttons to the given options.

As Ghostrail plays the role of a traffic monitor, it must be the server-side endpoint of SSL connections with the client side. Given that it runs in the same domain as the protected web application, we do not consider this point a serious issue. If needed, the communication between Ghostrail and the web application, as well as between Ghostrail and the replicas, can be encrypted again.

5.2 The Impact of Ghostrail on the Availability of the Protected Web Application

We evaluated whether Ghostrail has a negative impact on the web application's availability. A negative side effect can occur if Ghostrail fails to extract a regular reference that is accessed by the user in the next step. In that case, Ghostrail mistakenly classifies the user request as unexpected (false negative). The evaluation is threefold: First, we set up a demo web application that implements a broad range of modern web technologies, i.e., redirects, CSS, jQuery as a representative JavaScript library, dynamic page updates via AJAX, and the navigation to dynamically generated URLs. This approach is meant to find out whether there are general compatibility issues of Ghostrail with any web technology. We used Selenium [14] to direct an instance of Firefox and Chromium respectively. Each browser performed virtually 1,000 user actions, resulting in 20,648 requests overall (each user action can trigger several requests). Afterwards, we analyzed Ghostrail's log files and did not find any blocked request. Please note that every blocked request would be a false negative because the virtual users only clicked on links on filled forms – what we defined as compliant behavior.

Second, we set up Ghostrail as a reverse proxy for the Alexa Top 20 websites. We used Selenium again to make Firefox perform 200 user actions on each website. Overall, we recorded 18,319 requests with a false rejection rate of 17.57%. Our analysis showed that blocked requests contained customized elements. Some websites perform a kind of client fingerprinting, i.e., they read browser and system features that differ for Firefox and the replica and add such information to the requests. The replica proved able to simulate the more common User-Agent: string for client classification. Another source for blocked requests are client-side timestamps and random numbers generated by JavaScript and appended to requests. In these cases, the outcome of code execution differs for the browser and the replica. While we had to consider each web application as a black box, the application provider can configure Ghostrail more appropriately to avoid most of the false rejections, e.g. by adding a rule that ignores differing parameters if they match the expected pattern and if their processing may not cause harm. We avoid transmitting the random numbers and timestamps from client side to the replica for synchronization because this would allow a malicious user to inject arbitrary HTTP parameters.

Third, we accessed three websites manually to learn the perceivable impact of Ghostrail. This is important because the raw number of blocked requests does not make a point concerning the impact on the web application's availability.

- *Google Search:* The search function was usable without interference. Only the auto completion did not work due to differing request parameters.
- *Amazon:* We were able to search items, add them to our cart and checkout. However, we did not see product recommendations. The almost complete functionality of Amazon is particularly interesting because we experienced the highest number of falsely rejected requests ($\approx 60\%$). This result calls the significance of the raw number of false rejections into question.
- *Wikipedia:* We did not experience any issues on the availability.

We found that Ghostrail is able to allow workflows which span several domains. For instance, Ghostrail may protect an online shopping web application. When the user is redirected to a third-party cashier like PayPal, Ghostrail can not track the payment process (however, the cashier may run another instance of Ghostrail). Hence, the first request that leads the user back to the shopping application must be whitelisted as an application entry point. Instead of redirecting, a web application may include third-party content in its own pages. Then, the replica fetches the same content but does not provide cookies or authenticating HTTP parameters to avoid requests on behalf of the user.

5.3   Performance

Finally, we evaluated the performance impact of Ghostrail. We measured the HTTP round trip time between sending a request and receiving the response. We used the testbed with our demo application described above in order to avoid independent factors on the performance. The size of the served web pages ranges from 225KB to 450KB, and the round-trip overhead was between 250ms and 360ms. For applications with real-time requirements, e.g. online games, Ghostrail may only be an intermediate solution. For other applications, it is possible to scale the number of Ghostrail and replica instances with the load.

6   Related Work

The *Open Web Application Security Project (OWASP)* coined the term *Failure to Restrict URL Access* [15] to describe a similar vulnerability as our control-flow weakness. However, it is more focused on access control flaws. Workflows and control-flow integrity play a tangential role in the description.

With existing approaches, every change on the web application either needs a manual change on the policy definition [16, 17] or a new pre-release learning phase to derive the policy automatically [18–21]. Their policies can never be sound because training phases always miss unusual scenarios and manual policy definition requires expert knowledge and is prone to human faults. Also, all such approaches must be fuzzy by design because they neglect the actual request context, e.g. HTTP parameters like an ID that change case-by-case but must not be changed by the user. Ghostrail is able to enforce exact parameter matching without a need for policy updates.

Depending on the business logic of the web application, changes on the client-side JavaScript code can cause damage to the application provider. Existing approaches statically analyze JavaScript to determine the expected sequence of requests [8] or check the web application for exploitable HTTP parameter pollution vulnerabilities [22]. Two approaches replicate client-side computation on server side to detect deviations: *NoTamper* [23] focuses on input validation of HTML forms, while *Ripley* [24] follows a similar approach to ours. It replicates client-side JavaScript events in a server-side replica. However, Ripley is only applicable during development but not for legacy applications. Also, it relies on a distributing compiler thus excludes non-fitting technologies. Technically, Ripley ignores mouse movements on client side and can not track respective events. As it uses event bubbling, it misses client-side events that redirect the browser. Ripley can not handle JavaScript code from different domains like common JavaScript libraries, mash-ups, and the `postMessage` API for communication between iframes. In that sense, Ghostrail is the consequent next step after Ripley because it covers modern application scenarios and all relevant user actions, thus makes less assumptions. Ripley and Ghostrail still share the same issues with randomness and timestamps.

An attacker exploiting a race condition vulnerability [7] can execute one function more often than intended by the application developer. Paleari et al. [2] describe an approach to detect race condition vulnerabilities in web applications.

7 Conclusion

We explained the complex problem of control-flow vulnerabilities and showed its high practical relevance by real-world examples, i.e., existing vulnerabilities and attacks. We identified the root causes in the attacker's possibility to craft arbitrary requests at any time together with the developer's assumption that users only follow provided links. Ghostrail overcomes this problem by the ad hoc generation of next step policies. It is the first approach that neither needs a repeated training phase nor a manual policy definition and covers the whole bandwidth of related vulnerabilities, including race conditions, HTTP parameter manipulation, unsolicited request sequences, and forceful browsing. Ghostrail is compatible with all modern web technologies including mash-up's and JavaScript libraries while it is applicable to all new and legacy web applications without any changes on the application code. For high-traffic applications, the induced load can be moved to any appropriate platform. In sum, we provided a thorough approach that provides guarantees to the developer concerning the sequences of incoming requests including the values of parameters. As a side effect, Ghostrail mitigates *Cross-Site Request Forgery (CSRF)* and *injection (XSS, SQLi)* attacks in most cases.

Acknowledgements. The research leading to these results was supported by the "Bavarian State Ministry of Education, Science and the Arts" as part of the FORSEC research association.

References

1. Braun, B., Pollak, C.v., Posegga, J.: A Survey on Control-Flow Integrity Means in Web Application Frameworks. In: Riis Nielson, H., Gollmann, D. (eds.) NordSec 2013. LNCS, vol. 8208, pp. 231–246. Springer, Heidelberg (2013)
2. Paleari, R., Marrone, D., Bruschi, D., Monga, M.: On Race Vulnerabilities in Web Applications. In: Zamboni, D. (ed.) DIMVA 2008. LNCS, vol. 5137, pp. 126–142. Springer, Heidelberg (2008)

3. Grossman, J.: Seven Business Logic Flaws That Put Your Website At Risk (White Paper), https://www.whitehatsec.com/assets/WP_bizlogic092407.pdf (last accessed January 23, 2014)

4. The New York Times: Thieves Found Citigroup Site an Easy Entry, http://www.nytimes.com/2011/06/14/technology/14security.html (last accessed January 23, 2014)

5. Tate, R.: Apple's Worst Security Breach: 114,000 iPad Owners Exposed, http://gawker.com/5559346/ (last accessed January 19, 2014)

6. Wang, R., Chen, S., Wang, X., Qadeer, S.: How to Shop for Free Online – Security Analysis of Cashier-as-a-Service Based Web Stores. In: IEEE S&P (2011)

7. OWASP: Race Conditions, https://www.owasp.org/index.php/Race_Conditions (last accessed January 23, 2014)

8. Guha, A., Krishnamurthi, S., Jim, T.: Using Static Analysis for Ajax Intrusion Detection. In: WWW (2009)

9. Joyent, Inc: Node.js, http://nodejs.org (last accessed January 22, 2014)

10. Hidayat, A.: PhantomJS, http://phantomjs.org (last accessed January 22, 2014)

11. Ilya Kantor: JavaScript Tutorial - Bubbling and capturing, http://javascript.info/tutorial/bubbling-and-capturing (last accessed January 22, 2014)

12. Fielding, R., Gettys, J., Mogul, J., Frystyk, H., Masinter, L., Leach, P., Berners-Lee, T.: HTTP/1.1. (RFC 2616)

13. Google: Gruyere, http://google-gruyere.appspot.com, (last accessed January 23, 2014)

14. SeleniumHQ: Browser Automation, http://docs.seleniumhq.org (last accessed January 23, 14)

15. OWASP: Failure to Restrict URL Access, https://www.owasp.org/index.php/Top_10_2010-A8-Failure_to_Restrict_URL_Access (last accessed January 23, 2014)

16. Abadi, M., Cardelli, L., Talaga, P.G., Chapin, S.J.: Enforcing Request Integrity in Web Applications. In: Foresti, S., Jajodia, S. (eds.) Data and Applications Security XXIV. LNCS, vol. 6166, pp. 225–240. Springer, Heidelberg (2010)

17. Braun, B., Gemein, P., Reiser, H.P., Posegga, J.: Control-Flow Integrity in Web Applications. In: Jürjens, J., Livshits, B., Scandariato, R. (eds.) ESSoS 2013. LNCS, vol. 7781, pp. 1–16. Springer, Heidelberg (2013)

18. Balzarotti, D., Cova, M., Felmetsger, V., Vigna, G.: Multi-Module Vulnerability Analysis of Web-based Applications. In: CCS (2007)

19. Cova, M., Balzarotti, D., Felmetsger, V., Vigna, G.: Swaddler: An Approach for the Anomaly-Based Detection of State Violations in Web Applications. In: Kruegel, C., Lippmann, R., Clark, A. (eds.) RAID 2007. LNCS, vol. 4637, pp. 63–86. Springer, Heidelberg (2007)

20. Felmetsger, V., Cavedon, L., Kruegel, C., Vigna, G.: Toward Automated Detection of Logic Vulnerabilities in Web Applications. In: USENIX Security (2010)

21. Li, X., Xue, Y.: BLOCK: A Black-box Approach for Detection of State Violation Attacks Towards Web Applications. In: ACSAC (2011)

22. Balduzzi, M., Gimenez, C.T., Balzarotti, D., Kirda, E.: Automated Discovery of Parameter Pollution Vulnerabilities in Web Applications. In: NDSS (2011)

23. Bisht, P., Hinrichs, T., Skrupsky, N., Bobrowicz, R., Venkatakrishnan, V.N.: NoTamper: Automatic Blackbox Detection of Parameter Tampering Opportunities in Web Applications. In: CCS (2010)

24. Vikram, K., Prateek, A., Livshits, B.: Ripley: Automatically Securing Web 2.0 Applications Through Replicated Execution. In: CCS (2009)

An Information Flow Monitor-Inlining Compiler for Securing a Core of JavaScript

José Fragoso Santos and Tamara Rezk

Inria
{firstname.lastname}@inria.fr

Abstract. Web application designers and users alike are interested in isolation properties for trusted JavaScript code in order to prevent confidential resources from being leaked to untrusted parties. Noninterference provides the mathematical foundation for reasoning precisely about the information flows that take place during the execution of a program. Due to the dynamicity of the language, research on mechanisms for enforcing noninterference in JavaScript has mostly focused on dynamic approaches. We present the first information flow monitor inlining compiler for a realistic core of JavaScript. We prove that the proposed compiler enforces termination-insensitive noninterference and we provide an implementation that illustrates its applicability.

1 Introduction

Client-side JavaScript programs often include untrusted code dynamically loaded from third-party code providers, such as online advertisers. This issue raises the need for enforcement mechanisms that isolate trusted code from code that comes from untrusted sources. Such mechanisms must prevent trusted programs from leaking confidential resources. Noninterference [13] is an expressive and elegant property that formally defines secure information flow, thus being commonly used as a soundness criteria for dynamic and static analyses that aim at enforcing secure information flow.

Due to the dynamic nature of JavaScript, research on mechanisms to check the compliance of JavaScript programs with noninterference has mostly focused on dynamic approaches. In practice, there are two main approaches for implementing a JavaScript information flow monitor: either one modifies a JavaScript engine so that it additionally implements the security monitor (as in [9]), or one inlines the monitor in the original program (as in [7, 11]). The second approach, which we follow, has the advantage of being *browser-independent*. We present the first compiler that inlines an information flow monitor for a subset of JavaScript that we call Core JavaScript. Core JavaScript includes the main standard features of the language, such as objects with prototypical inheritance and closures, as well as non-standard features, such as several unusual ways for interacting with the *global object* – a special object that binds global variables.

The proposed compiler is proven sound w.r.t. a standard definition of input-output termination insensitive noninterference for monitors. In this setting, attackers are assumed to be unable to observe the contents of intermediate memory

N. Cuppens-Boulahia et al. (Eds.): SEC 2014, IFIP AICT 428, pp. 278–292, 2014.

states or use divergent executions as a means of disclosing confidential resources. Informally, we prove that the execution of a compiled program only goes through if it is noninterferent; otherwise, the constraints inlined in the program by the compiler cause it to diverge. The paper is divided into two main sections. Section 2 presents an information flow monitored semantics for Core JavaScript that is proven *sound*, i.e. proven to enforce termination-insensitive noninterference. Section 3 presents an inlining compiler that rewrites Core JavaScript programs in order to simulate their execution in the monitor. The compiler is proven *correct*, meaning that the execution of a program goes through in the monitor *if and only if* the execution of its instrumentation by the inlining compiler goes through in the original semantics. We have implemented a prototype of the proposed compiler, which is available via at [1] together with a broad set of examples and a full version of this paper that includes the proofs of the main theorems.

1.1   Core JavaScript Syntax and Semantics

The syntax of Core JavaScript is given in Figure 1. Some expressions are annotated with one or two unique indexes for use by the compiler, which are omitted when not needed. In the examples, we use $o.p$ as an abbreviation for $o[\text{"p"}]$. Objects are the fundamental data type in JavaScript. Informally, an object can be seen as a collection of named values. At the semantic level, we model objects as partial functions from strings, taken from a set Str, to values. JavaScript values comprise: (1) primitive values (taken from a set $Prim$), (2) object references (taken from a set Ref), and (3) parsed function literals (for which we use the lambda notation: $\lambda x.\text{var } y_1, \cdots, y_n; e$). $Prim$ includes strings, numbers, and booleans, as well as two special values *null* and *undefined*. The strings in the domain of an object are called its *properties*. Some properties are internal and therefore can neither be changed nor read by programs. For clarity, these properties are prefixed with an "@". Every expression that creates an object in memory yields a free non-deterministically chosen reference that points to it. Hence, references can be viewed as pointers to objects. Given an object o, we use $\#o$ to denote the reference that points to it. Finally, a *memory* μ is a partial mapping from references to objects.

Notation. We use the notation: (1) $[p_0 \mapsto v_0, \cdots, p_n \mapsto v_n]$ for the partial function that maps p_0 to v_0, ..., and p_n to v_n resp., (2) $f[p_0 \mapsto v_0, \cdots, p_n \mapsto v_n]$ for the function that coincides with f everywhere except in p_0, ..., p_n, which are otherwise mapped to v_0, ..., v_n resp., (3) $f|_P$ for the restriction of f to P (provided it is included in its domain), and (4) $f(r)(p)$ for $(f(r))(p)$, that is, the application of the image of r by f (which is assumed to be a function) to p.

Function Calls and Variables. As in JavaScript, we model scope *via scope objects* [2,10]. Every function call triggers the creation of a scope object which maps its formal parameter as well as the variables declared in its body to their corresponding values. A scope object is said to be *active* if it is associated with the function that is currently executing. Furthermore, every scope object defines

$$
\begin{array}{llll}
e ::= & v^i & \text{value} & \mid \ \text{function}^i(x)\{\text{var } y_1, \cdots, y_n; \ e\} \ \text{function literal} \\
& \mid \ \text{this}^i & \text{this keyword} & \mid \ \{\}^i & \text{object literal} \\
& \mid \ e_0 \ \text{op}^i \ e_1 & \text{binary operation} & \mid \ e_0(e_1)^i & \text{function call} \\
& \mid \ x^i & \text{variable} & \mid \ e_0[e_1](e_2)^i & \text{method call} \\
& \mid \ x = e & \text{variable assignment} & \mid \ e_0, e_1 & \text{sequence} \\
& \mid \ e_0[e_1]^i & \text{property look-up} & \mid \ e_0 \ ?^{i,j} \ (e_1) : (e_2) & \text{conditional} \\
& \mid \ e_0[e_1] = e_2 & \text{property assignment} & &
\end{array}
$$

e, e_0, e_1 and e_2 represent expressions, i and j represent program indexes, x, y_1, ..., y_n represent variable names, and op represents binary operators.

Fig. 1. Syntax of Core JavaScript

a property @*scope* that points to the scope object that was active when the corresponding function literal was evaluated.

The sequence of scope objects that can be accessed from a given scope object through the respective @*scope* properties is called a *scope-chain*. The *global object*, which is assumed to be pointed by a fixed reference #*glob*, is the object that is at the end of every scope-chain and therefore it is the object that binds *global variables*. In order to determine the value associated with a given variable, one has to inspect all objects in the scope-chain that starts in the *active* scope object. This behavior is modeled by the semantic relation $\mathcal{R}_{Scope}$. If $\langle \mu, r_0, x \rangle \ \mathcal{R}_{Scope} \ r_1$, then r_1 is the reference that points to the scope object that is closest to the one pointed by r_0 in the corresponding scope-chain (whose objects are in the range of μ) and which defines a binding for variable x.

Function Literals and Variable Assignments. The evaluation of a function literal yields a reference to an object, called *a function object*, that stores its parsed counterpart. More specifically, since every function is executed in the environment in which the corresponding function literal was evaluated, every function object defines the following two properties: (1) @*code* that stores the parsed function literal and (2) @*fscope* that stores the reference that points to the scope object that was active when the corresponding function literal was evaluated. Assuming that the global object defines a variable *out* originally set to *null*, the evaluation of the program presented below on the left yields the value 0 and creates in memory the list of objects displayed below on the right:

$$
\begin{aligned}
&(\text{function}(x)\{ && o_s^0 = [@scope \mapsto \#glob, x \mapsto 0, g \mapsto o_g, h \mapsto o_h] \\
&\quad \text{var } g, h; && o_s^g = [@scope \mapsto \#o_s^0, x \mapsto 1] \\
&\quad g = \text{function}(x)\{h(2)\}, && o_s^h = [@scope \mapsto \#o_s^0, y \mapsto 2] \\
&\quad h = \text{function}(y)\{out = x\}, && o_0 = [@code \mapsto \lambda x.\text{var } g, h; \hat{e}, @fscope \mapsto \#glob] \\
&\quad g(1) && o_g = [@code \mapsto \lambda x.h(2), @fscope \mapsto \#o_s^0] \\
&\})(0); && o_h = [@code \mapsto \lambda y.out = x, @fscope \mapsto \#o_s^0]
\end{aligned}
$$

where (1) o_s^0, o_s^g, and o_s^h correspond to the scope objects associated with the invocation of the anonymous function, of function g, and of function h, respectively, (2) objects o_0, o_g, and o_h correspond to their respective function objects, and (3) $\hat{e}$ corresponds to the body of the anonymous function. After the execution of this program, the global object maps *out* to 0 and not to 1, because the scope object that is closest to o_s^h and which defines a binding for x is o_s^0 and not o_s^g (which does not belong to the scope-chain of o_s^h).

Object Literals and Property Look-ups. Core JavaScript features prototypical inheritance. This means that every object (except scope objects and function objects) defines a property *_prot_* that stores a reference to its prototype. When trying to look-up the value of a property p of an object o, the semantics first checks whether $p \in dom(o)$. If $p \in dom(o)$, the property look-up yields $o(p)$, otherwise the semantics checks whether the prototype of o defines a property named p, and so forth. The sequence of objects that can be accessed from a given object through the respective *_prot_* properties is called a *prototype-chain*. The prototype-chain inspection procedure is emulated by the semantic relation $\mathcal{R}_{Proto}$. If $\langle \mu, r, m, \Gamma, \Sigma \rangle \, \mathcal{R}_{Proto} \, \langle r', \sigma \rangle$, then r' is the closest reference to r in its corresponding prototype-chain (whose objects are in the range of μ) that defines a binding for m (we ignore, by now, the remaining elements of the relation, since they are used by the monitored semantics and not by the original semantics). The evaluation of an object literal yields a free non-deterministically chosen reference that points to a new object that only defines a property *_prot_* originally set to *null*. Hence, the evaluation of $o_0 = \{\}$, $o_0.p = 0$, $o_1 = \{\}$, $o_1._prot_ = o_0$, $o_1.p$ yields 0, because, although o_1 does not define property p, its prototype does. When looking-up the value of a property p in an object o, if p is not defined in the whole prototype-chain of o, instead of yielding an error, the semantics yields *undefined*. Therefore, the expression $o = \{\}$, $o.p$ evaluates to *undefined*.

Method Calls and the this *Keyword.* Functions whose references are assigned to properties of an object are called its *methods*. A function can be either invoked as a normal function or as a method. When calling a function as a method, the this keyword is bound to the corresponding object, otherwise it is bound to the global object. Therefore, every scope object defines a property @*this* (that was omitted in the first example) that holds the value of the this keyword in that scope. We further remark that given an object o, every method m accessible from o through its prototype-chain can be called as a method of o. Hence, suppose that in a memory μ, the global object defines two variables o_0 and o_1 that hold references to $[\_prot\_ \mapsto null, f \mapsto \#o_f]$ and $[\_prot\_ \mapsto \#o_0]$ respectively, where $\#o_f$ is the reference of a given function object. In the evaluation of expression $o_1.f(0)$, the semantics starts by creating a scope object in which property @*this* is set to $\#o_1$ and then proceeds with the evaluation of the body of f.

The remaining program constructs have the usual semantics, which can be understood from the formal definition. We make use of a big-step semantics for Core JavaScript with the following shape: $r \vdash \langle\langle \mu, e \rangle\rangle \Downarrow \langle\langle \mu', v \rangle\rangle$, where r is the reference of the active scope object, μ and μ' are the initial and final memories respectively, e the expression to be evaluated, and v the value to which it evaluates. Due to space constraints we choose not to give its formal definition here. Instead, we only present its monitored version, $\Downarrow_{IF}$ (Figure 2). In order to obtain $\Downarrow$ from $\Downarrow_{IF}$, one simply has to remove from $\Downarrow_{IF}$ the monitor constraints.

2   Monitoring Secure Information Flow

Specifying Security Policies. The specification of security policies usually relies on two key elements: a lattice of security levels and a labeling that maps resources to security levels. In the examples, we use $\mathcal{L} = \{H, L\}$ with $L \leq H$, meaning that resources labeled with level L (low) are less confidential than resources labeled with H (high). Hence, after the execution of a program, resources labeled with H are allowed to depend on resources originally labeled with L, but not the opposite, since that would entail an information leak. In the following, we always assume that $\leq$ and $\sqcup$ correspond to the order relation and the least upper bound on security levels respectively. A security labeling is a pair $\langle \Gamma, \Sigma \rangle$ where $\Gamma : \mathcal{R}ef \rightarrow \mathcal{S}tr \rightarrow \mathcal{L}$ maps each property in every object to a security level and $\Sigma : \mathcal{R}ef \rightarrow \mathcal{L}$ maps every reference to the *structure security level* [9] of the corresponding object. Hence, given an object o pointed to by a reference r_o, $\Gamma(r_o)(p)$ is the security level associated with o's property p and $\Sigma(r_o)$ is the structure security level of o. Notice that, as every variable is modeled as a property of a given scope object, Γ also maps variables to their corresponding security levels, treating variables and properties uniformly. In the examples, we assume that variables h and l are respectively labeled with levels H and L. The structure security level of an object can be understood as the security level associated with its domain. The need to associate a security level with the domain of every object arises because it is possible for a program to leak information *via* the domain of an object. For instance, after the evaluation of $o = \{\}$, h ? $(o.p = 0) : (null)$, $l = o.p$, the final value of the low variable l depends on the initial value of the high variable h. Precisely, when $h \in \{false, 0, null, undefined\}$, property p is not added to the domain of o and l is set to *undefined*, whereas in all other cases, both property p and variable l are set to 0. Finally, we observe that initial memories are assumed to include a global object for the binding of global variables. Accordingly, initial labellings apply both to the global object as well as the objects that are initially accessible through the global object.

Low-Equality. We introduce a notion of indistinguishability between memories that models the "power" of an attacker that can only observe resources up to a given security level σ, called low-equality, denoted by $\approx_{\beta,\sigma}$. Informally, two labeled memories are low-equal at level σ if they coincide in the resources labeled with levels $\leq \sigma$. Since references are non-deterministically chosen we need to be able to relate observable references in two different memories. To this end, we parametrize the low-equality relation with a partial injective function $\beta : \mathcal{R}ef \rightarrow \mathcal{R}ef$ [5] that relates observable references. The low-equality definition relies on a binary relation on values, named β-equality and denoted by $\sim_\beta$. β-*Equality:* two objects are β-equal if they have the same domain and all their properties are β-equal, primitive values and parsed functions are β-equal if they are equal, and two references r_0 and r_1 are β-equal if $\beta(r_0) = r_1$.

In the following, given a property labeling Γ, a reference r, and security level σ, we denote by $\Gamma(r)|_\sigma$, the set of observable properties in $\Gamma(r)$ at level σ: $\Gamma(r)|_\sigma = \{p \mid \Gamma(r)(p) \leq \sigma\}$.

Definition 1 (Low-Equality $\approx_{\beta,\sigma}$). *Two memories μ_0 and μ_1 are said to be low equal with respect to $\langle \Gamma_0, \Sigma_0 \rangle$ and $\langle \Gamma_1, \Sigma_1 \rangle$, security level σ, and function β, written $\mu_0, \Gamma_0, \Sigma_0 \approx_{\beta,\sigma} \mu_1, \Gamma_1, \Sigma_1$, iff for all references $r_0, r_1 \in dom(\beta)$ such that $r_1 = \beta(r_0)$, the following holds: (1) The observable domains coincide: $\Gamma_0(r_0)|_\sigma = \Gamma_1(r_1)|_\sigma = P$. (2) The objects coincide in their observable domains: $\mu_0(r_0)|_P \sim_\beta \mu_1(r_1)|_P$. (3) Either the domains of both objects are not observable, or they are both observable and completely coincide: $(\Sigma_0(r_0) \leq \sigma \vee \Sigma_1(r_1) \leq \sigma) \Rightarrow \Sigma_0(r_0) \sqcup \Sigma_1(r_1) \leq \sigma \wedge dom(\mu_0(r_0)) = dom(\mu_1(r_1))$.*

Monitored Semantics. The rules of the monitored semantic relation, $\Downarrow_{IF}$, defined in Figure 2, have the form $r, \sigma_{pc} \vdash \langle \mu, e, \Gamma, \Sigma \rangle \Downarrow_{IF} \langle \mu', v, \Gamma', \Sigma', \sigma \rangle$, where σ_{pc} is the security level of the execution context, $\langle \Gamma, \Sigma \rangle$ and $\langle \Gamma', \Sigma' \rangle$ are the initial and final labellings, and σ is the *reading effect* of e [13]. The remaining elements keep their original meaning in $\Downarrow$. The *reading effect* of an expression is defined as the least upper bound on (1) the levels of the resources on which the value to which it evaluates depends and (2) the level of the current context, σ_{pc}. The monitored execution of an expression e can be interpreted as an extension of the unmonitored execution of e that additionally performs the *abstract execution* of e on the abstract memory given by Γ. Hence, the computation of Γ' and σ precisely mirrors the computation of μ' and v. The monitored semantics makes use of a relation $\mathcal{R}_{NewScope}$, which models the storing of a new scope object in memory. Hence, if $\langle \mu, \Gamma, \Sigma, r_f, v_{arg}, r_{this}, \sigma_{pc}, \sigma_{arg} \rangle \, \mathcal{R}_{NewScope} \, \langle \mu', e, \Gamma', \Sigma', r', \sigma'_{pc} \rangle$, then: (1) μ' and $\langle \Gamma', \Sigma' \rangle$ are the memory and labeling obtained from μ and $\langle \Gamma, \Sigma \rangle$ by the allocation of the new scope object in the free reference r'; (2) r_f is the reference to the function that is going to be executed, e its body, v_{arg} the argument to be used, σ_{pc} the level of the context in which the function was invoked, σ_{arg} the reading effect of the actual argument, and r_{this} the reference to the object to be used as this; and (3) σ'_{pc} is the security level at which the execution of e takes place.

Among the possible techniques to design a purely dynamic sound information flow monitor, we choose to follow the *no-sensitive-upgrade* discipline [3]. Essentially, the monitor blocks executions that try to upgrade the value of low resources within high contexts. To illustrate the idea of this strategy, consider the following program: $h ? (l = 0) : (null)$. Suppose that the monitor allows the execution of this program to go through in an initial memory that maps h to 1 just raising the level of l to H (which constitutes a sensitive upgrade). If this same program is executed in a memory that maps h to 0; in the final memory, l is labeled with L and therefore it is visible. Hence, after executing this program starting from two indistinguishable memories, we obtain two memories that are distinguishable by an attacker at level L, meaning that the attacker has learned something about the confidential resources of the program.

Function/Method Calls, Conditional Expressions, and Function Literals. The only non-trivial part concerning the monitoring of these four types of expressions has to do with how the first three update the level of the execution context in which their subexpressions are evaluated. Observe that σ_{pc} must always be higher than or equal to the security levels of the resources that were used to decide: (1) which branch to take in a conditional expression whose code is still executing and (2) which function/method to execute in a function/method call expression whose execution is still being performed. E.g., consider the following expression:

$$f_1 = \mathsf{function}(x)\{l = 0\}, f_2 = \mathsf{function}(x)\{l = 1\}, h ? (f = f_1) : (f = f_2), f() \qquad (1)$$

Since the final value of the low variable l depends on the original value of the high variable h, this program does not abide by the security policy and is therefore considered *illegal*. Hence, independently of the branch taken in the execution of the conditional, in the evaluation of the corresponding expression, the monitor must be aware that the decision to take that branch depends on the value of a high variable. Analogously, when executing the body of the function assigned to f, the monitor must be aware that the fact that it is executing that function and not another does also depend on the value of a high variable. Hence, σ_{pc} must be upgraded to high both during the execution of the taken branch of the conditional and during the execution of the body of the function bound to f. Additionally, σ_{pc} must also take into account the level of the context in which the function literal corresponding to the function that is currently evaluating was itself evaluated. Consider the expression:

$$f = h ? (\mathsf{function}(x)\{l = 0\}) : (\mathsf{function}(x)\{l = 1\}), f() \qquad (2)$$

This program is illegal because after its execution, depending on the value of the high variable h, the low variable l can be either 0 or 1. To account for this type of leak, when a function literal is evaluated the level of the current context is stored in $\Gamma(r_f)(@fscope)$. Hence, every time the corresponding function is called, it is executed in a context whose level is set to be $\geq \Gamma(r_f)(@fscope)$.

Variable Assignments and Property Updates. In accordance with the no-sensitive-upgrade discipline, the monitor only allows a variable x (or a property p of an object o) to be upgraded in a context whose level is lower than or equal to its current level: $\sigma_{pc} \leq \Gamma(r_{pc})(x)$ (or $\sigma_{pc} \leq \Gamma(\#o)(p)$). Therefore, considering the expression given in Code Snippet (1), if f is a high variable, the assignments inside the branches of the conditional are allowed to go through. However, the assignment inside the body of the function bound to f is not, because the value of the execution context is high, whereas the level of the variable that is being updated is low. Notice, however, that, in the Rule [PROPERTY ASSIGNMENT] (for the case in which the property to be assigned is defined), the constraint is not $\sigma_{pc} \leq \Gamma(\#o)(p)$, but instead $\sigma_0 \sqcup \sigma_1 \leq \Gamma(\#o)(p)$. Observe that, since the monitor ensures that $\sigma_{pc} \leq \sigma_0$ and $\sigma_{pc} \leq \sigma_1$, the latter constraint subsumes the former. The need for this stricter constraint arises from the fact that in a property assignment, the assignment that actually takes place depends on the reading effects of (1) the expression that evaluates to the reference of the object of the property to be assigned and (2) the expression that evaluates to the actual property whose value is to be updated. Suppose, for instance, that variable o holds an object only containing low properties. Then, even if σ_{pc} is low, the expression $o[h] = 0$ is illegal, because depending on the value of h, it updates the value of a different low property. One cannot simply upgrade the level of the property to which h evaluates to H because that would constitute a sensitive upgrade, since for different values of h, an attacker at level L would see different properties disappearing from the observable domain of o.

Property Look-ups, Property Creation Expressions, and Object Literals. When a program looks up the value of a property p in an object o, if $p \notin dom(o)$, the security level associated with the property look-up expression must be equal to or higher than the structure security level of o, because this property look-up leaks information about its domain. In fact, since every property look-up searches the prototype-chain of the corresponding object, the security monitor has to take into account the structure security level as well as the level of property $\_prot\_$ of every object traversed during the prototype-chain inspection procedure (which corresponds to σ in $\langle \mu, r, m, \Gamma, \Sigma \rangle \, \mathcal{R}_{Proto} \, \langle r', \sigma \rangle$). For example, given a memory:

$$\mu = [\#o_0 \mapsto [p \mapsto 1, \_prot\_ \mapsto null], \#o_1 \mapsto [\_prot\_ \mapsto \#o_0], \#glob \mapsto [o_1 \mapsto \#o_1]] \quad (3)$$

and a labeling $\langle \Gamma, \Sigma \rangle$, such that Γ maps all properties in every object in the range of μ to L and $\Sigma = [\#o_0 \mapsto L, \#o_1 \mapsto H, \#glob \mapsto L]$, the reading effect of the expression $o_1.p$ must be H, because it leaks information about the domain of o_1 whose level is H. Naturally, when an object literal is evaluated, its structure security level is set to the level of the execution context, because the creation of the object is visible at that level. Finally, when creating a new property in an object o, the monitor checks whether the structure security level of o ($\Sigma(\#o)$) is at least as high as the reading effects of: (1) the expression that evaluates to $\#o$ (σ_0) and (2) the expression that evaluates to the name of the property to create (σ_1). Recall that both σ_0 and σ_1 are at least as high as the level of the execution context. Hence, the monitor does also implicitly require that $\sigma_{pc} \leq \Sigma(\#o)$. To illustrate the need for these constraints, consider the expression $o_0 = \{\}, o_1 = \{\}, h \; ? \; (h = o_0) : (h = o_1), h.p = 0, l = o_1.p$. This program is illegal, as the final value of the low variable l depends on the original value of the high variable h. In fact, since the level of h is not lower than or equal to the structure security level of any of the two objects, the monitor blocks the property creation.

Noninterferent Monitor. We say that a security monitor is noninterferent *iff* it preserves the low-equality relation. Informally, an information flow monitor is noninterferent *iff*, for any program e, whenever an attacker cannot distinguish two labeled memories before executing e, then the attacker is also unable to distinguish the final memories.

Theorem 1 (Non-Interferent Monitor). *For any expression e, memories μ and μ', respectively labeled by $\langle \Gamma, \Sigma \rangle$ and $\langle \Gamma', \Sigma' \rangle$, reference r, security levels σ_{pc} and σ, and function β s.t. $\mu, \Gamma, \Sigma \approx_{\beta, \sigma} \mu', \Gamma', \Sigma', r, \sigma_{pc} \vdash \langle \mu, e, \Gamma, \Sigma \rangle \Downarrow_{IF} \langle \mu_f, v_f, \Gamma_f, \Sigma_f, \sigma_f \rangle$, and $\beta(r), \sigma_{pc} \vdash \langle \mu', e, \Gamma', \Sigma' \rangle \Downarrow_{IF} \langle \mu'_f, v'_f, \Gamma'_f, \Sigma'_f, \sigma'_f \rangle$; then, there exists a function β' extending β s.t.: $\mu_f, \Gamma_f, \Sigma_f \approx_{\beta', \sigma} \mu'_f, \Gamma'_f, \Sigma'_f$. Moreover, if either $\sigma_f \leq \sigma$ or $\sigma'_f \leq \sigma$, then $v_f \sim_{\beta'} v'_f$.*

3   Monitor-Inlining

This section presents a new information flow monitor-inlining compiler for Core JavaScript, which instruments programs in order to simulate their execution in the monitored semantics presented in Section 2. This instrumentation rests on a technique that consists in pairing up each variable/property with a new one, called its *shadow* variable/property [7,11], that holds its corresponding security level. Since the compiled program has to handle security levels, we include them in the set of program values, which means adding them to the syntax of the language as such, as well as adding two new binary operators corresponding to $\leq$ (the order relation) and $\sqcup$ (the least upper bound).

In the design of the compiler, we assume the existence of a given a set of variable and property names, denoted by $\mathcal{I}_C$, that do not overlap with those available for the programmer. In particular, the compilation of every *indexed expression* requires extra variables intended to store the corresponding value and security level, to be later used in the compilation of other expressions that include it. Hence, we assume the set of compiler variables to include two indexed sets of variables $\{\$\hat{l}_i\}_{i\in\mathbf{N}}$ and $\{\$\hat{v}_i\}_{i\in\mathbf{N}}$, used to store the levels and the values of intermediate expressions, respectively. Given a variable x, we denote by $\$l_x$ the corresponding shadow variable. In contrast to variables, whose names are available at compile time, property names are dynamically computed. Therefore, we assume the existence of a runtime function $\$shadow$ that given a property name outputs the name of the corresponding shadow property. Given an expression e to compile, the compiler guarantees that e does not use variable and property names in $\mathcal{I}_C$ by (1) statically verifying that the variables in e do not overlap with $\mathcal{I}_C$ and (2) dynamically verifying that e does not look-up/create/update properties whose names belong to $\mathcal{I}_C$. To this end, the compiler makes use of a runtime function $\$legal$ that returns *true* when its argument does not belong to $\mathcal{I}_C$. For clarity, all identifiers reserved for the compiler are prefixed with a $. By making sure that compiler identifiers do not overlap with those of the programs to compile, we guarantee the soundness of the proposed transformation even when it receives as input *malicious programs*. Malicious programs try to bypass the inlined runtime enforcement mechanism by rewriting some of its internal variables/properties. E.g., the compilation of the expression $\$\hat{l}_h = L,\ l = h$ fails, as this program tries to tamper with the internal state of the runtime enforcement mechanism in order to be allowed to leak confidential information. Concretely, this program tries to transfer the content of h to l without raising the level of l by setting the level associated with variable h to low.

Besides adding to every object o an additional shadow property $\$l_p$ for every property p in its domain, the inlined monitoring code also adds to o a special property $\$struct$ that stores its structure security level. Hence, given an object $o = [p \mapsto v_0, q \mapsto v_1]$ pointed to by r_o and a labeling $\langle \Gamma, \Sigma \rangle$, such that $\Gamma(r_o) = [p \mapsto H, q \mapsto L]$ and $\Sigma(r_o) = L$, the instrumented counterpart of o labeled by $\langle \Gamma, \Sigma \rangle$ is $\hat{o} = [p \mapsto v_0, q \mapsto v_1, \$l_p \mapsto H, \$l_q \mapsto L, \$struct \mapsto L]$.

VALUE
$$r, \sigma_{pc} \vdash \langle \mu, v, \Gamma, \Sigma \rangle \Downarrow_{IF} \langle \mu, v, \Gamma, \Sigma, \sigma_{pc} \rangle$$

THIS
$$\frac{r_{this} = \mu(r)(@this) \qquad \sigma_{this} = \Gamma(r)(@this) \sqcup \sigma_{pc}}{r, \sigma_{pc} \vdash \langle \mu, \text{this}, \Gamma, \Sigma \rangle \Downarrow_{IF} \langle \mu, r_{this}, \Gamma, \Sigma, \sigma_{this} \rangle}$$

BINARY OPERATION
$$\frac{r, \sigma_{pc} \vdash \langle \mu, e_0, \Gamma, \Sigma \rangle \Downarrow_{IF} \langle \mu_0, v_0, \Gamma_0, \Sigma_0, \sigma_0 \rangle \qquad r, \sigma_{pc} \vdash \langle \mu_0, e_1, \Gamma_0, \Sigma_0 \rangle \Downarrow_{IF} \langle \mu_1, v_1, \Gamma_1, \Sigma_1, \sigma_1 \rangle}{r, \sigma_{pc} \vdash \langle \mu, e_0 \text{ op } e_1, \Gamma, \Sigma \rangle \Downarrow_{IF} \langle \mu_1, v_0 \text{ op } v_1, \Gamma_1, \Sigma_1, \sigma_0 \sqcup \sigma_1 \rangle}$$

VARIABLE
$$\frac{\langle \mu, r, x \rangle \mathcal{R}_{Scope} r_x \qquad r_x \neq null}{\begin{array}{c} v = \mu(r_x)(x) \qquad \sigma = \Gamma(r_x)(x) \sqcup \sigma_{pc} \\ \hline r, \sigma_{pc} \vdash \langle \mu, x, \Gamma, \Sigma \rangle \Downarrow_{IF} \langle \mu, v, \Gamma, \Sigma, \sigma \rangle \end{array}}$$

VARIABLE ASSIGNMENT
$$\frac{\begin{array}{c} r, \sigma_{pc} \vdash \langle \mu, e, \Gamma, \Sigma \rangle \Downarrow_{IF} \langle \mu_0, v_0, \Gamma_0, \Sigma_0, \sigma_0 \rangle \qquad \langle \mu_0, r, x \rangle \mathcal{R}_{Scope} r_x \\ r_x \neq null \qquad \sigma_{pc} \leq \Gamma_0(r_x)(x) \\ \Gamma' = \Gamma_0 [r_x \mapsto \Gamma_0(r_x) [x \mapsto \sigma_0]] \qquad \mu' = \mu_0 [r_x \mapsto \mu_0(r_x) [x \mapsto v_0]] \end{array}}{r, \sigma_{pc} \vdash \langle \mu, x = e, \Gamma \rangle \Downarrow_{IF} \langle \mu', v_0, \Gamma', \Sigma_0, \sigma_0 \rangle}$$

PROPERTY LOOK-UP
$$\frac{\begin{array}{c} r, \sigma_{pc} \vdash \langle \mu, e_0, \Gamma, \Sigma \rangle \Downarrow_{IF} \langle \mu_0, r_0, \Gamma_0, \Sigma_0, \sigma_0 \rangle \qquad r, \sigma_{pc} \vdash \langle \mu_0, e_1, \Gamma_0, \Sigma_0 \rangle \Downarrow_{IF} \langle \mu_1, m_1, \Gamma_1, \Sigma_1, \sigma_1 \rangle \\ \langle \mu_1, r_0, m_1, \Gamma_1, \Sigma_1 \rangle \mathcal{R}_{Proto} \langle r', \sigma' \rangle \qquad (v, \sigma) = \begin{cases} \langle \mu_1(r')(m_1), \sigma_0 \sqcup \sigma_1 \sqcup \sigma' \sqcup \Gamma_1(r')(m_1) \rangle & \text{if } r' \neq null \\ \langle undefined, \sigma_0 \sqcup \sigma_1 \sqcup \sigma' \rangle & \text{otherwise} \end{cases} \end{array}}{r, \sigma_{pc} \vdash \langle \mu, e_0[e_1], \Gamma, \Sigma \rangle \Downarrow_{IF} \langle \mu_1, v, \Gamma_1, \Sigma_1, \sigma \rangle}$$

PROPERTY ASSIGNMENT
$$\frac{\begin{array}{c} r, \sigma_{pc} \vdash \langle \mu, e_0, \Gamma, \Sigma \rangle \Downarrow_{IF} \langle \mu_0, r_0, \Gamma_0, \Sigma_0, \sigma_0 \rangle \qquad r, \sigma_{pc} \vdash \langle \mu_0, e_1, \Gamma_0, \Sigma_0 \rangle \Downarrow_{IF} \langle \mu_1, m_1, \Gamma_1, \Sigma_1, \sigma_1 \rangle \\ r, \sigma_{pc} \vdash \langle \mu_1, e_2, \Gamma_1, \Sigma_1 \rangle \Downarrow_{IF} \langle \mu_2, v_2, \Gamma_2, \Sigma_2, \sigma_2 \rangle \qquad \Gamma' = \Gamma_2 [r_0 \mapsto \Gamma_2(r_0) [m_1 \mapsto \sigma_0 \sqcup \sigma_1 \sqcup \sigma_2]] \\ \mu' = \mu_2 [r_0 \mapsto \mu_2(r_0) [m_1 \mapsto v_2]] \qquad m_1 \in \mu_2(r_0) \Rightarrow \sigma_0 \sqcup \sigma_1 \leq \Gamma_2(r_0)(m_1) \qquad m_1 \notin \mu_2(r_0) \Rightarrow \sigma_0 \sqcup \sigma_1 \leq \Sigma_2(r_0) \end{array}}{r, \sigma_{pc} \vdash \langle \mu, e_0[e_1] = e_2, \Gamma, \Sigma \rangle \Downarrow_{IF} \langle \mu', v_2, \Gamma', \Sigma_2, \sigma_2 \rangle}$$

FUNCTION LITERAL
$$\frac{\begin{array}{c} r_f \notin dom(\mu) \qquad \mu' = \mu [r_f \mapsto [@fscope \mapsto r, @code \mapsto \lambda x.e]] \\ \Gamma' = \Gamma [r_f \mapsto [@fscope \mapsto \sigma_{pc}, @code \mapsto \sigma_{pc}]] \qquad \Sigma' = \Sigma [r_f \mapsto \sigma_{pc}] \end{array}}{r, \sigma_{pc} \vdash \langle \mu, \text{function}(x)\{e\}, \Gamma, \Sigma \rangle \Downarrow_{IF} \langle \mu', r_f, \Gamma', \Sigma', \sigma_{pc} \rangle}$$

OBJECT LITERAL
$$\frac{\begin{array}{c} r_o \notin dom(\mu) \qquad \mu' = \mu [r_o \mapsto [\_prot\_ \mapsto null]] \\ \Gamma' = \Gamma [r_o \mapsto [\_prot\_ \mapsto \sigma_{pc}]] \qquad \Sigma' = \Sigma [r_o \mapsto \sigma_{pc}] \end{array}}{r, \sigma_{pc} \vdash \langle \mu, \{\}, \Gamma, \Sigma \rangle \Downarrow_{IF} \langle \mu', r_o, \Gamma', \Sigma', \sigma_{pc} \rangle}$$

FUNCTION CALL
$$\frac{\begin{array}{c} r, \sigma_{pc} \vdash \langle \mu, e_0, \Gamma, \Sigma \rangle \Downarrow_{IF} \langle \mu_0, r_0, \Gamma_0, \Sigma_0, \sigma_0 \rangle \qquad r, \sigma_{pc} \vdash \langle \mu_0, e_1, \Gamma_0, \Sigma_0 \rangle \Downarrow_{IF} \langle \mu_1, v_1, \Gamma_1, \Sigma_1, \sigma_1 \rangle \\ \langle \mu_1, \Gamma_1, \Sigma_1, r_0, v_1, \#glob, \sigma_0, \sigma_1 \rangle \mathcal{R}_{NewScope} \langle \hat{\mu}, \hat{e}, \hat{\Gamma}, \hat{\Sigma}, \hat{r}, \hat{\sigma}_{pc} \rangle \qquad \hat{r}, \hat{\sigma}_{pc} \vdash \langle \hat{\mu}, \hat{e}, \hat{\Gamma}, \hat{\Sigma} \rangle \Downarrow_{IF} \langle \mu', v, \Gamma', \Sigma', \sigma \rangle \end{array}}{r, \sigma_{pc} \vdash \langle \mu, e_0(e_1), \Gamma, \Sigma \rangle \Downarrow_{IF} \langle \mu', v, \Gamma', \Sigma', \sigma \rangle}$$

METHOD CALL
$$\frac{\begin{array}{c} r, \sigma_{pc} \vdash \langle \mu, e_0, \Gamma, \Sigma \rangle \Downarrow_{IF} \langle \mu_0, r_0, \Gamma_0, \Sigma_0, \sigma_0 \rangle \qquad r, \sigma_{pc} \vdash \langle \mu_0, e_1, \Gamma_0, \Sigma_0 \rangle \Downarrow_{IF} \langle \mu_1, m_1, \Gamma_1, \Sigma_1, \sigma_1 \rangle \\ r, \sigma_{pc} \vdash \langle \mu_1, e_2, \Gamma_1, \Sigma_1 \rangle \Downarrow_{IF} \langle \mu_2, v_2, \Gamma_2, \Sigma_2, \sigma_2 \rangle \qquad \langle \mu_2, r_0, m_1, \Gamma_2, \Sigma_2 \rangle \mathcal{R}_{Proto} \langle r_m, \sigma_m \rangle \qquad r_f = \mu_2(r_m)(m_1) \\ \langle \mu_2, \Gamma_2, \Sigma_2, r_f, v_2, r_0, \sigma_0 \sqcup \sigma_1 \sqcup \Gamma_2(r_m)(m_1) \sqcup \sigma_m, \sigma_2 \rangle \mathcal{R}_{NewScope} \langle \hat{\mu}, \hat{e}, \hat{\Gamma}, \hat{\Sigma}, \hat{r}, \hat{\sigma}_{pc} \rangle \qquad \hat{r}, \hat{\sigma}_{pc} \vdash \langle \hat{\mu}, \hat{e}, \hat{\Gamma}, \hat{\Sigma} \rangle \Downarrow_{IF} \langle \mu', v, \Gamma', \Sigma', \sigma \rangle \end{array}}{r, \sigma_{pc} \vdash \langle \mu, e_0[e_1](e_2), \Gamma, \Sigma \rangle \Downarrow_{IF} \langle \mu', v, \Gamma', \Sigma', \sigma \rangle}$$

SEQUENCE
$$\frac{r, \sigma_{pc} \vdash \langle \mu, e_0, \Gamma, \Sigma \rangle \Downarrow_{IF} \langle \mu_0, v_0, \Gamma_0, \Sigma_0, \sigma_0 \rangle \qquad r, \sigma_{pc} \vdash \langle \mu_0, e_1, \Gamma_0, \Sigma_0 \rangle \Downarrow_{IF} \langle \mu_1, v_1, \Gamma_1, \Sigma_1, \sigma_1 \rangle}{r, \sigma_{pc} \vdash \langle \mu, (e_0, e_1), \Gamma, \Sigma \rangle \Downarrow_{IF} \langle \mu_2, v_1, \Gamma_1, \Sigma_1, \sigma_1 \rangle}$$

CONDITIONAL
$$\frac{\begin{array}{c} r, \sigma_{pc} \vdash \langle \mu, \hat{e}, \Gamma, \Sigma \rangle \Downarrow_{IF} \langle \hat{\mu}, \hat{v}, \hat{\Gamma}, \hat{\Sigma}, \hat{\sigma} \rangle \qquad i = \begin{cases} 0 \text{ if } \hat{v} \notin \{0, false, undefined, null\} \\ 1 \text{ otherwise} \end{cases} \\ r, \sigma_{pc} \sqcup \hat{\sigma} \vdash \langle \hat{\mu}, e_i, \hat{\Gamma}, \hat{\Sigma} \rangle \Downarrow_{IF} \langle \mu', v, \Gamma', \Sigma', \sigma \rangle \end{array}}{r, \sigma_{pc} \vdash \langle \mu, \hat{e} ? (e_0) : (e_1), \Gamma, \Sigma \rangle \Downarrow_{IF} \langle \mu', v, \Gamma', \Sigma', \sigma \rangle}$$

NEW SCOPE
$$\frac{\begin{array}{c} r = \mu(r_f)(@fscope) \qquad \lambda x.\{\text{var } y_1, \cdots, y_n; e\} = \mu(r_f)(@code) \qquad r' \notin dom(\mu) \qquad \sigma'_{pc} = \sigma_{pc} \sqcup \Gamma(r_f)(@fscope) \\ \mu' = \mu [r' \mapsto [@scope \mapsto r, x \mapsto v_{arg}, y_1 \mapsto undefined, \cdots, y_n \mapsto undefined, @this \mapsto r_{this}]] \qquad \Sigma' = \Sigma [r' \mapsto \sigma'_{pc}] \\ \Gamma' = \Gamma [r' \mapsto [@scope \mapsto \sigma'_{pc}, x \mapsto \sigma'_{pc} \sqcup \sigma_{arg}, y_1 \mapsto \sigma'_{pc}, \cdots, y_n \mapsto \sigma'_{pc}, @this \mapsto \sigma'_{pc}]] \end{array}}{\langle \mu, \Gamma, \Sigma, r_f, v_{arg}, r_{this}, \sigma_{pc}, \sigma_{arg} \rangle \mathcal{R}_{NewScope} \langle \mu', e, \Gamma', \Sigma', r', \sigma'_{pc} \rangle}$$

Fig. 2. Monitored Core JavaScript Semantics

Formal Specification. The inlining compiler is defined as a function $\mathcal{C}$, given in Figure 3, that expects as input an expression e and produces a tuple $\langle \hat{e}, i \rangle$, where $\hat{e}$ is the expression that simulates the execution of e in the monitored semantics and i an index such that, after the execution of $\hat{e}$, $\$\hat{v}_i$ stores the value to which e evaluates in the monitored semantics and $\$\hat{l}_i$ its corresponding reading effect. Besides the runtime functions $\$shadow$ and $\$legal$, the compiler makes use of (1) a runtime function $\$check$ that diverges when its argument is different from *true*, (2) a runtime function $\$inspect$ that expects as input an object and a property and outputs the level associated with the corresponding prototype-chain inspection procedure, and (3) an additional binary operator hasOwnProp that checks whether the object given as its left operand defines the property given as its right one. During the evaluation of the instrumented code, the level of the execution context, σ_{pc}, is assumed to be stored in a variable $\$pc$. To this end, function literals are instrumented in order to receive as input the level of the argument and the level of the context in which they are invoked. Function/method calls are instrumented accordingly. Furthermore, the instrumented code of a function/method call must have access to both the return value of the original function/method and the level that is to be associated with that value. Therefore, every function literal returns an object that defines two properties: (1) a property $\$v$ where it stores the return value of the original function and (2) a property $\$l$ where it stores the level to be associated with that value. Each compiler rule precisely mimics the corresponding monitor rule. However, the compiler must also keep track of the variables in which the security level and the value of the expression to compile are stored during execution. This is done by assigning the value to which the expression evaluates to a new variable $\$\hat{v}_i$ and the security level to a new variable $\$\hat{l}_i$. The compilation of every variable/property assignment and sequence expression does not introduce additional variables because the corresponding value and reading effect are already available in the indexed variables introduced by the corresponding subexpressions.

Correctness. Definition 2 presents a *similarity relation* between labeled memories in the monitored semantics and instrumented memories in the original semantics, denoted by $\mathcal{S}_\beta$. $\mathcal{S}_\beta$ requires that for every object in the labeled memory, the corresponding labeling coincide with the instrumented labeling (except for some internal properties whose levels can be automatically inferred) and that the property values of the original object be similar to those of its instrumented counterpart according to a new version of the β-equality called $\mathcal{C}(\beta)$-equality. This relation, denoted by $\sim_{\mathcal{C}(\beta)}$, differs from $\sim_\beta$ in that it relates each parsed function with its corresponding compilation and in that it allows the domain of the instrumented object to be larger than the one of the original object.

Definition 2 (Memory Similarity). *A memory μ labeled by $\langle \Gamma, \Sigma \rangle$ is similar to a memory μ' w.r.t. β, written $\langle \mu, \Gamma, \Sigma \rangle \mathcal{S}_\beta \mu'$, if and only if $dom(\beta) = dom(\mu)$ and for every reference $r \in dom(\beta)$, if $o = \mu(r)$ and $o' = \mu'(\beta(r))$, then $\Sigma(r) = o'(\$struct)$ and for all properties $p \in dom(o) \backslash \{@scope, @this, @code\}$, $o(p) \sim_{\mathcal{C}(\beta)} o'(p)$ and $\Gamma(r)(p) = o'(\$l_p)$*

VALUE

$$\frac{\hat{e} = \$\hat{l}_i = \$pc,\ \$\hat{v}_i = v}{\mathcal{C}\langle v^i \rangle = \langle \hat{e}, i \rangle}$$

VARIABLE

$$\frac{x \notin \mathcal{I}_C \qquad \hat{e} = \$\hat{l}_i = \$pc \sqcup \$l_x,\ \$\hat{v}_i = x}{\mathcal{C}\langle x^i \rangle = \langle \hat{e}, i \rangle}$$

THIS

$$\frac{\hat{e} = \$\hat{l}_i = \$pc,\ \$\hat{v}_i = \mathsf{this}}{\mathcal{C}\langle \mathsf{this}^i \rangle = \langle \hat{e}, i \rangle}$$

BINARY OPERATION

$$\frac{\mathcal{C}\langle e_0 \rangle = \langle \hat{e}_0, j \rangle \qquad \mathcal{C}\langle e_1 \rangle = \langle \hat{e}_1, k \rangle \qquad \hat{e} = \hat{e}_0,\ \hat{e}_1,\ \$\hat{l}_i = \$\hat{l}_j \sqcup \$\hat{l}_k,\ \$\hat{v}_i = \$\hat{v}_j\ \mathsf{op}\ \$\hat{v}_k}{\mathcal{C}\langle e_0\ \mathsf{op}^i\ e_1 \rangle = \langle \hat{e}, i \rangle}$$

VARIABLE ASSIGNMENT

$$\frac{x \notin \mathcal{I}_C \qquad \mathcal{C}\langle e \rangle = \langle e', i \rangle \qquad \hat{e} = e',\ \$check(\$pc \leq \$l_x),\ \$l_x = \$\hat{l}_i,\ x = \$\hat{v}_i}{\mathcal{C}\langle x = e \rangle = \langle \hat{e}, i \rangle}$$

PROPERTY LOOK-UP

$$\frac{\begin{array}{c}\mathcal{C}\langle e_0 \rangle = \langle \hat{e}_0, k \rangle \qquad \mathcal{C}\langle e_1 \rangle = \langle \hat{e}_1, j \rangle \qquad e_{lev} = \$\hat{l}_i = \$\hat{l}_k \sqcup \$\hat{l}_j \sqcup \$inspect(\$\hat{v}_k, \$\hat{v}_j) \\ \hat{e} = \hat{e}_0,\ \hat{e}_1,\ \$check(\$legal(\$\hat{v}_j)),\ e_{lev},\ \$\hat{v}_i = \$\hat{v}_k[\$\hat{v}_j]\end{array}}{\mathcal{C}\langle e_0[e_1]^i \rangle = \langle \hat{e}, i \rangle}$$

PROPERTY ASSIGNMENT

$$\frac{\begin{array}{c}\mathcal{C}\langle e_0 \rangle = \langle \hat{e}_0, i \rangle \qquad \mathcal{C}\langle e_1 \rangle = \langle \hat{e}_1, j \rangle \qquad \mathcal{C}\langle e_2 \rangle = \langle \hat{e}_2, k \rangle \\ e_{enf} = \$\hat{v}_i\ \mathsf{hasOwnProp}\ \$\hat{v}_j\ ?\ \Big(\$check(\$\hat{l}_i \sqcup \$\hat{l}_j \leq \$\hat{v}_i[\$shadow(\$\hat{v}_j)])\Big) : \Big(\$check(\$\hat{l}_i \sqcup \$\hat{l}_j \leq \$\hat{v}_i.\$struct)\Big) \\ \hat{e} = \hat{e}_0,\ \hat{e}_1,\ \hat{e}_2,\ \$check(\$legal(\$\hat{v}_j)),\ e_{enf},\ \$\hat{v}_i[\$shadow(\$\hat{v}_j)] = \$\hat{l}_i \sqcup \$\hat{l}_j \sqcup \$\hat{l}_k, \$\hat{v}_i[\$\hat{v}_j] = \$\hat{v}_k\end{array}}{\mathcal{C}\langle e_0[e_1] = e_2 \rangle = \langle \hat{e}, k \rangle}$$

FUNCTION LITERAL

$$\frac{\begin{array}{c}\mathcal{C}\langle e \rangle = \langle \hat{e}_f, j \rangle \qquad e_{fbody} = \hat{e}_f,\ \$ret = \{\},\ \$ret.\$v = \$\hat{v}_j,\ \$ret.\$l = \$\hat{l}_j,\ \$ret \\ \{i_1, \cdots, i_k\} = indexes(e) \qquad e_f = \$\hat{v}_i = \mathsf{function}(x, \$l_x, \$pc)\{\mathsf{var}\ y_1, \cdots, y_n, \$\hat{v}_{i_1}, \$\hat{l}_{i_1}, \cdots, \$\hat{v}_{i_k}, \$\hat{l}_{i_k};\ e_{fbody}\} \\ \hat{e} = e_f,\ \$\hat{v}_i.\$struct = \$pc,\ \$\hat{v}_i.\$l_{@fscope} = \$pc,\ \$\hat{l}_i = \$pc,\ \$\hat{v}_i\end{array}}{\mathcal{C}\langle \mathsf{function}^i(x)\{\mathsf{var}\ y_1, \cdots, y_n;\ e\} \rangle = \langle \hat{e}, i \rangle}$$

OBJECT LITERAL

$$\frac{\begin{array}{c}e' = \$\hat{v}_i.\$struct = \$pc,\ \$\hat{v}_i.\$l_{proto} = \$pc \\ \hat{e} = \$\hat{v}_i = \{\},\ e',\ \$\hat{l}_i = \$pc,\ \$\hat{v}_i\end{array}}{\mathcal{C}\langle \{\}^i \rangle = \langle \hat{e}, i \rangle}$$

FUNCTION CALL

$$\frac{\begin{array}{c}\mathcal{C}\langle e_0 \rangle = \langle \hat{e}_0, j \rangle \qquad \mathcal{C}\langle e_1 \rangle = \langle \hat{e}_1, k \rangle \\ e' = \$\hat{l}_{ctx} = \$\hat{v}_j.\$l_{@fscope} \sqcup \$\hat{l}_j,\ \$ret = \$\hat{v}_j(\$\hat{v}_k, \$\hat{l}_k \sqcup \$\hat{l}_{ctx}, \$\hat{l}_{ctx}) \\ \hat{e} = \hat{e}_0,\ \hat{e}_1,\ e',\ \$\hat{l}_i = \$ret.\$l,\ \$\hat{v}_i = \$ret.\$v\end{array}}{\mathcal{C}\langle e_0(e_1)^i \rangle = \langle \hat{e}, i \rangle}$$

METHOD CALL

$$\frac{\begin{array}{c}\mathcal{C}\langle e_0 \rangle = \langle \hat{e}_0, j \rangle \qquad \mathcal{C}\langle e_1 \rangle = \langle \hat{e}_1, k \rangle \qquad \mathcal{C}\langle e_2 \rangle = \langle \hat{e}_2, l \rangle \\ e' = \hat{e}_0,\ \hat{e}_1,\ \hat{e}_2,\ \$\hat{l}_{ctx} = \$\hat{l}_j \sqcup \$\hat{l}_k \sqcup \$inspect(\$\hat{v}_k, \$\hat{v}_j) \sqcup \$\hat{v}_j[\$\hat{v}_k].\$l_{@fscope} \\ \hat{e} = e',\ \$ret = \$\hat{v}_j[\$\hat{v}_k](\$\hat{v}_l, \$\hat{l}_{ctx} \sqcup \$\hat{l}_l, \$\hat{l}_{ctx}),\ \$\hat{l}_i = \$ret.\$l,\ \$\hat{v}_i = \$ret.\$v\end{array}}{\mathcal{C}\langle e_0[e_1](e_2)^i \rangle = \langle \hat{e}, i \rangle}$$

SEQUENCE

$$\frac{\begin{array}{c}\mathcal{C}\langle e_0 \rangle = \langle \hat{e}_0, i \rangle \\ \mathcal{C}\langle e_1 \rangle = \langle \hat{e}_1, j \rangle \\ \hat{e} = \hat{e}_0, \hat{e}_1\end{array}}{\mathcal{C}\langle e_0, e_1 \rangle = \langle \hat{e}, j \rangle}$$

CONDITIONAL

$$\frac{\begin{array}{c}\mathcal{C}\langle e_0 \rangle = \langle \hat{e}_0, i \rangle \qquad \mathcal{C}\langle e_1 \rangle = \langle \hat{e}_1, j \rangle \qquad \mathcal{C}\langle e_2 \rangle = \langle \hat{e}_2, k \rangle \\ e_{cond} = \$\hat{v}_i\ ?\ \Big(\hat{e}_1,\ \$\hat{v}_t = \$\hat{v}_j,\ \$\hat{l}_t = \$\hat{l}_j\Big) : \Big(\hat{e}_2,\ \$\hat{v}_t = \$\hat{v}_k,\ \$\hat{l}_t = \$\hat{l}_k\Big) \\ \hat{e} = \hat{e}_0,\ \$\hat{l}_s = \$pc,\ \$pc = \$pc \sqcup \$\hat{l}_i,\ e_{cond},\ \$pc = \$\hat{l}_s, \$\hat{v}_t\end{array}}{\mathcal{C}\langle e_0\ ?^{s,t}\ (e_1) : (e_2) \rangle = \langle \hat{e}, t \rangle}$$

Fig. 3. Information Flow Monitor Inlining Compiler

The Correctness Theorem states that, provided that a program and its compiled counterpart are evaluated in similar configurations, the evaluation of the original one in the monitored semantics terminates *if and only if* the evaluation of its compilation also terminates in the original semantics, in which case the final configurations as well as the computed values are similar. Therefore, since the monitored semantics only allows secure executions to go through, we guarantee that, when using the inlining compiler, programs are rewritten in such a way that only their secure executions are allowed to terminate.

Theorem 2 (Correctness). *Provided that e does not use identifiers in $\mathcal{I}_C$, for any labeled and instrumented configurations $\langle \mu, e, \Gamma, \Sigma \rangle$ and $\langle \mu', e' \rangle$, function β, and reference r in μ, such that $\langle \mu, \Gamma, \Sigma \rangle \mathcal{S}_\beta \mu'$ and $\mathcal{C}\langle e \rangle = \langle e', i \rangle$, for some index i; there exists $\langle \mu_f, v_f, \Gamma_f, \sigma \rangle$ such that $r, \bot \vdash \langle \mu, e, \Gamma, \Sigma \rangle \Downarrow_{IF} \langle \mu_f, v_f, \Gamma_f, \Sigma_f, \sigma_f \rangle$ iff there exists $\langle \mu'_f, v'_f \rangle$ such that $\beta(r) \vdash \langle \langle \mu', e' \rangle \rangle \Downarrow \langle \langle \mu'_f, v'_f \rangle \rangle$, in which case: (1) $\langle \mu_f, \Gamma_f, \Sigma_f \rangle \mathcal{S}_{\beta'} \mu'_f$, (2) $v_f \sim_{\mathcal{C}(\beta)} v'_f$, and (3) $\sigma_f = \mu'_f(\beta(r))(\$\hat{l}_i)$.*

4   Discussion and Related Work

JavaScript Semantics. Since scope objects are assumed not to have a prototype and since we do not include the JavaScript with construct, Core JavaScript programs are syntactically scoped. This means that we could have modeled the binding of variables using substitution, as in other works targeting subsets of the whole language, as [8]. However, we have chosen to model scope using scope objects, as in [10], for two main reasons. First, we envisage to extend the model to deal with a larger subset of the language. Second, by modeling the binding of variables in the same way we model the binding of properties, we do not need to introduce an extra labeling function for the labeling of variables.

Monitoring Secure Information Flow. Information flow monitors can be divided in two main classes. *Purely dynamic* monitors (such as [3] and [4]) do not make use of any kind of static analysis. On the contrary, *hybrid monitors* (such as [12]) make use of static analyses to reason about the implicit flows that can arise due to untaken execution paths. Our choice for the inlining of a purely dynamic monitor has to do with the fact that the dynamic features of JavaScript make it very difficult to approximate the resources created/updated in untaken program branches. Hedin and Sabelfeld [9] have been the first to design an information flow monitor for a realistic core of JavaScript. Their monitor is purely dynamic and enforces the no-sensitive-upgrade discipline. This monitor has been designed in order to guide a browser instrumentation and not an inlining transformation. Furthermore, it differs from ours in that it labels values instead of variables/properties. Bichhawat et al. [6] have recently proposed a hybrid monitor that makes use of a sophisticated static analysis to minimize performance overhead [6].

Monitor-Inlining Transformations. Chudnov and Naumann [7] propose an information flow monitor inlining transformation for a WHILE language, which inlines the hybrid information flow monitor presented in [12]. Simultaneously,

Magazinius et al. [11] propose the inlining of a purely dynamic information flow monitor that enforces the no-sensitive-upgrade discipline for a simple imperative language that features global functions, a let construct, and an *eval* expression that allows for dynamic code evaluation. Both compilers pair up each variable with a *shadow* variable. We extend this technique to handle object properties by pairing up each property with a shadow property. The languages modeled in both [7] and [11] only feature primitive values and do not feature scope composition (in [7] there are no functions and in [11] every function is executed in a "clean" environment and does not produce side-effects). Hence, in both [7] and [11], the reading effect of an expression e corresponds to the least upper bound on the levels of the variables of e. Therefore, the instrumented code for computing the level of e is simply $\$l_{x_1} \sqcup \cdots \sqcup \$l_{x_n}$, where $\{x_1, \cdots, x_n\}$ are the variables that explicitly occur in e. In Core JavaScript (as in JavaScript) this does not hold. First, one can immediately see that expressions that feature property look-ups or function/method calls do not generally verify this property. Second, expressions may be composed of expressions that have side effects. Therefore, the level associated with the whole expression can actually be lower than the least upper bound on the levels of the variables that it includes. As an example, consider the expression $(x = y) + x$. Since $x = y$ evaluates to the value of y (besides assigning the value of y to x), the level of the whole expression only depends on the initial level of y. In order to handle these two issues, the inlining transformation must introduce extra variables to keep track of the values and levels of intermediate expressions. Finally, both [7] and [11] ignore the problem of malicious programs.

In summary, we have presented the first compiler for securing information flow in an important subset of JavaScript. The presented compiler is proven sound even when it is given as input malicious code that actively tries to bypass the inlined enforcement mechanism. A prototype of the compiler is available via [1] together with a broad set of examples that illustrate its applicability.

Acknowledgments. This work was partially supported by the Portuguese Government via the PhD grant SFRH/BD/71471/2010.

References

1. Information flow monitor-inlining compiler,
   http://www-sop.inria.fr/members/Jose.Santos/
2. The 5th edition of ECMA 262 June 2011. ECMAScript Language Specification. Technical report, ECMA (2011)
3. Austin, T.H., Flanagan, C.: Efficient purely-dynamic information flow analysis. PLAS (2009)
4. Austin, T.H., Flanagan, C.: Permissive dynamic information flow analysis. PLAS (2010)
5. Banerjee, A., Naumann, D.A.: Secure information flow and pointer confinement in a Java-like language. In: CSFW (2002)
6. Bichhawat, A., Rajani, V., Garg, D., Hammer, C.: Information flow control in WebKit's JavaScript bytecode. In: Abadi, M., Kremer, S. (eds.) POST 2014 (ETAPS 2014). LNCS, vol. 8414, pp. 159–178. Springer, Heidelberg (2014)

7. Chudnov, A., Naumann, D.A.: Information flow monitor inlining. In: CSF (2010)
8. Guha, A., Saftoiu, C., Krishnamurthi, S.: The essence of JavaScript. In: D'Hondt, T. (ed.) ECOOP 2010. LNCS, vol. 6183, pp. 126–150. Springer, Heidelberg (2010)
9. Hedin, D., Sabelfeld, A.: Information-flow security for a core of JavaScript. In: CSF (2012)
10. Maffeis, S., Mitchell, J.C., Taly, A.: An operational semantics for JavaScript. In: Ramalingam, G. (ed.) APLAS 2008. LNCS, vol. 5356, pp. 307–325. Springer, Heidelberg (2008)
11. Magazinius, J., Russo, A., Sabelfeld, A.: On-the-fly inlining of dynamic security monitors. In: Computers & Security (2012)
12. Russo, A., Sabelfeld, A.: Dynamic vs. static flow-sensitive security analysis. In: CSF (2010)
13. Sabelfeld, A., Myers, A.C.: Language-based information-flow security. IEEE Journal on Selected Areas in Communications (2003)

Authenticated Dictionary Based on Frequency

Kévin Atighehchi, Alexis Bonnecaze, and Traian Muntean

Aix Marseille University, CNRS, Centrale Marseille, ERISCS, I2M, UMR 7373,
13453 Marseille, France
{firstname.lastname}@univ-amu.fr

Abstract. We propose a model for data authentication which takes into account the behavior of the clients who perform queries. Our model reduces the size of the authenticated proof when the frequency of the query corresponding to a given data is higher. Existing models implicitly assume the frequency distribution of queries to be uniform, but in reality, this distribution generally follows Zipf's law. Therefore, our model better reflects reality and the communication cost between clients and the server provider is reduced allowing the server to save bandwith. When the frequency distribution follows Zipf's law, we obtain a gain of at least 20% on the average proof size compared to existing schemes.

Keywords: Authenticated dictionary, Data structure, Merkle tree, Zipf.

1   Introduction

Authenticated dictionaries are used to organize and manage a collection of data in order to answer queries on these data and to certify the answers. They have been heavily studied recently and have many applications including certificate revocation in public key infrastructure [4,7,10,16], geographic information system querying, or third party data publication on the Internet [5,2]. This last application is of great interest with the advent of cloud computing and Web services. For example, it is important that a user who consults a Web page can be confident of the authenticity of that page (or some of its contents).

Classical schemes involve three actors [22,8,9]: a trusted *source* which is generally the owner of the data, an untrusted provider also called *directory* and a set of *users* (also called clients). The directory receives a set of data from the source together with authentication information. These contents are stored by both the source and the directory but only the latter communicates with users. Therefore, as shown in Figure 1, users communicate directly with the directory to query the authentication information on a given data. This information contains a cryptographic proof and allows the users to authenticate the data.

Most of authenticated dictionaries use Merkle trees, red-black trees or skip-lists as data structures. These structures are closely equivalent in terms of cost of storage, communication and time [22]. They are well adapted as long as no distinction is made between data. However, in some situations, it may be useful to manage data as a function of some parameters. In the case of publications on the Internet, some pages are

N. Cuppens-Boulahia et al. (Eds.): SEC 2014, IFIP AICT 428, pp. 293–306, 2014.

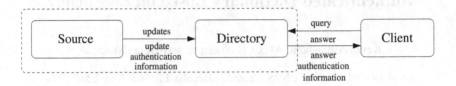

Fig. 1. The three-party authentication model

accessed more frequently, depending on user behavior. Some pages have a better reputation than others, and it may prove useful to order them following this criterion. in fact, any behavioural criterion could be taken into account.

In this paper, we introduce an authenticated dictionary scheme which takes into account the frequency of data being accessed. As regards Web traffic, it is well known that its frequency distribution follows Zipf's law [1,18,17,12,6,21]. More precisely, most traffic follows this law except for the traffic residue corresponding to very low frequencies. In fact, there is a drooping tail, which means that for these frequencies, the distribution decreases much faster than Zipf's law.

The paper is organized as follows. Section 2 contains background information regarding data structures and the dictionary problem. Section 3 introduces our scheme. We present the underlying data structures and the updating, searching and certification operations provided by the dictionary. In Section 4 we discuss the efficiency of our method, and show that, compared to existing schemes and when the frequency distribution follows Zipf's law, the reduction of proof size is better than 20%.

2   Background

2.1   Data Structures and Authentication

Data structures represent a way of storing and organizing data so that searching, adding or deleting operations can be done efficiently. A static structure has a size that cannot be changed and therefore it is not possible to delete or add any data a posteriori. However, the size of dynamic data structures can change allowing insertion and deletion operations. In this paper, the term *dynamic data structure* refers to any data structure which accepts insertion and deletion of data at any position. The term *append/disjoin-only data structure* refers to any data structure which accepts insertion and deletion at the end of the structure. Examples of dynamic structures [13] are hash tables, trees like 2-3 Trees, B-Trees or red-black trees, or other random structures like non-deterministic skip-lists [20].

In addition to these basic features, data structures can be used to construct authenticating mechanisms. Data structures based on rooted graphs are well adapted to deal with such mechanisms [22,8] since authenticating all the data covered by the graph just requires one single signature and some hash computations. An example of authenticated data structure is the static Merkle tree [14,15] of which the number of leaves is a power of 2. There exist variants accepting any number of leaves. Although these variants can still be considered as static, they can also be considered as append/disjoin-only data structures since structural changes can be done at the right side of the tree. This type of structure is suitable for time stamping [19,3]. In the following, we briefly detail one of these variants [19]. It is an almost balanced tree in which values of the internal nodes are calculated in the following way. Let $(e_1, e_2, \ldots, e_n)$ be the values of the leaves at the base of the tree. Values of nodes at the previous level are $(h(e_{2i+1}, e_{2i+2})_{i=0\ldots(n-2)/2})$ if n is even, and $(h(e_{2i+1}, e_{2i+2})_{i=0\ldots(n-3)/2}, e_n)$ otherwise. This process is repeated until a single value is obtained (this is the root node value). Adding an element e^* after e_n is a very simple operation. The value v of the root of the smallest (perfectly) balanced subtree to where e_n belongs is changed to $v' = h(v, e^*)$. Then, values of the internal nodes on the path from this root to the root of the tree are updated. The disjoin operation is just the inverse operation. Note that this structure is equivalent to a deterministic skip-list. Finally, one might add that static structures should always be preferred for their better complexity when there is no need for complex operations.

2.2 The Dictionary Problem

The authenticated dictionary problem has already been defined in the literature, for example in [22,8]. In this section, we summarize the main features of an authenticated dictionary. The source has a set S of elements which evolves over time through insertion and deletion of items. The directory maintains a copy of this set and its role is to answer queries from the users. A user may request a given element or may perform a membership query on S in order to know whether an item belongs or not to S. The user must be able to verify the attached cryptographic proof (in particular, public information about the source must be available).

Efficiency makes the difference between a good dictionary and a bad one. This efficiency can be measured in terms of computation cost, which is the time taken by the computation together with the cost of the hardware (memory space and bandwidth) used by the entities. The size of the proofs is perhaps the most important parameter since it plays a significant role on the interface bandwidth of the directory. Moreover, it may reduce the time for a user to verify the answer to a query. The time spent by the directory to answer a query is also an important parameter when the number of users is very large. Space used by the data structure as well as source to directory communication should be optimized. Finally, the time to perform an update should also be optimized.

In this paper, our objective is to reduce the average size of the proof. This improvement is done at the expense of a slightly greater need for memory and computation of both the source and directory.

3   A New Authenticated Dictionary Based on Frequency

So far, authentication schemes have relied on data structures like Merkle trees or skiplists. These data structures allow us to obtain small sizes of proof. In this sense, they seem to be optimal whenever each data has the same probability to be queried. However, in real life, users can make more queries on a given data than another. This means that the frequency of queries may be far from uniform. In the case of publication on the Internet, some Web pages are consulted more frequently than others. Taking into account this parameter, we introduce a scheme in which the size of authentication proof answering a query is smaller when the frequency of this query is higher. We obtain the following benefits:

- for the directory, we minimize on average the LAN/WAN interface bandwidth usage. This interface bandwidth represents a critical aspect because the number of simultaneous queries may be high.
- If the directory caches proofs which are frequently queried, the number of proofs being cached will be higher, improving at the same time efficiency.
- On average, for a given user, the LAN/WAN interface bandwidth and the number of calculations to verify a proof is reduced.

When the frequency distribution is uniform, it is preferable to use an almost balanced tree (or an equivalent data structure). However, when the frequency distribution is not uniform, there is no reason to use such a data structure. Rather, we should look for unbalanced tree structures in order to improve efficiency, in particular on the size and construction of proofs.

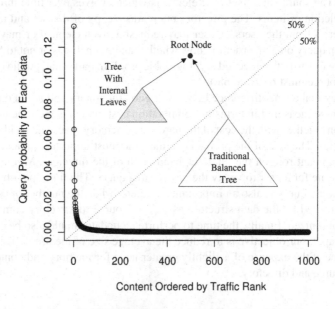

Fig. 2. Zipf's law and the tree T

We consider here a distribution which follows Zipf's law. Figure 2 shows that the distribution curve is close to the vertical axis for high frequency events whereas it is close to the horizontal axis for the many very low frequency events. The latter part of the curve (which corresponds to the lower tail) behaves like a uniform distribution. Therefore, if we had to construct an authenticated dictionary corresponding to the lower tail, we would certainly use a balanced tree or any equivalent data structure (denoted

T_2). However, for the rest of the distribution, we should use an unbalanced tree (denoted T_1), having its leaves ever closer to the root as frequency increases. Finally, in order to take into account the whole distribution, we propose to use a tree T whose root has T_1 as left child and T_2 as right child.

Since T does not arrange data in order of key identifiers but in descending order of frequencies, we need to use two other (non authenticated) structures, one ordering all the data according to frequencies and the other one ordering data according to key identifiers. Our scheme relies on the following data structures.

- We assume the use of two efficient dynamic binary trees which serve to organize and manage data. The first one, denoted A_1, ranks the $(u_i)_{i=1...n}$ in ascending order and allows us to search a given u_i and to retrieve its corresponding frequency. The searching operation only uses A_1 and is done in $O(\log(n))$. The second one, denoted A_2, is used to arrange frequencies in decreasing order and allows the rank of a given frequency to be retrieved.
- Authentication proofs are constructed using the third data structure, T. Its right child T_2, is a Merkle-like tree which processes data having very low frequencies. The left child, T_1 is a height-balanced tree with special properties: each node has three children, two of them being either parent nodes or leaves and the third one being exclusively a leaf. The structure T_1 is designed to reduce the size of proofs corresponding to high frequency data. The place of each leaf depends on the frequency of the data. The higher the frequency, the closer the leaf is to the root.

Even though the system uses more data structures than existing authenticated dictionaries, the global memory space taken by these structures is not significantly increased. In fact, adding structures is mainly equivalent to adding pointers which do not have a high memory cost.

Remark 1. For the sake of simplicity we assume that all the frequencies are distinct. We note that this is in fact the case if we consider the exact Zipf distribution. Furthermore, for the construction of the structure, we just consider absolute frequencies (an absolute frequency being the number of data access requests).

The next subsection presents some details about this authenticated data structure and assumes the use of A_1 and A_2.

3.1 Authenticated Data Structure Construction

Let n be the number of data. Considering the use of a cryptographic hash function H, let $\{u_1, u_2, \ldots, u_n\}$ be the set of hashed identifiers, let $\{c_1, c_2, \ldots, c_n\}$ be the set of hashed data and let $(f_1, f_2, \ldots, f_n)$ be the corresponding list of n frequencies. We denote by Π the permutation in $[1, \ldots, n+1]$ such that u_i has a frequency $f_{\Pi(i)}$.

In order to construct our tree T and its two children T_1 and T_2, we divide the data into two sets according to their frequencies, or more precisely in our case, according to the median of the frequency distribution. Each data corresponds to a leaf. Leaves of T_1 correspond to data having the highest frequencies $f_1, f_2, \ldots, f_k$ (ranked in descending order, where k is the smallest integer such that $\sum_{i=1}^{k} f_i \geq (\sum_{i=1}^{n} f_i)/2$. Leaves of T_2

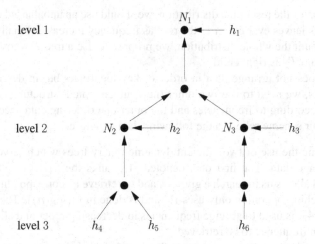

Fig. 3. Example of a tree T_1 for 6 elements. This diagram represents the flow of the computation of the nodes. Note that here the pairwise chaining for the computation of leaves is not depicted and that arrows denote the flow of information, not pointer values in the data structure.

correspond to the rest of the data. In practice, the number of leaves of T_2, denoted N_r, is much larger than that of T_1, denoted N_l. The tree T_2 is a Merkle tree for standard authenticated dictionaries. We also consider two special data, $\pm\infty$ both of frequency equal to zero which are used as sentinels in order to chain data according to their identity. The sentinel $+\infty$ is the last element of both lists and $f_{\Pi(n+1)} = f_{n+1} = 0$.

The source constructs the ordered sets

$$L^u = \{(u_1, f_{\Pi(1)}), \ldots, (u_n, f_{\Pi(n)}), (+\infty, 0)\}$$

and

$$L^f = \{(u_{\Pi^{-1}(1)}, f_1), \ldots, (u_{\Pi^{-1}(n)}, f_n), (u_{\Pi^{-1}(n)}, f_n), (+\infty, 0)\}.$$

In the first list the values u_i are ordered from the smallest to the largest, whereas the second list is ranked according to frequency. From these lists, the source calculates the tree T. Calculation of a leaf h_i is done as follows:

- $h_{\Pi(1)} = H(-\infty, u_1, c_1)$,
- $h_{\Pi(i)} = H(u_{i-1}, u_i, c_i)$ where $i \in [2, \ldots, n]$,
- $h_{\Pi(+\infty)} = H(u_n, +\infty, 0)$,

where 0 denotes empty content. Note that a pairwise chaining between the u_i (and $-\infty$, $+\infty$) is used when calculating the leaves, this device serves for constructing proofs of non-existence.

We determine i such that $2^i \leq N_l < 2^{i+1} - 1$. The calculation of nodes of T_1 is done as follows:

- $N_k = H(h_k, H(h_{2k}, h_{2k+1}))$ for $k \in [\![2^{i-1}, \lfloor \frac{N_l}{2} \rfloor[\![$;
- $N_{\lfloor \frac{N_l}{2} \rfloor} = H(h_{\lfloor \frac{N_l}{2} \rfloor}, H(h_{2\lfloor \frac{N_l}{2} \rfloor}, h_{2\lfloor \frac{N_l}{2} \rfloor+1}))$ if N_l is odd,
  $N_{\lfloor \frac{N_l}{2} \rfloor} = H(h_{\lfloor \frac{N_l}{2} \rfloor}, H(h_{2\lfloor \frac{N_l}{2} \rfloor}))$ otherwise;

- $N_k = H(h_k, H(N_{2k}, N_{2k+1}))$ for $k \in [\![2^{i-2}, \lfloor \frac{N_l}{4} \rfloor [\![$;
- $N_{\lfloor \frac{N_l}{4} \rfloor} = H(h_{\lfloor \frac{N_l}{4} \rfloor}, H(N_{2 \lfloor \frac{N_l}{4} \rfloor}, h_{2 \lfloor \frac{N_l}{4} \rfloor +1}))$ if $\lfloor \frac{N_l}{2} \rfloor$ is even,
  $H(h_{\lfloor \frac{N_l}{4} \rfloor}, H(h_{2 \lfloor \frac{N_l}{4} \rfloor}, h_{2 \lfloor \frac{N_l}{4} \rfloor +1}))$ otherwise;
- $N_k = H(h_k, H(h_{2k}, h_{2k+1}))$ for $k \in]\!] \lfloor \frac{N_l}{4} \rfloor, 2^{i-1} - 1]\!]$;
- $N_k = H(h_k, H(N_{2k}, N_{2k+1}))$ for $k \in [\![2^j, 2^{j+1} - 1]\!]$ and $j \in [\![0, i - 3]\!]$;

Leaves are listed in descending order of frequency, from the root to the base level and in a given level from left to right. Figure 3 shows the structure of T_1 for 6 data.

The calculation of nodes of T_2 is not detailed since T_2 is a Merkle-like tree. When the tree T is calculated, the source transmits the list of elements $(Id_i, c_i)_{i=1...n}$ together with the timestamped signature of the root node of T to the directory. Then, the directory is able to construct the data structures.

3.2 Proof Construction and Verification Algorithms

In order to construct a proof of existence or non-existence for a data of (hashed) identifier u, we first use A_1 to determine the frequency $f_{\pi(j)}$ which corresponds to the smallest u_j such that $u_j \geq u$. Then, we use A_2 to obtain the place $\pi(j)$ of this frequency. Suppose that $h_{\pi(j)}$ is a leaf of T_1. The binary representation of $\pi(j)$ is used to obtain the correct path in T_1 leading to the authentication proof. We consider a list P initially empty, which will contain the hashed values representing the proof. When we know the path, the construction of the proof is similar to the one used in a Merkle tree:

- The value of the root node of T_2 is added to P.
- The most significant bit of $\pi(j)$ is not considered but we consider the following one. If this bit is equal to 0, we add to P both the value of the right child node and of the internal leaf and we move to the left node. If this bit is equal to 1, we add to P both the value of the left child node and of the internal leaf and we move to the right node.
- The process is repeated for the next bit and so forth until the last bit of $\pi(j)$. Note that, at the end, if the data corresponds to an internal leaf, we add to P the hash of the concatenation of the two children (or the hash of the child, if there is just one child).
- In the case of a proof of existence, we add to P the value u_{j-1}. In the case of a proof of non existence, we add to P the values u_{j-1}, u_j and c_j.

All the other cases (and in particular the one where $h_{\pi(j)}$ belongs to T_2) can be easily handled and are left to the reader. The verification of the proof is done by the user and involves recalculating the root node of T from the value of the leaf corresponding to the data and hashes of the values of the proof. Note that the use of a commutative hash [8] for node calculation facilitates the calculation of the verification and slightly reduces the size of the proof.

3.3 Updating Algorithms

The source maintains its own copy of the authenticated dictionary and provides the directory with the necessary information for updating. Such information contains the type of operation to be made, the element $(Id, C(Id))$, and a signed timestamp of the new value of the root node of T. When updating the dictionary, dynamic data structures A_1, A_2 and T must be partially modified while maintaining the overall consistency of the system.

Updating T consists of updating either T_1 or T_2 or both T_1 and T_2 and recomputing the root node of T. We suppose that T_2 is an "append/disjoin-only" Merkle tree, that is to say a Merkle tree in which incremental insertions/deletions are made on the right side of the tree.

Remark 2. The use of a static structure for T_2 allows us to obtain a proof (at least) as short as would be the case with a dynamic structure. Moreover, deletion and insertion remain efficient since the position of the elements does not depend on any rank.

Insertion of an Element. Insertion of a new *pair element* (Id, c) where $H(Id) \notin (u_i)_{i=1...n}$, is done in T_2 since we consider the data to have zero frequency (it has never been queried before). The following operations must be done on T.

- We first determine the largest index j such that $u_j < H(Id) < u_{j+1}$.
- The existing leaf $h_{\Pi(j+1)} = H(u_j, u_{j+1}, c_{j+1})$ is changed to $h_{\Pi(j+2)} = H(H(Id), u_{j+1}, c_{j+1})$.
- A new leaf $h_{\Pi(j+1)} = H(u_j, H(Id), c)$ is created on the right side of the tree.
- Internal nodes corresponding to paths from each of these two leaves to the root node of T are recomputed.

Updating an Element. Here, we focus on the operation which changes the content of an existing element (Id, c) to c'.

- We find j such that $u_j = H(Id)$.
- We set $h'_{\Pi(j)} = H(u_{j-1}, u_j, c')$.
- We recompute the nodes of the path from the updated leaf $h'_{\Pi(j)}$ to the root node (these nodes may belong to either T_1 or T_2).

Content Reordering. When the frequency of an element has changed, T must be updated. There are three possibilities:

- The leaf belongs to T_1 and will stay in T_1.
- The leaf belongs to T_1 and will move to T_2.
- The leaf belongs to T_2 and will move to T_1.

In this paper, we focus on the first case, the two other cases are easier to deal with and are left to the reader. We describe an updating algorithm to maintain the frequencies in a certain descending order. For the sake of simplicity, we suppose that we just have to move one element of frequency f_m $(m > i)$ between f_i et f_{i+1}. We avoid the use of cyclic permutations since it would lead to update too many nodes (the cost would be in $O((m - i) \log(n))$). We prefer to use an algorithm that we call *min-max* which limits to one the number of changes at each level of the tree T_1. Let h be the depth of the tree. We denote by S_i $(i = 1 \dots h+1)$ the set of elements $(Id, C(Id))$ whose leaves belong to level i of the tree. Let $f(.)$ be the map which associates its frequency to a key identifier. At the same level, frequencies are not ordered but we must have:

$$\forall\, i = 1 \ldots h - 1,\ \forall\, Id_x \in S_i,\ Id_y \in S_{i+1}\ f(Id_x) \geq f(Id_y). \tag{1}$$

Suppose that the leaf authenticating an element $e = (Id, C(Id))$ belonging to level i must move up to level j $(i > j)$. This leaf is inserted at level j at the position of the leaf having the lowest frequency in this level. This last element is moved down to level $j + 1$ at the position of the leaf having the lowest frequency, and so on. The leaf having the lowest frequency at level $i - 1$ is moved up to the former position of e at level i. Finally, nodes which are on the path of the leaves that have been moved are recomputed back up the root of the tree. The algorithm is similar when $i < j$ except that the lowest frequency must be replaced by the highest frequency. If $i = j$, no change has to be done. If more than one frequency has changed, this algorithm can be applied for each change, albeit optimizations are possible but out of the scope of this paper.

Deletion of an Element. Here, we just outline the main steps of the deleting operation. Deleting an element leads to similar operations to that of reordering a leaf in T, with an updating of the pairwise chaining. Suppose that an element e is deleted at level i, the highest frequency element at level $i + 1$ is moved up to the position of e and its position will be taken by the element having the highest frequency at the next level, and so on until level h. At level h, the element at the right side is moved to the position left empty. Suppose that the frequency of e is f_i, then an updating of the pairwise chaining must be done. The new value of $h_{\pi(\pi^{-1}(i)+1)}$ is $H(u_{\pi^{-1}(i)-1}, u_{\pi^{-1}(i)+1}, c_{\pi^{-1}(i)+1})$. Furthermore, values of the ancestor nodes of leaves that have been moved have to be recomputed to restore the consistency of information.

4   Complexity Analysis

In this section, we analyze the complexity of the authentication part of our dictionary. We first concentrate on the size of a proof (of existence), then on the complexity of the proof construction and on the verification. Finally, we analyze the complexity of the updating operations. For the sake of simplicity, we express the operation cost in terms of the number of hash operations. We can then deduce the overall number of blocks processed by the hash function, which is approximately a multiple[1] of the number of hash evaluations.

Authentication Proof Size and Verification Run Time. In the following, we give the existence proof size in terms of the number of hash values needed to recompute the root node of T. The proof of non-existence for a hashed *identifier*, denoted u^*, is not detailed since this can be considered as a proof of existence for a particular hashed *identifier* u_i such that $u_{i-1} < u^* < u_i$ for a given $i \in [\![1, n + 1]\!]$. In this case the server has to provide to the client, in addition, the values of u_i and c_i. We detail different cases, the best case, the worst case and the average case. From the average proof size standpoint,

---

[1] In our system, the number of blocks processed in one evaluation of the hash function can vary: this is the tree arity of T_1 plus one (that is, 4) for a node evaluation of T_1, the tree arity of T_2 (that is, 2) for a node evaluation of T_2 and 3 for a leaf evaluation.

we discuss for which probability distribution it is preferable to use only T_1 or T_2, or the combination of both (T). Note that we express the verification complexity in terms of number of hash operations. In our construction, this number is close to the number of hash values contained in the proof.

Theorem 1. *Considering a number of elements $n \geq 1$, the authentication proof is of length 3 in the best case, and of length $\lceil \log(n - m) \rceil + 2$ in the worst case, where m is the Zipf distribution median.*

Proof. In the best case, the requested content is the most frequently viewed. The leaf corresponding to the requested *identifier* is then located at the root node of T_1. Assuming that the requested identifier corresponds to a hashed value u_i, the user needs the preceding hashed identifier u_{i-1}, plus the hash of the concatenation of the sibling nodes $H(N_2, N_3)$ (Both u_i and c_i are determined locally, once the content is downloaded), and finally the root node value of T_2. In the worst case, the requested content is located in the tree T_2 which is an almost balanced binary tree, the user needs the preceding hashed identifier u_{i-1} plus the siblings of the nodes along the path from the leaf to the root node, plus the root node value of T_1, for a total of at most $\lceil \log(N_r) \rceil + 2$ values.

Average Case. If the queries are uniformly distributed in the set of elements, there is no reason to use the tree T_1, due to the overhead of the internal nodes. In this case we should only use the almost balanced binary tree T_2 in order to have an average size for the authentication proof tightly upperbounded by $\lceil \log(n) \rceil + 1$. In order to show that the tree T_1 is useless in this case, let us determine the average proof size when we only use this tree. Consider n such that $n = 2^m - 1$. The proof size for an internal leaf belonging to a level i, for $i \in [\![1, m-1]\!]$, is $2(i-1) + 2$ hash values whereas it is $2(m-2) + 2$ for a base level leaf (level m). Take the derivative of the geometric series $\sum_{i=0}^{m-1} x^{i+1}$ and simplify the following average proof size of $\frac{1}{(2^m-1)}(\sum_{i=0}^{m-2}(2i+2)2^i + 2^{m-1}(2(m-2) + 2))$. We then deduce that, when using only T_1, the average proof size is close to $2\lfloor \log(n) \rfloor$ hash values.

By contrast, when the queries are distributed according to a geometric distribution of parameter $p = 1/2$ (which is close to a discrete equivalent of an exponential law), it is best to use only T_1. Indeed, by evaluating a geometric series, one can deduce that in such a case the average proof size is asymptotically 4 hash values.

As regards the Zipf distribution, it is preferable to use an authenticated data structure like T because frequencies do not decrease as fast as an exponential law. Zipf is based on harmonic series and therefore it is difficult to provide a bound of complexity that closely reflects reality. Consequently, we give in Table 1 numerical results by varying the dictionary size, along with the percentage gain compared to what is obtained with the use of a standalone Merkle-like data structure.

Proof Construction. If, for each node of the tree, hashes of the concatenation of left and right children are stored in memory, the construction cost is equal to the cost of a searching operation (expressed as the number of comparisons) which is in $O(\log(n))$. However, if these hashes have to be recalculated, the global cost is upper bounded by the number of hash calculations to be done on the path, which is itself upper bounded by the depth of the tree.

Table 1. Average proof size and verification cost results

Dictionary size	Merkle-like structure	Our system	Improvement
10^3	9.97	8.05	19.5%
$5 \cdot 10^4$	15.61	12.25	22.5%
$5 \cdot 10^5$	18.93	14.73	22.5%
10^6	19.93	15.46	22.5%

Update Complexity. We focus here on the updating of one element, in terms of hash computations.

Theorem 2. *When modifying the content of an element, the number of hash evaluations to update T is upper bounded by $\lceil \log(n) \rceil + 2$ where n is the overall number of elements in the dictionary.*

Proof. We update a leaf for a cost of one hash evaluation. Ancestor nodes of this leaf until the root node of T_1 (or T_2) need to be updated for a cost bounded by $\lceil \log(n) \rceil$. Finally the root node of T needs to be updated for a cost of one hash evaluation.

Theorem 3. *When inserting a new element of frequency $f = 0$, the number of hash evaluations is upper bounded by $2 \lceil \log(n) \rceil + 3$ where n is the overall number of elements after insertion.*

Proof. One pairwise link (one leaf) is changed in two pairwise links (2 leafs) for a cost of two hash function evaluations. The ancestor nodes of these two leaves, which can be located in T_2 or in T_1 and T_2, need to be computed (or re-computed) for an overall cost of at most $2 \lceil \log(n) \rceil + 2$ hash evaluations. Finally a last hash computation is needed to recompute the root node of T.

Theorem 4. *Assume that the absolute frequency of one element has changed and that this element which belongs to T_1 stays in T_1, the number of hash computations needed to meet the order property (1) is at most $\frac{\lfloor \log(n) \rfloor (\lfloor \log(n) \rfloor + 1)}{2}$.*

Proof. Let us suppose that the frequencies of the leaves from the root to the base level and from left to right are denoted f_1, f_2, ..., f_n. We consider the worst case which appears when a leaf of the base level needs to be moved at the root level, for instance if the frequency f_n is changed in f_n^* and $f_n^* > f_1$. Let h be the depth of the tree. In this scenario, by using the "min-max" choice criteria, we move the leaf h_n to the root level, while h_1 is moved down to the next level at the position of the leaf of lowest frequency. This last leaf is itself moved to the next level at the position of the leaf of lowest frequency, and so on, until the base level is reached. The lowest frequency leaf at level h is moved to the former position of h_n at level $h + 1$ (the base level). Overall, one leaf has been replaced at each level of the tree. Nodes along the path from changed nodes to the root node are updated. This non-optimal strategy leads to the following upper bound on the number of hash computations: $\sum_{i=1}^{h} i = \frac{\lfloor \log(n) \rfloor (\lfloor \log(n) \rfloor + 1)}{2}$

Theorem 5. *When deleting an element in T_1, by using the "min-max" choice criteria, the number of hash computations is in $O(\log(n)^2)$.*

Proof. Operations are similar to that of reordering an element, except that one leaf and its ancestor nodes need to be recomputed.

Search Complexity. The cost of a search operation is given in terms of comparisons. Search of a content: Since non authentifying structures use well known mechanisms, we do not describe the search algorithm. The content and frequency associated to a given u_i is obtained using A_1 and is done in $O(\log(n))$ comparisons. The rank of the frequency is obtained using A_2 and is also done in $O(\log(n))$ comparisons. Globally, the search of a leaf and the construction of the proof is done in $O(\log(n))$ comparisons. Search of an element: The cost is done in $O(\log(n))$ comparisons for insertion and modification of an element. The position of a leaf having a minimal (or maximal) frequency in a given level of the tree is done in $O(\log(n))$ comparisons.

Remark 3. From the previous analysis, we can deduce that reordering or deleting operations is done in $O(\log(n)^2)$ comparisons.

5   The Choice of the Structure

Our objective is to optimize the average proof size, avoiding the expensive worst cases. With our structure, the maximal proof length is bounded by $\lceil \log(n) \rceil + 2$. A dynamic Huffman tree gives slightly better results for the average case but the proof size in the worst case is in $O(n)$ for outlier (discrepant) samples. This worst case occurs for example when the distribution is exponential. An alternative is to use a dynamic Huffman tree for a small subset of data. This solution limits the expensive cost of the worst case. When considering a sample distant from Zipf's law, we may obtain a degenerate tree. In that case, the use of a length-limited Huffman tree [11] may be considered. Note that our structure has the advantage of simplicity (in particular, the construction of our tree is done in $O(n)$). Moreover, it provides all needed operations while keeping append/disjoin-only structures.

6   A Framework to Authenticate Http Responses

The aforementioned authenticated dictionary can be used for authentication of HTTP responses of a Web server [2] when the request distribution follows Zipf's law. The server returns either the requested page together with a 200 success response or a 404 error message and a proof of authenticity of the content of that page (or possibly a proof of non existence). In this context, u_i represents the hash of a url (Uniform Resource Locator) and c_i is the content of the corresponding page. However, it is important to note that in a dynamic site, a page has many contents which vary over time. Hence, it makes no sense to consider the hash of a page. When creating a page, one should define a scheme allowing authentication to be performed on the static fields which are of interest to the user.

7   Conclusion

We have proposed a model for authenticated dictionaries which takes into account the frequency of queries with the aim of obtaining a smaller proof size. This contrasts with the assumption made by existing dictionaries that the frequency distribution is uniform. Based on a frequency distribution following Zipf's law, we introduced a data structure with two components, each of which being nearly optimal for a portion of the distribution. We obtained an average gain of more than 20% on proof size while response time remains similar. In our complexity analysis, comparisons were made with a Merkle tree which is less costly than the dynamic structures used in [8]. However, since our system provides operations like insertion and deletion, it could also be compared to these dynamic structures, with the expectation that even greater gains would be realized.

In this paper, we have not discussed possible optimizations, including the use of length-limited Huffman trees, which will be developed in future papers.

References

1. Adamic, L.A., Huberman, B.A.: Zipf's law and the internet. Glottometrics 3, 143–150 (2002)
2. Bayardo, R.J.: Merkle tree authentication of http responses. In: In Proc. 14th WWW, pp. 1182–1183 (2005)
3. Blibech, K., Gabillon, A.: Chronos: an authenticated dictionary based on skip lists for timestamping systems. In: SWS, pp. 84–90 (2005)
4. Buldas, A., Laud, P., Lipmaa, H.: Accountable certificate management using undeniable attestations. IACR Cryptology ePrint Archive, 2000:27 (2000)
5. Devanbu, P., Gertz, M., Martel, C., Stubblebine, S.G.: Authentic Third-party Data Publication. In: Thuraisingham, B., van de Riet, R., Dittrich, K.R., Tari, Z. (eds.) 14th IFIP 11.3 Working Conference in Database Security. IFIP, vol. 73, pp. 101–112. Springer, Heidelberg (2000)
6. Easley, D., Kleinberg, J.: Power laws and rich-get-richer phenomena. In: Networks, Crowds, and Markets: Reasoning about a Highly Connected World. Cambridge University Press (2010)
7. Gassko, I., Gemmell, P.S., MacKenzie, P.D.: Efficient and fresh certification. In: Imai, H., Zheng, Y. (eds.) PKC 2000. LNCS, vol. 1751, pp. 342–353. Springer, Heidelberg (2000)
8. Goodrich, M.T., Tamassia, R.: Efficient authenticated dictionaries with skip lists and commutative hashing. Technical report, Johns Hopkins Information Security Institute (2001)
9. Goodrich, M.T., Tamassia, R., Schwerin, A.: Implementation of an authenticated dictionary with skip lists and commutative hashing 2, 68–82 (2001)
10. Kaufman, C., Perlman, R.J., Speciner, M.: Network security - private communication in a public world. Prentice Hall series in computer networking and distributed systems. Prentice Hall (1995)
11. Larmore, L.L., Hirschberg, D.S.: A fast algorithm for optimal length-limited huffman codes. J. ACM 37(3), 464–473 (1990)
12. Mahanti, A., Carlsson, N., Mahanti, A., Arlitt, M., Williamson, C.: A tale of the tails: Power-laws in internet measurements. IEEE Network 27(1), 59–64 (2013)
13. Mehta, D.P., Sahni, S. (eds.): Handbook of data structures and applications. Chapman & Hall/CRC (2005)
14. Merkle, R.: Protocols for public key cryptosystems. In: SIMMONS: Secure Communications and Asymmetric Cryptosystems (1982)

15. Merkle, R.C.: A certified digital signature. In: Brassard, G. (ed.) CRYPTO 1989. LNCS, vol. 435, pp. 218–238. Springer, Heidelberg (1990)
16. Naor, M., Nissim, K.: Certificate revocation and certificate update. IEEE Journal on Selected Areas in Communications 18(4), 561–570 (2000)
17. Nielsen, J.: Do websites have increasing returns (1997), http://www.nngroup.com/articles/do-websites-have-increasing-returns/
18. Nielsen, J.: A note about page popularity (2006), http://www.nngroup.com/articles/traffic-log-patterns/
19. Preneel, B., Van Rompay, B., Quisquater, J.J., Massiasand, H., Serret Avila, J.: Design of a Timestamping System (1999)
20. Pugh, W.: Skip lists: A probabilistic alternative to balanced trees (1990)
21. Saichev, A.I., Malevergne, Y., Sornette, D.: Theory of Zipf's Law and Beyond. Lecture Notes in Economics and Mathematical Systems. Springer (2009)
22. Tamassia, R.: Authenticated data structures. In: Di Battista, G., Zwick, U. (eds.) ESA 2003. LNCS, vol. 2832, pp. 2–5. Springer, Heidelberg (2003)

Géant-TrustBroker: Dynamic, Scalable Management of SAML-Based Inter-federation Authentication and Authorization Infrastructures

Daniela Pöhn, Stefan Metzger, and Wolfgang Hommel

Leibniz Supercomputing Centre, Munich Network Management Team
Boltzmannstr. 1, 85748 Garching n. Munich, Germany
{poehn,metzger,hommel}@lrz.de

Abstract. We present the concept and design of Géant-TrustBroker, a new service to facilitate multi-tenant ICT service user authentication and authorization (AuthNZ) management in large-scale eScience infrastructures that is researched and implemented by the pan-European research and education network, Géant. Géant-TrustBroker complements eduGAIN, a successful umbrella inter-federation created on top of national higher education federations in more than 20 countries world-wide. Motivated by experiences with real-world limits of eduGAIN, Géant-TrustBroker's primary goal is to enable a dynamic and highly scalable management of identity federations and inter-federations. Instead of eduGAIN's federation-of-federations approach, Géant-TrustBroker enables the on-demand establishment and life-cycle management of dynamic virtual federations and achieves a high level of automation to reduce the manual workload for the participating organizations, which so far is one of the most significant obstacles for the adoption of Federated Identity Management, e.g., based on the SAML standard. We contrast Géant-TrustBroker with other state-of-the-art approaches, present its workflows and internal mode of operations and give an outlook to how eduGAIN can be used in combination with Géant-TrustBroker to solve current AuthNZ problems in international research projects and communities.

Keywords: Federated Identity Management, SAML, Shibboleth, eduGAIN, Inter-Federation, Trust Management, Géant.

1 Introduction

Medium-sized and large organizations, such as universities, typically provide dozens of ICT services to their members, e.g., email, file, web collaboration, and print services as well as services specific for the organization and its business processes, e.g., exam management. Usually, a technical identifier – commonly referred to as username – is assigned to each member and all services can then be used by supplying one's username and some sort of credentials, such as a

N. Cuppens-Boulahia et al. (Eds.): SEC 2014, IFIP AICT 428, pp. 307–320, 2014.

password. While this procedure is common enough to be considered trivial for each individual user, the organization-wide management of an arbitrarily large number of users and their permissions for all the services can be challenging. Authorization models such as role-based access control (RBAC) and architectural concepts for centralized Identity & Access Management (I&AM) systems have solved most of the related challenges in theory and are successfully implemented in practice by many organizations, usually based on LDAP servers or relational database management systems that are used as user management backend.

Inter-organizational identity management becomes necessary either when an organization's member shall access external services, for example, because a service such as email has been outsourced to a third party provider, or when members of several organizations shall work together on a common project, such as a research project that involves multiple universities and industry partners. Federated Identity Management (FIM), based on standards such as SAML [3] or lightweight approaches like OpenID, assigns each user to her home organization, called Identity Provider (IDP), and technically ensures that services provided by another organization, referred to as Service Provider (SP), can be accessed by authorized users. The set of all IDPs and SPs that collaborate for a specific reason is commonly referred to as federation, and while federations in many industrial sectors consist of only very few members (only one IDP and one SP is not unusual), many national research and education networks (NRENs) operate large authentication and authorization infrastructures (AAIs), i.e., federations with hundreds of organizational members that include most of the country's higher education institutions and commercial scientific services providers.

While geographic and industrial-sector-specific borders for federations are not imposed by FIM technology itself, they have become a reality due to the historic evolution and growth of FIM use in both industry and higher education institutions: Most sectors and countries run their own federation, resulting in the problem that international and cross-sector collaboration is impeded: Neither a researcher from country A nor an industry partner from country B can access an ICT service operated by a university in country C based on existing AAIs. The only pragmatic solutions are to either create new local user accounts for all project participants, which obviously scales for small projects only, or to set up a new federation specific for the given project or community. Either solution increases the overall complexity for IDP and SP operators as well as for the users, who must either use separate credentials for each service or must be aware of which federations they are members of when accessing an external service.

Inter-FIM is the next evolutionary step and, so far, a young research discipline that still lacks resilient results. Enabling users from one federation to access services in other federations turned out to be a problem with conceptual, technical, and organizational aspects. Most issues stem from two characteristics of today's federations:

1. An organization's membership in a federation usually requires a contract, e.g., either with all other federation members or a central federation operator to ensure that all participants are obliged to certain behavior. For example,

IDPs must provide high quality user data to avoid SP misuse based on fake accounts, and SPs must commit themselves to honor privacy and data protection principles.

2. Federations must be built on common technical grounds, i.e., each member must use the same federation technology (e.g., SAML), and the data format used by all IDPs and SPs in the federation must be harmonized, resulting in the so-called federation schema that defines the syntax and semantics of information provided by IDPs about their users, such as name, email address, and language preferences.

The assumption that a world-wide federation could be built is utopian because no agreement on a common technology, membership criteria, and user data format could ever be achieved for tens of thousands of organizations [8]. A more promising approach is to integrate existing federations into a higher-level umbrella inter-federation: eduGAIN [1] is a successful attempt to set up an inter-federation for NRENs' country-specific AAIs that has been initiated by the pan-European research network Géant. It spans more than 20 federations already, but it grows slowly, supports only a minimalistic data schema, brings additional contractual complexity, and requires significant technical effort for each participating organization.

The limits experienced with eduGAIN in the real world have motivated a complementary and fundamentally different approach to enable Inter-FIM for international research projects and communities in the future. On the one hand, it is much more dynamic and scalable, but on the other hand it cuts back regarding formal contracts while still ensuring a suitable degree of reliability concerning the participant's behavior. While eduGAIN is a federation-of-federations, our new approach, named Géant-TrustBroker, creates dynamic, virtual federations that overcome many organizational and technical issues of other Inter-FIM approaches. In Section 2 we present the concept and goal of the Géant-TrustBroker service and contrast it with the current state of the art. Section 3 then details the Géant-TrustBroker Inter-FIM workflows. The paper is concluded by an outlook to how eduGAIN and Géant-TrustBroker will collude and a summary of the results achieved so far.

2   TrustBroker's Distinguishing Design and Related Work

FIM enables SPs to delegate user authentication to each user's IDP and to retrieve certain information about users, the so-called attributes, from this IDP. This workflow implies organizational and technical prerequisites:

- SP and IDP software, operated by different organizations, must be able to communicate with each other:
  - The communication endpoints of both services need to be known and technical information, such as X.509v3 certificates for digital signatures and encryption, must be available. This is commonly referred to as (IDP and SP) metadata.

- The syntax and semantics of exchanged data must be defined by a common data schema.
- SP and IDP must trust each other: The SP must be able to rely on the data provided by the IDP and the IDP must be confident that the personal data provided about its users is not misused. Traditionally, this requires written contracts, although more dynamic and easier to manage approaches like the Géant Code of Conduct [14] gain importance.

Because the scalability would significantly suffer if each SP had to bilaterally set these prerequisites up with each IDP, federations have successfully become a means to group all SPs and IDPs that share common properties, for example being related to a country's higher education infrastructure. Federations aggregate the metadata of all their participating SPs and IDPs, specify a common data schema, and provide a contractual framework that ensures basic properties for trusting each other.

Merging federations or putting them under the umbrella of an inter-federation is complex in practice due to the heterogeneity of the existing federations: Typically, both the federation data schemas and contract contents differ significantly even if they use the same FIM technology. Forcing all member organizations of a federation to change their data schema does not work in the real world, leading to inter-federation data schemas that are the common denominator of all involved federations, which in turn means that SPs, which require certain user attributes not included in the inter-federation data schema, cannot be used with their full functionality. The additional contracts required between federations and their members make the overall inter-federation more complex and cumbersome to manage. Yet, with major efforts eduGAIN successfully established such an inter-federation. However, in addition to the resulting problems outlined above another real-world problem has not been foreseen: Aggregating the XML-based SAML metadata from many national research federations leads to a huge inter-federation metadata file, whose processing becomes so cumbersome that many of the deployed SP and IDP software packages are slowed down to a crawl that must be either compensated through new hardware investments by all IDPs and SPs or leads to significantly reduced usability for the end users.

Géant-TrustBroker (GNTB) enables the exchange of user identity data across federation borders with the following key characteristics:

1. GNTB provides SP and IDP metadata in an on-demand manner: Instead of distributing the complete aggregated inter-federation metadata to all SPs and IDPs, GNTB provides IDPs only with the metadata of SPs used by at least one of their users and vice versa for SPs. This effectively avoids performance bottlenecks.
2. GNTB enables the exchange of data conversion rules in addition to the other metadata. Instead of supporting only a small set of common user attributes, this allows for the use of arbitrarily complex data schemas, while still ensuring that conversion rules must only be implemented once for each federation and not by each individual SP or IDP.

3. GNTB automates the technical integration of new metadata on the SP as well as on the IDP side when an IDP's user logs into an SP for the first time. This eliminates the manual workload for SP and IDP administrators and avoids waiting times for the end users before they can use a new SP.

The third property means that the technical setup of SP-to-IDP relationships can be fully automated, but it does not have to. Whether full automation is desired or not actually depends on the involved organizations' requirements for trust built on organizational measures:

- On the one hand, SPs of commercial services, which require payments and therefor liability, usually will not accept new users from previously unknown IDPs before they also have a complmentary, mutually signed contract. On the other hand, SPs of free-to-use services, such as a Wiki collaboration web server operated by a university for its research project partners, will prefer easy and quick account rollout for their users and a minimum amount of work to put into user management for the service.
- In practice, most IDP administrators will prefer a fully automated setup because up to now it is a very tedious task that is done anyway whenever one of their users requests access to a new SP. This holds true at least for the higher education sector, where the use of many external services is very common, e.g., due to many inter-organizational research projects. However, those IDP organizations, which are more restrictive about the use of external services, will not want full technical automation, at least not without an explicit manual approval step.

The first of the GNTB characteristics mentioned above regarding the metadata exchange is heavily influenced by related work. For example, most national research federations provide facilities for web-based management of SP and IDP metadata. One advanced example is the Resource Registry (RR) of the Switch federation SWITCHaai [4]: RR provides a web-interface for IDPs and SPs to register their metadata. It allows service providers to specify which of the federation schema attributes they actually use, a seemingly very basic information that is, however, not provided in most other research federations. In return, IDPs have the option to describe all attributes they actually offer [5]. Despite the wide range of provided functionalities, the webtool itself requires manual work for configuration and waiting time for the administrator to receive a basic attribute filter, which he can adapt.

Metadata aggregation and distribution has been designed and implemented by means of the Metadata Distribution Services (MDS) [16] in eduGAIN [1]. The metadata is first aggregated at the federational level, before MDS aggregates and signs the metadata for the whole inter-federation. Entities establish a static bilateral trust relationship, while the Interoperable SAML Profile [18] addresses the exchange of SAML messages. As huge metadata files affect performance and hardly any organization needs the metadata of all other inter-federation members for production – for example, an SP usually never needs information about all the other SPs in the inter-federation – Dynamic SAML (DSAML, [7]) and

Distributed Dynamic SAML [17], developed by Internet2, simplify the discovery of another entity, but does not solve the attribute conversion and attribute filter problems. For the initial trust establishment the metadata consumer validates the signature using a root certificate and establishes the trust. Despite the dynamic character, the metadata has to be published or registered at a central point, e.g. MDS. The Metadata Query Protocol by Young, currently submitted as IETF Draft [15], suggests how to retrieve metadata from entities using simple HTTP GET requests. It therefor solves the problem of huge aggregated metadata files, but otherwise has the same drawbacks as DSAML: attribute conversion, attribute filter and the initial trust establishment require manual work resulting in waiting time for users. The Metadata Query Protocol is one piece of the Metadata Exchange Protocol (MDX). Entities pick a registrar for their metadata and receive attributes from partner entities from one or more aggregators. Aggregators and registrars are linked in order to exchange metadata with each other, analogical to DNS. Similar to MDS, the PEER project [10] implemented a public endpoint entities registry that supports SAML but also other metadata. PEER can obtain metadata from an MDX implementation. Though PEER moves from a huge metadata aggregator to a central system, where administrators can register their domain, many manual steps are needed, e.g. to generate an attribute filter adjusted to the IDP or to establish technical trust between two entities.

3   TrustBroker Concept and Workflows

GNTB is basically a service to store and retrieve SP and IDP metadata as well as user attribute data conversion rules on demand. The main challenge is to seamlessly integrate the use of this functionality by both SPs and IDPs into standard FIM workflows; to this end, GNTB is tailored for SAML, which is the FIM standard most widely used in research federations, but it could be adapted to other FIM protocols without changing the core functionality.

We distinguish between management workflows and the so-called GNTB core workflow. Management workflows are used by SPs and IDPs to register, update, and delete their own metadata as well as conversion rules in the GNTB registry, similar to how they have to manage their metadata in their research federations. Registering one's metadata is required before the SP or IDP can make use of the GNTB-enhanced workflows: Although self-registration steps initially were and still could be integrated into a single core workflow, this turned out to make it unreasonably complex.

To explain the GNTB core workflow, depicted in Figure 1, let us assume that user Alice from IDP I in federation 1 wants to make use of a service located at SP S in federation 2. As often seen on SP websites, the login / user authentication form at S presents a list of IDPs, which S already knows. However, as I and S have no bilateral technical trust relationship established yet, Alice cannot choose I from that list and instead initiates the core workflow by choosing GNTB as her IDP. Using standard SAML mechanisms, Alice's web browser is redirected to the GNTB service; similar to federation's SAML IDP discovery services (also known as Where Are You From? service), GNTB then presents a list of the registered IDPs and Alice has to pick the one she wants to use; an account chooser application similar to OpenID's accountchooser.com or equivalent could be integrated as well. Her choice can be remembered, e.g., using cookies, if she always wants to use the same IDP, but account or IDP choosing functionality is increasingly requested by users with several accounts at different IDPs. GNTB passes the information about which IDP has been chosen back to S afterwards.

In the next step, S determines whether an user form IDP I is acceptable or the login should be aborted; for example, the SP could use a blacklist of unwanted IDPs or a whitelist containing only IDPs the SP has contracts with. Also, if Alice has chosen an IDP that is already known to S because she missed it in the list earlier, a regular FIM authentication workflow is started without any involvement of GNTB. If S confirms its interest in users from I, the GNTB core workflow continues as follows:

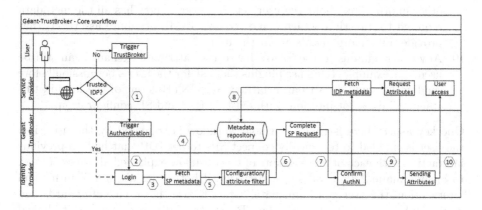

Fig. 1. GNTB's core workflow

1. S prepares a SAML user authentication request, but as it cannot communicate with I directly yet due to missing IDP metadata, it sends the request to GNTB, which temporarily stores it for use in step 7. This is necessary because GNTB must first trigger I to authenticate Alice and determine whether S is an acceptable SP. Otherwise, malicious users could add arbitrary IDPs' metadata to any SP and vice versa, even if they had no valid user account at these IDPs (flood protection).
2. GNTB redirects Alice for authentication to the login page of her IDP I; during this step and step 6, GNTB acts like an SP towards I.
3. In the case of successful authentication or if Alice is already logged in (i.e., a session exists), I fetches S's metadata and attribute conversion rules from GNTB. Otherwise the workflow is aborted showing an error message to Alice.
4. Based on this information retrieved from GNTB, I can automatically update its configuration by adding S's metadata.

5. For the creation of so-called attribute filters, i.e., rules about which user attributes I will send to S on request, I has to check whether it needs attribute conversion rules, which are part of the configuration file attribute-resolver.xml, and whether suitable rulesets are available at GNTB.

6. With Alice successfully authenticated and I completely set up for communication with S now, Alice is redirected back to GNTB, closing the sub-workflow started in step 2.

7. GNTB now redirects Alice back to I again, but uses S's request that was stored in step 1. Since Alice has already been authenticated at I in step 3, I can immediately send a SAML authentication assertion back to S, which also involves redirecting Alice's browser to S again.

8. Because SAML assertions, i.e., the data I sends to S, are usually digitally signed using public key encryption, S now needs to fetch I's metadata, which includes I's public key(s), from GNTB, and add it to its local configuration file of trusted IDPs in order to verify the signature.

9. S now knows that a valid user from I has logged into its service, but it has no other information about the user yet. However, S now has all the metadata required to directly contact I and request SAML attribute assertions that provide some more details about the user.

10. Any other add-ons to the SAML-based user attribute exchange can still be used. For example, IDPs use plugins that ask for the user's permission before sending personal data to an arbitrary SP. GNTB is out of the loop in this stage and does not interfere with existing IDP and SP configuration.

One key aspect here is that the whole workflow is triggered by the user, i.e., the user is enabled to technically connect SPs to her IDP that had no previous interaction with each other. Variants of the workflow explained above exist, e.g., to include manual approval steps. However, if both sides abstain from manual intervention, the user can immediately start to use the service afterwards and does not have to wait on both the SP and the IDP to set up the technical configuration, which we consider a significant improvement over the manual process that is used in all federations so far.

3.1 Variations of the Géant-TrustBroker Core Workflow

The GNTB core workflow as it has been shown in the previous section covers the primary use case GNTB has been designed for. Additionally, there are several variations of the workflow to handle the following special conditions and constellations:

1. IDP and SP already are members of the same federation.
2. IDP is connected to subordinate Attribute Authorities (AA).
3. SAML Entity Categories are used.
4. SP honors the Géant Code of Conduct.

In this section, we outline the effects of each of these variations. The core workflow is simplified when both the SP and the IDP are already members of the same federation (1) because no user attribute data conversion will be necessary and the required metadata will already be available at both the SP and the IDP. However, the IDP may not yet have been manually configured to send all of the required user attributes to the SP, so at least the IDP administrators could benefit from the automation that can be achieved using the GNTB workflow.

Variation (2) is intended for the growing number of cases in which SPs require information about users which the IDP cannot provide without querying a third party, usually referred to as AA. For example, the use of high performance computing resources via Grid middleware has been FIM-enabled, but Grid SPs typically require user attributes such as Grid user certificate distinguished names (DNs), which most universities do not store in their central I&AM system, so this information cannot be provided by the university's IDP. However, the IDP can retrieve these attributes from an AA; in this case, attribute conversion is necessary if the AA does not use the same data schema as the SP.

Variation (3) applies to SPs that use Entity Categories as described by REFEDS [12] and the Internet-Draft of the IETF Network Working Group [13]. SPs are categorized and IDPs can simplify their setup by applying their configuration to whole categories instead of individual SPs. Therefor, the Entity Category is stored at the GNTB along with the metadata and additional attribute information.

To facilitate the IDP-side trust building process, Géant recommends the use of the Code of Conduct (CoC) [14]. The CoC is a set of privacy and data protection obligations that is closely related to European data protection acts. Its basic idea is that SPs can signal that they honor the CoC and then IDPs can be configured to send personal user data to the SP without the formal requirement of written contracts that govern data protection measures. Variation (4) covers the use case that an IDP wants to check whether the SP honors the CoC, for example, to either reject SPs that do not use CoC or at least require a manual approval step.

3.2 Géant-TrustBroker Management Workflows

To simplify the GNTB core workflow, SPs and IDPs have to register their metadata and attributes information before the core workflow can be triggered for the first time by any user. Figure 2 shows this workflow for the SP side:

1. The SP has to create its metadata and specify required attributes. The XML-based data format for metadata is standardized by SAML and contains information about the necessary communication endpoints as well as the SP's server certificates, which are used for the verification of XML signatures and encryption purposes by the IDPs. Additionally, the SP can submit a list of required user attributes, which can be marked as either mandatory or optional; if an IDP cannot deliver one of the mandatory attributes, the user will not be able to use the service. A versioning storage backend is used in GNTB to track metadata changes because, e.g., certain IDP-side management workflows depend on whether an SP's metadata has changed since it was last retrieved. Write access to GNTB generally requires authentication

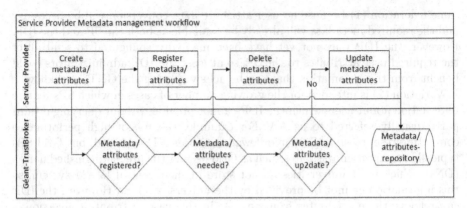

Fig. 2. Géant-TrustBroker management workflow for service provider metadata

to ensure that each SP and each IDP can only modify its own metadata. Similar to federation metadata management in most national research federations, technical contacts from SPs and IDPs need to register at GNTB and are assigned an identifier and credentials / keys for the GNTB API.

2. For a first-time setup, the SP uploads its metadata for registration at GNTB. Otherwise, the SP determines whether GNTB has the most recent version of the metadata and can otherwise update it. Metadata changes regularly, e.g., because the X.509v3 certificates contained have a limited validity period and then need to be replaced. Just like updating its metadata in each federation it is a member of, the SP is responsible for keeping its metadata up-to-date at GNTB.

3. If the SP does not want to further use GNTB, it could finally delete its data from the metadata/attribute repository. This cleanup step is optional because the SP must allow GNTB-based login to its service explicitly anyway. Also, GNTB removes outdated metadata entries periodically as well; for example, SP or IDP metadata with X.509v3 certificates whose validity period has expired cannot be used anymore and is purged so that no outdated information can be downloaded by IDPs.

The IDP metadata management workflow is very similar to this workflow and is therefor not described in detail here.

Whenever an SP updates its metadata, the IDPs that have users at this SP need to retrieve the update. Complementary, SPs need updated metadata from those IDPs their users are from. GNTB supports both a push- and a pull-model for transporting updated metadata. Because GNTB stores information about which IDPs have downloaded which SP metadata, they can send the update through a simple GNTB API call. Alternatively, GNTB can be configured as a standard Metadata Provider service in the IDP configuration, which results in the IDP software automatically polling for metadata updates, e.g., once per hour. Although the latter option causes a delay before the new SP metadata becomes active at the IDP, periodically downloading metadata is the most widely accepted

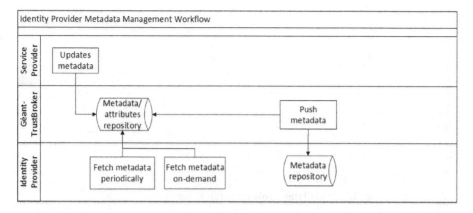

Fig. 3. Géant-TrustBroker workflow for conversion rules

and predominantly deployed method in today's research federations. It gives a higher degree of control that nothing important in the IDP configuration gets overwritten accidentally and is currently preferred by most IDP administrators. This workflow can be seen in Figure 3.

3.3 Géant-TrustBroker Workflow for Managing Conversion Rules

In international and cross-sector projects it is not unusual that an SP needs certain user attributes that are not used in the IDP's data schema, i.e., IDPs cannot provide these attributes without additional configuration. However, inter-federation schema discrepancies can often be mitigated using simple data conversion rules. In the simplest case, the attribute only has a different name in both involved schemas, e.g., *surname* vs. *lastname*, which can easily be mapped on a 1:1-basis. The most frequently required rule sets compose a new attribute out of several existing ones – for example, *fullName* is composed from *givenName* and *surname* – or use simple string operations to modify the syntax of existing attributes, e.g., the user's date of birth needs to be converted from *yyyy-mm-dd* to *mm/dd/yyyy* format. Although arbitrarily complex conversion rules could become necessary in theory, these three basic operations – mapping of attribute names, composing new attributes, and string operations for reformatting – are sufficient for almost all Inter-FIM real-world use cases as of today.

GNTB can optionally be used as a central conversion rule set repository by all registered IDPs. The intention is to enable the sharing of implemented conversion rules because usually other IDPs in the same national research federation can work with exactly the same conversion rules as all IDPs in the same federation are based on the same data schema. It therefor is sufficient if one IDP per federation implements conversion rules for a new SP and makes them available to the other IDPs. The workflow for sharing conversion rules is shown in Figure 4:

– The conversion rules are implemented and tested by the IDP administrator before the decision to share them is made.

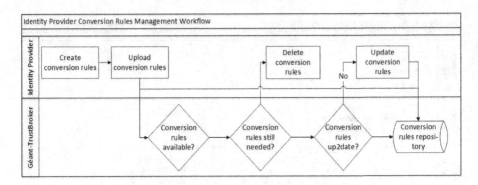

Fig. 4. Géant-TrustBroker workflow for conversion rules

- The IDP administrator uploads the conversion rule set to GNTB. Each rule contains metadata specifying for which SP or SP entity category the rule is intended and which source data schema it is built for. Most national research federation data schemas already have an official, globally unique identifier assigned to them. If no schema identifier is given, GNTB automatically assigns an IDP-specific identifier; this clearly limits automated re-use of the conversion rule, but administrators of other IDPs can still use it if they are confident that the sharing IDP uses the same data schema as they do. Write access to rules is restricted, so IDPs can create, modify, and delete their own conversion rules only for obvious reasons.

Sharing conversion rules on the one hand and re-using some other IDP's conversion rules on the other hand has several implications that must be considered:

- Instead of re-using existing conversion rules, another IDP in the same federation could implement and share conversion rules for the same SP, resulting in multiple, hopefully equivalent, conversion rule sets for the same purpose. During the automated integration of conversion rules at a third IDP, a decision on which rule set to use must be made automatically, defaulting to the newest rule set available. At the moment, GNTB only supports a manual cleanup of duplicates, but other mechanisms – such as a reputation rating system – can be implemented in the future.
- SPs can update their metadata or signal that they need additional or modified attributes. In this case, existing shared conversion rule sets might not work anymore or not cover the complete set of attributes required by the SP. If this happens, the affected shared rule sets are marked as *outdated* and the IDP administrators who shared them are notified. They have to update their shared rules to remove the *outdated* flag. By default, flagged rule sets are not automatically imported by other IDPs.

GNTB's IDP management workflow also ensures that updates of conversion rules that have automatically been added to the IDP configuration will be downloaded and integrated similar to changes in SP metadata. Because conversion rule sharing is a new and experimental functionality for IDPs, practical experience needs to be gained to determine the long-term feasibility and stability of this approach and which other issues may emerge.

4 Conclusion and Outlook

Géant-TrustBroker enables the on-demand, user-triggered exchange of SP and IDP metadata and related configuration data, such as user attribute data conversion rules, across identity federations' borders. It facilitates the fully automated technical setup of FIM-based AuthNZ data exchange and therefor significantly reduces the amount of manual implementation efforts required by both SP and IDP administrators. As a consequence, users can immediately start to use new federation-external services and do not have to wait until the SP and IDP administrators have finished this formerly manual setup process.

It must be kept in mind that a fully automated setup of FIM connections between organizations may not always be desired; especially commercial SPs, which require a written contract with IDPs to ensure, e.g., accountability and reliable payment, are not in the target group of our approach. Instead, the goal, as envisioned in the pan-European research and education network Géant, is to have both eduGAIN and Géant-TrustBroker available as management tools for inter-federations in eScience infrastructures. For SP-IDP-connections that require formal organizational trust building measures such as written contracts, eduGAIN will continue to be first choice. However, eduGAIN will be complemented by Géant-TrustBroker for use by multi-national and cross-sector research projects that want their members to access their distributed services easily and quickly without the previously usual organizational and technical overhead.

The Géant-TrustBroker core workflow, which is an extension of the standard SAML authentication and attribute queries, will be formally specified as an IETF Internet-Draft and submitted for standardization as IETF Request for Comments (RFC). The GNTB prototype and the implementation of the SP- and IDP-sided workflows for the FIM software package Shibboleth will be made available as open source and used for pilot operations in Géant in 2015.

Acknowledgment. The research leading to these results has received funding from the European Community's Seventh Framework Programme under grant agreement no 605243 (Multi-gigabit European Research and Education Network and Associated Services – GÉANT).

The authors wish to thank the members of the Munich Network Management (MNM) Team for helpful comments on previous versions of this paper. The MNM-Team, directed by Prof. Dr. Dieter Kranzlmüller and Prof. Dr. Heinz-Gerd Hegering, is a group of researchers at Ludwig-Maximilians-Universität München, Technische Universität München, the University of the Federal Armed Forces, and the Leibniz Supercomputing Centre of the Bavarian Academy of Sciences and Humanities.

References

1. Géant: eduGAIN Homepage (January 17, 2014),
   http://www.geant.net/service/eduGAIN/Pages/home.aspx
2. Hämmerle, L., Schofield, B.: eduGAIN - Are we there yet? (January 17, 2014),
   https://refeds.org/meetings/oct13/slides/
   eduGAIN-at-FIM4R-20131002-bas.pptx
3. Cantor, S., Kemp, J., Philpott, R., Maler, E.: Assertions and Protocols for the OA-
   SIS Security Assertion Markup Language (SAML) V2.0. OASIS Security Services
   Technical Committee Standard (2005)
4. SWITCH: SWITCHaai Resource Registry (January 17, 2014),
   http://www.switch.ch/de/aai/support/tools/resourceregistry.html
5. Hämmerle, L., Lenggenhager, T.: AAI Resource Registry Guide (January 17, 2014),
   https://www.switch.ch/aai/docs/AAI-RR-Guide.pdf
6. Solberg, A.: Dynamic SAML (January 17, 2014),
   https://rnd.feide.no/2010/02/18/dynamic_saml/
7. Harding, P., Johansson, L., Klingenstein, N.: Dynamic Security Assertion Markup
   Language. IEEE Security & Privacy 2(6), 83–85 (2008)
8. Young, I.A., La Joie, C.: Interfederation and Metadata Exchange: Concepts and
   Methods (2009), http://iay.org.uk/blog/2009/05/concepts-v1.10.pdf
9. FIN-CLARIN: The Language Bank of Finland - Language Archive Tools (January
   17, 2014), lat.csc.fi
10. Terena: PEER 0.11.0: Python Package Index (January 17, 2014)
    https://pypi.python.org/pypi/peer/0.11.0
11. Johannson, L.: pyFF Documentation - Federation Feeder 0.9.4 documentation
    (January 17, 2014), http://pythonhosted.org/pyFF/index.html
12. REFEDS: Entity Categories R&S (January 17, 2014),
    https://refeds.terena.org/index.php/Entity_Categories/R
13. Johansson, L., Young, I.A., Cantor, S.: The Entity Category SAML Entity Meta-
    data Attribute Types - draft-macedir-entity-attribute-00.xml (January 17 (2014),
    http://macedir.org/draft-macedir-entity-category-00.html
14. Géant: GANT Data Protection Code of Conduct (January 17, 2014),
    http://www.geant.net/uri/dataprotection-code-of-conduct/
    v1/Pages/default.aspx
15. Young, I. (ed.): Metadata Query Protocol - draft-young-md-query-01 (January 17,
    2014), http://datatracker.ietf.org/doc/
    draft-young-md-query/?include_text=1
16. eduGAIN (January 27, 2014), http://mds.edugain.org/
17. Harding, P., Johansson, J., Klingenstein, N.: Dynamic Security Assertion Markup
    Language: Simplifying Single Sign-On. IEEE Security & Privacy 6(2), 83–85 (2008),
    doi:10.1109/MSP.2008.31
18. Solberg, A. et. al: Interoperable SAML 2.0 Web Browser SSO Deployment Profile
    (January 17, 2014), http://saml2int.org/profile/current

Efficient Identity-Based Signature from Lattices

Miaomiao Tian* and Liusheng Huang

School of Computer Science and Technology,
University of Science and Technology of China
miaotian@mail.ustc.edu.cn

Abstract. Identity-based signature is an important technique for light-weight authentication. Recently, many efforts have been made to construct identity-based signatures over lattice assumptions since they would remain secure in future quantum age. In this paper we present a new identity-based signature scheme from lattice problems. This scheme is more efficient than other lattice-based identity-based signature schemes in terms of both computation and communication complexities. We prove its security in the random oracle model under short integer solution assumption that is as hard as approximating several worst-case lattice problems.

Keywords: identity-based signature, lattice, performance.

1 Introduction

As the rapid development of networks, authentication between users is becoming increasingly important. In many scenarios, improving the performance of authentication is crucial. For example, in wireless sensor network and mobile social network, the battery life of devices is so short that complex authentication protocols are intolerable. Since digital signature is a main building block of authentication, reducing its complexity is an apparent approach towards meeting this demand. One way of reducing the complexity of signatures is to use identity-based signatures instead of regular signatures (which rely on certificates).

Identity-based signature (IBS) is a basic component of identity-based cryptography that was first introduced by Shamir [18] in 1984. As an alternative of traditional certificate-based cryptography, identity-based cryptography possesses an arresting advantage, i.e., it eliminates the onerous certificate management procedure in traditional certificate-based cryptography. To achieve the merit, each user in identity-based cryptosystem sets his identity (e.g. his e-mail address) as his public key (while in traditional certificate-based cryptosystem, users' public keys are random strings). The secret key of any user is generated by a trusted Private Key Generator (PKG) from PKG's secret key and the user's identity. Thanks to this advantage, IBSs are more preferable than regular signatures in many real-world applications.

---

* Corresponding author.

N. Cuppens-Boulahia et al. (Eds.): SEC 2014, IFIP AICT 428, pp. 321–329, 2014.

After Shamir's seminal work, several IBSs emerged (e.g. [9]), however fully practical implementations are recently proposed due to the work of [6]. In [6], Boneh and Franklin designed an efficient identity-based encryption scheme by utilizing bilinear pairings. Since then, many excellent proposals for IBS appeared based on pairings [11,8,5,15]. These IBS proposals are very efficient for practical applications, whereas they all substantially rely on the discrete logarithm problem that is facile for quantum computers [19]. In view of the recent progresses of quantum computer, looking for quantum-immune IBSs is no longer alarmist. To achieve this, new mathematical tool on which cryptographic schemes are built should be developed. Lattice seems to be our best option because cryptographic schemes based on lattices are supported by worst-case hardness assumption and conjectured to withstand quantum attacks. Moreover, lattice-based cryptographic schemes are also easy to implement since typical computations involved in them are only integer matrix-vector multiplication and modular addition. (See [16] for an overview on lattice-based cryptography.)

In 2010, Rückert [17] successfully constructed the first two (hierarchical) IBSs over lattice assumptions. One is secure in the random oracle model and the other is secure in the standard model. Later on, some other lattice-based IBSs also appeared, e.g., [20,12]). All of the IBS constructions followed the signature framework of Gentry, Peikert and Vaikuntanathan [10]. According to the framework, the signing key S of a user is a trapdoor of the function like $f_A(x) = Ax$ mod q, where A is a user-related matrix. Typically S is a short basis of the lattice defined by A. Armed with the signing key S, the user can run a preimage sampling algorithm for the function f_A to obtain a signature sig. For those lattice IBS schemes, the generation of users' signing keys requires lattice basis delegation technique [7,2,1]. Since the signing key size and the signature length will increase dramatically after lattice basis delegation, those IBSs would be inefficient in practice. In addition, the short basis (signing key) extraction algorithms involved in them are also very expensive, thus PKG will be overburdened.

Our Contributions. In this paper, we construct a new IBS scheme over lattice assumptions, which does not follow the signature framework of [10]. Actually, our IBS scheme adopts the rejection sampling technique of [13] and can be viewed as an identity-based version of Lyubashevsky's signature scheme [13]. Compared with other lattice-based IBS schemes, our scheme is much more efficient in terms of both communication and computation overhead. We prove the IBS scheme is secure against adaptive chosen message and identity attacks in the random oracle model under conventional short integer solution (SIS) assumption which, in turn, leads our IBS scheme to be secure under the worst-case hardness of approximating several classic lattice problems, by the results of [14].

Paper Organization. The remainder of this paper is organized as follows. Section 2 and Section 3 respectively give some preliminaries and an efficient signing key extraction algorithm to be used in this work. Section 4 provides our lattice-based IBS scheme. Section 5 concludes the whole paper.

2   Preliminaries

2.1   Notation

Throughout this paper, the security parameter is a positive integer n. For a positive integer k, $[k]$ denotes the set $\{1, \cdots, k\}$. Vectors are assumed to be in column form and are written as bold low-case letters, e.g., $\mathbf{v}$. The ith component of $\mathbf{v}$ is represented by v_i, and the ℓ_p norm of $\mathbf{v}$ is denoted by $||\mathbf{v}||_p$ (we will avoid writing p if $p = 2$). Matrices are represented by bold upper-case letters, e.g., $\mathbf{A}$. Let the ith column of $\mathbf{A}$ be $\mathbf{a}_i$ and define $||\mathbf{A}||_p = \max_i(||\mathbf{a}_i||_p)$. For a full rank square matrix $\mathbf{A}$, its Gram-Schmidt orthogonalization is denoted as $\widetilde{\mathbf{A}}$.

We say a function $f(n)$ is negligible if it is smaller than all polynomial fractions for sufficiently large n, and we use $\mathsf{negl}(n)$ to denote a negligible function of n. We say an event occurs with overwhelming probability if its probability is $1 - \mathsf{negl}(n)$.

The statistical distance between two distributions X and Y over some finite set F is defined as $\max_{e \subseteq F} |X(e) - Y(e)|$. We say that two distributions are statistically close if their statistical distance is negligible.

2.2   Lattices

An m-dimensional lattice Λ is a full-rank discrete subgroup of $\mathbb{R}^m$. In this paper, we focus on integer lattices, i.e., those lattices whose points have coordinates in $\mathbb{Z}^m$. Among these lattices are the "q-ary" lattices.

Definition 1. *For prime q, $\boldsymbol{u} \in \mathbb{Z}_q^n$ and $\boldsymbol{A} \in \mathbb{Z}_q^{n \times m}$, define the "$q$-ary" lattices as follows:*

$$\Lambda^{\perp}(\boldsymbol{A}) = \{\boldsymbol{e} \in \mathbb{Z}^m : \boldsymbol{A}\boldsymbol{e} = 0 \pmod{q}\},$$
$$\Lambda^{\boldsymbol{u}}(\boldsymbol{A}) = \{\boldsymbol{e} \in \mathbb{Z}^m : \boldsymbol{A}\boldsymbol{e} = \boldsymbol{u} \pmod{q}\}.$$

2.3   Gaussians on Lattices

The Gaussian function is a useful tool in lattice-based cryptography.

Definition 2. *For any $s > 0$ and $\boldsymbol{c} \in \mathbb{R}^m$, define the Gaussian function as:*

$$g_{s,c}(\boldsymbol{x}) = \exp(-\pi ||\boldsymbol{x} - \boldsymbol{c}||^2 / s^2).$$

Let $g_{s,c}(\Lambda)$ be a sum of $g_{s,c}$ over the lattice Λ. The discrete Gaussian distribution over Λ with center $\boldsymbol{c}$ and parameter s is defined as

$$G_{\Lambda,s,c} = g_{s,c}(\boldsymbol{x})/g_{s,c}(\Lambda).$$

For notational convenience, in the rest of the paper, $g_{s,0}$ and $G_{\Lambda,s,0}$ will be abbreviated as g_s and $G_{\Lambda,s}$, respectively.

The following facts about discrete Gaussian distribution are very useful in this work. They are from [14] and [10], respectively.

Lemma 1. *Let q prime and integer $m \geq 2n \log q$ and let Gaussian parameter $s \geq \omega(\sqrt{\log m})$. For any $u \in \mathbb{Z}_q^n$, we have:*

1. *For all but a q^{-n} fraction of $A \in \mathbb{Z}_q^{n \times m}$, $Pr[\, x \leftarrow G_{\Lambda^u(A),s} : ||x|| > s\sqrt{m}\,] \leq$ negl(n).*
2. *For all but a $2q^{-n}$ fraction of $A \in \mathbb{Z}_q^{n \times m}$, if $e \leftarrow G_{\mathbb{Z}^m,s}$, then the distribution of the syndrome $t = Ae \pmod{q}$ is statistically close to uniform over $\mathbb{Z}_q^n$.*

2.4 Hardness Assumption

The security of our signature scheme rests on the hardness of SIS problem [3].

Definition 3. *Given an integer $q > 0$, a matrix $A \in \mathbb{Z}_q^{n \times m}$ and a real γ, the SIS problem is finding a vector $v \in \mathbb{Z}^m \backslash \{0\}$ such that $Av = 0 \pmod{q}$ and $||v|| \leq \gamma$.*

For the hardness of SIS problem, Micciancio and Regev [14] have showed that, for any polynomial-bounded m, γ and for any prime $q \geq \gamma \cdot \omega(\sqrt{n \log n})$, solving SIS on the average is as hard as approximating some intractable lattice problems such as the shortest lattice vector problem in the worst case.

2.5 Short Bases of Lattices

Short basis of a lattice is an important concept in many lattice-based cryptographic schemes. Here, we recall two useful theorems on short lattice bases. The first theorem is adapted from Lemma 3.5 of [4] that shows a recent result on how to generate a short basis of an approximate uniform lattice. The second theorem comes from [10] that is about how to use a short lattice basis to solve a kind of SIS problems.

Theorem 1. *Let $q \geq 3$ be odd and $m > 5n \log q$. There is a probabilistic polynomial-time (PPT) algorithm TrapGen(q, n) that outputs a matrix $A \in \mathbb{Z}_q^{n \times m}$ and a basis $B \in \mathbb{Z}^{m \times m}$ of $\Lambda^\perp(A)$ such that A is statistical close to uniform, and $||B|| \leq O(n \log q)$ and $||\tilde{B}|| \leq O(\sqrt{n \log q})$ with overwhelming probability.*

Theorem 2. *Let $m \geq n$ be an integer and q be prime. Let $\Lambda^\perp(A)$ be a lattice defined by matrix $A \in \mathbb{Z}_q^{n \times m}$ and B be a basis of $\Lambda^\perp(A)$. If $s \geq ||\tilde{B}|| \cdot \omega(\sqrt{\log n})$, then for any $u \in \mathbb{Z}_q^n$, there is a PPT algorithm SamplePre(A, B, s, u) that outputs a vector $v \in \Lambda^u(A)$ from a distribution that is statistically close to $G_{\Lambda^u(A),s}$.*

2.6 Discrete Normal Distribution

This work will also make use of the discrete normal distribution.

Definition 4. *For any $\sigma > 0$ and $c \in \mathbb{Z}^m$, define the continuous normal distribution as:*

$$\rho_{\sigma,c}^m(x) = (2\pi\sigma^2)^{-\frac{m}{2}} \exp(-\frac{||x - c||^2}{2\sigma^2}).$$

Let $\rho_{\sigma,c}^m(\mathbb{Z}^m)$ be a sum of $\rho_{\sigma,c}^m$ over $\mathbb{Z}^m$. The discrete normal distribution over $\mathbb{Z}^m$ centered at $c \in \mathbb{Z}$ with parameter σ is defined as

$$D_{\sigma,c}^m(x) = \rho_{\sigma,c}^m(x)/\rho_{\sigma,c}^m(\mathbb{Z}^m).$$

In the rest of the paper, we will abbreviate $\rho_{\sigma,0}^m$ and $D_{\sigma,0}^m$ as ρ_σ^m and D_σ^m.

The following lemma shows two basic properties of such distributions [13,14].

Lemma 2. *For any $\sigma > 0$ and positive integer m, we have:*

1. $Pr[x \leftarrow D_\sigma^1 : |x| > 12\sigma] < 2^{-100}$.
2. $Pr[\boldsymbol{x} \leftarrow D_\sigma^m : ||\boldsymbol{x}|| > 2\sigma\sqrt{m}\,] < 2^{-m}$.

Lyubashevsky [13] also shows the following interesting fact on the distribution.

Lemma 3. *For any $\boldsymbol{v} \in \mathbb{Z}^m$ and positive real α, if $\sigma = \omega(||\boldsymbol{v}||\sqrt{\log m})$, we have*

$$Pr[\boldsymbol{x} \leftarrow D_\sigma^m : D_\sigma^m(\boldsymbol{x})/D_{\sigma,v}^m(\boldsymbol{x}) = O(1)] = 1 - 2^{\omega(\log m)},$$

and more specifically, if $\sigma = \alpha||\boldsymbol{v}||$, then

$$Pr[\boldsymbol{x} \leftarrow D_\sigma^m : D_\sigma^m(\boldsymbol{x})/D_{\sigma,v}^m(\boldsymbol{x}) < e^{12/\alpha+1/(2\alpha^2)}] > 1 - 2^{-100}.$$

2.7 Rejection Sampling Technique

The core idea of rejection sampling technique for a signature scheme is to make the distribution of the outputted signatures is independent of signing key. To achieve this goal, rejection sampling technique works as follows. When signing a message, a signer with signing key s first chooses a random y from some distribution and computes the candidate signature sig that is in the form of y adding to (or multiplying by) some function of s. Let the target distribution of the outputted signatures be f which is independent of s, and let the distribution of all candidate signatures be g which may be related to s. If $f(x) \leq Mg(x)$ for all x and some real $M > 0$, then the candidate signature sig can be output with probability $f(\text{sig})/(Mg(\text{sig}))$. By [21], we know if the signer follows the above process, then the distribution of the outputted signatures is f and the expected number of times this process will output a signature is M.

As an example of how to use the rejection sampling technique, consider the signature scheme of Lyubashevsky [13]. Its target distribution is D_σ^m. To sign a message μ, first select a random $\mathbf{y}$ from D_σ^m and compute $\mathbf{z} = \mathbf{y} + \mathbf{Sc}$, where $\mathbf{S}$ is a signing key and $\mathbf{c}$ is a hash value on the inputs of $\mathbf{y}$ and μ. The candidate signature is $(\mathbf{c}, \mathbf{z})$. Notice that the $\mathbf{z}$'s distribution is $D_{\sigma,\mathbf{Sc}}^m$ and, by Lemma 3, $D_\sigma^m(\mathbf{y})/D_{\sigma,\mathbf{Sc}}^m(\mathbf{y}) \approx e$. Therefore, according to the rejection sampling technique, we know there exists a small $M(\approx e)$ such that if we output the candidate signature $(\mathbf{c}, \mathbf{z})$ with possibility $\min(1, \frac{D_\sigma^m(\mathbf{z})}{MD_{\sigma,\mathbf{Sc}}^m(\mathbf{z})})$ then $\mathbf{z}$'s distribution is D_σ^m (in this case, by Lemma 2, we have $||\mathbf{z}|| \leq 2\sigma\sqrt{m}$ with a high probability) and the expected number of running the signing process is no more than M.

3 Matrix Sampling Algorithm

In our construction, we need an efficient algorithm to extract each user's signing key that is a short matrix $\mathbf{S}$ satisfying $\mathbf{AS} = \mathbf{U} \pmod{q}$ for some user-defined matrix $\mathbf{U}$. We address this problem by introducing the algorithm SampleMat that is an extension of the preimage sampling algorithm SamplePre of [10].

The algorithm SampleMat$(\mathbf{A}, \mathbf{B}, s, \mathbf{U})$ works as follows.

1. Input $\mathbf{A} \in \mathbb{Z}_q^{n \times m}$ and $\mathbf{U} \in \mathbb{Z}_q^{n \times k}$, a basis $\mathbf{B}$ of $\Lambda^\perp(\mathbf{A})$ and parameter $s \geq \|\widetilde{\mathbf{B}}\| \cdot \omega(\sqrt{\log n})$.
2. For each $i \in [k]$, run algorithm SamplePre$(\mathbf{A}, \mathbf{B}, s, \mathbf{u}_i) \to \mathbf{s}_i \in \mathbb{Z}^m$.
3. Output $\mathbf{S} = [\mathbf{s}_1, \cdots, \mathbf{s}_k] \in \mathbb{Z}^{m \times k}$.

By Theorem 2, we know, for any $\mathbf{u} \in \mathbb{Z}_q^n$, the algorithm SamplePre$(\mathbf{A}, \mathbf{B}, s, \mathbf{u})$ will sample a vector $\mathbf{v} \in \Lambda^{\mathbf{u}}(\mathbf{A})$ from a distribution that is statistically close to $G_{\Lambda^{\mathbf{u}}(\mathbf{A}), s}$. Therefore, we can easily check that the output $\mathbf{S}$ of the above algorithm SampleMat$(\mathbf{A}, \mathbf{B}, s, \mathbf{U})$ satisfies $\mathbf{AS} = \mathbf{U} \pmod{q}$ and its distribution is statistically close to $G_{\Lambda^{\mathbf{u}_1}(\mathbf{A}), s} \times \cdots \times G_{\Lambda^{\mathbf{u}_k}(\mathbf{A}), s}$ (thus $\|\mathbf{S}\| \leq s\sqrt{m}$ with overwhelming probability by Lemma 1). As a result, we have the following lemma.

Lemma 4. *Let $m \geq n$ and $k \geq 2$ be positive integers, and let q be prime. Let $\Lambda^\perp(\boldsymbol{A})$ be a lattice defined by matrix $\boldsymbol{A} \in \mathbb{Z}_q^{n \times m}$ and $\boldsymbol{B}$ be a basis of $\Lambda^\perp(\boldsymbol{A})$. If parameter $s \geq \|\widetilde{\boldsymbol{B}}\| \cdot \omega(\sqrt{\log n})$, then for any $\boldsymbol{U} \in \mathbb{Z}_q^{n \times k}$, there is a PPT algorithm SampleMat$(\boldsymbol{A}, \boldsymbol{B}, s, \boldsymbol{U})$ that outputs a matrix $\boldsymbol{S} \in \mathbb{Z}^{m \times k}$ from a distribution that is statistically close to $G_{\Lambda^v(\boldsymbol{A}), s}$ such that $\boldsymbol{AS} = \boldsymbol{U} \pmod{q}$ and $\|\boldsymbol{S}\| \leq s\sqrt{m}$ with overwhelming probability, where $G_{\Lambda^v(\boldsymbol{A}), s} = G_{\Lambda^{\boldsymbol{u}_1}(\boldsymbol{A}), s} \times \cdots \times G_{\Lambda^{\boldsymbol{u}_k}(\boldsymbol{A}), s}$.*

4   An Efficient IBS Scheme from Lattices

We here give the description of our efficient IBS scheme based on lattices.

4.1   Construction

Our IBS construction involves a few parameters defined below:

- prime $q \geq 3$, real M, $m > 5n \log q$, k, λ are all positive integers.
- bound $\widetilde{L} = O(\sqrt{n \log q})$, Gaussian parameter $s = \widetilde{L} \cdot \omega(\sqrt{\log n})$, $\sigma = 12s\lambda m$.

The IBS scheme works as follows.

Setup(n). Given a security parameter n, do the following:

1. Run TrapGen(q, n) to output an approximate uniform matrix $\mathbf{A} \in \mathbb{Z}_q^{n \times m}$ along with a basis $\mathbf{B} \in \mathbb{Z}_q^{m \times m}$ of $\Lambda^\perp(\mathbf{A})$ such that $\|\widetilde{\mathbf{B}}\| \leq \widetilde{L}$.
2. Select two hash functions $H : \{0, 1\}^* \to \{\mathbf{v} : \mathbf{v} \in \{-1, 0, 1\}^k, \|\mathbf{v}\|_1 \leq \lambda\}$ and $H_1 : \{0, 1\}^* \to \mathbb{Z}_q^{n \times k}$.
3. Output the public parameters $params = \{\mathbf{A}, H, H_1\}$ and PKG's secret key $SK = \mathbf{B}$.

Extract$(params, SK, ID)$. Given the public parameters $params$, PKG's secret key $SK = \mathbf{B}$ and an identity $ID \in \{0,1\}^*$, run algorithm Sam-
pleMat$(\mathbf{A}, \mathbf{B}, s, H_1(ID))$ to obtain a signing key $sk_{ID} = \mathbf{S}_{ID} \in \mathbb{Z}^{m \times k}$ for
the user with identity ID. The correctness of $\mathbf{S}_{ID}$ can be verified by check-
ing if $\mathbf{A}\mathbf{S}_{ID} = H_1(ID)$ and $\|\mathbf{S}_{ID}\| \leq s\sqrt{m}$.

Sign$(params, \mu, sk_{ID})$. Given the public parameters $params$, a message $\mu \in$
$\{0,1\}^*$ and a signing key $sk_{ID} = \mathbf{S}_{ID}$, do the following:

1. Select a random $\mathbf{y} \leftarrow D_\sigma^m$.
2. Compute $\mathbf{h} = H(\mathbf{A}\mathbf{y}, \mu)$ and $\mathbf{z} = \mathbf{S}_{ID}\mathbf{h} + \mathbf{y}$.
3. Output $\text{sig} = (\mathbf{h}, \mathbf{z})$ with probability $\min(1, \frac{D_\sigma^m(\mathbf{z})}{MD_{\sigma, \mathbf{S}_{ID}\mathbf{h}}^m(\mathbf{z})})$. If nothing is
   outputted, repeat the algorithm Sign$(params, \mu, sk_{ID})$.

Verify$(params, \text{sig}, \mu, ID)$. Given the public parameters $params$, a signature
$\text{sig} = (\mathbf{h}, \mathbf{z})$, a message μ and an identity ID, output 1 if and only if
$\mathbf{h} = H(\mathbf{A}\mathbf{z} - H_1(ID)\mathbf{h}, \mu)$ and $\|\mathbf{z}\| \leq 2\sigma\sqrt{m}$.

4.2 Correctness

Theorem 3. *The identity-based signature scheme above satisfies correctness.*

Proof. According to the construction of the IBS scheme, we know that

$$\mathbf{A}\mathbf{z} - H_1(ID)\mathbf{h}$$
$$= \mathbf{A}\mathbf{z} - \mathbf{A}\mathbf{S}_{ID}\mathbf{h}$$
$$= \mathbf{A}(\mathbf{z} - \mathbf{S}_{ID}\mathbf{h})$$
$$= \mathbf{A}\mathbf{y}$$

Therefore, we have $H(\mathbf{A}\mathbf{z} - H_1(ID)\mathbf{h}, \mu) = H(\mathbf{A}\mathbf{y}, \mu) = \mathbf{h}$.

By simply combining the rejection sampling technique described in Section
2.7 with Lemma 3, we know the distribution of $\mathbf{z}$ is very close to D_σ^m. Therefore,
by Lemma 2, we have $\|\mathbf{z}\| \leq 2\sigma\sqrt{m}$ with probability at least $1-2^{-m}$.

4.3 Efficiency

The most efficient (presently known) lattice-based IBS schemes are those ones
that are secure in the random oracle model, e.g., the IBS schemes[1] proposed respectively by Rückert [17] and Tian et al. [20]. We now compare the performance
of our IBS scheme to that of the two schemes.

Table 1 lists the comparison on the communication overhead of the three schemes
for the same security parameter n, where the constant c is the bit length of all identities in Rückert's scheme with random oracle, $\bar{s} = s\sqrt{(c+1)m}\omega(\sqrt{\log n})$ and
$\hat{s} = s \cdot m\omega(\log^{3/2} n)$ are extended Gaussian parameters, and other parameters are

---

[1] Notice that these IBS schemes are both generalized ones, i.e., they may have more
than two hierarchies. For comparability, we here set their hierarchy depth as 2 (including the PKG).

Table 1. Comparison of several lattice-based IBS schemes

Scheme	Signing key size	Signature size
Rückert [17] with RO	$(m(c+1))^2 \log(\bar{s}\sqrt{(c+1)m})$	$m(c+1)\log(\bar{s}\sqrt{(c+1)m}) + n$
Tian et al. [20]	$m^2 \log(\hat{s}\sqrt{m})$	$m \log(\hat{s}\sqrt{m}) + n$
This work	$mk \log(s\sqrt{m})$	$m \log(12\sigma) + \lambda(\log k + 1)$

the same as those in Section 4.1. Since $m \gg k$ and $n \gg \lambda(\log k + 1)$ for reasonable security (e.g., 512 bits or more), one can easily check that the signing key size and the signature length of our scheme are both much smaller than those of Rückert's scheme as well as those of Tian et al.'s scheme.

In terms of computation complexity, we can see that the signing and verification algorithms of our scheme are very simple because they only take matrix-vector multiplication, integer addition and hash operations, whereas signing a message in the schemes of Rückert and Tian et al. both need to run the more complicated algorithm SamplePre. Moreover, the signing key extraction algorithm in our scheme is the algorithm SampleMat, which is much faster than the algorithm RandBasis used in the extraction algorithms of Rückert and Tian et al.'s schemes.

Therefore, we can conclude that our IBS scheme is more efficient than other lattice-based ones in terms of both communication and computation overhead.

4.4   Security

Theorem 4. *The proposed identity-based signature scheme is existential unforgeable against adaptive chosen message and identity attacks in the random oracle model, assuming the hardness of SIS problem.*

The proof of Theorem 4 will appear in the full version of this paper.

5   Conclusion

In this paper, we presented the first lattice-based IBS scheme that dose not employ the signature framework of [10]. We proved its security in the random oracle model under the SIS assumption. Our IBS scheme is more efficient than others based on lattices. We believe the ideas and techniques used in this work will also be helpful for designing other lattice-based signatures.

Acknowledgements. This work was partially supported by the National Natural Science Foundation of China (No. 61202407), the Basic Perspective Project of SGCC (No. XXN51201304253), and the Natural Science Foundation of Jiangsu Province of China (No. BK2011357).

References

1. Agrawal, S., Boneh, D., Boyen, X.: Efficient lattice (h)ibe in the standard model. In: Gilbert, H. (ed.) EUROCRYPT 2010. LNCS, vol. 6110, pp. 553–572. Springer, Heidelberg (2010)

2. Agrawal, S., Boneh, D., Boyen, X.: Lattice basis delegation in fixed dimension and shorter-ciphertext hierarchical ibe. In: Rabin, T. (ed.) CRYPTO 2010. LNCS, vol. 6223, pp. 98–115. Springer, Heidelberg (2010)
3. Ajtai, M.: Generating hard instances of lattice problems. In: STOC 1996, pp. 99–108. ACM (1996)
4. Alwen, J., Peikert, C.: Generating shorter bases for hard random lattices. Theory of Computing Systems 48(3), 535–553 (2011)
5. Barreto, P.S.L.M., Libert, B., McCullagh, N., Quisquater, J.-J.: Efficient and provably-secure identity-based signatures and signcryption from bilinear maps. In: Roy, B. (ed.) ASIACRYPT 2005. LNCS, vol. 3788, pp. 515–532. Springer, Heidelberg (2005)
6. Boneh, D., Franklin, M.: Identity-based encryption from the weil pairing. In: Kilian, J. (ed.) CRYPTO 2001. LNCS, vol. 2139, pp. 213–229. Springer, Heidelberg (2001)
7. Cash, D., Hofheinz, D., Kiltz, E., Peikert, C.: Bonsai trees, or how to delegate a lattice basis. In: Gilbert, H. (ed.) EUROCRYPT 2010. LNCS, vol. 6110, pp. 523–552. Springer, Heidelberg (2010)
8. Choon, J.C., Cheon, J.H.: An identity-based signature from gap diffie-hellman groups. In: Desmedt, Y.G. (ed.) PKC 2003. LNCS, vol. 2567, pp. 18–30. Springer, Heidelberg (2002)
9. Fiat, A., Shamir, A.: How to prove yourself: practical solutions to identification and signature problems. In: Odlyzko, A.M. (ed.) CRYPTO 1986. LNCS, vol. 263, pp. 186–194. Springer, Heidelberg (1987)
10. Gentry, C., Peikert, C., Vaikuntanathan, V.: Trapdoors for hard lattices and new cryptographic constructions. In: STOC 2008, pp. 197–206. ACM (2008)
11. Hess, F.: Efficient identity based signature schemes based on pairings. In: Nyberg, K., Heys, H.M. (eds.) SAC 2002. LNCS, vol. 2595, pp. 310–324. Springer, Heidelberg (2003)
12. Liu, Z., Hu, Y., Zhang, X., Li, F.: Efficient and strongly unforgeable identity-based signature scheme from lattices in the standard model. Security and Communication Networks 6(1), 69–77 (2013)
13. Lyubashevsky, V.: Lattice signatures without trapdoors. In: Pointcheval, D., Johansson, T. (eds.) EUROCRYPT 2012. LNCS, vol. 7237, pp. 738–755. Springer, Heidelberg (2012)
14. Micciancio, D., Regev, O.: Worst-case to average-case reductions based on gaussian measures. SIAM J. Computing 37(1), 267–302 (2007)
15. Paterson, K.G., Schuldt, J.C.N.: Efficient identity-based signatures secure in the standard model. In: Batten, L.M., Safavi-Naini, R. (eds.) ACISP 2006. LNCS, vol. 4058, pp. 207–222. Springer, Heidelberg (2006)
16. Regev, O.: Lattice-based cryptography. In: Dwork, C. (ed.) CRYPTO 2006. LNCS, vol. 4117, pp. 131–141. Springer, Heidelberg (2006)
17. Rückert, M.: Strongly unforgeable signatures and hierarchical identity-based signatures from lattices without random oracles. In: Sendrier, N. (ed.) PQCrypto 2010. LNCS, vol. 6061, pp. 182–200. Springer, Heidelberg (2010)
18. Shamir, A.: Identity-based cryptosystems and signature schemes. In: Blakely, G.R., Chaum, D. (eds.) CRYPTO 1984. LNCS, vol. 196, pp. 47–53. Springer, Heidelberg (1985)
19. Shor, P.W.: Polynomial-time algorithms for prime factorization and discrete logarithms on a quantum computer. SIAM J. Computing 26(5), 1484–1509 (1997)
20. Tian, M., Huang, L., Yang, W.: Efficient hierarchical identity–based signatures from lattices. Int. J. Electronic Security and Digital Forensics 5(1), 1–10 (2013)
21. Von Neumann, J.: Various techniques used in connection with random digits. J. Research Nat. Bur. Stand., Appl. Math. Series 12(1), 36–38 (1951)

Context-Aware Multifactor Authentication
Based on Dynamic Pin

Yair H. Diaz-Tellez[1], Eliane L. Bodanese[1], Theo Dimitrakos[2], and Michael Turner[2]

[1] School of Electronic Engineering and Computer Science, Queen Mary University of London,
London, United Kingdom
{y.diaz-tellez,eliane.bodanese}@qmul.ac.uk
[2] Security Futures Practice, BT Innovate and Design, British Telecommunications
Ipswich, United Kingdom
{theo.dimitrakos,michael.turner}@bt.com

Abstract. An innovative context-aware multi-factor authentication scheme based on a dynamic PIN is presented. The scheme is based on graphical passwords where a challenge is dynamically produced based on contextual factors and client device constraints while balancing security assurance and usability. The approach utilizes a new methodology where the cryptographic transformation used to produce the Dynamic PIN changes dynamically based on the user input, history of authentications, and available authentication factors at the client device.

Keywords: authentication, dual ciphers, context-aware, dynamic PIN.

Introduction

User authentication is a means of identifying a user and verifying his identity. Different authentication methods exist, e.g. token-based, biometric-based, and knowledge-based. Each method has its own properties, (dis)advantages, and applications. Text passwords are a widely used method because of convenience and usability; however, they are vulnerable to key logging, shoulder-surfing, dictionary, and social engineering attacks. Graphical passwords are an alternative as they can mitigate the above-mentioned attacks. One approach to increase assurance is multi-factor authentication. However, not all transactions require the same assurance level. An adequate level depends on criticality, sensitivity, context, and the risk involved. Additionally, there are trade-offs among variables such as assurance, performance, and usability.

This work proposes an innovative context-aware multi-factor authentication scheme based on a Dynamic PIN. The scheme produces a graphical challenge based on context, client device constraints, and risk associated, while balancing assurance and usability. Also, a methodology is proposed where the crypto-function used to produce the Dynamic PIN changes dynamically. A PIN is generated without any predictable backward and forward correlation making practically infeasible for an attacker to predict the next PIN. The approach leverages on the fact that users commonly use various types of client devices that incorporate authentication factors

N. Cuppens-Boulahia et al. (Eds.): SEC 2014, IFIP AICT 428, pp. 330–338, 2014.
© IFIP International Federation for Information Processing 2014

(e.g. SIM cards, biometric readers, etc.), sensors, and APIs, which can be integrated in the authentication process to modulate security assurance, and to optimize it using context.

Section 2 presents related work. The scheme consists of two functional phases: **registration and setup**: the user creates an account and registers different information (section 3); and **challenge and dynamic PIN**: a challenge and Dynamic PIN are generated (section 4). Section 5 presents the conclusions and future work.

Related Work

The proposed scheme considers how the properties of graphical passwords[1] can be adjusted at runtime balancing assurance vs. usability. In [2], a PIN-based mechanism is presented that uses a secret sequence of objects to analyze security vs. usability. This work does not consider the use of contextual information to influence the generation of the challenge. Several frameworks have been proposed that make use of context [3, 4]. [5] introduces the notion of implicit authentication that consists in authenticating users based on behavioral patterns. [6] presents a framework that combines passive factors (e.g. location) and active factors (e.g. tokens) in a probabilistic model for selecting an authentication scheme that satisfies security requirements; however, it does not consider client device constraints.

Security tokens, implementable on hardware[7] and software[8], typically generate a one-time-password (OTP)[9] in response to the user typing a PIN. Several token-based systems feature a fixed function that outputs the OTP [10-14]. The proposed system is effectively a software-based security token that produces an OTP, i.e. the Dynamic PIN; and additionally, the crypto-function used changes itself dynamically improving the pseudo-randomness of the scheme.

Registration and Setup

Registering Authentication Factors. The scheme uses authentication factors that may be available on the client device, e.g. SIM number, or fingerprint. For each factor, the server creates a record and associates a secret seed generated ly, $(af_{name_i}, af_{value_i}, af_{seed_i})$ with af_i an authentication factor. For example, (IMSI, 464989052765867, 4596). A vector of secret seeds is pushes into the device. An authentication token is computed by $AuthNToken = PBKDF2(concat((af_{value_i} + af_{seed_i})))$. PBKDF2, a Key Derivation Function, is used to derive a key strong against brute force attacks. A token vector is defined as $AuthNTokenVector = AuthNToken_1, AuthNToken_2, ... AuthNToken_m$, where m is the number of authentication factors registered for a device. The client must recreate the same token calculated at the server side. Notice that the value af_{value_i} is obtained at runtime.

Registering the Image-Based Password(s). The user is presented with a selection of image categories, $\mathbb{C} = \{C_1, C_2, C_3, \dots\}$. Each category consists of image objects grouped by common characteristics easy to understand, e.g. icons. Let category $C = (o_1, o_2, o_3, .. o_n) \in \mathbb{C}$ be a set of n objects. A seed is randomly generated for each object o_i. Let $seedsVector = (seed_1, seed_2, seed_3, .. seed_n)$ be the vector of seeds with $(o_i, seed_i) \in (C \times seedsVector)$. Each $seed_i$ is of 2 bytes length and represented as 4 hexadecimal digits (0-F). The user selects a subset of objects as his secret password: $secretSequence \subset C$. For $|n| \gg |secretSequence|$ a brute force attack can become increasingly difficult as the number of combinations and permutations increases.

Registering Device Parameters. This includes form factor parameters about the device(s): type of device, display size, authentication interfaces – e.g. biometrics. These are used to specify at runtime an adequate customization of the image challenge.

Challenge and Dynamic PIN Generation

Overview. Steps: (i) the server generates a random pin string (RPS) and the graphical challenge. The RPS is used as part of the dynamic pin generation algorithm. The challenge is constructed by combining a subset of secret and non-secret images based on device constraints, context, and level of assurance required. Due to lack of space, it is assumed the communication channel between client and server is secured. A key exchange protocol, e.g. Diffie Hellman, can be easily incorporated in the scheme. (2) the user is asked to recognize the subset of secret images; (3) a crypto-function is computed dynamically based on different variable elements of information including user input, authentication factors, and history of authentication attempts; (4) the crypto-function is then used to generate the dynamic pin; (5) the client device sends the dynamic pin to the server for validation.

4.1   Generation of the RPS and the Context-Based Image Challenge

In this section, first the random pin string (RPS) and the image challenge are introduced. Then, a rules-based mechanism used to parameterize and generate the challenge based on runtime context information, device constraints, and risk is presented.

Random Pin String (RPS). The RPS is a synchronization value used during the computation of the dynamic pin. The RPS is a pseudo-randomly generated string of 160 bytes in length: $RPS = RPB_1 RPB_2 RPB_3 \dots RPB_{159}, \text{ where } RPB_i \text{ is a byte}$.

Image Challenge. The image challenge is the set $ChallengeImages = (SecretImages \cup NonSecretImages), \text{with cardinality } |q + p|$ where: (i) $SecretImages \subset secretSequence, \text{with cardinality } |SecretImages| = q$, a subset of images selected from the $secretSequence \subset C$ that contains the image password objects selected by the user at registration; and (ii) $NonSecretImages = C \setminus SecretSequence, \text{with cardinality } |NonSecretImages| = p$, , where the relative complement of $secretSequence$ in C is the set of elements in C, but not in $secretSequence$: $C \setminus secretSequence = \{o \in C \dashv | o \notin secretSequence\}$.

Security Strength of the Challenge and Usability. Fig. 1(a) shows an example of a challenge represented as a grid of icons where $q = 5$, $p = 20$, and $n = 25$ (the greyed images represent the secret).

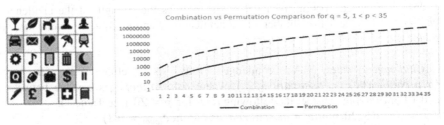

Fig. 1. (a) Example of an image challenge, (b) Combination vs. Permutation Functions

The security strength of the challenge depends on the values of p and q, and on the mode in which the user is asked to recognize the secret images. In the combination mode images are recognized in any order: $n!/(n-q)!\,(q)!$. In permutation mode images are recognized according to the sequence registered: $n!/((n-q)!)$. In both cases, $n = q + p$. Fig. 2(b) illustrates, in logarithmic scale, the speed at which the number of possible combinations (and therefore the security strength) for a challenge with $q = 5$ increases for different values of p ($1 < p < 35$) for the permutation and combination modes. As illustrated, permutation mode provides higher security over combination mode. However, such increase in security is inversely proportional to usability since it is easier for the user to recognize the 5 secret images without having to recall the exact sequence.   Table 1 compares the modes for different p and q.

Table 1. Comparison combination vs. permutation for different p and q

Chart Area	p	n	Combination mode	Permutation mode
	20	24	10626	255024
5	20	25	53130	6375600
6	20	26	230230	1.66E+08
4	30	34	46376	1113024
5	30	35	324632	38955840
6	30	36	1947792	1.4E+09

Rules-Based Challenge Generation, Usability vs Security Assurance. A challenge is generated at runtime taking into account: client device constraints, contextual factors and risk associated, the level of authentication assurance required, and usability.

Client device constraints. A client device constraint is defined as a tuple ($device\_id, parameter, p$) where p (see Table 1) is an estimate of the size of the challenge. For instance, a laptop has a larger screen than a smartphone and can display a challenge with a larger number of image objects $n = q + p$,

    1.   ($smartphone_{abc}, screen_{size} = 5$ inch, 20)

Contextual rules. This refers to contextual factors that carry a level of risk. A contextual rule is defined as a tuple ($context_{parameter_1}, ..., context_{parameter_x}$,

$risk\_level$) where $risk_{level}$ is a value between 0 and 1. For example, consider an employee authenticating to a corporate server and the following contextual rules:

2.   ($location = HOME, time = ANY, risk_{level} = MEDIUM = 0.5$)

In the proposed system, the level of risk defines the strength of the challenge – *challenge rules*; and the number of authentication factors required –*authentication factor rules*.

Challenge rules. A challenge rule is defined as a tuple $(q, p, challenge_{mode}, assurance_{level})$. where $assurance_{level}$ is a value between 0 and 1 For example consider the following rules for $p = 20$ (see Table 1):

3.   ($5, 20, mode = unordered, assurance_{level} = 0.3$)
4.   ($6, 20, mode = unordered, assurance_{level} = 0.5$)
5.   ($4, 20, mode = ordered, assurance_{level} = 0.5$)

Notice that rules 4 and 5 are given the same $assurance_{level}$. This is because the number of possible combinations and permutations for these two rules are of similar order of magnitude, 230230 and 255024(see Table 1).

Authentication factor rules. An authentication factor rule is defined as a tuple $\left(number_{authentication\,factors}, risk_{level}\right)$ and indicates the number of authentication factors required given some risk level. For instance:

6. $\left(authentication_{factors} = 1,\ risk_{level} = LOW = 0.2\right)$
7. $\left(authentication_{factors} = 2,\ risk_{level} = MEDIUM = 0.5\right)$

Example. Assume rules (1) and (2) are applicable. In such case, then rules (4) and (5) would hold true, i.e. p=20 and $assurance_{level} \geq risk_{level}$. And between (4) and (5), (4) would be the optimal choice since it mitigates the present level of risk and provides the best option in terms of usability, i.e. unordered recognition mode. Rule (4) enforces p=20 and q=6 to generate the challenge. Similarly, rule (7) would hold true, i.e. $assurance_{level} \geq risk_{level}$, and enforces the use of at least two authentication factors, i.e. the challenge itself, and an additional factor, e.g. IMSI.

4.2   User Response to the Challenge

The user responds to the challenge by selecting the secret images. The algorithm then retrieves the secret images' seeds and performs an XOR operation over them whose result is a pin of 4 hexadecimal digits (hex_i) in length: $UserPIN = seed_{1'} \oplus seed_{2'} \oplus seed_{3'} \oplus ... \oplus seed_{|secretImages|} = hex_1 hex_2 hex_3 hex_4$, where each element $seed_{i'}$ corresponds to an element $seed_i \in seedsVector$ (i.e. $seed_{i'} \xrightarrow{f} seed_i$). The value $UserPIN$ along with the value RPS are taken as input parameters to the cryptographic transformation that calculates the dynamic pin.

4.3   Computation of the Cryptographic Transformation Function

A Substitution Box (S-Box) is a component used in cryptosystems to perform substitutions in a way that relations between output and input bits are highly non-linear.

This protects against cryptanalysis. An S-Box designed to be resistant to linear and differential cryptanalysis is the Rijndael S-Box[15]. The design was made balancing security and computational efficiency. The security strength of crypto-algorithms based on S-Boxes can be improved by changing the S-Box dynamically (e.g. Blowfish). This makes more difficult to carry out an attacks without knowing what S-Box to associate to a given output. To increase the pseudo-randomness of the dynamic PIN, it is proposed to use an S-Box that can be obtained dynamically, complies with strong security design criteria and crypto-properties, and that can be generated using a deterministic technique based on parameters known to both client and server. Barkan et al. [16] show that by replacing the irreducible polynomial and the affine transformation in the Rijndael S-Box it is possible to produce dual ciphers with the same cryptographic properties of the original S-Box. This result is used here to propose an indexing technique that allows selecting different dual ciphers, i.e. S-Boxes. In the next subsections the mathematical definitions that support the formulation of the indexing technique are presented along with the proposed indexing function(s).

Rijndael S-box[15]. The Rijndael S-box is an algebraic operation that takes in an element of the Galois Field $GF(2^8)$ and outputs another element of $GF(2^8)$, where $GF(2^8)$ is viewed as the finite field $\frac{GF(2)[X]}{(X^8+X^4+X^3+X+1)}$ of polynomials over the finite field $GF(2)$ reduced modulo by the polynomial $X^8+X^4+X^3+X+1$. The operation has 2 steps: (i) find the multiplicative inverse of the input over $GF(2^8)$ (0 is sent to 0); and (ii) apply the affine transformation $Ax + b$ where x is the result of the first step, (in Rijndael) A is a specific 8×8 matrix with entries in $GF(2)$ and b is a specific vector with 8 entries in $GF(2)$, both specifically chosen to make it resistant to linear and differential cryptanalysis. Elements in $GF(2^8)$ are represented as bytes and transformations can be pre-computed and represented as a lookup matrix.

Dual Ciphers[16]. Two ciphers E and E' are called Dual Ciphers if they are isomorphic, that is to say there exists three invertible transformations f, g, h such that $E_K(P) = f(E'_{g(K)}(h(P)))$ $\forall P, K$, where P is the plain text and K is the key. Different cipher can be created from an original cipher while keeping the original's algebraic properties because of the isomorphism.

Square Dual Cipher of the Rijndael S-box[16]. If the constants of the Rijndael S-box (denote the Rijndael S-box E) are replaced such that: (i) it is replaced A with A^2 where A^2 is not simply the square of the matrix, it is equal to QAQ^{-1} where Q is an 8×8 matrix chosen such that $Qx = x^2$ for all x. As a side result this also means that $QAQ^{-1}x = (Ax)^2$; and (ii) b is replaced with b^2. Hence it can be shown that these transformations result in a dual cipher (let it be denoted E^2). It can be seen that $A^2x + b^2 = QAQ^{-1}x + Qb = Q(A(Q^{-1}x) + b)$. Hence making these transformations (and creating the square dual cipher) is equivalent to applying a pre and post matrix multiplication on the original Rijndael S-box. This same transformation can be applied to E^2 to obtain E^4 and similarly for $E^8, E^{16}, E^{32}, E^{64}$ and E^{128} ($E^{256} = E$).

Modifying the Polynomial of the Rijndael S-box[16]. Recall that the first operation of the Rijndael S-box is to find the multiplicative inverse of the input over $GF(2^8)$. There are a total of 30 irreducible polynomials of degree 8, of which the Rijndael selected $X^8+X^4+X^3+X+1$. As different fields $GF(2)[X]/f(X)$ for different irreducible polynomials $f(X)$ of the same degree are isomorphic, there exist a linear transformation which can be represented as a binary matrix R such that R takes an element of the Rijndael case and outputs an element of the new case with the changed polynomial. The matrix R is of the form $R = (1, a, a^2, a^3, a^4, a^5, a^6, a^7)$ where $a^{i'}s$ are computed modulo the new irreducible polynomial. Hence R can be used in the same way as Q was used in the previous: applying a pre and post matrix multiplication on the original Rijndael S-box $R(S(R^{-1}x))$. As there are 30 irreducible polynomials, each of which has the 8 squared ciphers this totals $8 \times 30 = 240$ different dual ciphers. In the book of Rijndaels [17] the 240 dual ciphers of Rijndael are presented including the matrices Rs and the $R^{-1}s$. Here they are used in the following way on the original Rijndael S-box to create a new S-box: $S_{new}(X) = R \times SRijndael(R^{-1} \times X)$, with $SRijndael$ the original Rijndael S-Box matrix.

Indexing the Dual Ciphers of the Rijndael S-box. In the proposed scheme, an indexing technique is used for the 240 distinct dual ciphers of Rijndael (in [18] the number of possible dual ciphers has been extended to 9120). An indexing function is defined, i.e. $index_{new}$, to determine what dual cipher, out of the 240, to use to generate a new S-Box, i.e. $S_{new}(X)$. $index_{new}$ takes as input authentication tokens $AuthNToken_i$, the seeds associated to $SecretImages$ and $NonSecretImages$, and the index value of the last successful authentication. The proposed indexing function has two variants dependent recognition mode: permutation or combination.

Let $DualCipherMatrices = ((R_1, R_1^{-1}), (R_2, R_2^{-1}), ..., (R_{240}, R_{240}^{-1}))$ be the vector of Dual Ciphers' matrices $(R_{index}, R_{index}^{-1})$ where $0 \leq index < 240$. The two indexing function are defined as follows: (combination mode) $index_{new} = (index_{current} + \sum_{i=1}^{l} AuthNToken_i + \sum_{SecretImages} seeds + \sum_{NonSecretImages} seeds) \bmod 240$; and (permutation mode) $index_{new} = (index_{current} + \sum_{i=1}^{l} AuthNToken_i + \sum_{k=1}^{q=|SecretImages|} k \times seed_k + \sum_{NonSecretImages} seeds) \bmod 240$, with $t_{index_{current}} < t_{index_{new}}$, *with time t*.

In permutation mode each $seed_k$ is multiplied by the index k forcing the result to depend on order. Both variants of $index_{new}$ output an integer between 0 and 239 that is used to select $(R_{index_{new}}, R_{index_{new}}^{-1}) \in DualCipherMatrices$, and to determine the new S-Box transformation: $S_{new}(X) = R_{index_{new}} \times SRijndael(R_{index_{new}}^{-1} \times X)$. $S_{new}(X)$ takes as input a byte and outputs another byte.

4.4   Generation of Dynamic PIN (*DynPIN*)

The dynamic pin, *DynPIN*, is generated by performing iterative substitutions through the transformation function, $S_{new}(X)$, using the values $UserPIN$ and RPS.

Recall that $UserPIN = hex_1 hex_2 hex_3 hex_4$, where $0 \ll hex_i \ll F$, is 2 bytes long, that is, each hexadecimal digit hex_i is a nibble (half byte), and that $RPS = RPB_1 RPB_2 RPB_3 ... RPB_{159}$, is 160 bytes long. Each byte RPB_i is composed by a more significant and a less significant part, *nibble* RPB_i^H *and nibble* RPB_i^L. The dynamic pin is defined $DynPIN = byte_1 byte_2 byte_3 byte_4$.

Each $byte_i$ digit is computed as the result of a chain of 7 substitutions between $UserPIN$ (2 bytes long) and 2 bytes of RPS, and 7 iterations through the s-box $S_{new}(X)$. Fig. 2 shows the sequence of substitutions to produce $byte_1$. In the diagram each arrow indicates one iteration through $S_{new}(X)$. During each iteration, $S_{new}(X)$

takes as input one byte consisting of two nibbles: a hexadecimal digit of $UserPIN$ and a nibble of RPB_i; and outputs a new byte, hereafter S_i. The following are the 7 iterations performed to generate $byte_1$:

$$S_{new}(hex_1, RPB_0{}^H) = S_1$$
$$S_{new}(S_1{}^H, RPB_0{}^L) = S_2$$
$$S_{new}(S_2{}^L, hex_2) = S_3$$
$$S_{new}(S_3{}^H, hex_3) = S_4$$
$$S_{new}(S_4{}^L, RPB_1{}^H) = S_5$$
$$S_{new}(S_5{}^H, RPB_1{}^L) = S_6$$
$$S_{new}(S_6{}^L, hex_4) = S_7 = b.$$

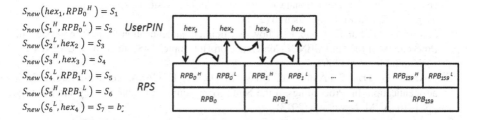

Fig. 2. Chain of substitutions and S-Box iterations to generate $byte_1$ of $DynPIN$

The same process is repeated for the other digits, $byte_2, byte_3, and\ byte_4$, but using a different starting byte of RPS for each digit. To achieve this, the RPS is split into 4 quarters (each one 40 bytes long), and the previous digit ($byte_{i-1}$) of $DynPIN$ viewed as an integer, 0 to 255, and reduced modulo 40, is used to determine a starting byte in RPS. The starting byte in RPS for $byte_i$ is calculated as follows: $Z = (40 * j) + Y$, where $Y = |(byte_{i-1})_{10}|_{40}$. Z is the starting byte in the RPS used to calculate $byte_2$ ($j = 1$), $byte_3 (j = 2), and\ byte_4 (j = 3)$. Thus the starting byte in the RPS is randomized within each quarter block of the RPS. Once all the digits are computed, the dynamic pin is sent to the server for validation. The server executes the same algorithm and verifies the dynamic pin sent by the user.

Conclusions and Future Work

This paper presented a context-based multi-factor authentication system based on a dynamic PIN. A novel crypto-function has been proposed that changes dynamically based on the user input, history of authentications, and authentication factors at the client device. The dynamic aspect of the crypto-function increases the pseudo-randomness of the scheme and provides strong protection against cryptanalysis. The scheme generates a challenge based on context, takes into account risk and tunes assurance vs. usability criteria. In addition to the standard client-server workflow scenario, the proposed scheme has been implemented as a software security token that displays the Dynamic PIN and the user types it on a web interface. The synchronization between client and server via the web interface uses QR-Codes and the client device's camera. The prototype is being validated.

References

1. Xiaoyuan, S., Ying, Z., Owen, G.S.: Graphical passwords: a survey. In: 21st Annual Computer Security Applications Conference, pp. 10 pp. 472 (Year)
2. Catuogno, L., Galdi, C.: A Graphical PIN Authentication Mechanism with Applications to Smart Cards and Low-Cost Devices. In: Onieva, J.A., Sauveron, D., Chaumette, S., Gollmann, D., Markantonakis, K. (eds.) WISTP 2008. LNCS, vol. 5019, pp. 16–35. Springer, Heidelberg (2008)

3. Bardram, J.E., Kjær, R.E., Pedersen, M.Ø.: Context-Aware User Authentication – Supporting Proximity-Based Login in Pervasive Computing. In: Dey, A.K., Schmidt, A., McCarthy, J.F. (eds.) UbiComp 2003. LNCS, vol. 2864, pp. 107–123. Springer, Heidelberg (2003)

4. Corner, M.D., Noble, B.D.: Protecting applications with transient authentication. In: Proceedings of the 1st International Conference on Mobile Systems, Applications and Services, pp. 57–70. ACM, San Francisco (2003)

5. Jakobsson, M., Shi, E., Golle, P., Chow, R.: Implicit authentication for mobile devices. In: Proceedings of the 4th USENIX Conference on Hot Topics in Security, p. 9. USENIX Association, Montreal (2009)

6. Hayashi, E., Das, S., Amini, S., Hong, J., Oakley, I.: CASA: context-aware scalable au-thentication. In: Proceedings of the Ninth Symposium on Usable Privacy and Security, pp. 1–10. ACM, Newcastle (2013)

7. http://www.safenet-inc.com/products/data-protection/two-factor-authentication/gold-challenge-response/

8. Aloul, F., Zahidi, S., El-Hajj, W.: Two factor authentication using mobile phones. In: IEEE/ACS International Conference on Computer Systems and Applications, AICCSA 2009, pp. 641-644 (Year)

9. Lamport, L.: Password authentication with insecure communication. Commun. ACM 24, 770–772 (1981)

10. Dodson, B., Sengupta, D., Boneh, D., Lam, M.S.: Secure, Consumer-Friendly Web Authentication and Payments with a Phone. In: Gris, M., Yang, G. (eds.) MobiCASE 2010. LNICST, vol. 76, pp. 17–38. Springer, Heidelberg (2012)

11. Gianluigi, M., Pirro, D., Sarrecchia, R.: A mobile based approach to strong authentication on Web. In: International Multi-Conference on Computing in the Global Information Technology, ICCGI 2006, p. 67 (2006)

12. Wen-Bin, H., Jenq-Shiou, L.: Design of a time and location based One-Time Password authentication scheme. In: 2011 7th International Wireless Communications and Mobile Computing Conference (IWCMC), pp. 201–206 (2011)

13. Soare, C.A.: Internet Banking Two-Factor Authentication using Smartphones (2012)

14. Eldefrawy, M.H., Khan, M.K., Alghathbar, K., Kim, T.-H., Elkamchouchi, H.: Mobile one-time passwords: two-factor authentication using mobile phones. Security and Communication Networks 5, 508–516 (2012)

15. Daemen, J., Rijmen, V.: AES Proposal: Rijndael. Submitted to the Advanced Encryption Standard (AES) contest (1998)

16. Barkan, E., Biham, E.: In How Many Ways Can You Write Rijndael? In: Zheng, Y. (ed.) ASIACRYPT 2002. LNCS, vol. 2501, pp. 160–175. Springer, Heidelberg (2002)

17. Barkan, E., Biham, E.: The book of Rijndaels. Cryptology ePrint Archive, Report 2002/158 (2002), http://eprint.iacr.org/2002/158

18. Raddum, H.: More Dual Rijndaels. In: Dobbertin, H., Rijmen, V., Sowa, A. (eds.) AES 2005. LNCS, vol. 3373, pp. 142–147. Springer, Heidelberg (2005)

Authorship Attribution for Forensic Investigation with Thousands of Authors

Min Yang and Kam-Pui Chow

Department of Computer Science, Faculty of Engineering
The University of Hong Kong, Hong Kong
{myang,chow}@cs.hku.hk

Abstract. With the popularity of computer and Internet, a growing number of criminals have been using the Internet to distribute a wide range of illegal materials and false information globally in an anonymous manner, making criminal identity tracing difficult in the cybercrime investigation process. Consequently, automatic authorship attribution of online messages becomes increasingly crucial for forensic investigation. Although researchers have got many achievements, the accuracies of authorship attribution with tens or thousands of candidate are still relatively poor which is generally among 20%~40%, and cannot be used as evidence in forensic investigation. Instead of asserting that a given text was written by a given user, this paper proposes a novel authorship attribution model combining both profile-based and instance-based approaches to reduce the size of the candidate authors to a small number and narrow the scope of investigation with a high level of accuracy. To evaluate the effectiveness of our model, we conduct extensive experiments on a blog corpus with thousands of candidate authors. The experimental results show that our algorithm can successfully output a small number of candidate authors with high accuracy.

1 Introduction

With the development of Internet technologies and online social network, web services (e.g., emails, blogs, forums and micro-blogs) become a means by which new ideas and information spread rapidly. However, since people on the virtual space do not need to provide their real identities, accurate automatic authorship attribution of anonymous documents is increasingly requisite in various cyber-criminal scenarios, including online fraud detection, terror message origination, article counterfeit and plagiarism detection. Authorship attribution techniques can assist law enforcement to discover criminals who supply false information in their virtual identities, and collect digital evidence for cybercrime investigation.

Automatic authorship attribution is a problem of computationally inferring the author of an anonymous text or text whose authorship is in doubt[15]. Generally, authorship attribution approaches fall into two major categories: the profile-based approaches and the instance-based approaches[3,4,14,22]. For the profile-based approach, a single representation (i.e., profile) is produced for each

N. Cuppens-Boulahia et al. (Eds.): SEC 2014, IFIP AICT 428, pp. 339–350, 2014.
© IFIP International Federation for Information Processing 2014

author using training data. Each text of unknown authorship is then compared with the profile of each author and is assigned to the most likely one. The profile-based approach is able to handle very short texts since they concatenate all the texts by the same author. For the instance-based approach, it produces one representation per training text, and a classification model is built to estimate the most likely author of a anonymous text. Compared with the profile-based approach, the instance-based approach is easier to combine different text representation features, and it is more robust when the size of candidate authors set is large. Further study[12] shows that profile-based and instance-based approaches could be complementary to each other, and combining these two approaches can significantly improve the performance of author attribution.

Most of the previous works on authorship attribution focus on formal texts with only a few possible authors by applying statistics [3] and machine learning approaches [4,14,22]. Unfortunately, this version of the authorship attribution problem dose not often arise in the real world. Recently, researchers have turned their attention to informal texts (e.g., emails and social blogs) and tens to thousands of authors [17,11,19,16,12,10,20]. For example, Koppel et al. [10] use similarity-based methods along with multiple randomized feature set to achieve high precision when the set of known candidates is extremely large (many thousands). To conquer the challenge that there are not enough labeled examples to construct an accurate classifier, some semi-supervised learning approaches for authorship attribution have been proposed. These approaches usually use the test data as unlabeled examples to improve the classification model [7,12]. Considering the content of documents and the interests of authors, the author-topic model has been used for authorship attribution [20], which yield a state-of-the-art performance in terms of classification accuracy when tens or thousands of candidate authors are taken into account.

Although researchers have got many achievements, the accuracies of authorship attribution with tens or thousands of candidate are still relatively poor, which are generally among 20%~40% [16,10,20]. The traditional authorship attribution approaches cannot be used as evidence in forensic investigation since a quite accurate prediction is required for digital forensics, and it is useless in the sense that we could never confidently assert that a given text was written by a given user. In this paper, we propose a novel hierarchical authorship attribution algorithm combining both profile-based and instance-based approaches to reduce the size of the candidate authors and narrow the scope of investigation with a high level of accuracy. First, we apply profile-based paradigm to build two classifiers with different feature sets for gender and age attribution respectively. And then, a authorship attribution classifier is built using the probabilities distribution of gender and age attribution obtained in the previous step as prior. With this classifier, we can obtain a small number of the most possible authors from thousands of candidate authors with a high level of accuracy that is higher than a threshold (e.g., 95%). At last, we output a set of most possible authors with probabilities. Extensive experiments have been conducted to verify the proposed approach on real-world blog dataset.

The rest of this paper is organized as follows. In Section 2, we review related work in authorship attribution. In Section 3, we introduce our model and algorithm used in this paper. In Section 4, we presents the experiment data and experimental setting. In Section 5, the experiment results are showed and discussed. Finally, Section 6 concludes the paper and indicates some future works.

2 Related Work

In resent years, plenty of statistical and machine learning techniques have been proposed for authorship attribution using different kinds of features [13,1]. Stamatatos details most of the existing techniques for automatic authorship attribution in [21]. Generally speaking, authorship attribution approaches can be classified into two groups: profile-based approaches and instance-based approaches. Profile-based approaches concatenate training texts per author in one single text file. An unseen text is, then, compared with each author file, and the most likely author is estimated based on a distance measure. For example, Keselj, et al.[9] propose a widely used n-grams profile-based method, which is based on building a byte-level n-gram author profile of an author's writing. Frantzeskou et al. [6] proposed a novel and simple distance, called simplified profile intersection (SPI), which simply counts the amount of common n-grams of the two author profiles. This approach to authorship identification of source code provide better results than other distances. In order to utilize the differences between the training texts by the same author, the majority of the modern authorship attribution approaches are instance-based, which consider each training text sample as a unit that contributes separately to the authorship attribution. Such as, Burrows [2] presents principal components analysis with word frequencies to analyze authorship, and the results show a high level accuracy. Peng et al. [18] extend the naive Bayes algorithm for authorship attribution with statistical language models. Halteren [8] proposes a method that borrows some elements from both profile-based and instance-based approaches.

To conquer the challenges that there are not enough labeled examples to construct an accurate classifier, some semi-supervised learning approaches have been proposed since it is possible to use the test sets as unlabeled examples and use some information from them to improve the classification model [7,12]. Guzman et al. [7] propose a self-learning method that is specially suited to work with just a few training examples to tackle the problem that lacks of training data with the same writing style. That method considers the automatic extraction of the unlabeled examples from the web and its iterative integration into the training data set. Kourtis and Stamatatos [12] apply a co-training learning approach for authorship attribution by combining the Common N-Grams (CNG) [9] model and a Support Vector Machine classifier based on character n-grams. Its main idea is to combine the outputs of these classifiers in the test set and augment the training set with additional document.

Most of the previous works consider the simple version of the authorship attribution problems, and focus on formal texts with only a small, closed set of candidate authors. In order to apply authorship attribution in real life data, some large candidate sets with informal texts have been considered by researchers recently. Luyckx and Daelemans [16] propose a memory-based learning approach in doing authorship attribution with many authors and limited training data, and the results show the robustness of the memory-based learning approach when compared to eager learning methods such as SVMs and maximum entropy learning. Madigan et al. [17] conduct experiments on a collection of data released by Reuters consisting of 114 authors using sparse Bayesian logistic regression. This proposed algorithm shows promising performance as a tool for authorship attribution with high-dimensional document representations. Different from the approaches mentioned above, our algorithm take author's profile information (e.g., age and gender) into consideration, which is motivated by the analysis conducted by Schler et al. in [19] indicating significant differences in writing style and content between male and female bloggers as well as among authors of different ages. In addition, instead of asserting that a anonymous text was written by a given user, our authorship attribution algorithm proposes to reduce the size of the candidate authors and narrow the scope of investigation with a high level of accuracy.

3   The Proposed Method

In this section, we describe a novel authorship attribution algorithm combining both profile-based and instance-based approaches to reduce the size of the candidate authors and narrow the scope of investigation with a high level of accuracy. Generally, the proposed algorithm consists of two phase, as shown in Figure 1. In the first phase, we apply profile-based paradigm to build two classifiers with different feature sets for gender and age attribution, respectively. The probability distribution of gender and age can be used as a prior for the next phase. In the second phase, a logistic regression classifier is built using the probability distribution of gender and age as prior based on instance-based paradigms. With this classifier, we can obtain a small number of the most possible authors from thousands of candidate authors with a high level of accuracy that is higher than a threshold.

3.1   Features Selection

In this work, we consider differences in male and female authors and differences among authors of different ages. Broadly speaking, two different kinds of potential distinguishing features can be considered: content-based features and style-based features . This is motivated by the observation that different people might tend to write about different topics as well as to express themselves differently about the same topic. For style-based features, we consider individual parts-of-speech and function words, which is described by Eggins in [5]. Content-based features are simple content words, and we apply unigrams in this work. For gender, we choose 2000 features with greatest information gain for gender.

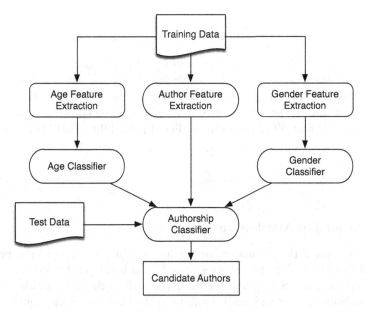

Fig. 1. Algorithm Overview

And for age, we choose 2000 features with greatest information gain for age. Similarly, 2000 features with greatest information gain for author are selected to train the classifier for authorship attribution.

3.2 Age and Gender Attribution

For each author, we concatenate all his documents and extract both content-based features and style-based features from them. To present the document with extracted features, we represent a document as a numerical vector $X = (x_1, \ldots, x_i, \ldots, x_n)$, where n is the number of features and x_i is the relative frequency of feature i in the document. Once labeled training documents have been represented in this way, we can apply machine-learning algorithms to learn classifiers that assign new documents to categories. In this paper, we use logistic regression [13] to learn two classifier that classify texts according to author's gender and age, respectively. Logistic regression is widely used for classification problems recently, and the independent variables do not have to be normally distributed, or have equal variance in each group. What's more, logistic regression is more than just a classifier. Instead, it can make stronger and more detailed predictions such as the predicted probabilities. Consider a binary supervised leaning problem, where were given a set of instance-label pairs $\{(x_i, y_i) \mid i = 1, \ldots, n\}$. Here, $x_i \in R^M$ is an M-dimensional feature vector, and $y_i \in \{0, 1\}$ is the class label. Formally, the logistic regression model which predicts the conditional probability distribution of the class label y given the input feature vector x is that

$$\Pr(Y = 1|X; \beta_0, \beta) = \pi(x; \beta_0, \beta) = \frac{1}{1 + \exp(-(\beta_0 + x \cdot \beta))} \tag{1}$$

Where $\beta \in R^M$ is the coefficient vector of X, and β_0 is the intercept term. $\pi(x; \beta_0, \beta)$ is the probability of the outcome of interest. For multi-class classification problem, we can still use logistic model. Assume Y can take k values, instead of having one set of parameters β_0 and β, each class c will have its own parameters $\beta_0^{(c)}$ and $\beta^{(c)}$, then the predicted probability distribution will be

$$\Pr(Y = 1|X; \beta_0^{(c)}, \beta^{(c)}) = \pi(x; \beta_0^{(c)}, \beta^{(c)}) = \frac{1}{1 + \exp(-(\beta_0^{(c)} + x \cdot \beta^{(c)}))} \tag{2}$$

3.3   Authorship Attribution

After we obtained the estimator for gender and age, we can use the predicted probabilities for gender and sex as a prior for authorship attribution.

Given documents S for an unknown author, given the information of all candidate authors' gender and age information, the probability distribution for authorship attribution is given by

$$p\,(author = i|S, gender, age\_class) \propto p\,(author = i|S) \cdot p\,(gender(i)|S) \cdot p\,(age\_class(i)|S) \tag{3}$$

where the first term acts like a likelihood, and the second and third terms served as priors.

$p\,(author = i|S)$ is estimated with an instance-based approach, i.e. we estimate the likelihood for each instance documents separately, and multiply the probabilities together to get the combined probability

$$p(author|S) \propto \prod_i p(author|S_i) \tag{4}$$

4   Experiments

4.1   Dataset Description

The Blog Authorship Corpus consists of 678,161 blog posts of 19,320 bloggers gathered by Schler et al. [19] from blogger.com in August 2004. There are approximately 35 posts and 7250 words per person. The blog posts can be about any topic, but the large number of authors ensures that every topic is likely to interest at least some authors. The (self-reported) age and gender of each author is known and for each age interval the corpus includes an equal number of male and female author based on the author's reported age, we label each blog in our corpus as belonging to one of three age groups: 13-17 (42.7%), 23-27 (41.9%) and 33-47 (15.5%).

Algorithm 1. Hierarchical Author Identification

- Given N documents written by K authors $\boldsymbol{X} = \{x_1, \ldots, x_N\}$ and their authorship labels $\boldsymbol{y} = \{y_1, \ldots, y_N\}$, where $y_i \in \{1, \ldots, K\}$.
- For each author $i \in \{1, \ldots, K\}$, we have $gender(i) \in \{M, F\}$ and $age\_class(i) \in$ {teenagers, young adults, middle-aged}.
- Gender attribution
  - Extract features $\boldsymbol{X}^{(g)}$ for gender classifier using stylistic features and content-based features selected by information gain for gender
  - Use $\boldsymbol{X}^{(g)}$ and $\boldsymbol{y}^{(g)} = \{gender(y_1), \ldots, gender(y_N)\}$ to train a gender classifier with profile-based paradigm
  - Given documents $\boldsymbol{S}$ from an unknown author, the gender classifier can estimate the probability distribution $p(gender|\boldsymbol{S})$ for $gender \in \{M, F\}$.
- Age class attribution
  - Extract features $\boldsymbol{X}^{(a)}$ for age classifier using stylitic features and content-based features selected by information gain for age class
  - Use $\boldsymbol{X}^{(a)}$ and $\boldsymbol{y}^{(a)} = \{age\_class(y_1), \ldots, age\_class(y_N)\}$ to train an age classifier with profile-based paradigm
  - Given documents $\boldsymbol{S}$ from an unknown author, the gender classifier can estimate the probability distribution $p(age\_class|\boldsymbol{S})$ for $age\_class \in$ {teenagers, young adults, middle-aged}.
- Authorship attribution
  - Use $\boldsymbol{X}$ and $\boldsymbol{y}$ to train an authorship classifier using instance-based pradigm
  - Given documents $\boldsymbol{S}$ from an unknown author, the authorship classifier can estimate the probability distribution $p(author|\boldsymbol{S})$ using 4.
  - For any author i, calculate thhe posterior probability with author's gender and age class distribution as prior using 3.
  - Output M authors $\{a_1, \ldots, a_M\}$ who have highest posterior probability. The number M of authors to output is chosen to ensure $\sum p(author = a_i) > threshold$.

Since some blogs in this corpus are meaningless for authorship attribution, such as advertisements and lyrics of songs, we first remove the authors who wrote smaller than 20 blogs. And then, we use Akismet[1] to remove the potential spams among these authors. Finally, we obtain 2,077 prolific authors with their full posts as our training data. The statistics of the dataset is shown in Table 1.

4.2 Experimental Setup

In the experiments, data preprocessing was performed on both data sets. First, the texts are tokenized with a natural language toolkit NLTK[2]. Then, we remove non-alphabet characters, numbers, pronoun, punctuation and stop words from

---

[1] http://akismet.com/

[2] http://www.nltk.org

Table 1. Dataset statistics

Age	Gender		
	Female	Male	Total
13~17	335	348	683
23~27	543	503	1046
33~47	170	178	348
Total	1048	1029	2077

the texts. Finally, WordNet stemmer[3] is applied so as to reduce the vocabulary size and settle the issue of data spareness.

For all experiments, we perform ten-fold cross validation, and the results are evaluated using classification accuracy, i.e., the percentage of test documents that were correctly assigned the author. What's more, L1-regularized logistic regression is used to train the classifiers, which is well-suited for large-scale text classification. Here, LIBLINEAR[4] is used as the implementation of logistic regression classifier. We experiment with cost parameter valued from the set $\{0.01, 0.1, 1, 10\}$, until no accuracy improvement was obtained.

5   Experimental Results

In this section, we present and discuss the experimental results in details.

5.1   Gender and Age Attribution Results

For gender attribution, we consider it as a binary classification problem with the class label female and male. Accuracies of gender attribution are shown in the first line of Table 2. From Table 2, we observe that the proposed algorithm can obtain 85.1% accuracy with the combined features, which is 3.2% higher than that using style-based features and 5.9% higher than that using content-based features.

For age attribution, we label each blog in our corpus as belonging to one of three age groups {teenagers, young adults, middle-aged}, based on author's reported age. The age attribution problem in this paper can be treated as a multiclass L1-regularised logistic regression problem. Results for age attribution are shown in the second line of Table 2. Similar to gender attribution, we can gain the best performance with 80.1% accuracy using both style and content features.

---

[3] http://wordnet.princeton.edu

[4] http://www.csie.ntu.edu.tw/~cjlin/liblinear/

Table 2. Accuracies of gender and age attribution using various feature sets

Task	Style features	Content features	Style and content features
Gender attribution	81.9%	79.2%	**85.1%**
Age attribution	70.5%	78.3%	**80.1%**

Based on the results in Table 2, we can summarize that authors' gender and age information might be highly helpful for authorship attribution because of the high accuracies of gender and age attribution on the blog dataset. With the probability distribution gained from gender and age attribution, most of the candidate authors who have different profiles (i.e., gender and age) with the author of anonymous documents, can be filtered in authorship attribution.

5.2   Authorship Attribution Results

To evaluate the effectiveness of our approach, we compared the proposed algorithm with standard logistic regression and Disjoint Author-Document Topic Model (DADT) used in [20], utilizing the same features. We report the classification accuracies in Table 3. As an easy observation, the proposed hierarchical authorship attribution algorithm significantly outperforms the other algorithms that are widely used for authorship attribution. For example, The accuracy of our algorithm is 3.7% higher than DADT model and 7.4% higher than standard logistic regression, validating the effectiveness of the proposed algorithm.

Table 3. Accuracies of three authorship attribution algorithm

Algorithm	Style features	Content features	Style and content feature
Logistic regression	23.6%	27.4%	32.1%
DADT	**30.5%**	31.3%	35.8%
Proposed algorithm	29.2%	**32.6%**	**39.5%**

Although our algotithm achieves state-of-the-art performance compared to the existing model for authorship attribution, it cannot produce a practicable and authentic result for forensics in real life. Hence, instead of classifying a given text to a specific author with relatively low accuracy, we seek to output a small number of potential candidate authors with a high level of accuracy. The experiment result of our proposed hierarchical authorship attribution is described in Figure 2. With the accuracy of 96.5%, we can narrow down the size of candidates authors from 2,000 to 20. Furthermore, we can get 100% accuracy

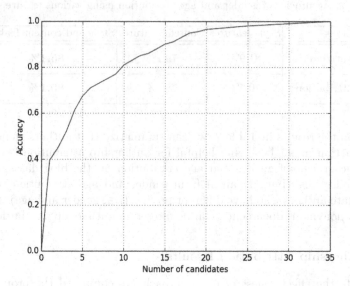

Fig. 2. Accuracy with different number of candidate authors

when choosing 35 candidate authors from the original experimental dataset. These results show that our model can help investigator to narrow the scope of investigation with a high level of accuracy. The advantages of our approach comes from its capability of taking the probability distribution gained from gender and age attribution, as prior knowledge to filter many easily confused candidate authors.

6   Conclusions and Future Work

In this paper, we introduce a hierarchical classifier which combines profile-based and instance-based paradigms to automatic authorship attribution in cases with a large number of informal texts from thousands of authors. Instead of predicting a author with relatively low accuracy, we seek to reduce the size of the candidate authors and narrow the scope of investigation with a high level of accuracy. The mainly advantage of our approach comes from its capability of taking the probability distribution gained from gender and age attribution, as prior knowledge to filter many easily confused candidate authors. Extensive experimental results indicate that our algorithm can successfully output a small number of candidate authors with high accuracy. For example, we can choose 20 potential candidate authors from 2000 candidates with the accuracy of 96.5%, and the probability of each candidate authors can be output to assist the investigators.

Our approach performed well for closed-set tasks, while it cannot be applied to open-set tasks in which the true author of an anonymous text might not be one of the known candidates. In the future, we will devote our effort to extend the proposed hierarchical classifier to handle the open-set tasks by assessing classification confidence. Another possible research direction is to deal with the imbalance problem where a relatively small number of text at least for some candidate authors compared to other candidates.

References

1. Abbasi, A., Chen, H.: Applying authorship analysis to extremist-group web forum messages. IEEE Intelligent Systems 20(5), 67–75 (2005)
2. Burrows, J.F.: An ocean where each kind: Statistical analysis and some major determinants of literary style. Computers and the Humanities 23(4-5), 309–321 (1989)
3. Coifman, R.R., Victor Wickerhauser, M.: Entropy-based algorithms for best basis selection. IEEE Transactions on Information Theory 38(2), 713–718 (1992)
4. De Vel, O., Anderson, A., Corney, M., Mohay, G.: Mining e-mail content for author identification forensics. ACM Sigmod Record 30(4), 55–64 (2001)
5. Eggins, S.: Introduction to systemic functional linguistics. Continuum International Publishing Group (2004)
6. Frantzeskou, G., Stamatatos, E., Gritzalis, S., Katsikas, S.: Effective identification of source code authors using byte-level information. In: Proceedings of the 28th International Conference on Software Engineering, pp. 893–896. ACM (2006)
7. Guzmán-Cabrera, R., Montes-y-Gómez, M., Rosso, P., Villaseñor-Pineda, L.: A Web-Based Self-training Approach for Authorship Attribution. In: Nordström, B., Ranta, A. (eds.) GoTAL 2008. LNCS (LNAI), vol. 5221, pp. 160–168. Springer, Heidelberg (2008)
8. Van Halteren, H.: Author verification by linguistic profiling: An exploration of the parameter space. ACM Transactions on Speech and Language Processing (TSLP) 4(1), 1 (2007)
9. Kešelj, V., Peng, F., Cercone, N., Thomas, C.: N-gram-based author profiles for authorship attribution. In: Proceedings of the Conference Pacific Association for Computational Linguistics, PACLING, vol. 3, pp. 255–264 (2003)
10. Koppel, M., Schler, J., Argamon, S.: Authorship attribution in the wild. Language Resources and Evaluation 45(1), 83–94 (2011)
11. Koppel, M., Schler, J., Argamon, S., Messeri, E.: Authorship attribution with thousands of candidate authors. In: Proceedings of the 29th Annual International ACM SIGIR Conference on Research and Development in Information Retrieval, pp. 659–660. ACM (2006)
12. Kourtis, I., Stamatatos, E.: Author identification using semi-supervised learning. In: CLEF 2011: Proceedings of the 2011 Conference on Multilingual and Multimodal Information Access Evaluation (Lab and Workshop Notebook Papers), Amsterdam, The Netherlands (2011)
13. Lee, S.-I., Lee, H., Abbeel, P., Ng, A.Y.: Efficient l¯ 1 regularized logistic regression. In: Proceedings of the National Conference on Artificial Intelligence, vol. 21, p. 401. AAAI Press, MIT Press, Menlo Park, Cambridge (1999, 2006)
14. Li, J., Zheng, R., Chen, H.: From fingerprint to writeprint. Communications of the ACM 49(4), 76–82 (2006)
15. Love, H.: Attributing authorship: An introduction. Cambridge University Press (2002)

16. Luyckx, K., Daelemans, W.: Authorship attribution and verification with many authors and limited data. In: Proceedings of the 22nd International Conference on Computational Linguistics, vol. 1, pp. 513–520. Association for Computational Linguistics (2008)
17. Madigan, D., Genkin, A., Lewis, D.D., Argamon, S., Fradkin, D., Ye, L.: Author identification on the large scale. In: Proc. of the Meeting of the Classification Society of North America (2005)
18. Peng, F., Schuurmans, D., Wang, S.: Augmenting naive bayes classifiers with statistical language models. Information Retrieval 7(3-4), 317–345 (2004)
19. Schler, J., Koppel, M., Argamon, S., Pennebaker, J.W.: Effects of age and gender on blogging. In: AAAI Spring Symposium: Computational Approaches to Analyzing Weblogs, pp. 199–205 (2006)
20. Seroussi, Y., Bohnert, F., Zukerman, I.: Authorship attribution with author-aware topic models. In: Proceedings of the 50th Annual Meeting of the Association for Computational Linguistics: Short Papers-Volume 2, pp. 264–269. Association for Computational Linguistics (2012)
21. Stamatatos, E.: A survey of modern authorship attribution methods. Journal of the American Society for Information Science and Technology 60(3), 538–556 (2009)
22. Zheng, R., Qin, Y., Huang, Z., Chen, H.: Authorship analysis in cybercrime investigation. In: Chen, H., Miranda, R., Zeng, D.D., Demchak, C.C., Schroeder, J., Madhusudan, T. (eds.) ISI 2003. LNCS, vol. 2665, pp. 59–73. Springer, Heidelberg (2003)

Detection and Labeling of Personal Identifiable Information in E-mails

Christoph Bier and Jonas Prior

Fraunhofer Institute of Optronics,
System Technologies and Image Exploitation IOSB, Karlsruhe, Germany
{christoph.bier,jonas.prior}@iosb.fraunhofer.de

Abstract. The protection of personal identifiable information (PII) is increasingly demanded by customers and data protection regulation. To safeguard PII a organization has to find out which incoming communication actually contains it. Only then PII can be labeled, tracked, and protected. E-mails are one of the main means of communication. They consist of unstructured data difficult to classify. We developed an automated detection system for PII in e-mails and connected it to a usage control infrastructure. Our concept is based on previous findings in the area of spam detection. We tested our approach with a data set in a customer service scenario. The evaluation shows that the utilization of Bayes-classification is very promising to detect PII.

1 Introduction

The European data protection regulation (95/46/EC) requires enterprises, e.g., telecommunication providers, to comply with the clients' privacy rights, to ensure the protection of personally identifiable information (PII) and to fulfill the right to information. The right to information entitles the data subject to request from the data controller information on origin, transfer, and purpose of processing of his PII at any time. Thus, the usage and processing of PII needs to be safeguarded and controlled by detection, labeling and tracking. With the tremendous growth of data, it is not feasible to do that ad hoc. As a solution, usage control and provenance tracking methods [1] are proposed in recent research. But one of the major and yet unsolved problems remains: How does one know which received or created data contains PII? How can privacy policies and PII come together? Up to now, this is mostly done manually. But it is not yet possible to detect unstructured PII and annotate them with policies automatically.

As one of the most frequently used means of communication between clients and companies, especially in customer service, e-mails offer a rich source of PII. Many of them contain highly confidential customer data like banking accounts, usage patterns or contractual data, while many others like internal e-mails and newsletters do not. Overall, PII in e-mails is heterogeneous and therefore difficult to identify.

N. Cuppens-Boulahia et al. (Eds.): SEC 2014, IFIP AICT 428, pp. 351–358, 2014.

In this paper we present a model that can recognize e-mails containing PII and annotate them with policies (section 2). Our idea is to apply spam filter technologies to the classification of PII in incoming e-mails.

We design an integrated model of PII detection, usage control and provenance tracking, that can attach and enforce policies for sensitive data in order to protect them. A prototype is developed as part of a mail user agent to show the general feasibility of our idea (section 3). An extensive evaluation based on realistic test data shows that our approach is reasonably justified and promising (section 4).

2   Classification

PII are heterogeneous and differ from scenario to scenario. Therefore, an automatic learning system has to be developed to detect e-mails containing PII. The classification of such e-mails is a binary text classification problem meaning that there is one class with PII and one without PII. The issue is equivalent to the spam filter problem where e-mails need to be classified in good (ham) or bad ones (spam).

A frequently used algorithm for binary text classification is the Naive Bayes classifier. *Naive* refers to the assumption that the occurrence of the features, in this case the words of the e-mail, are distributed independently. But this assumption does not hold for textual data. The Naive Bayes classifier estimates a probability for each class based on previously classified data. The best class is the one with the highest probability (*maximum a posteriori*) [2]. Thus, for each class a probability is calculated. The prior knowledge $P(c_j)$ of each class is multiplied by the product of all $P(a_i|c_j)$. $P(a_i|c_j)$ is the conditional probability that the term a_i occurs in class c_j based on previously classified data.

$$c_{map} = \arg\max_{c_j \in C} P(c_j) \prod_{i=1}^{n} P(a_i|c_j) \tag{1}$$

Naive Bayes is the basis of most spam filters [3]. The most widely used model of spam filters is based on Graham's and Robinson's ideas [4, 5]. Robinson extended Graham's work by customizing the conditional probability $P(a_i|c_j)$ in order to deal with rare words that occur only in one class. Furthermore, he used the Fisher method to combine the conditional probabilities into a χ^2-distribution with *2n* degrees of freedom. In his model, an e-mail can be classified as *unsure* when the classifier is not sure about the correct class. The conditional probabilities for the classes c_{ham} and c_{spam} are combined into a χ^2-distribution $\chi_{2n}^2 = -2\ln(\prod_{i=1}^{n}(P(a_i|c_{spam})))$.

For the second class a χ^2-distribution can be defined by replacing $P(a_i|c_{ham})$ with $1 - P(a_i|c_{spam})$ because it is $P(a_i|c_{ham}) = 1 - P(a_i|c_{spam})$ due to the binary classification task. The inverse χ_{2n}^2-function χ_{2n}^{-2} is applied to both χ^2-distributions to calculate a score for each class (H and S). The Equation for score H is $H = \chi_{2n}^{-2}(-2\ln(\prod_{i=1}^{n}(P(a_i|c_{spam}))))$.

Finally the two scores are combined into a single score $I = \frac{1+H-S}{2}$ with values between 0 and 1.

We use this approach and substitute the two classes *ham* and *spam* with *PII* and *noPII*. The classifier learns from e-mails marked as *PII* or *noPII* and the calculation of the scores I remains the same. The classification of the e-mails then is done by defining two thresholds t_{noPII} and t_{PII}:

$$class = \begin{cases} \text{PII} & \text{if } t_{PII} > I > 0 \\ \text{unsure} & \text{if } t_{noPII} \geq I \geq t_{PII} \\ \text{noPII} & \text{if } 1 > I > t_{noPII} \end{cases} \qquad (2)$$

If the classification returns the class *unsure.* then the user has to do the classification manually. If $t_{noPII} + t_{PII} = 1$, then there is no third class *unsure.*

3 Architecture

The scenario of privacy policies requires to combine the classification of textual information proposed in the foregoing section with usage control and provenance tracking technologies. Hence, we have developed an overall architecture described in the first part of this section forming the framework for these components. Following, the structure of the PII-detector is clarified. An instantiation shows the practical applicability of our approach.

The Usage Control and Provenance Architecture. Our PII-detector is embedded in an architecture to enable usage control and provenance tracking of the sensitive data contained in detected e-mails. A basic usage control architecture consists of a policy enforcement point (PEP), a policy decision point (PDP) and a policy information point (PIP). The PEP is integrated in each application or system where policies have to be enforced in. Every time an event (like "copy" or "delete") is detected, the PEP informs the PDP and asks if the event is allowed or not. The PDP decides this request based on the deployed policies. In the case of data-centered policies [6], the PDP asks the PIP if the container (e.g., files, e-mails) mentioned in the event contains data referred to in one of the deployed policies. If the PDP allows the event to happen, the information flow model of the PIP is updated. Provenance tracking takes advantage of the information flow state represented by the PIP and provides comprehensive information to the person concerned (data subject) [1].

The process of introducing a PII-containing e-mail to the infrastructure is as follows: First, the policy of the container is deployed at the PDP. Second, representations of the containers holding the newly detected PII are created at the Provenance Storage Point (ProSP). Additional meta information (e.g., sender e-mail address) is provided. Third, the PIP is informed about a new representation, connecting the container and the data ID.

The PII-Detector as Part of a Mail User Agent. The processing of incoming e-mails is handled by the mail user agent (e.g., Mozilla Thunderbird) in which the PII-detector is integrated by taking advantage of the agent's plug-in framework. The PII-detector is responsible for three tasks: *Detect* e-mails containing PII based on the previous described classification model, *label* the e-mails classified as sensitive, and *inform* the usage control infrastructure. For detection, the message body of a new incoming e-mail is tokenized in its single words. The header of the e-mail is omitted, because the potentially sensitive sender and receiver addresses do not provide any information about the sensitivity of the content itself. Furthermore a rule-based classification on header fields (e.g. messages from sender A contains always PII) could lead to a high percentage of false classified e-mails. Next, an analyzer calculates probabilities for each word and combines them with the Fisher method (see section 2). Based on the calculated scores, the e-mail is marked as an e-mail containing PII or not. Finally, the tokens of the new incoming e-mail are added to the existing training data. E-mails clasified as containing PII are labeled by adding a special tag to the header of the e-mail. This labeling is shown to the user via the graphical interface of the mail user agent. By one click, the user can correct the decision made by the classifier.

To show the benefit of our approach, we *instantiated* the PII-detector as the Thunderbird (TB) extension *Thunderbayes4PII*. A PEP for TB has already been developed [7]. Furthermore, spam filter implementations are available. Our implementation is built on *Thunderbayes++*.[1] We selected it because it integrates SpamBayes,[2] an one-to-one implementation of the methodology of Robinson and Graham. We adapted SpamBayes such as only the body and the subject of a message are analyzed for classification. In addition, we replaced the classes *ham* and *spam* by *PII* and *noPII*. Moreover, spam-specific components were deactivated and the GUI was adapted to the PII-detection task.

4   Evaluation

We evaluate the performance of the previously described PII-detector to detect e-mails with PII with a test data set consisting of e-mails with (class *PII*) and without PII (class *noPII*). Our use case is the e-mail communication between customers and the customer support of a telecommunication company. Unfortunately, there are no publicly available e-mails with PII. Hence, we used public data sets which we transformed to an appropriate test set by adding PII.

We crawled the messages of customers from the *Service Forum* of *Deutsche Telekom AG*,[3] where customers ask questions concerning telecommunication services, bills or orders. Although these messages are public, they represent communication between a customer and customer service. Furthermore, the style of writing in these messages is similar to e-mail communication. However, these messages do not contain any PII to identify the customer. Therefore we added artificially generated PII to create a realistic data set for the class *PII*. Depending on the content of the messages, we added PII such as the full address, a customer/access/invoice/order/phone number or banking account data.

---

[1] ThunderBayes++ Google Code Project
   https://code.google.com/p/thunderbayes/
[2] SpamBayes Project Website http://spambayes.sourceforge.net/
[3] Deutsche Telekom AG Service Forum http://forum.telekom.de

Table 1. Data Sources

Class PII	Class noPII
	E-mails from the authors' mailbox
Messages from Deutsche	E-mails from ENRON data set[4]
Telekom Forum	E-mails about internet marketing[5]
	E-mails from internet advertisement
	platform (Zanox[6] and Affilinet[7])

For class *noPII* we selected e-mails from the authors' mailbox, e-mails about telecommunication, internet advertisements and marketing. Moreover, e-mails from the *Service Forum* of the Deutsche Telekom not containing PII were chosen. Likewise, we added e-mails from the ENRON data set, which represents internal communication of a company. Table 1 provides an overview of the selected sources.

The messages from the *Service Forum* were converted into an e-mail format. The e-mails are written in German language, except the e-mails from the ENRON data set, which were translated from English to German. For the evaluation, we used 500 e-mails belonging to class *PII* and 500 e-mails belonging to class *noPII* whereby the data set consists of 1000 e-mails in total. We used a confusion matrix to create measures to evaluate the performance of the classifier [8]. True Positives (TP) and True Negatives (TN) refer to the number of elements, which are classified correctly while False Positives (FP) are predicted as positives, but are actually negatives. False Negatives (FN) are predicted as negative elements which are actually positives. Unsure Negative (UN) and Unsure Positive (UP) are the e-mails, which are classified as *unsure*. The confusion matrix in table 2 summarizes TP, FP, FN, TN, UN and UP.

Table 2. Confusion Matrix

		Predicted class		
		PII	noPII	unsure
Actual	**PII**	TP	FN	UP
class	**noPII**	FP	TN	UN

The True Positive Rate ($TPR = \frac{TP}{TP+FN+UP}$) specifies the fraction of e-mails containing PII, which are classified correctly. True Negative Rate ($TNR = \frac{TN}{TN+FP+UN}$) specifies the fraction of e-mails containing no PII, which are classified correctly. The False Positive Rate ($FPR = \frac{FP+UN}{TN+FP+UN}$) specifies the fraction of e-mails containing no PII, which are classified incorrectly. The False

---

[4] Enron Data http://enrondata.org/

[5] ServiceReport http://servicereport.eu

[6] Zanox AG, http://www.zanox.com

[7] Affilinet GmbH, http://www.affili.net

Negative Rate ($FNR = \frac{FN+UP}{TP+FN+UP}$) specifies the fraction of e-mails containing PII, which are classified incorrectly. The Error rate measures the fraction of incorrectly classified e-mails in total.

$$Error = \frac{FP + FN + UN + UP}{TP + FP + TN + TP + UN + UP} \tag{3}$$

Accuracy describes the fraction of the correctly classified e-mails in total.

$$Accuracy = \frac{TP + TN}{TP + FP + TN + TP + UN + UP} \tag{4}$$

We performed a *n-fold* cross-validation to evaluate the performance of our detection system. This means that the data set was split into n subsets. n-1 of them are used for training the PII-detector, the remaining subset was the test data to evaluate it. This was repeated n times, each time with a different training and test set. The average of the results of all evaluations is the performance of the model. We performed an evaluation for $n=5$ and $n=10$. This means, the training data in the *10-fold* cross-validation consisted of 900 e-mails and the test data of 100 e-mails. In the *5-fold* cross-validation the ratio was 800 e-mails for training and 200 e-mails for testing.

Furthermore, the thresholds t_{PII} and t_{noPII} were varied. We started with $t_{PII} = 0.1$ and $t_{noPII} = 0.9$ and increased t_{PII} in each iteration by 0.1 and at the same time decreased t_{noPII} by 0.1 (see figure 1).

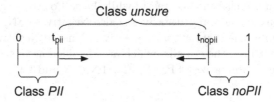

Fig. 1. Variation of t_{PII} and t_{noPII}

Table 3 shows the average results of each iteration. The results of the cross-validation show, that the PII-detector classified e-mails from class *PII* correctly and did not misclassify any e-mails with PII for $t_{PII} \geq 0.4$. The PII-detector misclassified e-mails from the class *noPII* for some values of t_{noPII}. The e-mails from the class *PII* seem to be a homogeneous class and differ strongly from most e-mails of the class *noPII*.

The results of the evaluation show that our proposed system can detect e-mails with PII very well and has an accuracy of more than 95%. The artificial inclusion of PII in the Telekom data set has not influenced the quality of the evaluation. The classification of the Bayes filter was in all e-mails based on key words in proximity to the PII, but not on the PII itself. Nevertheless, it should be considered that the quality of the PII-detector depends on the quality of the training data. Furthermore, the training and test data consists of e-mails in German language. The results could differ in other languages.

Table 3. Cross-Validation $n=10$ and $n=5$

Parameter		Results n=10					Results n=5				
t_{PII} t_{noPII}		Err.	Acc.	TNR	FNR	TPR	FPR	Err.	Acc.	TNR	FNR	TPR	FPR
0.1	0.9	0.062	0.938	0.882	0.006	0.994	0.118	0.061	0.939	0.882	0.004	0.996	0.118
0.2	0.8	0.050	0.950	0.902	0.002	0.998	0.098	0.051	0.949	0.898	0.000	1.000	0.102
0.3	0.7	0.048	0.952	0.906	0.002	0.998	0.094	0.048	0.952	0.904	0.000	1.000	0.096
0.4	0.6	0.046	0.954	0.908	0.000	1.000	0.092	0.047	0.953	0.906	0.000	1.000	0.094
0.5	0.5	0.045	0.955	0.910	0.000	1.000	0.090	0.047	0.953	0.906	0.000	1.000	0.094

5 Related Work

Text classification is mostly done by learning algorithms. According to the literature, the results of evaluation and comparison of different classification models (Support Vector Machines, k-Nearest-Neighbours, Decision Trees, Naive Bayes, ...) on textual data has shown that Support Vector Machines performed best in the evaluations [9–11]. Still, Naive Bayes classifiers have the advantage to learn new data incrementally.

Access & Usage Control systems need policy specification languages [12]. Usage control can be understood as an extension of access control to the future [13]. Usage control is concerned with how data can be used when it has been accessed to. Usage control systems have been instantiated for several kinds of layers such as Thunderbird [7], Firefox [14], and Windows [15].

Provenance tracking originates in scientific computing community [16]. But in recent work it is also discussed how provenance can improve transparency in the context of privacy [1]. PII is especially relevant in large, unstructured data sets. Hence, a system like the one proposed in this work is a prerequisite to utilize usage control and provenance tracking for the purpose of privacy improvements.

6 Conclusion

We developed a system that is able to detect e-mails with PII. It is embedded into a usage control and provenance architecture. To our knowledge, it is the first approach to detect PII automatically and annotate them with policies. We performed a soundly evaluation for a realistic data set and the results have shown that our PII-detector has an accuracy of over 95%, indicating that the approach is promising. Up to now, our evaluation is limited to the German language. Further evaluations with data sets in other languages are suggested.

Future work could encompass extending our PII-detector to other data sources like Word documents. In some cases it could be also interesting to have more than two classes, like PII of different degrees of sensitivity.

Acknowledgment. This work was partially funded by Fraunhofer Gesellschaft Internal Programs, Attract 692166.

References

1. Bier, C.: How Usage Control and Provenance Tracking Get Together - A Data Protection Perspective. In: IEEE Security and Privacy Workshops (SPW 2013), pp. 13–17 (2013)
2. Manning, C.D., Raghavan, P., Schütze, H.: Introduction to information retrieval. Cambridge University Press, Cambridge (2008)
3. Zdziarski, J.: Ending Spam: Bayesian Content Filtering and the Art of Statistical Language Classification. No Starch Press (2005)
4. Graham, P.: A plan for spam (2002), http://www.paulgraham.com/spam.html (last accessed January 15, 2014)
5. Robinson, G.: A statistical approach to the spam problem. Linux Journal (107) (March 2003), http://www.linuxjournal.com/article/6467 (last accessed January 15, 2014)
6. Pretschner, A., Lovat, E., Büchler, M.: Representation-Independent Data Usage Control. In: Garcia-Alfaro, J., Navarro-Arribas, G., Cuppens-Boulahia, N., de Capitani di Vimercati, S. (eds.) DPM 2011 and SETOP 2011. LNCS, vol. 7122, pp. 122–140. Springer, Heidelberg (2012)
7. Loerscher, M.: Usage Control for a Mail Client, Master thesis (2012)
8. Han, J., Kamber, M., Pei, J.: Data mining: concepts and techniques. Morgan Kaufmann (2012)
9. Joachims, T.: Text categorization with support vector machines: Learning with many relevant features. In: Nédellec, C., Rouveirol, C. (eds.) ECML 1998. LNCS, vol. 1398, pp. 137–142. Springer, Heidelberg (1998)
10. Zhang, T., Oles, F.J.: Text categorization based on regularized linear classification methods. Information Retrieval 4, S.5–S.31 (2001)
11. Aas, K., Eikvil, L.: Text categorisation: A survey. Technical report, Norwegian Computing Center, Oslo (1999)
12. Pretschner, A., Schutz, F., Schaefer, C., Walter, T.: Policy Evolution in Distributed Usage Control. In: Proc of the 4th Int. WS on Security and Trust Management (STM 2008), pp. 109–123. Elsevier (2008)
13. Park, J., Sandhu, R.: The UCON ABC usage control model. ACM Transactions on Information and System Security 7(1), 128–174 (2004)
14. Kumari, P., Pretschner, A., Peschla, J., Kuhn, J.M.: Distributed Data Usage Control for Web Applications: A Social Network Implementation. In: Proc of the 1st ACM Conf on Data and application security and privacy (CODASPY), San Antonio, TX, pp. 85–96 (2011)
15. Wüchner, T., Pretschner, A.: Data Loss Prevention based on data-driven Usage Control. In: Proceedings of the IEEE 23rd International Symposium on Software Reliabilitiy Engineering (ISSRE 2012), pp. 151–160 (2012)
16. Simmhan, Y.L., Plale, B., Gannon, D.: A survey of data provenance in e-science. ACM Sigmod Record 34(3), 31–36 (2005)

A Preliminary Study on User's Decision Making towards Retweet Messages

Nor Athiyah Abdullah[1], Dai Nishioka[1], Yuko Tanaka[2], and Yuko Murayama[1]

[1] Graduate School of Software & Information Science, Iwate Prefectural University,
152-52, Sugo, Takizawa, Iwate, Japan.
athiyah@comm.soft.iwate-pu.ac.jp,
{nishi_d,murayama}@iwate-pu.ac.jp
[2] National Institute of Informatics, Research Organization of Information and Systems,
2-1-2 Hitotsubashi, Chiyoda-ku, Tokyo, Japan
yuko-tanaka@nii.ac.jp

Abstract. Twitter was used to a great extent by government, media and individuals to obtain and exchange information real time during emergency. In ambiguous situation where information is crucial, some misinformation may creep in and spread around by retweet. This paper discusses on Twitter issues in emergency situation. A survey was conducted to investigate user's decision making after one read retweet messages in Twitter. As the result of the factor analyses, we grouped the 28 question items into three categories: 1) Desire to spread the retweet messages as it is considered important, 2) Mark the retweet messages as favorite using Twitter "Favorite" function, and 3) Search for further information about the content of the retweet messages.

Keywords: retweet, emergency, social media, decision making, Twitter.

1   Introduction

The social media allow people to interact freely, engaging in a conversation and build relationship using words, audio, pictures and videos. With social media, everybody can involve in reporting news, and therefore the ideas of "citizen reporter" occur where several events discovered by social media users. Compared to Facebook, 63.9% of the respondents in a survey by MMD laboratory [1] state that Twitter help them gather information about the disaster. There are several motivations on why user tend to depend on social media during emergencies, such as convenience, technology and ability barrier, prior experience, quality of the information, mass sending ability, and time and cost effective [2, 3].

Although there were many research about the potential of social media role and usage in emergency domain have been reported, few of them focused on how to combat misinformation transmission in social media. Previous research highlighted the need to study on people behavior after one read the crisis information and how people share information in social media [4]. Previous studies reveal the relationship between ambiguity, importance, anxiety, distance, feelings (valence and arousal) with information sharing behavior in disaster [4, 5, 6, 7, 8, 9].

N. Cuppens-Boulahia et al. (Eds.): SEC 2014, IFIP AICT 428, pp. 359–365, 2014.
© IFIP International Federation for Information Processing 2014

There are four phases of the emergency management process: mitigation, preparedness, response and recovery. The use of social media is crucial in between preparedness and response phases where understanding on the information available and how to utilize it was seen as enormously important in emergency. Citizen supplying information to online system, such as by uploading disaster photos or updating information on affected people is crucially helpful in response phase [10]. Accordingly, our motivation study is towards the reducing of misinformation spreading at response phases, focusing on the public who may or may not directly affected in a disaster on spreading disaster-related information so that actions can be taken immediately to help reducing the disaster impact. Therefore, we conduct a survey to investigate what is the user's action after they read the retweet messages. The findings of this paper present the preliminary study on user's decision making towards spread message in general. In the future, we plan to investigate further focusing on information spreading in emergency situation.

The rest of the paper is organized as follows. In section 2, we explain the social media issues within the emergency domain. Next in section 3, we discuss the research method. We elaborate our results and the discussion of findings in section 4. Finally, in section 5, we conclude our work and future work.

2   Background of the Study

2.1   The Social Media Issues in Emergency

In recent years, several studies have focused on the potential use of social media sites for mass collaboration in emergency response and rescue during emergency situation [2, 11, 12, 13]. There have been several studies in the literature reporting the effectiveness of social media in providing information about the disaster such as during The Great East Japan Earthquake [3, 14, 15], The Hurricane Sandy [12, 16], The Australian country fire authority [17], and plane crash in Hudson River [18]. Disaster communication, as part of emergency management indicates three essential elements needed when dealing with real incidents, which are speed, rhythm and trust [19]. During disaster, when formal channel such as television and newspaper did not provide enough information, information from "citizen reporter" fill the information seeking gap [13]. Author [14] noted that the centrality of mass media increase as the ambiguity in social environment increases. Previous studies highlighted trusted information as one of the greatest problems with social media use during emergencies [2, 3, 6, 11, 13, 16]. Furthermore, other studies in the literature indicate the potential of social media on misinformation and rumor transmission that can create panic situation in emergencies [4, 7, 12, 13]. Misinformation can create panic situation during disaster, as people are strongly rely on social media as one of the most reliable information channel in disaster [7, 13, 15].

2.2   The Transmission of Misinformation in Twitter during Emergencies

Recently, Twitter has more than 230 million of active users monthly with 500 million tweets are sent per day [20]. Retweet is a way which users can be in a conversation and act as the building blocks for information sharing with potentially providing larger audience [21, 22]. Research by Gupta et al. [12] discovered that 86% of tweets with fake images URLs were retweets during 2012 Hurricane Sandy. The presence of URL increased the intention to spread the tweets although the URL did not have correct hyperlink function [8, 23]. In a different study, [24] gave a summary review on numbers of favorite and retweet numbers of false rumors spread in Twitter after the 2011 Japan earthquake. Based on the numerical analysis from the data collected, several misleading information spread after the disaster got high retweet number by users.

Research in rumor transmission started since WWII where in wartime, rumor transmission tend to happen when individuals distrust the news they heard [9]. The reason people transmit rumors is motivated by three psychological motivations which are: fact finding, relationship enhancement and self enhancement [25]. If false information is widely transmitted, it may cause people to change their belief and opinion [4]. Several action has been taken to reduce misinformation from spreading such as "rumor control" section on FEMA website (http://www.fema.gov), Twitter account (@IsTwitWrong) to criticize fake images spread by retweet, and official authorities account on Twitter to engage with citizen through social media channel during disaster [12,15]. Thus, with the concern to examine why people make decision to retweet, we first investigate what is the user's action and state of mind after they read retweet message. Accordingly, we conduct a survey and report our findings in the next section.

3   The Questionnaire Design and Demographic Information

The questionnaire designed in Japanese language with 48 question items. The questions are divided into three parts with 7-likert scale answer. Likert scale is usually used in questionnaire to obtain respondents degree of agreement with a statement [26]. The first part related to the questions of whether one sees retweet messages or not. The second part related to the questions of user's possible actions other than retweet. Meanwhile, the third part of the question related to the questions of whether one performs retweet or not, after they read the retweet messages. Figure 1 illustrates the scope of the questionnaire design in this study. The tweet posted by user A has been retweet by user B. Then, user C who read the retweet message from user B might take an action towards the spread message to their followers, and the information circulated. In this survey, our focus is to investigate user C decision making after they read the retweet message.

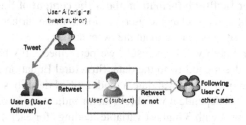

Fig. 1. The questionnaire design

The survey was held on 10 and 11 December, 2012. Total of 133 students who are Twitter user (mean age = 20.5, male = 94) from Iwate Prefectural University, Japan participated in the paper based survey.

For the analysis part, we perform Exploratory Factor Analysis (EFA) with maximum likelihood method. Factor analysis is used for data reduction and to group a large set of intercorrelated variables together under a small set of underlying variables. We eliminate the question items that have problems with floor effect (4 items), Cronbach alpha value (3 items), and questions that are not indicate positive actions user shall take towards retweet messages (13 items). Therefore, out of 48, only 28 question items remain for the analyses. Then, we perform Confirmatory Factor Analysis (CFA) with Structural Equation Modeling (SEM) to specify the relationship between variables and factors.

4   Results and Findings

4.1   The Exploratory Factor Analysis (EFA) and Confirmatory Factor Analysis (CFA) Result

We analyze 28 question items which related to user's positive action taken towards retweet message. The result of the factor analysis found that 3 factors derived. The three factors were explained by 52.415% (Cumulative) as a total. To confirm the reliability of measurement, Cronbach's coefficient alpha of each subscale factor 1, factor 2 and factor 3 are .930, .862, and .787 respectively. For the reliability test, the value of .70 and above is acceptable in most of the social science research situation. Table 1 shows the factor loadings for each factor.

We identified the following factors as the factors related to user's decision making towards retweet messages:

Factor 1: Desire to spread the retweet messages as it is considered important: This factor consists of 21 items regarding user willingness to take action towards the retweet messages by forwarding it, if they think the retweet message is important to be spread. The message could be positive, negative matter, call for action, "Pls RT" messages or the presence of URL link.

Factor 2: Mark the retweet messages as favorite using Twitter "Favorite" function: This factor consists of 3 items related to user's decision to use the Twitter favorite function (star symbol) to mark the retweet messages as favorite.

Factor 3: Search for further information about the content of the retweet messages: This factor consists of 4 items related to user's action to make further search if their interest sprung on the message content or about the tweet author.

To enhance the reliability of EFA result, we performed CFA to confirm the initial model of EFA provides a good fit to the data. Structural Equation Modeling (SEM) is a confirmatory technique used to validate a model. SEM describes the relationship between a set of observed dependent variables (factor indicators) and a set of continuous latent variables (factors) with 3 highest variable loadings for each factor (Figure 2).

Table 1. The Factor Pattern Matrix

Question Item	Factor 1	Factor 2	Factor 3
40	.853	-.287	.005
35	.797	-.042	-.012
28	.770	.048	-.021
38	.695	-.206	.139
31	.687	.085	-.003
26	.661	.124	.002
27	.658	.081	-.074
42	.645	-.034	.127
41	.633	-.077	-.032
9	.613	-.137	-.016
32	.581	.245	-.131
30	.576	.117	-.185
36	.565	-.157	.094
16	.563	.153	.014
34	.547	.082	-.022
5	.460	.146	-.009
17	.442	.299	-.007
20	.426	.215	.223
29	.423	.106	.273
24	.414	-.024	.128
8	.382	.049	.023
13	-.067	.940	.020
14	-.195	.861	.039
15	.032	.739	.056
18	-.081	-.067	1.054
19	-.050	.104	.825
12	.123	.129	.368
7	.152	.134	.276
Cumulative %	37.882	45.792	52.415
Cronbach's coefficient alpha	0.930	0.862	0.787

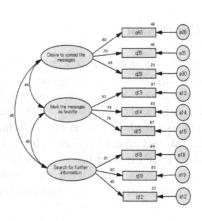

Fig. 2. The SEM diagram

We got the values as follows: Goodness of Fit Index (GFI) = .950, Comparative Fit Index (CFI) = .981, RMSEA = .057, AIC = 76.236. For GFI and CFI, the value of .95 and above indicates good model fit of the data [27]. Meanwhile, for the Badness of Fit, the RMSEA value less than .05 indicate close fit model. The lower value of AIC reflects better fitting model for model comparison. Hence, based on the result obtained, our model is a good fit model of the data.

4.2   Discussion and Future Work

In case of disaster, people often retweet and spread tweets they find in twitter trending topics, regardless of whether they follow the user or not [11]. We present our findings on one action towards spread message and as a result, we extracted 3 factors indicate user's decision making towards retweet message: 1) Desire to spread the retweet messages as it is considered important, 2) Mark the retweet messages as favorite using Twitter "Favorite" function, and 3) Search for further information about the content of the retweet messages. Most users tend to spread any messages that they think is important for others to know. However, not all information is accurate during disaster. Individuals were more likely to spread crisis information when they have negative feelings such as scared, worried, anxious, angry or nervous [4]. The present finding also support Tanaka et al. [7] study which concluded that regardless of the tweet type, the more important user evaluate the tweet, the higher they intend to transmit the messages. This paper present our preliminary study findings on user's decision making towards spread message in general. Although all subjects in the survey are Twitter users, some of them might not experience the real disaster situation. Therefore, the for the future work, we plan to improve the questionnaire focusing on emergency related situation and conduct a user survey with greater number of subjects for various groups.

5   Conclusion

In this paper, we raised our concern on misinformation spreading issue using social media in emergencies by investigating user's decision making towards retweet message. We conduct a survey in Japan to investigate what action user will take towards retweet messages. The following points emerged from the present investigation: 1) Users tend to spread the retweet messages they saw, regardless it is any kind of message; positive, negative, jokes, or call for action, if they think it is important for others to know, 2) User's retweet behavior in emergencies might be different from the normal situation because in emergency where information is critical, user might transmit misinformation to make sense of their uncertainty.

References

1. Mobile Marketing Data (MMD) Report: Survey on social media use after the Great East Japan Earthquake (2011) (in Japanese), http://mmd.up-date.ne.jp/news/detail.php?news_id=799 (accessed December 14, 2013)
2. White, C., Plotnick, L., Kushma, J., et al.: An online social network for emergency management. Int. J. Emergency Management 6(3/4), 369–382 (2009)
3. Peary, B.D.M., Shaw, R., Takeuchi, Y.: Utilization of Social Media in the East Japan Earthquake and Tsunami and its Effectiveness. Journal of Natural Disaster Science 34(1), 3–18 (2012)
4. Chen, R., Sakamoto, Y.: Perspective matters: Sharing of Crisis Information in Social Media. In: Proc. of the 46th Hawaii International Conference on System Sciences (HICCS-46), pp. 2033–2041 (2013)
5. Chen, R., Sakamoto, Y.: Feelings and Perspective matter: Sharing of Crisis Information in Social Media. In: Proc. of the 47th Hawaii International Conference on System Sciences (HICCS-47), pp. 1958–1967 (2014)
6. Tanaka, Y., Sakamoto, Y., Matsuka, T.: Toward a Social-Technological System that Inactivates False Rumors through the Critical Thinking of Crowds. In: Proc. of the 46th Hawaii International Conference on System Sciences (HICCS-46), pp. 649–658 (2013)
7. Tanaka, Y., Sakamoto, Y., Matsuka, T.: Transmission of Rumor and Criticism in Twitter after the Great Japan Earthquake. In: Proc. of the 34th Annual Conference of the Cognitive Science Society, pp. 2387–2392 (2012)
8. Tanaka, Y., Sakamoto, Y., Honda, H.: The Impact of Posting URLs in Disaster-related Tweets on Rumor Spreading Behavior. In: Proc. of the 47th Hawaii In-ternational Conference on System Sciences (HICCS-47), pp. 520–529 (2014)
9. Allport, G.W., Postman, L.: The Psychology of Rumor. Henry Holt and Company, New York (1947)
10. Hiltz, S.R., et al.: The Domain of Emergency Management Information. In: Van de Walle, B., Turoff, M., Hiltz, S.R. (eds.) Information Systems for Emergency Management, New York. Advances in Management Information Systems, vol. 16 (2010)

11. Raue, S., Azzopardi, L., Johnson, C.W.: #trapped!: Social media search system requirements for emergency management professionals. In: Proc. of the 36th International ACM SIGIR Conference on Research and Development in Information Retrieval, pp. 1073–1076 (2013)

12. Gupta, A., Lamba, H., Kumaraguru, P., et al.: Faking Sandy: Characterizing and identifying fake images on Twitter during Hurricane Sandy. In: Proc. of the 22nd International Conference on World Wide Web (WWW 2013 Companion), pp. 729–736 (2013)

13. Hagar, C.: Crisis informatics: Perspectives of trust–Is social media a mixed blessing?. Student Research Journal 2(2) (2012), http://scholarworks.sjsu.edu/slissrj/vol2/iss2/2/. (accessed September 13, 2013)

14. Jung, J.: Social media use and goals after the Great East Japan Earthquake. First Monday 17(8) (2012), doi: 10.5210/fm.v17i8.4071

15. Acar, A., Muraki, Y.: Twitter for crisis communication: Lessons learned from Japan's tsunami disaster. Int. J. Web Based Communities, 392–402 (2011)

16. Chatfield, A.T., Scholl, H.J., Brajawidagda, U.: #Sandy Tweets: Citizens' Co-Production of Time-Critical Information during an Unfolding Catastrophe. In: Proc. of the 47th Hawaii International Conference on System Sciences (HICCS-47), pp. 1947–1957 (2014)

17. UK Government: Using Social Media in Emergencies: Smart Practices (2012), https://www.gov.uk/government/uploads/system/uploads/attachment_data/file/85946/Using-social-media-in-emergencies-smart-tips.pdf (accessed January 9, 2014)

18. Curtis, A.: The Brief History of Social Media (2013), http://www.uncp.edu/home/acurtis/NewMedia/SocialMedia/SocialMediaHistory.html (accessed January 8, 2014)

19. Murayama, Y., Saito, Y., Nishioka, D.: Trust Issues in Disaster Communication. In: Proc. of the 46th Hawaii International Conference on System Sciences (HICCS-46), pp. 335–342 (2013)

20. Twitter, Inc.: About Twitter, Inc., https://about.twitter.com/company (accessed January 14, 2014)

21. Boyd, D., Golder, S., Lotan, G.: Tweet, Tweet, Retweet: Conversational aspects of Retweeting on Twitter. In: Proc. of the 43th Hawaii International Conference on System Sciences (HICCS-43), pp. 1–10 (2010)

22. Tinati, R., Carr, L., Hall, W., et al.: Identifying communicator roles in twitter. In: Proc. of the 21st International Conference Companion on World Wide Web (WWW 2012 Companion), pp. 1161–1168 (2012)

23. Zarella, D.: The Science of Retweets (2009), http://danzarrella.com (accessed November 29, 2013)

24. Mukai, M.: Research on a Model for Decision Making in Retweet which caused Spreading of False Rumor in Emergencies. Master Dissertation, Iwate Prefectural University (2012) (in Japanese)

25. DiFonzo, N., Bordia, P.: Rumor Psychology: social and organizational approaches. American Psychological Association, Washington (2007)

26. Bertram, D.: Likert Scales (2007), http://www.al-huda.net/2012/PA/2014/topic-dane-likert.pdf (accessed March 16, 2014)

27. Brown, G.: An Introduction to Confirmatory Factor Analysis (CFA) and Structural Equation Modeling, SEM (2011), https://www.academia.edu/1680329/An_Introduction_to_Confirmatory_Factor_Analysis_CFA_and_Structural_Equation_Modeling_SEM_ (accessed January 7, 2014)

Behavior Analysis of Web Service Attacks

Abdallah Ghourabi, Tarek Abbes, and Adel Bouhoula

Higher School of Communication of Tunis SUP'COM, University of Carthage, Tunisia
{abdallah.ghourabi,adel.bouhoula}@supcom.rnu.tn,
tarek.abbes@isecs.rnu.tn

Abstract. With the rapid development of Internet and its services, cyber attacks are increasingly emerging and evolving nowadays. To be aware of new attacks and elaborate the appropriate protection mechanisms, an interesting idea is to attract attackers, then to automatically monitor their activities and analyze their behaviors. In this paper, we are particularly interested in detecting and learning attacks against web services. We propose an approach that describes the attacker's behavior based on data collected from the deployment of a web service honeypot. The strengths of our approach are that (1) it offers a high interaction environment, able to collect valuable information about malicious activities; (2) our solution preprocesses the set of data attributes in order to keep only significant ones (3) it ensures two levels of clustering in order to produce more concise attack scenarios. In order to achieve these contributions, we employ three analysis techniques: Principal Component Analysis, Spectral Clustering and Sequence Clustering. Our experimental tests allow us discovering some attacks scenarios, such as SQL Injection and Denial of Services (DoS), that are modeled in Markov chains.

Keywords: Honeypot, Web Service, Attacker's Behavior, Clustering, Data Analysis.

1 Introduction

The Web Service technology is increasingly used in companies due to its simplicity and interoperability. It is based on several standards such as SOAP and XML for exchanging information between applications in heterogeneous environments through the Internet. Among the security problems of Web Services are the exchanged data that can convey many threats to the target system. To address these security issues, administrators have to carefully supervise the execution and utilization of web services. The Honeypot technology constitutes an ideal solution to ensure this kind of monitoring. It allows discovering new attacks methods, intrusion scenarios and attackers' objectives and strategies. In this context, we have proposed in an earlier work [3] a honeypot solution, called WS Honeypot, designated to attract and monitor web service attacks.

Honeypots are very useful for collecting valuable information about the attackers and their techniques. However, the volume of collected data increases rapidly due to frequent and repetitive data. The large amount of data complicates the

N. Cuppens-Boulahia et al. (Eds.): SEC 2014, IFIP AICT 428, pp. 366–379, 2014.

analysis task and overwhelms rapidly the human analyst. Thus, a manual tracking of attackers' activities on the honeypot seems to be very difficult and tedious work. To improve the performance of the data analysis in our WS Honeypot, we propose in this paper an automatic approach to analyze the collected data and describe attackers' behaviors on the honeypot. Our approach combines 3 analysis techniques: Principal Component Analysis to select the features to be extracted from the captured data; Spectral Clustering to cluster the collected requests and Sequence Clustering to regroup the similar activities performed by the attackers and describe their behavior.

The remaining parts of the paper are organized as follows: Section 2 reviews the related works. Section 3 defines the analysis techniques used in our approach. Section 4 presents the architecture of our analysis approach and describes the working principle of the implemented algorithms. Section 5 reports our experimental results. Finally, we conclude the paper in Section 6.

2   Related Work

The approach proposed in this paper is positioned among other related works that aim to characterize attacks in the honeypots. Despite the common purpose, these works have used various analytical techniques. For instance, Pouget and Dacier [8] proposed a simple clustering approach to analyze the data collected from the honeypot project Leurre.com. Their objective is to characterize the root causes of attacks targeting their Honeypots. The aim of this algorithm is to gather all attacks presenting some common characteristics (duration of attack, targeted ports, number of sent packets, etc.) based on generalization techniques and association-rule mining. Resulting clusters are further refined using Levenshtein distance. The final goal of their approach is to group into clusters, all attacking sources sharing similar activity fingerprints, or attack tools. Alata et al. [1] presented some results obtained from their project CADHo (Collection and Analysis of Data from Honeypots). The purpose of this project is to analyze the data collected from the environment Leurre.com and to provide models for the observed attacks. They proposed simple models describing the time-evolution of the number of attacks observed on different honeypot platforms. Besides, they studied the potential correlations of attack processes observed on the different platforms taking into account the geographic location of the attacking machines and the relative contribution of each platform in the global attack scenario. The correlation analysis is based on a linear regression models. Thonnard and Dacier proposed a framework for attack patterns' discovery from the honeynet collected data [11]. The aim of this approach is to find, within an attack dataset, groups of network traces sharing various kinds of similar patterns. In this work, the authors applied a graph-based clustering method to analyze one specific aspect of the honeynet data (the time series of the attacks). The results of the clustering applied to time-series analysis enable to identify the activities of several worms and botnets in the traffic collected by the honeypots.

Compared to above works, our approach offers two main advantages. Firstly, we use the Principal Component Analysis to select the pertinent features unlike other works where this selection is done manually. Secondly, to cluster observed attacks, we employ a sequence clustering method which allows tracking the transition between the attacker's activities taking into account the order of realization.

3 Data Analysis Techniques

To analyze the large amount of data collected from the honeypot, several techniques of data analysis can be applied, such as statistics, data mining and machines learning. Generally, researchers apply such methods to data for two main reasons: to better understand the existing data and to predict something about new data [7]. In this paper, we propose a hybrid approach composed of three analysis techniques (Principal Component Analysis, Spectral Clustering and Sequence Clustering) to analyze the data collected from our WS Honeypot and describe the behavior of the captured attacks. Before presenting our approach, we devote this section to introduce these three techniques.

3.1 Principal Component Analysis

The Principal Component Analysis (PCA) is a data analysis method used for dimensionality reduction and multivariate analysis. The central idea of principal component analysis is to reduce the dimensionality of a data set consisting of a large number of possibly correlated variables, while retaining as much as possible of the variation present in the data set [4]. This is achieved by transforming these variables into a smaller number of uncorrelated variables called principal components. This transformation is defined in such a way that the first principal component is a linear combination of the original variables with the largest possible variance. The second principal component is the linear combination of the original variables with the second largest variance and orthogonal to the first principal component, and so on [12].

To describe the principle of PCA, let us consider a set of observations $(x_1, x_2, ..., x_n)$ where each observation is represented by a vector of length m. The dataset is represented by a matrix X of dimensions $n \times m$. The transformation into principal components is mainly based on the eigenvalues and the eigenvectors of the covariance matrix C (formed from X). We suppose that $(\lambda_1, u_1), (\lambda_2, u_2), ..., (\lambda_m, u_m)$ are the pairs (eigenvalue, eigenvector) of the covariance matrix C. We choose the k eigenvectors having the largest eigenvalues. Afterwards, we form a $m \times k$ matrix U whose columns consist of the k eigenvectors. The representation of the data by principal components is made by projecting the original data onto the k-dimensional subspace according to the following rule [12]:

$$y_i = U^T(x_i - \mu)$$

Where $\mu = \frac{1}{n}\sum_{(i=1)}^{n} x_i$ and y_i is a k-dimensional vector that represents the projection of the original m-dimensional data vector x_i.

3.2   Spectral Clustering

Clustering is an unsupervised learning method that seeks to assign a set of objects into homogeneous groups (called clusters). Several algorithms can be used to cluster data such as k-means, hierarchical clustering, spectral clustering, etc. In recent years, spectral clustering has become one of the most popular modern clustering algorithms. It is simple to implement and very often outperforms traditional clustering algorithms such as the k-means algorithm [6]. Unlike other clustering algorithms, the spectral clustering algorithm is based on the concept of similarity between each pair of points instead of distance.

Given a set of data points $x_1, ..., x_n$, the similarity matrix may be defined as a matrix S, where S_{ij} represents a measure of the similarity between all pairs of data points x_i and x_j. The main goal of clustering is to divide the data points into several groups in a way that the data points of the same group exhibit similar properties. To do that, the Spectral clustering represents the data in the form of the similarity graph $G = (V, E)$. Each vertex V_i in this graph represents a data point x_i. Two vertices are connected if the similarity S_{ij} between the corresponding data points x_i and x_j is positive or larger than a certain threshold, and the edge is weighted by S_{ij} [6].

After constructing the similarity graph, the next step is to find a partition of the graph in a way that the edges between different groups have very low weights and the edges within a group have high weights. The basic idea is to calculate the graph Laplacian matrix L, and to extract the k (number of clusters to construct) first eigenvectors of L. These eigenvectors allow obtaining a projection space with a smaller dimension (k dimensions). Afterwards, a clustering algorithm (e.g. k-means) can be applied to assign each data point into a cluster among the k ones.

3.3   Sequence Clustering

The role of sequence clustering is to group a set of sequences in such a way that sequences in the same group (cluster) are more similar to each other than to those in other clusters. The working principle of a sequence-clustering algorithm differs depending on the used implementation. In our work, we are particularly interested in Microsoft Sequence Clustering algorithm [10] which is included in the data mining tools of Microsoft SQL Server.

Microsoft Sequence Clustering

The Microsoft Sequence Clustering algorithm is a hybrid algorithm that uses Markov chain to analyze the sequences and partitions them using the Expectation Maximization (EM) method of clustering. The Markov chain can be defined as a mathematical system that describes the transition probabilities between a set of states. In Microsoft Sequence Clustering algorithm, each generated cluster is associated to an n-order Markov chain.

To describe the basic principles of this algorithm, consider the case of a first-order Markov chain. For an observed sequence, the probability of belonging to a given cluster is in effect the probability that the observed sequence was produced by the Markov chain associated with that cluster [2]. Consider a sequence $x = x_1, x_2, ..., x_l$ of length l, the probability of belonging to a given cluster C_k is calculated using the following formula:

$$p(x|C_k) = p(x_1, C_k). \prod_{(i=2)}^{l} p(x_i|x_{(i-1)}, C_k) \qquad (1)$$

where $p(x_1, C_k)$ is the probability that x_1 is the first state in the Markov chain associated with the cluster C_k and $p(x_i|x_{(i-1)}, C_k)$ is the transition probability of state $x_{(i-1)}$ to x_i in the same Markov chain. To calculate the parameters of this model, the Microsoft Sequence Clustering implements the iterative algorithm Expectation and Maximization (EM).

4   Automatic Analysis of Web Service Honeypot Data

The data collected from a honeypot contains interesting information about the attacker and his activities. This information is useful to understand the hackers' strategies and to learn the modus operandi of their attacks. To obtain a better knowledge, an exhaustive analysis of collected data is very important. In this paper, we propose an automatic approach to analyze attacks traces collected from the deployment of a Web service Honeypot called WS Honeypot, previously presented in [3].

WS Honeypot is a high interaction honeypot that simulates the behavior of a Web service. The role of this honeypot is to attract and monitor attackers targeting web service applications. WS Honeypot provides real web services to ensure a real interaction with attackers. The services offered by the honeypot can be deployed by using two technologies, Axis and .Net. The approach proposed in this paper aims at describing the behavior of attacks captured by WS Honeypot, using several analysis techniques.

4.1   WS Honeypot Data Analysis Workflow

The overall architecture of our approach is shown in Figure 1. The WS Honeypot captures the SOAP messages sent by the attackers. Afterwards, we extract from each SOAP message its characteristic parameters (Feature extraction). Then, we apply a statistical method called "Principal Component Analysis" to select the most relevant features that ensure reliable identification of attacks. Thus, we obtain a dataset of observations (DS1) incorporating significant parameters extracted from captured SOAP messages. The next step consists in applying a spectral clustering on dataset DS1 in order to cluster the captured SOAP messages into homogeneous groups; each group is supposed to represent a message type. As each SOAP message sent by the user is designated to perform an activity in the web service, we consider in the following that each resulting cluster

Fig. 1. Data analysis workflow in WS Honeypot

represents an activity type that an attacker can accomplish with different manners at the WS Honeypot. Hence, the spectral clustering analysis allows us to characterize the session of an attacker by determining his activity types in the honeypot in a period of 24 hours. These data are stored on a second dataset DS2 called "session characteristics". The final step of our analysis process consists in applying a sequence clustering on the second dataset DS2 in order to form homogeneous clusters. Each cluster is designed to describe the attacker's behavior for each attack type. The cluster, containing related activity types, can be modeled by a Markov chain to outline the attack scenario.

4.2 Features Selection and Extraction

Features selection and extraction is a preprocessing step, which is very important in our approach. It allows the selection of relevant features to be extracted from the SOAP messages in order to improve the performance of the clustering process. Although the choice of these features can be made manually based on expert knowledge, the use of automated algorithms for feature selection is very interesting to obtain better results. In the case of our approach, we employ a statistical method called "Principal Component Analysis" to select the most pertinent features.

The selection process is as follows: Firstly, we prepare a preliminary list of all possible features that we can extract from a SOAP message. Then, we apply the PCA algorithm on a set of instances representing some SOAP messages according to the chosen features. Finally, we exploit the results of PCA to reduce the preliminary list of features and keep only those which are relevant.

Preliminary List of Features

First of all, we describe all features that we are able to extract from a SOAP message. The Web service requests are formatted in XML language and encapsulated in SOAP messages with the use of HTTP as a transport protocol. A malicious user, trying to attack the Web service, can inject a malicious content in the SOAP message in order to exploit the target. Therefore, the inspection of the SOAP messages contents is essential to identify attacks. Moreover, we extract extra parameters characterizing the SOAP exchange and the amount of consumed resources for processing. This list includes the source IP address of the sender machine, the destination IP address, the encoding type, the header size, the overall size of the request, the protocol type, the port number, the input parameters of the web service operations and some information related to

Table 1. List of initial features

No	Feature	Description
1	Src_IP	source IP address
2	Dest_IP	destination IP address
3	Protocol	type of used protocol
4	Port	destination port number
5	Soap_msg_size	size of the SOAP message
6	Soap_header_size	size of the header
7	Soap_request_type	request type
8	Soap_response_type	response type
9	Encoding	used encoding type
10	Operation	called operation name
11	in1	input for parameter number 1
12	in2	input for parameter number 2
13	in3	input for parameter number 3
14	in4	input for parameter number 4
15	in5	input for parameter number 5
16	in6	input for parameter number 6
17	in7	input for parameter number 7
18	in8	input for parameter number 8
19	in9	input for parameter number 9
20	in10	input for parameter number 10
21	Time	request processing time
22	Mem	memory occupation
23	CPU	request CPU usage

the request processing (execution time, memory and CPU usage). We present in Table 1 the preliminary list of the selected features during this step.

Selection of Pertinent Features

The objective of this step is to apply the Principal Component Analysis (PCA) method in order to reduce the list of preliminary features described in Table 1 by eliminating useless features. For this purpose, we collect several types of SOAP requests. In addition to normal requests, we gather others messages with malicious code causing several attacks such as SQL/XML injection, denial of service, parameter tampering, etc. From each SOAP message, we extracted the features described in Table 1 and we stored them in a dataset. Each instance (observation) of the dataset is designed to characterize a SOAP request. On this dataset, we applied a PCA algorithm implemented in Tanagra software [9].

The PCA replaces the old axes with new axes (called factorial axes). The latter are associated with new variables (called principal components) obtained by linear combinations of old variables. To interpret the results, we report in Table 2 the obtained factorial axes, the associated eigenvalues, the proportion of inertia (data dispersion) explained by each factorial axis and the cumulative inertia. For the choice of factorial axes (or principal components) to be retained, we are based on the Kaiser criterion [5] which consists in only retaining the axes that have an eigenvalue greater or equal to 1 (i.e. the first 6 axes). Nevertheless, as the axes 7 and 8 have an eigenvalue very close to 1, we also retained them. From Table 2 we can see that the first 8 factorial axes dispose 77.84% of the available information.

Table 2. Factorial axes issued from PCA

Axis	Eigen value	Proportion (%)	Cumulative (%)
1	2,770407	17,32 %	17,32 %
2	2,182733	13,64 %	30,96 %
3	1,689447	10,56 %	41,52 %
4	1,524927	9,53 %	51,05 %
5	1,230749	7,69 %	58,74 %
6	1,105892	6,91 %	65,65 %
7	0,989987	6,19 %	71,84 %
8	0,960595	6,00 %	77,84 %
9	0,844701	5,28 %	83,12 %
10	0,802064	5,01 %	88,13 %
11	0,419877	2,62 %	90,76 %
12	0,350289	2,19 %	92,95 %
13	0,332850	2,08 %	95,03 %
14	0,301130	1,88 %	96,91 %
15	0,267431	1,67 %	98,58 %
16	0,226920	1,42 %	100,00 %
17	0,000000	0,00 %	100,00 %
...			

The last step in this process consists in projecting the original data on the 8 first factorial axes and determining the variables that correlate better with these axes. Based on this projection, we selected 12 variables that have a high correlation with the factorial axes: Operation, Soap_msg_Size, Mem, CPU, Time, in1, in2, in3, in4, in5, in6, and in7. This analysis show that these 12 variables are the most important (and hence the most relevant) compared to the rest of variables.

The selected variables (features) are used to construct the first dataset "SOAP message content" noted DS1. From each SOAP request captured by the WS Honeypot, we extract the 12 features to characterize the request and we store them in the dataset DS1.

4.3   SOAP Messages Clustering

Intruders employ different methods to penetrate the target system. When exploiting web services, they have several ways to succeed an attack (SQL injection, Path traversal, XML Injection, DoS, etc.). Thus, clustering similar attacks is useful to characterize the different categories of intrusion. For this process, we used the spectral clustering algorithm. To cluster the collected SOAP messages (requests), we apply the clustering algorithm on the first dataset DS1 of "SOAP messages content". The execution of spectral clustering algorithm includes essentially three steps: construction of the similarity matrix S, extracting the k first eigenvectors from the Laplacian matrix L, and partitioning the data.

Construction of Similarity Matrix

The first step in spectral clustering is to construct a similarity matrix that measures the similarity between the data points of our dataset DS1. We construct a graph where pairs of objects are connected by links weighted by similarity values. The final objective is to find a partition of the graph such that edges between different groups have a very low weight (similarity) and the edges within a group have a high weight. Since SOAP messages are viewed as a set of string, we choose the Levenshtein distance instead of the Euclidean distance to compute the similarity. Having two strings, the chosen distance is equal to the minimum number of edits needed to transform one string into the other, with the allowable edit operations being insertion, deletion, or substitution of a single character. Once we calculate this value, the resulting similarity function is a Gaussian measure $S_{ij} = exp(\frac{-d^2(x_i, x_j)}{2\sigma^2})$, where d is a distance function (Levenshtein distance) and σ is a user specified scaling factor. At the end of this step, we obtain a similarity matrix $S \in R^{n \times n}$, where n is the size of the objects set.

Extracting the k First Eigenvectors

The next step of spectral clustering is to construct the similarity graph $G = (V, E)$ based on the similarity matrix S. V denotes the set of vertices V_i representing the data point x_i; E is the set of edges connecting the pairs of vertices. In the case of our implementation, each data point x_i contains the characteristic parameters of each SOAP message captured by the WS Honeypot.

Afterwards, we need to calculate the graph Laplacian matrix L and extract the k (number of clusters to construct) first eigenvectors $(u_1, ..., u_k)$ of L as described in Subsection 3.2. These eigenvectors allow obtaining a projection space with smaller dimensions (equal to k). We use these vectors $(u_1, ..., u_k)$ as a set of columns to obtain a matrix U whose rows will be classified in the next and final step.

For the choice of the number of clusters k, we refer to the idea presented by U. Luxburg [6], which is based on the eigengap heuristic. Here, the goal is to choose the number k in such a way that all the $\lambda_1, ..., \lambda_k$ eigenvalues are very small, but λ_{k+1} is relatively large.

Data Partitioning

At the final step of spectral clustering, we consider each row of the matrix U as a point in R^k and we cluster it via K-means (in our case) or other algorithm. Finally, we assign the original object x_i (SOAP message i) to cluster j if and only if row i of the matrix U is assigned to cluster j.

4.4   Sequence Clustering

Web service attacks are not always too simple as sending a single request containing malicious parameters. Attackers are now looking for solutions to generate more complicated attacks that are performed on several steps, hence involving multiple Web service requests. For example, the denial of service attack is performed by submitting multiple requests from one or several sources in the same time. In other cases, an attacker must initiate other attacks in order to succeed his final attack. To follow and characterize the entire attack scenario, the security expert needs to monitor the interaction between the attacker and the system. For this reason, we choose in our approach to monitor the entire sessions captured by the WS Honeypot. The proposed idea consists in collecting the sequence of activities occurred during a user session and applying a clustering algorithm to form homogenous clusters. We define a session as the set of SOAP requests submitted to the WS Honeypot from one source during a period not exceeding 24 hours. Each formed cluster is designed to describe the behavior of attackers that have performed similar activities in the honeypot.

The sequence clustering algorithm is applied on the second dataset "session characteristics", noted DS2. Each instance of the dataset contains: the source IP address of the session, the sequence of activities performed during the session and the average inter-arrival time. The sequence of activities is created based on the results of spectral clustering. Knowing that each cluster formed by the spectral clustering represents an activity type, we can determine the sequence of activities in each session by checking each received request to which activity cluster is belonging. For example, suppose that during a given session we captured 5 SOAP requests (req1, req2, req3, req4 and req5). After the spectral clustering, we concluded that req1, req2 and req3 are belonging to Cluster 1 because they are very similar. On the other hand, req4 and req5 belong respectively to Cluster 2 and Cluster 3. The sequence of activities related to this session is then equal to {A1, A1, A1, A2, A3}.

The sequence clustering method used in this approach is based on Microsoft Sequence Clustering algorithm described in Subsection 3.3. In this clustering process, we collect all the sequences of activities captured from the WS Honeypot and we form homogenous clusters. Each cluster is supposed to describe the attacker's behavior for an attack type. In some clusters we can find several attacker sequences. This means that these attackers have performed similar activities in the honeypot. Each resulting cluster is represented by a Markov chain. The chain is used to describe the attacker's behavior and the transitions between the activities that s/he has carried out.

5   Experimental Results

5.1   Experimental Data

The experimental tests described in this section are performed on the data collected from the deployment of our WS Honeypot on Internet. The period of deployment has lasted five months starting from February 2012 until June 2012. The honeypot was configured to simulate a Web service for online shopping. This type of service attracts many attackers especially those seeking for confidential information like credit card numbers and user passwords.

To enrich the data upon which WS Honeypot can work and give it the opportunity to receive other types of attack, we have chosen to simulate multiple attacks and to use some tools of penetration test and vulnerabilities discovery in order to attack the WS Honeypot. In this way, the overall data collected from the honeypot were coming from different sources:

- Real traffic from the Internet
- Fuzzing penetration testing tool (WSFuzzer)
- Web vulnerability scanner (Acunetix)
- Simulated attacks from different sources

Table 3. Dataset Characteristics

Dataset size	Number of captured requests	Number of sources	Number of sessions	Protocol distribution
38.7 MB	2317	113	451	SOAP (96%) Other (4%)

In total, we have collected an amount of data equal to 38.7 MB, which are generated by 2317 requests coming from 113 different IP sources. In Table 3, we give a brief summary of the collected dataset.

5.2 SOAP Messages Clustering

Most often, attackers send SOAP requests with malicious contents in order to attack a web service. The purpose of these requests is to generate harmful activities on the target service. The content and the nature of a malicious request depend on the attack type and goal. For example, the added code within a SOAP request to launch an SQL injection attack differs from that used in an XSS (Cross-site scripting) attack. To assign each SOAP request to an attack class, we employed the spectral clustering. The goal of this clustering is to categorize the activities performed by the attacker during its interaction with the WS Honeypot.

Table 4. Example of groups formed by the Sectral Clustering

Group number	Malicious sequence	Probable attack type
Group 1	0 or 1=1 ' or 0=0 – " or 0=0 – or 0=0 – ' or 0=0 ' or 1=1– " or 1=1- ' or 'x'='x 0 or 1=1	SQL injection
Group 2	
 
 
 ' /'	Meta-Character Injection
Group 3	../../../../../../../../../../etc/passwd%00 ../../../../../../../../../../etc/passwd ../../../../../../../../../../etc/shadow%00 ../../../../../../../../../../etc/shadow \..\..\..\..\..\..\..\..\..\passwd ../../../../../../../conf/server.xml	Path Traversal
Group 4	AAAAAAAAAAAAAAAAA AAAAAAAAAAAAAAAA AAAAAAAAAAAAAAAAAAA......AA AAAAAAAAAAAAAAAAAAAAAAA BBBBBBBBBBBBAAAAAAAA.....AAA BBBBBBBBBBBBBBBBBBBBBBBBBB BBBBBBBBBBBBBB	Unknown
...		

To test this technique we applied the spectral clustering over our collected dataset. In Table 4, we describe the result of this task by presenting some formed groups (clusters) and the malicious content found in these groups.

5.3 Description of the Attacker's Behavior

All activities performed by the users in the WS Honeypot, whatever malicious or not, are stored in our datasets. To characterize these activities, we firstly apply a spectral clustering. For example, if an attacker sent a SOAP request to the honeypot and the clustering process reveals that the request belongs to group 1 (in Table 4), we can conclude that the attacker performed the activity type 'A1', i.e. it is most likely to be an SQL injection. Afterward, we determine the list of activities for each user within the same session, and we apply a sequence clustering on the constructed dataset.

In Table 5, we present some examples from the obtained results. Among the clusters formed by the sequence clustering, we describe Cluster 5 and Cluster 12. In cluster 5, we find 6 similar sequences of 6 different attackers. There are 3 types of activity: A1, A8 and A10. The attacker number 1 has performed during the same session the following activities: A1, A1, A8, A8 and finally A10. A1 means an SQL injection; A8 and A10 refer to 2 variants of parameters tampering attack. To describe the behavior of the intruder in this cluster, we employ the Markov chain. In this chain, the states represent the activities types and the links describe the transition probabilities between these states. By analyzing the Markov Chain derived from Cluster 5, we can conclude that the attack

Table 5. Example of clusters obtained from sequence clustering

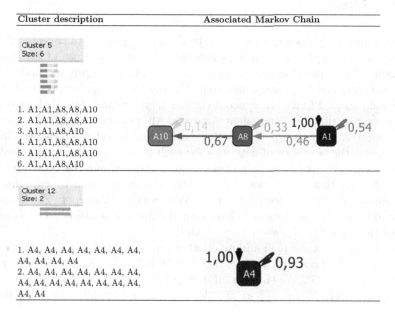

Cluster description	Associated Markov Chain
Cluster 5 Size: 6 1. A1,A1,A8,A8,A10 2. A1,A1,A8,A8,A10 3. A1,A1,A8,A10 4. A1,A1,A8,A8,A10 5. A1,A1,A1,A8,A10 6. A1,A1,A8,A10	A10 —0,14— ; —0,67— A8 —0,33— ; 1,00 ; A1 —0,54— ; —0,46—
Cluster 12 Size: 2 1. A4, A4, A4, A4, A4, A4, A4, A4, A4, A4, A4 2. A4, A4, A4, A4, A4, A4, A4, A4, A4, A4, A4, A4, A4, A4, A4, A4	1,00 ; A4 ; 0,93

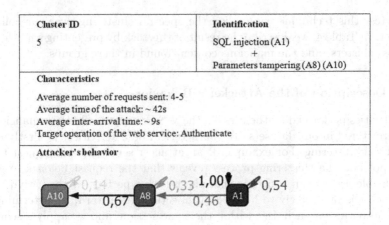

Fig. 2. Example of a Cluster signature

begins with the activity A1 (which may be repeated several times) and then passes to A8 and A10 with a given transition probability. In Cluster 12, there are 2 sequences formed by the activity A4. Here, A4 designates the submission of a large SOAP request with a repetitive content. An attacker, who generates at several times this type of activity, essentially aims to conduct a denial of service attack.

Each cluster can be summarized by a signature describing the attack process. For example, we present in Figure 2 the attack signature of Cluster 5.

6   Conclusion

In this paper, we proposed an analysis method to explore data collected from a web service honeypot. The analysis process is based on the use of a statistical technique "Principal Component Analysis" and two clustering methods: Spectral Clustering and Sequence Clustering. The described approach is divided into three main steps. Firstly, we selected the pertinent features from collected data by the use of Principal Component Analysis. Afterwards, we applied a spectral clustering to extract groups of activities sharing common characteristics. Finally, we gathered the sequence of activities for each attack session and we used the sequence clustering to form homogeneous groups describing the behavior of attackers having similar attitudes. We evaluated our approach by experimental tests applied on data collected from our Web Service Honeypot. The obtained results describe the attacker's behavior in the form of a Markov Chain representing the transition between its activities.

As a future work, we plan adding another functionality to automatically construct enriched attacks signatures to be used by Intrusion Detection and Prevention Systems (IDPS). We envisage also expanding the detection features of our Honeypot so that it can support attacks targeting web applications in general.

References

1. Alata, E., Dacier, M., Deswarte, Y., Kaniche, M., Kortchinsky, K., Nicomette, V., Pham, V.H., Pouget, F.: Collection and analysis of attack data based on honeypots deployed on the Internet. In: First Workshop on Quality of Protection, Security Measurements and Metrics, Milan, Italy (2005)
2. Ferreira, D., Zacarias, M., Malheiros, M., Ferreira, P.: Approaching Process Mining with Sequence Clustering: Experiments and Findings. In: Alonso, G., Dadam, P., Rosemann, M. (eds.) BPM 2007. LNCS, vol. 4714, pp. 360–374. Springer, Heidelberg (2007)
3. Ghourabi, A., Abbes, T., Bouhoula, A.: Design and implementation of web service honeypot. In: 19th International Conference on Software, Telecommunications and Computer Networks, Split, Croatia (2011)
4. Jolliffe, I.T.: Principal Component Analysis, 2nd edn. Springer, NY (2002)
5. Kaiser, H.F.: The application of electronic computers to factor analysis. Educational and Psychological Measurement 20, 141–151 (1960)
6. Luxburg, U.: A Tutorial on Spectral Clustering. Statistics and Computing 17(4), 395–416 (2007)
7. Maloof, M.A.: Machine Learning and Data Mining for Computer Security: Methods and Applications. Springer (2006)
8. Pouget, F., Dacier, M.: Honeypot-based Forensics. In: AusCERT Asia Pacific Information Technology Security Conference (AusCERT 2004), Brisbane, Australia (2004)
9. Rakotomalala, R.: TANAGRA: a free software for research and academic purposes. In: Proceedings of EGC 2005, RNTI-E-3, vol. 2, pp.697–702 (2005)
10. Tang, Z., MacLennan, J.: Data Mining with SQL Server 2005. Wiley (2005)
11. Thonnard, O., Dacier, M.: A framework for attack patterns' discovery in honeynet data. Digital Investigation 8, S128–S139 (2008)
12. Wang, W., Battiti, R.: Identifying Intrusions in Computer Networks with Principal Component Analysis. In: Proceedings of the First International Conference on Availability, Reliability and Security (2006)

BANKSEALER: An Online Banking Fraud Analysis and Decision Support System

Michele Carminati[1], Roberto Caron[1], Federico Maggi[1],
Ilenia Epifani[2], and Stefano Zanero[1]

[1] Politecnico di Milano, Italy
Dipartimento di Elettronica, Informazione e Bioingegneria
{michele.carminati,roberto.caron,federico.maggi,stefano.zanero}@polimi.it
[2] Politecnico di Milano, Italy
Dipartimento di Matematica
ilenia.epifani@polimi.it

Abstract. We propose a semi-supervised online banking fraud analysis and decision support approach. During a training phase, it builds a profile for each customer based on past transactions. At runtime, it supports the analyst by ranking unforeseen transactions that deviate from the learned profiles. It uses methods whose output has a immediate statistical meaning that provide the analyst with an easy-to-understand model of each customer's spending habits. First, we quantify the anomaly of each transaction with respect to the customer historical profile. Second, we find global clusters of customers with similar spending habits. Third, we use a temporal threshold system that measures the anomaly of the current spending pattern of each customer, with respect to his or her past spending behavior. As a result, we mitigate the undertraining due to the lack of historical data for building of well-trained profiles (of fresh users), and the users that change their (spending) habits over time. Our evaluation on real-world data shows that our approach correctly ranks complex frauds as "top priority".

Keywords: fraud detection, bank fraud, anomaly detection.

1 Introduction

The popularity of Internet banking has led to an increase of frauds, resulting in substantial financial losses [15,4]. Banking frauds increased 93% in 2009–2010 [6], and 30% in 2012–2013 [8].

Internet banking frauds are difficult to analyze and detect because the fraudulent behavior is dynamic, spread across different customer's profiles, and dispersed in large and highly imbalanced datasets (e.g., web logs, transaction logs, spending profiles). Moreover, customers rarely check their online banking history such regularly that they are able to discover fraud transactions timely [15].

We notice that most of the existing approaches build black box models that are not very useful in manual investigation, making the process slower. In addition, those based on baseline profiling are not adaptive, also due to cultural and behavioral differences that vary from country to country. Instead of focusing on

N. Cuppens-Boulahia et al. (Eds.): SEC 2014, IFIP AICT 428, pp. 380–394, 2014.
© IFIP International Federation for Information Processing 2014

pure detection approaches, we believe that more research efforts are needed toward systems that *support* the investigation, and we had the unique opportunity to work on a real-world, anonymized dataset.

In this paper we propose BANKSEALER, an effective online banking semi-supervised decision support and fraud analysis system. BANKSEALER automatically ranks frauds and anomalies in bank transfer transactions and prepaid phone and debit cards transactions. During a training phase, it builds a local, global, and temporal profile for each user. The local profile models past user behavior to evaluate the anomaly of new transactions by means of a novel algorithm that uses the Histogram Based Outlier Score (HBOS). The global profiling clusters users according to their transactions features via an iterative version of Density-Based Spatial Clustering of Applications with Noise (DBSCAN). For this, we use Cluster-Based Local Outlier Factor (CBLOF). This approach allows to handle undertraining, which is particularly relevant for new users, which lack of training data. The temporal profile aims to model transactions in terms of time-dependent attributes. For this, we design a series of thresholds and measure the anomaly in terms of the percentage gap from the thresholds once they are exceeded. We handle the concept drift of the scores with an exponential decay function that assigns lower weights to older profiles.

We tested the BANKSEALER on real-world data with a realistic ground truth (e.g., credential stealing, banking trojan activity, and frauds repeated over time) in collaboration with domain experts. Our system ranked fraud and anomalies with up to 98% detection rate. Given the good results, a leading Italian bank is deploying a version of BANKSEALER in their environment to analyze frauds.

In summary, our main contributions are:

- a general framework for online semi-supervised outlier-detection based on the marginal distribution of the attributes of the user's transactions.
- a combination of different models to discover different types of frauds. The scores calculated by BANKSEALER have a clear statistical meaning, aiding the analyst's activity. Our approach is adaptive to non-stationary sources and can deal with concept drift and data scarcity.
- We developed an automatic decision support system for banking frauds, evaluated it in real-world setting, and deployed it to a large national bank.

2   Online Banking Fraud Detection: Goals and Challenges

Our goal is to support the analysis of (novel) frauds and anomalies by analyzing bank transfer logs, prepaid cards and phone recharges. From an analysis of the literature (summarized in §6) and a real-world dataset obtained from a large national bank (described in §4.1), we found peculiar characteristics that make the analysis of these datasets particularly challenging: skewed and unbalanced distribution of the attribute values, high number of nominal attributes, high cardinality associated with some of attributes (e.g., IP and IBAN take several thousands of distinct values). We also noticed the prevalence of users who perform a low number of transactions—an issue not considered in the literature.

Given the scarcity of labeled datasets, such a system must be able to work in an unsupervised or semi-supervised fashion. This conflicts with the requirement of the system being able to provide "readable" evidence to corroborate each alert. These peculiarities have remarkable implications for the typical statistical and data mining methods used in the outlier detection field.

3   Approach and System Description

BANKSEALER characterizes the users of the online banking web application by means of a local, a global and a temporal *profile*, which are built during a training phase. As depicted in Fig. 1, the training phase takes as input a list of *transactions*. As summarized in Tab. 1 we take into account three types of transactions. Each type of profile (i.e., local, global, temporal) extracts different statistical *features* from the transaction attributes (e.g., average, minimum, maximum, actual value), according to the type of model built.

BANKSEALER works both under semi-supervised and unsupervised assumptions by using a sample of the unlabeled dataset as training data. In the first case, the assumption is that the training data contains only legitimate transactions. In the second case, which is more realistic, the assumption is that the training dataset contains frauds, although these are a minority. As shown by [5,13], we can safely assume that the data in input contains frauds but, due to the fact that they are rare, the learned model is unbiased.

Once the profiles are built, BANKSEALER processes new transactions and ranks them according to their anomaly score and the predicted risk of fraud. The *anomaly score* quantifies the statistical likelihood of a transaction being a fraud w.r.t. the learned profiles. The *risk of fraud* prioritizes the transactions by means of anomaly score and amount.

BANKSEALER is not a classifier: It provides the analysts with a ranked list of fraudulent transactions, along with the anomaly score of each user. Top-ranked transactions have higher priority. As described in §1, the rationale behind this design decision is that analysts must investigate reported alerts in any case: Therefore, the focus is on collecting and correctly ranking evidence that support the analysis of fraudulent behavior, rather than just flagging transactions.

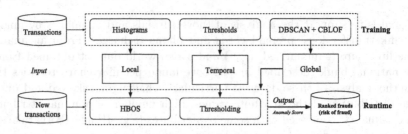

Fig. 1. BANKSEALER architecture

Table 1. List of attributes for each type of transaction. "CC_ASN" is the country code of the autonomous system of the client's IP. "Card type" takes values such as "Mastercard" or "VISA". Attributes in **bold** are hashed for anonymity needs.

DATASET	ATTRIBUTES
Bank Transfers	Amount, CC_ASN, IP, **IBAN**, IBAN_CC, Timestamp, **Recipient**
Phone recharges	Amount, CC_ASN, IP, Phone operator, **Phone number**, Timestamp
Prepaid Cards	Amount, Card type, Card number, CC_ASN, IP, Timestamp

3.1   Local Profiling

The goal of this profiling is to characterizes each user's individual spending patterns. During training, we aggregate the transactions by user and approximate each feature distribution by a histogram. More precisely, we calculate the empirical marginal distribution of the features of each user's transactions. This representation is simple, readable and effective.

At runtime, we calculate the anomaly score of each new transaction using the HBOS [7] method. The HBOS computes the probability of a transaction according to the marginal distribution learned. As described in §3.1, we improved the HBOS to account for the variance of each feature and to allow the analyst to weight the features differently according to the institution's priorities.

Training and Feature Extraction. The features are the actual values of all the attributes listed in Tab. 1. During training we estimate the marginal distribution of each feature using uni-variate histograms in a way similar to what is done in HBOS [7,17,13]. However, we do not consider correlation between features in order to gain lower spatial complexity and better readability of the histograms. Uni-variate histograms are indeed directly readable by analysts who get a clear idea of the typical behavior by simply looking at the profile. In addition, they easily allow to compute the anomaly score as the sum of the contributions of each feature, giving an intuitive justification of the resulting anomaly score. For *categorical attributes* (e.g., IP, CC), we count the occurrences of each category. For *numerical attributes* (e.g., Amount, timestamp) we adopt a static binning and count how many values falls inside each bin. After this, we estimate the marginal frequency of the features, computing the relative frequency.

Runtime and Anomaly Score Calculation. We score each new transaction using HBOS [7]. It considers the relative frequency of each bin to quantify the log-likelihood of the transaction to be drawn from the marginal distribution. In other words, for each feature t_i of the transaction t we calculate $\log \frac{1}{\text{hist}_i(t_i)}$, where hist_i indicates the frequency of the i-th feature. The resulting values are summed to form the anomaly score $\text{HBOS}_i(t)$. The logarithm makes the score less sensitive to errors caused by floating point precision. To account for the higher relevance of frauds in high-amount transactions, we multiply the anomaly score by the transaction amount.

Feature Normalization, Weighting and Rare Values. One of the main drawbacks of the original HBOS is that it does not take into account the variance of the features. For example, if Alice typically uses the banking web application from 5 distinct IPs and Bob from 2, the HBOS for Alice would be much lower than the HBOS for Bob. However, their activity is equally legitimate. To avoid this problem we apply a min-max normalization [9, pp. 71–72] to the histogram, where the minimum is zero, and the maximum is the highest bin.

In addition to the normalization, we added a weighting coefficient w_i to each feature to allow the analyst to tune the system according to the institution's priorities. In our experiments, however, we fixed all the weights at 1, except for IP and IBAN, which were fixed at 0.5 because of their high variance.

When a feature value has never occurred during training for a user (i.e., zero frequency within the local profile), the respective transaction may be assigned a high anomaly score. However, a user may have just changed his spending habits legitimately, thus causing false positives. To mitigate this, we calculate the frequency of unseen values as $k/1 - f$, where f is the frequency of that value calculated within a particular cluster, if the global profiling is able to find a cluster for that user. Otherwise, f is calculated on the entire dataset. This method quantifies the "rarity" of a feature value with respect to the global knowledge. The parameter k is an arbitrarily small, non-zero number. In our experiments we set it to 0.01.

Profile Updating. We update the histograms using an exponential discount factor, expressed in terms of the time window W and its respective sampling frequency. Every month we recursively count the values of the features in the previous months discounted by a factor $\lambda = e^{-\tau/W}$, where $W = 365$ days (up to 1 year). The rationale is that business activities are typically carried out, throughout an entire year, with a monthly basis. The parameter τ/W influences the speed with which the exponential decay forgets past data. In our case we empirically we set $\tau = 5$, because it seemed to best discount past data with respect to time and sampling windows.

Undertrained and New Users. An undertrained user is a user that performed a low number of transactions. In BANKSEALER this value is a parameter, which empirically we set at $T = 3$ as this is enough to get rid of most of the false positives due to undertraining.

For undertrained users, we consider their global profile (see §3.2) and select a cluster of similar users. For each incoming transaction, our system calculates the anomaly score using the local profile of both the undertrained user and the k nearest neighbor users (according to the Mahalanobis distance as detailed in §3.2). For new users, we adopt the same strategy. However, given the absence of a global profile, we consider all the users as neighbors.

3.2   Global Profiling

The goal of this profiling is to characterize "classes" of spending patterns. During training, we first create a global profile for each user. Then, we cluster the resulting profiles using an iterative version of the DBSCAN. Finally, for each global profile we calculate the CBLOF score, which tells the analyst to what extent a user profile is anomalous with respect to its closest cluster. The global profile is also leveraged to find local profiles for undertrained or new users. The rationale is that users belonging to the same cluster exhibit spending patterns with similar local profiles.

Training and Feature Extraction. Each user is represented as a feature vector of six components: total number of transactions, average transaction amount, total amount, average time span between subsequent transactions, number of transactions executed from foreign countries, number of transactions to foreign recipients (bank transfers dataset only). To find classes of users with similar spending patterns, we apply an iterative version of the DBSCAN, using the Mahalanobis distance [11] between the aforementioned vectors.

To mitigate the drawbacks of the classic DBSCAN when applied to skewed and unbalanced datasets such as ours (i.e., one large cluster and many small clusters), we run 10 iterations for decreasing values of ε from 10 to 0.2, which is the maximum distance to consider two users as connected (i.e., density similar). High values of this parameters yield a few large clusters, whereas low values yield many small clusters. At each iteration, we select the largest cluster and apply DBSCAN to its points with the next value of ε. The smaller clusters at each iterations are preserved. We stop the iterations whenever the number of clusters exhibits an abrupt increase (i.e., a knee). In all of our experiments, we empirically observed that this happens at 0.2. As a result, we obtain a set of clusters, which contain similar user profiles.

Anomaly Score Calculation and Updating. The global profile is used to assign each user profile a global anomaly score, which tells the analyst how "uncommon" their spending pattern is. For this, we compute the unweighted-CBLOF [2] score, which considers small clusters as outliers with respect to large clusters. More precisely, the more a user profile deviates from the dense cluster of "normal" users, the higher his or her anomaly score will be. The CBLOF anomaly score is the minimum distance of a user profile from the centroid of the nearest largest cluster. CBLOF takes only two parameters (α and β), which we evaluated empirically by considering as "normal" the 90%-percentile of the user profiles. The clustering is re-run according to the sampling frequency (i.e., 1 month). Moreover, we update the CBLOF anomaly score using an exponential discount, as described in §3.1.

3.3   Temporal Profiling

The goal of this profiling is to deal with frauds that exploit the repetition of legitimate-looking transactions over time (e.g., frequent wire transfers of amounts that not violating the local or global profile). We construct a temporal profile for each user having a sufficient amount of past transactions. During training, we aggregate the transactions of each user over time and calculate the

Table 2. Amount transferred for each dataset and scenario

Fraud scenario	Amount transferred (€)		
	Bank transfers	Phone recharges	Prepaid cards
1: Information Stealing	10,000–50,000	250–255	750–1,000
2: Transaction Hijacking	10,000–50,000	250–255	750–1,000
3: Stealthy Fraud very low amount	50–100	5–10	50–100
low amount	100–500	10–25	100–250
medium amount	500–1,000	25–50	250–500

sample mean and variance of the numerical features. These are used as thresholds during runtime to calculate the anomaly score as the delta.

After a first training, updating profiles and anomaly scores is necessary because users may change their spending habits. We use a time window, which size can be easily chosen given the hardware resources available, as show by our experiments. Within such time window, the features of the transactions are aggregated with a daily sampling frequency.

Training and Feature Extraction. For each user, we extract the following aggregated features: total amount, total and maximum daily number of transactions. During training, we compute the mean and standard deviation for each feature, and set a threshold at mean plus standard deviation to classify transactions as anomalous. Undertrained users are excluded from temporal profiling because occasional transactions have a high variance, unsuitable for this kind of analysis. The anomaly scores are updated as in the global profile (i.e., exponential discount to account for evolving spending habits).

Runtime and Anomaly Score Calculation. xAt runtime, according to the sampling frequency, we calculate the cumulative value for each of the aforementioned features for each user. Then, we calculate the delta between each cumulative value and the respective threshold. Positive deltas are summed up to form the anomaly score.

4   Experimental Evaluation

The goals of our evaluation is to measure (1) the effectiveness and (2) the computational resource requirements of BANKSEALER in correctly ranking fraudulent transactions never seen before among the top.

4.1   Dataset Description and Fraud Scenarios

We obtained 3 months of anonymized data collected from a large national consumer bank between April and June 2013: we used 2 months for training and 1 month for testing, as suggested in [9, pp.359–364].

The dataset consists of 371,137 *bank transfers* (47,650 users), the money transfers made from any account of the bank to any other account, 54,141 *prepaid cards* transactions (16,093 users), the transactions to top up credit on prepaid cards, and 34,986 *phone recharge* transactions (8,415 users), the transactions to refill prepaid cellphone accounts. The dataset is unlabeled, but it contains no known frauds as confirmed by the bank we collaborate with.

The evaluation of BANKSEALER is particularly difficult because, like any unsupervised analysis tool, it produces novel knowledge. In addition, no frauds were known or reported at the bank in the 3 months of observation. Therefore, we relied on domain experts (bank operators) to enrich our testing dataset with generated frauds based on three fraud scenarios that, based on their experience, well replicate the typical real attacks performed against online banking users. We focus on the most important and challenging fraud schemes nowadays, those driven by banking trojans (e.g., ZeuS, Citadel) or phishing.

Scenario 1: Info Stealing. The trojan modifies the login form to deceive the victim into entering an one time password (OTP) along with the login credentials. This information is used by the fraudster to execute a transaction (with a high amount) towards a his account, where the victim never sent money to. We test both the case of the connection coming from a national and foreign IP address. To inject the fraud, we randomly choose a victim from the testing dataset and used a random timestamp for the transaction.

Scenario 2: Transaction Hijacking. The trojan, not the fraudster, hijacks a legitimate bank transfer by manipulating the victim's browser. The challenge is that the connection comes from the victim's computer and IP address. Moreover, we execute the fraudulent transaction within ten minutes from a real one, to emulate a session hijacking.

Scenario 3: Stealthy Fraud. The strategy of the fraudster is to execute a series of low–medium amount transactions, repeated daily for one month during working hours, to better blend in. We analyze three cases (very low, low and medium daily amounts). We use the same number of users of the previous scenarios, each performing 30 fraudulent transaction.

For the bank transfers dataset, the money can be transferred to a national or foreign account, whereas for the phone recharges and prepaid debit cards the money is charged on an unknown card. Tab. 2 shows the amounts for each dataset and scenario.

4.2 Evaluation Approach and Metrics

After training, we inject n fraudulent transactions (or users) in the testing dataset. Then, we use the local profiles to rank transactions, and the temporal profiles to rank users, according to the respective anomaly scores. The global profiles are used to mitigate undertraining.

We analyze the top n transactions or users in the ranking, where n is the number of injected transactions (or users). In our case, n accounts for 1% of the

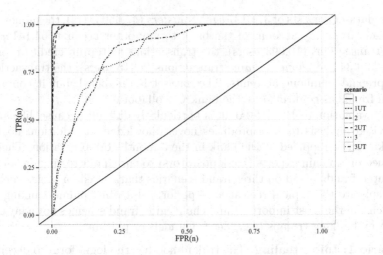

Fig. 2. True positive rate (TPR) and false positive rate (FPR) for $n \in [1, N]$, where N is the size of the testing dataset. The label "UT" stands for "undertraining". In **Scenario 1** and **2** BANKSEALER detects about 98.26% of the frauds with 99.98% of precision (0.19% FPR). **Scenario 3** (users) is the most challenging because of stealthy, small-amount frauds: BANKSEALER still detect 69.73% fraudulent users with 83.10% of precision (14.03% FPR).

testing dataset. Depending on the specific scenario, a fraud may trigger either the local or temporal profile, or both. Either way, thanks to the presence of both profiling, the analyst is able to notice the fraud. We count as true positives the number of fraudulent transactions (or users) in the top n positions, and the remainder ones (to the whole n) are either false positives or negatives.

The **overall results** are summarized in Fig. 2. BANKSEALER outperforms the state of the art. For instance, [15] detects up to 60–70% of the frauds with an unreported precision. Remarkably, the effect of undertraining is negligible.

Experiment 1: Well-trained Users. We first tested BANKSEALER without the noise due to non well-trained users (i.e., we removed users with less than 3 transactions from the dataset). All test are repeated 10 times and the results are averaged to avoid biases.

As Tab. 3 shows, the combination of local and temporal profiles guarantees that frauds are ranked high at either transaction level, thanks to the local profiles, or user level, thanks to the temporal profile.

The results on the information stealing frauds (**Scenario 1**) are very promising. Transaction hijacking frauds (**Scenario 2**) are particularly challenging, because the malware does not alter the overall amount of transactions performed: It leverages existing transactions by diverting them to a different recipient. The IP address is one of those usually used by the user and, in the case where the recipient fraudulent account is national, these transactions blend in quite easily. It is likely that with more training data these features will become more significant. However, even for this last case, thanks to the temporal profile anomaly

Table 3. Experiment 1 results on transactions and users. Blank cells indicate inapplicable dataset-scenario combinations (e.g., phone recharge transactions have no IBAN, phone recharge or prepaid card transactions are only nation-wise).

Fraud scenario	Correctly ranked frauds (%)					
	Bank transfers		Phone recharges		Prepaid cards	
	Transactions	Users	Transactions	Users	Transactions	Users
1: Information Stealing foreign IP and IBAN	**98**	57	**96**	87	**95**	68
foreign IP, national IBAN	**91**	57				
national IP, foreign IBAN	**98**	57	87	**95**	67	**96**
national IP and IBAN	**91**	57				
2: Transaction Hijacking foreign	**75**	58				
national	22	**58**	83	**89**	71	**77**
3: Stealthy Fraud foreign, very low amount	**73**	64				
foreign, low amount	**68**	67				
foreign, medium amount	69	**73**				
national, very low amount	42	**64**	64	97	**99**	93
national, low amount	37	**67**	94	**99**	92	**97**
national, medium amount	42	**72**	95	**99**	94	**98**

score BANKSEALER correctly ranked 58% of the frauds, up to 89% in the case of the phone recharges dataset. Indeed, if we consider the action of refilling phones or prepaid cards, we expect users to do this only towards a few fixed numbers or cards. This means that a recharge towards an unknown phone number or card is always anomalous, even if the transaction amounts is low and the IP address of the connection is one of those commonly used by the user.

Stealthy frauds (**Scenario 3**) are also challenging: the local profile performs well when the recipient account is foreign, or with phone recharge and prepaid card frauds. Interestingly, stealthy frauds involving very low amounts (50–100€) are correctly ranked better than transactions involving low amounts (100–500€). The reason is because the very-low amounts are rarer in the dataset, and thus obtain higher anomaly scores.

Experiment 2: Undertrained and New Users. We evaluated the capabilities of the global profile to lookup a good replacement local profile for undertrained and new users. We proceeded similarly to what we did in the previous experiment, injecting 1% of fraudulent transactions, but we spread the injections evenly across well trained, undertrained, and new users.

Tab. 4 summarizes the percentage of correctly ranked transactions overall, for well-trained users only, for undertrained uses only, and finally for new users only. Performance is similar to the previous experiment, even if the percentage of correctly ranked frauds are obviously a little lower due to the additional noise.

The fact that undertrained sometimes obtain better ranking than well-trained users, especially when in the attack scenario the frauds are masked to be similar to common transactions, is an artifact due to the fact that in undertrained users' profiles even frauds designed to appear as legitimate transactions can

Table 4. Experiment 2 results on well-trained, undertrained, new users only, and overall. As in Tab. 3, blank cells indicate inapplicable dataset-scenario combinations.

Fraud scenario		Correctly ranked frauds (%)										
		Bank transfers				Phone recharges				Prepaid cards		
		Overall	Well trained	Undertrained	New	Overall	Well trained	Undertrained	New	Overall	Well trained	Undertrained	New
1: Information Stealing	foreign IP and IBAN	96	98	99	92	80	99	99	43	80	85	94	59
	foreign IP, national IBAN	75	81	95	52								
	national IP, foreign IBAN	95	97	93	88	76	97	100	29	73	81	96	42
	national IP and IBAN	73	84	93	41								
2: Transaction Hijacking	foreign	63	43	91	51								
	national	24	13	57	3	40	29	83	6				
3: Stealthy Fraud	foreign, very low amount	52	40	91	22								
	foreign, low amount	56	38	92	39								
	foreign, medium amount	61	42	93	49					32	18	73	6
	national, very low amount	27	13	68	1	16	3	42	4	56	45	94	28
	national, low amount	29	14	71	2	19	5	51	0	59	40	91	47
	national, medium amount	34	19	78	3	19	2	56	0	72	64	94	59

receive a high score if the (few) transactions already observed for them are very different from the injected ones. Frauds injected in new users, instead, are ranked incorrectly when are designed to be similar to legitimate transactions. This is due to the fact that, for new users, transactions are tested against the average profile of all transactions in the dataset, and thus transaction with common attributes will receive low scores.

In the experiments on the phone recharges dataset, we obtain a slightly lower percentage of correctly ranked frauds than those in Tab. 3. On the other hand, for the stealthy fraud (**Scenario 3**) the percentages are considerably lower. A factor is the huge number of undertrained users in the phone recharges dataset (2,932 transactions for well trained users vs. 11,505 transactions in total). Similar considerations hold for the prepaid cards dataset, in particular for the higher percentage of correctly ranked frauds with undertrained users.

Experiment 3: Performance and Resource Requirements. To test the performance of BANKSEALER, we measured both the computational requirements at runtime (as this is a constraint for the practical use of the system in production), and peak memory requirements at training time (as this is a constraint on the dimension of the dataset that can be handled).

For computational power requirements, we tested the time to analyze one day and one month of data, both with and without the handling of undertrained and new users explained in §3.1. Our experiments have been executed on a desktop-class machine with a quad-core, 3.40Ghz Intel i5-3570 CPU, 8GB of RAM, running Linux 3.7.10 x86_64. Processing times are taken using the *time* library. The results are listed in Tab. 5. As we can see, the processing time varies on the basis of the context being tested, and there is a significant difference

Table 5. Computation time required at runtime under various conditions. In the typical use case, the system works on a daily basis, thus requiring 6 minutes (worst case).

Testing interval	Elapsed time		
	Bank transfers	Phone recharge	Prepaid cards
1 day, no undertrained/new users	$1'00''$	$0'18''$	$0'07''$
1 day, undertrained/new users	$4'00''$	$0'24''$	$0'10''$
1 month, no undertrained/new users	$6'00''$	$0'30''$	$0'12''$
1 month, undertrained/new users	$93'00''$	$2'30''$	$1'00''$

induced by the handling of undertrained/new users. In production BANKSEALER will analyze transactions day by day. Therefore, the maximum time required would be 4 minutes per day for the bank transfers context. In conclusion, we believe that BANKSEALER could be suitable for online fraud monitoring.

We tested the scalability of the system by measuring the RAM consumption at training time, which is the most memory-intensive phase. We used the bank transfers dataset, the largest one. We relied on memory-profiler and psutil . As Fig. 3 shows, the peak RAM consumption increases linearly with the number of days and quadratically with the number of users. This is expected, as the most memory-intensive data structure is the distance matrix, a square matrix of the size of the number of users.

5 Discussion

The main barrier in this research field is the lack of publicly available, real-world frauds and a ground truth for validation. Indeed, we had to resort to synthetically generated frauds. The absence of non-anonymized text fields does not allow us to analyze, for instance, their semantics. In future extensions, BANKSEALER will

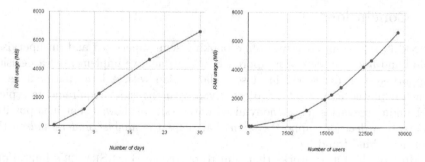

Fig. 3. RAM requirements for increasing values of W (left) and users profiled (right)

compute the models on the bank side and export privacy-preserving statistics for evaluation.

The prototype is also constrained by the RAM consumption of the clustering phase. This technical limitation can be mitigated in two possible ways. First, a triangular data structure to store the distance matrix. Second, a parallel version of DBSCAN [16], which splits the dataset on multiple machine.

6   Related Work

Fraud detection, mainly focused on credit card fraud, is a wide research topic, for which we refer the reader to [5,14,4].

Limiting our review to the field to banking fraud detection, supervised approaches based on contrast patterns and contrast sets (e.g., [3]) have been applied. Along a similar line [1] proposed a rule-based Internet banking fraud detection system. The proposed technique does not work in real time and thus is profoundly different from ours. Also, supervised techniques require labeled samples, differently from BANKSEALER.

The unsupervised approach presented in [15] is interesting as it mitigates the shortcomings of contrast pattern mining by considering the dependence between events at different points in time. However, [15] deals with the logs of the online banking web application, and thus does not detect frauds as much as irregular interactions with the application. Among the unsupervised learning methods, [12] proposed an effective detection mechanism to identify legitimate users and trace their unlawful activities using Hidden Markov Model (HMM)s. [10] is based on an unsupervised modeling of local and global observations of users' behavior, and relies on differential analysis to detect frauds as deviations from normal behavior. This evidence is strengthened or weakened by the users' global behavior. The major drawback of this approach is that the data collection must happen on the client side, which makes it cumbersome to deploy in large, real-world scenarios. In general, a major difference between existing unsupervised and semi-supervised approaches and BANKSEALER is that they do not give the analyst a motivation for the analysis results, making manual investigation and confirmation more difficult.

7   Conclusions

BANKSEALER is an effective online banking semi-supervised and unsupervised fraud and anomaly detection approach, with which we implemented a decision support system developed in close collaboration with a large national bank, which deployed it in a pilot project. Even with the strict requirements typical of banking scenarios (e.g., anonymized datasets), we showed that it is possible to create a decision support system that helps the analyst *understanding* the reasons behind frauds.

Most of the future works that aim to overcome BANKSEALER's limitations require more detailed datasets, which are often difficult to obtain due to privacy restrictions. Some examples are the semantic analysis of the text attributes, improvements of the temporal profile, and the estimation of the number of transactions required to fully train a profile.

A short-term work is to consider the feedback given by the analyst, which however requires careful evaluation because of the possible biases that an analyst may introduce. To this end, we currently deployed BANKSEALER in a real world environment, to collect the feedback of banking analysts on the detected anomalies.

Acknowledgements. The research leading to these results has received funding from the European Union Seventh Framework Programme (FP7/2007-2013) under grant agreement n 257007, as well as from the TENACE PRIN Project (n. 20103P34XC) funded by the Italian Ministry of Education, University and Research.

References

1. Aggelis, V.: Offline Internet Banking Fraud Detection. In: ARES, pp. 904–905. IEEE Computer Society (2006)
2. Amer, M., Goldstein, M.: Nearest-Neighbor and Clustering based Anomaly Detection Algorithms for RapidMiner, 1–12 (August 2012)
3. Bay, S.D., Pazzani, M.J.: Detecting Group Differences: Mining Contrast Sets. Data Mining and Knowledge Discovery 5(3), 213–246 (2001)
4. Bolton, R.J.: David: Statistical fraud detection: A review. Statistical Science 17 (2002)
5. Chandola, V., Banerjee, A., Kumar, V.: Anomaly detection: A survey. ACM Comput. Surv. 41, 15:1–15:58 (2009)
6. Fossi, M., Egan, G., Haley, K., Johnson, E., Mack, T., Adams, T., Blackbird, J., Low, M.K., Mazurek, D., McKinney, D., Wood, P.: Symantec Internet Security Threat Report trends for 2010. Technical report, Symantec (April 2011)
7. Goldstein, M., Dengel, A.: Histogram-Based Outlier Score (HBOS): A Fast Unsupervised Anomaly Detection Algorithm (2012)
8. Haley, K., Wood, P.: et al.: Internet Security Threat Report 2013, 18 (2013)
9. Han, J., Kamber, M.: Data mining: concepts and techniques, 2nd edn. Morgan Kaufmann (2006)
10. Kovach, S., Ruggiero, W.: Online banking fraud detection based on local and global behavior. In: ICDS 2011: The Fifth Intl. Conf. on Digital Society, pp. 166–171 (2011)
11. Mahalanobis, P.C.: On the generalized distance in statistics. In: Proc. of the National Institute of Science of India, 49–55 (1936)
12. Mhamane, S., Lobo, L.: Internet banking fraud detection using HMM. In: 2012 Third Intl. Conf. on Computing Communication Networking Technologies (ICCCNT), pp. 1–4 (2012)
13. Noto, K., Brodley, C., Slonim, D.: FRaC: a feature-modeling approach for semi-supervised and unsupervised anomaly detection. Data Min. Knowl. Discov. 25(1), 109–133 (2012)
14. Phua, C., Lee, V.C.S., Smith-Miles, K., Gayler, R.W.: A Comprehensive Survey of Data Mining-based Fraud Detection Research. CoRR abs/1009.6119 (2010)

15. Wei, W., Li, J., Cao, L., Ou, Y., Chen, J.: Effective detection of sophisticated online banking fraud on extremely imbalanced data. World Wide Web 16(4), 449–475 (2013)
16. Xu, X., Jäger, J., Kriegel, H.P.: A Fast Parallel Clustering Algorithm for Large Spatial Databases. Data Min. Knowl. Discov. 3(3), 263–290 (1999)
17. Yamanishi, K., Takeuchi, J.I., Williams, G., Milne, P.: On-Line Unsupervised Outlier Detection Using Finite Mixtures with Discounting Learning Algorithms. Data Min. Knowl. Discov. 8(3), 275–300 (2004)

Security Assessment of Payment Systems under PCI DSS Incompatibilities

Şerif Bahtiyar, Gürkan Gür, and Levent Altay

Provus - A MasterCard Company
Progress R&D Center, Ayazaga, 34396, Istanbul, TR
{serif.bahtiyar,gurkan.gur,levent.altay}@provus.com.tr

Abstract. With the ubiquitous proliferation of electronic payment systems, data and application security has become more critical for financial operations. The Payment Card Industry Data Security Standard (PCI DSS) has been developed by the payment industry to provide a widely-applicable and definitive security compliance among all components in electronic payment infrastructure. However, the security impact of PCI DSS incompatibilities and relevant security assessment approaches for such cases are yet to be investigated in a comprehensive manner. Therefore, in this paper we present a security assessment framework for payment systems under PCI DSS incompatibilities. Moreover, we analyze a case study to evaluate our proposal and to provide some guidelines to security experts for assessment of PCI DSS compliance.

Keywords: Payment system security, Security assessment, PCI DSS, Risk analysis, Data and applications security.

1 Introduction

Electronic payments have been the driver of instant and ubiquitous economic transactions particularly for the last two decades. Moreover, sector statistics indicate that cash and check payments are declining while electronic payment methods are gradually taking over [1, 2]. Therefore, this profound trend of electronic payment proliferation has brought forth an inevitable consequence regarding security: the reliance of this infrastructure on information and computing systems with data and application security becoming more critical for financial operations. The payment related data such as the confidential data of payers and transactional records stored and transmitted in these systems are subject to various attacks and security threats. Taking these matters into consideration, the Payment Card Industry Data Security Standard (PCI DSS) has been developed by the payment industry to facilitate a widely-applicable and definitive security compliance for electronic payment infrastructure [3–5].

PCI DSS defines the essential *requirements* serving some determined *objectives* and mainly focusing on the most valuable asset in a payment system: cardholder data (CHD). It has been growing in volume and coverage since its inception with additional guidelines and best practices published by PCI Security

N. Cuppens-Boulahia et al. (Eds.): SEC 2014, IFIP AICT 428, pp. 395–402, 2014.

Standards Council (SSC). However, the security impact of PCI DSS incompat-ibilities and security assessment approaches considering the system context are yet to be investigated in a comprehensive manner. Although there are some assessment procedures, they are typically costly and require complicated and intense effort by the assessor and assessee. Therefore, in this paper we devise a security assessment framework for electronic payment systems focusing on PCI DSS incompatibilities. We evaluate our model using a case study representing payment industry context. The proposed model, *Hierarchical Context-based Se-curity Assessment (HCOSA)*, is a simple yet effective method providing insights to institutions on their security level in addition to inherent security assessment functionality.

2   Payment Systems and PCI DSS

Payment can be described as the transaction of the financial value between the buyer and seller. Modern electronic payment systems are based on *Transaction Processing* (also known as *Transaction Switching*). This activity involves process-ing, transmission, and storage of cardholder related data at various constituents in the payment network. In addition to PCI DSS, well-known compliance stan-dards in data security ISO 27001 and EI3PA have common goal controlling and protecting sensitive data. PCI DSS and EI3PA differ from ISO 27001 being more standardized and regulated specifically to CHD and consumer credit informa-tion, respectively. Additionally, ISO 27004, BIP 0074:2006, and NIST SP800-55 Revision 1 have been standardized, with the aim of measuring the effectiveness and verifying the implementations of mentioned standards.

The main goal of an attacker in payment systems regarding data security is to capture CHD and exploit it. In terms of information security aspects, most attackers endanger Integrity and Confidentiality attributes of the payment sys-tem [6]. Based on the resulting damage, relevant threats can be classified into two main categories, namely *exposure* or *disruption of CHD*. Disruption of CHD has been largely mitigated by EMV standard and thus rarely faced [7]. But the exposure of CHD is still an open issue for payment systems due to PCI DSS incompliant parties. Thus, PCI DSS focuses on decreasing the probability of the occurrence of CHD exposure in payment systems [8].

In Table 1, we list PCI DSS objectives and the related security dimensions and threats. For instance, Objective (1) (O1) states that a compliant institution should provide a robust network environment against unauthorized modification or destruction of the CHD and Cardholder Data Environment (CDE) which leads to better integrity [9]. Under O2, CHD should be transmitted securely across networks. In that regard, encryption provides the confidentiality and integrity of CHD. For computational environment, O3 implies deployment of antivirus software which again serves to the integrity and confidentiality objectives. O4 requires the configuration of access control and limited access based on desig-nated roles. Moreover, it requires the system to uniquely identify, authenticate, log and control system access. However, O5 and O6 contain elements that are less

Table 1. PCI DSS requirements with key security objectives and threats

Objectives	Directly Related to	Sample Threat types
Build and Maintain a Secure Network	Availability: prevention against data delays or removal	Merchant website and processor gateway outages
Protect CHD	Confidentiality: protection against unauthorized data disclosure	− Data theft − Eavesdropping for accessing and decoding CHD
Maintain a Vulnerability Management Program	Integrity: prevention against unauthorized data modification	− Account tampering − Payment fraud
Implement Strong Access Control Measures	Authenticity: authentication of data source and modifier	− Internal theft − Physical acquisition of CHD
Regularly Monitor and Test Networks	Accountability	Any potential security threat
Maintain an Information Security Policy	Nonrepudiation: prevention against any one party from reneging on an agreement	Any potential security threat

intuitive. The former item contains a requirement for intrusion detection and/or prevention functions whilst the latter addresses a range of security management functions, including matters such as incident response and management of third party relationships.

With omnipresent threats to the payment networks and the necessity of cost-efficient and timely security assessment of related systems, simple and effective security assessment is crucial. However, PCI DSS requirements are generally difficult to define in measurable and quantitative terms, which makes the security assessment of an organization according to these objectives a challenging task. Therefore, we propose HCOSA for PCI DSS in this work, focusing on streamlined and effective security assessment functionality for PCI DSS actors. This approach allows for a continuous and repeatable compliance assessment for PCI DSS.

3   Proposed Methodology: Hierarchical Context-Based Security Assessment (HCOSA) for PCI DSS

We devise a security assessment methodology regarding PCI DSS and factors on the security of a payment-related system, namely Hierarchical Context-based Security Assessment (HCOSA). We assess the security of card holder data within an organization according to incompatibilities to PCI DSS requirements based on this approach. Security information flow and participating parties for the assessment are shown in Fig. 1. Actually, PCI has defined 12 PCI DSS requirements (Ri) under 6 objectives, where the objectives have been used to group and explain the requirements more precisely. For example, PCI DSS O1 contains R1

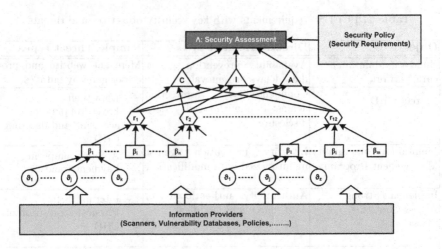

Fig. 1. Information flow for security assessment based on PCI-DSS

and R2 that are related to availability of systems as shown in Table 1. PCI DSS R1 is *Install and maintain a firewall configuration to protect cardholder data.*

In real life, systems have three main security objectives, namely confidentiality, integrity, and availability. Almost always, the objectives have different weights according to facts of organizations. For instance, availability is more significant than integrity for some services of financial institutions, which we have observed. Therefore, we compute the security assessment of an organization according to confidentiality, integrity, and availability requirements of CHD with Equation 1. Actually, a more granular security assessment formula may be constructed by considering many dependencies but this will increase the complexity of assessment with minor contribution to accuracy, which may be inapplicable in real life context.

$$\Lambda(t) = \kappa_c C(t) + \kappa_i I(t) + \kappa_a A(t). \tag{1}$$

Explanations of parameters used in all equations are provided in Table 2 and the values of parameters are within $[0, 1]$. In Equation 1, if $\Lambda(t) = 1$ or close to one, the security of CHD is high according to PCI DSS and the security policy of the organization, where $\sum \kappa_{x \in \{c,i,a\}} = 1$. Coefficients $\kappa_{x \in \{c,i,a\}}$ represents weights of confidentiality, integrity, and availability according to the security policy of an organization that contains CHD. On the other hand, we compute the three security objectives with $C(t) = \sum_{x=1}^{12} dc_x r_x(t)$, $I(t) = \sum_{x=1}^{12} di_x r_x(t)$, and $A(t) = \sum_{x=1}^{12} da_x r_x(t)$, where $\sum_{\forall x} dy_x \in \{dc_x, di_x, da_x\} = 1$. Specifically, we compute values of the three objectives according to satisfactions of each PCI DSS requirement and their dependencies related to the each security objective. For instance, assume that an organization partially satisfies PCI DSS Requirement 1 (R1), where the $r_1(t) = 0.53$. Assume also that $C(t)$ depends on that PCI DSS requirement with $dc_1 = 0.34$. Thus, the total effect of the PCI DSS requirement for the computation of $\Lambda(t)$ is $dc_1 \cdot r_1(t) = 0.159$.

Table 2. Model parameters and their descriptions

Parameter	Description
$\Lambda(t)$	Security assessment
$C(t)$	Assessed confidentiality
$I(t)$	Assessed integrity
$A(t)$	Assessed availability
κ_c	Weight of confidentiality
κ_i	Weight of integrity
κ_a	Weight of availability
$r_x(t)$	The effect of PCI-DSS requirement x
dc_x	Dependency coefficient of PCI-DSS requirement x related to confidentiality
di_x	Dependency coefficient of PCI-DSS requirement x related to integrity
da_x	Dependency coefficient of PCI-DSS requirement x related to availability
$\beta_{x,y}(t)$	Effect of sub requirement y of PCI-DSS requirement x
$v_j(x,y,t)$	Effect of vulnerability j to subrequirement y of requirement x

Organizations may partially or fully satisfy any subrequirement of a PCI DSS requirement. However, if a subrequirement of a PCI DSS requirement is not satisfied, which means $\beta_{x,y}(t) = 0$, the organization is then incompatible with that PCI DSS requirement, $r_x(t) = 0$. Moreover, each PCI DSS requirement consists of many subrequirements. Therefore, we compute the satisfaction of each PCI DSS requirement by considering effects of the subrequirements with $r_x(t) = \prod_{\forall y} \beta_{x,y}(t)$.

A subrequirement is compatible if it is resistant to potential vulnerabilities related to this subrequirement. Total effect of related vulnerabilities is the sum of effect of all vulnerabilities, which can be at most one. For this reason, we compute the compatibility of a subrequirement according to effects of potential vulnerabilities as following.

$$\beta_{x,y}(t) = 1 - \min\left(1, \sum_{\forall j} v_j(x,y,t)\right). \tag{2}$$

The impact of a vulnerability is determined according to information obtained from automated tools, such as scanners, vulnerability databases, security policies, and logs of security devices like firewalls and intrusion detection systems. For the sake of brevity, we do not present the impact of specific measurements about vulnerabilities and alternative measurements, such as the indicator of weakness in a firewall, in details. The impact of vulnerability and its measurement is challenging to determine since it is very context-dependent. Moreover, the gathered information needs to be pre-processed and evaluated for a consistent analysis. For instance, the impact factor of each requirement can be evaluated according to statistics on past breaches [10] and affected security objective due to the inadequate related requirement [11]. Thus, we focus on the assessment framework itself in this work and determining values of the coefficients are out of scope of our paper.

4   Updating Firewalls in a Financial Institution

In this section, we present a case study for elaborating on HCOSA related to a financial institution managing its firewalls under PCI DSS compliance. The purpose of this case study is to show the effects of updating firewalls and routers and PCI DSS incompatibilities related to the updates. In this case study, we have simulated the network of this institution using MATLAB to evaluate HCOSA.

Let us consider a financial institution that has more than ten thousand employees at different physical locations over the world. The field of activity of the corporation is the processing of electronic payments that are carried out with various payment cards. Therefore, CHD is a very sensitive data for such corporation, which should be protected.

The internal (trusted) network of the corporation consists of all trusted networks in different physical locations and it contains CHD in addition to other information. A trusted network is connected to the internal network via the Internet (i.e., untrusted network). The perimeter security of a trusted network is established with firewalls, intrusion detection systems, intrusion prevention systems, and configurations of routers against attacks coming from the Internet.

The internal network of the institution is updated regularly according to various criteria, such as employees who leave or join, new security threats discovered, and technological improvements. The firewalls and routers are also maintained according to these updates. Additionally, the institution has PCI DSS certificate and it should preserve the certificate to carry out its business. On the other hand, changes related to firewalls and routers should comply with PCI DSS requirements. Specifically, PCI DSS requirement 1 (R1) is directly related to changes or configurations of firewalls and routers, stating the action *"Install and maintain a firewall configuration to protect cardholder data"* [3].

HCOSA is a multi-layered framework and considers subrequirements of a PCI DSS requirement for security assessment. R1 has five subrequirements and each subrequirement is related to different tasks of firewalls and router operation and maintenance. For instance, subrequirement 1.1 has seven tasks. Therefore, vulnerabilities related to each task affect the security of the corporation. In HCOSA, sources of vulnerability information are scanners, vulnerability databases, and other sources whose main tasks are to find security vulnerabilities. Actually, determining security vulnerabilities and their effects are complex tasks. In this case study, therefore, we assume that relevant vulnerabilities are known. Then we set their effects to subrequirements in an illustrative way to evaluate the proposed model.

In high-level evaluation, the security of an institution satisfies or not satisfies the PCI DSS requirements. In low-level evaluation, on the other hand, it is impossible to formally prove and verify the security of an ICT system. For this reason, if a subrequirement has a satisfaction ratio over a predefined threshold, the subrequirement is considered as *satisfactory*. In this case study, we assume that subrequirements are evaluated daily and a subrequirement is expected to have $\beta_{x,y} \geq 0.9$ for four consecutive days. If a subrequirement fails to satisfy this expectation, a maintenance process for firewalls and routers is initialized to

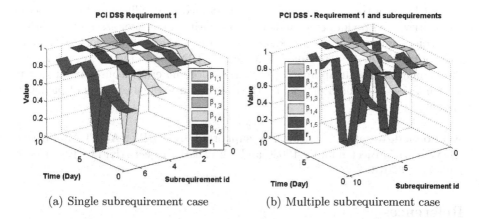

(a) Single subrequirement case   (b) Multiple subrequirement case

Fig. 2. The relationship among PCI DSS Requirement 1 and a major change in (a) a subrequirement (b) various subrequirements

improve security. However, some maintenance may have considerable negative effect for day five as shown in Fig. 2(a). There may be many reasons causing this negative effect. Simply, the lack of adequate qualified security experts, unexpected state of modifying network topology related to firewalls and routers in a complex network are some of them and they may result in unsatisfied subrequirement(s). Actually, the network in question is highly dynamic and compliance to PCI DSS may fluctuate over time. These fluctuations may be negligible if they satisfy the predefined threshold as shown for $\beta_{1,1}, \beta_{1,2}, \beta_{1,3}, \beta_{1,5}$ in Fig. 2(a).

Maintaining firewalls and routers regarding a subrequirement may affect only the subrequirement and its PCI DSS requirement as in Fig. 2(a) or it may affect many subrequirements and the PCI DSS requirement as in Fig. 2(b). For instance, the maintenance process to improve security level of subrequirement 4, $\beta_{1,4}$, is carried out in day five in this case study. The security level of $\beta_{1,4}$ is improved after the maintenance process but security levels of subrequirements $\beta_{1,2}$ and $\beta_{1,5}$ drop considerably as shown in Fig. 2(b). Therefore, the maintenance process related to firewalls and routers has been carried on until day seven to construct a system that satisfies all subrequirements of PCI DSS R1.

The case study shows that any change in the network of a financial corporation that contains CHD should be investigated carefully related to PCI DSS incompatibilities. Since such networks are very large, complex, and dynamic environments, the investigation has to be done in an automated way. HCOSA can be applied in network infrastructure to monitor and assess security of an organization related to PCI DSS in a continuous and repeatable process.

5 Conclusion

In this work, we investigate security assessment for PCI DSS requirements in payment systems. We devise a security assessment approach for PCI DSS in a context-based setting. We focus on PCI DSS incompatibilities and their effects on security. We provide some guidelines to security experts for assessment of PCI DSS compliance. In future work, we plan to extend our framework to include more advanced dependency models among PCI DSS requirements and improve the evaluation for our approach considering more heterogeneous contexts, such as evaluation of vulnerabilities and their effects in various contexts of payment systems.

Acknowledgments. This work is supported by EUREKA ITEA2 Project ADAX with project number 10030 and TEYDEB Project AKFiS with project number 1130018.

References

1. Liu, J., Xiao, Y., Chen, H., Ozdemir, S., Dodle, S., Singh, V.: A survey of payment card industry data security standard. IEEE Communications Surveys and Tutorials 12(3), 287–303 (2010)
2. Choo, K.K.R.: New payment methods: A review of 2010-2012 FATF mutual evaluation reports. Computers & Security 36, 12–26 (2013)
3. Payment Card Industry (PCI) Data Security Standard: Requirements and security assessment procedures. (November 2013),
   https://www.pcisecuritystandards.org/security_standards/documents.php/
4. Peterson, G.: From auditor-centric to architecture-centric: SDLC for PCI DSS. Information Security Technical Report 15(4), 150–153 (2010)
5. Ataya, G.: PCI DSS audit and compliance. Information Security Technical Report 15(4), 138–144 (2010)
6. Verizon Risk Team: Verizon Enterprise Risk and Incident Sharing Metrics Framework (2013), http://www.verizonenterprise.com/resources/
   whitepapers/wp_verizon-incident-sharing-metrics-framework_en_xg.pdf
7. Trustwave's SpiderLabs: Global security report (2013),
   https://www2.trustwave.com/2013GSR.html
8. Ogundele, O., Zavarsky, P., Ruhl, R., Lindskog, D.: The implementation of a full EMV smartcard for a point-of-sale transaction and its impact on the PCI DSS. In: Privacy, Security, Risk and Trust (PASSAT), 2012 International Conference on Social Computing (SocialCom), pp. 797–806 (September 2012)
9. Rowlingson, R., Winsborrow, R.: A comparison of the payment card industry data security standard with ISO17799. Computer Fraud&Security 2006(3), 16–19 (2006)
10. Baker, W., Hutton, A., Hylender, C.D., Pamula, J., Porter, C., Spitler, M.: 2011 data breach investigations report (2011), http://www.verizonbusiness.com/
    resources/reports/rp_databreach-investigations-report-2011_en_xg.pdf
11. Bradley, T., Chuvakin, A., Elberg, A., Koerner, B.J.: PCI Compliance: Understand and implement effective PCI data security standard compliance. Syngress Publishing (2007)

PriMan: Facilitating the Development
of Secure and Privacy-Preserving Applications

Andreas Put, Italo Dacosta, Milica Milutinovic, and Bart De Decker

KU Leuven, Dept. of Computer Science, iMinds-DistriNet
Celestijnenlaan 200A, 3001 Heverlee, Belgium
{firstname.lastname}@cs.kuleuven.be

Abstract. Security and privacy are essential in today's information-driven society. However, security technologies and privacy-enhancing technologies (PETs) are often difficult to integrate in applications due to their inherent complexity and steep learning curve. In this paper, we present a flexible, technology agnostic development framework that facilitates the integration of security and privacy-preserving technologies into applications. Technology-specific configuration details are shifted from the application code to configuration policies. These policies are configured by domain experts independently from the application's source code. We developed a prototype in Java, called PriMan, which runs on both desktops and Android based devices. Our experimental evaluation demonstrates that PriMan introduces a low and acceptable overhead (e.g., less than one millisecond per operation). In addition, we compare PriMan with other, freely available solutions. PriMan facilitates the integration of PETs and security technologies in current and future applications.

Keywords: Software Architecture, Security, Identity Management, Framework.

1 Introduction

Security and privacy are requirements that keep gaining importance in today's information-driven world. Every system or application connected to the Internet has to be sufficiently secured. However, information leaks and security breaches are commonplace, even though many can be prevented by the proper use of proven security and privacy technologies. For example, the Open Web Application Security Project (OWASP) has identified a list of important vulnerabilities for mobile applications [1]. Among the top vulnerabilities on this list are: insecure data storage, insufficient transport layer protection, poor authorization and authentication, etc. Developers, however, need to have knowledge of various technical concepts (e.g., security protocols, key management, cryptographic algorithms, etc.) to correctly implement technologies that mitigate these vulnerabilities. Furthermore, deploying and configuring PETs and security technologies requires additional expertise. As a result, it is challenging for average developers to implement adequate security and privacy mechanisms in their applications.

N. Cuppens-Boulahia et al. (Eds.): SEC 2014, IFIP AICT 428, pp. 403–416, 2014.

Another problem is that many security and privacy mechanisms are coded directly into applications and, hence, mixed with the business logic. This practice hinders code reusability, as large modifications to the code base are typically required to reuse mechanisms from one application into another one. In addition, these large modifications increase the possibility of errors and security and privacy weaknesses.

In this paper we present PriMan, a framework developed within the MobCom project[1] [2], that facilitates the integration of security and privacy technologies for authentication and protection of data while in transit (over communication channels) or being stored. The abstractions made by PriMan shift the technology-specific configuration details from the application code to configuration policies. Developers thus only work with abstract components, the interface of which is common for every technology used underneath.

A developer can use the framework to initialize a connection or to store an object, while the configuration policy defines which type of connection is used (e.g., HTTP or HTTPS) and how the object is stored (e.g., in a file or in an encrypted database). In addition, the framework simplifies application code, as the framework itself performs many of the common tasks associated with each operation. These features make it well suited for rapid prototyping, or even to test the effects of different technologies on applications. PriMan uses a lightweight and modular architecture. Its thin middleware layer resides between the application code and the different technology libraries, introducing a low performance overhead. Our benchmarks show that PriMan adds an overhead of less than one millisecond per operation. Moreover, PriMan's architecture is designed to run not only on servers but also mobile devices.

In short, we make the following contributions:

- We defined abstractions that capture common features and traits over several sets of technologies in such a way that they are independent from their underlying algorithms and/or cryptographic components. Although the technology specific features are hidden by these abstractions, they still can be specified in configuration policies.
- We designed and implemented a PriMan prototype in Java, which includes a full-fledged implementation of the Idemix anonymous credential system [3, 4]. We evaluated the efficiency of our framework by measuring how much overhead it introduces. We also compare PriMan to the CARL framework [5] and to ABC4Trust [6].
- We integrated privacy-preserving authentication policies with support for anonymous and traditional credentials (e.g., Idemix and X.509 certificates[7]). These policies allow service providers to easily specify what a client needs to prove in order to gain access to a service. Clients can inspect these policies before authentication in order to analyse what information they reveal to the service provider.

---

[1] *The Mobile Companion (MobCom)* project's main goal is to transform mobile devices such as smartphones into powerful, flexible and user-friendly tools to manage our identities in a privacy-friendly way.

2   The PriMan Framework

PriMan is an application development framework that focuses on security, privacy, flexibility and ease of use. The latter is mainly geared towards application developers, as they are the targeted users of the framework. Firstly, the framework offers PETs and security technologies to developers. Secondly, it provides a technology-agnostic API, i.e., code written with PriMan is completely independent from the actual technologies used underneath. The framework configures at runtime which components are used (e.g., X.509 or Idemix) by following configuration policies, which also contain the specific configuration details of the chosen technology. This concept is similar to the separation of document content from its style for web pages (i.e., HTML and CSS). By separating application code from configuration details, developers can focus on writing application logic without concerns about the details of the underlying technologies. Moreover, by relying on configuration policies, PriMan facilitates changes to current technologies or switching among different technologies (e.g. X.509 to Idemix). Furthermore, PriMan automatically performs common development tasks, reducing the programming work left to the developer.

2.1   Abstractions

PriMan defines abstractions over sets of technologies to create an intuitive and technology-agnostic API. This section explores these abstractions for two of the framework's components: the connection and credential components.

The starting point for making these abstractions is: what are the common, high level concepts and operations of a set of technologies, i.e., which high level operations do developers expect from these technologies. For example, for the set of connection technologies (table 1), the common concepts are *connections* and *connection listeners*, the latter being an object which listens for incoming connections. The specific configuration details for each technology are abstracted by *connection parameters*, which are created from configuration policies. After a connection is established, it can be used to send or receive data and finally, it can be shut down.

For example, TCP sockets are one of the simplest connection technologies, however, a significant amount of configuration options are possible. Input and output streams are used to write and read data from a socket, and the technology-specific parameters like hostname, port or time-out values are selected from a configuration policy.

As authentication is an important task in many systems, the credential component is a major part of PriMan. Table 2 shows the most important abstractions produced for this component. The table shows how three credential providers (X.509, Idemix and username-password) implement these abstractions. First, to create new credentials, an issuer has to be set up, which involves generating and installing the necessary cryptographic keys. For X.509 an issuing keypair

Table 1. The most important abstractions defined by PriMan's Connection component are listed in the first column. The second and third column list how these abstractions are implemented by the TCP and SSL providers.

Abstraction	TCP socket	SSL socket
Create Connection and listen (server) — create connection to server (client)	Open TCP socket and Listen (server) — create TCP connection (client)	Open (SSL) socket using an SSL Certificate and listen (server) — create SSL connection (client)
Send data	Send object through socket	Send object through SSL socket
Receive data	Receive obj. through socket	Receive obj. through SSL socket
Close connection	Clear and close TCP socket	Clear and close SSL socket
Connection params.	Port, address, timeout	Port, address, timeout, cert.-store file, type and password

and certificate is required. Similarly, an issuing keypair is required for Idemix. A username-password credential does not require a cryptographic keypair or an issuing certificate. Therefor, their issuer parameters are empty. The issuance of new credentials is a protocol between the issuer and the client, which requires an established connection. Framework connection objects are used to establish these connections and to send or receive data, independent of the technology used underneath.

Once credentials have been issued, they can be used to create proofs of certain claims. X.509 and passwords only support one claim: "I own this credential" (this certificate or this username). Idemix-claims are more complex[2] and defined in a proof specification. Each credential component creates and verifies the (cryptographic) proof of a claim in its own particular way. With X.509 certificates, a signature of a nonce or challenge is created and verified, while an Idemix proof consists of several parts: a proof of knowledge of a CL-signature [8], and the zero-knowledge proofs [9] for all predicates contained in the claim. Proving ownership of a username can be simply done by sending the corresponding password or a one-way function thereof to the verifier, who can verify whether it matches a stored copy.

PriMan's abstractions have been derived empirically in a two-step process. First, the common traits, concepts and operations of a set of technologies are identified and a first version of the abstractions is created. Second, these abstractions are validated in practice by developing applications with them. After this, a new iteration of this process is performed using the feedback gathered in the second stage, until the API stabilizes. In a following stage, the API will be validated and tested in a more formal manner and larger setting.

---

[2] In contrast to X.509, Idemix can hide the attributes not required in an authentication. In addition, it supports predicate proofs, in which (in)equality of attributes can be proven with other attributes or constants, without revealing the exact values of these attributes.

Table 2. The most important abstractions defined by PriMan's credential component are listed in the first column. The second and third column list how these abstractions are implemented by the X.509 and Idemix providers. The fourth column shows how to the same abstractions apply to the most used credential of all, the username-password pair.

Abstraction	X.509	Idemix	Passwords
Create Issuer	Create self-signed cert. or use existing cert. to create issuer	Create Idemix keypair	Do nothing
Issuer params.	Type, sign/hash algo, values keystore file and password	Location of idemix public parameters	
Issue credential (Server)	Use certificate and the client's cert. request to generate a new certificate	Use keypair and key-value pairs to interactively issue a new Idemix cred.	Store (salted) password hash
Get new cred. (Client)	Generate keypair and create cert. request	Use the user secret to interactively issue cred.	Create username and password
Issuance params.	Type, sign/hash algo, values keystore file and password	Location of idemix public parameters, values	Username-password
Claim	X.509 certificate	Idemix proof specification	The username
Create proof of a claim	Sign a nonce with the private key of the cert.	Generate Idemix proof with regard to a nonce	Password
Verify proof	Verify the signature with public key of the cert.	Verify the Idemix proof w.r.t. the proof spec.	Match password with stored one

2.2   Framework Architecture

Three main concepts are integral to PriMan's architecture: *Managers, Service Providers* and *Core Classes* (Figure 1).

Managers. A manager is the main access point to PriMan's functionality, and is situated in the *framework layer*. It forms part of the interface to a set of technologies, e.g., the connection manager allows a developer to set up a communication channel of a particular technology. The manager offers a technology-agnostic interface; the technology which is actually used, depends on the method parameters it receives from the *application layer*. These parameters often include a configuration policy, which specifies the technology-specific configuration details for the technology provider below. Furthermore, Managers provide a flexible mechanism responsible to select the appropriate provider.

Core Classes. The core classes are the technology-agnostic abstractions of the different technology-specific concepts. Core classes consist mostly out of abstract classes and interfaces and thus, their main feature is the definition of one well-fitting API, which is independent from algorithms or components used underneath.

Service Providers. A service provider is an implementation of a specific technology such as X.509 or Idemix credentials. Each service provider implements a specific interface related their associated technology, the *Service Provider Interface* (SPI). In addition, they contain the implementations of the core classes associated with the provider's technology. The layer between PriMan's API and a technology's library is made as thin as possible, which

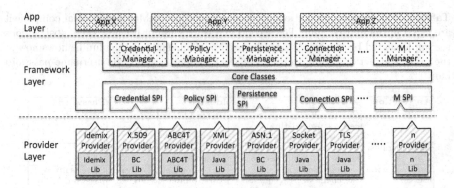

Fig. 1. Applications using PriMan are layered in three parts. The application-specific code resides in the *App Layer*. The technology-agnostic API for the application code is defined in the *Framework Layer*. Finally, the technology-specific implementations which plug into the framework reside in the *Provider Layer*.

significantly reduces the framework's overhead. This is done using the wrapper software design pattern, in which each method call is mapped to one or more operations of the software library that provides the implemented technology. Due to the framework's abstractions, providers often map one framework operation to multiple method calls of the technology library. This approach decreases the chances of developers' mistakes, as most of the low level details remain hidden for the developer while a significant part of the work is performed by the framework.

The manager can address its providers uniformly because each provider associated with a certain manager complies to the same SPI. This architecture provides a flexible plug-in mechanism, through which plug-ins (providers) can be loaded or unloaded at run-time.

2.3   Framework Components

The PriMan framework without any providers is just an empty shell. The framework defines the abstractions over sets of technologies and provides a plug-in mechanism for loading these providers, which are implementations of the defined abstractions. PriMan's pluggable architecture is well suited to deploy applications on mobile devices as well as desktops. Heavyweight components could be exchanged for more lightweight ones suitable for mobile platforms. The downside of such a plug-in architecture is that it introduces some additional overhead. However, this runtime overhead is can be significantly reduced by preloading service providers.

The PriMan framework is a good tool to perform rapid prototyping of applications. A developer can easily change the used technologies in her set-up, without having to recompile the code by simply changing one of the configuration policies. In doing so, the performance effects of different technologies (e.g., using Idemix instead of X.509) on these applications can be analyzed.

2.4   Implementation

We implemented the above architecture using the Java programming language. Java greatly simplifies the development of a mobile version of PriMan, as the Android operating system uses Java as its native programming language. Most of PriMan's desktop-version code can be reused in the mobile version. In addition, most framework providers can be plugged into the Android version of PriMan, if they do not depend on platform dependent features.

At the time of writing, ten different providers have been implemented for Desktop and Android platforms. The Idemix [4] and X.509 [7] credential systems, the CARL authentication policy language [5] and ABC4Trust presentation policies [6, 10], the XML and PEM/ASN.1 persistence provider [11], and the TCP and SSL connection providers. For Android, the framework supports two secure file encryption providers: one based on Android's secure keyring and one based on a tamper proof module.

3   Functional Evaluation

To evaluate PriMan's capabilities, we considered the following scenario. A municipal library offers inhabitants of the city access to its online portfolio. Citizens own a digital version of their identity card (eID) that contains an Idemix credential and can be managed on a smartphone. To access the library's online content, users need to use their credential to prove they live in the city. In addition, to access adult content, users need to prove that they are older than 18.

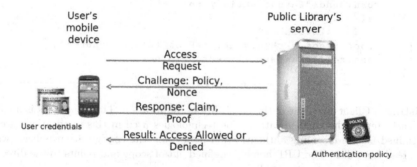

Fig. 2. Both client and server follow an interactive authentication protocol. The client uses her credentials to build a proof that satisfies the server's authentication policy.

The protocol (figure 2) follows the guidelines for authentication using anonymous credential systems set by ABC4Trust's architecture for developers [6]. First, the server will send an authentication policy and a nonce to a connecting user. The authentication policy states that the user must prove that she owns a government issued credential, that she lives in the city and that she is older then eighteen. Such authentication policies clearly improve the user's privacy, as users can inspect these policies, learning what personal information will be revealed to whom, before any information is disclosed during the authentication. If she can do so, the user will construct a claim that satisfies the authentication policy, and create a proof of this claim. The server now verifies whether or not this claim satisfies the authentication policy and whether the proof is valid. If both tests succeed, the client may access the requested content, otherwise, access will be denied.

```
1  //INITIALIZATION
2  Priman priman = Priman.getInstance();
3  ConnectionManager cmgr = priman.getConnectionManager();
4  ServerPolicyManager spMgr = priman.getServerPolicyManager();
5  PersistenceManager pMgr = priman.getPersistenceManager();
6  CredentialManager cMan = priman.getCredentialManager();
7  priman.loadConfiguration(home.resolve("priman.conf"));
8  //INITIALIZE CONNECTION
9  ConnectionParameters cparams =
10     pMgr.load(home.resolve("clientParams.xml"));
11 Connection conn = cmgr.createConnection(cparams);
12 conn.send("ACCESS-REQUEST");
13 //GET POLICY AND NONCE
14 String polStr = (String)conn.receive();
15 Nonce nonce = (Nonce)conn.receive();
16 ServerPolicy sp=spMgr.parsePolicy(polStr);
17 //CREATE CLAIM USING USER CREDENTIALS AND POLICY
18 Claim claim = sp.getClaim(pMgr.getCredentials());
19 if(claim == null){//CANNOT SATISFY POLICY?
20     conn.send("Cannot satisfy policy");
21 } else{
22     //GENERATE/SEND PROOF
23     Proof proof = cMan.generateProof(claim,  nonce);
24     conn.send(cMan.serializeProof(proof));
25 }
```

Listing 1. Client side code of the public library application. The framework is involved in each step of the authentication. The technologies used in this applications are determined by the incoming authentication policy and the configuration policies which are read from disk. The URI 'home' is defined out of scope and points to the directory containing the configuration policies.

Listing 1 shows the Java code required to implement the client side of this application with PriMan. First, the framework is initialized, and the managers are loaded (2-7). Then, the connection manager is used to set up the connection, using the configuration policies, which are read from a file (9-11). Thereafter, an access request is sent through the newly created connection, and an authentication policy and a nonce is sent back. PriMan parses this policy (12-16).

The policy defines which types of credential are allowed in the proof and, therefore, defines the proof. At this point, we can clearly identify one of the strengths of PriMan. *Because all technology-dependent details are absent in the application code, the developer is not concerned with what type of credential is actually used.* Whether it is a username-password, an Idemix or an X.509 credential, it will make no difference in the application code.

Using the authentication policy, a claim is created (18), which will later be used to generate a proof (23). In this scenario, the claim specifies that the user lives in a certain city, that she is older than eighteen and that she will prove this using her Idemix eID. However, depending on the authentication policy, the claim could require other facts (e.g., the fact that the user is female), or it could even specify that the user knows a password associated with a given username. While generating the proof, the credential manager will use the claim object to determine which technology and, thus, which provider is needed. However, the API also exposes the functionality to inspect the claim: which type it is, which credentials are used, what information will be disclosed, etc. . Finally, the client serializes and sends the proof to the service provider, which only needs to verify it before it can grant or deny the user access. By doing this verification, the server will only learn whether or not the client could satisfy the authentication policy.

Using PriMan, the scenario illustrated above would take little over forty lines of code to implement both the client and server side. Due to space constraints, the server-side code is not listed, but it is similar to the client-side code. Note that PriMan not only allows the developer to easily construct these complex scenarios, but also facilitates the substitution of the currently used technology for another, simply by modifying configuration policies.

4   Discussion

4.1   Design Decisions

This section discusses the design decisions and their impact with relation to *usability* from a developer's point of view and *performance*.

Usability. By providing a usable, technology-agnostic abstractions, the additional cost of integrating PETs and security technologies in applications becomes negligible. However, special attention has been invested in determining what information and operations are to be exposed by the technology-agnostic abstractions. These abstractions work in cooperation with configuration policies, which specify exactly which framework components are used and provide technology-specific parameters to these components. Developers are not required to write these policies themselves, as these policies can be written by domain experts, independently from the source code, or retrieved from an online repository. In addition, a policy creation tool can greatly increase the usability of these configuration policies for developers. Such a tool could receive as input a high level description of the desired properties of an application, like the privacy, availability or performance properties, and return as output the optimal combination of configuration policies.

Table 3. The Framework overhead and Idemix library execution time for prove and verify operations on a desktop (D) and smartphone (M). Two types of proof were evaluated: ownership of a credential with three hiden attributes (3,0) and with three revealed attributes (3,3). The mean times for 100 samples are listed in milliseconds with the standard deviation between parentheses.

	Prove D	Verify D	Prove M	Verify M
(3,0) Idemix	91 (5.4)	80 (4.9)	337.92 (10.52)	289.46 (8.73)
(3,0) Overhead	0.16 (0.09)	0.14 (0.02)	0.61 (0.08)	0.38 (0.04)
(3,3) Idemix	71 (2.7)	66 (3.2)	262.42 (8.63)	240.06 (4.73)
(3,3) Overhead	0.17 (0.1)	0.12 (0.01)	0.65 (0.06)	0.31 (0.03)

Performance. The framework's core consists mostly of abstract classes and interfaces. Almost all the logic is contained in the framework providers, which implement these abstract classes. They are implemented by the framework's providers, which only translate the incoming operations, defined by the abstract classes, to one or more operations of a technology-providing library (e.g., the Idemix library). Thereafter, the output of the technology-providing library is wrapped and returned in a PriMan object. This procedure is simple, and only introduces little overhead.

Table 3 shows the amount of overhead caused by the framework in milliseconds. These tests were performed on a machine with an Intel Core i5 @ 2.5 GHz with 4GB of RAM and on a Samsung Galaxy S3 smartphone. The implementation of PriMan is written in Java, uses the Idemix library (v. 2.3.4) and the tests were performed on Java SE 1.7 for Mac OS and Android version 4.1.2. For this test, the Idemix provider has been chosen because it is the most complex of PriMan's providers. It requires the most work and, hence, the most time to translate method calls from and to the Idemix library. 100 samples were taken, of which the mean execution times are listed with the standard deviation between parentheses.

As the results clearly show, the overhead caused by both the prove and verify tasks is negligible for both desktop and mobile, with no single overhead value larger than 0.2 ms and 0.7 ms respectively. In addition, the framework does not behave different on a smartphone, where each operation, including the framework's overhead, takes three to four times longer.

4.2   Comparison

CARL. We ran several benchmarks to compare the performance overhead of PriMan with the CARL framework [12]. To our knowledge, this is the only open, freely available available framework that combines authentication policies with the Idemix credential system. The setup for these tests is identical to the one used in the previous test and both frameworks use the same Idemix library. For every test, both the client-side and the server were run on the same machine.

Both the PriMan and CARL framework were used to implement an application that uses the authentication scheme similar to the one shown in figure 2.

Table 4. Performance comparison between PriMan and the CARL framework. PriMan performs its tasks consistently faster than the CARL framework. Because both frameworks use the same Idemix library, the generation and verification times are nearly the same. The mean times from 100 samples are listed in milliseconds, with the corresponding standard deviation between parentheses.

	CARL	PriMan
Claim/Proof generation (user)	2658 ms	799 ms
Policy parsing	1845 ms (203)	15 ms (1)
Claim generation	58 ms (3)	24 ms (2)
Idemix proof generation	755 ms (21)	760 ms (23)
Verification (server)	1152 ms	549 ms
Idemix proof verification	554 ms (19)	534 ms (12)
Policy verification	587 ms (10)	15 ms (2)

The actors in this scheme are the same: a client, who manages credentials on his device and wants to authenticate to a server. The client's six credentials are all anonymous Idemix credentials with a 2048-bit modulus and four to six attributes. When the client requests access to the server, the latter sends an authentication policy (in the CARL policy language). The client parses this policy, and tries to build a claim using the local credentials that can satisfy the initially sent authentication policy. If this is possible, a proof of this claim is created and sent to the server. This proof is verified by the server, which also checks if this proof satisfies the authentication policy.

The figures in table 4 clearly show that PriMan is consistently more efficient than CARL. 100 separate runs of the protocol were performed, of which the mean execution times are listed with the standard deviation between parentheses. The Idemix proof generation and verification times are similar for both frameworks, which is to be expected because the same idemix library is used. For the other subtasks, PriMan is more efficient due to three reasons. First, PriMan does not work with an intermediate, technology independent claim representation, which means that no "claim transformation" needs to be performed. This transformation step is performed by CARL in both the *claim generation* and *policy verification* step. Secondly, PriMan parses the policy to a simple but efficient internal representation, which means that parsing, claim generation and claim verification requires much less work. CARL, on the other hand uses a very extensive and elaborate parsing library, which causes the policy parsing time to explode. Finally, the layer between PriMan's API and the Idemix library is much thinner compared to the CARL framework. All these factors add up and result in a framework which supports the same features as CARL, but 2 to 3 times faster.

ABC4Trust. The goal of the ABC4Trust [10] project is to improve the federation and interchangeability of technologies that support trustworthy, privacy-preserving Attribute Based Credentials (ABC), or anonymous credentials. ABC4Trust has defined a common, unified architecture for ABC systems, and develops an open reference implementation of ABC systems to deploy in actual pilots.

PriMan similarly defines abstractions that cover multiple technologies and systems under a common, unified architecture. However, the abstractions made by PriMan cover not only anonymous credential technologies, but also other kinds of credential technologies like X.509 certificates and the username-password pair. In addition, PriMan targets data storage and the protection of communication channels.

Nevertheless, PriMan and the ABC4Trust architecture are not mutually exclusive. The architecture defined by ABC4Trust can fit in the abstractions of PriMan, i.e., a provider can be implemented which implements this architecture. The advantage of this is that applications written with PriMan can be made compatible with systems based on the ABC4Trust architecture. Because Priman does not use its own technology-independent format, but wraps a translation layer around existing formats, messages from/to an ABC4Trust application can be interpreted by a PriMan application. The framework thus remains compatible with the technologies it implements.

5 Related Work

The PriMan framework is inspired by a framework developed within the ADAPID project [13] ("Advanced Applications for the Belgian eID card"). This framework offers a unified interface for the Belgian eID card and X.509 certificates. In contrast to ADAPID, the focus of PriMan is to facilitate the integration of PETs and security technologies in applications. In addition, PriMan also focusses on performance, usability and support for mobile devices.

Much work has already been performed in the field of privacy preserving identity management. The requirements of such systems are investigated in [14–16]. The European project ABC4Trust [10, 6] builds on this work by defining a common, unified architecture for anonymous credential systems. This work is validated by several pilot projects in which authentication is performed using anonymous credential systems.

Privacy-friendly identity management should allow for anonymous yet accountable transactions, which can be provided by using anonymous credential systems. First, the client and the service provider must agree on an authentication policy. Various privacy preserving policy languages for attribute based credentials have been proposed [5, 6, 17]. After receiving a policy, the user employs her credentials to prove that the information contained therein satisfies the authentication policy. Second, further constraints can even be made on the downstream usage of this information by the service provider or other third parties [6, 17, 18].

An authentication framework has been made available that combines the Idemix credential system with the CARL authentication policy [5], but this framework introduces a lot of overhead and is not suitable for mobile devices. PriMan supports the same CARL authentication policies, but it introduces almost no computational overhead and it is optimized for mobile devices. The PriMan implementation of CARL supports authentication using Idemix, but also authentication using all other supported credential systems. Due to PriMan's technology-agnostic API it does not matter which technology is used underneath as every technology provides an implementation for the same set of operations.

A similar project, Opaak [19], implements the Idemix credential system and offers a set of authentication protocols which developers can easily integrate in their applications. Like PriMan, Opaak recognises the importance of mobile devices and supports Android. However, the scope of PriMan is bigger than that of Opaak. PriMan aims at offering the tools to build secure, privacy-friendly applications from start to finish; from credential storage mechanisms and the set-up of connections, to credential systems and various types of policies.

6 Conclusions and Future Work

This paper presents PriMan, a flexible framework that facilitates the development of secure, privacy-preserving applications by offering high-level technology-agnostic abstractions. Through its configuration policies, PriMan allows applications to seamlessly switch between different technologies. In addition, PriMan's API removes the need for developers to learn the specific details of a new technology. Furthermore, little work is required to integrate a new technology in the framework because of its flexible and extensible design.

PriMan has an efficient and modular implementation which allows it to run on a wide range of devices. It supports mobile devices and brings, among other components, a full-fledged anonymous credential system to these platforms.

We have implemented privacy-preserving authentication policies that can be used in combination with the credential systems supported by PriMan. These policies allow users to learn and review what information they will reveal during an authentication. The performance results show that PriMan's design introduces only a small amount of performance overhead.

One of the goals of PriMan is to facilitate the development of advanced, but privacy preserving application. The framework accomplishes this by offering a simple and intuitive technology-agnostic API. It is our intention to further investigate and validate the usability of this API, and its accompanying configuration policies. Furthermore, the framework could support various other policy types with which access control can be regulated and framework tasks automated. E.g., a user could specify what personal information contained in credentials can be revealed to which entities. The vocabulary and grammar of such a language, and the usability thereof are still open questions.

Acknowledgements. This research was funded by the IWT-SBO Project Mob-Com: A Mobile Companion (https://www.mobcom.org).

References

1. OWASP: OWASP Mobile Security Project — Top Ten Mobile Risks (2013),
   https://www.owasp.org/index.php/OWASP_Mobile_Security_Project
2. MobCom Project: MobCom: A Mobile Companion (2013),
   http://www.mobcom.org/
3. Camenisch, J.L., Lysyanskaya, A.: An efficient system for non-transferable anonymous credentials with optional anonymity revocation. In: Pfitzmann, B. (ed.)
   EUROCRYPT 2001. LNCS, vol. 2045, pp. 93–118. Springer, Heidelberg (2001)
4. Specification of the Identity Mixer cryptographic library – version 2.3.2, IBM Research – Zurich (2010)
5. Camenisch, J., Mödersheim, S., Neven, G., Preiss, F.S., Sommer, D.: A card requirements language enabling privacy-preserving access control. ACM (2010)
6. Camenisch, J., Krontiris, I., Lehmann, A., Neven, G., Paquin, C., Rannenberg, K.:
   H2. 1-abc4trust architecture for developers. Heartbeat (2012)
7. Housley, R., Ford, W., Polk, W., Solo, D.: Rfc 2459 - internet x.509 public key
   infrastructure certificate and CRL profile (1999)
8. Camenisch, J.L., Lysyanskaya, A.: Signature schemes and anonymous credentials from bilinear maps. In: Franklin, M. (ed.) CRYPTO 2004. LNCS, vol. 3152,
   pp. 56–72. Springer, Heidelberg (2004)
9. Rackoff, C., Simon, D.R.: Non-interactive zero-knowledge proof of knowledge and
   chosen ciphertext attack. In: Feigenbaum, J. (ed.) CRYPTO 1991. LNCS, vol. 576,
   pp. 433–444. Springer, Heidelberg (1992)
10. ABC4Trust Project: ABC4Trus EU Project - Official Website (2013),
    https://www.abc4trust.eu/
11. Housley, R.: RFC 5652 - Cryptographic Message Syntax, CMS (2009)
12. Preiss, F.-S.: Credential-Based Authentication Framework With Built-In Ready-
    To-Use Identity Mixer Support (2011),
    http://www.zurich.ibm.com/~frp/com.ibm.zurich.authn.cb/
13. adapID Project: advanced applications for electronic IDentity cards in Flanders
    (2009), http://www.cosic.esat.kuleuven.be/adapid/
14. Camenisch, J., Shelat, A., Sommer, D., Fischer-Hübner, S., Hansen, M., Krase-
    mann, H., Lacoste, G., Leenes, R., Tseng, J.: Privacy and identity management
    for everyone. ACM (2005)
15. PrimeLife Project: PrimeLife - Bringing sustainable privacy and identity manage-
    ment to future networks and services (2013), http://primelife.ercim.eu/
16. Hansen, M., Berlich, P., Camenisch, J., Clauß, S., Pfitzmann, A., Waidner, M.:
    Privacy-enhancing identity management. Information Security Technical Report
    (2004)
17. Hansen, M., Schwartz, A., Cooper, A.: Privacy and identity management. IEEE
    Security Privacy 6(2), 38–45 (2008)
18. Bichsel, P., Camenisch, J., Preiss, F.S.: A comprehensive framework enabling data-
    minimizing authentication. ACM (2011)
19. Maganis, G., Shi, E., Chen, H., Song, D.: Opaak: using mobile phones to limit
    anonymous identities online. ACM (2012)

Managing Employee Security Behaviour in Organisations: The Role of Cultural Factors and Individual Values

Lena Connolly[1], Michael Lang[1], and Doug Tygar[2]

[1] Business Information Systems, National University of Irelaand Galway, Ireland
y.connolly1@nuigalway.ie
[2] Electrical Engineering and Computer Science,
University of California, Berkeley, US

Abstract. An increasing number of information security breaches in organisations presents a potentially serious threat to the privacy and confidentiality of personal and commercially sensitive data. Recent research shows that human beings are the weakest link in the security chain and the root cause of a great portion of security breaches. In the late 1990's, a new phenomenon called "information security culture" has emerged as a measure to promote security-cautious behaviour of employees in organisational settings. The concept of information security culture is relatively new and research on the subject is still evolving. This research-in-progress paper contributes to our understanding of this very important topic by offering a conceptualisation of information security culture. Additionally, this study indentifies factors that instigate adverse employee behaviour in organisations.

Keywords: Information Security, Information Security Culture, Organisational Culture, National Culture, Employee Behaviour, Individual Values.

1   Introduction

With the arrival and the widespread of the Internet and the personal computer, the Information Age has swiftly replaced the era of industrialisation and the knowledge-driven economy transformed the way various industries run their operations. The automobile industry is an obvious illustration of this shift – a new car today is less and less a manufacturing product and more a smart machine that uses computer technology to combine safety, emissions, entertainment and performance. Technological advances rely on knowledge, and knowledge turns into information once it is shared. Therefore, information is a valuable asset for a lot of organisations. As online presence has also developed into a key business value, many companies have been pushed to move their operations on the Web along with this information, stored and managed by computerised information systems.

While online presence entails a myriad of benefits such as reduced costs and an extended customer base, major risks are involved, including the potential loss or violation of vital information. Protecting these assets is the highest ranked priority for

N. Cuppens-Boulahia et al. (Eds.): SEC 2014, IFIP AICT 428, pp. 417–430, 2014.

many businesses as their very existence depends on certain information. The consequences of lost information may vary from a breach of privacy for customers to complete disruption of business operations for organisations. While information predators have become more sophisticated, many legitimate businesses are either not aware or neglect the fact that the consequences of an information security breach can be rather dramatic. A recent attack on Loyaltybuild, a company that manages customer loyalty schemes across Europe, is an evident example of negligence. Attackers exploited enormous weaknesses in Loyaltybuild's security system, leading to the loss of personal information of more than 1.5 million customers. As was revealed later, the company kept sensitive information in an unencrypted form [1].

A number of critical measures to manage information security breaches in organisations have been highlighted within the literature, including reliable internal processes and good corporate governance as well as technical and socio-cultural measures [2]. Historically the use of technical controls has prevailed over socio-cultural solutions in organisational settings. However, in the late 1990s, Information Systems (IS) researchers have brought attention to the latter because technical controls are powerless to manage all types of security violations. For instance, a technical control is unable to prevent employees from writing passwords down. Besides, empirical studies show that although businesses are spending more on technology-based solutions, the number of information security breaches is actually on the rise [3].

In the late 1990's, the new concept of Information Security Culture (ISC) has emerged as a measure that promotes security-cautious behaviour of staff [4]. In a general sense, ISC can be defined as the "behaviour in an organisation that contributes to the protection of data, information and knowledge" [5]. A more comprehensive definition of ISC is that put forward by da Veiga and Eloff [2] as:

> "attitudes, assumptions, beliefs, values and knowledge that employees/stakeholders use to interact with the organisation's systems and procedures at any point in time".

Since its arrival, research on the topic of ISC has rapidly expanded. A great number of ISC theories and assessment instruments have been developed by IS scholars. ISC has been described using theories adapted from various disciplines including psychology [6], economics [7], behavioural sciences [8] and management [9]. Most commonly, ISC has been explained using organisational culture theories, Schein's [10] model been the most predominant [2].

Although prior research on ISC greatly contributes to the body of IS research, a number of areas require further investigation [4,11]. In particular, there is little information about what constitutes or conceptualises security culture [12]. A literature review conducted in the course of this research also has revealed a dearth of quantitative studies in the area of ISC. Furthermore, prior research in the information security area demonstrates that studies that include organisational culture generally lack strong theoretical foundations for linking organisational culture values to information security outcomes [13]. Moreover, Dinev et al. [14] point out to the lack of cross-cultural research in the IS field. This research-in-progress paper aims to address the aforementioned research gaps and accomplish the following objectives:

1. Identify the factors that impact upon employee behaviour with regards to information security in organisational settings using an exploratory research approach.

2. Test the relationships between these factors and employee security behaviour using a confirmatory research approach.

This paper is organised as follows. We first present a theoretical framework that guides this study followed by a definition of culture adopted in this research. This is followed by research methodology and preliminary results of qualitative data analysis. The paper then wraps up by outlining future research directions, and alluding to some of the limitations and challenges that lie ahead for us.

2   Theoretical Framework

We submit that various cultural aspects should be taken in consideration when studying adverse behaviour of employees in organisational settings. Numerous national and organisational culture scholars have demonstrated the effect of cultural aspects on human behaviour. For example, Hofstede [15] compares culture with an onion consisting of multiple layers; values are the inner layer of the onion and the core element of culture. They are invisible until they become evident in behaviour. Furthermore, Hofstede [16] and Spector [17] demonstrate a connection between national culture values and employees' compliance with authority and organisational policies and rules.

Typically, organisational culture researchers define culture as a "set of shared values, beliefs, assumptions and practices that shape and direct members attitude and behaviour in the organisations" [4, p.88]. Kilmann [18] describes culture as a separate and hidden force that controls behaviours and attitudes in organisations. A study conducted by Porter and McLaughlin [19] further demonstrates the significant role that organisational climate plays in shaping employee behaviour.

The notion of ISC culture has been also linked to human behaviour. For instance, Kraemer and Carayon [20] stress that ISC emerges from the way in which people behave towards information and the security thereof. In particular, ISC influences behaviour in such a way that employees develop "good" practices based on security standards and policies of a particular organisation. Schlienger and Teufel [21] emphasise the importance of establishing ISC as important measure to address the "human error" factor.

We propose a theoretical model that combines De Long and Fahey's *taxonomy of organisational culture* [22], Wallach's *organisational culture model* [23], Hofstede's original *taxonomy of national culture* [16] and Schwartz's *Theory of Motivational Types of Values* [24] as presented in Figure 1.

In IS research, organisational and national culture have been predominantly measured in terms of values [25]. Following Leidner and Kayworth's catalogue of organisational and national culture taxonomies [25], a variety of cultural frameworks has been examined in order to choose appropriate models for this research. Wallach's comprehensive *framework of organisational culture* [23] was selected to form the organisational culture part of our model. Wallach identified and defined three distinct organisational cultures, - *bureaucratic, innovative* and *supportive*, - covering almost all the values outlined by Leidner and Kayworth [25]. Additionally, Wallach's model has been adapted in quantitative [33] as well as cross-cultural [27] studies in IS research. Wallach's Organisational Culture Index will be used in this research to measure organisational culture.

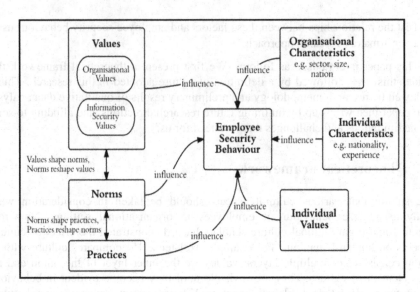

Fig. 1. Theoretical framework

To date, Hofstede's taxonomy of cultural values [16] has been the most popular conceptualisation of national culture. Hofstede defines culture in terms of four values – *power distance, uncertainty avoidance, individualism-collectivism* and *masculinity-femininity*. Hofstede's scores of cultural values will be used as the measure of culture because they have been subject to more checks of internal validity, external validity and reliability than the measures used in any other cross-cultural study. Additionally, Hofstede's research is the largest study of cultural values ever undertaken both in terms of number of countries and number of respondents [28]. National culture needs to be considered in terms of its impact on organisations and also individuals.

To test the influence of individual values on behaviour with regards to information security, the *Theory of Motivational Types of Values* by Schwartz [24] was chosen. Schwartz's model is viewed as the most comprehensive approach, covering 56 values grouped into 10 categories. The *Theory of Motivational Types of Values* demonstrates strong generalisability as it has been successfully tested in more than 60 countries [26].

2.1   Culture

For the purpose of this research, culture is viewed as a phenomenon that can be observed at multiple levels in an organisation. Culture is reflected in three levels – values, norms and practices [22].

At the deepest level, culture consists of values, which are embedded tacit preferences about what the organisation should strive to attain and how it should do so. For instance, if an organisation values customer confidentiality, employees will treat customer information with extra caution by following data protection requirements outlined by this organisation.

Norms generally stem from values, but they are more observable [22]. For instance, if rules with regards to customer confidentiality are breached, a termination of employment may be a norm in an organisation that puts high emphasis on customer confidentiality.

Practices are the most visible symbols and manifestations of a culture. In the context of information security, this level is related to the implemented security measures and processes [29].

Values, norms, and practices are interrelated: values are revealed in norms that, in turn, shape specific practices. While values shape norms and practices, sometimes managers will change practices and norms in an attempt to reshape values over time. Values, norms and practices directly influence employee behaviour [22].

3 Research Methodology

This study follows Clark and Creswell's [30] Sequential Exploratory Mixed Method approach consisting of a qualitative phase to be subsequently followed by a quantitative phase. Data collection for the qualitative phase of this study was carried out using semi-structured interviews. The interview guide was built on Wallach's taxonomy of organisational culture. Additionally, general questions about ISC were asked in order to tease out ISC values. Interview guide topics including corresponding values and questions are demonstrated in Table 1.

Table 1. Interview guide topics

Topics	Values	Examples of questions
Information Security Culture values, norms and practices	unknown	What information security values are promoted in your organisation? In your opinion how well confidential information is protected in your organisation?
Orientation to rules	Procedural, regulated, cautious	Is it acceptable to break rules in your organisation?
Hierarchy vs. Equality	Hierarchical, power-oriented, ordered, structured vs. equality, collaboration, personal freedom	Is it common in your organisation to socialise with management?
Competitive environment	Driving, challenging, enterprising	Is competition between colleagues promoted in your organisation?
Employee welfare	Stimulating, encouraging	How satisfied are you with a benefit system provided by your organisation?
Friendliness vs. Pressure	Relationships-oriented, trusting, good place to work vs. results-oriented, pressurised	Is it acceptable to have non-work related chats in your organisation?
Sociability	Sociable	Do you socialise with your colleagues?

Overall seven organisations were interviewed, all based within the United States. Initially, we planned to conduct two interviews in each organisation – one with an executive and another with an employee to gather various views. However, the subject of information systems security is rather sensitive, therefore access to potential interviewees was restricted. In total, nine interviews were conducted. All interviews were recorded and transcribed using a professional service. To preserve confidentiality, all companies have been assigned aliases when referred to herein.

The methodology adopted for the qualitative phase of this study is based on the constant comparative method according to Maykut and Morehouse [31] who draw on the work of Glaser and Strauss [32] and Lincoln and Guba [33] in their development of this methodological framework. "In the constant comparative method the researcher simultaneously codes and analyses data in order to develop concepts; by continually comparing specific incidents in the data, the researcher refines these concepts, identifies their properties, explores their relationships to one another, and integrates them into a coherent explanatory model" [34].

4   Findings

In the first phase of qualitative data analysis, Open Coding, we identified and labeled discrete incidents of data related to cultural values, norms and practices. An example of our coding is shown in Table 2.

Table 2. Interview guide topics

Example excerpt from interview at RetCo, October 2012	Open Coding
We use several different levels of rules in the organisation. We have policies that are very high level statements and those are informed by our kind of company values and then we have below the policies we have standards, so information security standards and privacy standards, that we follow and then underneath that we have specific practices and procedures and those are very rigid, those are if you're going to do a certain thing you need to follow a procedure and those are all published and accessible to all of our employees on an intranet website so there's no question about if people want to learn how to do something or learn what those are that's readily available in addition to a lot of training that informs employees about them as well. So that's kind of the hierarchy and then in some cases we have even published and maintained some guidelines on how to do certain things and recommendations on security, not just at work but in the home too, so employees are given information on how to protect themselves at home on information security and those are more guidelines of course because we don't have controls over what people do at home but we feel that if people are practising good safe practices at home it's going to translate over at the work environment as well	Values: • *Information Security* • *Individual Privacy* Norms: • *Keeping information secure* • *Following procedures* Practices: • *Policy* • *Education*

In further data analysis, the initial codes were grouped into organisational and information security values, norms and practices following De Long and Fahey's *taxonomy of organisational culture* [22]. Consistent with Wallach's *model of organisational culture* [23], eight organisational values have been identified: *hierarchy, rule-orientation, pressure, stimulation, sociability, relationships, equality*, and *drive*. In accordance with Schwartz's *Theory of Motivational Types of Values*, three individual values have been defined: *achievement, benevolence, conformity*, and *self-direction*. Additionally, a self-defined classification of Information Security Culture has emerged containing four values: *information security* (high vs. low), *information confidentiality* (high vs. low), *rule-orientation*, and *equality*. Each of these ISC values are briefly described below, along with examples of how these values are manifested in interview data.

4.1   Information Security Culture Taxonomy

Information Security (High). Modern organisations accumulate huge volumes of information including sensitive information. The breach of this information first leads to its exposure and then may result in a breach of privacy and financial losses. Security of a computer-based information system should, by design, protect the confidentiality, integrity, and availability of the system that contains sensitive information [35].

CloudSer is a software company that provides cloud and virtualisation software and services. Therefore, protecting customer information is a high priority for this organisation. A Software Engineer of CloudSer was clear about the company's standpoint with regards to information security:

> "Everybody understands that security is a big concern from a lot of aspects, so I would tend to think they [information security rules] are working ... Information security is a central function across the organisation."

RetCo, a company that manages retirement and health plans, also puts high emphasis on information security due to sensitive nature of the information they store. A RetCo Security Officer states:

> "We use several different levels of rules in the organisation. We have policies that are very high level statements and those are informed by our company values, and then below the policies we have standards. So we have information security standards and privacy standards that we follow, and then underneath that we have specific practices and procedures, and those are very rigid ... And then in some cases we have even published and maintained some guidelines on how to do certain things and recommendations on security, not just at work but in the home too, so employees are given information on how to protect themselves at home on information security, and those are more guidelines, of course, because we don't have controls over what people do at home, but we feel that if people are practising good safe practices at home, it's going to translate over at the work environment as well."

Information Security (Low). On the contrary, EducInst, a higher education institution, has a different attitude towards information security. Although the organisation seems to have in place various security measures, e.g. technical controls, education and training, and ISP, information security is not a priority in EducInst. For instance, although ISP exists, employees are not aware of its presence, and education and training is poorly organised. The interviewee commented:

> "There is a formal set of rules and practices are online, and they're far too detailed to discuss here … [For example, we have] very specific rules about personally identifiable information such as a social security number. So if you send me a resumé, it's got lots of personally identifiable information on it, I have to be very careful to protect that and not store it in an unencrypted form on my computer, otherwise I'm in breach of those rules. And that's actually a State law, so it's not just an EducInst rule. A State law that's largely ignored by most people here, but it's on the books … In EducInst, information security values are way, way, way down on the list. People give lip service to it … What's officially on the books and what the actual practice is, those are two different things."

Information Confidentiality (High). Understandably, companies that acquire and store confidential information, must prioritise information confidentiality. An unauthorised use and disclosure of confidential data leads to dramatic consequences for individuals and organisations. The goal of confidentiality is to ensure that information is not accessed by an unauthorised person [36].

CloudSer has a large customer base and retains confidential information of their clients. Keeping this information secure is of most important value as its disclosure may damage companies' ability to run business. A Software Engineer of CloudSer says:

> "…any company which is providing software, which other companies rely on or possesses, like details about company, the customers enterprise deployment, you need to value that trust, so you can't break some rules with respect to that. We have 300,000 customers, some of those customers are competitors of the other guys. So let's just hypothetically say I have Pepsi and Coke as my customers, right…I can't tell Pepsi what Coke is doing, I can't tell Coke what Pepsi is doing. So our customers trust us with that information knowing that we might as well be serving Pepsi. So, yeah, there are certain rules that you cannot break without getting fired."

Due to its nature of business, RetCo holds a lot of personally identifiable information (PII). Therefore, information confidentiality is highly prioritised by this organisation as stated by their Security Officer:

> "We have security standards and practices around encryption, such as what type of encryption is approved to use in the environment, what has to be encrypted, and to what level, and also how these encryption keys are handled and managed in the organisation. We have policies

and practices around physical access to the computer room, and so we have certain levels of access and certain approval processes in place like who can access our protected areas, and what levels of approval have to happen, and we have things in place like not just card key electronic access, but we have things like Iris scanner technology to get in to the computer rooms and things of that nature, and, of course, we've got these practices and procedures and processes that are in place to support that physical access."

Information Confidentiality (Low). Although EducInst also possesses PII, our informant revealed that this organisation is not particularly concerned about information confidentiality of their customers:

"As I said, I think things tend to be fairly casual in terms of protecting people's privacy. For example you know, let me give an example. So protecting credit card numbers, right. So people's credit card numbers are floating all around this organisation. If you were interested in stealing a lot of credit card numbers, it would be so easy to do in this organisation. Again, just because of the casualness with which people treat information ... Let me give you an example, at EducInst we are rolling out a new system for paying disbursements. We have a chief privacy officer who is supposed to be in charge of protecting privacy at EducInst. But my secretary was able to use that system to find out things like the Provost's credit card number, or names of all the students who'd been treated for genital warts, or the names of a police officer who had to undergo a psychological help after an incident. She pointed these problems out to the chief privacy officer, and the chief privacy officer could do squat about them ... So my point is that we have all the stuff on the book, and there's State laws about it, but it's largely ignored because it's not a value of the organisation."

Equality. CloudSer and RetCo are two companies that emphasise employee input with regards to information security measures. At CloudSer and RetCo, employees are encouraged to provide feedback about information security rules. According to both interviewees, based on employees' comments, rules can be changed. In these organisations everyone has equal voice and ability to speak up regardless of rank or position. It's a highly collaborative and opinionated environment where employees at all levels are easy to approach [23]. A Software Engineer at CloudSer explained that:

"For the security measures they bring about, they introduce it to the employees before its roll out, they test it out, and then they take employee feedback to see if it's too intrusive or too restrictive for that matter. So it's generally participative, but I haven't really seen any security measure being repealed because employees do not like it ... Generally, people do accept that [security rules are] there for a good reason, unless it's like prohibitively restrictive which it's not the case in my company"

A Security Officer at RetCo adds:

> "I think a lot of times employees having this open dialogue, they can change the rules by bringing things up. I've seen it happen in the past, where the enterprise will make a decision to lock computers, the keyboards on computers, after a certain amount of time, when the computer is idle, and that's because people may get up and walk away from their computer, and they want to lock the screen and make sure that nobody else can walk by and access the information. So employees feeling empowered to challenge or to at least bring up the issues, have made a lot of changes in their user environments because of that. So, for example, if it's 10 minutes of inactivity and the computer locks, the screen lock, employees have complained and said, 'you know, it's really closer to 20 before we really are not working on it', and so the policies have been changed based upon the use of the users and them providing that feedback."

Rule-Orientation. In the rule-oriented organisations, rules are very important and are not allowed to break. These companies are procedural, regulated, and cautious and put high emphasis on following information security policies and procedures [26]. A Security Officer at RetCo reveals:

> "It's not acceptable to break rules in our organisation. Mostly because most of our rules are derived from regulations and laws so that's something that is not normally accepted in the organisation …We use several different levels of rules in the organisation. We have policies that are very high level statements, and those are informed by our company values, and then below the policies we have standards, so information security standards and privacy standards, that we follow, and then underneath that we have specific practices and procedures, and those are very rigid, those are if you're going to do a certain thing, you need to follow a procedure."

A Security Consultant at FinCo adds:

> "If there is a rule in place, the rule is in place for a reason and you don't break it, you request an exception and you have to talk to the right people to request an exception. So you never just break a rule … The security practices are fairly extensive for SOX and GLBA compliant environment, so we have to be audited for both of those on a yearly basis, although actually we go through audits I think twice a year. And then we have an internal audit office that basically does audits twice a year as well, to make sure that we're going to be able to pass those Federal Mandated Audits … So we pretty much follow best practices that are mandated."

4.2   Interpretation and Further Propositions

In most organisations interviewed for this study, employees circumvent information security rules. Following De Long and Fahey's [22] framework of organisational culture, organisational values, norms and practices have to be aligned and this alignment encourages behaviour that is in accordance with organisational values. However, in companies where dysfunctional behaviour was recorded, our results are inconsistent with De Long and Fahey's framework. For instance, while these organisations put high value on information security, conflicting practices (e.g. *lack of education*) and norms (e.g. *casualness in terms of protecting confidential information, circumventing rules, nobody ever reads policy because it is too big, policy is not taught, rules are hard to implement,* and *screw-ups are tolerated*) were recorded. Based on this analysis, we suggest that:

Proposition 1: *A misalignment between values, norms and practices leads to employee non-compliance with an organisation's information security rules and practices.*

Further analysis revealed that clash of organisational culture values may also lead to employee adverse behaviour. For instance, TechCorp encourages employees to take risks and at the same time puts high emphasis on following procedures. In CivEngCo, higher management enforces hierarchical structure and utilises power and control in managing employees while front-line managers value equality and collaboration. Therefore, whilst employees' various opinions and new ideas are supported by lower level management, executives are resistant to except initiatives and change old processes. As a result, ambitious employees lose motivation and respect for the organisation and circumvent information security rules. Therefore, we propose that:

Proposition 2: *A conflict between organisational culture values leads to employee non-compliance with an organisation's information security rules and practices.*

Moreover, we observed that possibly employees' individual values influence behaviour with regards to information security. For instance, two employees who work for the same organisation and share identical status and nature of work, have different attitude towards information security rules. IT Corp is bureaucratic in nature and enforces religious obedience to procedures which sometimes hurt employees' productivity. Employee 1 is ambitious and hard-working but still accepts the procedure-oriented environment (individual value of *conformity*). On the contrary, Employee 2 circumvents information security rules because they are too restrictive (individual value of *self-direction*). Therefore, we conclude that incongruence between organisational and individual values leads to employee non-compliance with security rules and hence, the following proposition is derived:

Proposition 3: *A conflict between individual values and organsiational values leads to employee non-compliance with an organisation's information security rules and practices.*

5   Conclusions and Future Work

In the literature, human beings have been referred as "the weakest link in the security chain". While the importance of technical controls to prevent the "human error" factor is absolutely undeniable, technology is unable to manage all types of human violations. A socio-cultural approach addresses this problem by having a direct affect on human behaviour. Prior research has emphasised the significance of socio-cultural measures. However, there are areas that require further enquiry. This research-in-progress is an attempt to address a research gap in the area of ISC.

In the next stage of our research, we conduct further qualitative data analysis (based on a European sample, for comparative purposes), and will then develop a survey instrument based on qualitative findings. The original purpose of the qualitative phase is to develop research hypothesis, which then can be tested in the quantitative phase. In the near future, we also to plan extend this research by adding other environments including important emerging digital economies in regions such as East Asia, the Indian subcontinent, Brazil, and the former Easter Bloc. This work may allow us to better model the notion of adversarial behaviour in different regions. Therefore, from the standpoint of information security, this research has potential to make a valuable contribution to theory and practice.

In terms of shortcomings and limitations, studies that involve culture tend to be rather complex. As Straub et al. [37] put it, "culture has always been a thorny concept and an even thornier research construct". Furthermore, studies that include several cultural aspects tend to be even more complex. In particular, it may be hard to separate effects of national and organisational cultures in organisational settings due to similar characteristics. For example, hierarchy in an organisation can be a result of a bureaucratic culture of this organisation or a societal norm of the country where this organisation is located. Quantifying the concept of culture is another challenge that is anticipated in this project. In order to measure culture in a meaningful way, a value-based approach will be employed. Taking in consideration the aforementioned complexities, we would therefore welcome feedback and suggestions from other researchers who may have encountered this same difficulty or are contemplating similar avenues of enquiry.

References

1. Pope, C., Edwards, E.: Over 1.5 million affected by Ennis data breach. The Irish Times (2013), http://www.irishtimes.com/news/consumer/over-1-5-million-affected-by-ennis-data-breach-1.1592128
2. Da Veiga, A., Eloff, J.H.P.: A framework and assessment instrument for information security culture. Computers & Security 29, 96–207 (2010)
3. Von Solms, B.: Information Security – The Third Wave? Computers & Security 19, 615–620 (2000)
4. Lim, J.S., Chang, S., Maynard, S., Ahmad, A.: Exploring the Relationship between Organizational Culture and Information Systems Security Culture. In: Proceedings of the 7th Australian Information Security Management Conference, pp. 87–97. Edith Cowan University (2009)

5. Kuusisto, T., Ilvonen, I.: Information security culture in small and medium size enterprises. Frontiers of E-Business Research (2003),
   http://www.ebrc.info/kuvat/431-439.pdf
6. Boss, S.R., Kirsch, L.J., Angermeier, I., Shingler, R.A., Ross, R.W.: If Someone Is Watching, I'll Do What I'm Asked: Mandatoriness, Control, and Information Security. European Journal of Information Systems 18, 151–164 (2009)
7. Van Niekerk, J.F., von Solms, R.: Information security culture: A management perspective. Computers & Security 29, 476–486 (2010)
8. Ajzen, I.: Attitudes, Personality, and Behavior, 2nd edn. Open University Press, Berkshire (2005)
9. Ray, C.A.: Corporate Culture: The Last Frontier of Control? Journal of Management Studies 23, 287–297 (1986)
10. Schein, E.H.: Organizational Culture and Leadership: The Dynamic View. Jossey-Bass, San Francisco (1985)
11. Malcomson, J.: What is security culture? Does it differ in content from general organisational culture? In: Proceedings of the 43rd Annual International Carnahan Conference on Security Technology, pp. 361–366 (2009)
12. Alnatheer, M., Chan, T., Nelson, K.: Understanding and measuring information security culture. In: Proceedings of Pacific Asia Conference on Information Systems (2012)
13. Hu, Q., Dinev, T., Hart, P., Cooke, D.: Managing employee compliance with information security policies: The critical role of top management and organizational culture. Decision Sciences 43, 615–660 (2012)
14. Dinev, T., Goo, J., Hu, Q., Nam, K.: User behaviour towards protective information technologies: the role of national cultural differences. Information Systems Journal 19, 391–412 (2009)
15. Hofstede, G.: Culture's Consequences: International Differences in Work-related Values. Sage Publications, Thousand Oaks (2001)
16. Hofstede, G.: Culture's Consequences: International Differences in Work-related Values. Sage Publications, Thousand Oaks (1980)
17. Spector, P.E.: Behavior in Organizations as a Function of Employee's Locus of Control. Psychological Bulletin 91, 482–497 (1982)
18. Kilmann, R.H.: Managing Your Organization's Culture. Nonprofit World Report 3, 12–15 (1985)
19. Porter, L.W., McLaughlin, G.B.: Leadership and the organizational context: Like the weather? The Leadership Quarterly 17, 559–576 (2006)
20. Kraemer, S., Carayon, P.: Computer and Information Security Culture: Findings from Two Studies. In: Proceedings of the Human Factors and Ergonomics Society 49th Annual Meeting, pp. 1483–1487 (2005)
21. Schlienger, T., Teufel, S.: Information security culture: The socio-cultural dimension in information security management. In: Proceedings of the IFIP TCII 17th International Conference on Information Security, pp. 191–201 (2002)
22. De Long, D., Fahey, L.: Diagnosing cultural barriers to knowledge management. Academy of Management Executive 14, 113–127 (2000)
23. Wallach, E.D.: Individuals and Organizations: The Cultural March. Training and Development Journal 37, 29–36 (1983)
24. Schwartz, S.H.: Universals in the content and structure values: Theoretical advances and empirical tests in 20 countries. Advances in Experimental Social Psychology 25, 1–65 (1992)

25. Leidner, D.E., Kayworth, T.: Review: A review of culture in information systems research: Toward a theory of information technology culture conflict. MIS Quarterly 30, 357–399 (2006)
26. Myyry, L., Siponen, M., Pahnila, S., Vartiainen, T., Vance, A.: What Levels of Moral Reasoning and Values Explain Adherence to Information Security Rules? An Empirical Study. European Journal of Information Systems 18, 126–139 (2009)
27. Lok, P., Crawford, J.: The effect of organisational culture and leadership style on job satisfaction and organisational commitment: A cross-national comparison. Journal of Management Development 23, 321–338 (2004)
28. Shane, S., Venkataraman, S., MacMillan, I.: Cultural Differences in Innovation Championing Strategies. Journal of Management 21, 931–952 (1995)
29. Vroom, C., von Solms, R.: Towards Information Security Behavioural Compliance. Computers & Security 23, 191–198 (2004)
30. Clark, V.L.P., Creswell, J.W.: The Mixed Methods Reader. Sage Publications, Thousand Oaks (2008)
31. Maykut, P., Morehouse, R.: Beginning Qualitative Research: A Philosophic and Practical Guide. The Falmer Press, London (1994)
32. Glaser, B.G., Stauss, A.L.: The Discovery of Grounded Theory. Aldine, Chicago (1967)
33. Lincoln, Y., Guba, E.: Naturalistic Inquiry. Sage Publications Inc., Beverly Hills (1985)
34. Taylor, S.J., Bogdan, R.: Introduction to Qualitative Research Methods: The Search for Meanings. Wiley, New York (1984)
35. Gordon, L.A., Loeb, M.P.: The Economics of Information Security Investment. ACM Transactions on Information and System Security 5, 438–457 (2002)
36. Joshi, J.B.D., Aref, W.G., Ghafoor, A., Spafford, E.H.: Security models for Web-based Applications. Communications of the ACM 44 (2001)
37. Straub, D., Loch, K., Evaristo, R., Karahanna, E., Strite, M.: Toward a theory-based measurement of culture. Journal of Global Information Management 10, 13–23 (2002)

Organizational Transformation and Information Security Culture: A Telecom Case Study

Gurpreet Dhillon[1], Romilla Chowdhuri[1], and Cristiane Pedron[2]

[1] Virginia Commonwealth University, Richmond, USA
{gdhillon,syedr2}@vcu.edu
[2] University of Lisbon, Portugal
cdpedron@gmail.com

Abstract. When two companies merge, technical infrastructures change, formal security policies get rewritten, and normative structures clash. The resultant changes typically disrupt the prevalent security culture as well. In this paper we use ET Hall's (1959) theory of cultural message streams to evaluate the disruptions in security culture following a merger. Findings from our analysis would be beneficial to researchers to theorize about security culture formulation during a merger. At a practical level decision makers would find the analysis useful for engaging in strategic security planning.

Keywords: Security Culture, Organizational Transformation, Formal & Informal security.

1 Introduction

The merger of the companies cause significant challenges in terms of integrating their technical infrastructure, policies and procedures, and normative aspects related to how work gets done. The changes also have a consequent effect on the security and integrity of the enterprise. Previous research shows (see [2], [8]), that structural and business process related changes indeed make an organizational vulnerable. Research also shows that building and sustaining a good security culture is extremely important in times of radical change. In this paper we use E.T. Hall's theory of cultural messages [4] to evaluate information security consequences of an organizational transformation.

In the extant literature, security culture is deemed important for the protection of organization's information assets. Various definitions of security culture have been proposed. For example, Dhillon [2] defines it as behavior, values, and assumptions that ensure information security. Helokunnas and Kuusisto [5] define security culture as a system in which attitude, motivation, knowledge, and mental model about information security interact. With respect to organization's information assets, researchers express the need for coherent security culture that focuses beyond the technical and formal controls [2], [7], [9], [10]. Recent literature review by Ramachandran et al. [6] indicates that very few studies focus on security culture. Moreover cultural conflict in information security has not been studied very well.

N. Cuppens-Boulahia et al. (Eds.): SEC 2014, IFIP AICT 428, pp. 431–437, 2014.

2   Case Description and Analysis

In this study we adopt an interpretive case study research approach [11]. Data was collected primarily through semi-structured interviews and informal conversations. Participants were the employees at different management level in the two merging companies. The participation was voluntary and each interview lasted about 60 minutes. Majority of the data was collected over an eight-month period while the merger was in progress.

The setting of the case study is an Organizational Customer and Relationship Management (OCRM) project that was launched due to the merger of the two companies - AirTelco and Relicom. The project aims to support the business goals of the transformed organization by integrating the CRM systems of the two merged organizations. Both AirTelco and Relicom belong to a business group that is greatly projected in Europe and has diversified business portfolio. Relicom was the industry leader of landline phones. The company offered its customers a wide range of services and solutions that cover more than the normal fixed network services like data communications, broadcasting, video conferencing, and broadband solutions. AirTelco was the market leader of the mobile segment. Its main goal is technological innovation and customer orientation. The differences in the strategic focus of the two companies stem from how they originated. While AirTelco was a product of a competitive market space, Relicom grew up in a monopolistic market. These differences in origin were evident in the approaches that the two companies had adopted towards technological innovation and customer management.

The cultural map analysis is performed using E.T. Hall's ten streams of cultural messages. The interpretations about the impact on information security are drawn by reflexive thinking in relation to cultural messages and data provided by the participants. Per our analysis, *gender* did not emerge to be significant. The summary of the analysis is presented in Table 1.

Interaction. The OCRM project affected the interactions between the higher management and operational teams. Inclined towards technological innovations, AirTelco employees occupied dominant technology positions whereas Relicom employees occupied managerial roles. This segregation of technological and managerial roles not only created division of power and space but also caused a lack of clarity in terms of privacy and security of customer data that resided on OCRM servers.

Association. As the two organizations had different approaches towards customer management, a sense of sub-communities caused resistance towards adopting OCRM. In addition, lack of governance structures further increased the distance in security culture.

Subsistence. Although employees were trained for using OCRM, no knowledge about the changes OCRM instigated in the business processes was disseminated. OCRM was of little to employees in overcoming their comfort zones. Additionally, the legal and regulatory differences prevented the integration of some of the databases, leading to information availability and integrity issues.

Territoriality. The OCRM system defined new work boundaries for AirTelco and Relicom employees. Relicom employees felt that they were forced to follow the division and space determined by AirTelco employees. Work remained compartmentalized, formal boundaries changed and new group boundaries emerged. Such hostility between groups makes them prone to social engineering attacks.

Temporality. The requirements for the design and implementation of OCRM system were collected in just five weeks. Additionally, AirTelco employees had a laid back attitude in dealing with day to day issues whereas Relicom employees were more aggressive. There were frequent changes in the process and people involved in requirement gathering. As a result, employees were inventing unique ways of getting work done faster.

Learning. Few employees were selected to give training to other employees. However, the manuals put together by trainers were based on what they wanted others to know. Training between AirTelco and Relicom was not synced. Relicom for example knew more about wireless products and services relative to AirTelco. Training was limited to technical knowledge; employees were not made aware of the security policies.

Table 1. Cultural Analysis Mapping

Direct Organizational Intervention through the OCRM system	Implications for Security
Interaction: Communication patterns changed because people from both companies need to work together formally and informally.OCRM forces AirTelco and Relicom to cross sell and be customer responsive.	Lack of clarity in terms of security and privacy. New organization had limited grip on protection of critical company and customer data.
Association: Prior to merger, AirTelco and Relicom had multiple groupings and perspectives for CRM implementation. Conflicts were rampant. Merger of two companies results in "them" vs. us" attitude.	Conflict among groups was rampant. This resulted in lack of agreement on the kind of controls that were to be established. Absence of formal associations caused a lack of shared vision which is detrimental to system success. There was no sense of ownership about customer data.
Subsistence: Prior to the merger, AirTelco employees had very little interest in customer service because a) it was difficult to cross sell products/services b) performance was loosely linked to employee earnings. Following the merger, however lack of customer responsiveness and inability to sell telecom services would result in reprimands. At the same time OCRM made sales and service efforts easier.	While the merger took place, the databases of the two companies cannot be merged because of legal and regulatory reasons. This results in issues pertaining to management of security, data integrity, and availability.
Territoriality: Following the merger, Relicom employees felt that they had to follow the divisions and space allocations of AirTelco. Merger brought two companies to share resources and equipment. The manner in which they approached work remained compartmentalized.	A lack of clarity of business processes, formal and informal spaces creates issues regarding 'social obligations' and 'responsibilities' that go beyond the law of the letter. Typically such environments can be excellent candidates for social engineering attacks/manipulations.

Table 1. (*Continued.*)

Temporality: Requirements for the new OCRM were collected in just 5 weeks and every few weeks the process and responsibilities changed. AirTelco had a more laid back attitude in dealing with issues, problems and customer complaints, while Relicom was more aggressive.	One of the biggest concerns with respect to temporality is flawed assumptions leading to incorrect specification. The flawed or buggy systems are not only costly and time consuming to fix, but also pose significant security hazards. Frequent changes in routines results in human error, which is a serious security threat.
Learning: Learning was undertaken in 'train the trainer' mode. The training program was technical in nature. Employees were however left to themselves to articulate the training content. In many instances new products and services were offered without adequate training or making employees aware about such products or services.	The nature and scope of training impacts the kind of a policy that is developed. If the new company wanted to create well balanced security policies, their training should go beyond the technical edifice. However, this was not the case. While employees seemed to be well versed with the technical, products, and services, they were unsure if the processes were broken or routines were inappropriate. This is a serious security threat because of exclusive reliance on the technical fix.
Recreation and Humor: Post merger the company created a "stock market" for ideas where employees could invest their virtual money.	Creating homogeneous culture for ensuring security is always preferred. The new AirTelco/Relicom organization did a good job in creating such an environment. However, there was no means for them to ensure continuous improvement and integrating cultural process back for a sustained cultural integration. Failure to do so usually causes disillusionment and results in employees abandoning their integrative efforts - a serious security concern.
Defense: OCRM enforces formal controls on employees. Employees were expected to comply with the inbuilt controls.	The manner in which the changes panned out or were interpreted resulted in discordance between different stakeholders. Employees seemed to be at the mercy of the newly established routines. While this was necessary at the lower end of the organization, managers themselves felt that OCRM imposed an over-engineered solution. Increased possibility of employees circumventing control, which is a major security issue.
Exploitation: The organization (post-merger) has created a "laboratory of new ideas". Employees from different divisions are encouraged to brainstorm and test the efficacy of new ideas.	While the intent of the laboratory was very good, it received mixed reviews. In some cases employees felt involved, but in others they seemed to be disillusioned. Organizations need to ensure sustainability and correct direction of such innovative arrangements in order to ensure correct exploitation, else there is a risk of failure/abuse.

Recreation and Humor. To facilitate cultural homogeneity between employees, senior management encouraged employees to discuss investment options. However, there was no effort made to improve such interaction. Failure to do so usually causes disillusionment and results in employees abandoning their integrative efforts.

Defense. Although, inbuilt controls in OCRM ensured security, these formal controls imposed restrictions on employees and forced them to work as per defined processes. Employees learned to circumvent the system to ensure that the work gets done as per their way.

Exploitation. A "laboratory" setting was created to allow employees discuss innovative ideas. In some cases employees felt involved, but in others they seemed to be disillusioned. Although innovative ideas were generated and implemented, few of them were pushed through because of the power of the people who promoted those ideas.

3   Discussion

The case study presents an interesting basis for interpreting silent messages and hence the prevalent security culture. Based on our analysis we identify several principles that form the basis for good information security management.

1.   Good information security management is a function of effective communication structures.

While the need for establishing communication structures may seem intuitive, the importance of such structures in ensuring good information security cannot be underestimated. It was Giddens [3] who proposed that two disembedding mechanisms exist - tokens and expert systems. For Giddens tokens is any media of interchange that could be passed from one place to the other such as physical artifacts, conceptual structures or information. In the context of the merger between AirTelco and Relicom, while the OCRM system could have been a token, there clearly was significant confusion regarding how the system could be used to ensure customer responsiveness. On the contrary, the system imposed its own way of working and hence created confusion amongst the stakeholders. In the literature, the importance of tokens has been noted as significant as they ensure a common basis for establishing a communication structure (see [2], [3]).

The second disembedding mechanism noted by Giddens [3] is that of expert systems- a collection of people who have specialized knowledge. While the merger between AirTelco and Relicom went ahead and various systems were inherited, there was no effort whatsoever in establishing expert systems. Hence conflict among groups was rampant, which resulted in lack of agreement on the kind of controls that should be established.

2.   Information security management is a consequence of how business processes are redesigned taking into consideration the informal, formal, and technical aspects.

Hall [4] argues, "Change is a complex circular process. It proceeds from formal to informal to technical to new formal, with the emphasis shifting rather rapidly at certain junctures" (pg 93). It is interesting to note that both AirTelco and Relicom recognized the importance of creating a homogeneous culture, which would ensure security. The new AirTelco/Relicom organization indeed did a good job in creating such an environment. However, there was no means for them to ensure continuous improvement and integrating cultural process back for a sustained cultural integration. Failure to do so usually causes disillusionment and results in employees abandoning their integrative efforts - a serious security concern. As Hall notes change is a complex and a circular process and there is a need to continuously evaluate and reevaluate how formal changes impact the informal and subsequently get institutionalized. Typically organizations stop the change management process at this juncture. Majority of security breaches however occur post implementation of the technical edifice. There typically is another set of redefinition of formal structures following a technical implementation, and many failures become obvious at this point.

3. *Organizational stability relies on having well defined formal and informal group boundaries thus reducing friction and confusion.*

As discussed before, a major concern is the scope of change and how such changes affect stakeholder groups and current boundaries. By clearly defining roles and responsibilities, management can reduce animosity among stakeholders and streamline business processes to achieve maximum project benefit. Understanding formal and informal business processes is critical to an organization's ability to create new opportunities through project development. Any rancor and conflict because of such issues can be a cause of significant concern. Institutions that are unable to clearly demarcate the formal and informal boundaries typically result in confusing the roles and responsibilities see [1]. In our case study organization a lack of clarity of business processes, formal and informal spaces created issues related to 'social obligations' and 'responsibilities' that go beyond the law of the letter. Typically such environments can be excellent candidates for social engineering attacks and manipulations.

4. *Balancing the informal, formal and technical controls is essential to prevent over-engineered solutions.*

It goes without saying that a technical solutions to mergers and management of security are essential. Simply implementing a customer relationship system and hoping that communication needs can be addressed is not sufficient. What is required is linking technical solutions to the formal rules and obligations of various stakeholders. This necessitates the need for formal structures that support the technical edifice. Managing security after all is a holistic activity and there is a need to maintain integrity amongst the formal and the technical components. Finally the more pragmatic and normative aspects need to be evaluated as well. Ongoing education and training programs form the basis for building a security culture and a common belief system.

4   Conclusion

In this paper we presented the cultural analysis of two organizations undergoing merger and identified the impact of such transformations on the pertinent information security culture. We used E.T. Hall's [4] theory of silent messages to interpret the impact of radical organizational transformation on information security. The analysis allowed us to define the principles of information security in the context of organization transformations. We believe that these principle set the ground for further theorizing about culture and information security. These principle could also help practitioners to plan for information security management during such transformations.

References

1. Backhouse, J., Dhillon, G.: Structures of responsibility and security of information systems. European Journal of Information Systems 5(1), 2–9 (1996)
2. Dhillon, G.: Managing information system security. Macmillan, London (1997)
3. Giddens, A.: The consequence of modernity. Stanford University Press, Stanford (1990)
4. Hall, E.T.: The silent language, 2nd edn. Anchor Books, New York (1959)
5. Helokunnas, T., Kuusisto, R.: Information security culture in a value net. In: Engineering Management Conference, IEMC 2003 on Managing Technologically Driven Organizations: The Human Side of Innovation and Change, pp. 190–194. IEEE Press, New York (2003)
6. Ramachandran, S., Rao, V.S.C., Goles, T., Dhillon, G.: Variations in Information Security Cultures across Professions: A Qualitative Study. Communications of the Association for Information Systems 33, 163–204 (2013)
7. Ruighaver, A.B., Maynard, S.B., Chang, S.: Organizational Security Culture: Extending the End-user Perspective. Computers & Security 26, 56–62 (2007)
8. Segev, A., Porra, J., Roldan, M.: Internet security and the case of Bank of America. Communications of the ACM 41(10), 81–87 (1998)
9. Von Solms, B.: Information Security—The Third Wave? Computers & Security 19, 615–620 (2000)
10. Vroom, C., Von Solms, R.: Towards Information Security Behavioral Compliance. Computers & Security 23, 191–198 (2004)
11. Walsham, G.: Interpreting information systems in organizations. John Wiley & Sons, Chichester (1993)

A Holistic Approach for Cyber Assurance of Critical Infrastructure with the Viable System Model[*]

Theodoros Spyridopoulos[1], Ioanna-Aikaterini Topa[2], Theo Tryfonas[1], and Maria Karyda[2]

[1] Cryptography Group, University of Bristol, UK
[2] Department of Information and Communication Systems Engineering
University of the Aegean, Greece
{th.spyridopoulos,theo.tryfonas}@bristol.ac.uk,
icsdm12018@icsd.aegean.gr, mka@aegean.gr

Abstract. Industrial Control Systems (ICSs) are of the most important components of National Critical Infrastructure. They can provide control capabilities in complex systems of critical importance such as energy production and distribution, transportation, telecoms etc. Protection of such systems is the cornerstone of essential service provision with resilience and in timely manner. Effective risk management methods form the basis for the protection of an Industrial Control System. However, the nature of ICSs render traditional risk management methods insufficient. The proprietary character and the complex interrelationships of the various systems that form an ICS, the potential impacts outside its boundaries, along with emerging trends such as the exposure to the Internet, necessitate revisiting traditional risk management methods, in a way that treat an ICS as a system-of-systems rather than a single, one-off entity. Towards this direction, in this paper we present enhancements to the traditional risk management methods at the phase of risk assessment, by utilising the cybernetic construct of the Viable System Model (VSM) as a means towards a holistic view of the risks against Critical Infrastructure. For the purposes of our research, utilising VSM's recursive nature, we model the Supervisory Control and Data Acquisition (SCADA) system, a most commonly used ICS, as a VSM and identify the various assets, interactions with the internal and external environment, threats and vulnerabilities.

1 Introduction

Industrial Control Systems (ICSs), have been a fundamental part of Industry automation for many years. They are typically used to control industrial processes, such as power production, oil extraction, transportation, telecommunications etc. [1]. Those processes have a direct impact on the National Critical Infrastructure (CI) [2], making their protection against cyber-attacks a process of national significance. Effective Cyber-Security Risk Assessment methods are vital in order to manage security risks against the ICSs.

Assessing and managing cyber-security risks in traditional IT systems has followed certain well established techniques [3–6]. Nevertheless, the complexity and the interconnectivity of Industrial Control Systems (ICSs) hinder the application of traditional

---

[*] This work was supported by the Systems Centre and the EPSRC funded Industrial Doctorate Centre in Systems (Grant EP/G037353/1).

N. Cuppens-Boulahia et al. (Eds.): SEC 2014, IFIP AICT 428, pp. 438–445, 2014.

cyber-security risk management methods. In many cases though, the methods applied are adaptations of the conventional methods for managing cyber-security risks within the environment of an organisation [7], therefore addressing only part of the threat landscape and certainly mostly the traditional IT components, as opposed to sensor/actuator or other control elements [8]. For that reason, new methods are being developed. However, the majority of these lack the perspective of resilience [8], while in many cases the identification of the threats and vulnerabilities is conducted in each domain of the ICS separately, omitting the interactions between the various assets or threats. As a consequence they tend to protect the various domains of the system independently, applying overwhelming security measures driven by the worst case scenarios [8]. This way, even though the system is considered secure, cost-efficient risk mitigation strategies can not be identified. Therefore, novel holistic cyber-security risk assessment and management approaches that can overcome the drawbacks of past approaches have to be explored.

Towards this direction, we propose a conceptual framework for the enhancement of the cyber-security risk assessment in ICSs, adopting principles of the Viable System Model (VSM) [9]. We use the VSM to model the cyber-assets and functions within an ICS and identify the way cyber-threats against them affect the *viability* of the system, taking into account the various interactions that take place.

The rest of the paper is structured as follows. In Section 2 we discuss related work in the field of cyber-security risk assessment in Critical Infrastructure. Section 3 presents the basic background on the VSM. The description and analysis of our proposed model are given in Section 4. Finally, Section 5 discusses conclusions drawn from our work.

2 Related Work

Cyber-security risk assessment constitutes a fundamental element for the protection of ICSs. According to [8], Critical Infrastructure risk assessment methods are divided into two distinct categories, the sectoral methods, which refer to those who treat each sector separately in the risk assessment process, and those that follow a systemic approach examining the CIs as interconnected networks. Most existing methods fall into the first category. In order to cope with ICS, those methods have been extended. Nevertheless, they have limitations when they are applied in cross-sectoral environments. Furthermore, in most methods of both categories resilience concerns are not addressed or exist only implicitly. Our model falls into the second category, utilising the VSM as a vehicle for the identification and description of the cyber assets and cyber-security risks. The inherent scalable nature of VSM ensures resilience while its systemic behaviour allows the investigation of the emerging interconnections.

The authors in [10] examine Critical Infrastructure as Complex Adaptive Systems. They represent ICSs as large sets of components that interact with each other while synergies emerge through those interactions. They introduce the notion of interacting agents where each agent carries data regarding its location, capabilities and memory. However, the modelling and simulation of such models poses significant challenges and thus has not been taken into account for the risk assessment process. Since our model is based on the VSM, a model that has already been tested against the viability management of an ICS, it poses no similar challenges. In [11] the authors present a simulation environment for SCADA security analysis and assessment. However, even though their work takes into account the interdependencies to an extend and provides resilience, it is purely focused on the network communications between different parts of system, without taking into account several cyber-threats that are not network-driven.

In another approach [12] the authors combine Survivability System Analysis (SSA) with Probabilistic Risk Assessment (PRA) in order to develop a new approach towards risk management in power substations that inherits the strengths of both. The principles of survivability analysis used in their work resemble the viability concept adopted in the VSM that we use in our work. However, this work lacks the ability to thoroughly explore the emerging inter- and intra- disciplinary interactions.

3   Basic Background on the VSM

Our research mostly focuses on the risk assessment process in ICSs. We have combined the traditional risk assessment methodology with principles of the Viable System Model, providing a new way of thinking towards the "cyber-asset identification" and "cyber-threat assessment" steps within a typical cyber-security risk assessment process, as described e.g. in [3]. In this section we provide background information relevant to the Viable System Model and its application to the cyber domain. The Viable System Model was originally designed by Stafford Beer to model the viability of an organisation [13, 14]. Beer studied the human organism and constructed an organisational model for enterprises based on the methods used by the central and autonomic nervous systems to manage the operations of the organs and muscles. The model divides the organisation into three fundamental parts, i.e. Management, Operations and the Environment. The Operations part entails all the operations that take place inside the organisation while the management part controls the smooth operation of the system, ensures its stability, facilitates its adaptation to the future trends and structures the policies of the organisation. The environment entails all external entities that exchange data with the system. A general view of the model is shown in Figure 1. Beer suggests that we should model an organisation in the way the human body works, in a way that is not so strict and solid as the pyramid but flexible to adapt to changes caused by the environment. As seen in Figure 1, the VSM is composed of six different systems, each one of a distinct role.

System 1: Operational units within the organisation.

System 2: Attenuation of oscillations and coordination of activities via information and communication.

System 3: Management of the primary units. Provision of synergies.

System 3*: Investigation and validation of information flowing between Systems 1-3 and 1-2-3 via auditing/ monitoring activities.

System 4: Management of the development of the organisation; dealing with the future and with the overall external environment.

System 5: Balancing present and future as well as internal and external perspectives; ascertaining the identity of the organisation and its role in its environment; embodiment of supreme values, norms and rules of the system

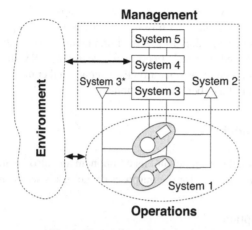

Fig. 1. The Viable System Model

Each operation in System 1 can communicate with the rest of the operations of System 1 and the external environment for exchange data. Their overall function is coordinated by System 2 and controlled by System 3 which is also responsible for the provision of synergies. System 3* is responsible to conduct audits upon System 1 to check if System's 3 directions and commands are implemented properly and address the existence of any issues to System 3. System 4 communicates with the external environment so that it can deal with the future trends and identify the various changes that take place in the external environment. It is in contact with System 3 in order to deliver the changes that have to be done and with System 5 which forms the upper level of management that deals with the system's policies and role inside the environment. System 5 is connected with System 3 since it monitors the homoeostasis between System 4 and System 3. Furthermore, System 5 has the responsibility to deliver the ethos of the organisation and take long term decisions that will be passed to System 3 in order to direct System 1 on how to implement them. Also, System 5 has to know the current state of the Organisation, through reports from System 3, in order to take a long term decision. An interesting characteristic of the VSM is its recursive nature. Each operation in System 1 forms a VSM subsystem with its own operational and management parts.

The VSM has already been used in the cyber-security domain, as a framework for examining the impacts of attacking organisations [15]. The authors utilised the VSM in order to identify the weak points within an organisation by modelling cyber-attacks as attacks against the various systems of the model. This way they managed to explore the impact of an attack based on the systems it affected. However, their work bears certain limitations as it only focuses on one VSM model, disregarding its recursive nature. Neither does it provide information regarding the VSM's relationship with the environment as well as other organisations.

In another approach [16] the authors use the VSM to model Information Security Governance establishing a baseline of the current information security operations system. In their work they model the cyber-security mechanisms of an organisation as a VSM, mapping the various protection mechanisms on the VSM depending on the way they function. However, their research focuses exclusively on the protection mechanisms, omitting information regarding the cyber-assets and impact assessment of a cyber-attack. This is because they follow the implementation of a standard (ISO27001) and thus a checklist-based approach. In our work we use the VSM differently, modelling the cyber-assets of the system as operational or managerial components of a VSM, and examining the impact of a cyber attack upon it.

4   Proposed Model

In this Section we detail our model and its component and also an analysis of the VSM and how we utilise its features for the purposes of the risk assessment in ICSs.

4.1   Model Description

For the purpose of our research, we use VSM to model the assets of the system and the emerging relationships between those assets and the internal and external environment. Considering those relationships as another type of asset, we identify the threats against them and examine the vulnerabilities of the system that can be exploited by the identified threats. Since VSM was originally used to model the viability of a system, identifying the threats against the security of its system-components and their relationships equates to identifying the threats against the viability of the system. Therefore, in order to identify threats against the organisation we can do this by identifying the possible threats against the viability of the system as presented in [15]. In each of the six systems of the VSM we identify the threats that can:

- make the system unavailable to the rest of the systems disrupting its connection to them (Denial of Service attack),
- corrupt the connection of the system to the rest of the systems by sending false data to them (Man in the Middle attack),
- render the system unavailable to its external environment (Denial of Service attack),
- corrupt the connection of the system to its external environment (Man in the Middle attack),
- disclose or corrupt data transferred from/to the system to/from the external environment or another system inside the organisation (data theft, data tampering),
- disclose or corrupt data that reside within the system (data theft, data tampering),
- make its subsystems or suprasystem unavailable,
- corrupt the connection with its subsystems or suprasystem,
- alter or disclose the data transferred to its subsystems or suprasystem.

Afterwards we explore the vulnerabilities that can be exploited by the threats identified in the previous step. The rest of the risk assessment process follows the traditional methodologies. Figure 2 illustrates our proposed risk assessment process. The first step of the process includes the construction of the VSM of the upper level organisation and it is repeated for every subsystem until the lowest level of the organisation where operations are performed by hardware. This way, all the possible assets and interactions are taken into account. At this point it is important to note that in order to identify all the assets and map them to the VSM as operational or management systems, knowledge from people within the ICS is also required. Managers form the upper management levels of the ICS along with engineers from the operational levels have to be consulted.

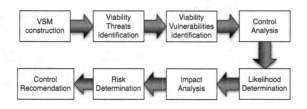

Fig. 2. VSM Risk Assessment Process

4.2 Model Analysis

In general, the proposed process starts with the construction of the VSM of the upper organisational levels. A general VSM model addressing the most common upper level functions that can be found in an ICS, such as Finance, Sales and Marketing, Production, Legal Services, IT, Human Relations etc., can be seen in Figure 3.

All departments of System 1 are coordinated through regular meetings between the activities directors, an action that forms System 2, and organised by the executive director (System 3). The Quality Control Direction forms System 3*, which is responsible for the monitoring and auditing activities on the various departments. System 4 and System 5 are defined as the Marketing and Forward Planning Direction and the Management Board respectively. At a first glance, VSM at this level has nothing to offer to the cyber-security risk assessment. However, the lack of a System (for instance System 3*) may result in significant effects to the subsystems of the various departments of System 1, or a less effective Forward Planning Direction may result in missing critical security news. Thus, even at this level certain threats against cyber security of the ICS that derive from poor organisation of the ICS can be identified. In the context of VSM, the viability of the whole system is inextricably linked with the viability of its subsystems, therefore, each unit should function as a VSM in itself. Applying recursively the VSM in every department of the ICS and delving deeper into the lower levels can reveal more threats against cyber security. In Figure 4, after applying VSM recursively we reach the SCADA system-level. At this level all operations consist of hardware components, known as *field devices*. The impact of a successful cyber-attack there is much higher, because it can affect directly the function of the whole ICS. The VSM helps us identify all the interactions between the various field devices and the control/management equipment/department. Furthermore, interconnections with the external environment can also be identified. For example cyber-threats can origin from trusted insiders carrying knowingly or not compromised equipment, e.g. a malware-infected flash drive, or a compromised mobile device etc. As part of the environment we can find other ICSs that exchange data or services with the ICS under attack. The investigation of those interconnections provides the ability to examine the impact of a cyber-attack on other ICSs.

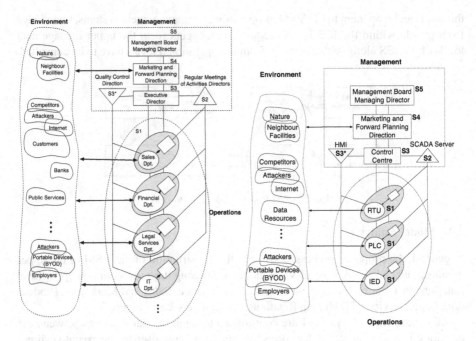

Fig. 3. VSM General Model of the Upper Organisational Level of an ICS

Fig. 4. Applying the VSM on the SCADA system

5   Conclusion

Risk assessment is an essential part of the protection process of Critical Infrastructure. There is a wide variety of risk assessment tools that are currently being used, however the complexity of these systems poses major challenges to the traditional approaches. Existing methods struggle to manage the dependencies in such environments, and resilience remains in most cases an unsolved issue.

In this paper we have used the Viable System Model in order to identify the relationships between the different parts within and outside the Critical Infrastructure system, scope the area of concern with respect to 'cyber' and construct a whole-system view of the assets, threats and vulnerabilities within that scope. Our work enriches the identification steps of conventional risk assessment methods. The VSM approach yields improved results as a diagnostic tool and so combined with a risk management method it can provide system resilience at multiple hierarchical levels. This approach takes into consideration organisational issues (management, coordination etc.) that play a vital role in the ability of a system to mitigate cyber-threats and could otherwise be overlooked.

As part of future work we are currently investigating agent-based modelling techniques where each agent embodies certain characteristics based on its position within the VSM. Furthermore, we aspire to develop novel risk management tools based on VSM, rather than using it as part of traditional methods. This requires the development of a quantitative risk evaluation process that will make use of the findings of the VSM to compute risks. Further work will focus on the development of a game theoretic model that tackles this issue.

References

1. Stouffer, K., Falco, J., Scarfone, K.: Guide to industrial control systems (ics) security. NIST Special Publication 800(82) 16–16
2. European Commission: Council directive 2008/114/ec of 8 december 2008 on the identification and designation of european critical infrastructures and the assessment of the need to improve their protection. Official Journal of the European Union (2008)
3. Peltier, T.R.: Information security risk analysis. CRC Press (2005)
4. Stoneburner, G., Goguen, A.Y., Feringa, A.: SP 800-30. risk management guide for information technology systems. Technical report, National Institute of Standards & Technology, Gaithersburg, MD, United States (2002)
5. Alberts, C.J., Dorofee, A.: Managing information security risks: the OCTAVE approach. Addison-Wesley Longman Publishing Co., Inc. (2002)
6. Karabacak, B., Sogukpinar, I.: Isram: information security risk analysis method. Computers & Security 24(2), 147–159 (2005)
7. Stouffer, K., Falco, J., Kent, K.: Guide to supervisory control and data aquisition (scada) and industrial control systems security. Recommendations of the National Institute of Standards and Technology (NIST). Special Publication, 800–82 (2006)
8. Georgios, G., Roberto, F., Muriel, S.: Risk assessment methodologies for critical infrastructure protection. part i: A state of the art. EUR - scientific and technical research reports, JRC.G.6-Security technology assessment (2012)
9. Espejo, R., Harnden, R.: The viable system model: interpretations and applications of Stafford Beer's VSM. Wiley, Chichester (1989)
10. Rinaldi, S.M., Peerenboom, J.P., Kelly, T.K.: Identifying, understanding, and analyzing critical infrastructure interdependencies. IEEE Control Systems 21(6), 11–25 (2001)
11. Chunlei, W., Lan, F., Yiqi, D.: A simulation environment for scada security analysis and assessment. In: 2010 International Conference on Measuring Technology and Mechatronics Automation (ICMTMA), vol. 1, pp. 342–347. IEEE (2010)
12. Taylor, C., Krings, A., Alves-Foss, J.: Risk analysis and probabilistic survivability assessment (rapsa): An assessment approach for power substation hardening. In: Proc. ACM Workshop on Scientific Aspects of Cyber Terrorism(SACT), Washington, DC, vol. 64 (2002)
13. Beer, S.: Brain of the firm: the managerial cybernetics of organization. J. Wiley, New York (1981)
14. Beer, S.: The heart of enterprise. John Wiley & Sons, Chichester (1994)
15. Hutchinson, B., Warren, M.: Information warfare: using the viable system model as a framework to attack organisations. Australasian Journal of Information Systems 9(2) (2007)
16. Alqurashi, E., Wills, G., Gilbert, L.: A viable system model for information security governance: Establishing a baseline of the current information security operations system. In: Janczewski, L.J., Wolfe, H.B., Shenoi, S. (eds.) SEC 2013. IFIP AICT, vol. 405, pp. 245–256. Springer, Heidelberg (2013)

Privacy Design Strategies*
(Extended Abstract)

Jaap-Henk Hoepman

Radboud University Nijmegen
P. O. Box 9010, 6500 GL Nijmegen, The Netherlands
jhh@cs.ru.nl

Abstract. In this paper we define the notion of a privacy design strategy. These strategies help IT architects to support privacy by design early in the software development life cycle, during concept development and analysis. Using current data protection legislation as point of departure we derive the following eight privacy design strategies: MINIMISE, HIDE, SEPARATE, AGGREGATE, INFORM, CONTROL, ENFORCE, and DEMONSTRATE. The strategies also provide a useful classification of privacy design patterns and the underlying privacy enhancing technologies. We therefore believe that these privacy design strategies are not only useful when designing privacy friendly systems, but also helpful when evaluating the privacy impact of existing IT systems.

1   Introduction

Privacy by design [5] is a system design philosophy that aims to improve the overall privacy[1] friendliness of IT systems. Point of departure is the observation that privacy (like security) is a core property of a system that is heavily influenced by the underlying system design. As a consequence, privacy protection cannot be implemented as an add-on. Privacy must be addressed from the outset instead. The fundamental principle of privacy by design is, therefore, that privacy requirements must be addressed throughout the full system development process. In other words starting when the initial concepts and ideas for a new system are drafted, up to and including the final implementation of that system. Privacy by design is gaining importance. For example, the proposal for a new European data protection regulation [10] explicitly requires data protection by design and by default. It is therefore crucial to support developers in satisfying these requirements with practical tools and guidelines.

As explained in Section 2, an important design methodology is the application of so called software design patterns. These design patterns refine the system architecture to achieve certain functional requirements within a given set of constraints. During software development the availability of practical methods to protect privacy is high during

---

* This research is supported by the research program Sentinels (www.sentinels.nl) as project 'Revocable Privacy' (10532). Sentinels is being financed by Technology Foundation STW, the Netherlands Organization for Scientific Research (NWO), and the Dutch Ministry of Economic Affairs. This research was (partially) conducted within the Privacy and Identity Lab (PI.lab, www.pilab.nl).

[1] In this paper we focus on data protection, and treat privacy and data-protection as synonyms.

N. Cuppens-Boulahia et al. (Eds.): SEC 2014, IFIP AICT 428, pp. 446–459, 2014.

actual implementation, but low when starting the project. Numerous privacy enhancing technologies (PETs) exists that can be applied more or less 'off the shelf'. Before that implementation stage, privacy design patterns can be used during system design. Significantly less design patterns exist compared to PETs, however. And at the start of the project, during the concept development and analysis phases, the developer stands basically empty handed.

This paper aims to close this gap [13,26]. Design patterns do not necessarily play a role in the earlier, concept development and analysis, phases of the software development cycle. The main reason is that such design patterns are already quite detailed in nature, and more geared towards solving an implementation problem. To guide the development team in the earlier stages, we define the notion of a privacy design strategy. Because these strategies describe fundamental, more strategic, approaches to protecting privacy, they enable the IT developer to make well founded choices during the concept development and analysis phase as well. These choices have a huge impact on the overall privacy protection properties of the final system.

The privacy design strategies developed in this paper are derived from existing privacy principles and data protection laws. These are described in section 3. We focus on the principles and laws on which the design of an IT system has a potential impact. By taking an abstract information storage model of an IT system as a point of departure, these legal principles are translated to a context more relevant for the IT developer in section 4. This leads us to define the following privacy design strategies: MINIMISE, HIDE, SEPARATE, AGGREGATE, INFORM, CONTROL, ENFORCE and DEMONSTRATE. They are described in detail in section 5.

We believe these strategies help to support privacy by design throughout the full software development life cycle, even before the design phase. It makes explicit which high level decisions can be made to protect privacy, when the first concepts for a new information system are drafted. The strategies also provide a useful classification of privacy design patterns and the underlying privacy enhancing technologies. We therefore believe that these privacy design strategies are not only useful when designing privacy friendly systems, but that they also provide a starting point for evaluating the privacy impact of existing information systems.

2   Software Development

Software architecture encompasses the set of significant decisions about the organisation of a software system[2], including the selection of the structural elements and their interfaces by which a system is composed, the behaviour as specified in collaborations among those elements, the composition of these structural and behavioural elements into larger subsystem, and the architectural style that guides this organisation.

Typically, the development of a software system proceeds in six phases: concept development, analysis, design, implementation, testing and evaluation. In fact, these phases are often considered a cycle, where after evaluation a new iteration starts by

---

[2] Based on an original definiton by Mary Shaw, expanded in 1995 by Grady Booch, Kurt Bittner, Philippe Kruchten and Rich Reitman as reported in [19].

updating the concept as appropriate. In this paper we distinguish design strategies (defined in this paper), design patterns and concrete (privacy enhancing) technologies as tools to support the decisions to be made in each of these phases. The design strategies support the concept development and analysis phases, the design patterns are applicable during the design phase, and the privacy enhancing technologies are useful during the implementation phase.

2.1 Design Patterns

The concept of a *design pattern* is a useful vehicle for making design decisions about the organisation of a software system. A design pattern

> "provides a scheme for refining the subsystems or components of a software system, or the relationships between them. It describes a commonly recurring structure of communicating components that solves a general design problem within a particular context." [3]

Typically, the description [11] of a design pattern contains at least its name, purpose, context (the situations in which it applies), implementation (its structure, components and their relationships), and the consequences (its results, side effects and trade-offs when applied). Many design patterns exist, at varying levels of abstraction.

A classical software design pattern is the *Model-View-Controller*[3], that separates the representation of the data (the model) from the way it is represented towards the user (the view) and how the user can modify that data (using the controller). Few privacy design patterns have been *explicitly* described as such to date. We are aware of the work of Hafiz [14,15], Pearson [23,22], van Rest *et al.* [30], and a recent initiative of the UC Berkeley School of Information[4]. Many more *implicit* privacy design patterns exist though, although they have never been described as such. We will encounter them in our discussion of the patterns corresponding to the privacy design strategies we develop below.

2.2 Design Strategies

Because certain design patterns have a higher level of abstraction than others, some authors also distinguish *architecture patterns*, that

> "express a fundamental structural organisation or schema for software systems. They provide a set of predefined subsystems, specify their responsibilities, and include rules and guidelines for organising the relationships between them."[5]

---

[3] Originally formulated in the late 1970s by Trygve Reenskaug at Xerox PARC, as part of the Smalltalk system.
[4] http://privacypatterns.org/
[5] See http://best-practice-software-engineering.ifs.tuwien.ac.at/ patterns.html, and The Open Group Architecture Framework (TOGAF) http://pubs.opengroup.org/architecture/togaf8-doc/ arch/chap28.html

The *Model-View-Controller* pattern cited above is sometimes considered such an architecture pattern. The distinction between an architecture pattern and a design pattern is not always easily made, however. Moreover, there are even more general principles that guide the system architecture. We choose, therefore, to express such higher level abstractions in terms of *design strategies*. We define this as follows.

> A design strategy describes a fundamental approach to achieve a certain design goal. It favours certain structural organisations or schemes over others. It has certain properties that allow it to be distinguished from other (fundamental) approaches that achieve the same goal.

Whether something classifies as a strategy very much depends on the universe of discourse, and in particular on the exact goal the strategy aims to achieve. A *privacy design strategy* is a design strategy that achieves (some level of) privacy protection as its goal.

Design strategies do not necessarily impose a specific structure on the system although they certainly limit the possible structural realisations of it. Therefore, they are also applicable during the concept development and analysis phase of the development cycle[6].

2.3 Privacy Enhancing Technologies

Privacy Enhancing Technologies (PETs) are better known, and much more studied. Borking and Blarkom *et al.* [1,29] define them as follows.

> "Privacy-Enhancing Technologies is a system of ICT measures protecting informational privacy by eliminating or minimising personal data thereby preventing unnecessary or unwanted processing of personal data, without the loss of the functionality of the information system."

This definition was later adopted almost literally by the European Commission [8].

In principle, PETs are used to implement a certain privacy design pattern with concrete technology. For example, both 'Idemix' [4] and 'u-prove' [2] are privacy enhancing technologies implementing the (implicit) design pattern *anonymous credentials*. There are many more examples of privacy enhancing technologies, like 'cut-and-choose' techniques [7], 'onion routing' [6] to name but a few.

3   The Foundations of Data Protection

We aim to derive privacy design strategies from existing data protection laws and privacy frameworks. We therefore briefly summarise those here.

In the European Union, the legal right to privacy is based on Article 8 of the European Convention of Human Rights of 1950. In the context of data protection, this right has been made explicit in the 1995 data protection directive [9], which is based on the privacy guidelines of the Organisation of Economic Co-Operation and Development (OECD) from 1980 [21].

---

[6] We note that the notion of a privacy design strategy should not be confused with the foundational principles of Cavoukian [5] or the concept of a privacy principle from the ISO 29100 Privacy framework [17].

3.1 The OECD Guidelines

The OECD guidelines, of which the US fair information practices (FIPs) [28] — *notice, choice, access* and *security* — are a subset, define the following principles.

- The collection of personal data is lawful, limited, and happens with the knowledge or consent of the data subject (*Collection Limitation*).
- Personal data should be relevant to the purposes for which they are to be used, and be accurate, complete and kept up-to-date (*Data Quality*).
- The purposes of the collection must be specified upfront (*Purpose Specification*), and the use of the data after collection is limited to that purpose (*Use Limitation*).
- Personal data must be adequately protected (*Security Safeguards*).
- The nature and extent of the data processing and the controller responsible must be readily available (*Openness*).
- Individuals have the right to view, erase, rectify, complete or amend personal data stored that relates to him (*Individual Participation*).
- A data controller must be accountable for complying with these principles (*Accountability*).

3.2 Data Protection in Europe

The OECD principles correspond roughly to the main provisions in the European data protection Directive of 1995 [9]. For example, Article 6 states that personal data must be processed fairly and lawfully, must be collected for a specified purpose, and must not be further processed in a way incompatible with those purposes. Moreover the data must be adequate, relevant, and not excessive. It must be accurate and up to date, and kept no longer than necessary. These provisions express a need for purpose limitation, data minimisation, and data quality.

Other articles of the Directive deal with transparency and user choice. For example, article 7 requires unambiguous consent from the data subject, while article 10 and 11 require data controllers to inform data subjects about the processing of personal data. Article 12 gives data subjects the right to review and correct the personal data that is being processed about them. Finally, security as a means to protect privacy is addressed by article 17, that mandates adequate security of processing.

We note that the European data protection directive covers many more aspects, that are however less relevant for the discussion in this paper. The directive is currently under review. A proposal for a regulation to replace it has been published [10], and an amendment was recently adopted by the European Parliament. This regulation is still in flux and under heavy debate, but it contains the following rights and obligations that are relevant for our discussion in this paper.

- A controller must implement data protection by design and by default (art. 23).
- A controller must be able to demonstrate compliance with the regulation (art. 5, and also art. 22).
- Data subjects have the right to be forgotten and to erasure (art. 17).
- Data subjects have the right to data portability, allowing them 'to obtain from the controller a copy of data undergoing processing in an electronic and structured

format which is commonly used and allows for further use by the data subject'
(art. 18).
- A data controller has the duty to issue a notification whenever a personal data
breach occurs (art. 31 and 32).

3.3 The ISO 29100 Privacy Framework Perspective

In the full paper [16] we also include the ISO 29100 Privacy framework [17] in our
analysis, but due to space constraints this is omitted from this extended abstract.

3.4 Summary of Requirements

Not every legal requirement can be met by designing an IT system in a specific way.
Legitimacy of processing is a good example. If the processing is illegitimate, then it will
be illegitimate irrespective of the design of the system. We therefore focus our effort on
studying aspects on which the design of an IT system has a potential impact. These are
summarised in the list below.

- Purpose limitation (comprising both specification of the purpose and limiting the
use to that stated purpose).
- Data minimisation.
- Data quality.
- Transparency (Openness in OECD terms).
- Data subject rights (in terms of consent, and the right to view, erase, and rectify
personal data).
- The right to be forgotten.
- Adequate protection (Security Safeguards in OECD terms).
- Data portability.
- Data breach notifications.
- Accountability and (provable) compliance.

These principles must be covered by the privacy design strategies that we will derive
next. Whether this is indeed the case is analysed in section 6.

4 Deriving Privacy Design Strategies

A natural starting point to derive privacy preserving strategies is to look at when and
how privacy is violated, and then consider how these violations can be prevented.
Solove's taxonomy [25], for example, identifies four basic groups of activities that affect privacy: information collection, information processing, information dissemination
and invasions. This is in fact similar to the distinction made between data transfer, storage and processing by Spiekermann and Cranor [26]. This general subdivision inspired
us to look at IT systems at a higher level of abstraction to determine where and how
privacy violations can be prevented.

In doing so, we can view an IT system as an information storage system (i.e., database
system) system. Many of today's systems, like classical business or government administration systems, are database systems. The same holds for social networks. Current

data protection legislation [9] is pretty much written with such a database model in mind. In a database, information about individuals is stored in one or more tables. Each table stores a fixed set of attributes for an individual. The columns in the table represent this fixed set of attributes. A row is added for each new individual about whom a record needs to be stored. Sometimes, data is not stored at the level of individual persons, but is instead aggregated based on certain relevant group properties (like postal code).

Within the legal framework described in section 3, the collection of personal data should be proportional to the purpose for which it is collected, and this purpose should not be achievable through other, less invasive means. In practice, this means that data collection should be *minimised*. This can be achieved by not storing individual rows in a database table for each and every individual. Also the collection of attributes stored should correspond to the purpose, leading to fewer columns being stored. Data collected for one purpose should be stored *separately* from data stored for another purpose. Linking of these database tables should not be easy. When data about specific individuals is not necessary for the purpose, only *aggregate* data should be stored. Personal data should be properly protected, and *hidden* from other parties. A data subject should be *informed* about the fact that data about her is being processed, and she should be able to request modifications and corrections where appropriate. In fact the underlying principle of information self-determination [31] dictates the she should be in *control*. Finally, the collection and processing of personal data should be done in accordance to a privacy policy, that should be actively *enforced*. The current proposal for the revision of the European privacy directive (into a regulation) also stresses the fact that data controllers should be able to *demonstrate compliance* with data protection legislation. The data controller has the burden of proof with respect to compliance and must, for example, run and document a privacy impact assessment (PIA).

Given this analysis form the legal point of view, we distinguish the following eight privacy design strategies: MINIMISE, SEPARATE, AGGREGATE, HIDE, INFORM, CONTROL, ENFORCE and DEMONSTRATE. A graphical representation of these strategies, when applied to a database system, is given in Figure 1.

5   The Eight Privacy Design Strategies

We will now proceed to describe these eight strategies in detail. We have grouped the strategies into two classes: data-oriented strategies and process-oriented strategies. The first class roughly corresponds to the privacy-by-architecture approach identified by Spiekermann and Cranor [26], whereas the process-oriented strategies more-or-less cover their privacy-by-policy approach.

5.1   Data Oriented Strategies

Strategy #1: MINIMISE. The most basic privacy design strategy is MINIMISE, which states that

> The amount of personal data that is processed[7] should be restricted to the minimal amount possible.

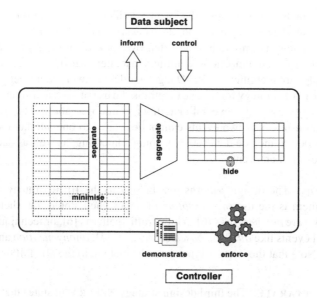

Fig. 1. The database metaphor of the eight privacy design strategies

This strategy is extensively discussed by Gürses *et al.* [13]. By ensuring that no, or no unnecessary, data is collected, the possible privacy impact of a system is limited. Applying the MINIMISE strategy means one has to answer whether the processing of personal data is proportional (with respect to the purpose) and whether no other, less invasive, means exist to achieve the same purpose. The decision to collect personal data can be made at design time and at run time, and can take various forms. For example, one can decide not to collect any information about a particular data subject at all. Alternatively, one can decide to collect only a limited set of attributes.

Design Patterns. Common design patterns that implements this strategy are *select before you collect* [18] , *anonymisation* and *use pseudonyms* [24].

Strategy #2: HIDE. The second design strategy, HIDE, states that

> Any personal data, and their interrelationships, should be hidden from plain view.

The rationale behind this strategy is that by hiding personal data from plain view, it cannot easily be abused. The strategy does not directly say from whom the data should be hidden. And this depends on the specific context in which this strategy is applied. In certain cases, where the strategy is used to hide information that spontaneously emerges from the use of a system (communication patterns for example), the intent is to hide the information from anybody. In other cases, where information is collected, stored or

---

[7] For brevity, and in line with Article 2 of the European directive [9], we use data processing to include the collection, storage and dissemination of that data as well.

processed legitimately by one party, the intent is to hide the information from any other party. In this case, the strategy corresponds to ensuring confidentiality.

The HIDE strategy is important, and often overlooked. In the past, many systems have been designed using innocuous identifiers that later turned out to be privacy nightmares. Examples are identifiers on RFID tags, wireless network identifiers, and even IP addresses. The HIDE strategy forces one to rethink the use of such identifiers. In essence, the HIDE strategy aims to achieve unlinkability and unobservability [24]. Unlinkability in this context ensures that two events cannot be related to one another (where events can be understood to include data subjects doing something, as well as data items that occur as the result of an event).

Design Patterns. The design patterns that belong to the HIDE strategy are a mixed bag. One of them is the use of *encryption* of data (when stored, or when in transit). Other examples are *mix networks* [6] to hide traffic patterns [6], or techniques to unlink certain related events like *attribute based credentials* [4], *anonymisation* and the use of *pseudonyms*. Note that the latter two patterns also belong to the MINIMISE strategy.

Strategy #3: SEPARATE. The third design strategy, SEPARATE, states that

> Personal data should be processed in a distributed fashion, in separate compartments whenever possible.

By separating the processing or storage of several sources of personal data that belong to the same person, complete profiles of one person cannot be made. Moreover, separation is a good method to achieve purpose limitation. The strategy of separation calls for distributed processing instead of centralised solutions. In particular, data from separate sources should be stored in separate databases, and these databases should not be linked. Data should be processed locally whenever possible, and stored locally if feasible as well. Database tables should be split when possible. Rows in these tables should be hard to link to each other, for example by removing any identifiers, or using table specific pseudonyms.

These days, with an emphasis on centralised web based services this strategy is often disregarded. However, the privacy guarantees offered by peer-to-peer networks are considerable. Decentralised social networks like Diaspora[8] are inherently more privacy friendly than centralised approaches like Facebook and Google+.

Design Patterns. No specific design patterns for this strategy are known.

Strategy #4: AGGREGATE. The fourth design pattern, AGGREGATE, states that

> Personal data should be processed at the highest level of aggregation and with the least possible detail in which it is (still) useful.

Aggregation of information over groups of attributes or groups of individuals, restricts the amount of detail in the personal data that remains. This data therefore becomes less

---

[8] http://diasporafoundation.org/

sensitive. When the information is sufficiently coarse grained, and the size of the group over which it is aggregated is sufficiently large, little information can be attributed to a single person, thus protecting its privacy.

Design Patterns. Examples of design patterns that belong to this strategy are the following: *aggregation over time* (used in smart metering), *dynamic location granularity* (used in location based services), and *k-anonymity* [27].

5.2 Process Oriented Strategies

Strategy #5: INFORM. The INFORM strategy corresponds to the important notion of transparency:

> Data subjects should be adequately informed whenever personal data is processed.

Whenever data subjects use a system, they should be informed about which information is processed, for what purpose, and by which means. This includes information about the ways the information is protected, and being transparent about the security of the system. Providing access to clear design documentation is also a good practice. Data subjects should also be informed about third parties with which information is shared. And data subjects should be informed about their data access rights and how to exercise them.

Design Patterns. A possible design patterns in this category is the *Platform for Privacy Preferences (P3P)*[9]. *Data breach notifications* are also a design pattern in this category. Finally, Graf *et al.* [12] provide an interesting collection of privacy design patterns for informing the user from the Human Computer Interfacing perspective.

Strategy #6: CONTROL. The control strategy states that

> Data subjects should be provided agency over the processing of their personal data.

The CONTROL strategy is in fact an important counterpart to the INFORM strategy. Without reasonable means of controlling the use of one's personal data, there is little use in informing a data subject about the fact that personal data is collected. Of course the converse also holds: without proper information, there is little use in asking consent. Data protection legislation often gives the data subject the right to view, update and even ask the deletion of personal data collected about her. This strategy underlines this fact, and design patterns in this class give users the tools to exert their data protection rights.

CONTROL goes beyond the strict implementation of data protection rights, however. It also governs the means by which users can decide whether to use a certain system, and the way they control what kind of information is processed about them. In the context of social networks, for example, the ease with which the user can update his privacy

---

[9] http://www.w3.org/P3P/

settings through the user interface determines the level of control to a large extent. So user interaction design is an important factor as well. Moreover, by providing users direct control over their own personal data, they are more likely to correct errors. As a result the quality of personal data that is processed may increase.

Design Patterns. We are not aware of specific design patterns that fit this strategy.

Strategy #7: ENFORCE. The seventh strategy, ENFORCE, states:

A privacy policy compatible with legal requirements should be in place and should be enforced.

The ENFORCE strategy ensures that a privacy policy is in place. This is an important step in ensuring that a system respects privacy during its operation. Of course the actual level of privacy protection depends on the actual policy. At the very least it should be compatible with legal requirements. As a result, purpose limitation is covered by this strategy as well. More importantly though, the policy should be enforced. This implies, at the very least, that proper technical protection mechanisms are in place that prevent violations of the privacy policy. Moreover, appropriate governance structures to enforce that policy must also be established.

Design Patterns. Access control is an example of a design patterns that implement this strategy. Another example are *sticky policies* and privacy rights management: a form of digital rights management involving licenses to personal data.

Strategy #8: DEMONSTRATE. The final strategy, DEMONSTRATE, requires a data controller to

Be able to demonstrate compliance with the privacy policy and any applicable legal requirements.

Table 1. Mapping of strategies onto legal principles

	Purpose limitation	Data minimisation	Data quality	Transparency	Data subject rights	The right to be forgotten	Adequate protection	Data portability	Data breach notification	(Provable) Compliance
MINIMISE	o	+								
HIDE		+					o			
SEPARATE	o						o			
AGGREGATE	o	+								
INFORM				+	+				+	
CONTROL					o	+		+		
ENFORCE	+	+				+	+			o
DEMONSTRATE										+

Legend: +: covers principle to a large extent. o: covers principle to some extent.

This strategy goes one step further than the ENFORCE strategy in that it requires the data controller to prove that it is in control. This is explicitly required in the new draft EU privacy regulation [10]. In particular this requires the data controller to be able to show how the privacy policy is effectively implemented within the IT system. In case of complaints or problems, she should immediately be able to determine the extent of any possible privacy breaches.

Design Patterns. Design patterns that implement this strategy are, for example, *privacy management systems* [20], and the use of logging and auditing.

6   Conclusions and Acknowledgements

We have derived eight privacy design strategies from an IT system perspective, taking the legal requirements as point of departure. The coverage of these legal principles by the design strategies is summarised in Table 1 (using the detailed description of each strategy in section 5).

As discussed before, not every legal data protection principle can be covered by a privacy design strategy, simply because the design of the system has no impact on that principle. Some data protection principles, like purpose limitation, are only partially covered by some of the strategies. Realising purpose limitation in full also requires procedural and organisational means.

With respect to design pattern coverage, we first observe that design patterns may belong to several design strategies. For example the *use pseudonyms* design pattern both implements the MINIMISE strategy and the HIDE strategy. In the course of our investigations we also observed huge differences between design strategies in terms of the number of design patterns known to implement them. For the strategies MINIMISE and HIDE, a large number of design patterns exist. This is not surprising, given the focus of most research in privacy enhancing technologies on these aspects of privacy protection. For the SEPARATE and CONTROL strategies on the other hand, no corresponding design patterns are known.

This paper discusses work in progress. In particular, further research will be performed to classify existing privacy design patterns into privacy design strategies, and to describe these design patterns in more detail. Moreover, we have identified several implicitly defined design patterns (like *attribute based credentials*) that arise from our study of existing privacy enhancing technologies. Further developments and collaboration in this line of research will also be documented on our Wiki[10]. We would very much welcome contributions from the research community.

I would like to thank the members of the Privacy & Identity Lab[11] for discussions and valuable feedback. In particular I am grateful to Ronald Leenes, Martin Pekarek and Eleni Kosta for their detailed comments and recommendations that greatly improved this paper.

---

[10] http://wiki.science.ru.nl/privacy/
[11] http://www.pilab.nl

References

1. Borking, J.: Der identity-protector. Datenschutz und Datensicherheit 20(11), 654–658 (1996)
2. Brands, S.: Rethinking Public Key Infrastructures and Digital Certificates; Building in Privacy, 1st edn. MIT Press (2000) ISBN 0-262-02491-8
3. Buschmann, F., Meunier, R., Rohnert, H., Sommerlad, P.: Pattern-Oriented Software Architecture, A System of Patterns, vol. 1. John Wiley & Sons (1996)
4. Camenisch, J.L., Lysyanskaya, A.: An efficient system for non-transferable anonymous credentials with optional anonymity revocation. In: Pfitzmann, B. (ed.) EUROCRYPT 2001. LNCS, vol. 2045, pp. 93–118. Springer, Heidelberg (2001)
5. A. Cavoukian.: Privacy by design – the 7 foundational principles. Technical report, Information and Privacy Commissioner of Ontario (January 2011) (revised version)
6. Chaum, D.: Untraceable electronic mail, return addresses, and digital pseudonyms. Commun. ACM 24(2), 84–88 (1981)
7. Chaum, D., Fiat, A., Naor, M.: Untraceable electronic cash. In: Goldwasser, S. (ed.) CRYPTO 1988. LNCS, vol. 403, pp. 319–327. Springer, Heidelberg (1990)
8. Communication COM (2007)228 from the Commission to the European Parliament and the Council. On Promoting Data Protection by Privacy Enhancing Technologies (PETs) (Not published in the OJC) (2007)
9. Directive 95/46/EC of the European Parliament and of the Council of 24 October 1995. On the protection of individuals with regard to the processing of personal data and on the free movement of such data. OJ CL 281, 0031–0050 (1995)
10. Proposal for a Regulation of the European Parliament and of the Council. On the protection of individuals with regard to the processing of personal data and on the free movement of such data. OJ C 102, 24 (2012)
11. Gamma, E., Helm, R., Johnson, R., Vlissides, J.: Design Patterns: Elements of Reusable Object-Oriented Software. Addison-Wesley (1994)
12. Graf, C., Wolkerstorfer, P., Geven, A., Tscheligi, M.: A pattern collection for privacy enhancing technology. In: The 2nd Int. Conf. on Pervasive Patterns and Applications (PATTERNS 2010), Lisbon, Portugal, November 21–26 (2010)
13. Grses, S., Troncoso, C., Diaz, C.: Engineering privacy by design. In: Conference on Computers, Privacy & Data Protection, CPDP 2011 (2011)
14. Hafiz, M.: A collection of privacy design patterns. In: Proceedings of the 2006 Conference on Pattern languages of Programs, PLoP 2006 pp. 7:1–7:13. ACM, New York (2006)
15. Hafiz, M.: A pattern language for developing privacy enhancing technologies. In: Softw. Pract. Exper. (2011), doi:10.1002/spe.1131.
16. J.-H. Hoepman.: Privacy design strategies, eprint arXiv:1210.6621 (October 2012), A preliminary version was presented at the Amsterdam Privacy Conference (APC 2012) and the Privacy Law Scholars Conference (PLSC 2013)
17. ISO/IEC 29100. Information technology – Security techniques – Privacy framework. Technical report, ISO JTC 1/SC 27
18. Jacobs, B.: Select before you collect. Ars Aequi 54, 1006–1009 (2005)
19. Kruchten, P.: An ontology of architectural design decisions. In: Bosch., J. (ed.) Proc. of the 2nd Groningen Workshop on Software Variability Management, Groningen, The Netherlands (2004)
20. Casassa Mont, M., Pearson, S.: An adaptive privacy management system for data repositories. In: Katsikas, S., López, J., Pernul, G. (eds.) TrustBus 2005. LNCS, vol. 3592, pp. 236–245. Springer, Heidelberg (2005)
21. Organisation of Economic Co-Operation and Development. OECD guidelines on the protection of privacy and transborder flows of personal data (1980)

22. Pearson, S., Benameur, A.: Decision support for design for privacy: A system focused on privacy by policy. In: PrimeLife/IFIP Summer School 2010: Privacy and Identity Management for Life, Helsingborg, Sweden (August 2010) (to appear)

23. Pearson, S., Shen, Y.: Context-aware privacy design pattern selection. In: Katsikas, S., Lopez, J., Soriano, M. (eds.) TrustBus 2010. LNCS, vol. 6264, pp. 69–80. Springer, Heidelberg (2010)

24. A. Pfitzmann, M. Hansen.: Anonymity, unlinkability, undetectability, unobservability, pseudonymity, and identity management – a consolidated proposal for terminology (version v0.34 August 10, 2010), http://dud.inf.tu-dresden.de/ Anon_Terminology.shtml

25. Solove, D.J.: A taxonomy of privacy. University of Pennsylvania Law Review 154(3), 477–564 (2006)

26. Spiekermann, S., Cranor, L.F.: Engineering privacy. IEEE Trans. Software Eng. 35(1), 67–82 (2009)

27. Sweeney, L.: k-anonymity: A model for protecting privacy. International Journal of Uncertainty, Fuzziness and Knowledge-Based Systems 10(5), 557–570 (2002)

28. US Federal Trade Commission. Privacy online: Fair information practices in the electronic marketplace, a report to congress (2000)

29. van Blarkom, G.W., Borking, J.J., Verhaar, P.: PET. In: van Blarkom, G.W., Borking, J.J., Olk, J.G.E. (eds.) Handbook of Privacy and Privacy-Enhancing Technologies - The Case of Intelligent Software Agnets, ch. 3, pp. 33–54. College Bescherming Persoonsgegevens, The Hague (2003)

30. van Rest, J., Boonstra, D., Everts, M., van Rijn, M., van Paassen, R.: Designing privacy-by-design. Presented at the Annual Privacy Forum 2012, Limmasol, Cyprus (2012)

31. Westin, A.: Privacy and Freedom. Atheneum, New York (1976)

Distance Computation
between Two Private Preference Functions

Alberto Blanco, Josep Domingo-Ferrer, Oriol Farràs, and David Sánchez

Universitat Rovira i Virgili
Dept. of Computer Engineering and Mathematics
UNESCO Chair in Data Privacy
Av. Països Catalans 26
E-43007 Tarragona, Catalonia
{alberto.blanco,josep.domingo,oriol.farras,david.sanchez}@urv.cat

Abstract. We consider the following problem: two parties have each a
private function, for example one that outputs the party's preferences on
a set of alternatives; they wish to compute the distance between their
functions without any of the parties revealing its function to the other.
The above problem is extremely important in the context of social, political or business networks, whenever one wishes to find friends or partners
with similar interests without having to disclose one's interests to everyone. We provide protocols that solve the above problem for several types
of functions. Experimental work demonstrates that privacy preservation
does not significantly distort the computed distances.

Keywords: Private distance computation, privacy, social networks, utility functions, preferences, user profiles, private matching.

1 Introduction

Shyness often has a rational component. Getting to know a stranger normally
requires us to disclose some of our privacy to that stranger. Indeed, in a fair
relationship there is normally a tit-for-tat approach, in which each of the parties
must disclose something in order to learn something. It would be more privacy-
preserving and less risky if two parties could determine whether they have similar
interests without *prior* disclosure of such interests to each other. Of course, the
more similar their interests turn out to be, the greater the *posterior* mutual
disclosure: in the extreme case, if their interests turn out to be at distance 0,
total mutual disclosure occurs.

In game-theoretic terms, the above problem can be expressed as two players
being interested in determining how close their utility functions are without
disclosing these utility functions to each other. In particular, this allows forming
coalitions with homogeneous interests without prior utility disclosure.

Solving this problem is very relevant in many practical situations:

- In social networks, users could find friends or other users to follow who share
  their interests, without being forced to disclose their own private interests

N. Cuppens-Boulahia et al. (Eds.): SEC 2014, IFIP AICT 428, pp. 460–470, 2014.

(*e.g.* religion, sexual orientation, health condition, etc.). For example, in the social network PatientsLikeMe [12] users currently need to disclose their diseases in order to find users with similar ailments, a privacy loss which could be mitigated by our approach.

- Grooming attacks in social networks could be hindered to a good extent with our approach. Note that the groomer would need to guess the victim's interests in order to become her/his friend.
- Targeted consumer profiling could be also made possible. A company could create dummy users of a social network with the profile of the consumers it is looking for. In this way, the company could identify communities of potential consumers with the desired profile, without encroaching on the privacy of people who do not fit the profile being sought.
- In commercial transactions, parties could determine whether the values they assign to a collection of goods are similar, without prior disclosure of their chosen value(s). For example, in some cases a company may be interested in associating with companies with *dissimilar* interests, in order to form a complementary partnership, rather than associating with companies with too similar interests, which may be regarded as competitors.
- In job recruitment, companies and candidates would be able to confidentially determine to what extent the corporate vision is shared by each candidate. Thanks to the privacy-preserving mechanism, a lot of different factors could be included in the evaluation, without the company being forced to reveal its strategic goals to unsuccessful candidates or the latter needing to disclose their views.

1.1 Contribution and Plan of this Paper

We present in this paper privacy-preserving protocols that allow computing the distances between various types of functions. After that, we report on experimental work that shows that privacy preservation does not cause a significant distortion in the computed distance.

Section 2 defines several cases of privacy-preserving distance computation between functions, depending on the nature of the function and the type of distance being considered. Section 3 describes a protocol for privacy-preserving distance computation based on set intersection. Section 4 reports on experimental work. Section 5 describes related work. Conclusions and future research lines are summarized in Section 6.

2 Taxonomy of Distance Computation between Functions

The protocol to compute the distance between two functions in a privacy-preserving way depends on the nature of the functions and the way the distance is to be measured. We next discuss several cases.

2.1 Case A: Counting Common Qualitative Preferences

In this case, the interests or preferences of each player are characterized as binary features on various independent topics. For example, in a social networks like Facebook, users are asked to provide their opinions on different topics as "like" or "do not like". In PatientsLikeMe [12], users are requested to detail their medical histories as binary selections from sets of alternatives (diseases, symptoms, etc.).

We can consider the preferences or profile of a player as a set containing his/her opinions or personal details. Let this set be X for the first player C and Y for second player S. Then the distance between the interests of C and S can be evaluated as the multiplicative inverse of the size of the intersection of X and Y, that is $1/|X \cap Y|$, when the intersection is not empty. If it is empty, we say that the distance is ∞.

Clearly, the more the coincidences between X and Y, the more similar the preferences of both players, and the smaller the distance between them.

2.2 Case B: Correlating Qualitative Preferences

As in the previous case, the players' preferences are expressed as qualitative features. However, if these features are not independent (*e.g.* related diseases) or they are not binary (*e.g.* expressed as free textual answers to questionnaires), the distance between the players' profiles cannot be computed as the size of the intersection between their sets of features. For example, if C suffers from anorexia and S from bulimia, there is some coincidence between them because they both present eating disorders. This coincidence must be captured by the resulting distance.

Assume we have a correlation function $s : E \times E \mapsto \mathbb{Z}_+$ that measures the similarity between the values in the sets of features of C and S, where E is the domain where the sets of features of both players take values. For nominal features (*e.g.* disease names), semantic similarity measures can be used for this purpose [13]; for numerical features that take values over bounded and discrete domains (*e.g.* ages, zip codes), standard arithmetic functions can be used. Assume further that both players know this function s from the very beginning.

Here the distance between the set X of C's features and the set Y of S's features can be computed as

$$1/(\textstyle\sum_{x \in X} \sum_{y \in Y} s(x,y))$$

when the denominator is nonzero. If it is zero, we say that the distance is ∞.

2.3 Case C: Quantitative Preference Functions

In this case, we want to compute the difference between two quantitative functions over the same domain, which define the preferences or profiles of the two players. We assume that they are integer functions. That is, C has a private preference function $f : E \to \mathbb{Z}$ and S has a private preference function $g : E \to \mathbb{Z}$.

A way to measure the dissimilarity between f and g is to compute $d(f, g) = \sum_{i=1}^{t} |f(x_i) - g(x_i)|$, where $D = \{x_1, \ldots, x_t\}$ is a representative discrete subset of elements from E.

This scenario fits well the usual way of learning, modeling and managing social network user profiles in the literature [1,16,21]. It consists in associating a vector of weights to each user, where each weight expresses the preference of the user on a certain topic (*e.g.* sports, science, health, etc.). Users are thus compared according to the distance between their vectors of weights.

3   Computing Distances Based on Set Intersection

It will be shown further below that the above three cases A, B and C can be reduced to computing the cardinality of set intersections. Hence, we first review the literature for solutions to secure two-party computation of set intersection cardinality.

Secure multiparty computation (MPC) allows a set of parties to compute functions of their inputs in a secure way without requiring a trusted third party. During the execution of the protocol, the parties do not learn anything about each other's input except what is implied by the output itself. There are two main adversarial models: honest-but-curious adversaries and malicious adversaries. In the former model, the parties follow the protocol instructions but they try to obtain information about the inputs of other parties from the messages they receive. In the latter model, the adversary may deviate from the protocol in an arbitrary way.

We will restrict here to a two-party setting in which the input of each party is a set, and the desired output is the cardinality of the intersection of both sets. The intersection of two sets can be obtained by using generic constructions based on Yao's garbled circuit [20]. This technique allows computing any arithmetic function, but for most of the functions it is inefficient. Many of the recent works on two-party computation are focused on improving the efficiency of these protocols for particular families of functions.

Freedman, Nissim, and Pinkas [4] presented a more efficient method to compute the set intersection, a *private matching scheme*, that is secure in the honest-but-curious model. A private matching scheme is a protocol between a client C and a server S in which C's input is a set X of size i_C, S's input is a set Y of size i_S, and at the end of the protocol C learns $X \cap Y$. The scheme uses polynomial-based techniques and homomorphic encryption schemes.

Several variations of the private matching scheme were also presented in [4]: an extension of the malicious adversary model, an extension of the multi-party case, and schemes to compute the cardinality of the set intersection and other functions. Constructing efficient schemes for set operations is an important topic in MPC and has been studied in many other contributions. Several works such as [2,3,5,10,15] present new protocols to compute the set intersection cardinality.

We now proceed to specifying protocols to deal with cases A, B and C above. In all cases, the distance between the private preferences of the two parties is computed using a protocol that yields the cardinality of a set intersection.

3.1   Case A

C inputs X and S inputs Y, and they want to compute $|X \cap Y|$ without revealing their own set.

In the protocol specified below, C inputs $X = \{a_1, \ldots, a_s\} \subseteq E$, S inputs $Y = \{b_1, \ldots, b_t\} \subseteq E$, where s and t are known, and finally C learns $|X \cap Y|$. For S to learn also $|X \cap Y|$, the protocol below should be run a second time (sequentially or concurrently) with the roles of C and S being exchanged.

We will use the protocol described in [4] for the cardinality of the set intersection, that is secure in the honest-but-curious model. The homomorphic encryption scheme we use is the Paillier cryptosystem [11]. The protocol exploits the property that, given three elements m_1, m_2, m_3, it is possible to efficiently compute $Enc(m_1 + m_2)$ and $Enc(m_1 \cdot m_3)$ from $Enc(m_1)$, $Enc(m_2)$, and m_3. We assume that C and S agree on a way to represent the elements of E as elements of the Enc function. They also agree on a special string m. The protocol is outlined next.

Step 1 C chooses the secret-key parameters, and publishes its public keys and parameters.

Step 2 C computes the polynomial $p(x) = \prod_{i=1}^{s}(x - a_i)$.

Step 3 C sends $Enc(p_0), \ldots, Enc(p_s)$ to S, where p_i is the coefficient of degree i of p.

Step 4 S picks a random element $r_j \in \mathbb{Z}_n$ for every $1 \leq j \leq t$. S computes $Enc(r_j \cdot p(b_j) + m)$ for $1 \leq j \leq t$. Then S sends these ciphertexts to C.

Step 5 C decrypts the received ciphertexts. The result of each decryption is m or a random element.

If the size of the domain of Enc is much larger than $|X|$, the scheme computes $|X \cap Y|$ with high probability: indeed, the number of times that m is obtained in the last step indicates the number of common elements in X and Y. Observe that C learns $|X \cap Y|$, but C does not learn any additional information about Y or $X \cap Y$ (in particular, C does not learn the elements of these sets). Moreover S cannot distinguish between cases in which C has different inputs.

3.2   Case B

Here, C inputs X and S inputs Y, two sets of features, and they want to know how close X and Y are without revealing their set. In the protocol below, only C learns how close X and Y are; for S to learn it as well, the protocol should be run a second time (sequentially or concurrently) with the roles of C and S being exchanged.

We assume that the domain of X and Y is the same, and we call it E. The closeness or similarity between elements is computed by means of a function s. In particular, we consider functions $s : E \times E \to \mathbb{Z}_+$. Observe that Case A is a particular instance of this Case B in which $s(x, x) = 1$ and $s(x, y) = 0$ for $x \neq y$.

Let Y be the input of S. For every $z \in E$, S computes $\ell_z = \sum_{y \in Y} s(z, y)$. Observe that ℓ_z measures the overall similarity of z and Y. Let $Y' = \{z \in E : \ell_z > 0\}$. It is common to consider functions satisfying $s(z, z) > 0$ for every $z \in E$, and so in general $Y \subseteq Y'$.

A protocol for such a computation can be obtained from the previous protocol, by replacing Step 4 with the following one:

Step 4' For every $z \in Y'$, S picks ℓ_z random elements $r_1, \ldots, r_{\ell_z} \in \mathbb{Z}_n$ and computes $Enc(r_j \cdot p(z) + m)$ for $1 \leq j \leq \ell_z$. Then S sends all these ciphertexts to C.

Thus, for every $z \in Y'$, S sends ℓ_z ciphertexts. In Step 5 C will recover m from these ciphertexts only if $z \in X$. Hence, at the end of the protocol the total number of decrypted messages that are equal to m is

$$\sum_{x \in X} \ell_x = \sum_{x \in X} \sum_{y \in Y} s(x, y),$$

that is, the sum of similarities between the elements of X and Y. This clearly measures how similar X and Y are. At the end of the protocol, C knows $|Y'|$ and S knows $|X|$. Besides that, C and S cannot gain any additional knowledge on the elements of each other's set of preferences.

3.3   Case C

Here C inputs a private function f and S inputs a private function g, and they want to know how close these functions are without revealing them to each other.

The value $d(f, g)$ will be computed in a vectorial setting. We assume that $f, g : E \to \mathbb{Z}_+$. Note that if f or g take negative values, then C and S can define $f' : E \to \mathbb{Z}_+ : x \mapsto f(x) + c$ and $g' : E \to \mathbb{Z}_+ : x \mapsto g(x) + c$ for some large enough constant $c \in \mathbb{Z}_+$. Observe that $d(f, g) = d(f', g')$.

Given $D = \{x_1, \cdots, x_t\} \subseteq E$ publicly known, C defines the vector $\mathbf{u} = (u_1, \ldots, u_t) \in \mathbb{Z}_+^t$, where $u_i = f(x_i)$ for $i = 1, \ldots, t$, and S defines $\mathbf{v} = (v_1, \ldots, v_t) \in \mathbb{Z}_+^t$, where $v_i = g(x_i)$ for $i = 1, \ldots, t$. The problem described in Section 2.3 can be reduced to computing $\|\mathbf{u} - \mathbf{v}\| = \sum_{i=1}^t |u_i - v_i|$.

Given $\mathbf{u}$ and $\mathbf{v}$, we define the sets $X = \{(i, j) : u_i > 0 \text{ and } 1 \leq j \leq u_i\}$ and $Y = \{(i, j) : v_i > 0 \text{ and } 1 \leq j \leq v_i\}$. Following the protocol for computing the cardinality of the set intersection presented above, C and S can compute $|X \cap Y|$ in a private way (the protocol needs to be run twice with the roles of C and S being exchanged in the second run). Observe that

$$|X \cap Y| = |\{(i, j) : u_i > 0 \text{ and } v_i > 0 \text{ and } 1 \leq j \leq \min\{u_i, v_i\}\}|$$
$$= \sum_{1 \leq i \leq t} \min\{u_i, v_i\}.$$

According to [4], in addition to learning $|X \cap Y|$, during the protocol $\mathcal{S}$ learns $|X|$ and $\mathcal{C}$ learns $|Y|$. Hence both $\mathcal{C}$ and $\mathcal{S}$ can compute

$$|X| + |Y| - 2|X \cap Y| =$$

$$= \sum_{i=1}^{m} \max\{u_i, v_i\} + \min\{u_i, v_i\} - 2\sum_{i=1}^{m} \min\{u_i, v_i\} =$$

$$= \sum_{i=1}^{m} \max\{u_i, v_i\} - \min\{u_i, v_i\} = \sum_{i=1}^{m} |u_i - v_i| = \|\mathbf{u} - \mathbf{v}\|$$

in a private way.

4   Experimental Analysis

This section illustrates the applicability of the proposed protocols to compare profiles of social network users in a privacy-preserving way.

Empirical work was based on 16 Twitter users selected among the most relevant ones from WeFollow [18] and WhoToFollow [19]. These web sites rank and classify Twitter users in a set of categories. As done in [16,17], we took the two 2012 most influential users for each of the following eight categories: Arts, Health, Shopping, Science, Computers, Sports, Society and Business.

Both client and server use the following computing environment: Asus S56C computer with an Intel core i7 3517U 8GB RAM DDR3 1600Mhz, running Ubuntu 13.10 and Java7 (opendjk-1.7). The size of the keys used is 1024 bits. The implementation of the Paillier cryptosystem is the one in [14], which we patched to evaluate polynomials using Horner's method.

We profiled each Twitter user by following the procedure described in [16]. In a nutshell, we extract the noun phrases from the user's most recent set of 100 tweets, and we classify them in the above eight categories. Then, the contribution of each noun phrase to the corresponding category is measured as its informativeness, computed from its distribution in the Web. The aggregated contributions of all the noun phrases of a category measure the interest of the user in the category topic. Profiles are thus represented by a set of vectors containing eight normalized weights, each one quantifying the interest of the user in each of the eight categories. For example, the profile of the Twitter user CERN, which corresponds to the European Center for Nuclear Research, is: {Arts=15.1%, Health=0.27%, Shopping=1.79%, Science=47.93%, Computers=7.5%, Sports=5.45%, Society=10.65%, Business=11.31%}, which shows a clear preference for Science-related topics. Thus, user profiles can be seen as preference functions that can be completely represented by a discrete set of eight quantitative features. This fits the case C discussed above, whose privacy preserving protocol is presented in Section 3.3.

To evaluate the suitability of the privacy-preserving protocol in terms of accuracy, we first computed the pairwise distance d between all 16 user profiles as described in Section 2.3: $d(f, g) = \sum_{i=1}^{m} |f(x_i) - g(x_i)|$, where $x_i \in \{$Arts,

Health, Shopping, Science, Computers, Sports, Society, Business}, and f and g represent the profiles of two different users by assigning the user's weight to each input category x_i. Then, we computed the same pairwise distances using the privacy-preserving protocol described in Section 3.3.

Since our protocol assumes that the functions f and g to be compared output integer values, in a first experiment we rounded weights to the nearest integer. To measure the accuracy of the results, we computed the average error between the distances obtained by straightforward (non-private) computation and the distances obtained by our privacy-preserving distance computation. Such an average error was 1.69% with a standard deviation of 2.25%. This shows that our protocol does not cause a significant distortion in spite of the rounding needed to accommodate values.

On the other hand, the average run time for a privacy-preserving distance computation was 36.7 seconds, whereas it was negligible for a non-private computation. From direct analysis of the protocol (Section 3.3), it can be seen that the run time for a privacy-preserving distance computation depends on the number of weights to be compared (eight) and on the ranges of such weights. Since we rounded percentages to be integers between 0 and 100, the range of weights was 100.

In situations in which reducing the response time is especially important, one may sacrifice some accuracy to speed by using an integer representation with a smaller range. For example, by dividing all weights by 10 and rounding to the nearest integer, we reduce the weight range to 10, which in turn reduces the required number of encryption/decryption steps in the set intersection protocol by an order of magnitude. We did this and we obtained an average run time of 2.7 seconds per privacy-preserving distance computation. However, the average error with respect to non-private distances was 18.49% with a standard deviation of 17.8%, which illustrates how the (lack of) accuracy in the input discretization impacts on the (lack of) accuracy of the output.

Last but not least, we examined scalability. Figure 1 shows the growth of the computing times for $\mathcal{C}$ and $\mathcal{S}$ as the size of X and Y grow. The linear behavior is clear, with $\mathcal{S}$ having a higher computational load than $\mathcal{C}$. More on computational complexity is discussed in Section 5 below.

5   Related Work

We consider the problem of computing the distance between two private utility or preference functions. In the proposed cases, we deal with discrete or discretized domains, which allows us to lean on the literature on private record matching. In this type of matching, the problem is slightly different: it consists of matching the records of the same entity (individual, company, etc.) distributed across different data sets, while keeping those data sets private to their owners. There are three main approaches in the private record matching literature: sanitization-based, cryptographic and hybrid.

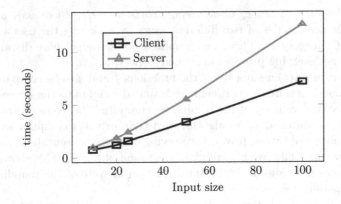

Fig. 1. Execution time of the client $\mathcal{C}$ and the server $\mathcal{S}$ for different input sizes

In *sanitization-based* methods, matching is performed on perturbed versions of the private data sets, in order to protect them against disclosure; a survey of perturbation/sanitization methods and record linkage methods can be found in [6]. This class of methods is usually computationally efficient but it incurs an obvious accuracy toll: matching on perturbed data sets is less accurate than matching on the original data sets. Indeed, false positive and false negative matches can appear.

Cryptographic methods are based on secure multiparty computation and they achieve privacy without accuracy loss. As mentioned above, we follow this approach, as we use MPC to compute the cardinality of set intersection, specifically the protocol in [4]. Our approach could be easily adapted to use other set intersection cardinality protocols in the literature, such as the ones mentioned at the beginning of Section 3 ([2,3,5,10,15]).

The communication complexity of our protocol is $O(i_{\mathcal{C}} + i_{\mathcal{S}})$, where $i_{\mathcal{C}}$ and $i_{\mathcal{S}}$ are the sizes of $\mathcal{C}$'s input and $\mathcal{S}$'s input, respectively. $\mathcal{C}$'s computation complexity is $O(i_{\mathcal{C}} + i_{\mathcal{S}})$, while $\mathcal{S}$'s computation complexity is in fact $O(i_{\mathcal{C}}i_{\mathcal{S}})$, but it can be reduced to $O(i_{\mathcal{C}} \log \log i_{\mathcal{S}})$ [4]. The computational complexity of the scheme in [3] is linear in $i_{\mathcal{C}} + i_{\mathcal{S}}$. Other protocols like the ones presented in [10] do not differentiate the users $\mathcal{C}$ and $\mathcal{S}$: both receive the set intersection cardinality at the end of the protocol.

There are also solutions for the private computation of the set intersection cardinality of $n > 2$ sets from n parties, and constructions that are secure in the malicious adversary model [2,3,4,5,10,15]. In a private matching scheme, the size of the inputs is known by both parties. Some techniques presented in [2] allow hiding the size of the inputs, but the communication and computation complexity of the resulting protocol is higher.

Hybrid methods try to achieve a trade-off between the sanitization-based and cryptographic methods, to retain as much accuracy as possible while keeping computational complexity reasonable. The idea is to use a blocking phase that operates over sanitized data in order to rule out pairs of records that do not satisfy the matching condition. Then cryptographic MPC matching is applied only to blocks of both data sets which contain pairs of candidate matches. Methods following this approach are [7] (where k-anonymity is used as sanitization), [8] (where differential privacy is used as sanitization) and [9] (which refines [8]). The approach proposed in our paper could also be adapted to the hybrid approach, as the final MPC stage of this approach can also be implemented via set intersection.

6 Conclusions and Future Research

Computing the distance between the private preference functions held by two different parties is very relevant in a number of applications. We have motivated several application scenarios in which the private functions express the preferences or profiles of the parties or, in game-theoretic terms, the utility of the players. These scenarios include finding friends or partners with similar interests in social networks, hindering grooming attacks, etc.

We have defined the problem for several types of private functions and, for each function type, we have given a protocol that solves the problem based on two-party secure computation of the cardinality of a set intersection. Empirical work shows that preserving the privacy of the preferences does not meaningfully affect the accuracy of the distances obtained.

Future work will involve designing a protocol to compute the distance between two private functions based on their *whole* domain E, rather than on a discrete subset D. This general approach will require dealing with continuous domains.

Acknowledgments. This work was partly supported by the Government of Catalonia under grant 2009 SGR 1135, by the Spanish Government through projects TIN2011-27076-C03-01 "CO-PRIVACY", TIN2012-32757 "ICWT", IPT-2012-0603-430000 "BallotNext" and CONSOLIDER INGENIO 2010 CSD2007-00004 "ARES", and by the European Commission under FP7 projects "DwB" and "Inter-Trust". J. Domingo-Ferrer is partially supported as an ICREA Acadèmia researcher by the Government of Catalonia. The authors are with the UNESCO Chair in Data Privacy, but they are solely responsible for the views expressed in this paper, which do not necessarily reflect the position of UNESCO nor commit that organization.

References

1. Abel, F., Gao, Q., Houben, G.-J., Tao, K.: Semantic enrichment of Twitter posts for user profile construction on the social web. In: Antoniou, G., Grobelnik, M., Simperl, E., Parsia, B., Plexousakis, D., De Leenheer, P., Pan, J. (eds.) ESWC 2011, Part II. LNCS, vol. 6644, pp. 375–389. Springer, Heidelberg (2011)
2. Blanton, M., Aguiar, E.: Private and oblivious set and multiset operations. In: ASIACCS 2012, pp. 40–41. Springer (2012)

3. De Cristofaro, E., Gasti, P., Tsudik, G.: Fast and private computation of cardinality of set intersection and union. In: Pieprzyk, J., Sadeghi, A.-R., Manulis, M. (eds.) CANS 2012. LNCS, vol. 7712, pp. 218–231. Springer, Heidelberg (2012)

4. Freedman, M.J., Nissim, K., Pinkas, B.: Efficient private matching and set intersection. In: Cachin, C., Camenisch, J.L. (eds.) EUROCRYPT 2004. LNCS, vol. 3027, pp. 1–19. Springer, Heidelberg (2004)

5. Hohenberger, S., Weis, S.: Honest-verifier private disjointness testing without random oracles. In: Danezis, G., Golle, P. (eds.) PET 2006. LNCS, vol. 4258, pp. 277–294. Springer, Heidelberg (2006)

6. Hundepool, A., Domingo-Ferrer, J., Franconi, L., Giessing, S., Schulte Nordholt, E., Spicer, K., de Wolf, P.-P.: Statistical Disclosure Control. Wiley (2012)

7. Inan, A., Kantarcioglu, M., Bertino, E., Scannapieco, M.: A hybrid approach to private record linkage. In: Proc. IEEE 24 Intl. Conf. Data Eng.-ICDE 2008, pp. 496–505 (2008)

8. Inan, A., Kantarcioglu, M., Ghinita, G., Bertino, E.: Private record matching using differential privacy. In: Proc. of the 13th Intl. Conference on Extending Database Technology-EDBT 2010, pp. 123–134 (2010)

9. Inan, A., Kantarcioglu, M., Ghinita, G., Bertino, E.: A hybrid approach to private record matching. IEEE Transactions on Dependable and Secure Computing 9(5), 684–698 (2012)

10. Kissner, L., Song, D.X.: Privacy-preserving set operations. In: Shoup, V. (ed.) CRYPTO 2005. LNCS, vol. 3621, pp. 241–257. Springer, Heidelberg (2005)

11. Paillier, P.: Public-key cryptosystems based on composite degree residuosity classes. In: Stern, J. (ed.) EUROCRYPT 1999. LNCS, vol. 1592, pp. 223–238. Springer, Heidelberg (1999)

12. PatientsLikeMe, http://www.patientslikeme.com

13. Sánchez, D., Batet, M., Isern, D., Valls, A.: Ontology-based semantic similarity: A new feature-based approach. Expert Systems with Applications 39(9), 7718–7728 (2012)

14. The Homomorphic Encryption Project (thep), https://code.google.com/p/thep/ (accessed March 17, 2014)

15. Vaidya, J., Clifton, C.: Secure set intersection cardinality with application to association rule mining. Journal of Computer Security 13(4), 593–622 (2005)

16. Viejo, A., Sánchez, D., Castellà-Roca, J.: Preventing automatic user profiling in Web 2.0 applications. Knowledge-based Systems 36, 191–205 (2012)

17. Viejo, A., Sánchez, D., Castellà-Roca, J.: Using profiling techniques to protect the user's privacy in Twitter. In: Torra, V., Narukawa, Y., López, B., Villaret, M. (eds.) MDAI 2012. LNCS, vol. 7647, pp. 161–172. Springer, Heidelberg (2012)

18. WeFollow, http://wefollow.com

19. WhoToFollow, http://whotofollow.net

20. Yao, A.C.-C.: How to generate and exchange secrets. In: FOCS 1986, pp. 162–167 (1986)

21. Zoltan, K., Johann, S.: Semantic analysis of microposts for efficient people to people interactions. In: RoEduNet 2011, p. 14 (2011)

Privacy-Preserving Implicit Authentication

Nashad Ahmed Safa[1], Reihaneh Safavi-Naini[1], and Siamak F. Shahandashti[2]

[1] University of Calgary, Canada
{rei,nasafa}@ucalgary.ca
[2] Newcastle University, UK
siamak.shahandashti@ncl.ac.uk

Abstract. In an implicit authentication system, a user profile is used as an additional factor to strengthen the authentication of mobile users. The profile consists of features that are constructed using the history of user actions on her mobile device over time. The profile is stored on a server and is used to authenticate an access request originated from the device at a later time. An access request will include a vector of recent features measurements on the device that will be matched against the stored features to accept or reject the request. The features however include private information such as user location or web sites they have visited. In this paper we propose *privacy-preserving implicit authentication* which achieves implicit authentication without revealing unnecessary information about the users' usage profiles to the server. We propose an architecture, give formal security models, and propose constructions with provable security. We consider two security models, namely for cases where the device behaves semi-honestly or maliciously.

Keywords: Implicit Authentication, User Privacy, Homomorphic Encryption, Provable Security, Behavioural Features.

1 Introduction

In mobile applications such as mobile commerce, users often provide authentication information using Mobile Internet Devices (MIDs) including cell phones and notebooks. In most cases however, password authentication is the primary method of authentication. The weaknesses of password-based authentication systems, including widespread usage of weak passwords, have been widely studied (see e.g. [25] and references within). In addition to these weaknesses, limitations of user interface on MIDs results in an error prone process for inputting passwords, encouraging even poorer choices of password by users.

To strengthen authentication, two-factor authentication has been proposed. The second factor, when based on extra hardware such as SecureID tokens, have additional cost and limit their wide application. An attractive method of strengthening password systems is *implicit authentication* [13] which effectively adds a second factor to authentication. The idea is to use the history of device usage to construct features, that are used to provide a second factor for verifying an access request from a user with a claimed identity. Experiments in [13]

N. Cuppens-Boulahia et al. (Eds.): SEC 2014, IFIP AICT 428, pp. 471–484, 2014.
© IFIP International Federation for Information Processing 2014

showed that features extracted from device history can be effectively used to distinguish users. Although the approach is applicable to any computing device, it is primarily used to enhance security of mobile users carrying MIDs.

The user profile includes private information including (i) device data, such as GPS location data and WiFi/Bluetooth connections, (ii) carrier data, such as information on cell towers connected to the device, or Internet access pattern, and (iii) cloud data, such as calendar entries. The profile is stored at the carrier to ensure that a compromised device cannot be used to impersonate the legitimate user. This profile however includes private and potentially sensitive user data, that must be protected.

The aim of this paper is to address this problem: we propose an efficient method of privacy preserving implicit authentication systems, and model and prove its security.

We consider a network-based implicit authentication system where user authentication is performed collaboratively by the *device* (the MID), and the *carrier* (network service provider). *Application servers* will use the result of this authentication to grant access to users and do not directly participate in the authentication protocol.

Our implicit authentication protocol generates a score that will be used to accept to reject the user. The score is obtained through secure two party computation between the device and the carrier. User data is encrypted and stored at the carrier and is used by the interactive protocol to compute the authentication. Data privacy against a semi-honest carrier is guaranteed because the user data is stored in encrypted form. Calculating the score is by a specially designed secure two party computation protocol. Secure two party protocols can be implemented through general constructions using secure circuit evaluation, e.g. [27,11], or fully homomorphic encryption [9]. These general constructions however will be inefficient in practice.

Because no data is stored on the MID, user data stays protected even if the device is lost or stolen.

1.1 Our Contributions

The main contribution of this paper is proposing a profile matching function that uses the statistics of features to accept or reject a new sample presented by a user, and providing a privacy preserving protocol for computing a score function for a newly presented data. We assume the user profile is a vector of features, each corresponding to a random variable, $(V_1, \ldots, V_n)$, with an associated probability distribution. The distribution of V_i is stored as the set of values of the variables in the last ℓ_i successful logins. A new login attempt generates a vector of values, one for each feature. The verification function must decide if this vector indeed has been generated by the claimed user. Our proposed verification algorithm takes each feature separately and decides if the presented value is from the claimed user. The final verdict is reached by combining the decisions from all features. To determine if a new value presented for a feature v_i matches the model (stored distribution of the feature), we will use a statistical decision making approach that uses the *Average Absolute Deviation (AAD)* of the distribution. We use AAD to define an interval around the read value v_i given by $[v_i - AAD(V_i), v_i + AAD(V_i)]$ and determine the concentration of the stored values in the user profile that falls within this Interval: if the number is higher than a specified threshold, then the authentication algorithm accepts the reading. AAD and standard deviation are commonly used measures for estimating the spread of a distribution. Our verification algorithm effectively measures similarity of the presented value with "most common" readings of the variable. Using AAD allows more efficient private computation.

Constructing User Profiles. A user profile is a feature vector $(V_1, \ldots, V_n)$, where feature V_i is modelled by a vector of ℓ_i past samples. The vector can be seen as a sliding window that considers the latest ℓ_i successful authentication data. Using different ℓ_i is allowed for better estimation of the feature distribution. Possible features are the frequency of phone calls made or received by the user, user's typical locations at a particular time, commonly used WiFi access-points, websites that the user frequently visits, and the like. Some features might be dependent on other ones. For example, given that the user is in his office and it is lunch time, then there is a higher chance that he receives a call from home. We do not consider dependence of features and in selecting them make special care to select those that appear independent.

We note that usage data such as application accesses and past WiFi connections could enhance performance and usability of the device and applications. However to use such data securely as part of the authentication system, the data must be stored securely at the carrier to be protected from malicious parties who may get hold of the device. In practice a user can be given a choice to use certain device-collected data for authentication and so for such data.

Privacy-Preserving Authentication. All user profile data is stored in encrypted form on the carrier and the decryption keys are only known by the device. To find the authentication score for each feature, the device and the carrier have to perform a secure two-party computation that outputs the authentication score to the carrier, and nothing to the device. We propose a 3-round protocol between the device and the carrier that allows the carrier to "securely" calculate the score. To provide the required efficiency, we have to sacrifice some privacy in the sense that although the actual data samples are not leaked, the protocol does expose structural information related to the relative order of data samples. We give a formal definition of this notion of privacy which guarantees that no information other than the relative order of samples is revealed by a secure protocol. We then prove the security of the protocol, according to the definition, against semi-honest adversaries.

The paper is organized as follows. We discuss the related work in the field of behavioural authentication in Section 1.2. Section 2 contains the preliminaries needed for our scheme. System architecture, the adversarial model, and a basic implicit authentication protocol not guaranteeing privacy are presented in Section 3. We give details of our proposed protocols for semi-honest and malicious devices in Section 4. Security proofs and a detailed discussion on the efficiency of our proposed protocol are provided in the full version of this paper [21].

1.2 Related Work

The privacy problem in implicit authentication was noted in [13]. The three approaches proposed for enhancing privacy are: (i) removing unique identifier information; (ii) using pseudonyms; and (iii) using aggregate data instead of fine grained data. All these methods however have limited effectiveness in protecting users' privacy while maintaining usefulness of the system. It is well known that user data with identification information removed can be combined with other public data to re-identify individuals [24], and fixed pseudonyms does not prevent linkability of records [15]. Finally coarse aggregates result in inaccurate authentication decisions.

Further discussion on related work e.g. on privacy-preserving biometric systems [16,18,19,22] and implicit authentication systems using accelerometers [6], gait recognition [14], user location [5,23,7,4], and fingerprints [26] can be found in full version of this paper [21].

2   Preliminaries

Our constructions use homomorphic encryption and order preserving symmetric encryption. In the following we first give an overview of these primitives.

Homomorphic Encryption (HE). We use here an *additive homomorphic public key encryption scheme* [20,8] which supports addition and scalar multiplication in the ciphertext domain. Let $E_{pk}^{HE}(\cdot)$ denote such an encryption algorithm. Given encryptions of a and b, an encryption of $a + b$ can be computed as $E_{pk}^{HE}(a + b) = E_{pk}^{HE}(a) \odot E_{pk}^{HE}(b)$, where $\odot$ represents an efficient operation in the ciphertext space. The existence of the operation $\odot$ enables scalar multiplication to be possible in the ciphertext domain as well; that is, given an encryption of a, an encryption of ca can be calculated efficiently for a known c. To simplify the notation, we use $+$ for both the operations $+$ and $\odot$. As an instantiation, we use Paillier Cryptosystem [20,8] in which $E_{pk}^{HE}(x+y) = E_{pk}^{HE}(x)E_{pk}^{HE}(y)$ and $E_{pk}^{HE}(cx) = E_{pk}^{HE}(x)^c$. Paillier Cryptosystem is semantically secure under the decisional composite residuosity assumption [20,8].

Order Preserving Symmetric Encryption (OPSE). Order preserving symmetric encryption (OPSE) was introduced in [3]. A function $f : D \to R$ is order preserving if for all $i, j \in D$: $f(i) > f(j)$ if and only if $i > j$. A symmetric encryption scheme having plaintext and ciphertext space D, R is order preserving if its encryption algorithm is an order preserving function from D to R for all keys; i.e., an OPSE maps plaintext values to ciphertext space in such a way that the order of the plaintext values remains intact. The construction provided in [3] has been proven secure in the POPF-CCA (pseudorandom order preserving function against chosen-ciphertext attack) model. More details on the security model and encryption system are given in the full version of this paper [21].

Secure Two-Party Computation. In a secure two-party computation, two parties A and B with private inputs x and y, respectively, compute a function $f(x, y)$ ensuring that, *privacy* and *correctness* are guaranteed. Privacy means that neither A nor B learns anything about the other party's input. Correctness means that the output is indeed $f(x, y)$ and not something else. To formalize security of a two-party protocol, the execution of the protocol is compared to an "ideal execution" in which parties send their inputs to a trusted third party who computes the function using the inputs that it receives. Informally, a protocol is considered secure if a real adversary in a real execution can learn "the same" amount of information as, or can "change the protocol output" not more than what an ideal adversary can do in the ideal model.

Security of two-party protocols is considered against different types of adversaries. In the *semi-honest* model (a.k.a. honest-but-curious model), the adversary follows the protocol specification but tries to learn extra information from the protocol transcript. A *malicious* (a.k.a. dis-honest) adversary however follows an arbitrary strategy (bounded by polynomial time algorithms) and can deviate from the protocol specification.

There are a number of generic constructions for secure two party computation, e.g. [27,11], however they have proven to be too inefficient in practice, specially in resource-restricted devices. An alternative approach to realize specific secure two-party protocols is based on homomorphic encryption (HE). In this approach, one party sends its encrypted inputs to the other party, who then computes the specific desired function in the encrypted domain using the homomorphic properties of the encryption system. Paillier's additively homomorphic cryptosystem [20] and Gentry's fully homomorphic scheme [10] are the commonly used tools in this approach.

Average Absolute Deviation. In our protocol we use a model of feature comparison that uses average absolute deviation. The *median* of a data set is the numeric value separating the higher half of distribution from the lower half. The *average absolute deviation (AAD)* of a data set is the average of the absolute deviations and characterizes a summary of statistical dispersion of the data set. For a set $X = \{x_1, x_2, \ldots, x_N\}$ with a median denoted by $\text{Med}(X)$, AAD is defined as $AAD(X) := \frac{1}{N} \sum_{i=1}^{N} |x_i - \text{Med}(X)|$.

Notation. Throughout the paper we use E_{pk}^{HE} and D_{sk}^{HE} to denote the encryption and decryption algorithms of a homomorphic encryption scheme such as Paillier Cryptosystem with public and secret key pair (pk, sk). For the OPSE algorithm we use E_k^{OPSE} and D_k^{OPSE} to refer to the encryption and decryption with key k. Key generation algorithms are denoted by $KeyGen^{HE}$ and $KeyGen^{OPSE}$, respectively for HE and OPSE schemes.

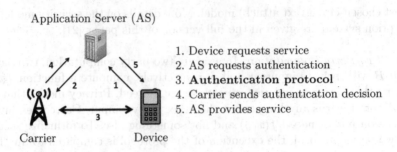

1. Device requests service
2. AS requests authentication
3. **Authentication protocol**
4. Carrier sends authentication decision
5. AS provides service

Fig. 1. The System Architecture

3   System Model

Fig. 1 gives the working of the system we consider in practice. The authentication process is between the device and the carrier. In a typical scenario, an application server receives a service request from a device. The user information is forwarded to the carrier that will engage in the authentication protocol with the device. At the completion of the protocol, the results are sent to the application server, and if successful, the device (user) will receive the requested service.

The focus of this paper is on the device and carrier authentication. We assume other communication channels are secure and the information will be communicated safely across these channels. User data is stored in encrypted form at the carrier. The device records user's data, encrypts it and sends it to the carrier. No data used to develop the user profile in implicit authentication is stored on the device. This ensures that if the device is compromised, the adversary cannot learn the user profile and simulate its behaviour.

We only consider the data that is collected by the device to be included in the user profile. The information collected by the carrier is known to the carrier and is not included. Selection of an appropriate set of features that allow distinguishability of users is outside the scope of this paper. The goal of this paper is to provide privacy for user features that are used as part of the user's profile.

Trust Assumptions and the Adversarial Model. We assume that the carrier correctly follows the protocol but may try to learn the users' data. This is a reasonable assumption given the stature and reputation of carriers and difficulty of tracing the source of data leakage. We assume the device is used by the user for a period of time before being compromised. This is the period during which the user profile is constructed. We consider two types of adversaries. Firstly, we consider a less sophisticated adversary that tries to use a stolen device without tampering with the hardware or the software and so the device is assumed to follow the protocol. This also corresponds to the case that the authentication program resides in a tamper proof [12,17] part of the device and cannot be modified by the adversary and so a captured device follows the protocol but takes input data from the adversary. We assume the program can be read by the device holder, but cannot be changed. In the second case, the device behaves in a malicious way and may deviate from the protocol to succeed in an authentication scenario.

In both cases the system must guarantee privacy of the user: that is, neither the carrier nor the adversary in possession of the compromised device should learn the user's profile data. A stolen device used by an active malicious user must also fail in authentication.

3.1   Authentication without Privacy

A user profile consists of *features*. A feature is a random variable that can be sampled by the device and in combination with other features provides a reliable means of identifying users. We denote feature i by the random variable V_i that is sampled at each authentication request, and if the authentication is successful, is stored by the carrier and used as part of the distribution samples for evaluation of future authentication requests. The variable distribution for the i-th feature is approximated as $V_i = (v_i(t_1), v_i(t_2), \ldots, v_i(t_{l_i}))$. Here, $v_i(t_j)$ is the feature value at time t_j and l_i is a system parameter. As discussed before, we only consider independent features.

The *user profile* $\mathcal{U}$ is a tuple of features; that is $\mathcal{U} := (V_1, V_2, \ldots, V_n)$, where n is the total number of features. A *sampled feature vector* is denoted as $(v_1(t), v_2(t), \ldots, v_n(t))$ where $v_i(t)$ is the current instance of the variable V_i. Given a user profile and a new set of measured samples (for features), the scoring algorithm first calculates individual feature scores, and then combines them to generate a total score which is compared to a threshold. Authentication is considered successful if the score is higher than the threshold. The scoring algorithm works as follows.

We assume the final authentication score is obtained as a combination of authentication scores that are calculated for each feature separately. The *scoring function* for each variable estimates if the new sample belongs to the distribution that is represented by a set of samples from previous successful authentications. For a feature V_i we define our scoring function as follows:

$$s_i(t) = \Pr[\, b_l^i(t) \leq V_i \leq b_h^i(t) \,], \text{ where}$$

$$b_l^i(t) = v_i(t) - \text{AAD}(V_i) \quad \text{and} \quad b_h^i(t) = v_i(t) + \text{AAD}(V_i) \,.$$

Here, $AAD(V_i)$ represents the average absolute deviation of data in the set V_i.

The probability $\Pr[\, b_l^i(t) \leq V_i \leq b_h^i(t) \,]$ is approximated by counting the number of elements of V_i that fall between $b_l^i(t)$ and $b_h^i(t)$ and dividing the count by the number of all elements, i.e. l_i.

As will be shown in Section 4, the choice of $AAD(V_i)$ allows the carrier to perform the required computation on encrypted data. The scoring function estimates the likelihood of the new sample belonging to the distribution by counting the number of the previously recorded values of a feature that conform with, i.e. are within a determined interval of, the new sample.

To obtain the combined score of n features, various methods might be used depending on the authentication policy. A simple and popular method in this regard is the weighted sum of the scores as $a(t) := w_1 s_1(t) + \cdots + w_n s_n(t)$, where w_i represents the weight assigned to the i-th feature and $a(t)$ is the combined authentication score.

In summary, the authentication protocol proceeds as follows: The carrier has a user profile which consists of the sample distributions of the user features. The device sends a set of sampled behavioural data to the carrier. The carrier retrieves the sample distribution for each feature and calculates the feature scores. Then it combines the individual feature scores and compares the combined score with a threshold to make an authentication decision.

4   Privacy-Preserving Authentication

At the heart of the authentication protocol is the score computing algorithm. It basically takes two inputs: the stored distribution and the fresh device sample, and it produces a feature score. All the computation takes place at the carrier side, given the two inputs above, where the former is stored by the carrier, and the latter is provided by the device. Both inputs are in plaintext. In this section, we focus on this algorithm and provide a two-party score computing protocol that is able to calculate the feature score from *encrypted* profiles stored at the carrier and *encrypted* fresh samples provided by the device, where the keys to encryptions are only known to the device.

We chose to provide private protocols for score computation on the *feature score* level, as opposed to the *combined score* level, for two reasons: first, different carriers might have different authentication policies, and hence different score combination formulas, and our formulation choice leaves the choice of combination method open; second, we consider it an overkill to require that the carrier only finds out about the combined score and nothing about the individual scores, and indeed solutions for such an overkill are likely to be inefficient for practice.

In the following we propose a protocol between a device and a carrier that enables the carrier to calculate a feature score for the device, while provably guaranteeing that no information about the stored profile at the carrier is revealed to the device other than the AAD of the stored feature values, and no information about the fresh feature value provided by the device is revealed to the carrier other than how it is ordered with respect to the stored profile feature values.

4.1   A Protocol Secure against Honest-but-Curious Adversaries

Let $HE = (KeyGen^{HE}, E^{HE}, D^{HE})$ be a homomorphic encryption scheme, such as Paillier, and $OPSE = (KeyGen^{OPSE}, E^{OPSE}, D^{OPSE})$ be an order-preserving symmetric encryption scheme. The protocol Π_{PI} we propose consists of four phases: system setup, precomputation, authentication, and AAD update. The protocol works as follows:

System Setup. Performed once for each device, $KeyGen^{HE}$ and $KeyGen^{OPSE}$ are run to generate the HE key pair (pk, sk) and the OPSE key k_2. Public parameters of the two encryption systems HE and OPSE, including pk, are communicated to the carrier.

Precomputation. At any point during the life of the system, the carrier has stored an accumulated user profile containing $\left(E_{pk}^{HE}(v_i(t_j)), E_{k_2}^{OPSE}(v_i(t_j)) \right)$ for $j = 1, \ldots, l_i$. Before the start of the authentication protocol, the carrier precomputes $E_{pk}^{HE}(AAD(V_i))$ as follows. It first computes:

$$E_{pk}^{HE}(AAD(V_i) \cdot l_i) = \sum_{j=1}^{l_i} \left| E_{pk}^{HE}(v_i(t_j)) - E_{pk}^{HE}(\mathrm{Med}(V_i)) \right|,$$

where $\mathrm{Med}(V_i)$ denotes the median element of V_i and can be found using the OPSE ciphertexts stored in the profile. Then the constant factor l_i is removed using the scalar multiplication property of the homomorphic encryption HE. In Paillier cryptosystem, this is done by raising $E_{pk}^{HE}(AAD(V_i) \cdot l_i)$ to the power of l_i^{-1}, where l_i^{-1} is precomputed once and stored along with l_i as system parameters.

Authentication. Device samples the features (i.e. user data) using its modules. For each feature value $v_i(t)$, $1 \leq i \leq n$, at time t, device computes a pair of encrypted values, $e_i(t) = (E_{pk}^{HE}(v_i(t)), E_{k_2}^{OPSE}(v_i(t)))$. The HE ciphertext allows the carrier to perform necessary computations, namely addition and scalar multiplication, in the encrypted domain, while the OPSE ciphertext helps the carrier find the order information necessary to the computation.

Device sends $e_i(t)$ values to the carrier. Using these values, carrier calculates $E_{pk}^{HE}(b_l^i(t))$ and $E_{pk}^{HE}(b_h^i(t))$ as follows:

$$E_{pk}^{HE}(b_l^i(t)) \leftarrow E_{pk}^{HE}(v_i(t)) - E_{pk}^{HE}(AAD(V_i))$$

$$E_{pk}^{HE}(b_h^i(t)) \leftarrow E_{pk}^{HE}(v_i(t)) + E_{pk}^{HE}(AAD(V_i))$$

where $V_i = \{v_i(t_1), \ldots, v_i(t_{l_i})\}$ and $E_{pk}^{HE}(AAD(V_i))$ is pre-computed as discussed.

Carrier however does not know the order of the newly generated encrypted values with respect to the stored ciphertexts in the user profile. To find the order, carrier interacts with the device: carrier first sends $E_{pk}^{HE}(b_l^i(t))$ and $E_{pk}^{HE}(b_h^i(t))$ (for all features) back to the device. Device decrypts the ciphertexts using the decryption function D_{sk}^{HE} and gets $b_l^i(t)$ and $b_h^i(t)$, and then encrypts the result to find $c_l^i(t) = E_{k_2}^{OPSE}(b_l^i(t))$ and $c_h^i(t) = E_{k_2}^{OPSE}(b_h^i(t))$, respectively, using the OPSE scheme. Device sends $c_l^i(t)$ and $c_h^i(t)$ back to the carrier.

Carrier computes the individual score $s_i(t)$ as the number of the OPSE ciphertexts $E_{k_2}^{OPSE}(V_i)$ in the profile that satisfy $c_l^i(t) \leq E_{k_2}^{OPSE}(V_i) \leq c_h^i(t)$. Note that this condition is equivalent to $b_l^i(t) \leq V_i \leq b_h^i(t)$.

The same process is used for all features. The final authentication score is then calculated using the score combination method, e.g. the weighted sum method described earlier. Finally, the final calculated score determines if implicit authentication is successful or not. If implicit authentication is not successful, the device is challenged on an explicit authentication method, e.g. the user is logged out of a service and prompted to log in anew by providing a password.

AAD Update. If implicit authentication is successful, or if it is unsuccessful however the device subsequently succeeds in explicitly authenticating itself, then the AAD needs to be updated using the new encrypted features provided in the authentication phase. The current feature history includes a vector of size l_i. The new feature is added to this vector first, and then, depending on the carrier's strategy, the oldest feature might be discarded to keep the vector size constant. In both cases, recalculating the AAD only needs constant-size differential calculations and there is no need to recompute AAD from scratch (which instead would be linear in the size of the vector). The reason is that when the median is shifted, for almost half of the existing feature values, the absolute deviation increases by the difference of the old and new medians, and for almost all of the rest of the existing feature values, the absolute deviation decreases by the same value, and these almost totally cancel each other out. Only a few calculations are needed eventually to account for the few that do not cancel out, plus the possible discarded feature, and the new feature.

Complexity. We discuss the computation complexity of the precomputation, authentication, and update phases of our protocol in the full version of this paper [21]. We implement Paillier and OPSE to confirm computation benchmarks in the literature, and calculate concrete running times for our protocol. In particular, we show that authentication takes *less than 300 milliseconds* on a typical device as a background process, and hence our protocol is able to protect user privacy with an insignificant computation overhead cost.

Security. We discuss the security of our protocol considering honest-but-curious devices and carriers in the full version of this paper [21]. We provide a formal definition of privacy for our protocol against honest-but-curious devices and carriers. The definition intuitively guarantees that by participating in the protocol, the device only learns the AAD of the usage data stored at the carrier side, and the carrier only learns little beyond the order information of the current sample with respect to the stored data. We argue that the AAD and order information learned during the protocol reveal little about the actual content of the data in question, and hence our definition guarantees a high level of privacy. Eventually, in the full version of this paper [21], we prove the following theorem guaranteeing the privacy of our protocol:

Theorem 1. *Protocol Π_{PI} is provably secure against honest-but-curious devices and honest-but-curious network carriers.*

4.2 Securing the Protocol against Malicious Devices

In the above version of the protocol, secure against honest but curious adversaries, in the authentication phase the carrier interacts with the device as follows:

the carrier sends homomorphic ciphertexts $E_{pk}^{HE}(b_l^i(t))$ and $E_{pk}^{HE}(b_h^i(t))$ to the device and the device is expected to reply back order-preserving ciphertexts of the same plaintexts, i.e. $E_{k_2}^{OPSE}(b_l^i(t))$ and $E_{k_2}^{OPSE}(b_h^i(t))$. These order-preserving ciphertexts are subsequently used to compare the values of $b_l^i(t)$ and $b_h^i(t)$ in the order-preserving ciphertext space with the feature values and find out how many feature values lie between $b_l^i(t)$ and $b_h^i(t)$. However, a malicious device cannot be trusted to return correctly formatted order-preserving ciphertexts. In the following, we propose a modified version of the protocol secure against malicious devices. We call this modified version Π_{PI*}.

First, we note that the device cannot be forced to use an honest feature value $v_i(t)$ to start with. In the absence of a trusted hardware such as tamper-proof hardware, the device may enter the interaction with the carrier on any arbitrary input. Even with the recent advances in smartphone technology, e.g. ARM's TrustZone [1], the device cannot be prevented to change the sensor readings unless the whole algorithm is run in the so called Trusted Execution Environment (TEE). However, the device can be required to show that the ciphertext $E_{pk}^{HE}(v_i(t))$ is well-formed. To enforce this requirement, we require that the device sends an interactive proof of knowledge of the corresponding plaintext $v_i(t)$ along with the ciphertext $E_{pk}^{HE}(v_i(t))$. Proofs of knowledge of plaintext exist for most public key encryption schemes. For Paillier encryption, a concrete proof protocol can be found in [2], which can be made non-interactive using the well-known Fiat-Shamir heuristic.

Apart from inclusion of the above proof of knowledge, further modification is required to make the protocol secure against malicious devices. The main idea here is as follows: instead of asking the device for order-preserving ciphertexts, the ability to interact with the device is used to directly compare $b_l^i(t)$ and $b_h^i(t)$ with the feature values, only using the homomorphic ciphertexts. In each round of interaction $b_l^i(t)$ (resp. $b_h^i(t)$) is compared with an element of the feature vector. The relative position of $b_l^i(t)$ (resp. $b_h^i(t)$) within the elements of the feature vector can be hence found in $\log l_i$ rounds of interaction following a binary search algorithm.

Assume that in one round the carrier wishes to compare $b_l^i(t)$ with $v_i(t_j)$. The carrier has homomorphic encryptions of both, i.e. $E_{pk}^{HE}(b_l^i(t))$ with $E_{pk}^{HE}(v_i(t_j))$, and hence can calculate $E_{pk}^{HE}(b_l^i(t) - v_i(t_j))$. The carrier is interested in knowing whether $b_l^i(t) - v_i(t_j)$ is positive, negative, or zero. The carrier chooses k random values and encrypts them using the homomorphic encryption scheme. It also randomises $E_{pk}^{HE}(b_l^i(t) - v_i(t_j))$ using scalar multiplication by either a positive or a negative random blinding factor. The carrier finally shuffles all the $k + 1$ ciphertexts, including the k random cipheretxts and the blinded version of $E_{pk}^{HE}(b_l^i(t) - v_i(t_j))$, and sends them all to the device. The device decrypts all the received ciphertexts and replies back to the carrier with $k+1$ responses indicating whether each of the received ciphertexts decrypt to a positive, negative, or zero plaintext. The carrier knows what the response should be for the k random ciphertexts. Hence, it will first check whether all such responses are as expected.

If they are, then the carrier deducts whether $b_l^i(t) - v_i(t_j)$ is positive, negative, or zero, by reversing the effect of the random blinding factor.

The idea in the above interaction is that since all the $k + 1$ challenges look random (and hence indistinguishable) to the device, a malicious device has at most $\frac{1}{k+1}$ chance of cheating and not getting caught. k is a parameter of the protocol and controls a trade-off between complexity and security. The larger k is, the less chance there is for a malicious device to cheat, but at the same time the higher the complexity of the protocol is.

Note that even if the device manages to cheat and not get caught, it does not gain any meaningful advantage in impersonating a legitimate user since the $b_l^i(t) - v_i(t_j)$ value is blinded before being sent to the device. Blinding changes the sign of the $b_l^i(t) - v_i(t_j)$ value with 50% probability. A malicious device therefore is not able to tell which behaviour, being honest or cheating, works in its favour.

Complexity. We discuss the computation complexity of the modified protocol in the full version of this paper [21]. In particular, we show that an authentication failure is discovered in *less than 4 seconds* after the first feature reading is reported by the device.

Security. We discuss the security of our protocol considering malicious devices in the full version of this paper [21]. We provide a formal definition of privacy for our protocol against maliciously-controlled devices. The definition intuitively guarantees that even if the device is maliciously controlled, it will not be able to learn any information more than what it would learn during an honest execution of the protocol. Eventually, in the full version of this paper [21], we prove the following theorem guaranteeing the privacy of our protocol:

Theorem 2. *Protocol $\Pi_{PI}*$ is provably secure against maliciously-controlled devices (with probability at least $\frac{k}{k+1}$), and is provably secure against honest-but-curious carriers.*

Conclusion

In this paper we proposed a privacy preserving implicit authentication system that can calculate authentication score using a realistic scoring function. We argued that using user behaviour as an additional factor in authentication has attractive applications. We showed that by relaxing the notion of privacy, one can construct efficient protocols that ensure user privacy and can be used in practice. The low computation and communication complexity of our proposed protocol in the case of semi-honest adversary makes it executable almost in real-time for carrier and modern MIDs. We also provided a modification to the basic protocol to ensure security in the case of a malicious device. Our proposed protocol in this case, has a complexity that grows logarithmically with the size of the user profile. We argued that this translates into a reasonable time-frame for implicit authentication with protection against malicious devices. A complete implementation of the system will be our future work.

References

1. ARM TrustZone,
   http://www.arm.com/products/processors/technologies/trustzone
2. Baudron, O., Fouque, P.-A., Pointcheval, D., Stern, J., Poupard, G.: Practical Multi-Candidate Election System. In: Proc. 20th ACM Symposium on Principles of Distributed Computing, pp. 274–283. ACM (2001)
3. Boldyreva, A., Chenette, N., Lee, Y., O'Neill, A.: Order-Preserving Symmetric Encryption. In: Joux, A. (ed.) EUROCRYPT 2009. LNCS, vol. 5479, pp. 224–241. Springer, Heidelberg (2009)
4. Čapkun, S., Čagalj, M., Srivastava, M.: Secure Localization with Hidden and Mobile Base Stations. In: Int'l Conf. on Computer Communication, INFOCOM 2006 (2006)
5. Čapkun, S., Hubaux, J.-P.: Secure Positioning of Wireless Devices with Application to Sensor Networks. In: INFOCOM 2005: 24th Annual Joint Conf. of the IEEE Computer and Communications Societies, vol. 3, pp. 1917–1928. IEEE (2005)
6. Chang, K.-H., Hightower, J., Kveton, B.: Inferring Identity Using Accelerometers in Television Remote Controls. In: Tokuda, H., Beigl, M., Friday, A., Brush, A.J.B., Tobe, Y. (eds.) Pervasive 2009. LNCS, vol. 5538, pp. 151–167. Springer, Heidelberg (2009)
7. Chiang, J.T., Haas, J.J., Hu, Y.-C.: Secure and Precise Location Verification Using Distance Bounding and Simultaneous Multilateration. In: 2nd ACM Conference on Wireless Network Security, pp. 181–192. ACM (2009)
8. Damgård, I., Jurik, M.: Generalisation, A Simplification and Some Applications of Paillier's Probabilistic Public-Key System. In: Kim, K. (ed.) PKC 2001. LNCS, vol. 1992, pp. 119–136. Springer, Heidelberg (2001)
9. Gentry, C.: A Fully Homomorphic Encryption Scheme. PhD thesis, Stanford University (2009)
10. Gentry, C., Halevi, S.: Implementing Gentry's Fully-Homomorphic Encryption Scheme. In: Paterson, K.G. (ed.) EUROCRYPT 2011. LNCS, vol. 6632, pp. 129–148. Springer, Heidelberg (2011)
11. Goldreich, O., Micali, S., Wigderson, A.: How to Play Any Mental Game - A Completeness Theorem for Protocols with Honest Majority. In: Proc. 19th ACM Symposium on Theory of Computing, pp. 218–229. ACM (1987)
12. Haubert, E., Tucek, J., Brumbaugh, L., Yurcik, W.: Tamper-Resistant Storage Techniques for Multimedia Systems. In: Electronic Imaging 2005, pp. 30–40. International Society for Optics and Photonics (2005)
13. Jakobsson, M., Shi, E., Golle, P., Chow, R.: Implicit Authentication for Mobile Devices. In: Proc. of the 4th USENIX Conf. on Hot Topics in Security. USENIX Association (2009)
14. Kale, A., Rajagopalan, A., Cuntoor, N., Krüger, V.: Gait-Based Recognition of Humans Using Continuous HMMs. In: Proc. 5th IEEE Int'l Conf. on Automatic Face & Gesture Recognition, pp. 336–341. IEEE (2002)
15. Krumm, J.: Inference Attacks on Location Tracks. In: LaMarca, A., Langheinrich, M., Truong, K.N. (eds.) Pervasive 2007. LNCS, vol. 4480, pp. 127–143. Springer, Heidelberg (2007)
16. Leggett, J., Williams, G., Usnick, M., Longnecker, M.: Dynamic Identity Verification via Keystroke Characteristics. International Journal of Man-Machine Studies 35(6), 859–870 (1991)

17. Möller, S., Perlov, C., Jackson, W., Taussig, C., Forrest, S.R.: A Polymer Semiconductor Write-Once Read-Many-Times Memory. Nature 426(6963), 166–169 (2003)
18. Monrose, F., Rubin, A.: Authentication via Keystroke Dynamics. In: Proceedings of the 4th ACM Conference on Computer and Communications Security, pp. 48–56. ACM (1997)
19. Nisenson, M., Yariv, I., El-Yaniv, R., Meir, R.: Towards Behaviometric Security Systems: Learning to Identify a Typist. In: Lavrač, N., Gamberger, D., Todorovski, L., Blockeel, H. (eds.) PKDD 2003. LNCS (LNAI), vol. 2838, pp. 363–374. Springer, Heidelberg (2003)
20. Paillier, P.: Public-Key Cryptosystems Based on Composite Degree Residuosity Classes. In: Stern, J. (ed.) EUROCRYPT 1999. LNCS, vol. 1592, pp. 223–238. Springer, Heidelberg (1999)
21. Safa, N.A., Safavi-Naini, R., Shahandashti, S.F.: Privacy-Preserving Implicit Authentication. Cryptology ePrint Archive, Report 2014/203 (2014), http://eprint.iacr.org/2014/203
22. Shahandashti, S.F., Safavi-Naini, R., Ogunbona, P.: Private Fingerprint Matching. In: Susilo, W., Mu, Y., Seberry, J. (eds.) ACISP 2012. LNCS, vol. 7372, pp. 426–433. Springer, Heidelberg (2012)
23. Singelee, D., Preneel, B.: Location Verification Using Secure Distance Bounding Protocols. In: IEEE International Conference on Mobile Adhoc and Sensor Systems Conference, pp. 840–846. IEEE (2005)
24. Tan, K., Yan, G., Yeo, J., Kotz, D.: A Correlation Attack Against User Mobility Privacy in a Large-Scale WLAN Network. In: Proc. of the 2010 ACM Workshop on Wireless of the Students, by the Students, for the Students, pp. 33–36. ACM (2010)
25. Tsai, C.-S., Lee, C.-C., Hwang, M.-S.: Password Authentication Schemes: Current Status and Key Issues. IJ Network Security 3(2), 101–115 (2006)
26. Wang, D.-S., Li, J.-P.: A New Fingerprint-Based Remote User Authentication Scheme Using Mobile Devices. In: Int'l Conf. on Apperceiving Computing and Intelligence Analysis (ICACIA 2009), pp. 65–68. IEEE (2009)
27. Yao, A.C.-C.: How to Generate and Exchange Secrets. In: 27th Annual Symposium on Foundations of Computer Science, pp. 162–167. IEEE (1986)

Trusted Computing to Increase Security and Privacy in eID Authentication

Jan Vossaert[1], Jorn Lapon[1], Bart De Decker[2], and Vincent Naessens[1]

[1] KU Leuven, Department of Computer Science, Technology Campus Ghent
Gebroeders Desmetstraat 1, 9000 Ghent, Belgium
{firstname.lastname}@cs.kuleuven.be
[2] KU Leuven, Department of Computer Science, iMinds-DistriNet
Celestijnenlaan 200A, 3001 Heverlee, Belgium
{firstname.lastname}@cs.kuleuven.be

Abstract. Smart cards are popular devices for storing authentication credentials, because they are easily (trans)portable and offer a secure way for storing these credentials. They have, however, a few disadvantages. First, most smart cards do not have a user interface. Hence, if the smart card requires a PIN, users typically have to enter it via an untrusted workstation. Second, smart cards are resource constrained devices which impedes the adoption of advanced privacy-enhancing technologies (PETs) such as anonymous credentials.

This paper presents a new solution that addresses these issues. It allows users to enter their PIN via the workstation and securely transfer it to the smart card. The solution further extends existing smart card assisted authentication technology based on X.509 credentials with privacy-preserving features such as multi-show unlinkability and selective disclosure. The system can, hence, be used to improve the privacy properties of these rolled-out infrastructures. The solution relies on a secure execution environment running on the workstation. We have put our solution into practice and implemented a prototype.

1 Introduction

With an increasing number of online services, the need for reliable secure authentication grows ever stronger. Hence, many governments are issuing eID cards that enable citizens to authenticate and prove several personal properties. This allows the user to establish a secure authenticated session with a remote service provider. The remote service provider can control access to his service based on the released information. These eID systems are often implemented using a smart card to protect the credentials of the user.

These systems, however, also have multiple drawbacks. First, as with many smart card based systems, the user typically enters his PIN via the workstation. This allows malware on the workstation to intercept the PIN which may lead to further abuse. Second, many systems use X.509 credential technology to authenticate the user. This type of credential, however, does not offer the same privacy preserving features as anonymous credential systems.

N. Cuppens-Boulahia et al. (Eds.): SEC 2014, IFIP AICT 428, pp. 485–492, 2014.

This paper presents a strategy that tackles these issues. The *contribution* of this paper is twofold. First, it presents a solution that allows users to securely enter their PIN via a workstation to activate the authentication credentials on their smart card. The solution further extends existing smart card assisted authentication technology based on X.509 credentials with privacy-preserving features such as multi-show unlinkability and selective disclosure. It can, for instance, be used to increase the privacy and security of existing electronic identity infrastructures [10]. It applies the secure virtualization technologies contained on the workstation to realize a Secure Execution Environment (SEE). Second, a prototype of this system is presented to validate our solution. For the prototype, a CCID[1] stack is added to an existing framework for building SEE applications.

2   Related Work

Several European countries are issuing governmental eID cards [10]. Many countries use a smart card that contains the credentials of the user. The user enters a PIN to activate the credentials. As most smart card readers do not have a secure pin-pad, the PIN is typically entered via the keyboard of the workstation. This introduces a security risk as the PIN can be intercepted by malware running on the workstation. Many countries use standard X.509 credentials for user authentication. A signed set of attributes is embedded in or linked to the authentication certificate. This approach does not offer the privacy preserving features (i.e. anonymous/pseudonymous authentication and selective disclosure) that anonymous credentials do. A few exceptions, such as the German eID system and the system proposed in [11], do provide similar privacy preserving features.

Anonymous credential systems such as Idemix and U-Prove allow users to authenticate in a privacy preserving manner. Users can choose not to release any information but the fact that they hold a valid credential. Furthermore, they allow users to prove unlinkable provider specific pseudonyms. Users can also select which attributes will be disclosed to the service provider. Several efforts have been done to port these computationally expensive systems to run on a smart card. While in [2,1] a basic version of the Idemix system is implemented on a smart card, [9] and [13] respectively provide a full implementation of U-Prove and Idemix on a smart card. Although there are still some barriers for using anonymous credential systems (e.g. there is no universally good revocation strategy [6]), these advances make anonymous credential systems an increasingly viable option for rolling out electronic identity infrastructures. However, most existing systems still rely on X.509 credentials. The system presented in this paper can be applied to improve the privacy properties of these existing systems. Systems using anonymous credentials can also benefit from the proposed systems for securely handling the PIN input and for correctly informing the user about the pending transactions (e.g. what information is released to whom).

---

[1] CCID is a standard for communication between a host and a smart card reader.

3   Background

TCG Trusted Computing. Nowadays, commodity computers are equipped with a Trusted Platform Module (TPM). This is a hardware module attached to the computer's motherboard, extending the system with a set of security features. One of these features is the measurement of the state of the system. To this end, the TPM contains several Platform Configuration Registers (PCRs). These are cleared upon power up and can only be modified using the extend operation, performed inside the TPM. This operation requires two parameters: a PCR register and a value. This value is typically the hash of a binary software component. The result of this operation is a new PCR value, being the hash of the value currently contained in the register and the *value* to extend.

Based on this state, the TPM also supports a number of additional operations. Data can be encrypted with the seal operation and only if the system resides in the state specified during the seal operation can the data be decrypted (unseal). Additionally, the quote command returns a proof of the state (*quote*) which a third party can verify (verifyQuote) asserting that the system runs in a specific (trusted) state. The TPM specification supports both attestation based on an RSA key pair and Direct Anonymous Attestation (DAA) [4]. If the latter is used, no uniquely identifying information is released.

Secure Execution Environment. While TPMs have been built-in in workstations for several years, more recent is the adoption of SEE technologies such as Intel TXT and AMD SVM. These technologies cooperate with the TPM to allow the execution of measured code independently of previously executed software.

McCune et al. presented a framework called *Flicker* [8] that uses these technologies to isolate security critical code from applications and run it in a secure environment. The main, possibly untrusted, OS is temporarily suspended after which the sensitive Piece of Application Logic (*PAL*) is securely executed. When the execution of the sensitive code is completed, the OS resumes execution. The framework supports data transfer between the main OS and the *PAL*. The TPM operations can be used to assert to a remote party that certain data was generated by a trusted *PAL*. In [12] and [3] this framework is respectively extended to allow USB-UHCI and secure user interaction (i.e. input via the keyboard and output via the monitor). The user can only trust the displayed information if he is assured that it has been generated by a trusted *PAL*. Brasser et al. [3] proposed an enrollment procedure during which a user-specific picture is sealed to the state of the trusted *PAL*. This is done in a trusted enrollment environment (e.g. on a freshly installed workstation, not yet connected to the Internet) so that an attacker cannot obtain the picture of the user. Since only the trusted *PAL* can access the picture, the user is assured that the trusted *PAL* is running if the correct picture is shown. In [12] the enrollment procedure is realized using a smartphone on which the user can select his authentication picture. This allows the user to establish trust in a *PAL* running on a workstation that is (possibly) infected by malware or untrusted software.

4 Design

This section lists the different actors, followed by the requirements and a description of the system. Finally, a detailed description of the protocols is presented.

4.1 Roles

We assume a user U working on a workstation that runs a legacy operating system (OS) and supports SEE technologies for running a trusted application (PAL). A smart card reader is attached to the workstation. The user also carries a smart card (C), from a rolled-out eID infrastructure, that contains an X.509 credential. This is used to authenticate the user to a remote service provider (SP). The user needs to unlock the credential on his smart card using his PIN.

4.2 Requirements and Adversary Model

Requirements

R_1 Malware running on the workstation cannot intercept the PIN of the user.
R_2 Malicious software cannot mislead the user into approving malicious authentication attempts or disclosing more information than desired by the user.
R_3 The user can select which attributes are disclosed to the service provider.
R_4 The service provider is assured that the attributes released during authentication are certified by a trusted CA.

Adversary Model. We assume an attacker that can manipulate the user's operating system and application. Regarding the secure execution environment, simple hardware attacks (e.g. via DMA, memory dump) are taken into account but invasive, side-channel attacks and shoulder surfing are considered out of scope. With respect to the cryptographic capabilities of the attacker, we follow the Dolev-Yao attacker model: attackers can not break cryptographic primitives, but they can perform protocol-level attacks.

4.3 General Approach

The user authenticates towards a remote service provider via a workstation using his smart card. Instead of using the X.509 credentials on the smart card to authenticate towards the service provider, they are used to authenticate towards a trusted PAL running on the workstation. To this end, the public key of the CA (pk_{ca}) is embedded in the PAL binary. The PAL is started to handle the input of the PIN and the authentication. This protects the PIN from being intercepted by malware running on the workstation. The PAL verifies the authentication of the smart card and can, subsequently, selectively attest the obtained attributes towards the service provider using the *quote* functionality of the TPM. Since the TPM's DAA capabilities are used, no information but the disclosed attributes, the fact that the user had a valid credential and that the filtering was performed by a trusted application is released. This allows multi-show unlinkability if the user doesn't disclose uniquely identifying information. The *PAL* not only acts as an authentication proxy between the eID and *SP*, it also gives the user control over which attributes are released to *SP*. This prevents malware on the workstation from misleading the user into approving malicious transactions.

4.4   Protocols

Prerequisites. The SEE technologies on the workstation are enabled and the TPM has been certified (i.e. obtained a DAA credential). The service provider obtained the PCR state of the trusted *PAL*. The state of the *PAL* is certified by a trusted third party. The user has gone through an enrollment phase with the workstation during which his authentication image (img_u) is sealed to the state of the trusted *PAL*, resulting in an encrypted image enc_{img}.

Authentication. Figure 1 presents the protocol for authenticating the user towards a remote service provider. First, the user requests access to a protected resource from the service provider (1). The provider responds with an authentication request containing its certificate, the attribute request and an attestation challenge (2). Subsequently, the *PAL* is started and the attribute request is passed as a parameter, together with (enc_{img}) and the certificate of the service provider (3). The *PAL* now unseals enc_{img} (4). The user is subsequently informed by the *PAL* regarding the pending authentication and requested to enter his PIN. Meanwhile, the user's unique image is shown to indicate that the trusted environment is running (5). The user can, hence, trust the information shown on the display. To acknowledge the authentication, the user enters his PIN (6). The *PAL* now unlocks the credentials on the smart card using the PIN and sends a challenge to the smart card (7). If the PIN verification succeeds (8), the card signs the challenge and transfers the resulting signature and the certificate ($cert_u$) to the *PAL* (9-10). The *PAL* now verifies the authentication (11-12). If the verification succeeds, the *PAL* extracts the requested attributes ($atts$) from $cert_u$ (13). The *PAL* *extends* its state with the requested attributes and the certificate of the service provider (14). The *PAL* ends its execution and returns the user's attributes to the regular OS, that resumes its operation (15). The OS now performs a *quote* operation on the state resulting from the *PAL* execution (16). This quote attests towards *SP* that a trusted *PAL* obtained the user's attributes from a valid smart card (i.e. the *PAL* state is extended with the user's attributes) and that the user was shown the correct information about the service provider (i.e. the *PAL* state is extended with the service provider's certificate). The resulting quote is sent to *SP* along with $atts$ (17). The service provider verifies the quote and, hereby, checks the authenticity of the received attributes (18). Upon success, access is granted (19).

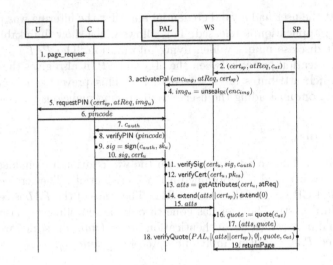

Fig. 1. Privacy friendly authentication using X.509 credentials

5   Validation

This section validates and illustrates the feasibility of our approach by developing a prototype for the Belgian eID infrastructure [5]. The Belgian eID [5] contains an X.509 credential that is used for user authentication. The middleware implements a PKCS#11 interface that other applications can use to support eID authentication. Several service providers use the eID infrastructure to handle user authentication. To test the compatibility with these existing service providers, the prototype is forced to release the entire authentication certificate. Adding the privacy-preserving parts of the protocol does not pose any additional technical challenges but requires some additional logic at the service provider.

A smartphone is used in the enrollment procedure during which the user seals an authentication image to the state of the trusted *PAL*. The PKCS#11 module of the existing middleware has been modified so that the operations requiring a verified PIN are delegated to the trusted *PAL*. For the *PAL* application, a CCID driver was implemented on top of the USB-UHCI stack. This allows the *PAL* to communicate with the eID inserted in the smart card reader. The *PAL* further contains a minimal version of the eID middleware to unlock and use the credentials on the eID.

Our prototype adds a total of 2641 lines of code to the *Flicker* framework, preserving a minimal Trusted Computing Base (TCB). Although adding the selective disclosure part of the protocol will slightly increase the TCB, it will remain sufficiently small to suggest that it can be formally verified. The whole authentication process takes about seven seconds compared to about two seconds for the regular authentication process. The main bottleneck are the TPM operations. Hence, the performance can be increases significantly by using a virtual TPM [7], while maintaining the same security properties.

The prototype has been tested with existing Web-based service providers. No modification of the browser or service provider are required. The privacy-preserving functionality, however, does require adding some additional logic to the service provider. A similar approach can be taken for other European eID cards as many (e.g. Italy, Spain and Portugal) use a design similar to the Belgian eID.

6 Evaluation

Requirements Review. During authentication the user is assured that the trusted application is running by displaying the personal image. Since the user only enters his PIN if the correct image is shown, the *PAL* is in full control of the workstation during the input of the PIN. Hence, malware running in the OS cannot intercept the PIN (cfr. R_1). Similarly, the user is assured that the provided information about the pending authentication is correct. The *PAL* binds the authentication proof to the service provider shown to the user by extending its state with the provider's certificate (cfr. R_2). During authentication of the eID to the *PAL*, the latter obtains all of the user's attributes contained on the card. The *PAL* filters the received information and only releases the attributes approved by the user (cfr. R_3). The *PAL* verifies the authenticity of the smart card via a challenge-response protocol. The *PAL* only continues the authentication if a valid smart card is used. Via the attestation protocol, the service provider is assured that a trusted *PAL* checked the validity of the smart card and filtered the attributes (cfr. R_4).

Security and Privacy Considerations. The *PAL* is trusted by both the user and the service provider to correctly execute the specified protocol. The functionality of the *PAL* is kept to the minimum. The small TCB decreases the chance of bugs and suggests that formal verification is possible. Moreover, the *PAL* can be updated by distributing a new binary to the workstation and the new certified state to the mobile and providers. Subsequently, the previous version is revoked.

Identity cards that have been stolen or otherwise compromised can be revoked. This has no impact on the *trusted PIN input* system as the service provider receives the authentication certificate and can, hence, check the revocation status. In the *privacy friendly authentication* system, however, the service provider only receives the attributes released by the *PAL*. The *PAL*, therefore, is responsible for checking the revocation status of the card. In case the revocation list contains a limited number of serials, it can be passed along to the *PAL* as an argument. In case the revocation list is too large, the *PAL* generates a nonce that is transferred to an OCSP server together with the serial of the eID. The nonce should be transferred via the regular OS to the OCSP server to ensure that the *PAL* doesn't have to contain networking drivers which would bloat the TCB. The response is subsequently transferred back to the *PAL* that can now verify the revocation status of the card.

7   Conclusion

This paper presented a system that can be applied to increase the security and privacy of smart card based authentication systems that use X.509 credentials. It allows users to securely enter their pincode via the workstation to activate the authentication credentials on the smart card. The system further realizes privacy enhancing features such as multi-show unlinkability and selective disclosure. A prototype using the Belgian eID card is presented, illustrating the feasibility of the system. The system applies SEE technologies included in most workstations.

References

1. Bichsel, P., Camenisch, J., De Decker, B., Lapon, J., Naessens, V., Sommer, D.: Data-minimizing authentication goes mobile. In: De Decker, B., Chadwick, D.W. (eds.) CMS 2012. LNCS, vol. 7394, pp. 55–71. Springer, Heidelberg (2012)
2. Bichsel, P., Camenisch, J., Groß, T., Shoup, V.: Anonymous credentials on a standard Java Card. In: Proceedings of the 16th ACM Conference on Computer and Communications Security, CCS 2009, pp. 600–610. ACM (2009)
3. Brasser, F.F., Bugiel, S., Filyanov, A., Sadeghi, A.-R., Schulz, S.: Softer smartcards - usable cryptographic tokens with secure execution. In: Keromytis, A.D. (ed.) FC 2012. LNCS, vol. 7397, pp. 329–343. Springer, Heidelberg (2012)
4. Brickell, E., Camenisch, J., Chen, L.: Direct anonymous attestation. In: Proceedings of the 11th ACM Conference on Computer and Communications Security, CCS 2004, pp. 132–145. ACM, New York (2004)
5. De Cock, D., Wouters, K., Preneel, B.: Introduction to the belgian EID card. In: Katsikas, S.K., Gritzalis, S., López, J. (eds.) EuroPKI 2004. LNCS, vol. 3093, pp. 1–13. Springer, Heidelberg (2004)
6. Lapon, J., Kohlweiss, M., De Decker, B., Naessens, V.: Analysis of revocation strategies for anonymous idemix credentials. In: De Decker, B., Lapon, J., Naessens, V., Uhl, A. (eds.) CMS 2011. LNCS, vol. 7025, pp. 3–17. Springer, Heidelberg (2011)
7. McCune., J., Li., Y., Qu., N., Zhou., Z., Datta., A., Gligor., V., Perrig, A.: Trustvisor: Efficient TCB reduction and attestation. In: Proceedings of IEEE Symposium on Security and Privacy, pp. 143–158 (2010)
8. McCune, J.M., Parno, B.J., Perrig, A., Reiter, M.K., Isozaki, H.: Flicker: An execution infrastructure for TCB minimization. SIGOPS Oper. Syst. Rev. 42(4), 315–328 (2008)
9. Mostowski, W., Vullers, P.: Efficient U-Prove implementation for anonymous credentials on smart cards. In: Rajarajan, M., Piper, F., Wang, H., Kesidis, G. (eds.) SecureComm 2011. LNICST, vol. 96, pp. 243–260. Springer, Heidelberg (2012)
10. Naumann, I., Hogben, G.: Privacy features of european eID card specifications (2009), http://www.enisa.europa.eu
11. Vossaert, J., Lapon, J., De Decker, B., Naessens, V.: User-centric identity management using trusted modules. In: Camenisch, J., Lambrinoudakis, C. (eds.) EuroPKI 2010. LNCS, vol. 6711, pp. 155–170. Springer, Heidelberg (2011)
12. Vossaert, J., Lapon, J., De Decker, B., Naessens, V.: Client-side biometric verification based on trusted computing. In: De Decker, B., Dittmann, J., Kraetzer, C., Vielhauer, C. (eds.) CMS 2013. LNCS, vol. 8099, pp. 34–49. Springer, Heidelberg (2013)
13. Vullers, P., Alpár, G.: Efficient selective disclosure on smart cards using idemix. In: Fischer-Hübner, S., de Leeuw, E., Mitchell, C. (eds.) IDMAN 2013. IFIP AICT, vol. 396, pp. 53–67. Springer, Heidelberg (2013)

Author Index

Printed in the United States
by Bookmasters

Printed in the United States
By Bookmasters